HERBERT MORRISON

Bernard Donoughue (Lord Donoughue of Ashton) was educated at Oxford, where he gained a First and a Doctorate of Philosophy, and at Harvard, USA. He was a Lecturer in Politics for eleven years at the London School of Economics and Political Science, a partner in a leading firm of city stock-brokers, a director at a merchant bank, and on the editorial staff of *The Times*, *Sunday Times*, *Sunday Telegraph*, and *The Economist*. He was Head of the Policy Unit at 10 Downing Street and Senior Policy Advisor to Prime Ministers Wilson and Callaghan, 1974–79; was elevated to the House of Lords in 1985; and served as Tony Blair's Minister for Farming and Food in 1997–99. His main interests are in music, literature, politics and horseracing. He has published four books on history and politics and is currently a Visiting Professor of Government at the London School of Economics and Political Science.

Also by Bernard Donoughue

British Politics and the American Revolution
The People Into Parliament: An Illustrated History of the Labour Party
On the Treadmill: Presidents and Prime Ministers at Work (with Robert J. Thompson)
Prime Minister: The Conduct of Policy Under Harold Wilson and James Callaghan

G. W. Jones (George Jones) M.A., D.Phil. (Oxford) has been Professor of Government at the London School of Economics and Political Science since 1976. He is the author of a number of books and articles on central and local government. He was a member of the Layfield Committee on Local Government Finance (1974–76) and of the National Consumer Council (1991–99). In 1999 he was appointed to the Advisory Panel on Beacon Councils, and awarded the OBE.

Also by G. W. Jones

Borough Politics
West European Prime Ministers
The Government of London
At the Centre of Whitehall

HERBERT MORRISON

Portrait of a Politician

Bernard Donoughue
and G.W. Jones

Foreword by
Peter Mandelson

**PHOENIX
PRESS**

5 UPPER SAINT MARTIN'S LANE
LONDON
WC2H 9EA

To Carol Donoughue and Diana Jones

A PHOENIX PRESS PAPERBACK

First published in Great Britain
. by Weidenfeld & Nicolson in 1973
This paperback edition published in 2001
by Phoenix Press,
a division of The Orion Publishing Group Ltd,
Orion House, 5 Upper St Martin's Lane,
London WC2H 9EA

A CIP catalogue record for this book is available
from the British Library.

Printed and bound in Great Britain by
Clays Ltd, St Ives plc

ISBN 1 84212 441 2

Contents

PART TWO 1940–1965

Illustrations

Foreword

My grandfather was born over a hundred years ago. His heyday in office was in the 1930s and '40s. He retired from politics in 1959 when, true to his principles, he declined a hereditary peerage and settled for a new-fashioned life one instead. He did little else in his remaining years apart from preside over the British Board of Film Censors and fight the replacement of the London County Council by the GLC.

So why look at his life again now? Because Morrison is one of Labour's forgotten heroes. Morrison was Labour's first and greatest leader of the London County Council, the Home Secretary who sustained London through the Blitz, the dominant figure on the NEC in masterminding Labour's 1945 victory, and the man who as Deputy Prime Minister in the Attlee cabinet can take more credit than anyone else for driving through that government's domestic and legislative programmes.

But, first and foremost he was the quintessential political organiser, responsible more than anyone else for rebuilding the party after the 1931 disaster. He created Labour's political base in London where he was not just an office holder, from 1915 to 1962, but the London Labour Party's dynamic force and inspiration, whether on the conference platform, with his sleeves rolled up at the election HQ, or on the dance floor of the Friday night social at the Co-op Women's Guild. He even instigated competitive choir singing among the CLPs! At conference last year I met an elderly delegate from Peckham who still treasured fond memories of Herbert.

There is therefore a certain historical injustice about Labour's treatment of Morrison. Also there is the relevance of his story to the present day. My grandfather was a consistent moderniser throughout his political career. He championed Labour's nation-wide, classless appeal. Of all Labour's leaders in the 1945 government, he understood best the need for political parties constantly to renew their policies and appeal. But before I expand on Morrison's politics and the lessons of his experience for today, let me reflect as a practising politician on Morrison the man and his career.

This biography's authors quote Fenner Brockway describing him as 'gauche and rough hewn' but adding 'there was no keeping down his energy, his smartness, his knack of getting things done, his cocksureness'. I think that is as good a summary of his character as any.

His self-confidence, not to say cockiness, marked him out, although he had nothing like the education and intellectual assurance of a modern-day Blair. If anything, his tireless devotion to politics made him more the Gordon Brown of his generation, though the Chancellor's relentless commitment has not yet extended, as Morrison's did, to sleeping on a camp bed in the office! There is also a bit of John Prescott in Morrison, a bluff working-class character who melded ideas and organisation into a distinctive political identity, rather as the deputy leader does today. I feel very proud of him.

All this I have learned from the biography between these covers. It is a far cry from my childhood memories of my grandfather.

I do not know exactly how old I was when my mother told me one day after school that I was unlikely ever to see him again. I think I was about ten or eleven and I was very taken aback. He was not well, she said, his one eye was failing him and it would not be possible for him to drive across London to see us anymore. Couldn't we go to visit him in the House of Lords instead, I asked. Afraid not, was the firm reply.

To understand this, you have to understand the circumstances of my grandfather's second marriage. Edith met him on a golf-course and married him two years after my grandmother died in 1953. (Unfortunately I never knew this reserved but reputedly gentle lady who had taste and poise.) Edith was a buxom Lancashire woman who voted Conservative. From the moment they tied the knot my grandfather's family, friends and colleagues were put into the background. Unfortunately this included my mother, his only child, and his grandsons, Miles and me.

Every once in a while, Grandpa would drive himself across London from Eltham to Hampstead Garden Suburb to visit us for Saturday lunch. My memories are dim but I can remember waiting impatiently, walking up to the front gate to catch the first glimpse of his white Morris car turning the corner into Bigwood Road. He heaved himself out, a great shock of white hair emerging first, a colourful bow-tie following. He sat at table, white napkin tucked into his collar, and then smoked a cigar. He liked cigars and we would bring him a box back from holiday every summer. A sit-down and snooze would follow lunch and soon he would be off back to Eltham.

Apart from picture postcards sent to Miles and Peter from different parts of the world, this was my only contact with him. I do not remember how my mother was with him or what we talked about. However, I have a feeling he did not keep his views about Harold Wilson to himself as the Wilsons were our neighbours and Grandpa regarded him with disapproval. I do not recall amusing anecdotes or gales of laughter coming from him. Nor do I remember tension surrounding him. He was more a legend than a grandad in my family.

Visitors would talk about him, occasionally there would be something in the newspapers and on the television or radio about him but otherwise he was not a presence in our home. In retrospect, I can see that my mother was affectionate but rather distant from him. It would have been nice to have had his attention but this never quite happened.

Grandpa died in March 1965, two months after Churchill (I remember doing scrapbooks about both of them in quick succession). I must have become quite political by then because at his funeral I was thrilled that George Brown was there representing the government. We went down the garden path to the front door of the house in Eltham to which we had never been invited. I met Edith for the first time. Standing in the hallway was Mr Brown himself and as we were introduced he boomed at me that Herbert would have been shocked to see me wearing a blue tie at his funeral. Grandpa was no longer in a position to be shocked by anything, but I was. Miles did not care and my father, typically, was greatly amused by the incident which he would be able to treasure for future story-telling occasions.

The Salvation Army band played at the funeral and everything was arranged and provided for by the Co-op. Grandpa went as he had lived. My mother did not allow me to take more time off school to attend his memorial service in Westminster Abbey. And we had no further contact with Edith other than her leaving some personal belongings of his for us to collect from Aunt Edie's in Brighton. Much to our embarrassment she turned up years later signing letters to *The Times* on behalf of the right-wing Freedom Association. It would not have been so bad, my mother said, had she not signed herself (Lady) Morrison of Lambeth. Grandpa would have been aghast.

I wish I had more joyous memories of him. What sticks is the stoic look on my mother's face that Saturday evening when I ran into the kitchen to tell her of the ITN newsflash announcing Grandpa's death. If I had not fully realised it before, I knew then he was special. No doubt there was a variety of reasons for my mother telling me not to talk about him at school. Partly, she disapproved of people trading on their families and she would always discourage boastfulness. But also she would have wanted to protect me. At school she felt she had suffered at the hands of unkind teachers and been subjected to playground mockery because of her politician father.

For whatever reason, I was for many years reluctant to tell people who my grandfather was, despite my immersion in politics and the Labour Party from the age of fifteen onwards. I first read extensively about his life and career when this biography was published in the year I went up to university. By that time, in 1973, Labour government was taken for granted, punctuated by spells of Tory administration. I did not think deeply about his early role because there was little remaining sense of the struggle from which the party had emerged in the first half of the century. Nor was there much anticipation of the struggles that would threaten the party's existence just seven years later, at the beginning of the 1980s. It was in this period that my own political views hardened significantly and that I started to think more profoundly about the sort of Labour Party I wanted to support: a mass party, representative of its supporters, espousing mainstream social democratic values, with policies that were capable of being implemented in the real world.

Consciously or not, I was absorbing the outlook of my grandfather. As I look back on this period now, I believe I was increasingly modelling my own views and values on his. Ten years on, I wanted not only to think like him but to follow in his footsteps as well. In government since 1997 I have thought about his career more extensively than in my entire previous life. In the cabinet office, like him, I experienced the thrill of being at the centre of government but also the frustrations of not being in a department with executive responsibilities. In later ministerial assignments I have led departments in ways that are similar to his – his care for detail, his desire to inspire as well as to manage, his respect for civil service experience and his love of the party.

I may not have acquired his greatness but in so much of my behaviour I really am my grandfather's grandson.

Morrison bestrode Labour politics from the 1920s to the 1950s. His career was anything but ephemeral. Yet when today's Labour politicians pay tribute to their saints and martyrs, Attlee is still the hero of 1945, Nye the creator of the NHS, Cripps the essence of moral rectitude, Bevin the architect of the post-war international order. Dalton has less kudos with the wider party but is still honoured on the social democratic right as the patron of his proteges Gaitskell and Crosland. Morrison is the unfairly forgotten figure of Labour's 'finest hour'.

The best contemporary indicator of Morrison's prominence (though it would not be today) is perhaps his thirty-three years of service on the National Executive Committee, stretching between 1920 and 1955. There were, however, two revealing one-year breaks, which give us hints as to why he never made it to the very top. The first was when, as a result of Bevin's intervention in denying him the Transport Workers' block vote, he was defeated by the near-alcoholic Greenwood for the party treasurership in 1943. The second was when he was unceremoniously booted out of the constituency section along with Dalton in the great Bevanite surge at the 1952 Morecambe conference.

Morrison's service on the NEC was longer than that of any of his distinguished colleagues and rivals. Attlee was a member of the NEC for a mere twenty-one years. He was elected for the first time at the 1934 conference. Attlee was seen as a sensible chap, neither too far to the right or left, and the following year the parliamentary party was to choose him rather than Morrison as leader after the 1935 election. Dalton was first elected in 1926 and served continuously from 1928 until he shared Morrison's fate at Morecambe in 1952. Cripps rebelliously held his place on the party's executive from 1934 but was expelled from the party between January 1939 and February 1945 and subsequently concentrated on his career in the cabinet.

As for Nye Bevan, the member of the Big Six of the 1945 government who has most closely approached beatification, he was not elected to the NEC until 1944, serving continuously apart from one break, until his premature death in 1960. The break came in 1954 when Gaitskell's rising star, hitched to the block votes of the big union barons, smashed Bevan's ambitions for the treasurership, foreshadowing the humiliation that Gaitskell was to inflict on both Bevan and my grandfather in the 1955 leadership election.

The only surviving Labour politicians who come close to Morrison in NEC service are the contrasting pair of Jim Callaghan (1957–80) and Tony Benn (1959–92). Morrison's greatest Labour movement contemporary, Ernest Bevin, in sharp contrast, never served on Labour's NEC. As General Secretary of the Transport Workers, and a Labour cabinet minister from 1940 onwards, he exercised his often decisive influence in other ways, usually to Morrison's disadvantage.

Labour's view of Morrison suffered from the party's vicious factionalism in the 1950s. This was the era of the great Bevanite split when Labour's unity was broken apart on the altar of Nye Bevan's ego. The left cast Morrison as a right-wing anti-hero, the man who presided over the cabinet in Attlee's absence when their champion resigned over NHS charges. Worse still, Morrison had thwarted Nye's ambition to be Foreign Secretary. But the right, too, abandoned Morrison when, with almost military discipline, they transferred their loyalty to the young pretender, Hugh Gaitskell. He was the new, fresh hope, the symbol of a new generation, well-educated and articulate but, it is often forgotten, far more accommodating towards the trade unions than Morrison had ever been.

When Attlee finally stood down from the leadership in 1955 – purposely delaying, it is always said, in order to benefit Gaitskell at the expense of the ageing Morrison - the younger man ran away with the prize. Morrison was bitter at the ingratitude of his colleagues, particularly those who owed their position as MPs to his patronage and influence. But he was past his prime and should have realised it. Everyone in active politics has to be conscious of their 'sell-by' date. He should have known that, in politics, people will support you for what you can do for them in the future, not for what you have achieved for them in the past. Loyalty in politics is always a complex calculus of affection and utility.

There is however another reason why I believe Morrison has so far failed to capture the imagination of succeeding political generations. It's to do with the way that party managers and political strategists are perceived. I understand the problem because our political backgrounds are rather similar.

Morrison came up through the party. His stomping grounds were Lambeth (where he was a leading political activist), Hackney (where he was a powerful mayor, then MP), Woolwich (his LCC seat) and Lewisham (which he represented from 1945 onwards). He operated for much of his early political life from the London Labour Party office which was then on Westminster Bridge Road.

My political apprenticeship was served as a Lambeth councillor in Stockwell. Some of the local children went to a primary school named after my grandfather and their parents frequented the Lord Morrison of Lambeth pub on the Wandsworth Road. From 1985 I operated from Labour's office in the Walworth Road virtually opposite Herbert Morrison House, then the London Labour headquarters.

Morrison loved the Labour Party which is why he stuck with it through the disaster of 1931 just as I did during Labour's worst moments in 1981. And we both played our part in rebuilding Labour's potential as an election-winning organisation – he in the 1930s, myself in the 1980s rescuing Labour not just from the ruins of defeat but from the edge of a precipice that threatened its extinction. We both, in our different ways, in different eras, obeyed Keir Hardie's famous injunction to the early Labour Party to 'look first to the register'.

Those of us who care deeply about political organisation and strategy are unfairly open to the charge that we are little interested in ideas and policy, and even worse, lack any real convictions. Morrison had to put up with this nonsense, particularly in the latter part of his political life. Perhaps it is a fault on our own part that those of us who are fully committed to the party as an institution don't feel the need to wear our convictions on our sleeve. Certainly my grandfather, after he had got over his early Marxist phase, did not spend a lot of time indulging himself in political philosophy.

But he was driven throughout his whole political life by a passion to make Britain a more just and efficient society. He fought for those values that unite the whole at the centre-left in each succeeding generation: genuine opportunity for all and a fairer distribution of life- chances. He shared the determination to do all in our power to extend to the many the freedom to make meaningful choices that in his day was confined to a tiny few and still today remains far from universal.

Morrison was throughout his life interested in the practical improvements the state could bring to ordinary people's lives, almost always based on the strong partnership he advocated between central and local government. His pockets were always stuffed with policy papers setting out his latest plan or scheme. Not for him the empty gesture or the emotional spasm.

He was deeply fascinated by what today we would call questions of delivery. In London he fashioned a forceful model of local government - rather like the system of powerful mayors and cabinets we are developing today which delivered high quality public services and amenities. Until, that is, the excesses of the ultra-left destroyed his legacy in the late 1970s and early 1980s and made Labour fearful of strong local government for a generation.

We are still paying a price today for that loss of confidence in public services, the low status of local government and the disconnection in the public mind between tax and spend. That is why our present-day message of investment in public services must be combined with detailed and credible plans for improvement, innovation and reform.

Morrison began his political life very differently from how he ended up. Early in the last century, he was a convinced revolutionary. As a young member of the hard-left Social Democratic Federation he once spied the figure of Philip Snowden, then a leading ILP figure and later Chancellor of the Exchequer, walking with his wife. Morrison, then employed as a shop assistant and grocery deliverer, hastily scribbled a note which he thrust into Snowden's hand: 'When, Mr Philip Snowden, will you move this resolution in the Commons – "That in the opinion of this House there is no real remedy for the problems of poverty short of Socialism"? Cease talking reform and advocate social revolution. From Unattached.' The young ideologue did not wait for a reply.

But the self-taught Morrison soon progressed from Marx's set texts to the business of reading agendas and chairing meetings, skills for which he became known far and wide in Labour circles. He struggled up from nothing. Politicians are rarely made like that any more. From the outset he soaked up others' education and surrounded himself with cleverer people throughout his political career. By the 1920s he was a councillor and mayor of Hackney and soon to be a Member of Parliament. But his reputation had been made since 1915 as the secretary of the London Labour Party. He was so attached to this role that even as a minister he insisted that he be seconded to government and not replaced as secretary. His first post was as Minister of Transport in MacDonald's 1929 administration where he drew up the London Passenger Transport Act, the beginning of the capital's integrated transport system. The great defeat of 1931 saw him out of Parliament. Had Attlee not clung on in Limehouse it is inconceivable that he rather than Morrison would have emerged as party leader, but when both were contesting the post in 1935 Attlee had the advantage of a parliamentary seat between 1931 and 1935.

Morrison had further established himself by then as Labour's first leader of the London County Council. There are unnamed memorials to his leadership across London: the green belt, and housing estates which still stand as models of good quality public housing in comparison with the socially-engineered monstrosities of the 1960s and '70s; Waterloo Bridge, replaced after Morrison took a pickaxe to the collapsing original in the face of central government's refusal to sanction borrowing for the new construction; the South Bank, which emerged from the Festival of Britain he fathered in 1951. LCC-originated schools, parks and amenities cover the capital. This was the high tide of municipal socialism that Morrison pioneered.

County Hall, now a Japanese-owned hotel thanks to Mrs Thatcher, was the centre of his life. Back and forth across Westminster Bridge he walked between his office-cum-home and Parliament in the pre-war years before settling into Whitehall as Minister of Supply from May 1940. Morrison 'delivered the goods' according to Anthony Eden and Beaverbrook praised his 'efficiency and competence'. But it was as Home Secretary that he came into his own. The journalist Hannen Swaffer claimed he urged Beaverbrook to tell Churchill in October 1940 that 'cockneydom was on the verge of revolt', that the communists were about to march on Whitehall and that Morrison must be put in charge of the Blitz because ' he is the only man that Londoners trust . . . if London runs, the war will be lost'.

London did not run, and the war was won.

The war was a turning point for Morrison in many ways because he was able to turn himself from an essentially municipal into a fully national figure. He did this not just through an increasingly adept use of the media to project himself and his political vision but by using his substantial influence inside the political system to shape detailed policies for the post-war world. He was an inspiring personality. In speeches and articles he repeatedly addressed ideas for building a better society which sought to leave behind the class divisions and economic stagnation of the 1930s. Churchill intensely disliked such boat-rocking, but that did not stop Morrison. He spoke of the need for a more egalitarian society, with universal education providing opportunity for all and comprehensive provision for welfare, health and social security to put an end to poverty. He was attacked in the *Daily Mail* for making 'political' speeches. But he was not to be deflected and continued on the themes of industrial organisation and the relationship between the state and business, and the promotion of greater international economic co-operation as part of a wider United Nations organisation.

It was natural that Morrison should be put in charge of the preparations for the Labour Party's coming election campaign. On the NEC in the 1930s he had already done a great deal to help reconstruct the Labour Party as a credible alternative government after the disaster of 1931. His watchful eye (he had been blind in the other since birth) was trained on every aspect of policy and organisation. With Hugh Dalton he took over manifesto planning, and the emerging policy ideas were drawn together with the nuts and bolts of local activity and propaganda in the election committee that Morrison chaired. This paved the way for the 1945 victory. Nobody rivalled his experience or challenged his authority; he relished the fight and was thoroughly at home driving the party machine.

Once the election was won, Morrison continued in government in much the same role. He became Lord President of the Council and Leader of the House of Commons, co-ordinating economic and domestic policy and driving Labour's huge legislative programme through Parliament. As Deputy Prime Minister he was the government's anchorman. He carried on in much the same capacity until Bevin's withdrawal through ill health in 1951. By then, Attlee had experienced recurrent illness, Stafford Cripps had retired, other cabinet members were either fading or falling out with each other, and things were starting to look and feel ragged. Morrison himself had never fully recovered his elan after the thrombosis he suffered in 1947. So when in 1951 he went to relieve Bevin, whose stature and popularity with officials had grown during his time in the Foreign Office, the auguries were not good. Morrison found himself in unfamiliar territory at a time when the cabinet was becoming increasingly fractious during Attlee's absence in hospital.

There are different judgements that can be made about his brief spell at the Foreign Office, but it was not a happy berth for him. Distracted by the need to manage rebellious colleagues in the cabinet, it did not receive his full attention. But the confiscation of Britain's Persian oilfields was a major foreign policy challenge, and when the spies Burgess and Maclean defected their escape was a huge, and avoidable, embarrassment. To Foreign Office officials he was not their beloved Ernie, and if Morrison let himself down the Foreign Office did not lift much of a finger to break his fall.

Within fifteen years of leaving office Morrison had died, disappointed at not becoming Labour leader. Readers of this book can judge his personal and professional attributes as a politician and minister. I would cite just three.

First, throughout his time in municipal and national politics his legendary campaigning prowess revolved around the issues of the day, the social improvements, the economic reorganisation, the international co-operation demanded by the condition of the people. The articles, speeches and pamphlets he churned out invariably consisted of demands for change. Whether he was advocating municipal enterprise in Hackney, comprehensive housing plans on the LCC, or social ownership in government, Morrison had a bold prescription for every ill – and he was always banging out the message. He had a marvellous gift for the telling turn of phrase – the much-derided sound bite of the modern political era- and was not afraid of using pro-fessional presentational help. In one LCC election he attacked the Tories as the party of 'Mr Dilly, Mr Dally and Mr Can't' whose only motto was 'Something Saved, Nothing Done'. His urgings to 'Go to it' and 'Keep at it' became the slogans of the munitions factories during the war.

At the time of his first contest for the party leadership in 1935, Kingsley Martin, editor of the *New Statesman*, backed him as being 'dynamic, open to ideas, keen to argue and above all keen that the party should succeed and win'. Tawney told Martin that Morrison was in reality more radical than he sounded, which explains the support he gained from the left-wing intellectual Harold Laski and the near-communist D.N. Pritt. Never bound by con-vention or old ideas, Morrison, it was said, built his leadership on a kind of 'democratic cajolery which was very different from Bevin's autocratic bullying'.

A second attribute marked him out from Bevin in another way. Whereas the great Transport Workers' leader saw Labour as the trades unions' instrument, Morrison was insistent that the party had to represent interests that extended far beyond those of the organised working-class. As a young man Morrison reached branch office in his union, the National Union of Clerks, between 1910 and 1913. But after opposing a union motion at a Labour conference he was severely censured and he resigned.

He drew two lessons from this experience. The first was that trades unions were limited by their pursuit of sectional interests rather than wider political objectives, and that no action by unions could ever be indifferent to the wider community interest. And the second was that for any organisation to attempt to make instructions binding on representatives was a breach of basic democratic principle. He applied this standard to every part of political life, not least to local government where he more than anyone laid down the principle of councillors' independence from party control.

The third attribute I would mention is the way Morrison treated the views of his civil servants and constantly surrounded himself with experts and intellectuals who could challenge and enhance his position. He was one of the few politicians of his generation to be deeply interested in the effectiveness of the machinery of government. On leaving office he took up a visiting fellowship at Nuffield College, Oxford, to write *Government and Parliament: A Survey from the Inside*.

James Callaghan recently gave me his first edition of the book, presented and signed by the author, and told me a story illustrating Morrison's devotion to British parliamentary practice. Callaghan had been his substitute delegate at the first meeting of the Council of Europe in Strasbourg in 1949. Morrison went home after a week, leaving Callaghan with instructions to make sure that the procedure committee which was devising the rules of the Council should adopt the British House of Commons as its model and Erskine May as its bible. According to Callaghan, as the committee was chaired by a Belgian senator with an Italian as the rapporteur and Reynaud, the former French P.M, pulling the strings, he failed on all counts!

Morrison drew great plaudits from his officials. His permanent secretary at the Ministry of Transport described him as 'a brilliant administrator'. At the Home Office, Morrison praised his civil servants for their efficiency and humanity, 'for the way in which even under the pressures of the war's darkest days they never lost sight of the liberal principles which are at the heart of the British political system'. In the Lord President's office, Max Nicholson, the official closest to him, said of Morrison that he was 'the most professional minister I have ever worked for . . . he told officials they must give him their honest views even if wholly in conflict with his own. But if he overruled them they must then go off and do what he decided.' Today, that is probably as good a model as any for a minister to emulate.

But what lessons does Morrison have to teach New Labour today?

One striking lesson is that throughout his political life my grandfather believed Labour should have a broad appeal across the social classes. He was an inveterate ambassador for the Labour cause in hitherto hostile territories. He persuaded many middle-class, well-educated people to join the party and put themselves forward as candidates because he saw that this would benefit the party. And in 1945 he made the extraordinarily bold step of forsaking his own safe seat to take on a Tory-held constituency because he felt this was the sort of place where Labour had to prove it could win.

This was his New Labour message of 1945. 'For many years I have counselled the socialist party that, if it is ever to secure an independent stable parliamentary majority, it must gain and keep the support, not only of the politically conscious organised workers, but also of the large number of professional, technical and administrative workers of whom there are many in East Lewisham. It is because I have confidence in the reasoned appeal the socialist party can make to all sections of the community, manual workers and black coats alike, that I have decided to go to East Lewisham . . . emphasising by this action my conviction that the soundest socialist appeal is that which is most universal in its scope.'

This is as good an encapsulation as any of what Tony Blair calls one-nation socialism, and I share it. But it represents a point of view about the overall political approach of the centre-left that is not universally shared. There is a debate about the left's electoral tactics and strategy that never goes away. It was not long into the history of Tony Blair's Government that the argument came to be heard that Labour needed to appeal more to its traditional heartlands and to put forward policies and positions specifically tailored to reflect the supposed interests of its 'core vote'. Like Morrison, I strongly support policies that meet the requirements of the needy and vulnerable but not to the exclusion of other groups in society. As a general political approach, therefore, I reject a core-vote strategy on grounds of both tactics and principle.

Firstly there is a good deal of myth surrounding the concept of Labour's 'core vote'. The radically changed social class structures of today are self-evident. However even in Morrison's time, when the manual working-class accounted for a clear majority of the electorate, about half of it did not vote Labour in the elections of the 1930s. Secondly people's concerns transcend the boundaries of class. Voters want competence in their government; above all, they want economic prosperity and security, and decent public services that they can rely on. They will vote for the party that seems to them most on their side in securing these goals, but the 'side' they think of is that of the people broadly defined, not some 'core vote' or class interest. Thirdly people look to their politicians to present a practical but compelling vision of the country's future, not cheap populist attacks on imaginary class enemies opposed to a 'core vote'.

For me, this is about far more than electoral tactics. It's about how social democrats achieve lasting change in society. Take the example of New Labour's relationship with business. We have sought to take business with us in all our major decisions. Some critics say this has blunted our radicalism.

My reply is that it has facilitated a rebalancing of the labour market which business accepts and which at the same time represents a major extension of employee rights.

But it is not just business that the one-nation approach suggests New Labour should embrace. I love the Labour Party but I am not chauvinistic about it. I do not believe that it contains a monopoly of all wisdom or that it should behave as an exclusive sect. That is why we must not retreat from building a broad-based progressive alliance that unites the radical majority in our country behind our values and ideas.

A second, still relevant lesson of my grandfather's life is that throughout it he was a moderniser. When Minister of Transport in 1929 he battled to create London Transport out of disparate and competing private companies. At County Hall in the 1930s, he brought into being high quality public housing, parks and other amenities. Before 1945 he was the chief architect (although not the author) of Labour's manifesto, 'Let us face the future'. After the war, he gave his name to the concept of nationalisation which brought the coal, railway, gas and electricity industries into public ownership.

Of course, the reader may pause at this point to query how someone who masterminded Britain's nationalisation programme can be described as a moderniser. The answer goes to the heart of what I mean by a 'moderniser'.

A moderniser in my book is a person who in his or her time makes the right choices for the future of either the Labour Party or Britain, who grasps the nettle of what needs to change, who has a clear sense of strategy in making their modernising choices a reality in government, and who is a master of both politics and strategy as well as being bold, decisive and prepared where necessary to break free from convention in securing change.

Nationalisation of the basic utilities was, in my view, the right policy for Britain in the 1940s – rather than sixty years later. And the programme was pushed through in an imaginative, practical way.

There was a long political progression from Morrison's early beliefs as an ardent Marxist activist in the Social Democratic Federation before the First World War, to the Deputy Prime Minister who legislated in the 1945 government for the nationalisation of basic industries on grounds of productive efficiency.

Early socialists argued for public ownership on the grounds that private ownership and the capitalist system were inherently wasteful and unjust. They envisaged a wholesale 'socialist transformation' of society in which production would be based on need, not profit. This conviction that the system of production needed to be transformed was for them the distinguishing characteristic of their socialism, as set out in Clause IV of the party's 1918 constitution. It set them apart from the progressives and radicals of the Edwardian Liberal Party who genuinely yearned for a society of greater fairness and social justice, but lacked the distinguishing socialist belief that it was necessary to transform the capitalist system of production in order to make this possible. Within the

Labour Party, this belief in the necessity for socialist transformation was strengthened by the economic crisis of the early 1930s and the collapse of the MacDonald government in the face of it. The party dallied with quasi-revolutionary positions that foreshadowed Militant Tendency motions of the 1980s calling for 'nationalisation without compensation of the three hundred monopolies'.

It was against this background that my grandfather's achievement as a moderniser has to be judged. The fall of the MacDonald government was for him more of an agonising personal wrench than proof that the fundamental tenets of the 'parliamentary road to socialism' had been called into question.

However, the experience of 1931 convinced him that Labour had to work out a practical policy for production rather than simply await the mystical moment of socialist transformation, which for many people in the party (who, unlike Morrison, came from strongly nonconformist traditions) was seen as a kind of secular Second Coming. In this endeavour Hugh Dalton was a crucial partner with Morrison on the NEC, particularly in bringing on board a generation of young economists, like Douglas Jay, Evan Durbin and Hugh Gaitskell, who understood the lessons of emerging Keynesian thinking. Together they developed the concept of economic planning as an altern-ative to wholesale nationalisation; they introduced new ideas such as the relevance of competition policy to tackling monopolies and restrictive practices; and they made the argument for public ownership of a limited number of basic industries on grounds of industrial efficiency and their strategic importance.

In the circumstances of the late 1930s, this case for limited public ownership on grounds of efficiency was persuasive. The coal industry suffered from chronic problems of over-capacity throughout the inter-war years; the private owners were unwilling to invest because of competition from marginal pits; and the social consequences of immiseration in the coalfield districts were a stain on British society. Nationalisation offered the only way out – and this conviction was magnified by the impact of the war which left the coal industry in crying need of investment and modernisation. The same could be said of the railways.

Gas and electricity were newer industries with multitudinous private and municipal undertakings trying to meet a huge expansion of demand. There were big efficiencies to be realised by a programme of investment in building national grids which enabled power supplies to become both more secure and cheaper as the result of production in fewer, larger scale plants. There is little evidence that this would have happened without nationalisation.

Morrison's particular contribution was to devise structures of governance that were designed to implement this particular vision of public ownership. Because the purpose was to promote greater efficiency, his main concern was to see that the newly nationalised industries were well-managed. He drew heavily from his experience of setting up London Transport during the

MacDonald government. In his view, if the industries were to be efficient, management had to be of high quality and its independence from outside pressures had to be bolstered. So to the annoyance of many on the left, he thought it a virtue to recruit proven managers from the old private sector companies; the faults of the past were the result not of their failings as individuals but of the inefficient structures of private ownership.

He resisted strenuously Bevin's attempts to give the trades unions an automatic seat on the new company boards – the directors' first loyalty should be to the boards, not to any outside interest – although he did not hesitate to appoint individual trade unionists whom he felt could make a big contribution. The outstanding example was Bevin's great rival and enemy in the trade union movement, the TUC General Secretary, Walter Citrine, who became a living legend as chairman of the nationalised electricity industry.

He also believed that nationalised industry management had to be free of political interference. Ministers should operate at 'arm's length' from boards and he was very resistant to parliamentary scrutiny of the nationalised industries in any form (in later life opposing the establishment of the Select Committee on Nationalised Industries).

Morrison's principles for the management of nationalised industries were a long way from the vague notions of socialisation in which many in the Labour Party believed. And he attracted party criticism for them, particularly when it became known that he had resisted the extension of nationalisation to the steel industry. In that sense he was a moderniser, and a brave one.

Did his concept of nationalisation stand the test of time? I would argue that for the first twenty-five to thirty years the balance sheet was on the whole favourable. National grids were built. The industries did show the capacity to modernise, with coal, electricity and the railways undergoing huge and painful restructuring particularly in the 1960s. The conversion to natural gas was a technical achievement of a high order. The industries on the whole enjoyed good industrial relations, and working conditions, particularly with regard to health and safety, greatly improved.

But increasingly costly mistakes were made, often as a direct result of the political interference from which my grandfather strove so hard to protect nationalised industry management – not just through the mucking-up of industry finances as ministers struggled to control prices but also through the implementation of wider industrial policies, for example the disastrous attempt to build a wholly British-designed nuclear reactor. The basic failing of nationalisation was that ultimately it did not succeed in keeping ministers at 'arm's length'. This was compounded when the trade unions pressurised Labour ministers, especially in the 1970s, to interfere in board decisions in order to serve sectional interests.

It is dangerous to speculate what Morrison would have thought of Margaret Thatcher's privatisation policies had he lived to see them. There would undoubtedly have been great sadness, but he would probably have recognised an element of inevitability given that the system of governance that, as a great moderniser in his time, he had established had outlived its original purpose.

In his own day, however, it was towards the end of the post-war administration that Morrison's modernising instincts became controversial. Before others woke up to the shift, he sensed that people were beginning to see Labour as behind the times. Although in the 1950 and 1951 elections Labour's core supporters rallied in their millions to the party responsible for full employment and the new NHS, other voters associated Labour's planning and nationalisation with austerity and rationing. What had seemed fresh and urgent in 1945 began to look unnecessary and even oppressive.

The man most closely identified with Labour's new policies in 1945 was by 1950 arguing that Labour needed a new sort of programme that reflected the changing social face of Britain in a post-austerity world. But he was preaching to an unsympathetic party. To those on the left, many of whom already felt that the government had been insufficiently bold, Morrison seemed to be advocating a crude retreat from public ownership and state control. Loyalists, on the other hand, could see nothing wrong with continuing with the policies they been pursuing since 1945. The manifesto was being delivered-what more was required? Morrison knew that a fresh agenda was needed. But he was tired, like all the other senior members of the government. They had been in government effectively since 1940. He never put flesh on the bones.

Writing this foreword nearly four years into what I hope and believe will prove the first term of a long period of Labour government, this is the essential Morrison maxim we must never ignore: delivery and renewal must go hand in hand.

It is certainly true that Tony Blair's government is renewing the public's collective memory about Labour. This fresh memory owes much to the success with which we have combined enterprise and fairness as the hallmarks of our political approach. We cut corporation tax and cut poverty. We introduce tough competition law and introduce the minimum wage. We create a small business service and lift children out of poverty. We give support to high-tech start-ups and to single parents. In each area of policy, from introducing the minimum wage to widening industrial competition, we constantly strive to further both efficiency and social justice.

The old negative memories of Labour are passing. Gone is the 'winter of discontent', to be replaced by low inflation, low mortgage rates and social security bills under control. Gone is the IMF crisis, to be replaced by record sums available for investment. Gone is opposition to the sale of council houses, to be replaced by the patient-centred NHS. Gone is the advocacy of unilateralism, to be replaced by the willingness to deploy troops as peace-keepers in support of a just and stable international order.

But a government that rests on its laurels is a government that is nearing the end of its life. That's why New Labour must avoid the 1950–51 experience; we must use our period of office to pick up steam rather than coast without a clear sense of purpose.

Britain faces a permanent challenge to secure a sustainable increase in its economic growth rate. And, linked to this, while securing minimum standards of employment protection, this century must see a new concept of job security based on employability and changing patterns of work.

There are other challenges, too, that Morrison would readily recognise.

Throughout his political life Morrison was a committed internationalist. In the 1950s he recognised, more quickly than the bulk of the party at that time, that the best expression of internationalism in the post-war environment was to be strongly pro-European. Labour has come a long way since then and, today, is a gut European party. A commitment to Europe is of central importance to any modern social democratic project because it is vital to Britain's prosperity, security and strength. The nation-state can no longer fulfil this task alone. In my view, in the modern world you can still be a Conservative and a pro-European but you can't be a social democrat and be anti-European. On that, I'm absolutely convinced my grandfather would agree.

Similarly in relation to social policy. It has been relatively straightforward for Labour to make families with low incomes better off by means of redistributive policies. But the deeply complex problems of urban and neighbourhood disintegration pose problems of a more fundamental kind: endemic fears that crime is rising and that criminals go unpunished, that responsibility to others and common decency are under threat, and that families are breaking down in a society where 'anything goes'. These fears are not irrational: they are realities that do as much to undermine social cohesion and inclusion as poverty and unemployment. The challenge is to address not just the poverty of individual expectations for families trapped on welfare benefits, but the poverty of hope that comes from broken and demoralised communities.

This is a challenge that Herbert Morrison, as city manager, public sector reformer and investor in local communities, would immediately recognise. Crucial to any solution is the revival of a culture of civic leadership together with community responsibility and self-help.

In my grandfather's day there was confidence in local democracy. Our objective today should be to rebuild that confidence. In the last quarter century the scope for civic leadership, for civic innovation, has become too limited. The mayoral and cabinet agenda being developed should be seen as a new beginning for local government. Just as in schools and hospitals, our maxim should be 'intervention in inverse proportion to success'. If local democrats demonstrate sustained performance and responsible service delivery, they should be able to keep their independence and earn further freedoms. In enacting this principle, we could signal a radical departure from the centralising policies of previous administrations and provide an excellent bequest to future generations.

This would also enable future Herbert Morrisons to come through from local seed-beds of democracy and make a real difference. That Labour should have finally learned the lessons of his own life would give my grandfather great joy. And for me it would be his finest memorial.

Peter Mandelson
January 2001

Preface

When Lord Morrison died in 1965 he left his papers to Nuffield College, Oxford. To the surprise of those who earlier remembered a large collection of documents, the papers now constituted only one suitcase-full, much of this printed material of little historical interest. Lady Morrison explained that about twenty box files were burned when they moved house in 1960. Ethel Donald, Morrison's close friend and personal secretary for nearly forty years, stated in a letter to the Warden of Nuffield, Mr D. N. Chester, that 'all the documents – private and governmental, which I had filed for so many years – were destroyed – much to my sorrow and dismay. The history of a lifetime went up in smoke because of supposed difficulties in finding storage room in the new house.'

The problem facing the literary executors was how to ensure that a satisfactory analysis could be made of Morrison's major contribution to British political and administrative developments, as well as of the man himself, when his papers and published *Autobiography* were so inadequate.

The solution was to mount a study of Morrison while people who knew him and had worked with him were still alive. Their recollections – even allowing for the defects of personal memory – would to a considerable extent make up for the deficiencies of Morrison's own papers. Accordingly the Warden, with the approval of Lady Morrison, invited us to undertake the official biography.

We decided on a clear demarcation of effort. George Jones was responsible for Part One, dealing with Morrison's life up to 12 May 1940 when he joined Churchill's wartime coalition as Minister of Supply, and Bernard Donoughue was responsible for Part Two, describing his life after that date. Although the two sections were written separately, we have worked closely together in preparing the book and especially when interviewing over three hundred former friends, enemies, associates and working colleagues of Morrison. We were in complete agreement in our view of the man and accept joint responsibility for the whole work. This book is long, but Morrison's active public life ranged over sixty years and it would have been impossible in a brief study to do justice to his important contributions in London local government, in Parliament, in the Cabinet, in the development of public corporations and, above all, in the growth of the Labour Party at all levels. Although he began life without privileges of wealth or education, he became one of the select few who have made an impact on the lives of all of us in twentieth-century Britain.

Bernard Donoughue
George Jones
June 1972

Preface to 2001 Edition

Herbert Morrison was a remarkable twentieth-century politician and Labour minister. Yet he often seems best remembered for two regrettable misquotations and for being Peter Mandelson's grandfather. The quip by Ernest Bevin, about someone being his own worst enemy, 'Not while I'm alive he ain't', usually has Morrison as the fallguy, but in fact it was Aneurin Bevan, as is clear from Alan Bullock's *Ernest Bevin: Foreign Secretary 1945–1951* (London: Heinemann, 1983), page 77. And Morrison never said or wrote 'We'll build the Tories out of London': if anyone can find an authoritative source that proves otherwise, we offer a prize of a free lunch with us at the LSE where we are still teaching a seminar on the British Executive after over 30 years connection with the School.

Peter Mandelson, who was playing with his toys when one of us interviewed his mother, Morrison's daughter, explains in the new Foreword the influence his grandfather has played in his life and career. Although they have many basic differences of character and lifestyle, we can present here only what seem striking similarities between them and even stimulation to Peter's political approach and ambitions. Despite some big differences between them, he seems to have been following in Morrison's footsteps, and seeking to do even better in seeking to modernise the Labour party and Britain. If Peter's career is completely to follow Morrison's, then ending as a blind film censor should provide much gaiety to the nation.

Morrison was a formidable national politician: in the 1930s the Transport minister who integrated London's buses and the tube; in the War the Home Secretary who raised morale in the blitz, preserved civil freedoms and gave his name to the most effective indoor bomb shelter; and for five years after the War virtually Deputy Prime Minister who managed through Cabinet and Parliament the Labour Government's massive legislative programme on the welfare state and nationalisation. He felt he should have been Leader of the Labour Party and Prime Minister, contending for the leadership in 1935, 1945 and 1955. He was Foreign Secretary for a brief and uninspiring period in 1951, distracted perhaps by his beloved Festival of Britain, the successful Dome venture of the day, though his passionate support for Swedish social democracy and for the fledgling democratic state of Israel, showed that he was not without interests abroad.

He was the leading moderniser in the Labour Party, active on its National Executive Committee from the 1920s until the 1950s. Scourge of communists and the extreme left, he felt Labour would always be in opposition, and unable to do anything constructive, if parading outdated left-wing ideology and based on the working class alone. He sought to win over the middle class, even exchanging in 1945 his solid Labour seat for a suburban marginal one, to show he put his career where his rhetoric was.

In championing the Labour Party, he deployed the most modern techniques of public relations and used the media to promote its cause. He urged prudence in public expenditure, reminding Labour that the poor paid taxes and felt their burden more than did the rich. He argued that Labour must demonstrate its capacity to govern. In opposition he planned for government, valuing a disciplined party, with a moderate programme and effective organisation. His style of party leadership was to give a lead and not just to follow his followers. He respected public opinion and gave priority to consumers rather than trades unions – he had written a pamphlet calling for a Citizens' Charter in 1921. He was keen to use the talents of women, appointing them to positions women had never held before, as on the Fire Brigade Committee of the London County Council and the Metropolitan Water Board 'to stir that lot up.'

He was a great champion of local government as the most responsive provider of efficient local services to the public. He began his governmental career as Mayor of Hackney in 1920, and was Leader of the London County Council from 1934 to 1940. While there he campaigned for good public housing to replace the slums and to provide electricity in all homes. He was an advocate of town planning and started London's green belt. He showed that one did not need directly elected mayors to produce active, well-known leaders who could champion their localities against central government. Morrison demolished the outdated Waterloo bridge and erected in its place the best bridge in London: all in the face of central government opposition. Sometimes the centralisers defeated him as with Bevan's establishment of the bureaucratic monstrosity of the National Health Service in place of Labour's promised health service based on local government. He would have been distressed at New Labour's treatment of local government as simply an agent of central government.

He was the architect of Labour's programme of nationalisation, creating the Morrisonian public corporation as the form of organisation to run Britain's public industries and utilities. He hoped it would enable managers to be dynamic entrepreneurs, following ministerial directions only on matters of strategic significance. He would have been disappointed at the later inefficiencies and contempt for the consumer of many nationalised industries and services, but would have been even more aghast at privatisation and the array of regulators who, he felt, would stifle managerial enterprise.

He was a consummate party strategist and tactician, not only winning the 1934 LCC election after Labour's collapse of 1931 but gaining an even bigger majority in 1937, and he masterminded a massive Labour victory in the general election of 1945. He gloried in representative democracy as a way of promoting the public interest, and would have resisted those who sought to replace it with populist arrangements behind whose façade lurk special interests.

Morrison respected traditional ways of governing, which he felt could be used by Labour to achieve its objectives. He was superb at using officials and civil servants, seeking their professional advice, after which he would make his own political judgment. He opposed the establishment of select committees as mischief-making rivals to the real elected government, preferring to set up party committees of backbenchers to occupy their time and take their minds off plotting. He was worried about Labour politicians falling for the enticements of corruption and sleaze offered by business interests and sectional groups. He urged Labour councillors and MPs to stay at arm's length from contractors and potential contractors, and devised some of the earliest codes and standards of good practice.

Morrison made enemies, because he gave a lead and was successful at challenging sectarians and sectional interests, including some trades unions, whom more devious politicians might have stroked. It was ironical that one dubbed 'as artful as a barrel-load of monkeys' was himself so distrusted that he never achieved his great and almost obsessive aim of becoming leader of his party – and hence sadly judged his own remarkable political career as a failure.

We felt it worthwhile to reissue our biography, with its text unchanged, to celebrate a man who helped shape the Labour Party, whose modernising approach is an important element in New Labour, who had great national and local achievements to his name, and who can still teach us today some important lessons about politics and government. He was also personally a fascinating and complex character, whose life and career can enlighten us about the strange people who pursue political office, and the damage this pursuit inflicts on their private lives. His story also shows how little has changed at the top in politics: Labour cabinets were never happy bands of colleagues. While his life enables us to see Peter Mandelson's own career in context, perhaps he illuminates our understanding of others too. He was above all an achiever, and he left many aspects of British public life the better for his activities.

Bernard Donoughue
George Jones
November 2000

Acknowledgements

Many people have helped us to write this book; a mention of some of their names here is but a small sign of our gratitude. We would like to thank the Warden of Nuffield College and Lady Morrison of Lambeth for asking us to undertake this task, for allowing us complete freedom and for being ready at all times with advice when we required it. We must record our thanks to the Nuffield Foundation which awarded us one of their small grants to help us travel around the country and interview many of Lord Morrison's contemporaries. The London School of Economics and Political Science over the period of our study put at our disposal the services of a number of able research assistants who engaged in a variety of tedious but essential chores for which we are most grateful. We would also like to thank the Warden and his colleague at Nuffield College, Mr P. M. Williams, together with Professor P. W. Campbell of the University of Reading, Professor P. J. O. Self of the London School of Economics and Political Science, Leslie and Freda Stone and Elly Shodell, for reading the draft and for commenting on it so carefully.

We wish to thank the great number of publishers and authors whose works we have cited and from which we have drawn quotations. The Librarians of the British Library of Economics and Political Science; Nuffield College, Oxford; the Beaverbrook Library; and Churchill College, Cambridge, provided us with excellent facilities and gave us access to and permission to quote from collections in their libraries. We owe a debt to a number of librarians in London who allowed us access to their collections at Lambeth, Hackney and in the City at the Guildhall Library. A variety of organizations with which Lord Morrison was associated made their archives freely available to us; for this service we must thank the Labour Party, the London Labour Party, the Woolwich Labour Party, the Hackney Borough Council, the Greater London Council, the London Boroughs' Association, the Metropolitan Water Board, the Lee Conservancy Catchment Board, the South-Eastern Electricity Board and the British Board of Film Censors. We must thank the Keeper of the Public

Record Office for access to governmental records of the period, especially Cabinet and departmental papers. We also thank the literary executors and the official biographers of Hugh Gaitskell and Ramsay MacDonald for generously allowing us access to their papers. Mr R. Boon kindly gave us use of a collection of papers relating to Morrison (described in references as Morrison–Boon papers). For the many press sources we have used we must thank the Curator of the British Museum and his staff at the Newspaper Library, Colindale, and the Librarians of the *Daily Express* and the *Evening News*. Mr H. G. Pearson, the Department Records Officer at the Home Office, and his colleague Mr P. Bradshaw were always most helpful and we are in great debt to them. We must also thank Mr S. S. Wilson for his kind assistance.

Above all we must thank the large number of people whom we interviewed about Morrison. With one exception, everyone we approached agreed to talk to us, and we very much enjoyed and appreciated the helpful reception we were given. Without their co-operation this book could not have been written. Many of them also showed us papers and letters which were valuable supplements to their memories. Other people kindly wrote to us about their recollections and when we have used them as a source we have cited them in the notes.

Finally we record our thanks to our wives Carol Donoughue and Diana Jones for putting up once again with the trials and tribulations that so disrupt family life when an enterprise of this kind is undertaken.

Abbreviations

ABC	Aerated Bread Company
ARP	Air Raid Precautions
ASLEF	Associated Society of Locomotive Engineers and Firemen
BDF	Brixton Discussion Forum
CM	*Council Minutes*
H and KG	*Hackney and Kingsland Gazette*
HS	*Hackney Spectator*
ibid.	in the same place
ILP	Independent Labour Party
IMTA	Institute of Municipal Treasurers and Accountants
JIC	Joint Industrial Council
LCC	London County Council
LCS	London Co-operative Society
LLP	London Labour Party
LNER	London and North-Eastern Railway Company
loc. cit.	in the place quoted
LPCR	*Labour Party Annual Conference Report*
LSE	London School of Economics and Political Science
MR	Municipal Reform
NAC	National Administrative Council (of the ILP)
NATSOPA	National Society of Operative Printers and Assistants
NCL	National Council of Labour
NEC	National Executive Committee (of the Labour Party)
NUC	National Union of Clerks
NUGMW	National Union of General and Municipal Workers
NUR	National Union of Railwaymen
op. cit.	in the work quoted
OTC	Officers' Training Corps
PLP	Parliamentary Labour Party

PPS	Parliamentary Private Secretary
RACS	Royal Arsenal Co-operative Society
SDF	Social Democratic Federation
SDP	Social Democratic Party
TGWU	Transport and General Workers' Union
TUC	Trades Union Congress
UN	United Nations
WTA	Workers' Travel Association

PART ONE
1888–1940

Section I: The Making of a Politician 1888–1918

Chapter 1

The Beginning[1]

When Herbert Stanley Morrison was born on 3 January 1888 he seemed healthy enough; but within three days he was totally blind in his right eye. Instead of sparkling blue, its centre was a grey blob. He was handicapped and disfigured for life. Apparently the midwife failed to clean his eye thoroughly after birth, thus allowing an infection to destroy it. The effects of her negligence were to shape his life, as much as did his parents and his childhood background. Yet despite this disaster he could claim 'my one eye served me well'.[2]

Morrison's mother, Priscilla Caroline Lyon, daughter of a carpet fitter, was a genuine Cockney, born and brought up within the sound of Bow Bells in the East End of London. She had been a maidservant at the London Hospital, Mile End Road, working in the wards and at a near-by boarding-house for doctors, where the landlady, Mrs Morrison, was the widow of a Customs official. Her son, Henry, met Priscilla. He was captivated and threw over the girl to whom he was already engaged. They were married at St Peter's Parish Church, Stepney, in January 1872. She was twenty-three and he was twenty-two.

Henry Morrison was also a Cockney and like his wife spoke in a strong London accent. His distant forebears may have left Scotland to seek their fortunes in London, but he did not come from Scotland. His first job had been as a brass moulder, but when the fumes injured his chest he was advised to seek an outdoor occupation. In 1873, therefore, he enrolled as a police constable in the Metropolitan Police Force at the Brixton station, in south London. He was tall and powerful, with a handsome bearded face reminiscent of Edward VII. A dominating, authoritarian personality, he was a strong Tory who supported the established social and political order with such devotion that he regarded criticism of it as wicked. He valued an ordered society divided into classes, and his highest good was a steady job, through which, he believed, by hard work and thrift, a man might rise from one class to another; his greatest fear was a lapse into the worthless, insecure proletariat. He was loyal to the Crown and a keen upholder of the law. During the late 1880s and early 1890s the increasingly assertive trade union movement and the proponents of the newfangled socialism organized many demonstrations, marches and strikes in London, which meant extra duties for the metropolitan police, loss of rest days, but no extra pay. Henry Morrison played his part in defending the Queen's Peace against these people, whom he regarded as irresponsible anarchists. He had helped to form a solid barrier of policemen across an entrance to Trafalgar Square in 1886, when the crowd, prevented from attending a trade union meeting, ran amok along Pall Mall. And in July 1888 he was on duty during the strike of the match girls at Bryant and May's.

In the home he was stern and domineering: a difficult man for his children or visitors to get to know. Henry was not a cruel man: he rarely hit his children, but he was not warm or close to them. A daughter-in-law claimed that 'one thought twice before approaching him'. He seemed at times irritable and touchy, at others sunk in depression. His weakness for alcohol was such that his wife feared that he would lose his job, and she would send young Bert (as Herbert was known until 1911) to keep an eye on his father as he sat in a nearby public house, and to tell her when he had had enough. Bert was terrified lest his father should notice him as he peeped around the door or jumped up to look through the glass.

Bert's mother was a quite different personality. To him she embodied all motherly virtues, and on her death he wrote in his diary that she was the 'holiest, perfectest, purest mother the earth has ever shown'. His earliest memory of her was as a 'stout, comfortable-looking woman . . . serving beef with a magnificent batter pudding and getting me to drink milk'. She was warm and affectionate to her children, never too busy to comfort them or play with them, often to the neglect of her household chores. When Bert and his sister Edie came home from school in the winter, she would warm their frozen hands in her armpits. She organized games for the children around the kitchen range, and she had a penchant for practical jokes. She would attach thread to a sweet or a coin which she placed on the garden path, and, when one of the children tried to pick it up, she would jerk the cord. She also joined with the children in sing-songs. Her husband rarely played with them. He just sat in his chair asleep, or sulking, as if jealous of the fun they were having or resentful of his wife's closeness to the children.

He had, perhaps, two grievances against his wife. It was family gossip that he would have been promoted to the rank of sergeant if he had been prepared to move to Blackheath, but his wife refused to leave the area she had come to love so well. He remained a constable and this rankled. Secondly, she resisted his frequent demands for sexual intercourse when his shift-work brought him home in the morning or afternoon and when he was under the influence of drink. By 1888 she had borne him seven children in under ten years. Her figure was plump; and she was tired by the problems of looking after a large family.

She wanted no more. Henry perhaps vented some of his frustration on his offspring.

Bert had four sisters and two brothers. Florence, who died soon after birth, he never knew. The eldest was Harry, born on 5 May 1878. After failing as a grocer, he became a clerk at Whitbread's brewery, where he remained until retiring as a chief clerk. Minnie was the eldest sister; she served behind the counter of a sub-post office, and died in her twenties. Lucy, the third sister, remained a spinster. She started work as a waitress at a café and became a manageress of a grocery and dairy products shop. Frank began as a butcher's boy and ended up owning a number of butcher's shops in south London. Although Bert kept in touch with them all later, he was never on such close terms with them as with his sister, Edith, born just over two years before him. As children they played and went almost everywhere together. When their mother died, Edie took over the responsibilities of running the house and looking after her father and Bert. In character and temperament she was like her mother, and Bert loved her deeply, remaining close to her all through his life. He visited her often at her home in Brighton, and she paid close attention to his career, always ready to comfort him in difficult times. She married a compositor, who was killed in the First World War. For the rest of her life she reared her family and watched over her brother.

The occupations of his family indicate clearly the class from which Morrison came, the lower middle class. His father was in a steady, secure job and, with a wage around thirty shillings a week, was fairly well paid, at least in comparison with many working and lower middle class people. His uniform was provided, his holidays were with pay, he had a rent allowance, a pension was assured and he was looked up to in this most respectable position. The area in which they lived, Brixton, the hub of Lambeth, near to the main highways of Brixton Road and Brixton Hill, was lower middle class, inhabited by other policemen, even detectives, clerks in the City or at main railway stations, commercial travellers, skilled mechanics and assistants from West End shops. Charles Booth classified Ferndale Road, where Bert was born, as 'fairly comfortable', but it was close to very working class areas of 'poverty' or 'moderate poverty', such as Walworth, North Lambeth or Kennington where Charlie Chaplin was growing up at the same time. To the south were 'well-to-do' and 'comfortable' areas, so that from their mid-way position the Morrisons could observe what they could aspire to as well as that to which they feared to fall.[3] They felt that they were 'a cut above their neighbours'. Edie said 'we felt we were something' and Morrison recalled that 'the modest Morrison home was the envy and admiration of the neighbours'. Morrison described the life as hard, since the upkeep of a large family ate deeply into his father's pay; yet it cannot be said that they were poverty-stricken. Morrison said 'we did not know what it was to go really hungry'; they had meat and milk, never went without shoes and occasionally had pocket money: a farthing every Saturday, shared with another boy, for clearing out the back yard.[4] Photographs of the family taken in the 1890s show no evidence of hardship, and at Minnie's wedding carriages were hired to take guests to and from the church.

The house in which Bert was born, 240 Ferndale Road, was apparently a double-fronted detached house, larger than the common single-fronted terraced houses near by.[5] Half-way up its windows were brass rods for net curtains, a sure sign of respectability. Also in the house lived the owner, George Hancock, a milkman, who kept his horse and cart in sheds at the bottom of the garden. Mrs Morrison helped him, scalding the churns in her copper boiler and assisting with the book-keeping. His round prospered and he used his profits to buy houses in the area. In 1895 he gave the Morrisons, as a reward for their services, a house in Mordaunt Street, No. 39, only a few minutes' walk from their previous home. He gave it on condition that when the parents died it went to Bert, of whom he was very fond. They would play and go out on the rounds together and Bert would ride on the horse. His early days at Ferndale Road, before he went to school, were the happiest of his childhood. Most exciting was the fire station next door. He went there often, to clamber over the engines and to dress up in the firemen's helmets and boots. In Ferndale Road itself were a variety of small businesses and shops; and across the road from their home was a sweet-shop where Bert and Edie would spend their precious farthings on caramels, which they would take turns to suck, and 'jumbo-chains' – long pieces of liquorice. Most fascinating was the farthing lucky dip, a box into which they would plunge their hands and collect some trinket.

The house in Mordaunt Street was single-fronted, in the middle of a terrace, with three bedrooms upstairs, two main rooms downstairs which became one when a partition was moved back, a kitchen and scullery, and a small back garden. This house was quite suitable for the smaller family which the Morrison household became as the children left home and took jobs. Expenses were less; there was no rent to pay and fewer mouths to feed. The high spot of the week was Sunday evening when all the brothers and sisters together with their friends assembled. The partition was folded back and musical instruments were distributed. There was a piano: another sign of a respectable home. Bert joined in, at first banging the lid of a saucepan. They played and sang the popular ballads of the day. Their father rarely joined in the jollifications, but would 'do the miserable act'.

Their mother would take Bert and Edie to the music-hall, to the gallery at the Brixton Theatre or the Empress Hall. At Christmas their father would take them to the Old Vic for a pantomime. In his top hat and frock coat, looking the image of the Prince of Wales, he would force his way to the head of a queue, brandishing his stick and bellowing 'make way'. There were also the family holidays to Ramsgate, at the same back-street boarding-house at the same time each year. Bert loved to watch the minstrels on the sands and listened again and again to their sketches and songs. A regular feature of Sundays was a visit to grandmother Morrison at her hospital boarding-house, where there were delicious rock cakes and brandy snaps. At home Bert found an atmosphere of comfort and affection; he was cuddled and fussed. He was to search for it again for the rest of his life. At home the only jarring note was his father. When he went to school, however, he found a cruel world.

In 1893 he started at the Stockwell Road Board School, a few minutes' walk from his home. He was terrified and had to be dragged there by Edie. He gripped the railings and had to be pulled away. The school had opened in 1877: a barrack-like building, holding 470 students with fifty to a class. The ground floor was for infants up to age seven, the next floor for girls and the top for boys. It made a lasting impression on him. 'That school of mine – I can see it, feel it, smell it now. Dark paint, heavy walls, a feeling that the roof was falling on you.' Sunlight was so scarce that gas-jets burned all day in the class-rooms; he was frightened by their flickering across gaudy but grim biblical pictures. The smell of gas, mixed with that of urine from the small lavatories, pervaded everything. Beating was common. He recalled: 'There was a general impression that small boys could absorb knowledge quite efficiently through the nether portions of the anatomy.' After being appointed stair monitor, Bert slid down the banisters, was caught, caned six times and deprived of his first position of responsibility. In 1924 he said that he had never loved those school-days and that he dreaded chemistry and algebra, but he was never guilty of 'hopping the wag',[6] i.e. playing truant.

When he was eleven he was transferred to the St Andrew's Church of England School, Lingham Street, since Stockwell Road had no upper standard VII for boys. The school was as gloomy as his first, and had few amenities: one small playground, one drinking tap and trough lavatories. At the end of each afternoon the whole school assembled in the hall, 'and in the sullen twilight of a winter's afternoon we would intone the somewhat dreary hymn, "The day thou gavest, Lord, is ended" '. For religious knowledge Bert won his only prize. He was ever indebted to this school for introducing him to literature. He had to learn many poems, which he found valuable, for 'no one can become word-perfect in Gray's *Elegy*, which was a set piece for recitation, without in time responding to the beauty of the lines'. He loved reading and was a frequent borrower from the school library. The most memorable event of his school career was being chosen as the school's orator to deliver a formal speech on Trafalgar Day. Twelve of the most likely candidates were lined up in the playground, each declaimed, and Bert was chosen: his first attempt at public speaking. Just when he was beginning to appreciate school and learning, he had to leave, a fortnight after he was fourteen, on 17 January 1902, having obtained his labour certificate to say he was a satisfactory student. In 1960 Morrison said: 'I shall always be grateful for my elementary education – that is, all there was of it. I know I am a bit of an inverted snob, but I am rather proud of it. I don't have any grievance against the education system that kept me out of the secondary schools which hardly then existed – I was just born at the wrong time. But they taught me the three R's, and they taught me to like reading which is one of the greatest blessings of life.'[7]

Of these days Morrison wrote: 'I tended to be more solitary than others because of the blindness in one eye. Children can be heartless and cruel about physical defects, and the fact that I could not see as easily and quickly as they could often meant that I was left out of the more active games and was thrown on my own resources. They called me "one eye" and "ball of fat".'[8] He also suffered from fallen arches which further limited his agility. It is always difficult for a policeman's son to be accepted fully as a member of a gang of schoolboys, and virtually impossible for one with a blind eye and flat feet. He was also gullible. They would dig a hole in a garden path, cover it with sticks and lead him into it. He did not allow himself to be consumed by self-pity, but remained defiant in the face of their wounding insensitivity. He never spoke of his humiliations at home and tried to be on good terms with the boys who hurt him so much. Most often he would look on while they played, and he was only invited to join in when it was impossible otherwise to make up a team. Then he asserted himself, claiming that the cricket bat was not the proper weight or length, and if he was bowled out, he would invariably dispute it and persist in staying in. He was so determined that the boys found it impossible to argue with him. One said 'if he had an idea on anything no one could convince him'.

Not fully a part of any group of boys, he turned to girls and children younger than himself. Girls tended to take pity on him and to fuss him, and in turn he was affectionate. They would sit together on doorsteps and talk, or walk around the streets or ride on a tram. He liked to take the neighbours' children for walks in their prams, or collect their parents' shopping. Most often he was alone, roaming around the streets, roller-skating down the roads, running errands, like fetching the family's bread in a pillow case. At times he gave expression to a mischievous sense of fun, inherited from his mother. His favourite trick was to tie thread to a number of door knockers and to contrive to bang them simultaneously, then from a hiding-place he loved to watch the inhabitants as they opened their doors at the same time to find no one there.

When alone he loved to read. He devoured the comics he could buy from the sweet counters. Most cost only a halfpenny and were frowned on by teachers and parents. He also read the more respectable adventure stories of Henty, Ballantyne and Fenn, which he bought in cheap editions or borrowed from the school library. He read, with great pleasure at their vivid language and sound, W. T. Stead's *Penny Poets*, and he revelled in the pocket novelettes of Edie's, where wicked landlords menaced beautiful heroines. To get money to buy a precious book, he would deceive his parents. Once a week his mother would send him to Lambeth Baths for his weekly scrub, giving him a penny for his return fare. He usually walked to save it, and sometimes failed to have the bath. He was absorbed in his reading. His schoolmates found him 'studious'. His father was annoyed. 'Put it on the fire,' he would shout, fearing perhaps that Bert would strain his one good eye and become wholly blind.

Morrison later summed up his childhood. 'I was moody, lacked self-confidence. I was unhappy and I kept apart from the other youngsters. I became introspective. You know what that means – it may crack you up or it may make you determined to stand on your own.' He said to himself: 'You've got to stand on your own feet.'[9] In 1946 a journalist, after interviewing Morrison, wrote: 'This isolation drove him into himself. . . . It drove him to self-assertion.'[10]

Having left school, Bert had to find a job. His first choice was to be a compositor like Edith's boy-friend. But his father opposed for fear that his eye would be damaged. Bert then suggested going as a clerk at some City firm, like the sons of a policeman who lived near, but again his father refused, and for the same reason. The upshot was that he went to work for his brother Harry and his sister-in-law Kitty in a small grocery and provision store they had just opened in Streatham. Harry's ambitions had also been frustrated by his father who had forbidden him to seek a career on the stage. Bert's work was to sweep and tidy the shop, run messages, make up and deliver orders. His wages were five shillings a week and he lived in. He described this situation as 'not too bad'. Harry and Kitty were good companions and full of fun. She recalled Bert as 'dreamy'; his mind seemed far away from making up the orders as he weighed the soda or sugar. He was still pestered by boys who shouted at him through the shop window or as he took out the orders. She often had to chase them away. She felt that the hostility of these boys was the source of his drive. It was as if he said: 'I'll show you. I'll get further than you.'

His brother's shop failed to prosper and it had to close down, so Bert in 1903 went to work as an errand boy for the Brixton branch of Walton, Hassell and Port, grocers and wine and spirit merchants. It was near his home and so he returned to live at Mordaunt Street. He earned seven shillings a week, but the work was harder than at his brother's. The orders were heavier and he had to deliver them over longer distances. He had to carry baskets which weighed thirty to forty pounds fully laden or push them in a hand cart. He trudged the streets well into the night. His feet and ankles ached painfully, because of his fallen arches and through wearing shoes that were ill fitting. He said: 'What was on my mind was my feet.'[11] At the end of the day he took up to three-quarters of an hour to drag himself home over a journey which normally took ten minutes. When he was free he would queue for the gallery at a music-hall or theatre in Brixton. He was particularly thrilled by the music and plot of *Tannhäuser*, performed by the Carl Rosa Opera Company, and he searched for the book to read the story. He also loved to go to the melodramas at the Elephant and Castle Theatre.

While he was at the Brixton shop he first became interested in politics, around the age of sixteen. At home politics were rarely discussed; the family followed the father's unquestioning Conservatism. Bert's political consciousness was first awakened by street orators. He had been attracted to the great preachers whose thunderings from the pulpits crammed the churches. He recalled seeking out whichever church on Sunday night had some famous preacher. He also sought out street orators on evenings and Sundays at their sites in Brockwell Park or Rushcroft Road. He listened most attentively to the temperance reformers,[12] whose descriptions of the evils of drink struck a chord. He saw with his own eyes the degradation brought about by excessive drinking. On his way home from the shop he would stand outside public houses and watch the drunks come out. Outside the Atlantic Hotel, Brixton: 'One night there was a fight: a man was knocked down and a dark fluid made its way down the pavement to the gutter. I was really alarmed – it must be that the man's head had cracked and this was blood. But I was wrong: he had had a bottle of stout in his pocket; the fluid was stout, not blood.'[13] This incident so shocked him that he began to wonder why working people who really could not afford it spent so much on drink. He decided that the reason was because of their bad housing conditions; 'extreme poverty, with its slums, boredom and helplessness' drove men and women to the gin palace and beer bar. His interest in social conditions was aroused.

At about the same time another orator[14] played a most important part in shaping Bert's development. He gave Bert 'The Best Advice I Ever Had'.[15] The orator earned some extra money by 'reading' heads at sixpence a consultation. Phrenology was at that time regarded by many as a respectable science, and parents often consulted phrenologists about their children's future careers. One Friday night in Rushcroft Road, outside the Tate Library and opposite the Town Hall, Morrison listened as the speaker concluded his harangue with an appeal that phrenology 'would tell you about yourself'. Morrison had just sixpence to last out the week. He hesitated, then went forward, taking a gamble which he instantly regretted, yet which he later felt changed his life. The 'man of science' spent what seemed an interminable period measuring and feeling Morrison's head and then spoke: 'You haven't a bad head. Not a bad head at all. A good head in fact. A head out of the ordinary. There's something in you that hasn't come out yet. You must let it out. Until it comes out, you will never be happy. 'Once it comes out, you will discover all sorts of things that you don't suspect today. I saw you "mooning" just now. That's what I mean. You only "moon" because you can't understand what's in you. That's what's making you lonely. I'll bet you are lonely, aren't you? Good. Then study.'

'Why study?' queried the young Morrison.

'Because,' replied the man, speaking slowly, 'you'll be a man some day and I shall be proud to have had you on this box. If you will only use your time well, you have a great future. You are an idealist. From your head, you may one day be Prime Minister. That ridge above your eyes – that's originality. A full and rounded forehead – memory.

'What do you read?' he asked.

'Boy's stories, *Deadwood Dick, Mysterious Gutch, Eastern Vengeance.*'

'Better read rubbish than nothing, for it's good to read. But why not try better stuff? History, economics, biography and so on. Try it. You should get good literature into that promising head of yours. You've got a good head.'[16]

The impact of this confrontation on Bert was tremendous.[17] He had had no encouragement from his home or school, but now the renowned orator and scientist had told him that if he studied he could be Prime Minister. Books became even more of a passion. Out of his wages he saved a few pence a week to buy them; he borrowed them from the local library and haunted the reading rooms. He began with Macaulay's *History of England.* Then he tried Green's *Readings from English History* which 'fired my imagination. Through it I became aware for the first time of social problems, and I began to wonder how the conditions I saw around me in London could be improved.' He read social studies of the industrial revolution and the working class. 'Questions of bad housing, high rents and inadequate education took on a real meaning for me. The thrill of learning seized me – one of the greatest joys I had ever known.'

This reading drove him to socialism.[18] He was not born into it, nor bred in it, nor was there any sudden revelation. It was a gradual intellectual conversion. His commitment was sealed in October 1906 when he joined the most active socialist organization in the area where he lived, the Brixton branch of the Independent Labour Party. He joined because it seemed to be about to achieve something. The General Election of 1906 had returned twenty-nine Labour Members of Parliament and the ILP was active in local government with members on many councils, including Lambeth. He left it within three months, because he felt it was not socialist enough. Following Robert Blatchford's line in *Clarion*, he believed that Labour MPs were identical to Liberals, propounding mere palliatives.[19] He switched to the Social Democratic Federation which had an active branch near the shop in Pimlico, to which he was transferred.

He was around nineteen when he was promoted to be a junior shop assistant, the second hand, at Walton, Hassell and Port's branch at Lupus Street, near Victoria Station. His wages were at first eight shillings a week, rising to ten shillings when he became first hand, and he lived in. At the start his principal task was to keep the shop clean. The bugbear of his life was the almost daily cleaning of the enormous plate-glass window. Although he spent hours scraping and wiping he could never get it properly clean: a perpetual disappointment. He also served behind the counter, and had 'the pleasure of meeting various types of the human race, from prostitutes to la-di-da ladies'.[20]

Pimlico presented a varied cross-section of people: most of the customers were working men and women, skilled, unskilled or out of work. There was also a number of the shabby-genteel who insisted on calling Pimlico 'South Belgravia' and behaved in the shop in a grand manner, imitating their social idols in real Belgravia. Although the work was demanding, he was brisk and cheerful. Packaged goods were rare and most things, like sugar, tea and coffee, had to be weighed and wrapped, which required considerable manual dexterity. Mental acumen was also needed to calculate the costs. A particularly difficult operation was to measure exactly the right amount of treacle to be tapped from a large and grimy canister into a customer's receptacle. The manager was kindly, but was a stickler for neat appearance. He expected the assistants' aprons always to be spotlessly white. This presented Bert with a problem, especially when serving black treacle, for some invariably found its way to his apron. Bert had also to deliver goods over long distances in a truck which took considerable pushing, even when unladen, and before delivery he had to canvass for orders.

He was greatly honoured when the manager granted his request to be allowed to dress the window. 'I think that most of all I enjoyed my efforts at window-dressing. I regarded it as an art, and if anyone had dared to say it wasn't, I would have defended fiercely my opinion. For from it, I got all the joy of creation. I had done it all myself, and could step back on the pavement and get from my window all the satisfaction and all the divine doubt of an artist. To me it was not a mundane arrangement of goods and price-tickets. To me it was an expression of proportion, of colour, of balance.'[21] He became the star window dresser. In that task he revealed his aim in whatever job he undertook – to bring order to chaos. His first instinct was: 'Let's make it tidy.'[22]

The hours at the shop were long: from 8 a.m. to 9.30 p.m. on Mondays, Tuesdays and Wednesdays; to 10 p.m. on Fridays; to midnight on Saturdays and to 5 p.m. on Thursdays, the early closing day, when he would rush off to queue for the gallery at a theatre. Sunday was a day off, when no meals were provided at the shop, and Bert went home. During the rest of the week all meals were provided by the manager's wife. The manager and his family lived on the second floor. Bert shared a room on the top, third floor, at the front with John Pretty who was first hand when he began.[23] They could not see to the street below, since a brick wall jutted up in front of the window. The room held two single beds, some chairs, a wash-stand and basin, and by each bed was a tin trunk for their belongings. Bert's trunk, which he always carefully locked, contained a number of little tin boxes in which he kept his money; sixpence for holidays, sixpence for clothes, sixpence for books, all were carefully saved each week. And in the trunk were his precious books. Pretty's most vivid memory of Morrison was his passion for reading. At night after undressing he would get into bed, light a candle, put it on his trunk and read until the early hours. 'Why don't you pack it in?' Pretty would say, to no avail. Pretty recalled him reading books by Blatchford and Chiozza Money. Morrison himself has told of his reading at this time. After his long day at the shop he would walk to Wilton Road near by, to a branch of Lockhart's Dining Rooms, a working-class café, and would remain there for an hour over a halfpenny mug of cocoa, reading and reading, as the aroma of sausages and onions wafted by. The manager became difficult. 'He started, when I ordered cocoa, giving me tea or coffee and I really wanted cocoa. He said nothing and I said nothing. But, having guessed the trouble, out of my limited means I also ordered a penny cheese cake. Thereupon I got a half-penny cup of cocoa regularly.'[24] At closing time he would return to the shop to be in bed by midnight, reading until sleep hit him. 'I rose in the morning an hour earlier than usual. After dressing in my heatless room above the grocer's shop, I wrapped myself in a blanket and read as much as I could before the grocer's wife called me to breakfast.'[25] Sometimes it was so cold that concentration was impossible and he was so tired that he had to read sections over many times. He read on trains, at libraries and at home. Edith said 'he always had his head stuffed in a book'.

From this time until 1912, a period of about five years, he read, with an intensity never again to be achieved, a wider range of books than he would ever tackle again. The works of Chiozza Money were especially influential: his articles in the *Morning Leader*, and his book *Riches and Poverty*, a five-shilling purchase which Morrison claimed made him a socialist. He read Blatchford's *Merrie England* and *Britain for the British*, Kropotkin's *Appeal to the Young* and *Fields, Factories and Workshops*, Marx's first nine chapters of *Capital* and his *Communist Manifesto*. He read Engels and Kautsky, in Twentieth Century Press translations. The works of Ernest Belfort Bax were eagerly devoured, for he was an idol of young men in the SDF. He also read works by Huxley, Darwin, Lecky and Spencer whose *First Principles* impressed him. He liked Ruskin and Arnold whose *Culture and Anarchy* and *Literature and Dogma* he regarded as two of the four books he would most advise the young to read:[26] the others being Green's *History of England* and the *Poems and Songs of Robert Burns*. He read the fiction and essays of G. B. Shaw, H. G. Wells, Arnold Bennett, Jack London, Frank Norris, John Galsworthy, G. K. Chesterton and Hilaire Belloc, and he liked books on London, its history and government. Most of the books were published in cheap editions at sixpence or a shilling each. Relying for information on what to read from socialist magazines like *Clarion*, *Justice* and the *Labour Leader*, he would comb the book shops and libraries. He said 'reading was my further education'. It awakened his imagination and made him a critic of every facet of society. He also attempted at this time to learn languages, buying elementary grammar books in French, German and Russian, but he never got beyond the first few pages.[27] In later life he always emphasized the importance of reading, listing the books he read at this time with pride.

He was very serious minded. He kept a diary for a few years, 1905, 1906 and 1907, which contained few personal entries. Most items were about politics. During parliamentary sessions he summarized in six to eight lines the business of the day, noting the significance of events, recording opinions and statements and commenting on the procedure. He jotted down notes about local government in London, the work of the LCC, the opening of a generating station or a new bridge. He copied out unemployment statistics from trade union returns. He covered international affairs too, such as the peace treaty which concluded the Russo-Japanese war.

Pretty, his room-mate, found Bert lacking in humour and obsessed with politics and socialism. He would ask him to come to football or cricket matches, but Bert refused, and in turn would try to persuade Pretty to come to some political meeting. He had no hobbies and showed no interest in girls. He was always on about how the country should be run, what the government and MPs should do, complaining that the government did not look after the interests of the working class. He once said to Pretty: 'Wouldn't you like to get on and get into Parliament?' Pretty replied: 'Whatever for? We're not educated. We can't speak.' Bert retorted that speaking should come simply to anyone. 'You give me a shilling and we'll get six others and hire a hall and hold a meeting.' This was done. He hired a hall in Effra Road, Brixton, and stuck a notice outside to announce the meeting. Only a handful turned up. Bert had organized his first meeting; the most famous political organizer in British politics had started his career inauspiciously. He also tried to get Pretty to sign a petition calling for trams to be allowed to cross the bridges over the Thames and not to stop at each end, and urged him to campaign for shorter hours in the shop. The manager knew about Bert's socialist beliefs and treated him with tolerant amusement.[28] Bert was easy to get on with and never lost his temper when needled. After Pretty left the shop, Bert took his place as first hand. He went with a new assistant on a day trip from Ramsgate to Boulogne, his first time abroad. He was sick all the way out, ate a peach at Boulogne, was sick all the way back, and once in England tucked into a plate of sumptuous boiled haddock which he felt was the finest English dish.[29]

Of his time at the shop in Pimlico, he said, 'it was a dog's life', but they were 'happy days'. He always recalled nostalgically the sawdust-covered floor and the smell of paraffin and firewood. He regarded his time spent as a shop assistant at all three shops as 'my apprenticeships'.[30] It gave him the chance to observe people and their oddities, the variety and inequality of the Edwardian street scene. 'You met the human race there. There were so many millions of people who were so very, very poor, and a few million were very, very rich, and I thought this was a raw deal and I'm going to alter it if I can with other people.'[31]

Chapter 2

The Politician Emerges

In July 1907 Bert joined the Westminster branch of the Social Democratic Federation. It consisted of about six to twelve members who met in the living-room of the house of Joe Butler, founder of the branch in 1906, who was Secretary of the Royal Army Clothing Union. Bert quickly struck up a friendship with H. J. Stenning, for a time the branch's Secretary. They formed the extreme wing of the branch, 'the impossibilists'. For instance in April 1908 the SDP* fought a parliamentary by-election in the Haggerston division of Shoreditch. Their candidate was a founder member, Herbert Burrows. To Bert and his cronies Burrows' election address[1] was reformist and gradualist. They called a special meeting of the branch and Bert moved a vote of censure, which was lost.[2] Also, one day while seeking orders along Brompton Road, Bert spied the figure of Philip Snowden,† limping along the pavement with his wife. He tore a sheet from his order book and hastily scribbled: 'When, Mr Philip Snowden, will you move this resolution in the Commons – "That in the opinion of this House there is no real remedy for the problems of poverty short of Socialism"? Cease talking reform and advocate social revolution. From "Unattached".' He thrust it into Snowden's hand and scampered away without waiting to observe the reaction.[3] With Stenning as chairman, Bert embarked upon his career of public speaking, from a barrel at the corner of Tachbrook Street and Warwick Street, within ten minutes' walk of his shop. Here he concluded his denunciatory speeches with the final words of Marx's *Communist Manifesto*: 'Workers of the World unite. You have nothing to lose but your chains.' He was never happier than

---

* In August 1907 the Social Democratic Federation changed its name to Social Democratic Party.

† Then a leading ILP figure and later Chancellor of the Exchequer in the Labour governments of 1924 and 1929–31.

when sending 'a shiver of fear down the backs of the petty bourgeoisie'.[4]

The branch was a pleasant social club for the young revolutionaries, and cheap too, membership costing only a few pence a month. To them socialism and revolution were everything. They called each other 'comrade' and felt dedicated to a cause. They were not religious. Bert's home was in no way devout. He had been packed off to Sunday School on Sunday mornings, so as to be out of the way of his mother preparing Sunday dinner, but he had dropped that when he started work. Now he was an atheist, believing that the materialist conception of history had no place for the supernatural. Indeed he objected to the SDP being open to people with religious beliefs. He liked to think of himself as 'an atheist monk', in the sense of being dedicated to his cause and abjuring all distractions of the flesh. He was ascetic, neither smoking nor drinking, both from conviction and poverty; and despite their appeal to him, he avoided girls, until the manager's daughter overcame his defences. He brought her home to meet his family and they liked her, and he had tea with her family on Sundays. Stenning was furious and told him to stop this nonsense which was interfering with his socialist work. Bert dutifully gave her up, much to the dismay of his family.

Just after his nineteenth birthday, in January 1907, soon after he came to the shop in Pimlico, his mother died. She had been an invalid for some time. She took to her bed and rarely went outside, except to stand at the front door and gaze into the street. Edith looked after the household, getting up at 6 a.m. to start the chores and not going to bed until midnight. She had to care for her mother, bandaging her ulcerated legs. Finally Mrs Morrison died, aged fifty-eight, after a bout of bronchial pneumonia. Her death probably contributed to Bert's intense emotionalism at this time.

In 1908 he found a better job. Putting aside his temperance principles, he became a telephone switchboard operator at the bottling stores of Whitbread's brewery, in Britannia Street, near King's Cross. His brother Harry had gone there as a clerk, and when the position became vacant suggested to Bert that he apply, and he sang Bert's praises. The job was landed. His wages shot up to thirty shillings a week, and the hours were shorter and more regular: from nine to six on week-days and till one on Saturdays. He had changed jobs so that he could have more time to work for the socialist cause, and he was proud to have risen to a white collar occupation.[5] He enjoyed the work. He would answer the phone with a cheery 'This is Whitbread's, bottlers of the best beer in the land', or 'We are Whitbread & Co., the largest beer bottlers in the world'.[6] Calls were not frequent and in his cubicle he would pore over his beloved books and write letters and articles to the Brixton press and socialist magazines. He would also hold long phone conversations with Stenning, discussing the latest book or article. When he heard someone coming he would quickly hide what he was doing and pretend to be on the job.

When he came to Whitbread's he was warned by Harry to be careful about his political activities lest he get the sack. So he adopted a pseudonym, H.

Marsden or Marsdon, under which he spoke or wrote to the press. He feared as much for Harry's job as his own, not wanting Harry to be dismissed as a result of finding a job for his brother. Within a year he was confident enough to come out in his own name. In June 1909 he had spoken at South Place as Marsden,[7] but in July at Vassall Road 'our Comrade Morrison spoke to a fair audience, delivering a fine address'.[8] In later years he spoke well of Whitbread's as employers; they never victimized him for his political activities.[9]

Moving to Whitbread's meant that he returned to live at home, where Edith looked after him and their father. She looked forward to Bert coming home in the evening. She wanted someone to talk to, but Bert would want only to read. He said: 'I was an unsocial Socialist.' With the family he was reticent about his socialist activities. Edith found it hard to know what he was doing. Perhaps he feared his father's reactions. Gradually, however, he became active in Brixton; he had spoken outdoors first in Pimlico, then he moved to pitches in Southwark back streets at East Street and Walworth Road; then he set up his soap-box in Brixton, in Effra Road. He was seen by neighbours, and the news spread, 'Have you heard Bert speaking?' It was quite an event in the street.[10]

Herbert's socialism was putting strains on his already tense relationship with his father. Now retired from the force he was drinking more and more, and his wife no longer mediated between them. Edith tried to calm their tempers, but failed. St John Ervine,* a friend of Bert's at this time, recalled a typical incident. 'Old Mr Morrison was a dyed-in-the-wool Tory. One night, when Herbert and I were going somewhere to uplift and reform something, he found that he had forgotten to bring a certain book with him, so he went to his home to pick it up. He was wearing a red tie, an enormity I could never bring myself to commit. I dislike symbols. As we came into the presence of Mr Morrison, the old man glared at his son's tie and exclaimed in wrath, "I see you've got that b—— rag round your neck again!" I fell out of the house as quickly as possible, followed by Herbert, and we both leant against some railings and hooted with laughter.'[11] It was no joking matter. A little later the Secretary of the Brixton SDP sent Bert an invitation card for a meeting, beginning 'Dear Comrade' and ending 'Yours fraternally'. His father saw it, tore it to pieces and threw it on the fire. 'Now Bertie, this has got to stop.' In reply Bert said: 'Dad, I'm not going to cause trouble in the home so I'll go and live elsewhere.'[12] He went upstairs, packed his bags and left, finding lodgings in an attic bed-sitting room near Streatham Station. He was bitter about his father at this time and told friends that his father had no time for a socialist son and had forced him to leave home.[13] Later in life his attitude to his father mellowed and he looked on Henry with more affection. He felt that his father had disapproved of his socialism not solely from political prejudice but because 'he honestly believed that his son would never get or keep a

---

* At this time a clerk in south London; later a dramatist and author.

B

good job if he persisted in his socialist ways', and that he was in for a particularly difficult time because of his one eye.[14]

The job at Whitbread's enabled him to fling himself for a period of over
four years, from 1908 to 1912, into the left-wing political life of Brixton and
south London. He transferred from the Westminster SDP to the Lambeth
branch, remaining a member until late 1909. It was an active branch, holding
ninety-two meetings between July and September 1908.[15] Bert was a regular
speaker at outdoor and indoor meetings, and wrote frequently in the local
press. His first long article was published in the SDP weekly *Justice* in 1909:
a somewhat congested and incoherent piece on the Lloyd George budget,
arguing that it was a 'business' and not a socialist budget, since the land
taxes still allowed landlords to continue fleecing the public.[16] He organized a
tour of slums to expose insanitary property.[17] In March 1909 he spoke to a
local discussion group, the Brixton Discussion Forum, on 'Capitalism: Its
Growth and Outcome'. It was a fiery appeal for revolution, and members
recalled his one eye glaring at the meeting.[18]

Bert was an active member of the Brixton Discussion Forum, being appointed
its Press Secretary in December 1908,[19] his first official appointment in any
organization. It met on Sunday mornings in an upper room of the Carlton
Hall, Tunstall Road, near the foot of Brixton Hill. It was Bert's equivalent of a
university. The range was great: political, social, economic, historical,
cultural, religious and philosophical. At the BDF new worlds and ideas were
opened to him. 'It was here that I came to grips with ideas which had hitherto
merely been printed words on a page. I was beginning to learn that it is not
enough to read. Unless knowledge thus gained is to remain sterile it is necessary to talk, argue and plan.'[20] The procedure of the Forum was for a speaker
to talk for fifteen minutes followed by five-minute contributions from others.
Morrison put a revolutionary Marxist line, liberally spiced with quotations
from Marx whose first volume of *Capital* he brought with him to the meetings.
Indeed he took *Capital* almost everywhere at this time, so that 'on one occasion somebody was heard to remark, "Here comes the class struggle." '[21]
He listened eagerly to the discussions and attacks on his views and quotations,
learning all the time and forming his more considered judgments. It was the
highlight of his week. Proud to be admitted to such an adult society he sought
to emulate his elders by purchasing a three-and-ninepenny bowler hat from
Dunn's, which he wore only for Forum meetings.

At the BDF he championed the working class against the oppression of
capitalism, which expropriated the surplus value produced by labour. The
solution was to expropriate the expropriators so that the wealth produced by
labour would be distributed to labour. That could be achieved only if the
means of production were owned by the state for the common good and not
by individuals for private profit. Since the capitalists would not yield their

power without a fight, parliamentary reforms were useless and a revolution was essential.[22]

Yet increasingly he became dissatisfied with the SDP as a vehicle to achieve these objectives. He first began to move away from it for tactical reasons. He wanted it to affiliate to the Labour Party, so as to permeate it with Marxist ideas. His branch rejected his proposal, not wishing to be identified with a reformist organization. 'You're not class-conscious,' Bert replied, 'but SDP conscious.'[23] He urged affiliation in *Justice*.[24] 'Outside the Labour Party we are mistrusted sectionalists; inside we are comrades in the working-class movement.' He feared that the SDP was becoming 'a political "nobody"'. 'Long enough have we been on the housetops repeating revolutionary phrases; it is about time we came down to earth and seriously considered how we are going to arrive at Social Democracy.' Gestures of defiance, 'hot air' and 'splutter' were no longer enough. In his earliest SDP days he had denounced toryism, liberalism, and labourism. Now he wanted to achieve something here and now. He criticized some members of the SDP for holding a torchlight procession through Clapham. 'Where did that get you? You only frightened people.'[25] He turned to the ILP and parliamentary democracy. In 1910 he joined the Brixton ILP branch. He said: 'The parliamentary struggle is worth taking a hand in.'[26] His view was: 'Send Labour representatives to Parliament and to local bodies. By the amendment of the law, let them make illegal the tyranny and robbery suffered by Labour.'

'By legal enactment we can make industries the property of the People instead of the rich.'[27] Revolution was out. The ILP was not 'a wicked fire eating organisation'; he was not eager for anyone else's blood. 'Our own blood might flow as a consequence, and that is undesirable. If we cannot convert the people by argument, we will give it up – unlike the Ulster Unionists.'[28]

Ramsay MacDonald* helped to woo Morrison away from revolution. At first Morrison assessed MacDonald as an insincere opportunist, indeed one of the 'Labour Fakers and Twisters'. Then at an annual conference of the ILP Morrison, hearing MacDonald speak for the first time, underwent a disturbing experience. He became convinced that MacDonald was sincere and that his views needed serious consideration. Gradually Morrison was won over to MacDonald's distrust of revolution which 'would destroy our forces and lead to reaction'. He was converted to MacDonald's 'Evolutionary Conception of Society on the Biological Analogy'.[29]

At this time Morrison was an inveterate open-air speaker, appearing at most of the sites in south London, such as South Place, Hercules Road, Kennington Triangle, Angell Road, Loughborough Junction station, Walworth Road and Clapham Common. Here he would stand on his soap-box and spout, often in the dim light from street lamps or public houses. In Brixton his two favourite

* Secretary of the Labour Party 1900–11, Treasurer 1912–24, Leader 1911–14 and 1922–31, and Labour's first Prime Minister, 1924 and 1929–31. At the time the outstanding ILP politician.

spots were in Brockwell Park and, for Sunday evenings, in Rushcroft Road. Brockwell Park was for south London a kind of Speakers' Corner. During the summer months thousands walked among the gardens and trees to be shouted at by speakers of every type: temperance reformers, tariff reformers, free traders, suffragettes, atheists, evangelists and cranks of all kinds. Morrison spoke at first for the SDP and then for the ILP. He had 'a cheeky, mischievous way of making points', 'saying simple things to people in a way they understood and liked'.[30] St John Ervine recalled that 'his power over a crowd was remarkable. Sheer good temper and ready street wit enabled him to soothe the most savage breast. I never once saw him nonplussed by an interrupter.' The facility had been acquired after considerable practice and many hard knocks. Friends helped him, including Stenning. James Mylles, the London area organizer of the ILP, 'guided, encouraged, and inspired me with the ideals and enthusiasm of those days'.[31] St John Ervine, five years older than Bert, was a great friend. They trained each other in the art of public speaking. One would deliberately heckle the other, not only to attract a larger crowd, but to pick holes in each other's arguments, and this made their speeches 'more cogent and forceful'.[32] Bert was so good at this that one night while he was heckling an SDP colleague, the poor man hissed out of the corner of his mouth: 'Shut up you little devil, you're overdoing it.' Even he could be floored. Once at Brockley Fields speaking for the Co-operative Movement: 'I pointed out that all the clothes I stood in came from a Co-operative store, whereupon a Cockney woman in the audience ejaculated, "And my God, you look like it." '[33] He was not always able to soothe a hostile crowd. Once he was nearly thrown into the duckpond at Clapham Common, and so he bought a book on judo and practised the holds on the small daughter of his landlady.[34]

He spoke for four or five nights a week, and two or three times on Sundays, battling against critics and apathy. He appealed in the columns of both *Justice* and the *Labour Leader* in 1910[35] to the comrades 'to carefully boycott Anti-Socialist open-air meetings during the season now commencing. It is no infrequent experience to a Socialist speaker to be addressing a very small audience, while, at an Anti-Socialist meeting a few yards away, there is a huge crowd. The cause is not to be found in the inferiority of the Socialist oration (that is, of course, unthinkable), but simply because some of the "comrades", instead of supporting their own meeting, will insist upon indulging in amateur heroics at the meeting of the "Antis", thereby securing for them a large audience which it would be otherwise impossible for them to attract.' A concern for political methods and tactics was in evidence even in his revolutionary phase.

During these outdoor speaking engagements he first met Clement Attlee, a young social worker from Toynbee Hall, whom he recalled speaking on ILP platforms in a quiet and modest manner, expounding and not denouncing.[36] Attlee spoke in London in a joint Fabian–ILP series of lectures on political history: his topic being Walpole.[37] Morrison also lectured on behalf of the

ILP to trade union branches: his three topics being 'the Labour Movement: its Growth and Outcome'; 'the Future of Trade Unionism'; and 'Labour and Politics',[38] which probably evoked more interest than Attlee's comments on an eighteenth-century politician. Their paths crossed again in 1911 and 1912 when both were nominated, unsuccessfully, for membership of the National Administrative Council of the ILP.[39]

Of his speaking Morrison said: 'I gradually developed the ability to mount the platform and speak without notes. I would have my general line of argument mentally prepared but I used to rely on the inspiration of the moment, the atmosphere of the meeting, or on the comments of that invaluable ally of a public speaker, the heckler, to direct my train of thought.'[40] He learned how to deal with the irrelevant jibe, the offensive personal insult and the blank obstinacy of a hostile audience.[41] It was 'a hard and sometimes disappointing apprenticeship'.[42]

Between 1910 and 1913 Herbert was active within his trade union, the National Union of Clerks. He was the chairman of the Brixton branch and its delegate to the Lambeth Labour Representation Committee, where he was minute secretary: his first official position in the Labour movement. He energized his branch, increasing its membership by seventy-five per cent in his first year.[43] He organized a campaign to recruit more members, holding meetings at the usual sites to advocate trade unionism. He wrote letters to the press appealing to clerks to join and sent out 'five hundred calendars advertising the branch – to local tobacconists, barbers, etc., and places where pen-pushers do collect'.[44] He tried to establish a federation of south London branches for joint social, athletic and propaganda work.[45] He made a special effort to organize the clerks of the Lambeth Borough Council, but failed to get his deputation, seeking higher wages, heard by the Council.[46]

He attended the union's annual conference at Leicester in 1913, speaking in favour of appointing an Assistant General Secretary, and not just a chief clerk, to be in charge of the office.[47] After shining at the conference he returned to give his branch an account of its proceedings. He seemed to be riding high, but the fall soon came. At a Labour conference he opposed a motion put forward by his union.* *The Clerk* of November 1913 records: 'After hearing a statement by Mr Morrison with regard to his action in opposing a NUC motion at a recent Labour Conference, he was censured, and tendered his resignation of the chairmanship of the branch, which was accepted with great regret.' The union's official history simply states that he 'never found himself really at home in the branch work and soon transferred his activity to other spheres'.[48]

His experience in the union taught him that Labour had to make an appeal wider than just to the working classes. He said: 'The struggle to make ends meet affects the clerical workers just as much as it does the mechanic'; he was often compelled 'to work under evil conditions. The ugly paw of

* The contents of the motion and the nature of the conference remain unknown.

unemployment is held over the head of the clerical worker'.[49] Clerks feel 'we are hanging on to the coat tails of the devil, although we have a vague conscious-ness that, in the end, he will ungraciously drop us in the deep'.[50] His experi-ence in the NUC may also have made him wary of involvement in trade union activities. Their scope was too limited: the pursuit of sectional objectives, not the achievement of power. And he may have been soured by the censure of his branch for not acting as a union delegate. He felt strongly that representa-tives should not be bound by instructions. After this period in the NUC he was never again to be active in the trade union movement. His world was to be that of political parties and local government.

Soon after joining the Brixton ILP in 1910 Bert became its chairman. It met at the Ruskin Hall, in Akerman Road, and about twenty of the forty mem-bers regularly attended. As chairman he was impressively efficient. He insisted on starting his meetings on time, arranged well-organized agenda and went through them with determination, keeping the members in order and their attention on the matters in hand. He gave a lead, yet in the end abided by the vote of the majority. He was drawn in 1911 by his friend, Willy Pogany, an artist who illustrated a de luxe edition of Omar Khayyam and the stories of the Wagnerian operas. According to Sir Frederic Osborn, he caught Mor-rison perfectly. He was presiding at a meeting, his hand on an agenda headed 'Officialism', his head cocked to one side, his quiff jumped up, and on his face a quizzical expression, with a tinge of fatherly superiority, as if saying to the meeting: 'I've done my best to persuade you; you must make up your mind; I know you're not really up to it, but I am ready to obey your democratic decision.' The title of the drawing was *Carried?*.* Stenning said of him: 'He always showed impatience at the dilatory business habits of the comrades. In those early days there was about him a sense of purpose.'

His reputation for organization spread quickly and in the later months of 1910 he was made Secretary of the South-West London Federation of the ILP, responsible for co-ordinating the work of the branches. He was able to achieve positions of responsibility so quickly because he was recognized as an outstandingly able organizer, head and shoulders above the other members. He had the time to do the jobs; he wanted to do them and there were few others who wanted to take them on.

He saw his role as being to vitalize the branches. He organized socials, especially in the Morris Hall, near Clapham Common. At these 'hops' he learned to dance and to enjoy himself, to become a 'social' socialist.[51] His rendering of the ballad 'Flora' was a great hit and another favourite was 'Oh, Trumpeter what art thou calling now?' which he sang robustly but somewhat out of tune. He became a very popular dancer, sometimes taking the floor in

* Morrison so liked the drawing that he had it made into postcards and distributed to friends. It appears as plate 26.

carpet slippers, and always with his red tie. After light refreshments he would often speak, without notes, in a genial and forthright manner, putting the ILP's case.[52] He arranged outings, for instance to Ashtead Woods on Whit Monday.[53] He organized demonstrations out-of-doors: ten in the year 1911–12. He regularly visited the branches, urging them to activity to win members, and he arranged for ILP speakers to be sent to trade union branches: twenty-nine in 1911–12.[54] He issued a monthly circular of information and advice to branches. 'I've always loved sending out circulars,' he said later.[55] In them he urged ILP members to win over trade unionists, to promote the ILP journal, the *Labour Leader*, and to help the party in local elections. He called on members 'immediately to put on their armour to go forth into battle'. Cyclists in particular were asked to give their services.[56] The Federation prospered, accumulating in 1912 a balance of over £100, so that it could give substantial grants to local branches putting up candidates in elections.[57]

His most famous enterprise was to organize two debates at the Memorial Hall in 1911: the first between Hilaire Belloc and Ramsay MacDonald, and the second between Bernard Shaw and G. K. Chesterton. Both were packed, and people were turned away from the doors. 'Everyone who is "anybody" in the London movement was present, and a good number of provincial "anybodies" were also there.'[58] The proceedings of the Belloc–MacDonald debate were published as a pamphlet, *Socialism and the Servile State*, with a foreword by Herbert Morrison, the first time he was published outside a newspaper or a magazine. He made for the Federation a profit out of the debates of over £100.[59] The *Labour Leader* queried 'Is any federation more enterprising?'[60]

He found his organizing work satisfying. He bought from Stenning for thirty shillings an ancient Yöst typewriter, and found a jettisoned flat-bed duplicator which he repaired. From his bed-sitting rooms in a number of lodgings he wrote his letters, the circulars, the agenda papers, reports and the press statements; he booked halls and duplicated tickets and arranged meetings. He had had no training in this. He just picked it up as he went along, relying on his own common sense and concern for tidiness and efficiency. He said: 'I was most anxious to make a success of this work.' It was a valuable rehearsal and proving period. 'I was learning a lesson that was to stand me in good stead in later years. I saw that the fight for socialism depended less on street corner rabble-rousing (though that had its use) and dramatic isolated action than on the slow but steady construction of an organization devoted to running a planned programme of propaganda, social work and organization.'[61] Through this work he came more and more to sympathize with the 'official gang' in the ILP both locally and nationally: men like Ramsay MacDonald and Philip Snowden.

As Secretary of the Federation he was a member of the London and Southern Counties Divisional Council of the ILP. He was a regular attender at its sessions and soon came to play a leading role.[62] Whenever the chairman was absent Morrison took his place. In 1916 he was appointed chairman, and with James Mylles, an old Brixton friend, as organizer, ran the Council until 1920, when he withdrew to concentrate his energies on the London Labour Party. On the Council Morrison seems to have been concerned mainly with procedure and organization. He was ever watchful to ensure that the ILP engaged in a variety of activities and that no improper behaviour occurred. On the Council Morrison confirmed his reputation as a first-class organizer.

His interest in local government was aroused at the same time as his concern with politics. His diary between 1905 and 1907 contained jottings about events in London government,[63] and he read works on the history of London, back even to Roman times. He studied the records of the vestries, districts and the Metropolitan Board of Works, which had preceded the London County Council and the Metropolitan Boroughs.[64] As he became more aware of the powers of local authorities, he saw that much of the social reform he desired could be implemented through them.* He began to attend meetings of the Lambeth Borough Council which met fortnightly on Thursday evenings. From the public gallery he listened to the debates, watching and learning how to handle an agenda – 'his favourite reading';[65] he noticed the importance of procedure and recognized the tricks of members and chairmen. Usually he was the only spectator. He was observed in the gallery by the editor of a struggling weekly local paper, *The Brixtonian*, who asked him to report the meetings for a fee of five shillings a time. Morrison jumped at the offer. 'After each meeting I would get down to making my report and finish by about one in the morning, getting up at seven so that I could drop it in the paper's offices on the way to work the next morning.'[66] He wrote his reports for about three years, until 1912; they were more lively than most contemporary accounts of council meetings. He tried to make the reader interested from the start. One began: ' "*Can't* we start from the beginning, Mr Mayor?" cried Alderman Townesend, in mental agony!'[67] He reserved his judgment on the value of the proceedings for letters to the press over his own name. He pointed out that he found they had 'a shamefully petty outlook'. 'Rates are regarded by the dominant party as essentially immoral things. . . . The Highways Committee keeps expenditure low; at various times, as a consequence, various cyclists use various forms of bad language, and their nervous systems are impaired. This is called economy. The cyclists have another name for it.' He attacked the public health department which limited its policies to 'the expedient minimum', while dangerous insanitary premises remained.[68]

The more he learned about the local government of London the more dissatisfied he became. A variety of services were under the control of separate

* The main local authorities in London at this time were the top-tier London County Council responsible for some services over all London, and twenty-eight Metropolitan Boroughs responsible for more localized functions.

and frequently conflicting authorities, like gas, electricity, water, transport, housing, public health, sanitation, police, the river, the docks. Such a tangle explained apathy and ignorance; many of the bodies were beyond the influence of effective public control, since they were not directly elected. He did not want to abolish the boroughs, but he felt that they should not be allowed to inhibit the development of London as a whole. 'We are not only citizens of Lambeth; we are citizens of London. We must beware of too much parish pump politics.' His answer was that the administrative area of London should be 'enlarged, simplified, unified'.[69] He ended an article in which he inter-viewed Frank Smith, one of the Labour members of the LCC, about its work with a prophetic conclusion: 'I feel convinced that the London Movement [Labour] will see the importance of the matter. Aye, the Great City! It will mean work. It will mean businesslike organization. But it's worth it! What think you ?'[70] He had a vision of Labour winning all London, and reforming the whole system.

He stood for the first time as a candidate at an election in November 1912 for the Vauxhall ward of Lambeth borough. Conscience-stricken as to his suitability to stand at the age of twenty-four, he finally agreed to be one of the six ILP candidates for six seats, facing opposition from both Progressives (Liberals) and Municipal Reformers (Conservatives). His first election address described him as 'Lambethian, bred and born. Has a first-hand knowledge of practical organising in the Labour movement. Chairman local branch of National Union of Clerks. Believes that business should be business; loves the work of organizing and administration. Tireless and persistent in his efforts.' A local paper commented that he had 'been busily taking lessons for the past year in the privileged gallery of the Town Hall in "how not to do it" '.[71]

Although he was the youngest candidate, although two of his colleagues were sitting members of the council, although some of the others had stood before, and although he was not even the official agent, he at once took the lead and organized the campaign.[72] His only previous experience of organizing an election had been in 1909 when he was sub-agent at a Labour committee room at an LCC by-election. The agent had encouraged Morrison, and from that time he read all he could about elections, acquiring a mastery of the intricacies of electoral law and procedures. In 1912 'he worked all out and all hours'; he got party workers out till midnight on the evening before the poll to deliver a last-minute leaflet. He insisted on a well-printed address which he designed and wrote himself. It was far superior to most election addresses of the time or even today, a little booklet really, containing photographs of the candidates with Morrison's profile carefully posed to hide his blind eye, and a photograph of a typical slum. It was clearly laid out, crisply written and presented all the vital information about the candidates and their meetings. It blamed the Municipal Reformers for the poor condition of Lambeth, its insanitary areas and slum property, its roads, continually out of repair, and the neglect of the poorer districts. The council was attacked for its failure to build low-rent houses and for its refusal to provide work for the unemployed. Labour urged the establishment of municipal depots to distribute pure milk, and higher wages and better conditions for employees of the council and its contractors. Included in the manifesto was a section on the subject on which Morrison was to be Labour's leading expert: London's traffic. 'We think there should be equal treatment as between trams and motor vehicles. The heavy motors tear up the roads, create a nuisance to the rate-paying shopkeepers, and generally destroy the safety and quietness of any neighbourhood wherein they travel, without contributing a single penny to the local rates for the up-keep of the roads they are continually destroying. On the other hand, the London County Council pay for the construction of the tram track, keep it in repair, and in addition, contribute to the rates of the Lambeth Borough Council.' Morrison's declaration concluded: 'The present industrial system makes the lot of the Workers one long struggle with poverty. We are wearied of this despotism, with all its inhuman consequences, and seek its overthrow. In its place we would substitute a Co-operative Commonwealth, wherein the necessities of all, and not of a few, would be the guiding principle.'

Morrison felt that the ILP would win the six seats. They had produced the best address, held the fullest-attended meetings and generally had run the most efficient campaign. But as the votes were counted his heart sank. Although the two sitting ILP members were returned, Morrison came bottom of the poll. 'I had failed abysmally. The lesson was, of course, valuable for a brash and over-optimistic young socialist.'[73] The defeat was later explained by the fact that since the poll closed at 8 p.m., there was not time to get the working men to vote as many had only just come home from work or were still at work. The system of triennial elections was also blamed, since it did not enable a strong local movement, fighting elections each year, to be built up. And finally, it was claimed that the absence of any effective public control over election expenses helped their opponents who were far richer than the ILP.[74] All in all it was a chastening experience: Morrison's first political disappointment.

Chapter 3

The Young Activist

In the autumn of 1912 Morrison left Whitbread's to be a circulation traveller for the new Labour daily paper established in October, the *Daily Citizen*.* Lord Brockway, then Fenner Brockway, editor of the *Labour Leader*, recalled suggesting Morrison for the job to Clifford Allen,† the secretary of the new paper in charge of the business side.[1] Morrison's wages rose by one pound a week to fifty shillings, and he was now working for a Labour cause.[2] His main loss was his leisure. His hours were long and irregular.[3] His task on the *Citizen* was to canvass for new readers, travelling around social-ist and trade union branches to persuade them to take the paper through circulation committees, six thousand of which were eventually set up.[4] He worked not just in London, but in the provinces too. He recalled the work as gruelling, rushing the papers to wherever there was a strike. The circulation rose splendidly while the strike lasted, but dropped back when it ended.[5] So successful was he that he was promoted to be deputy to the circulation manager, Mr Morgan, a dynamic, ebullient Welshman, who 'went at things like a bull in a china shop, while Herbert was left to pick up the pieces'.[6]

Herbert worked from the London office in Fleet Street, near Ludgate Circus, while the paper itself was printed in Manchester. His job now was to ensure that the copies were collected and distributed, which entailed a detailed knowledge of train times. He organized the dispatch of the papers by any means possible, cabs, cars, horse-drawn vans, trams. He incited the drivers to go hell for leather to catch the trains.[7] Young lads who regularly got there on time had a few coppers from his own pocket and much appreciative encourage-ment. If connections were missed, he never lost his temper; he would just ask how it happened and say 'try not to let it happen again'. He seemed in control, despite being surrounded by apparent confusion. He impressed people by his

* It was the official paper sponsored by the parliamentary leaders of the ILP, who disliked the *Herald*.

† Later Lord Allen of Hurtwood.

methodical routine; over his desk were lists of train times and his schedules of work for the week and the day, all neatly arranged.[8] He also dealt with publicity, designing and making up advertisements and posters. He assisted Morgan in some publicity stunts which included flying a balloon and kite which informed, '*Daily Citizen* every day, everywhere'. Brockway wrote of his time on the *Citizen*: 'he had a genius for organization, becoming the leader of his team of workers by natural ability, surmounting difficulties which baffled everyone else, mobilizing the rank and file of the Labour movement as reader-getters, and all the time as he went about his duties whistling, joking, laughing in characteristic Cockney lightheartedness.'[9] There were no proper hours. Once he worked non-stop from Sunday morning until Tuesday, and even then he went to bed for only a few hours.[10] 'My days in newspaper land were the hardest in my life. It was a terrible life.'[11]

His ambition was to be on the editorial side of the paper. He helped out when staff was short, reporting meetings. That was as close as he got. ' "I should have been there, too, if the damn paper hadn't shut down"; he said, with an outthrust of his chin.'[12] The itch to be a journalist was strong. From his teens 'he aimed at seeing himself in print',[13] writing letters and articles for the local press and then for socialist journals. Brockway liked his style and encouraged him to write for the *Labour Leader*. He said that 'Morrison had the capacity to write simply, in short, direct sentences that hit you between the eyes'. He was proud of his monthly ILP circular, almost a magazine in itself. He aped the mannerisms of journalists, while at the *Citizen*, using their jargon and smoking a pipe. In 1949 he said: 'Of course, if I had not got to where I am in politics, I believe I could have been a good newspaper editor.'[14]

His life was bound up with the paper. Its policy of taking advertisements for the army was criticized at a conference of the ILP London and Southern Counties Divisional Area. 'In a characteristic and clever speech' he explained that without such advertisements, the paper would collapse or have to be subsidized. But he failed to convince a majority.[15]

His final job at the *Citizen* was to act as secretary of a fund begun in 1915 to collect the 100,000 shillings needed to keep the paper in being. Its circulation was hit by the war, and a judicial decision prohibited trade unions from investing money in the *Citizen* without a ballot of their members. They began to withdraw. The paper had in fact lost money from the moment of its appearance. It was unable to compete effectively against the more readable *Herald* and its leadership was divided over its aims, whether it was to be a commercial venture or just propagandist.[16] Morrison's attempt to save the *Citizen* had no chance of success; only a quarter of the target was achieved. The paper died in March 1915,[17] and Morrison was out of work.

After leaving home, following the row with his father, Herbert lived in a succession of dingy bed-sitting rooms around Brixton, Clapham, Stockwell and Streatham, calling only occasionally to see his father. It was a somewhat miserable existence; he looked anaemic and ill fed; his clothes were shabby;

his elbows were holed and his cuffs frayed. He found solace at the homes of colleagues in the party, who invited him back in the evenings for a meal, often the only good meals of those days. In this warm atmosphere, fussed by the family, he would relax, sitting by the fire with his shoes off.[18] When he worked at the *Citizen* his boss, Morgan, suspecting that he was not having enough food, asked Herbert to lodge with him in Clapham. He accepted the offer and became one of the family. Mrs Morgan mothered him. He was a good companion, frequently engaging in frivolous banter. Sometimes a group from the *Citizen* would come in the evening to discuss current politics. Herbert would talk and talk, and would not be thrown off his stride by the striking of the Morgans' very loud clock at eleven or twelve.[19]

Leaving the Morgans he went to lodge with T. J. Fisher and his wife at Sternhold Avenue, Streatham. Fisher was an old colleague in the Brixton ILP and the National Union of Clerks. Here again he was coddled. Mrs Fisher took him in hand and tried to smarten him up. Some three years earlier she had insisted that if he was to meet important people he must be more presentable. She was adamant that he should call himself, and be called by others, 'Herbert' and not 'Bert' which she felt was too common. In 1910 'Bert' Morrison from the Brixton ILP was a delegate to the ILP's London Conference, and in the same year Morrison 'B' was listed in the register of the London and Southern Counties Divisional Council of the ILP; the 'B' however later had a line drawn through it, and an 'H' substituted. In 1911 he stopped using 'Bert' as his first name in press letters and on articles; from this time it went out of use, except to his oldest friends and family. Mrs Fisher always liked to feel that she had made *Herbert* Morrison. At the Fishers' he was a genial lodger. He liked to sing popular songs, while Mrs Fisher played the piano, a replica of the situation in the Morgan household. And all the time there was his organizing work to be done. He would stay up till the early hours, tapping at his typewriter.[20]

The children of these households remembered him with affection. Despite his cadaverous appearance he was looked on by them as an uncle, generous with gifts, ready to talk and full of fun. He would read bed-time stories and sing nursery rhymes, his favourites being contained in *The Dolly Ballads* by Robert Blatchford, which he had come across in 1907 and bought for himself as a Christmas present. He said he read it to 'many likkle girls and boys', who, like him, loved the childish talk and illustrations.[21]

His relations with unmarried women of around his own age were not as easy as with married women, older women or little girls. The bad eye made him 'a hideous little man', 'unprepossessing', 'one wouldn't look twice at him', 'boss-eyed Bertie', 'he didn't stand a chance'.[22] Beatrice Webb first met Morrison at this time at Fabian meetings where he 'interjected pert criticism'. He was 'cocky and self-assertive, with a marked Cockney accent; ugly in figure and colouring, with one eye gone wrong – altogether an unpleasing personality which did not look promising'.[23] However, he seemed to fancy himself with women and was flirtatious, but too pushing. Some detected in him a fear of women; although attracted to them he was afraid that they would lead him from his socialist work. One girl who got close to him in his late teens and early twenties was Nellie Harslett, a vivacious, intelligent and beautiful girl, adored by all the young men of her acquaintance, including Bert. Her father was the stage manager of a music-hall and her mother used to hold weekly soirées at their home, where people would discuss philosophical and metaphysical questions, after which Mrs Harslett would play the piano. It was a romantic atmosphere, and Nellie, a member of the SDP, brought Bert along. She liked him a great deal, but detected in him an inner conflict: he was fiercely attracted to women and wanted to marry and have lots of children, but he feared domestication. He told her that he wished he was a 'monk but not in a monastery'. She felt that she could have married him, but in the end rejected the idea, since she saw that marriage to him would be too difficult, for so set was he in his political purpose that he would never make concessions to his wife. She saw the two sides of him: the gay and light-hearted companion, and the unpleasant. He could be cruel, not mincing his words. Brusque and hurtful he would not forgive if he felt someone had gone against him.[24]

Politically he was all in favour of women, being a fervent champion of equal rights including the vote. He argued that they should be treated as human beings and not as domestic servants.[25] After some militant suffragette outrage in 1912 he condemned the hysteria of the anti-suffragists: 'Worse things happened when men were fighting for the suffrage.'[26] He wrote in the *Labour Leader* an ironical piece about a campaign for votes for men, a preposterous demand, for 'manly man will allow women to continue as his political and domestic guardians'. It was a law of nature that man's main job was to earn money for the family; he was more backward than woman, shown by the fact that he used more brute force, and he was not able to bear long-drawn-out pain, was more hysterical and had less self-control and got too easily excited. He observed two lovers: 'the balance of calmness and self-control is almost invariably in favour of the woman – A glance from a woman's eye; an accidental touch from her hand; a smile from her lips – these things will cause the average man to become temporarily insane. He loses his judgment and is liable to vote for the candidate with the prettiest smile.'[27] More seriously, he felt that 'when they become politically enfranchised, they will think more of and about themselves. They will demand and secure improved labour conditions. They will be much more interesting people to talk to as a whole; man has everything to gain and nothing to lose by the political and economic emancipation of women.'[28]

Nellie Harslett discovered an aspect of Bert's nature that was never to blossom: his aesthetic sense. She took him to her mother's soirées, and to the slightly more political evenings of J. F. Green at Herne Hill. After discussion there was singing: German *Lieder*, country ballads and Indian love lyrics.

Here Bert showed that he had an aesthetic sense; although not creative, he yearned to appreciate good music, poetry, drama and painting. This sense was squeezed out by his political activities which allowed him little time to read widely or to pay attention to the arts. He found satisfaction in the all-absorbing game of politics. He wanted to be close to the arts, and to be seen to be close, perhaps to impress Nellie and her companions. Sometimes, however, his other side burst through. As if to shock the more educated and sensitive, he would behave in a boorish manner, and people would feel that he lacked refinement. Some felt sick as he slobbered his way through a meal. These displays, noticed Nellie, occurred mainly when his companions made him feel inferior. She regarded him as a sad, lonely, complex figure.[29] But he was proud of being ordinary, of being typical of the 'common or garden people; the people who live in the respectable lower middle class suburb'. He shared their pleasures and challenged those socialists who looked down contemptuously on such attitudes: 'When I hear the sneers and regrets at the people's enjoyments and at the particular news stories which interest the man in the street, I sometimes think that there is more of the spirit of Socialism in the unconverted than there is in the converted.'[30]

His tastes were simple; he had no extravagances, other than books. He did not smoke (except while at the *Citizen*) or drink, and spent little on clothes; indeed he was indifferent to dress, in great contrast to the meticulous way in which he ordered his political affairs. He had no hobbies. Occasionally he went to the theatre to see a melodrama, and he once went to the Old Vic to hear *Lohengrin*. He wrote that when he felt lonely, 'I usually either go to bed or go to a picture palace.'[31] His only real relaxation was at the ILP socials where he flung himself with gusto into the dancing and singing. He read much, but less widely after 1912, narrowing his range to political and socialist works, government reports, agenda and minutes. Foreign affairs he paid scant attention to; his focus was on domestic issues, and increasingly on London.

Scotland, however, took his fancy, perhaps because he felt his origins lay in the clan Morrison, but more because of a trip he took in 1911. 'I went up to Dalry [Ayrshire] to do a week's propaganda work. I took with me an Everyman's edition of Burns. I read it in the train. I read it sitting by the roadside as I went around. I listened to the accents of the folk around me, and by the end of the week I was in. Or nearly.'[32] He became obsessed with Burns, even treating the readers of the Brixton press to a 'I am sorry, "but facts are chiels that winna ding an' downa be disputed" ',[33] and he wore a tartan tie. He returned speaking with a Scottish accent, which some interpreted as part of his then hero-worship of MacDonald.[34] Morrison modelled himself on him, adopting his stance on the platform. In his room he had a portrait of MacDonald hanging on the wall, like a sacred icon.[35]

He was not religious. The militant atheism of the SDP days mellowed into agnosticism, but he detested organized religion. In the *Labour Leader* he wrote: 'Christ proclaimed the brotherhood of man; the theologians have distorted the Gospel, have justified inequality, have written ponderously and at full length to prove that the church of their particular sect was the pure Church of God.'[36] In the war he noted: 'Christ said: Love one another. The Churches say: Kill one another.'[37]

To a contemporary he was 'a thin, pale-faced young fellow, clean-shaven, blue-eyed, and wearing spectacles. His dark brown hair, parted on the left, was swept across and upward, showing a broad high forehead. He was rather straight-lipped and had a habit of pressing his lips together so that the lower one seemed to protrude a little beyond the upper. His chin stood out pugnaciously too.'[38] To St John Ervine, 'His energy and ambition were tremendous.'[39] Lord Brockway wrote that: 'There was no keeping down his energy, his smartness, his knack of getting things done, his cocksureness', but he found Morrison 'gauche, awkward, crude, uncouth and rough hewn'.[40] A journalist who met him on the *Citizen* recalled: 'He meant everything he thought, and said it until the other fellow meant it as well.'[41]

During Morrison's time at Pimlico and Brixton a major issue was tariff reform or free trade. He was not a free trader, and denounced liberalism as unfettered competition; he proclaimed that tariff reform was coming, yet he was not enthusiastic for it. What was really needed was 'a constructive social policy, having for its ultimate aim the extinction of unemployment, and the raising of healthy and cultivated people'. The answer was 'the social ownership of land and capital'.[42]

Because of his interest in tariff reform he was invited by the Tariff Reform League to go to Germany, on a tour which it financed, to observe the benefits of protection. Accordingly he spent a week in July 1910 on a lightning visit to Hamburg, Berlin, Leipzig, Frankfurt and Cologne. Normally after these excursions working men wrote articles in their local papers explaining the advantages of protection, which they had seen with their own eyes. Morrison wrote four articles in the *Brixton Free Press*, which were quite different from those of previous visitors.[43] He pointed out the short time of the trip and that he was shown only factories where conditions were good. Conflicting information about wages was given him; and when he tried to get it sorted out, he was blocked. He saw poverty, slums, beggars and unemployed. In some ways things were better there: in other ways worse. He balanced various factors: hours worked, wages, different trades and industries, prices of various goods, and he criticized both the bigoted tariff reformers and the bigoted free traders. He analysed German industrial history, noting that its relative youth enabled it to learn much from Britain's mistakes. He feared, however, the 'paternalism' of German employers who provided 'baths, canteens and libraries', because it put great power in their hands. He admired German trade unions, because they spent money on facilities, while ours hoarded it. He disliked certain tyrannical facets of German society: the undemocratic franchise and press censorship. He admired the state railways, the big social insurance schemes and the enterprise of its local authorities. His final article on the lessons of his visit was the first comprehensive statement in print of his policy for this country: he was just twenty-two. He stated that 'something is wrong with England'. The chief social diseases were unemployment, sweated labour, physical deterioration, bad housing and ignorance. 'The enemy is National Inefficiency.' He submitted a set of 'business propositions' to make England commercially progressive. He advocated implementation of the Minority Report of the Royal Commission on the Poor Law, the planning of a ten-year public works programme which would concentrate on providing work in lean years; the establishment of Labour Exchanges and a national minimum wage. He urged a scheme of unemployment insurance through trade unions subsidized by the state, the reduction of excessive working hours, no employment of widows and children, and for those members of the working classes who would not work 'there should be a Detention Colony – not a prison, but a genuine reformatory and training place'. He called for maternity benefits, and free education from primary school to university. The state should own and run railways and canals, and local authorities should seek out insanitary dwellings and build houses, 'not barracks'.

He expanded and developed his ideas in 1911 in a remarkable series of articles in the *Labour Leader*.[44] Most took the form of imaginary conversations and dramatic confrontations. He created 'The Opponents of Socialism Ltd', who published the *Daily Irrepress*, to which a bejewelled lady contributed funds as insurance against the confiscation of her property. At the National Conference of the Opponents of Socialism, Mr Impossibilist, Mr Sentimento, Sir Black Patriot and Lord Coalrail put their reactionary views. These articles are the most entertaining that Morrison ever wrote. From them one can extract his political testament, the outcome of five years' reading, arguing, speaking and thinking.

He said later that he had learned his economics from the SDP and his politics from the ILP.[45] From the SDP he had acquired the belief that no long-lasting social reforms could be achieved without the acquisition by the state of the means of production and distribution. From the SDP he gained his belief in the materialist conception of history, the labour theory of surplus value, economic causation and the class struggle: a Marxist way of looking at society and its development. From the ILP he acquired the belief that necessary reforms, including the state's expropriation of shareholders, could be achieved through the parliamentary system by constitutional democratic means. After a brief flirtation with revolution in the SDP he became a devotee of parliamentary democracy, abhorring revolution with its consequences: chaos and tyranny. He was also influenced by the Webbs with their emphasis on organization and efficiency, and even by Lord Rosebery and other liberals who campaigned for National Efficiency. He admired the German Social

Democratic Party and powerful unions, and he was envious of state and municipal enterprise in Germany. Morrison selected from the many left-wing writers he had read during this period certain features which he amalgamated to form his own view of society and socialism. Although the items were not original, the blend bore the distinctive Morrisonian mark: a passion for efficiency, tidiness and order, and for business-like enterprise. The style was uniquely Morrisonian: practical, detailed, direct and clear, the whole enlivened by an ironical wit. He was a propagandist and organizer, believing that people could be persuaded if presented with a reasonable case in a reasonable way, and that socialists could win elections if a well-organized Labour Party could attract the voters' loyalty. He had reached this position by about 1911, and these views were to persist throughout his life.

During 1913 and 1914 he was a frequent contributor to the *Labour Leader* with his 'Straight Talks to the Workers': short snappy pieces, displaying a greater emotionalism than before. One example will illustrate:

> We shall not be happy till we've wiped their gentlemanly plundering and piracy from the social life of the world. We shall not be happy till every capitalist and landlord has been put out of action and decently industrious members of society have taken their places. We shall not be happy until the stomachs of the little ones have been replenished and glory has come to the soul of human kind.
>
> Let the rich do their damnedest, we fear them not! We'll give them a run for their money, and they won't find it a picnic either. If they'll come quietly we're agreeable, but, if they want war, then war it shall be![46]

In July 1914 he took stock of himself in an odd piece in *Labour Woman*.

> Fifteen years ago I believed that school was a fearful thing. Today I wish I were still at school. And I am.
>
> Fifteen years ago I loved to kiss my mother. Now I understand her, and would kiss her the more. But she is dead. . . .
>
> Fifteen years ago I played football in the street. Now I don't play football at all. I sell newspapers to the enthusiasts.
>
> Fifteen years ago I thought that pretty young ladies of twenty years were angels. Today, I don't believe that any girls are angels. I should not like angels as well.
>
> Fifteen years ago I believed that the consumption of beer in excess was a tragedy. I now believe it is a joke. A very poor joke.
>
> Fifteen years ago I conceived of parsons as very different to other men. Now I believe that parsons and men are much of a muchness. The best of the parsons *are* men.
>
> Fifteen years ago I thought that Ramsgate was the last word in holiday resorts; now I find that it isn't. Also that it is.
>
> Fifteen years ago I took very little girls and boys for halfpenny bus rides.

Today I take them to picture palaces. 'This here progress', says H. G. Wells through Mr Tom Smallways. 'It keeps on!'

Fifteen years ago I had no fairy god-mothers. Now I have several. And they are so kind to me.

Fifteen years ago all people were very human and fundamentally good. So they are today. Cheer-oh!

The sentiment of his last sentence was to come under heavy attack when the war began one month later.

Chapter 4
Time of Turmoil

When war broke out Morrison was working at the *Daily Citizen*. The day before, he had attended the big anti-war rally at Trafalgar Square. Now all he had worked for seemed shattered; terribly distressed he wrote bitter anti-war pieces each week in the *Labour Leader*. One, in the issue of 3 September, he had printed on postcards and distributed within the Labour movement. It said:

YOUR KING & COUNTRY NEED YOU!

'Your King and Country Need You!'

Ah! Men of the Country, you are remembered. Neither the King, nor the Country, nor the picture papers had really forgotten you. When your master tried to cut your wages down – did you think he knew of your beautiful brave heart? When were you unemployed – did you think your Country had forgotten you? When the military were used against you in the strike – did you wonder if your King was quite in love with you? Did you? . . . Ah! foolish one.

'Your King and Country Need You!'

Need hundreds of thousands of you to go to hell and to do the work of hell. The Commandment says: 'Thou shalt not kill.' Pooh! What does it matter? Commandments, like treaties, were made to be broken. Ask your parson: he will explain.

'Your King and Country Need You!'

Go forth, little soldier! Though you know not what you fight for – go forth! Though you have no grievance against your German brother – go forth and kill him! Though you may know he has a wife and family dependent upon him – go forth and slay him; he is only a German dog. Will he not kill you if he gets a chance? Of course he will.

He is being told the same story!

'His King and Country Need Him!'

Morgan, his boss, was so frightened that Herbert would be arrested for treason that he took him to Cornwall for a holiday. The police called while they were away, but nothing happened.[1] He returned and continued his attacks.[2] At the ILP annual conference of 1915 he opposed a proposal that soldiers should be allowed to form trade unions, since 'he objected to anything which would lead to the army being looked upon as a respectable profession'.[3]

A major concern of his was to preserve the unity of the Labour movement; he argued that anti-war agitation should be linked with campaigns on behalf of working class grievances. Up to the war he felt that things were going well with the movement. Trade unions were growing and linking up, getting a clearer conception of the Labour Party; 'the industrial and political solidarity of the workers was coming' – everything looked rosy, and now this. He hoped that in the end all would come back to the only war that mattered, the Labour war.[4] Without solidarity they would have to start at the bottom again and begin 'the tedious climbing'.[5] He did not participate actively in the No Conscription Fellowship, supported by Clifford Allen, because he felt it was not sufficiently working class, and he differed from many other ILP members in the anti-war movement, who supported guild socialism. He proclaimed that true industrial democracy could come only through political democracy.[6]

He was in despair. His political and personal hopes were dashed, for the *Citizen* collapsed in March 1915, and he was unemployed. Friends rallied to him. He became a part-time secretary to the second man in the ILP, a former leader-writer on the *Citizen* and frequent contributor to the *Labour Leader*, W. C. Anderson, MP for Sheffield, Attercliffe, son of a Scottish blacksmith, and former organizer for the National Union of Shop Assistants. Anderson was an opponent of the war, yet always expressed his hostility in a temperate way.[7] It was an act of kindness by Anderson to employ Morrison who knew no shorthand. Anderson wrote his letters in long-hand and Morrison typed them. Morrison also became a part-time traveller for the National Labour Press, the printers of much ILP and trade union material. His job was to canvass branches for orders, similar to his first work on the *Citizen*. But most important of all Dr Alfred Salter pushed him into the post of Secretary of the London Labour Party.

Salter was a fine doctor who practised amongst the poor of Bermondsey. There he organized a thriving ILP branch which he ruled with paternalist concern. He was a puritan, an ascetic, a non-smoker, teetotaller, vegetarian, a Quaker and the most pugnacious pacifist in London. While Morrison was organizing south London for the ILP, Salter, recognizing his talent, took him under his wing, recommended him for speaking engagements, and tried to persuade him to be his agent. Herbert refused, perhaps seeing that two such dominating people could not work together in one constituency.[8] Salter was Treasurer of the London Labour Party, and in April 1915 suggested that Morrison put his name forward as Secretary. Morrison wavered, wondering whether he had the ability to take it on, but Morgan told him to go for it. And so he let his name go forward.

The birth throes of the London Labour Party were prolonged. Many attempts had been made from the 1880s to bring together the conflicting sects and local movements of socialists and labour in London, but all failed until 1914.[9] Then the Secretary of the London Trades Council, Fred Knee, a member of the London Society of Compositors, managed 'to fuse warring and inharmonious elements into co-operation for a common end'.[10] Although a member of the British Socialist Party, formerly the SDP, he 'strove to show that revolutionary zeal could be combined with ability to deal with practical matters'. By diplomacy and bullying, this 'mighty atom' persuaded the London Trades Council on 12 March 1914 to convene a conference of delegates of unions and socialist societies to discuss yet again the formation of a London Labour Party. On 23 May 1914, 424 delegates met at the Essex Hall, Strand; 86 came from 197 socialist societies and 338 from 193 trade union bodies. Knee guided the meeting to the decision: 'that this Conference, representing Trade Unions, Trade Councils, and Federations, Local Labour Representation Committees, Independent Labour Party, British Socialist Party, Women's Labour League, Fabian Society, Co-operative Societies, Women's Socialist Circles and Women's Co-operative Guilds, do constitute itself the first session of the London Labour Party'. They appointed a provisional committee to draft a constitution which was approved by a conference on 4 July, and the first annual conference was held on 28 November 1914, when an executive committee was appointed, containing representatives of the various units composing the party: five from the BSP and eight from the ILP; the Secretary was Knee, the Chairman was the Chairman of the Trades Council, John Stokes, a member of the BSP and Secretary of the London Glassblowers' Union. The Treasurer was Salter. Tragedy struck. Knee died on 8 December. The LLP was without a Secretary until 27 April 1915 when Morrison was appointed, but only just. The BSP proposed Edwin Fairchild, a well-known lecturer and journalist; the ILP put up Morrison. At a show of hands Salter muttered 'Fairchild's got it', but by one vote Morrison had.[11] He was appointed part-time Secretary for the salary of one pound a week. The party's income for the first year 1914–15 was £119 1s 9½d; its expenditure £110 17s 6½d; for the second year £136 11s 1d and £117 4s 11½d respectively, from a total membership in 1914 of 134,951 and in 1915 of 151,549. Salter collected the money for the party and Morrison's salary out of contributions from ILP and trade union branches, and even from his own pocket. He found Morrison a place from which to run the party, 57 Upper Grange Road, Bermondsey, where Herbert worked from a table in the window of the front room. This was more congenial for him than the offices of the London Trades Council in Cowcross Street, near Smithfield Market, which had up till then been the headquarters of the LLP. He did his own typing and duplicating on the instruments he had used as organizer in south London for the ILP. Indeed the work was an extension of these activities.

From such small beginnings Morrison was to create the most powerful local political organization ever to exist in this country. For the rest of the war Morrison was at work building up this machine.

The object of the LLP was 'to educate our members in London questions and London Government', 'to assist in securing better organization in London's political Labour movement', and 'to formulate and make known a consistent Labour policy on London affairs'.[12] His main tool was his monthly *London Labour Party Circular*. The first was issued in October 1915, a single duplicated sheet: sixty copies in all. By May 1917 its circulation had increased to three hundred, and it became a four-page magazine. Its purpose was to keep the members in touch, informing them of Labour activities in London and providing them with facts and arguments to use in their localities. Tory and Liberal misdeeds were eagerly exposed with detailed information. He ransacked the agenda and minutes of the LCC and the borough councils and local government journals for the data he needed, which he presented with characteristic wit in 'sniplets': snappy items or stories.

His propaganda concentrated on attacking the economies of London local authorities, mainly on education, health and environmental services. He urged members to agitate against their reactionary councils and to advocate municipal enterprise. He himself lobbied ministers, MPs and local councils.

Morrison engaged in a whirlwind of activities. Immediately on assuming office he devoted himself to making the LLP a force in London. 'The London Labour Party will become dominant in London's public affairs – ultimately. The date will be fixed by our capacity for organization and the degree to which the rank-and-file is informed.'[13] He looked forward to the election to be held after the war. 'If Labour leaves capitalism in control of the Local Government machinery, all the Labour Governments in the world will not be successful in local administrative work. Electricity, housing, education, transit – in these and other great departments of public need the capitalists are preparing their offensive for the period of reconstruction; we shall commit a tragic blunder if we tamely submit to the municipal fortress being controlled by the enemies of popular ownership and control. . . .'[14] In 1915 he had written to all affiliated organizations asking them to nominate candidates. In 1917 he called on members to prepare for a possible election in March 1918; he told them to develop 'a "card index" frame of mind' and get down to details, such as arranging for expenses for the campaign.[15] His tactical sense was fully developed. He rejected a request from the British Socialist Party for a detailed electoral programme, since it would be impossible to keep up-to-date or meet particular local circumstances. More preferable was a broad statement of principles.[16] Winning elections was his object from the start. His main task during the war, however, was to keep together the party which had been so precariously formed. He sought to divert its attention from the war: 'Everybody knows that the Labour Movement has been split from top to bottom on the specific issue of the War. By avoiding this issue at Conferences, the London Labour Party has preserved a unity which would have been impossible in other circumstances. . . .'[17] By concentrating the party on domestic problems and tasks, Morrison preserved the LLP.

The war posed personal problems for Morrison. He is often thought of as having been a conscientious objector in the First War, but that was not strictly so. He was not against war in all circumstances. He was rather a 'political objector', against that particular war which he regarded as an imperialist and capitalist war brought about by commercial rivalry and secret diplomacy. He could not see a whit to choose between the contestants, and he especially objected to the British alliance with Russia which he had long opposed because of its oppressive regime. It was against international socialist principles to kill workers in order to help the Tsar. These views he propounded at meetings throughout the country; some were broken up by toughs, and at Hampstead he was dragged off his platform, taken to the pond, but he was not thrown in as the police arrived in time to carry him to safety.[18]

Morrison went to Leeds in June 1917 for a socialist anti-war convention. He sat in the Coliseum: one of a thousand delegates, but not a speaker. Here he heard MacDonald and Snowden call for peace. Their view was that the allies should call for self-determination by the peoples of Europe, which would stimulate the German people to put pressure on their government to end the war. A jarring note was struck by the delegate from the dockers' union, Ernest Bevin, who castigated the 'fatuous friends' of the ILP. He asked where they would stand if the German people put no pressure on their government. He saw no evidence that German Social Democrats were eager to strike against the war.[19] Although Morrison never referred to Bevin's speech, it must have been the first time that he had come across Bevin, and he could not have liked what he heard, since his hero, MacDonald, was being attacked. The convention passed a number of resolutions, hailing the Russian revolution of Kerensky, calling for socialist unity and seeking the establishment of thirteen district councils modelled on the Soviets. Morrison recalled: 'we departed, scratching our heads. It had been an anti-climax to all the exhilarating revolutionary talk, and most of us knew it.' In a few months, however, the hysterical conference and its unrealistic resolutions were largely forgotten.[20]

When conscription was introduced in 1916, he received his call-up papers. He could have escaped military service on medical grounds because of his blind eye, but he chose to make a stand. He appeared before the Military Service Tribunal at Wandsworth. He told them that he was a socialist by religion, a member of the ILP and that he had a deep conscientious objection to taking part in a war which was a product of capitalism.[21] Although at the start of the war he had criticized people who gave any assistance to it, including knitting helmets for the troops,[22] he now agreed to work in alternative service of benefit to the nation.[23] He offered to be a dustman in Wandsworth, for, he told the tribunal, it looked as if the borough needed some. The tribunal ordered him to work on the land; he agreed, much to the anger of many of his fellow objectors who preferred imprisonment to helping the war effort in any way. This moderate course brought him attacks from those who thought him a cowardly 'conchie' and from the objectors who saw him as a collaborator. But instead of the trenches or gaol, as he told a friend, 'I'm off to pick currants.'[24]

He went to work at Letchworth Garden City, thirty-seven miles from London, but linked to it by a frequent and fast train service.[25] He was employed by Mr J. J. Kidd who was a landscape gardener and nurseryman. Herbert was his assistant. This meant digging, working on the land and in greenhouses, and tidying people's gardens. He rode around Letchworth on a bicycle, with his spade, fork and rake over his shoulder. He was not very good at gardening – once pulling up some recently planted flowers and cabbages while leaving the weeds. Kidd was prominent in Letchworth left wing politics. A 'fiery socialist' and former secretary of the local SDP branch, he was very happy to give Morrison the job and leisure to carry out his duties as Secretary of the London Labour Party. Herbert had worried whether he should continue as Secretary when he was transferred to land work, but Salter had urged him to carry on.

Letchworth was a haven for conscientious objectors. Established in 1905 by Ebenezer Howard as a pioneering venture in a new type of living, it had attracted a variety of Utopians, socialists, anarchists, Tolstoyians, Quakers and cranks of all sorts, keen to begin a new life. A Miss Anne Lawrence built a college, the Cloisters, where people were taught handicrafts, making their own clothes and shoes, painting and cooking, so that they could live by the sweat of their brow and not by rent, interest or profit. In her bizarre castle the inmates slept in hammocks strung from columns in a circular building, quite open to the sky. Strange religious sects abounded and theosophy was strong. Letchworth was a centre of the underground for conscientious objectors on the run, and many hide-outs existed. Morrison could hardly have found a more satisfactory place in which to pass the war.

He lodged first with W. F. Moss, the general manager of the National Labour Press, who had first met Morrison when he worked on the *Citizen* and had given him a job as a representative when it had collapsed. Moss too was a pacifist. Morrison was as one of the family. He kept his LLP papers in a cupboard and was hard at it, dealing with correspondence, until the early hours. He brought to the house his current girl-friend, Rose Rosenberg, later Ramsay MacDonald's devoted private secretary: a girl on close terms with many of Labour's leading figures.[26] She was a gifted, vivacious woman, very interested in politics, who many felt would have been an ideal wife for Herbert, and she admitted that she could have married him. He seemed intoxicated by her, and loved to sing while she played the piano. In 'a cardboardy voice' he would intone that he was 'less than the dust beneath thy chariot wheels', and he whistled the Unfinished Symphony for weeks after she had played it to him. Together they attended music concerts given by Belgian refugees, and many were the happy evenings they spent together at the Moss household or at the home of his old friend, Frederic Osborn.

He then moved to the house of Peter Mylles, brother of his Brixton colleague James. Peter, a pacifist who taught printing at the Cloisters, had been gaoled for his beliefs, and Morrison came to lodge with his wife and family. Morrison also met at Letchworth another pacifist, Donald Daines, later his deputy and successor as Secretary of the LLP.

On Saturday nights at a temperance hall called the Skittles Inn there was folk dancing. Morrison flung himself enthusiastically into the proceedings, becoming very adept at country dancing. Here he met the woman who was to be his first wife. In his *Autobiography* he made no mention of her, although she appears in a single photo, without note;[27] he claimed that personal matters had no place in a political autobiography. Margaret 'Daisy' Kent was the star performer at the Skittles Inn, able to execute the most intricate movements with superb grace. She had a good figure, was slim, attractive, gracious and charming – 'the village-maiden type', reserved and unassuming. Morrison was impressed. He bounded awkwardly up to her, asked her to be his partner; she hesitated, smiled and accepted. The romance had begun. Rose was seen no more. People were amused; they could not understand what Daisy saw in this somewhat uncouth and cock-sure character, disfigured by his bad eye. Perhaps she was impressed by his energy. Some suggested that they were drawn together by their afflictions; he had a blind eye and she had a very obvious stammer. It is said that she was passive during Herbert's vigorous courtship, even putting his engagement ring on the mantelpiece for some months before deciding to accept it.

In almost every way she was different from Morrison. Like a figure from a painting by Burne-Jones or Rossetti, she dressed in an eccentric way, in flowing dresses, smocks and shirts, which she designed, made and coloured in striking combinations. She was artistic, indeed 'arty-crafty'. In her room was a loom for weaving cloth, and she loved to embroider. She liked the countryside and gardens, and was fond of dancing and music. She lived with her parents and brother in a detached three-bedroomed house in a pleasant rural setting. Her father, Howard Kent, a clerk at Euston Station, and her mother Annie had come to Letchworth in 1905 from Wood Green. Both were socialists, and were impressed by Morrison, and urged their daughter to accept him. She was eight years younger than Morrison, just twenty, having been born in September 1896. Now a secretary at the nearby Spirella corset factory, she had a sense of humour, which saw deeply into people, and, although very shy, was strong-willed. She persuaded Morrison to give up his pipe and become a non-smoker, converted him to vegetarianism and insisted that he be a teetotaller. This influence reinforced Morrison's earlier ascetic tendencies which had somewhat lapsed while he was at the *Citizen*. Morrison must have been in love with her. He cannot have married her in any way to advance his political career. Rose would have certainly been a better bet if that was his intention. At twenty-eight he was perhaps feeling he ought to be married; she was available, a challenge, representing much that he lacked and yet yearned for, and she did not actively rebuff him. So, they became engaged.

While at Letchworth Morrison involved himself in the work of the local ILP, attending their Sunday evening sessions at the Skittles Inn, when they heard such speakers as H. N. Brailsford, Ramsay MacDonald, E. D. Morel, George Lansbury, Sylvia Pankhurst, Bernard Shaw and G. D. H. Cole. Morrison spoke in his saucy and succinct style. He also conducted the affairs of the LLP from Letchworth. His light would burn in his room until very late as he typed and drafted, prepared his reports and circulars and wrote letters and articles. He persuaded the Kents to help with filling and addressing envelopes. He often went to London on LLP business; 'he kept the Party machine in motion'.[28]

While he was at Letchworth, his father died. After Herbert had left home, his father had been looked after by his daughters, Lucy and Edie, and by his daughter-in-law Kitty, who all found him increasingly difficult to manage as he drank more and more. He developed heart disease and died of an attack in November 1917 aged sixty-eight. On his death the house in Mordaunt Street became Herbert's. However, he felt that as a good socialist he could not be a property owner, and so he sold the house and divided the proceeds, about three hundred pounds, equally between himself, his brothers and sisters: a generous act, warmly acknowledged by his relatives.

'When the sirens and church bells proclaimed the Armistice I was digging for winter planting at Letchworth. I stopped digging, put my foot on my spade and experienced a quiet and profound emotion; relief that the carnage was over, sorrow for the fallen. It was my own two minutes' silence.'[29] With the war over; and with a little money saved, he could now marry and return to London. At the Hitchin Registry Office on 15 March 1919, he married Margaret. Her mother would have preferred a church wedding, but the couple were adamant. Herbert sold his bike for a pound to Margaret's brother and took her to live in London at 16 Clements Road, Bermondsey, in a house found for them by Dr Salter.

Although Herbert liked Letchworth, he felt he had to return to London. He was attracted by the idea of a garden city and from this time became the leading advocate within the Labour Party of the green belt around London, new towns and garden cities.[30] Margaret, lover of the rural setting, was terribly upset at coming to live in a grim and bug-infested house in Bermondsey. But Herbert said that if he was to serve the working class he had to live as one of them. However, it became too much for her, and they moved in 1920 to Clapton, in north Hackney, to a house which they shared with James Mylles and his family, who had moved from Brixton. Everything was set for Morrison to begin building up the London Labour Party and to take a part in the local government of Hackney.

Section II: London Politics and Towards a
Wider Stage in the 1920s

Chapter 5

On Hackney's Borough Council, 1920-1925

In November 1919 the Labour Party achieved surprising successes in the municipal elections all over the country. Seats which had long been held by Conservatives, Liberals and Independents fell to Labour. London was no exception. In November 1912, when the borough elections had last been held, Labour had won 46 of 1,362 seats; in November 1919 it won 572, and with its aldermen possessed over 600 members of London borough councils. It had a majority in 12 boroughs out of 28, and was the leading party in two others.[1] The swing to Labour was a national phenomenon, but in London one explanation for the victories was put about, which Morrison did little to dispute, namely that his efficiency as Secretary of the London Labour Party was responsible. Morrison had not been a candidate in his own borough of Hackney.* Although he attended meetings of the Hackney Labour Party, his main interest in 1919 and 1920 was in building up the London Labour Party. His vision was wider than Hackney. Indeed his interests were becoming national, since in 1920 he was first elected to the Labour Party's National Executive Committee.

In November 1919 Labour became the governing party in Hackney with a majority of two out of a council of seventy.[2] For its first Mayor the Labour Party went outside the council and chose a respected local man, Mr Payne, in order to preserve their flimsy majority. If they had chosen from their own ranks, a valuable vote would have been neutralized through his being made Mayor. The party stumbled through a somewhat undistinguished year, until in September 1920 Payne died. The party was racked by bitter wranglings about his successor. The claims of sitting members were strongly canvassed. But again it was decided not to jeopardize the slim majority; the choice was Morrison.

* In the 1920s Hackney, a metropolitan borough north of the Thames and adjoining the East End, had a population of about 220,000. Its composition was mixed, ranging from wealthy city merchants in the northern part to the working classes in the south, who worked in numerous small factories, notably clothing, furniture, footwear and engineering.

The local press was stunned; the *Hackney Spectator* called his nomination an 'insult to every man and woman in the borough'. It objected to his not being a native of Hackney and to his lack of experience of municipal life. He was not a member of the council, he never had been a member and on the only two occasions that he had stood for election, at Lambeth and North Southwark,[3] he had been beaten. The editorial urged that the Labour Party was not so bankrupt of ability that it had to bring in the party's paid organizer. This affair was 'an act of political jobbery of a very offensive and objectionable character', since with the Mayoralty went an allowance of £300 per annum. The paper also pointed out to ex-servicemen in the borough that he 'was one of those who throughout the war would not raise a finger to help to stop the on-rush of the hordes who were trying to destroy the free democracies and peoples, in whom he professes to believe'.[4]

The other paper was not so hostile. It recognized Morrison as 'a spare, fair-haired enthusiast with a genius for practical organization', and felt that 'if Hackney *must* have a Labour Mayor, there is no one who is better able than he to maintain the prestige of the office, as well as the high standard of duty set by its late holder', although it objected to the choice since his only contacts with the council were 'periodical visits to the strangers' gallery'.[5]

These criticisms were repeated in the council chamber on the day of his in-auguration, when his suitability was debated for nearly an hour. When the vote was taken fifteen Municipal Reformers (Conservatives) voted for another candidate, while forty-five Labour and Progressive (Liberal) votes were cast for Morrison. He then announced 'with fluency and determination' that he would be of service to all citizens and would 'endeavour to observe the im-partiality between the parties which should be the characteristic of a Mayor'. Both papers commented adversely on his 'sartorial equipment': 'his views were indicated by a glaring red tie – the outward sign of the full-blooded Socialist extremist'.[6] Within an hour of being made Mayor he faced his first difficult task, when a wily member of the opposition raised a tricky point of order, but Morrison made the correct ruling for, since he had been invited to accept the nomination, he had read many times the council's standing orders.[7]

At first he scorned ceremony; there was no formal reception for him when he was made Mayor. His mode of dress was to many an affront to dignity; he seemed to go everywhere in a brown Harris tweed suit, red tie and brown brogue shoes. He also followed the ruling of the organization of London Labour Mayors, inspired by George Lansbury,* not to wear resplendent scarlet mayoral robes. And when he attended dinners his vegetarianism and teetotalism encouraged jocular comments about his nut cutlets and ginger pop.[8] Some felt that he had lowered the tone of the Mayoralty, but Morrison retorted that he was unable to afford special clothes, and with serious un-employment in the borough he would not be ostentatious.

However during his Mayoralty an incident occurred which made him

* At the time active in the politics of Poplar; later leader of the Labour Party 1932–5.

change his mind about the trappings of ceremony. He visited a Christmas party where the children were looking forward to seeing the Mayor in his robes and chain. 'Their faces fell with disappointment and disillusion when I walked in wearing my usual brown tweed suit and only the chain. When I saw this childish reaction I said to myself, "We've made a mistake. The office matters more than the man; the children think we've let the position of mayor down." '[9] From then on he became concerned with the accoutrements of office. He insisted that the Town Clerk wear his black gown and wig in the council chamber, even on sweltering hot days. Morrison told him that such regalia gave prestige to local affairs, and that he did not want local government conducted in a street corner fashion.[10]

He performed the customary functions: the unveiling of the War Memorial; auction sales for charitable causes; visits to local institutions, like the infirmary, and to local events like boxing matches at the Baths, prize-givings at schools, anniversary services at churches, and banquets, like that of the local Chamber of Commerce. Never was there any criticism of his manner here. Morrison was adept at seeing what was expected of him as Mayor and he saw the value of favourable publicity for himself and the party. He impressed everyone as an impartial representative of the borough. He even met royalty without mishap, although he felt that when Queen Mary came to open a Salvation Army Mothers' Home she was shocked at his ubiquitous brown suit and red tie.[11] The main ceremonial occasion of his Mayoralty was a visit by the Prince of Wales. There was anxiety that a socialist would behave improperly in the presence of royalty.[12] In fact Morrison delighted the press, embarrassed his opponents and angered some of his supporters. His view was that he was Mayor of Hackney, of all its inhabitants and not just of a party, and that he should do what the citizens of Hackney wanted, which was to greet the King's son with a warm welcome. He ordered Union Jacks to be flown from the Town Hall and the Baths. On his way to the football stadium to meet the Prince he saw that there was no flag over the Baths. 'He had his car stopped and went personally into the building to instruct that the national flag should be hoisted in honour of the Royal visit.' Later 'the Prince was observed to be in pleasant conversation with Hackney's Labour Mayor, whose scarlet tie rivalled in prominence the mayoral insignia of office, and occasionally he would emphasise his remarks with familiar pats on the Mayor's arm'. In all, Morrison showed 'a proper appreciation of what was expected of him as chief citizen of a patriotic borough'.[13]

As chairman of the council Morrison performed with firmness and good humour, winning a reputation for calm efficiency. He had to be alert, since the opposition 'was up to everything' to trip him up. Normally he managed to keep tempers cool, but occasionally there was a flare-up.[14] Most often he was able to dispatch business briskly, ensuring that proper procedures were followed and all points of view heard.

Compared with most Mayors he was much more to the fore in policy-making; indeed, although William Parker was the nominal leader, Morrison during his Mayoralty soon became the real leader of the Labour Party on the Hackney council. His pre-eminence arose from his sheer ability, despite his youth, and from the fact that he had the time to devote himself to local government. He was a professional politician, the full-time paid Secretary of the London Labour Party, and his work on the Hackney council was an extension of his London Labour Party work; thus he could give more time to the council than any other member. The opposition certainly regarded Morrison as the leader and concentrated their fire on him. They called him the 'genius of the Council'.[15] They often mounted spiteful personal attacks. For instance the Town Clerk suggested that a telephone be installed in Morrison's house so that he could be in immediate communication with the Town Hall on any matter of urgency. Morrison had not initiated the idea and in committee had raised objections to the proposal. The opposition, however, complained that Morrison would want next a Rolls-Royce on the rates.[16]

The main problem which faced Hackney, and indeed the country, in 1920 and 1921 was unemployment. One of Morrison's first acts as Mayor was to create a distress fund for the unemployed of the borough. This recourse to charity, although to some demonstrating his practical sympathy with the unemployed, to others was a serious failing in a socialist. When he later praised the co-operation of every class and party in contributing to the fund, he widened further the rift between himself and the leaders of the militant unemployed.[17] They seized a local drill hall for their headquarters and took over some near-by houses which they held for a week; they fought with the police and even stole some borough council coal. They marched to the offices of the board of guardians* to protest against the low rates of relief and hurled threats and insults at those inside. Morrison disowned such direct action.[18] He wrote to the Prime Minister that he had set his face against disorder and illegality, and that the great bulk of organized labour adhered to 'democratic constitutionalism'.[19]

This fervour for constitutional behaviour brought him sharply into conflict with George Lansbury at Poplar. There the local Labour party had decided, without any consultation with the London Labour Party, that the local council should not levy rates for the precepts from the LCC and other local government bodies, as a protest against rising unemployment, the inadequacies of government action and the miserable scales of relief. Morrison regarded Poplar's action as not conducive to unity within the Labour movement. Such illegal action would paralyse the work of local government by dislocating services essential for the well-being of the people. In any case the government, not the LCC, was the enemy. He criticized Lansbury's policy as putting unreasonable burdens on working and lower middle class ratepayers, and he believed it would stand no chance of being endorsed by the electorate. He feared that Poplar's approach would provide a precedent for Labour's

---

* A locally elected body responsible for the relief of poverty.

opponents to go against the law if Labour was in power and they disagreed with Labour policy. He felt too that the central government would take reprisals against local authorities who undertook such action, supplanting them by central commissioners. Above all he felt it was dangerous to provoke chaos.[20]

When the Hackney council met to fix the rate for the year, a deputation from the unemployed was admitted and it appealed to the council to follow Poplar's example. Morrison rebuked the spokesman and asked him to withdraw. The public gallery erupted; Morrison was the butt of insults, the Red Flag was sung and he threatened to close the gallery. When quiet was restored he said 'conduct such as they had witnessed that night was not going to help the unemployed of the borough'. When the vote was taken only nine Labour rebels supported Poplar's example against forty-six for legality. To the militant unemployed Morrison was a 'washout'.[21]

To Morrison unemployment was a national problem, to be tackled by the central government and not by local authorities. Unemployment could not be really solved in a capitalist system. Only when the socialist Co-operative Commonwealth was established could unemployment be eradicated. However in the meantime the misery of unemployment could be alleviated. The government should pursue a peaceful foreign policy, particularly towards Ireland, Russia and Central Europe, ending blockades and providing credits, thus establishing 'open and friendly economic relations'. Foreign trade would be resumed, economic life revived and work restored to the jobless. The government had to provide from its resources work, or adequate maintenance and training. Local authorities, the borough councils and boards of guardians, with their puny resources could not be expected any longer to shoulder the heavy burdens which unemployment laid on them.

He advocated the provision of a series of useful public works* with ninety per cent of their cost borne by the national Exchequer and the remaining ten per cent by a municipal rate levied over the whole of London and not just by individual boroughs. Morrison felt that the existing system of local finance in London was grossly unfair. The rich boroughs with little unemployment contributed hardly at all towards the poor boroughs which had the most unemployed and therefore the largest expenditure. The answer was rate

---

* 'Housing, town planning and slum clearances, and the establishment of new towns or garden cities in the Home Counties, the further provision of schools, schemes for providing a more cheap and abundant public supply of electricity for commercial and domestic purposes, passenger traffic development, including tube extensions, reclamation of the foreshores of the River Lee [extension of main drainage facilities], and the putting into a state of efficiency of the banks and locks and other works of the River Thames, street widenings, construction and improvement of bridges and other public improvement schemes, transformation of neglected private, semi-private and public squares into pleasant public recreation grounds, improvement and development of the Port of London.' This list is constantly repeated in LLP policy statements and articles and speeches by Morrison in the 1920s.

equalization whereby resources and costs over the whole of London would be shared.

Hackney had done what it could to provide work, repairing many roads and painting public buildings, but such local works were not large enough to reduce significantly the numbers out of work. To impress on the government that it should take action to deal with a potentially dangerous situation Morrison organized what was the most dramatic incident of his Mayoralty, a journey to the Highlands of Scotland to beard Lloyd George in his hotel at Gairloch. In September 1921 a Cabinet Committee on Unemployment under the chairmanship of Sir Alfred Mond, the Minister of Health, had put forward proposals for grants to assist local authorities to provide work for the unemployed. Morrison rejected this approach, claiming that unemployment should be a national and not a local responsibility. Morrison sought an interview with the Prime Minister who was at Inverness; Lloyd George replied that his doctors forbade official interviews, and indeed no useful purpose would be served by such a meeting. Morrison, however, gathered seven other London Labour Mayors and together with Hackney's Borough Accountant as financial adviser travelled by train to Inverness only to find that Lloyd George had moved to a hotel at Gairloch thirty miles away. They hired a car and reached the hotel, where they found that Lloyd George had called post-haste the Cabinet Committee to meet the delegation. Morrison was selected as spokesman and forcefully put his case. Robin Cruikshank, later editor of the *News Chronicle*, described Morrison's performance as 'a combination of Cockney brashness and universal high-mindedness'. Lloyd George told Cruikshank: 'That was a most remarkable young man who spoke for the Mayors. I never heard a better marshalling of an argument. No rhetoric, no whir-r-rling of words, but a splendid organising of a case. Good! Very good! That young man will go far.'[22] The Prime Minister promised to examine Morrison's proposals, but would offer little else, except that boards of guardians might raise three-year loans, guaranteed by the government, and repay them from the rates. 'Desperate finance' replied Morrison, who concluded: 'If that is all you can give me, Sir, I am afraid we shall go away very disappointed and the outlook is pretty black for some time to come.' With the interview over the Mayors clambered into the car and dashed back to the station at Inverness. Although the militants looked on his trip as a stunt, Morrison was fairly pleased. He had publicized the plight of the unemployed and the inadequacy of the government's proposals.

In his last week as Mayor, Morrison was humiliated by the council. The Ministry of Health had written to the Town Clerk suggesting a meeting between borough and ministry representatives about equalization of London's rates. The Clerk took the letter to the Mayor who decided to deal with the matter. They both, together with the Borough Treasurer, went to the conference at the ministry. Later, when this meeting was reported to the Finance Committee, the Chairman protested that the Clerk should first have convened

C

a meeting of the Finance Committee or at least have consulted its Chairman. Morrison said: 'Have you finished? I move that you vacate the chair and that the Committee has no confidence in you.' And it was carried. The deposed Chairman took the battle into full council, moving that the Finance Committee's report about the meeting at the ministry be rejected, and he criticized both Morrison and the Clerk. As Mayor, Morrison deplored an attack on an official who could not reply and said that he himself bore all responsibility. His enemies claimed that he had treated the Chairman and his committee with contempt. There had been 'too much Morrison' and too little co-operation. Morrison replied that the remarks against him were made on personal and political grounds. He apologized in no way for his action and would do the same again. The report was rejected by twenty-nine votes to twenty-six which was regarded as a vote of censure on him.[23] The opposition felt they had ' "whipped" the Mayor so successfully that, almost in the last hour of that year, they brought him to his knees with a great thump'.[24]

On his last day as Mayor, however, Morrison was thanked for his services; his ability was praised, as were his zeal and devotion to the welfare of the borough; he was said to have performed his duties with great dexterity and at times with the exuberance of youth.[25] The new Mayor was William Parker, whose former position as leader Morrison now filled. Morrison later claimed of his time as Mayor 'it was an enjoyable and valuable year in my life'.[26] He had reached the topmost position in the council without any apprenticeship, and had made the most of all the opportunities it presented. He acquired a local base. He had built up a following amongst people in his own party and had won respect as a formidable opponent from his enemies. He had learned a great deal about Hackney and its system of local government, and he had come to know its leading citizens and officials, who appreciated his capacity for public business. He had shown that the Labour Party were not wild revolutionaries but were fair and fit to govern.

Although his public face was now well known in Hackney, his private life was obscure. On retirement from the Mayoralty Morrison made an uncharacteristic reference to his wife, praising her patience and fortitude. He said that his home life was tragic; he came home late every night, and was practically a lodger in the house, yet he was never met with a frown or a cross word. 'If she had gone to bed because it was so late, there was always a little love letter waiting for him on the table.'[27] His wife was unhappy in public life; withdrawn and nervous, she rarely went with him to public events, and when she did, was visibly ill at ease. She seemed 'a poor thing, not able to stand up for herself', 'a handicap to Morrison', 'a bit slow on the uptake', 'timid' and 'a strain to talk to'. Many who had made an initial effort to engage her in conversation never attempted it again, after waiting interminably as she 'splittered and spluttered her words out'.[28] During his Mayoralty she was pregnant and gave birth to their only child, Mary Joyce. The pregnancy and the need to care for the baby further kept Mrs Morrison out of public life. The delivery was painful, and she seems to have suffered a minor nervous breakdown, during which she refused to nurse the infant, and she developed an abhorrence of sexual relations. From that point, after just two years of married life, she apparently refused to have sexual intercourse with her husband. For another thirty-two years they lived together. Only those very close to them knew of the domestic unhappiness; to those who saw her from a distance she seemed, as she appeared in an official photograph taken during Morrison's Mayoralty, a graceful sylphlike creature, with a delicate, gentle, other-worldly-type prettiness. The china-smooth complexion concealed a disturbed waif married to the wrong man in the wrong environment. The moments of domestic bliss were rare. One, Morrison later revealed, was when his daughter was reluctant to take her milk and he counted to her in English, French and German to distract her.[29]

The Morrisons lived at Upper Clapton in north Hackney, a prosperous area of substantial houses inhabited in the main by wealthy families, even some City merchants. The setting was in parts rural, with cows grazing on Clapton Common, and near by were attractive walks along the banks of the River Lee.[30] The working class of Hackney lived in the south, in crowded mean streets of terraced houses, alleys and courts. Morrison's home was at 44 Warwick Road, a large three-storey house, with extensive wine cellars and spacious rooms, set in its own grounds and with its own driveway to the charming tree-lined road. He shared the house with the family of his colleague of pre-war days, James Mylles, who lived on the top floors, while the Morrisons had the ground floor as a self-contained flat. Mrs Morrison was responsible for its decoration; flowery materials in delicate pastel shades abounded; the atmosphere was chintzy and homespun. Sir Frederic Osborn recalled that she tried to bring something of Letchworth to the flat. To the teenage daughter of Mylles the Morrison household was happy; she detected no tension and heard no quarrels. Morrison was a cheerful and lively friend, very much an uncle to her. He was very forthcoming and extrovert, and still loved to play the piano and sing. The families were close and the relationships warm.

Morrison's family life was kept very separate from his public life. Hardly any party colleague went to his house and the Morrisons rarely entertained. He lived quite apart from the mass of his supporters and colleagues, in an area they regarded as 'the best part of Hackney' and '100% Tory'. However, some felt he was one of them for he appeared so frequently amongst them and made himself very well known at innumerable social gatherings. Here he entered into the jollifications with gusto, enjoying especially the dancing, folk, Morris and ballroom. But even when he was apparently relaxed an element of calculation intruded. He rationed the dances to one per person, and never concentrated on the gay young 'flappers', but flirted with the more elderly ladies. In this way he built up a core of devoted admirers, his 'key women', who formed the local women's sections of the party. He recognized their value as party workers on dreary but necessary chores, such as addressing and filling envelopes and compiling electoral lists. They formed a block of Morrison loyalists. He knew how to charm them and was proud to have them almost fighting each other to get a dance with him. When songs came to be sung he belted them out with a loud voice. He claimed that the Labour Party believed in 'getting together and enjoying songs and dances and making merry, because in this dreary world there was great need for it'.[31] Politics, however, predominated. A colleague recalled: 'The wards used to hold fortnightly parties for women and children and there were buns and tea and games. It was bedlam and Herbert used to speak on these occasions and was very good at it and exploited these parties to the full.'[32] He never had time for anything but politics – not for games, hobbies, friends, or family – or even widening his interests.[33] He had tried to learn French on gramophone records, but gave it up through lack of time. His spare time was spent on reading material connected with his political work.

Morrison had a fruitful relationship with the Town Clerk, R. H. Tee, who was appointed to Hackney at the start of Morrison's Mayoralty. They got on well together at once; they were of roughly the same age; they were both at the start of new careers and faced at least the suspicion of older men, and both were able, self-confident and enthusiastic, and did not suffer fools gladly. Tee, who remained Clerk of Hackney until 1941, said that Morrison 'was the best boss I ever worked for': 'the most able of the councillors'.

Tee said that Morrison's great quality as a political leader was that he was able to achieve the right relationship with his officials. Indeed Tee's descriptions of Morrison's handling of officials were identical with those of officials who worked for Morrison later at the LCC and in departments of central government. This knack must have been instinctive, since he had never had any training for such a role, and yet it was clearly present in this first position where he had officials under him. Morrison told Tee at the start of their partnership that he did not want officials to be 'yes-men'; he expected them to express themselves freely to him on any proposal, whether it was a matter of administrative detail or policy. In discussion he would always let the official have his say; he would raise points and argue to test the strength of a case. If he disagreed, he would say so with a quip, and never bore malice. He showed a capacity to assimilate a great number of facts and arguments quickly; he thoroughly mastered a subject so as not to be tripped up, and he could see to the core of a problem. After a matter had been thrashed out he reached his own decision, in a fair-minded way. His decisions were always firm; he did not 'wobble'. Officials felt that Morrison was open, straight and honest. Opposition members, too, felt 'you always knew where you were with him', yet 'you had to get up very early in the morning to get things past him'.

Morrison was aware of the delicate relationship between an elected member and an official. Tee once suggested that officials be allowed to attend party meetings so as to ensure that party members had full information before deciding party, and therefore council, policy. But Morrison retorted that officials, for their own protection, should not be mixed up in party squabbles. Officials had to advise members of all parties and to carry out loyally the policies of any party in a majority.

On the appointment of officials Morrison took an opposite view from George Lansbury. The latter felt that Labour needed politically sympathetic officials to carry out Labour policies. Morrison argued that it was better to be ignorant of the political views of officials. If not, then local government staff would be converted into 'the servants of a party or a political creed instead of the instrument of the will of the Council and the people as a whole'. It would encourage in officials attitudes of 'political servility and personal toadyism'. It would protect the incompetent and corrupt and discourage the efficient, while people would join the party simply to get jobs.[34]

Unlike most Labour representatives at this time Morrison was not suspicious of officials as class enemies. He respected their professional expertise. He supported proposals for higher salaries for officials, so that they were paid the proper rate for the job, whereas most Labour councillors objected to people with high salaries obtaining increases while so many other council employees were so poorly paid,[35] and the Municipal Reformers disliked higher salaries because they raised the rates. Morrison's view was that higher salaries were essential for the borough to attract first-rate officials on whose efficiency depended the running of the services. He said: 'If Labour wants to do things and to show the public that its programme of municipalization is good business then it must have able officials.'[36] Morrison displayed further sympathy for officials, when he urged them not to be 'stick-in-the-muds', sitting all day in their offices at Hackney, but to play a part in their national associations, such as their professional organizations, or the Association of Municipal Corporations or the various joint borough bodies in London. If they involved themselves in such activities, they would learn what other authorities were doing and thus Hackney itself would benefit. He showed particular kindness to Tee by encouraging him to complete his doctoral thesis and by arranging for him to have time off from council duties to do so.

Tee and Morrison had lunch together weekly when they discussed council business. Here Tee observed that Morrison was 'very raw socially', but willing to learn. He found in him no trace of meanness: 'he always stood his corner'. Despite their closeness, however, they never called each other by their first names; both felt it important to keep a little distant. Morrison called Tee 'Town Clerk', and Tee called Morrison 'HM' or 'Mr Mayor'. Tee was an important influence on Morrison, for Morrison was like a chameleon, quick to adopt the characteristics and ideas of those who impressed him. He found particularly attractive Tee's drive, perfectionism and mastery of council affairs.[37]

As Mayor, and then as leader of the council, Morrison behaved more like an American town manager or political boss than a traditional English Mayor. He gave a forceful lead. His methods were informal talks with key members and officials. The foundation of his influence was his meticulous reading of memoranda from officials and reports from committees. He was a member of the two committees which had an overview of the work of the local authority, namely Finance, and Establishment and General Purposes. He studied the minutes of all committees so that he could be in touch with all aspects of the council's work. He carried documents everywhere; his pockets always bulged with papers, and even at lunch he would prop up against a vase some paper that just had to be read. He also tried to conciliate potential opponents at an early stage. Although the opposition fought him bitterly in the council chamber, their leaders would meet him amicably in the Town Clerk's room, when he would seek to cajole them with humorous banter and 'smart alec talk'. 'He did not try to steam-roller them.'[38] After the clash with the former Chairman of Finance he usually paid great attention to managing his Labour colleagues. Having reached a decision he would seek to sell it to his own party. He would discuss it first with the chairmen of the committees concerned, the Chief Whip and those on whose loyalty he could depend. He would then rely on them to gather the support of their own cronies. The Chief Whip was of special significance. He rode around the borough on his bicycle slipping notes through doors or calling in for a cup of tea and a chat, always urging the Morrisonian view and listening to the opinions of the members, which he relayed back to the leader. Morrison often dropped into the whip's house in the evening for gossip about the state of the party and a meal.[39] Fully primed, Morrison knew where his strength and weakness lay, which arguments to stress, which anxieties to allay and which people were dangerous. At the party meeting Morrison gave a clear lead. Not as a rabble rouser, but in a reasonable style, he displayed a mastery of facts and arguments that seemed overwhelmingly convincing to the sensible and the moderate. A colleague said that he got his points home 'in a chummy style', not talking down to you but simply to you.[40] He invariably won a majority, but such management was no easy task.

The party on the council were men of little experience of local government, mainly working men and trade unionists who had to their amazement found themselves flung in 1919 into the council. They drew considerable derision from the opposition who regarded them as 'a rabble of nonentities', and even one of Morrison's colleagues said that they did not know 'their arses from their elbows'. Morrison himself told the Town Clerk that they were 'a poor lot', who had to be given a firm lead, and told what to do, how to do it and what not to do.[41] Some of them were inspired by Morrison's style; they recognized his ability, enthusiasm and wide knowledge. He was 'thorough, capable, shrewd, dynamic, not just a talker; he stood out from the others, knew what he wanted and how to get it: a driving force'. These ranks Morrison counted as his friends, and he welded them into a block of supporters. His leadership also consolidated a group of consistent opponents who regarded him as a dictator, intolerant, abrupt, impatient, never heeding their views and constantly going off on his own course. He was also disliked for his moderate views which seemed a betrayal of the working class; some doubted his adherence to the Labour movement for he was not a genuine working man and trade unionist, and lived apart from working people. They resented also perhaps his youth, and that he as a newcomer to Hackney should profess to know better than the older heads who had lived in Hackney all their lives. Morrison's leadership left no one neutral. One source of friction between Morrison and his Labour colleagues was that he took a much broader view. He never immersed himself solely in the intricacies of one particular service, but watched in a general way over them all, concentrating on fixing priorities. Such an approach brought him up against some chairmen who were narrowly devoted to the interests of their own committees.[42]

Leadership of the Labour members of the council was even more difficult because of their slim majority. Morrison used to pray none of the party would have 'flu, and that the Tories would catch it.[43] The thin majority was particularly irksome because some of the Labour members were inveterate haters of Morrison (two at least he claimed were communists). At no council meeting could he be sure of a majority.

In managing the press Morrison excelled. Although the two local papers never accepted his socialism, they respected him as a capable, sincere and sensible leader. Their initial hostility to him soon dispersed. By the end of Morrison's term of office, the *Hackney Spectator* described him as 'shrewd, keen, enthusiastic, and of wonderful ability, he has been the object of admiration by his bitterest political opponents'.[44] He knew how to use the local press to gain publicity for the party and for himself. He wrote frequent letters to the correspondence columns, and sent the papers advance copies of his speeches, and snippets from his talks to various gatherings. He kept the reporters and editors informed of his activities and was richly rewarded. Scarcely an issue went by without some reference to the doings or views of Herbert Morrison.

The major difference between Labour and the opposition on the Hackney council was about the scope of municipal enterprise. To Morrison the essence of socialism was the provision of services and goods to the public by public authorities and not by private enterprise, and a local authority was regarded by him as an admirable form of public organization for a wide range of activities. His main objective was to substitute municipal for private provision.[45] While Labour controlled Hackney, municipal enterprise was extended, and always in the face of bitter opposition. Council employees replaced contractors for the collection and disposal of refuse. The Corporation organized its own dances on Saturdays at municipal premises. The insurance business of the council was transferred from private companies to the joint local authority enterprise, Municipal Mutual Insurance Limited. And Morrison was a great advocate and a founder-trustee of the Municipal

Mutual Supply Ltd, a proposed joint local authority enterprise, which would act as a central supply department, buying in bulk machinery, tools and goods direct from manufacturers for use by individual local authorities, thus eliminating the middleman.

The most stunning example of successful municipal enterprise, to Morrison, was Hackney's electricity undertaking. Each year it earned substantial surpluses which were used to help reduce the rates; it was called 'the sheet anchor of the borough finances'. He often pointed to it as evidence of the capacity of municipal officials, under the direction of a committee, to run successfully a large trading undertaking. Morrison was a member of the Electricity Committee and had a close relationship with the borough's Electrical Engineer from whom he learned a formidable amount about electricity. They were responsible for the extension of the generating capacity of the Hackney electricity undertaking and for the decision to electrify the whole borough. Morrison felt that the success of its electricity undertaking could be repeated with other services.[46]

Housing was a great concern of Morrison. Labour at Hackney instituted a programme of building council houses and increased the number of notices served on private landlords to make them bring their properties into a decent state of repair. Labour saved the ratepayers twenty thousand pounds a year by replacing allowances to private landlords who collected their tenants' rates by the direct payment of rates by occupiers to the local authority. Morrison went on many deputations to ministers, urging increased grants for building and repairing houses, and urging that wartime rent controls should be maintained. He advocated that local authorities should be empowered to take over houses unoccupied for three months and let them to tenants, and to levy rates on property unoccupied for six months so as to give landlords an incentive to take in tenants. He also urged that the government should stop a trend which was causing anxiety in Hackney: the conversion of houses into factories.

Such projects as Labour undertook, Morrison justified as both humane and sound business propositions, efficiently and economically administered. The opposition fiercely criticized the Labour Party's management of the finances of Hackney, complaining that they had embarked on unnecessary and extravagant schemes. The council chamber echoed to the mutual accusations of financial incompetence. Comparative statistics of terrible complexity were bandied about to prove that Labour was economical or spendthrift. Morrison revelled in this type of debate, bewildering everyone with his tables of rate statistics, which he often then re-used in articles and letters to the press to show the efficiency of Labour boroughs. His most criticized financial manoeuvre came in 1922, prior to the November election, when the Labour Party managed to reduce Hackney's rate to the lowest in London, and lower than the last rate levied by the Municipal Reformers, by taking twenty-five thousand pounds from the electricity surplus. The opposition claimed it was an electioneering stunt, and Morrison later admitted it was an error, arguing that a surplus should be used to improve the service and to reduce costs for the consumers.[47]

At Hackney Morrison showed himself very much the friend of two forces which supported the Labour Party: the Co-operative Movement and trade unions. He publicized his patronage of the Co-operative Movement by frequently pointing out that he bought all that he could from the society's shop, even his notorious suits and ties. On the council he allowed the Co-operative Society to tender for the first time for contracts for certain supplies, much to the anger of the local shopkeepers. He advocated trade unionism too, urging all municipal employees to join their appropriate trade unions. With 100% membership attained they could then assert their strength 'with dignity, but firmness' through the recently established Whitley Council machinery of joint industrial councils.[48] Such collective bargaining brought order into industrial relations. When leader of the council, Morrison set up in Hackney a joint committee of council representatives and employees to discuss all manner of industrial relations problems, for Hackney had to be a model employer.[49]

He supported the trade unions over the wages to be paid to unemployed men occasionally employed by the council to do special work, often seasonal, like tree topping. The Municipal Reformers paid only seventy-five per cent of the trade union rate, arguing that more unemployed could be found work than if the full rate were paid. In reply Morrison criticized sweated labour and a wage not sufficient for bringing up a family.[50] But he was not an automatic champion of trade unions. When a clash arose between their demands and those of the wider community he put the latter first. In 1921, for example, when it was expected that a major coal and rail strike would paralyse the country, he wrote to the trade unions that the Labour councils had a duty to see that their people were fed, yet they wanted to be free of the charge of strike breaking. He sought co-operation between the town halls and the trade unions, whereby volunteers from local strike committees would ensure that essential supplies flowed freely.[51] The crunch never came for the strike was called off.

Morrison identified himself with two local causes which won him the support of people of all parties in Hackney. The River Lee flowed through Hackney, and was polluted by factories and local authorities higher up the river.[52] He urged the Conservancy Board and ministers to take action to clean up the Lee.[53] The local press and local organizations like the Rowing Club praised his efforts. But he achieved little. By 1925 he was sceptical whether the various local authorities could cope. He felt that a Greater London scheme of drainage was needed. His experience as Hackney's representative on the Conservancy Board, where he pressed Hackney's case, showed him the failings of bodies composed of representatives of local authorities.

He also defended another amenity of Hackney, its famous marshes granted to the people in 1892 in perpetuity as open space for their recreation. In the war, however, a small part had been taken by the government for a projectile factory. After the war the LCC, as trustees of the Hackney Marshes, decided to sell the factory site and not to return it as open space. Morrison became the leader of a local campaign for restoring the site to its original purpose. A citizens' committee was formed, a town's meeting held and Morrison was prominent in attacking the LCC, which he said 'have not attached proper importance to the opinions of the people of the borough itself. After all, the local Council are the guardians of the people of Hackney, and on local questions I would be inclined to take far more seriously the opinions of the Borough Council than the opinions of the London County Council.'[54] The LCC were unable to find a buyer for the land and in default let the land revert to open space.[55]

At the November 1922 municipal elections Labour's opponents, the Progressives and Municipal Reformers, mounted a concerted campaign, ensuring that there were no three-cornered contests. They condemned Labour for financial mismanagement, and portrayed the party as a coalition of communists, revolutionary socialists and a few political trade unionists. They presented themselves as the party of steady progress, of efficiency with the strictest economy. Labour concentrated on their own humane achievements, their concern for the underdog, their efficiency and their economy, revealed by the fact that Hackney's rates were the lowest in London. It was to no avail. All Labour candidates were defeated. Only five aldermen, including Morrison,* who were not due to retire for another three years, remained on the council as Labour representatives. Morrison's administration of Hackney looked as if it was decisively condemned by the electorate. Morrison's explanation was simple: 'Bad Labour organization; good Coalition organization. . . . Labour had a fine record of constructive Socialist work, but its weak electoral machine could neither find nor poll its supporters.'[56] The whip pointed out that the Labour Party in Hackney consisted really of the councillors and aldermen, and a few trade unionists, and that there was no significant band of supporters outside the council. Money was short and Morrison used to donate the expenses he recovered from the Conservancy Board to the party's election funds. He felt that the victories of 1919 were 'flukes' and that the defeats now were healthy, because they dispersed 'sawdust illusions' and showed that they must build up a strong organization. The local press was glad that Labour had taken a hand at the wheel: 'it was able to guide the thoughts of our civic fathers into fresh channels, and to indicate smooth sailing where hitherto nothing but rocks were supposed to exist.'[57]

Labour defeats were common over the whole country. There was a national swing to the coalition forces. In London Labour's share of the vote fell from 39 per cent to 35 per cent, although the number of those voting Labour rose. But the number voting Municipal Reform rose even more, and its share of

* He had been appointed to the aldermanic bench while he was Mayor.

the vote soared from 38 per cent to 57 per cent. It seemed to have gained most at the expense of the Progressives whose share of the vote collapsed from 23 per cent to eight per cent.[58] Hackney's result looks, therefore, in no way exceptional, especially when boroughs of similar social composition, like Fulham and Islington, witnessed shattering Labour defeats. But the Hackney result was exceptional in that Labour's share of the vote rose by about three per cent. It can be argued that, while Labour's share of the vote fell over London and in boroughs like Battersea, Camberwell, Islington, and even Poplar, it rose in Hackney because Morrison had made an impact.

Morrison was leader of the small Labour group on the Hackney council from 1922 to 1923. He had wondered whether to retire, but decided to remain, and he advised Labour aldermen in other boroughs to 'stay where they are, keep the flag flying and be in a position to secure inside information as to Borough Council policy'. They should stay also on behalf of those electors who had voted for the unsuccessful Labour candidates.[59] In the early years of opposition he was as assiduous in his duties as ever. He maintained an eye on all aspects of the authority's work from his membership of the Finance Committee. He turned up regularly to meetings and made skilful use of the procedures of the council, especially putting down motions and questions to obtain publicity for his criticisms of the council's policies, and calling for reports on topics to expose mismanagement. His Labour colleagues were overshadowed. When he was absent meetings were short; one lasted only seven minutes.[60]

He was concerned that the majority were not conducting business openly, particularly that business was decided at Monday night party meetings before matters had been discussed in council or committee. Such secrecy opened the door, he argued, to corruption. He complained that information was withheld from the opposition; even officials were not allowed to give him information without the permission of the party. He said: 'There is no encouragement to come to this place. There is nothing to do.'[61]

He had a keen eye for anything that smacked of graft. He showed himself a stickler for proper procedures for appointing staff. His concern for clean government seemed to some almost the obsession of a man who had started from nothing, was fearful that he might be tempted and allow himself to be bought and so kept on announcing that he was not for sale and would fight any would-be purchaser.[62] His view was that local government offered to working men and women with their low wages great temptations, and unscrupulous interests would not be reluctant to try to buy their influence. In the East End boroughs some major scandals were revealed and the Municipal Reformers in some areas gained an unsavoury reputation for malpractices with jobs and contracts. Morrison was most anxious that Labour's reputation should not be tarnished. Whenever even a whiff of such activities arose in

Hackney, he was to the fore in exposing it. As Mayor he had used his casting vote as Chairman of the Establishment Committee, in addition to his ordinary vote, to block the appointment of a person on whose behalf a certain councillor had taken great interest. He complained of councillors' canvassing for appointments and promotions.[63] In 1923 he forced the withdrawal of the new Deputy Medical Officer of Health, when he showed that the post had not been advertised and that the man had been a councillor at Hackney only eight months previously, when he should have been off the council for twelve months before being eligible for the appointment.[64] He uncovered the appointment to the Electricity Department of a relative of the Deputy Electrical Engineer, and that too without advertisement.[65] He felt strongly that members of the council should not use their position to grant themselves favours, as for instance when the Town Hall was hired to two members for a wedding reception,[66] and he urged Labour councillors not to become tenants of new municipal houses until the housing situation was easier, for fear that the voters would think improper influence had been used.[67]

The other themes he pressed home were those he had championed as leader of the council. Cuts in social services were fiercely opposed; he urged more expenditure on roads in working class areas; he condemned extravagant expenditure, on for instance a mural at the electricity showrooms and on high expenses for delegations to conferences.[68] He was most bitter when the majority copied his policy and used £20,835 of the electricity surplus to reduce the rates.[69] His final speech as a member of the council was to urge that direct labour and not contractors be used to redecorate council houses. He said 'he was glad that the last amendment he moved on the Council was for the sound and glorious principles of Socialism'.[70] His campaigns riled the majority, because they were so ably conducted. His speeches displayed a mastery of facts and arguments, and in any altercation which arose he remained cool, and became more witty and cutting the more he was provoked.[71]

His attendances at council meetings in 1924 and 1925 were not as regular as earlier and his questions and motions were fewer. The frustration of opposition, and of leading such meagre colleagues, convinced him that his time was better spent elsewhere. He had been elected to the LCC in 1922, and his work there took up more of his time. National politics beckoned. He was a member of the National Executive Committee of the Labour Party and was elected to Parliament for South Hackney in 1923. He was also absorbed deeply in his work for the London Labour Party. His sights went beyond Hackney. The main reason, however, why he left the Hackney borough council and did not stand for re-election was that he no longer qualified for membership, since in 1924 he had moved to Eltham. He said he felt that one should live in the borough on whose council one served. The opposition were full of glee at his departure. They had seen his failing interest: 'when he can't use this Borough Council for stunts he won't turn up because he's got bigger fish to fry.'[72]

Morrison's enemies made his final attendances at the council humiliating.

Morrison protested at their 'perpetual ignorant discourtesy'; 'some members', he said, 'are never happy unless they are howling me down!'[73] A blow came from Alderman Anning, a communist, who composed a twenty-five-verse poem, 'The Passing of 'Erb',[74] which was quoted at a council meeting to hoots of laughter. Only fragments survive.

> To say you came and conquered is not absolutely true,
> Or even as a leader struck terror to the Blue.
> Hackney called you to them, or, rather, Parker did;
> Was it a case for Socialism, or was it 300 quid?
> Some I know will miss you, will ponder your position;
> They will be your real staunch friends – members of
> the Coalition.

At the 1925 municipal elections in Hackney the verdict of 1922 was repeated. Not one Labour candidate was elected and the new council, now shorn of its Labour aldermen, was one hundred per cent Municipal Reform. As in 1922 Morrison put the result down to the superior organization of the opposition. However, compared with 1922, Labour's share of the vote had risen by about four per cent, which was slightly better than the rise of about three per cent in London as a whole,[75] and much better than in boroughs of a similar social composition like Battersea and Islington where Labour's share of the vote fell. As in 1922 Morrison seems to have made Labour somewhat more popular in Hackney than elsewhere in London.

Service on the Hackney council provided Morrison with opportunities to display his talents, and his experiences reinforced many of his earlier tendencies and attitudes – his adherence to constitutional procedures, his hatred of improper influence and his preference for collective as against private enterprise – but they also gave him new insights and caused him to alter some positions. There were six broad ways in which he learned important lessons. First he saw that a leader of a local authority, or any other group of men, could not be dictatorial; he had to work with and through colleagues who had to be coaxed. He also saw that it was unwise to be too closely involved with officials; there had to be a distance between them. Also, since a leader of a local authority had to work with colleagues, such as chairmen of committees, he would need them to be competent people whom he could trust. Such were not likely to be thrown up voluntarily by the electoral process. He saw that to collect together a team of able members of a local council he would have to go out and cajole those he wanted to come forward as candidates. The responsibilities of office moderated his views; he saw the limitations on authority: the myriad difficulties, legal, administrative and political, attached to different solutions. He acquired also a greater respect for the electorate. After he had suffered two overwhelming electoral defeats, in 1922 and 1925, instead of despising the voters, he seemed to defer to them even more, seeking always to present his policies to attract them. He saw that if the voters were not favourable then he, and the party, would have no opportunity to do the things they desired. Finally his experiences at Hackney showed him the serious limitations on the metropolitan boroughs as instruments to implement socialism. They had too few powers and covered much too small areas. His horizons were broadened; his view was no longer concentrated on Hackney. By the end of his time on the borough council he had come to recognize the drawbacks of the boroughs; the LCC was his objective now.

Chapter 6

At the London Labour Party, 1918-1929

A machine without high principles is a machine of no real value. And high principles without an efficient machine constitute but a voice crying in the wilderness. We have to make an efficient machine for a high moral purpose.[1]

Herbert Morrison

'The story of the rise of Labour in London is an epic in itself. And it is largely the story of the rise and growth of Herbert Morrison.'[2] Indeed he is the only Labour figure in British politics who reached the top ranks of the party through local government. The instrument which Morrison used was the London Labour Party. Although it had been created a few months before he became its Secretary, he forged it into a unique political machine. He was devoted to this organization above all others, since it was where he made his reputation and was the base from which he moved out to run the LCC and to play a role in national politics, on the National Executive of the Labour Party, as an MP and as a Cabinet Minister. With the LLP behind him Morrison could meet trade union bosses and upper class intellectuals on equal terms.

He was 'the life and soul of the party, its architect and inspirer, the man who cemented and welded it and kept it disciplined. As Secretary he ran the show; he initiated schemes, he conceived ideas, he drove people to do things, he inspired their activity.'[3] He was a 'Napoleon behind the type-writer'.[4]

Tables (a) to (d) in the appendices show Labour's spectacular rise from a meagre opposition group to be the governing party of London.[5] The membership of the LLP rose from 134,951 in 1914 to 371,260 in 1926; and, following an alteration in the methods of calculation in 1926, the local party membership of the LLP increased from 29,227 to 63,225 in 1939, and the trade union, co-operative and socialist society membership from 172,022 to 192,295. The income of the LLP's general account rose from £119 in 1914–15 to £3,946 in 1938–9, and its expenditure from £110 to £3,345.[6] The growth of the party and of Morrison's influence is reflected also in the expansion of LLP office space. On its creation the LLP headquarters were shared with those of the London Trades Council near Smithfield Market. Then they were wherever Morrison lodged, until in January 1920 the LLP acquired its first premises: two rooms at 15 Southwark Bridge Road, where 'much of our furniture came from surplus Army stocks, and looked like it'.[7] From then expansion was rapid: in March 1921 three rooms at 58 Theobalds Road; and in 1924 seven rooms at 12 Tavistock Place. Finally in August 1926 the LLP moved to the site which was to remain its headquarters until the late 1950s: the whole top floor of 258–262 Westminster Bridge Road, over a Lyons teashop, directly opposite County Hall and only four minutes' walk over Westminster Bridge to the Houses of Parliament. No more strategically situated position could have been found; from it Morrison could easily stride out to the LCC, Transport House, or the House of Commons.

The three most important forces which built up the LLP and enabled Morrison to gain fame were the national Labour Party, the trade unions, especially the Transport and General Workers Union of Ernest Bevin, and the Royal Arsenal Co-operative Society.

Between 1919 and 1921 Morrison was engaged in a wrangle with the Labour Party about its relationship with the LLP. Morrison claimed that the LLP was being neglected since it had no grant from head office. In October 1919 Morrison asked for money from the national party to extend the work of the LLP, and for offices in the same building as national headquarters. The reply was a refusal, on the grounds that if a grant was given to the LLP, other local parties would want one too, and that the present premises were fully occupied.[8] Head office feared that Morrison's ambitions would take the LLP beyond the control of the national party, and so his claims, even for a meagre forty pounds, were rejected. Morrison persisted.[9] After tortuous negotiations agreement was reached in 1921, whereby the National Executive would appoint a London District Organizer who would work from the LLP office. The NEC would pay his salary and a proportion both of the rent that had to be paid for larger offices and of charges for staff and furniture. In addition the NEC agreed to appoint a Woman Organizer, responsible for building up the work of the women's section, to work from the offices of the LLP.[10] Morrison was satisfied at the outcome of his pressure, but he continued to urge the NEC to give more; for instance in 1926 he sought an increased grant and a payment to cover the cost of the removal to Westminster Bridge Road. The NEC agreed to pay an extra fifty pounds a year, and fifty pounds for the removal.[11]

The first London District Organizer, appointed by the NEC in 1921, was Richard Windle, a native of Bermondsey and the agent at Walthamstow.

He remained at the LLP until 1929 when he was promoted to be Assistant National Agent.[12] He took over most of the work of creating and building up local Labour parties in London, which up to then Morrison had handled himself, urging trade unions to affiliate, giving legal and organizational advice, assisting in the selection of candidates for parliamentary elections, and above all guiding the local parties at general elections and by-elections. He was regarded as 'a prince among electioneers'.[13] Those who saw Windle in action called him 'the power behind Herbert's throne'.[14]

It is ironical that the man who is regarded as Morrison's worst enemy, Ernest Bevin, was also the financial mainstay of the LLP. Indeed Kingsley Martin* thought that the origin of Bevin's hatred of Morrison was because Morrison would not dance to the tune called by the man who paid the piper.[15] In October 1922 Bevin affiliated his new TGWU, over twenty-four thousand members, at twopence per person, to the LLP and, even more importantly, in the following year devised a new system of distributing trade union money to the party, which really put the LLP on a firm financial foundation. The national office of each trade union paid to the LLP head office a sum based on the total membership affiliated, and then the LLP according to an agreement with the trade union would allocate money to local parties. Thus the handling of the finance was centralized in place of the previous complicated and wasteful system whereby local branches of trade unions gave funds to local parties and to the LLP. The national offices of the trade unions could now keep a check on the money flowing out, while the LLP had an assured sum from a single source.[16] Another major paymaster was the London Society of Compositors, from whose ranks came the Chairman of the LLP, 1919–33, Thomas Naylor. Leading officials from other unions who contributed to party funds were also found places on the Executive. Morrison realized that the Labour Party depended on trade union money. He talked to Walter Citrine† about how best to approach the trade unions so as to get more funds flowing into the LLP.[17] Charles Brandon, a TGWU official, and later a Chairman of the LLP, described Morrison as a 'first class beggar'.[18]

Another major source of finance for the LLP was the Royal Arsenal Co-operative Society which affiliated in 1921, and always had at least one representative on the Executive. In return Morrison was a superb propagandist for the RACS. He frequently declaimed his devotion: 'So seriously do my wife and myself take our co-operative principles that not only are the bulk of our household needs purchased as far as possible at the Co-op, but the house itself has been decorated and a new fireplace constructed by the RACS. We bank with the Co-op and I am insured with the Co-op.'[19] Morrison was a genuine believer in the Co-operative Movement, and sought to encourage it to be more active in politics, pointing out that private traders backed the Conservatives who opposed the activities of the Co-op, for instance cutting them out of

* Editor of the *New Statesman*, 1931–60.
† General Secretary of the Trades Union Congress, 1926–46.

tendering to local government.[20] He included in the party journal *London News* a regular feature about Co-ops. Although the RACS supported the LLP, the London Co-operative Society never did, despite constant pleading by Morrison. Unlike the RACS, controlled by the loyalists of Woolwich, the LCS was dominated by communists and elements opposed to the Labour Party.

Morrison constantly urged local parties to recruit more members, not only to gain more activists who would act as propagandists for the party and win more votes, but also to increase the income of the party. Morrison paid great attention to individual subscriptions. Dr Alfred Salter was nominally the Treasurer of the LLP, yet he was not an active finder of funds. He was much more a guarantor of financial rectitude. With him as Treasurer no one was able to accuse the LLP of financial malpractice. Morrison was the active fund raiser. He created a special fund for anonymous donations and, through his colleagues with interests in the City, he would learn of people in business and in the professions who were sympathetic to Labour and prepared to give money if they could remain anonymous.

Morrison began as Secretary on a part-time basis at one pound a week. He continued at this rate for four years until the LCC elections of March 1919 when he was employed full-time on the campaign. Afterwards he remained full-time at five pounds a week. In December 1919 he had a rise to seven pounds and in June 1920 to eight pounds. In February 1921 he was given a salary of £420 a year, rising by annual increments of £20 to a maximum of £500.[21] Further benefits followed. In November 1921 the Executive agreed that it should pay half the cost of his phone bill, since he conducted so much business for the party from his flat, and in 1925 he was presented with a car by Alderman Emil Davies* to use on party business. Davies also offered to pay for its maintenance.

The staff at Morrison's disposal grew. At first he had relied on secretarial assistance at the London Trades Council. At Letchworth he found the Kent family eager to help with the chores, and there he discovered the man who was to be his deputy at the LLP and succeed him as Secretary. Donald Daines[22] had been active in the Norwich ILP and was an objector to the First War. He agreed to do work of national importance and was sent to a farm at Letchworth, where he struck up a friendship with Morrison. Daines helped him in his work as Secretary, and Morrison was so impressed that he promised to find Daines a full-time job at the LLP. After the war Daines helped Morrison at weekends on LLP work, and in December 1919, when the party was able to employ a clerical assistant for Morrison, Daines was appointed.

Morrison depended on Daines. To many he was Morrison's 'shadow'. He was plagued with asthma, and 'wasn't able to do very much really and what

* A financier and Labour's first alderman at the LCC.

he did was a great strain'. He was a most reticent and modest individual without political ambition. He had a more cultured mind than Morrison whom he sometimes criticized as being coarse-cut. He tidied up Morrison's articles, polishing the grammar and inserting literary allusions. Daines so captured the Morrisonian style that it was impossible to distinguish what Daines wrote from Morrison's own contributions. 'He could really see into Herbert's mind.' He drafted circulars and letters, and was responsible for making up the party journal. Morrison trusted him to keep the routine of the office ticking over, and Daines was content to stay in the background, happy to have found a niche which was not demanding; he was 'a good second-in-command'.[23]

In the 1920s more secretaries and clerical assistants were employed. By 1925 there were five clerks in addition to the two national officials. Then in 1926 there appeared a most formidable lady who was to be Morrison's private secretary for the rest of his life. Miss Ethel Donald was exactly what Herbert wanted: an efficient confidential secretary who would not interfere with his political activities. Miss Donald was disliked by the staff at the LLP. 'She lorded it over everyone, and was a damn dragon at times who stopped people getting to Herbert.'[24]

The staff were not the only people working at the LLP offices. Morrison encouraged members of the party to do voluntary work there, especially at election time when parcels had to be tied and items distributed all over London. He brought the daughters of party members from Hackney into the office and allocated them menial tasks, like licking stamps, answering the phone and sticking envelopes. They were there supposedly to learn office routine so as to fit them for secretarial work later.

In the very early days when the staff at the LLP were few and somewhat of a family Morrison would mix with them socially. 'On one occasion he invited all the staff to his flat in Hackney for an evening. After some food we all sat around while Herbert read *Pygmalion* to us. But the time went on and he was unable to finish it before we had to leave. He also took the staff once to some boat races organized by the Metropolitan Water Board and he often got some staff to exercise his red setter dog in Hackney.'[25] Such social contact became rare as the 1920s wore on.

Thus during the 1920s Morrison gathered around him a team of workers on whom he could depend. Under his leadership they carried out the responsibilities of maintaining the LLP. 'He didn't do the work himself. He organized others. He dished out the work and got on. He never sat in his room for long.'[26]

He created an impression of energy and drive on those who worked for him.[27] He would come in at any time, even very late, and expect the staff to work as enthusiastically as himself. He would never walk up the two flights of steps to the office, but would bound up two steps at a time, and he bustled about the office when he was there.[28] Morrison himself wrote in 1920 of the LLP headquarters, 'it is a business office where work is done and not a club for leisurely conversation'.[29] He was always in control. Indeed one secretary thought he had no emotions at all. 'He was insensitive to people. He was dedicated to Labour and politics; that was his life. He had no other interests and it was hard to talk to him about anything else. He didn't discuss himself very much and he was not really interested in people.' One secretary said: 'He would never say "thank you". It would not occur to him. He simply did not exist as a man.' He was jolly at socials, but even here he danced a lot because this enabled him not to have to get to know anyone really well. He was really friendless.

As head of the office staff, 'he always carried with him a little loose-leaf booklet into which he jotted down items wherever he was, about what he had to do. When he arrived at the office in the morning, he would call the staff individually to his room and check off on his pages the items that you had to deal with. As each was tackled, he would cross it off. Even if he wanted to tell you off, he jotted the points down on the paper beforehand. And I was often able to tell what was coming next by reading upside down the note on his desk. He expected hard work; he was a hard taskmaster.' The office was run very methodically. Charles Brandon said of Morrison: 'His great quality was tidiness. He pigeon-holed everything.' Lord Citrine said he 'had a passion for neatness and order'.[30] He was a lover of card indexes: on how LCC members had voted or lists of people to appeal to for money. Items had to be filed away so that one could find anything at a moment's notice. There was a drawer marked 'Executive', and before the Executive meeting, when Morrison wanted to draw up the agenda, he would take out the drawer and go through it: the same with a drawer marked *London News*. At the appropriate time he would bring out any item that he felt ought to be put in the next edition. He had an eye for detail. He would complain if the date on the calendar had not been adjusted correctly, or if a comma was put instead of a colon after 'Dear Sir'. His secretaries emphasized that, though he was a hard taskmaster for his staff, he drove himself as hard, if not harder: and his efficiency and drive inspired loyalty.

Morrison maintained contact with members of the party through his monthly circulars and the news sheet of the LLP, called in September 1918 the *London Labour Chronicle*. In addition to Morrison's editorial, his articles and brief items of information and advice, it carried regular features on party organization and on the LCC. Occasionally a famous figure, like Bernard Shaw or Ramsay MacDonald, would contribute. As its circulation mounted it expanded, took its first advertisements and carried its first photographs. In 1924 the LLP Executive decided to alter its format to that of a newspaper, and to change the title to *London News*. The dropping of 'Labour', argued the communists, was indicative of Morrison's efforts to win over the middle class to the detriment of the working class. But he replied that the new title was deliberately selected as the shortest and most easily remembered. It contained more articles, a greater range of topics, and there were now book reviews and cartoons.

London News provided Morrison with a monthly platform for his views. The atmosphere of the paper was Morrisonian. The openings were catchy: 'Now there's a queer thing.' The headings were striking: 'Points with Pith'; 'Phew!, Jackets Off'; 'Izzat so?' Morrison loved to cram articles with lists of facts to give a thorough backing to a case he was arguing. His concern for such specifics made some people condemn him as obsessed with detail. However he would retort that a mastery of detail was essential if one was to avoid being tripped up. At the start of the decade Morrison produced the editions almost single-handed. Since his days on the *Daily Citizen* he had had a desire to be a journalist; editing the *London News* fulfilled that ambition. So proud was he of his editorship that when he left the National Union of Clerks because it had become dominated by communists, he transferred to NATSOPA* on the basis of his work on *London News*.

He had hoped to extend his influence through a chain of Labour magazines, emanating from local Labour parties which he intended to supply with material. He formulated a scheme for ten or so papers, but had such a poor response from local parties that he came to see the attempt as premature, until local parties were stronger financially.[31] He wrote a fantastic number of articles for other Labour and socialist journals. His writings appear in the *Labour Magazine*, the *New Leader*, the *Social-Democrat*, the *Daily Herald*, and in the magazines of various trade unions and local parties. He also managed to find space in the capitalist press, since he wrote numerous letters to the correspondence columns. Each day he scanned the papers to spot items which would give him the excuse to reply. The *Star* was particularly sympathetic to Morrison. In its columns appeared frequent articles by Morrison and about him. He was close to its reporters and editors.[32] The *Star*, although Liberal, saw Morrison as a radical who wanted to improve London, and to a lesser extent he was also treated favourably by the other Liberal papers, the *Daily Chronicle* and the *Daily News*. Each week the names of Herbert Morrison and the London Labour Party were somewhere in print in London.

His many articles provided him with a supplement to his income. He was never as hard up as might appear from the salary he was paid, or as he often liked to make out, for on the side he was earning what must have been fairly substantial sums from his journalism. It was no wonder, then, that he never sought increases in his salary from the LLP. With his nominal salary he could portray himself as self-sacrificing and a humble earner, like so many of the party workers he mingled with.

* National Society of Operative Printers and Assistants.

The LLP subscribed to Durrant's press cuttings agency and each morning a batch arrived. Morrison went through them, and the morning newspapers, and then would dictate replies. The cuttings would be filed away into the relevant boxes. His method of composing articles was first to dictate to his secretary either straight out of his mind or from some scanty notes. They had then to be typed in double spacing and with large margins to allow him to alter them.[33] He also dictated in this style the thousands of circulars and letters which streamed from the office. His speeches at this time, however, were never written out. He just made notes and spoke impromptu. When one surveys the vast amount of writing and speaking that Morrison produced in the 1920s and 1930s one is forced to the conclusion that he was one of the most prolific politicians of the twentieth century. Almost every day he was composing some article or speech.

An important part of Morrison's work as Secretary of the LLP was to act as its spokesman before committees of inquiry or to ministers and their civil servants. For instance in 1919 he gave evidence to the Select Committee on Metropolitan Transport, in 1922 to the Royal Commission on London Government, in 1923 to the Sykes Committee on broadcasting and to an inter-departmental committee on public assistance. He went on numerous deputations to ministers, for instance in 1926 on poor law reform and in 1928 on the London floods. On such deputations he had many meetings with Neville Chamberlain, for whom he came to have a high regard, at least as a Minister of Health. Morrison impressed those who listened to him, for he had a command of the matter under consideration, and spoke briefly and to the point.

So effective was he that in 1923 Sidney Webb asked him to attend meetings of the Railway Rates Tribunal as representative of the Labour Party and the TUC. The Tribunal had been established under the 1921 Railways Act with the duty of fixing charges for the carriage of freight and for the fares of passengers. Over the next three years until the Tribunal issued its final judgment in December 1926, Morrison presented Labour's case, cross-examined railway representatives, and addressed the Tribunal on many occasions. He urged it to take account of the need for equity between different classes of users, to reduce the profits of the companies and to bring in lower charges and fares, especially for passengers and workmen. Although the final decision did not go as far as Morrison had pressed, he had success in reducing the companies' claims.[34] When the Tribunal began to sit again in 1929, Morrison was asked by the NEC to represent Labour again. Morrison refused because he could 'not now devote the necessary time to the task'.[35]

Morrison's goals were to make the London Labour Party an efficient organization, and to inspire party workers in the boroughs to create similarly efficient local organizations. His continuing message to the LLP was that in organizing activity could be found a deeply satisfying, indeed spiritual, experience. 'Let us not pant for the oratory of the speech-makers in the same manner as the drunkard thirsts for alcohol. The silent visionary with a card index beside him and a joyful heart within is not less important than they who move in the limelight.'[36] Intellectuals who failed to immerse themselves in party organization were criticized. 'We are sometimes tempted to pray that some folks [G. D. H. Cole] might do a little less research and lecturing and a little more of the rough and tumble work of the Labour Movement.'[37] His view was that work on the doorsteps of the voters won more votes for the party than speeches and research.[38]

Morrison's zeal for efficient organization had an almost Germanic quality. Indeed he very much admired the 'scientific intensity' of the organization of the German Social Democratic Party and tried to model the LLP on it, for example by undertaking a variety of social and cultural services for members, so that even their leisure pursuits could be carried out within party organizations.[39]

Morrison set up speakers' classes; he helped to organize a legal service by establishing throughout London a number of legal advice bureaux, served by lawyers who were Labour sympathizers, to advise citizens on their rights, notably in the fields of housing and rents, pensions, and poor law relief and life insurance. He drew up a panel of experts who were prepared to talk about a variety of topics and he arranged for them to visit party meetings. He made a special appeal to young people. In 1925 he created a Young People's Advisory Committee (on the lines of the women's section), and looked forward to the establishment of young people's sections by local parties. His view of a youth organization was that it should be limited. Young people were not to be involved in policy, but should equip themselves technically and intellectually for service to the party as adults.[40] In the 1920s few youth sections were created and they did very little.

In the 1920s Morrison became a kind of cultural impresario at the LLP. His view was that the LLP had to provide opportunities to satisfy the cultural aspirations of its members, and such comradeship would help to unify the party and make it a more efficient political organization. He wrote in 1925: 'The modern working class is not waiting for well-to-do people, however well-intentioned, to uplift them. We are going to uplift ourselves. . . . We are going to force the doors open, we are going to take our place at the feast of beauty. . . . There will be an Art of the People, produced by the people, played by the people, enjoyed by the people, for we will not be content with the commercialized stuff of modern capitalist society.'[41]

The first cultural activity organized by Morrison was the London Labour Choir in 1924. He established a choral union of eight local party choirs, who up till then had provided songs at party socials. He used them more and more at such gatherings, encouraged other parties to establish their own choirs and held an annual contest, at which Dr Ralph Vaughan Williams adjudicated.

By 1926 there were twenty London Labour choirs in the union, with a total of 635 members. So successful did it appear that Morrison sought to organize a Dramatic Federation on the same lines, beginning in 1925 with fifteen local Labour dramatic societies. In the following year the Dramatic Federation put on at the New Scala Theatre four performances of *The Insect Play* by the Brothers Čapek. Morrison urged party members to attend: 'From the lives of insects, the activities of humanity are satirized, the superficial lives of the idle rich exposed, whilst the ant scene is probably the greatest exposure of militarism which has been staged.' Also in 1925 he moved on to organize, along the same lines, a London Labour Symphony Orchestra, formed from local party groups.

However, Morrison became disillusioned. These activities were not financially self-supporting. *The Insect Play* had a deficit of a hundred pounds, and the Choral Union also ran up deficits. These enterprises used up a considerable amount of Morrison's time and that of the staff, circulating local parties, booking halls and printing tickets. He felt they would be better occupied in tasks directly related to party organization and electioneering.[42] Participation was disappointing. The number of choirs began to decline in 1926, and the local dramatic societies became play-reading circles and then fizzled out altogether, while the symphony orchestra never really got started. Morrison's ventures into culture were a brief distraction from the normal work of the party in the mid 1920s.

Each year from 1921 he organized the London Labour Fair, a bazaar and bring-and-buy sale, with sideshows and stalls, to raise money for the LLP. These were very successful. That in 1924 attracted six thousand people and made a profit of £731.[43] In the following year he organized the largest Fair yet, at the Crystal Palace, a Festival of Labour. It had all the elements from previous Fairs, speeches, choirs, dancing, dramatic displays, and various sports. However the profit was a mere sixteen pounds.[44] The most popular activities at the Festival were the sports, and after the Festival Morrison and the LLP decided to set up the LLP Sports Association, modelled on the previous cultural ventures, consisting of various local groups. The objective was to form leagues for football, cricket, tennis, darts, billiards, quoits and swimming. Only the football league seemed to succeed. By 1929, however, the Executive concluded that although eight hundred competitors were involved in the Sports Association it was a failure, for spectators were few, income meagre and the sports meetings had suffered a heavy financial loss. The officers had had to pass the hat around to pay the expenses.[45]

The most popular activity of the LLP was the Annual Reunion in January of each year. Here members gathered to dance, sing, play whist and enjoy a fancy dress contest. Morrison was a regular participant; he sang the songs fiercely and above all danced and danced. One party member who observed Morrison on such occasions felt that in some respects he seemed out of place. His clothes were odd; he tried to get the people to do folk dancing when they preferred 'Mother Brown'; and he never took a drink. He seemed to show puritanical disapproval of the boys who disappeared round the corner during the interval.[46]

However, the members of the women's sections vied with each other for his favours. While tripping around the floor he would tease them, holding them tightly, cuddling them, to the distaste of a few but to the delight of most. He would, whilst in the intimacy of the dance, urge them on to more activity in the party and try to recruit some to serve on their local councils or even on the LCC. His wife always came to the Annual Reunion where she sat out while Morrison moved through a succession of key women, reserving only the last waltz for her. People tried to talk to Mrs Morrison but gave up because of her stutter. Miss Donald, after joining the office, became a regular at the socials, always waiting in attendance on Morrison. Some tongues wagged about an *affaire*, but no one could produce evidence.

Morrison's attention to the ladies was not just because he liked their company. He realized that the women did most of the chores of party activity. Morrison made sure that women were represented on the Executive; he encouraged them to stand for local authorities, and he wrote leaflets and pamphlets appealing to women. The LLP formed a women's advisory committee for representatives from the women's sections, and organized for them conferences, weekend schools, and visits to the LCC and its establishments like the fire brigade. Morrison was idolized by the ladies, who thus formed a block of loyal workers. When he visited a particular locality for a meeting, he could rely on being entertained in the home of a member of the women's section. He was always trying to cadge a meal, even a bed for the night if he was far from home. His devoted 'key women' were honoured that they could look after the great Herbert. He basked in the warmth of the generous reception he was given, so different from the coldness of his own home.

In the early twenties Morrison helped to organize a number of demonstrations to protest against some enormity, often in co-operation with the London Trades Council and the Labour Party nationally, and often in Trafalgar Square. Morrison usually drafted the resolutions that were eventually passed by the gatherings. He organized rallies against intervention in Russia, the occupation of the Ruhr and the breaking off of diplomatic relations with Russia. Other protests called for the release of the Lord Mayor of Cork from Brixton Prison and the nationalization of the mines. He organized demonstrations on behalf of the unemployed and to celebrate Labour's cause on May Day. However, he became dissatisfied with such junkets. They won no votes and were valuable only as emotional outlets for the activists. And as with the May Day celebrations they could get out of hand and be taken over by communists. Instead he urged members to devote themselves to the more effective work of organization, and to visit people in their own homes, since governments were shifted on doorsteps rather than by marches.[47]

Morrison entered elections with gusto and thoroughness. His message to party members was that they should fight as many elections as possible. This was to him the only way to build up Labour as an independent political force.[48] From the earliest days he gave priority to fighting local elections. He said 'the Party will do well to concentrate the greater part of its attention on the municipal aspect of our work for some time to come. It is usual for Parliamentary representation to follow, and not to precede, the experience gained by participation in the administrative work of the municipal world.'[49]

The first elections in which the LLP was involved were those in 1919, for the LCC, boards of guardians and the boroughs. The party's activities in these campaigns provided the model for all future contests. In 1919 the LLP headquarters under Morrison's direction issued a stream of leaflets about the conduct of elections. They outlined the law, procedures to be followed, hints to agents and candidates, how to run committee rooms: and facts, figures and arguments to put on Labour's behalf. Policy statements, posters, model election addresses and press advertisements flowed from head office. In later years the amount grew and it became more sophisticated. The data were consolidated into pamphlets such as *Fifty Points for Municipal Electors, The Elector's Encyclopaedia and the Canvasser's Friend*, 'brief, bright and brotherly'. Longer and more detailed pamphlets were issued, dealing with special problems like transport, housing, electricity and health, or appealing to groups like teachers, doctors, white-collar workers and housewives. Morrison was in the thick of all this electioneering, for not only did he draft the electoral programme of the party, but he wrote most of the leaflets, advertisements, circulars and pamphlets himself. He designed the posters and thought up the slogans, for instance in 1923, 'the Protection you need is protection against the Profiteer', and in 1925, 'Keep out Messrs. Hardface and Gradgrind', and 'All the Bad Landlords are Voting Against Labour'. The 1928 elections for the LCC involved the LLP and Morrison far more than any other campaign of the 1920s. The LLP issued 1,600 sixteen-sheet posters, 11,000 double crown posters, 607,000 leaflets and 13,000 copies of a forty-four-page booklet *Shot and Shell for London Electors*, where Labour policy was effectively stated and 'Tory Nonsense Blown Sky-high'. Morrison had written to secretaries of local parties explaining the sorts of candidates who should be selected, and he emphasized the need for early preparations. He toured local parties and trade union branches giving lantern lectures on the LCC and its work, to kindle the enthusiasm of the party workers. He arranged conferences for candidates, agents and key party workers to discuss the campaign. He devised advertisements for the *Star* and the *Daily Herald*. He issued special editions of *London News* and wrote articles in Labour journals.

When all this frenzy of activity was over, Morrison's first message to the local parties was to prepare for the next LCC contest in 1931. He told them to select candidates as soon as possible so as to allow them to become known in the area, and to start raising finance for the campaign. The main enemy to be defeated, as he saw it, was 'King Apathy, His Satanic Majesty' who reigned in London elections. The LLP never let up in its electioneering activity; it became to Morrison almost an end in itself. He said that elections 'keep us busy and out of mischief'.[50]

When the campaigns were over, the LLP did not leave Labour members on public authorities to their own devices, but provided them with considerable assistance. This service began in 1919 following the unexpected Labour victories in the borough elections: 'that large numbers of the Labour representatives returned were without actual experience of municipal work, impressed upon us the urgent need of bringing our people together and placing at their disposal expert advice and information on municipal work, and of establishing machinery whereby a co-ordinated Party policy might be secured.'[51] To make Labour 'fit to govern',[52] Morrison organized conferences for Labour aldermen and councillors on the functions performed by local authorities. Here Morrison and leading party experts explained Labour policy and discussed difficulties which might arise. Morrison arranged for meetings, roughly quarterly, of delegates from local parties to discuss Labour's municipal policies in London. He asked that the agenda and minutes of all council meetings be sent to the LLP office so that he could extract from them items of interest to other boroughs. The Labour Mayors in London established the Metropolitan Labour Mayors' Association, of which Morrison was an honorary member. It met monthly as a forum for the exchange of experiences. Even as early as 1920 he could see that 'the office of the Party is being increasingly regarded as the place with which to communicate when questions of general London policy arise'.[53]

The local parties could not escape the presence of the LLP and Morrison. At least once a week some communication from Morrison reached them. He was as fond of circulars as he had been when ILP organizer in south London before the war. He created many: the *Municipal Circular*, *Organisation Points*, the *Councillor*, the *LLP Leaflets* and the *London Labour Party Chronicle*. He would explain how provisions of various bills, statutes and reports would affect local authorities; he would recommend publications for local members to read, arguments to use against their opponents, and model articles, advertisements and speeches. He would send them resolutions or letters which he asked them to sign and forward to the LCC, MPs and ministers, attacking or commending some course of action.

Some local members who disagreed with Morrison's policies or methods complained that he was the bully of the boroughs. Others, however, stressed that Morrison was not dictatorial.[54] He respected the views of the local parties, put his case and left it for them to decide. Indeed they welcomed his energy, and felt they were part of a bustling and well-informed organization.

Morrison was constantly travelling around the local parties in London, attending their meetings and socials, chatting up the local leaders and jollying them along. 'Herbert on the platform was a showman. If he addressed a working class audience he was very down to earth and homely. He would often imitate the husband with his backside to the fire giving out on some topic or the other.'[55]

Morrison was always eager to advise local parties on proper procedures. He was fascinated by the machinery and processes of political institutions, and his tidy mind was keen to check practices which blurred responsibilities.[56] In addition he wanted Labour members on public authorities, even if only in small minority groups, to organize themselves so efficiently that they could not be ignored. The first requirement was that they should act as a block. He urged Labour members on public bodies to meet together before the meeting to go through the agenda and decide on a common policy.[57] However he was adamant that Labour members who were JPs had to behave differently.* He favoured them meeting for 'mutual consultation with regard to problems that arise in the course of their duties'[58] and indeed organized three conferences of London Labour JPs for that purpose in 1926 and 1927,[59] but no decisions were to be reached for that 'would interfere with the judicial position of the Justices'. 'Each Justice must individually be responsible for the impartial administration of the law.'[60] Morrison was anxious to avoid the accusation that improper influence had been exercised.

He was concerned to achieve the right relationship between Labour members on a public body and their party outside. The model he commended was that of parliamentary practice, where the National Executive Committee and the Conference decided the broad principles and programme of the party and the Parliamentary Labour Party judged the best methods of applying the programme. In the local context the local party would settle the programme, and the group of Labour members on a council decide the best way to implement it. He was totally opposed to a local party or a trades council giving instructions to the group of elected members. 'Such a policy is fatal. I decline to admit that it is democratic, for a democracy which is based upon the practice of those with inside knowledge receiving instructions from those without such knowledge is an insult to democracy.' One danger of such a system was that the members of a council might be unable to express a view on a certain item until they had received their orders, which made good administration impossible.[61] Still, the outside party had a major role to play. Together with the group of council members it could devise the electoral policy and pass to the group suggestions and criticisms. In fact he commended the practices he followed for regulating relationships between the LCC Labour party and the Executive of the LLP. These two bodies never ex-

* Morrison was appointed a JP in February 1926 and was attached to the Blackheath Division whose court met at Catford. He never devoted much time to his judicial duties.

perienced the kind of struggles which took place in so many provincial towns in the 1920s,[62] largely because of Morrison.

Once elected to an authority Labour members were urged to follow the organization of the LCC Labour party. They should select a leader, whip and other officers, who would form a policy committee, akin to the Executive Committee of the PLP. This committee was to discuss policy proposals, put recommendations to the full group meeting and in an emergency act on behalf of the group. He stressed the democratic value of these group meetings. 'Our people will not be led if they have no voice in making policy.' Once the group had decided, it was for each member to vote in conformity with the majority, except on certain matters of conscience. Then a free vote could be allowed, on religious, moral and temperance matters. He also felt that free votes should be allowed wherever a councillor had to act in a judicial capacity or when he was responsible for appointing council employees.[63] If someone did feel deeply on other topics and had a different view from his colleagues, he would be allowed to abstain, but not to make an open attack on the majority decision. And such abstention should not become habitual otherwise the party would have to look closely at the individual.

He was concerned not to shackle leadership. He argued that, if in a debate new facts arose, the leader and whip should sound out members present and be free to change the line of the party. A leader might even have to reverse a party decision on the floor of the council chamber, in which case criticism should be reserved for the next party meeting and not indulged in during the council meeting itself. If leaders combined initiative and efficiency with a full regard to the rights of the rank and file, democratic leadership would succeed. His view of leadership was not that it was just a response to pressure from below. Leaders had to lead, subject at the end of the day to the authority of the party meeting.[64] He urged members to support their leaders.

Morrison believed that parties were appropriate to local government. He said that those 'who do not believe in the party system are too often the people who believe in shady practice in public administration'. He was eager to make Labour fit to govern and to do so meant ensuring that the party was not tainted with any suspicion of impropriety.

Morrison was always a most regular attender at any organization to which he belonged, but his attendance at Executive* meetings of the LLP was the most regular of all. Between 1916 and 1940 he missed only six meetings: because of other duties or illness. Morrison was the most constant attender. For most items on the agenda he would present a paper which laid out the nature of the problem under discussion, and normally put clearly his view. For each meeting Morrison also put in a report outlining his own activities

* It was elected at the annual conference by the constituent elements of the LLP, i.e. trade unions, local parties and socialist societies.

for the previous month, which listed what he had read, which meetings he had attended, what circulars and letters he had dispatched, whom he had consulted on what items, in addition to the latest membership figures.[65] Further, Morrison pushed into the Executive a constant flow of memoranda on policies. He wrote the first draft of all LLP policy statements, conference motions, Executive reports and election programmes, which were submitted to the Executive for its approval, and were sometimes amended, but only slightly. As the drafter of all such policy documents, Morrison was able to shape the policy of the LLP.

He never tried to railroad anything through, but he was skilful in fixing matters in advance. Before Executive meetings he would find out what people thought about a particular proposition and if enough of the influential figures were opposed he would not put it forward.[66] Dame Mabel Crout, who sat on the Executive, claimed that the Executive agreed invariably with what he suggested. Sir Isaac Hayward, also on the Executive, said that Morrison really led it; he never pushed his views down people's throats, but he won people by persuasion. Herbert's brother-in-law recalled that: 'Herbert would always go through an agenda most carefully, and mark when he wanted to speak, and note what he wanted to say and what he wanted to push.'[67]

The person Morrison had to manage above all was the Chairman: from 1919 to 1933 T. E. Naylor, General Secretary of the London Society of Compositors. Morrison said of him that 'he walks into a room as if he were not merely lost, but had given up hope of ever being found'.[68] He presided with calm repose over meetings of the Executive and many sessions of conference. He listened attentively to Morrison's guidance, to such an extent that enemies of Morrison described him as Morrison's 'spokesman and gramophone'.[69]

One of the greatest anxieties of the Executive was how to handle the annual conference. Morrison always drafted a set of motions for the Executive to commend to the conference and he gave guidance to the Executive about their reaction to motions suggested by other members of the party. When speakers had been selected to put the Executive's case he would brief them. Morrison would prepare a special agenda for the Chairman, and against each item were notes on what line to take and which speakers to call. 'Conferences were stage-managed by Herbert. He persuaded people to move this resolution or to speak for that cause or to vote that way.'[70]

Some conferences of the 1920s had been near-fiascos: that of 1925, for example, when the communists and their sympathizers disrupted the proceedings. To avoid a repetition Morrison persuaded the Executive to adhere to a strict time-table so that no longer would obstructionist elements 'indefinitely spin the proceedings out in order to get unrepresentative decisions at a late hour'.[71] His efforts succeeded. Ten years later he looked back on some of the conferences of the 1920s as rough-houses from beginning to end, with masses of silly points of order and interruptions.[72] He had brought order to the proceedings.

The most serious threat to Morrison's dominance of the LLP in the 1920s came from a group of Labour parties in the East End, associated with George Lansbury and the party at Poplar, which controlled the borough council and board of guardians. They pursued there a set of policies which Morrison felt damaged Labour's electoral appeal. They refused to levy the precepts of the LCC and other public authorities as a protest against the government's failure to tackle high unemployment and to equalize London's rates. The Poplar board of guardians paid to the unemployed of the borough higher scales of relief than either the government laid down or the unemployed had demanded, amounting by 1924 to £150,000 in illegal payments. The Poplar borough council also paid its employees wages much in excess of the rates negotiated through collective bargaining machinery. The Poplar Labour party gained considerable notoriety for spendthrift illegality. Morrison argued that the electorate would never trust authorities which spent the ratepayers' money so recklessly and displayed such contempt for constitutional behaviour. Their antics enabled the Tories to pose as protectors of the exploited citizens and as the true constitutional party. All over the country the spectre of 'Poplarism' was raised in local elections to frighten voters into the arms of the anti-socialist parties. He detected that the communists were behind 'Poplarism', providing the leaders who could win over the weak-minded and soft-hearted. Their purpose was to discredit the Labour Party and to encourage the growth of reaction so that they would be the only feasible opposition to the Tories. The left wing of the Labour Party failed to recognize the devious tactics of the communists and treated Morrison's analysis as a personal obsession.

Morrison's adherence to the constitutional path also brought him into conflict with some trade unionists. He rather scorned strikes, although he recognized their value in industrial disputes 'while capitalism lasts',[73] yet he was against their use in political disputes, save in the exceptional situation where it was necessary to coerce a government to act constitutionally or to follow the will of the majority. Such a case arose in 1920 when Morrison organized the London Council of Action to co-ordinate Labour opposition against the government's military intervention in Russia.[74] Generally he was 'an uncompromising opponent of direct action'.[75] He predicted that 'a general strike would fail. You would demonstrate not your strength, but your weakness.'[76]

The General Strike which Morrison had feared took place in May 1926. The Ministry of Health had issued a circular to local authorities outlining what local authorities should do to keep essential services in operation. Morrison would have nothing to do with this machinery which he saw as crude strike-breaking;[77] at the LCC the Labour Party refused to participate in the emergency committee responsible for maintaining food supplies, health and sanitation services, and urged co-operation with trade unions.

From the London Labour Party Morrison issued advice to party members in London 'to stand firm by our Trade Union members whilst at the same time giving the enemy no material with which to attack the Labour Party as being indifferent to the interests of the community'.[78] He urged local parties to arrange 'jolly social gatherings, primarily for the enjoyment of families directly involved in the dispute. We must all do our best to keep cheerful and jolly and to spread good comradeship during this time of difficulty.' He issued lists of Labour choirs, orchestras and dramatic societies, and he asked for the names of people who would distribute official party news bulletins.[79]

Morrison was keen to have his London Labour Party involved in some way. He was asked to attend a conference of the London district committee of trade unions, which he did, but it did not invite his further assistance. He spoke at about half a dozen strike meetings and sent two typists from the LLP office to the TUC, but it had plenty of secretarial assistance. Then after the strike had been going for a few days the General Council of the TUC asked him to take charge of and improve the Greater London Despatch Service. 'The interesting thing is that by the time I was called in and got into action, the first job that my revised despatch service had to discharge was to deliver the notice terminating the General Strike.' He said that he 'felt no grievance that I was left rather "kicking my heels" for quite a number of days'.[80]

Morrison was appalled at the inefficiency shown by the trade unions in the General Strike. They had not anticipated events, and worst of all they had neglected the political side of the movement.[81] About the only thing he could find to praise the unions for was their rejection of the Russian offer of £300,000. If it had been accepted the Tories would have had another stick with which to attack the Labour movement, and the Communist Party in Britain would ever after 'have flung it in our faces'.

He lost no time in punching home the lessons to be drawn from the General Strike. It was a weapon to be used only 'for the purpose of checking unconstitutional governments', against attempts to destroy democratic institutions or undermine the popular franchise. He pointed out that: 'a general strike beginning as an industrial struggle if carried to the bitter end, and if it is to be successful, must become a physical force, revolutionary struggle aiming at the forcible overthrow of the constitutional government and the seizing of power by the General Council of the Trades Union Congress. Nobody believes that the General Council contemplated or wished any such thing, and nobody with half a brain believes that in Great Britain such a policy could be successful.' The moral of it all was to build up the Labour Party. If there had been a Labour government it would have done everything possible to see that the miners had a fair deal.[82] The political, not the industrial, struggle was paramount.

Morrison wrote an analysis of the role of the Secretary and of his own characteristics in a memorandum to the Executive in 1929.[83] As General Secretary of a political party he required 'a sound general knowledge of political organization and the conduct of elections'. Being responsible for the central direction of London election campaigns, he must have 'technical and expert knowledge of publicity, advertising and the drafting of election literature'. As editor of *London News* he had to have 'ability as a journalist'. Since he was intimately concerned with local government matters at and between elections, he had to be 'expert in Local Government, familiar with Local Government law and practice and municipal problems, not only as regards the London County Council and the Metropolitan Borough Councils, but the various classes of extra-London local authorities and such central bodies as the Metropolitan Water Board, the London and Home Counties Joint Electricity Authority, the London and Home Counties Traffic Advisory Committee, etc. This, in turn, means that the Secretary should be familiar with the technical problems associated with the various branches of the public service in questions affecting the Metropolis, and should possess the confidence of the London Labour's hundreds of public representatives. . . . having regard to the many points at which London's interests are dealt with in Parliament and the need for Parliamentary action on behalf of the Party, the Secretary should possess knowledge of Parliamentary procedure and be able to communicate with Ministers and with the Labour Party in the House of Commons. . . . The Secretary must inevitably come into contact, not only with the leading people in the Party but local officers, the rank and file, trade union and co-operative officials, officers in the public service and others, and it is desirable that he should possess the capacity to "handle human material".' Finally, 'having regard to the wide administrative and financial responsibilities of the Party office, the Secretary requires considerable business ability'. The object of this review at that particular point of time was to convince the Executive that his services were so valuable that no one else could replace him and that they should not permanently fill the post of Secretary while he was a minister in the Labour government of 1929. It achieved its objective, and Morrison's services were retained in a temporary capacity, while Daines was raised to Acting Secretary with an extra hundred pounds per annum salary.

Morrison performed his secretarial duties with zeal. His life was one long round of meetings and committees, conferences, public gatherings, agitation, propaganda and organization. His energy transformed the puny organization of 1915 into the vigorous political machine of the late 1920s. When he started he was just a part-time Secretary with a box of papers in a bed-sitting room. By 1929 Labour had won a majority of parliamentary seats in London and he had made such a reputation as would propel him to ministerial office. Also the LCC seemed to be coming within his grasp.

D

Chapter 7

On the London County Council in the 1920s

Politics apart, the L.C.C. machine is a wonderful and beautiful thing.[1]

Herbert Morrison

In the 1920s the top tier of local government in London was the London County Council, covering a built-up area of 117 square miles and over four million inhabitants. It was responsible for those services that required an area bigger than that of the metropolitan boroughs, such as main drainage, fire brigade, parks and open spaces, education, street improvements, various licensing duties, slum clearance and housing, the ambulance service, and the operation of tramways.

Parties were active in the LCC from its creation. In 1889 the Progressives, an alliance of Liberals and Radicals, formed the majority; their opponents, the Moderates, who later changed their name to Municipal Reformers and were in effect Conservatives, took over control in 1907. Before the First War Labour had few members, only three in 1910 and one in 1913. Then in 1919 they shot up to seventeen facing eighty Moderates and forty-six Progressives.[2]

Morrison first stood as a candidate for the LCC in May 1920, at a by-election in North Southwark. Although Labour had never done well in this constituency and although the party itself was a meagre handful of supporters, Morrison was convinced that he could win. Here was the chance to display his renowned organizational abilities. Once adopted he took over the campaign. From his office streamed circulars, expounding not just his cause but listing the details of organization and procedures that he wanted followed, even going so far as to tell canvassers what to say on the doorstep: 'I have called on behalf of Mr Morrison the Labour candidate and I am anxious to know whether we may look on you as Labour supporters?' He wrote and designed his own leaflets, posters and election address. This portrayed him as 'A Worker for the Workers', with his chief slogan: 'Down with the Profiteers.'[3]

His main theme was municipal enterprise. He told party workers to 'tell the electors that by direct employment, Queensland's Labour Government did building work for £94,000 for which private "enterprise" wanted £117,000; that the same Govt. entered the meat business during the war and brought meat prices down by nearly one-half.' He sought a better health service, explaining: 'It is bad social conditions which makes Daddy Death so active in Southwark.' He advocated comprehensive housing plans, which would take into account women's views on design. He called for one London public traffic authority, a better education for bright children from poor families, reform of the rating system, and trade union conditions for employees of the council and its contractors. The word 'socialism' was absent.[4]

Morrison felt that his campaign was perfect. But the coalition Liberal candidate won, with a reduced majority. The only person surprised at the defeat was Morrison, who took it badly and dressed down the local workers after the count. They retorted that he should criticize those who had not helped, not those who had.[5] A former secretary in the party observed that Morrison 'was apt to forget that he depended in the Labour Party on voluntary labour, people who disliked being bossed about, and difficulties arose because he simply could not tolerate inefficiency'.[6] A teenage campaigner at North Southwark noted: 'It seemed to take him a long time to learn that simple folk often react unfavourably to being firmly put in their place from a great height.'[7]

Morrison's next attempt to enter the LCC was successful; in March 1922 at Woolwich East he was the first of two victorious candidates in this Labour stronghold.[8] This triumph marked the start of Morrison's close association with this distant part of south-east London, which was to remain for the rest of his life the area of London he loved best.

The Woolwich Labour Party was one of the earliest and most successful Labour parties in the country.[9] In 1903 Will Crooks was elected to Parliament for Woolwich and the party won a majority on the borough council, the first Labour local government majority in London. In 1904 it sent two Labour representatives to the LCC and nine to the board of guardians, and so became the first constituency in the kingdom to be represented on all elected bodies by Labour members. For the next seventy years Labour was never to lose its dominance in Woolwich. The Woolwich Labour Party pioneered individual membership years before it was recognized by the Labour Party constitution in 1918. Its organizers had seen the necessity for individual members, to attract personal interest and to bring in funds. Its membership long remained the highest of any local Labour party in the country, and with its wealth it was able to have its own party offices and staff, and to produce a newspaper, the Woolwich *Pioneer*.

The leadership of the Labour Party in Woolwich was impressive, and one man in particular made a great impact on Morrison: William Barefoot, one of the 'builders of the movement'.[10] Born in Woolwich in 1872, the son of a soldier, he left school at fourteen and became an office boy at the arsenal. Here he rose to work in the engineering room of the gun shop. In the 1890s he became an active member of the Associated Society of Engineers, took part in strikes and joined the ILP. First and foremost he was an organizer, for his own union and as Secretary of the Woolwich Trades Council. He saw the value of an independent Labour organization and led the Woolwich Trades Council to affiliate with the Labour Representation Committee on its foundation in 1900. He created a Parliamentary Committee of the Trades Council, invited Crooks to be the parliamentary candidate in 1902 and was his agent at the famous by-election of 1903. He then founded the Woolwich Labour Representation Association, 'probably the first local organization which incorporated the modern Labour Party scheme of individual membership of ward committees'. He left the arsenal and became Labour's full-time Secretary and Agent, organizing its great victories before the First War. He was the leader of the Woolwich council from 1912, and the town's first Labour JP in 1913. He edited the *Pioneer* from 1904 to 1922. He was 'the Governor of Woolwich' as Morrison called him,[11] and remained so until his death in 1941, following a collapse while speaking at a council meeting.

Morrison admitted that he was indebted to him.[12] Indeed, Barefoot's assistant from 1912 and successor in 1941, Mabel Crout, said that Barefoot 'guided Herbert when he was raw and young'.[13] Morrison regarded Barefoot as an ally on the London Labour Party Executive. At LLP conferences he made forceful speeches against Morrison's detractors, and arranged for Morrison to be adopted as the party's LCC candidate at Woolwich East.[14] There was no jealousy between these two powerful men, because Barefoot was content simply to rule the roost in Woolwich. He had no ambitions nationally or even for the LCC. Thus he was no rival to Morrison who was content to let Barefoot maintain a base for him at Woolwich, so that he could spend his time on LCC matters. He had greater confidence in the local leadership of the party in Woolwich than in Hackney.

That Labour should have been so dominant in Woolwich at such an early date is at first sight odd, for it had in the nineteenth century been a centre of Toryism and militarism, symbolized by its barracks and arsenal. The explanation for Labour strength, however, is fairly simple. The majority of the employed population worked at the arsenal where as skilled men, mostly engineers, they were highly unionized and highly political. The working class of Woolwich, the majority of the population, were no depressed proletariat, nor were they scattered among numerous small employers and thus hard to organize. They were successful in pressing their demands and their wages were high. During the Boer War, with much overtime required, their savings mounted, and many bought their own homes, a trend further encouraged by local authority loans for house purchase. In all London, Woolwich had most owner-occupiers among the working class. Such skilled men, with rising expectations, saw the advantages of collective action through trade unions in industrial affairs, and such men also saw the advantages of a separate Labour Party for political purposes: an extension of their commitment to their trade union.

A further feature of Woolwich was significant: its self-contained isolation from the rest of London. The majority of the population were employed within Woolwich, and there was little commuting into the centre, eight to nine miles away. Woolwich was very much a separate community with its own civic life, very untypical of London, and similar to isolated mining communities in Welsh valleys. A commitment to Labour was part of belonging to the community. At elections in Woolwich, as in other distinct communities, turn-out was high; indeed for years the polls at Woolwich were the highest in London. Voting, and voting for Labour, was a declaration of membership of the Woolwich community.

It was natural that Morrison should be attracted to Woolwich. He was given a safe seat, it is true, but Woolwich offered him more. There was Barefoot, and a congenial Labour party with sensible members like his running-mate for the LCC, Harry Snell, later Lord Snell, whom Morrison made first Labour Chairman of the LCC in 1934. Morrison looked up to this man, who came from the humble home of an agricultural labourer and had educated himself into a cultivated and philosophical gentleman.[15] Often when confronted with a problem Morrison would say: 'Now what would Harry Snell have done?'[16] Morrison's objective at the LLP was to create models of the Woolwich Labour Party throughout London. He admired Barefoot's machine. 'It was the pioneer of individual membership, of modern ward organisation, and of intensive, scientific political work . . . I am proud to be a member of the Woolwich Party.'[17]

Morrison was so taken with Woolwich that he went to live in its vicinity, at nearby Eltham. In 1923 the Morrison family moved from their flat in Clapton to a house at 272 Well Hall Road. Living at Eltham enabled Morrison to be close to his LCC constituency, while the Eltham railway station was only a few minutes' walk from his house, and from there within half an hour he could reach Waterloo or Charing Cross Stations. Eltham had the aspect at this time of a garden city. Its houses were well laid out, spaciously placed, with grass and trees abounding, while there was still open countryside around.[18] It looked and felt like Letchworth which his wife pined for. Also it enabled him to be close to the working class areas of Woolwich. It thus satisfied his public and private requirements. The house itself, part of a terrace and with three bedrooms, was leased from the local co-operative society. This particular co-op, the Royal Arsenal Co-operative Society, was one of the most successful in the country. It was the first co-operative society to affiliate to a local Labour party, the London Labour Party and the Labour Party nationally. On its governing body was the ubiquitous Barefoot. That Morrison was captivated by Eltham cannot be doubted. He remained there for the rest of his life.[19]

Woolwich voted for him, putting him at the top of the poll on the three occasions when he sought election to the LCC in 1922, 1925 and 1928. His campaign in 1922 was based on municipal enterprise, particularly in milk supply, coal supply and London traffic.[20] Although Morrison was returned for Woolwich East, the LLP made no gains on the LCC, simply maintaining its seventeen seats, while the Municipal Reformers gained fourteen from the Progressives.

Throughout the 1920s Morrison kept in close touch with the party at Woolwich, speaking and appearing often at various gatherings, He wrote regularly in the *Pioneer*, and the local press carried frequent items about his activities and views. At the LCC he raised matters relating to Woolwich in the same way as he did for Hackney, urging it to undertake public works in the Woolwich area to relieve unemployment, and seeking improvements to its parks and schools.[21] The leaders of the Labour party at Woolwich were proud to have him as their representative.[22]

Although Morrison was not elected to the LCC until March 1922, he had been the most influential figure in drawing up the Labour Party's election policy for the LCC. In July 1921 he had submitted a first draft to the LLP Executive after consulting the Chairman and the Treasurer. Then the Executive held a joint meeting with the LCC Labour Party to discuss the proposals. Morrison said: 'I am aiming at a brief, simple and direct statement of our principles.' Morrison's draft was accepted except for the section on housing policy over which there was some disagreement on phraseology. Morrison and the leaders of the LCC Labour Party met and settled the difficulty amicably. When the Executive approved the statement it was circulated to affiliated bodies and received its final approval at a special party conference in February 1922.[23]

Morrison shaped the manifesto from previous election programmes and conference resolutions, most of which he had originally drafted. It called for the major reorganization of local government in London, with the abolition of the variety of *ad hoc* agencies. The burden of rating on householders would be reduced by larger national grants and the full rating of government properties, empty properties and site values. Under Labour the LCC would undertake a large programme of house building at low rents, and seek to create a regional plan for building new towns on garden city lines in the home counties. All London passenger transport facilities would be owned and operated by the LCC which would also take over gas, electricity and water supplies, and coal, bread, fish, meat and milk supplies, slaughter-houses and markets, and set up a bank. There would be no poverty bar on an able child receiving a good education, for higher grants would be paid. The LCC would be a model employer, adopting trade union conditions for its employees and for those of its contractors, who in any case were to be eliminated wherever practicable. Finally the health services of London were to be improved; municipal management and control of a wide range of medical and welfare services were to replace provision through the Poor Law. In sum it pursued 'a collectivist policy in its municipal work for the purpose of promoting the welfare of the people and in order to combat the insidious activities of trusts and combines'.[24] Morrison's themes were very much a repetition of those urged by the Progressives around the turn of the century. They too had advocated the unification of London government, the municipal ownership of public utilities and monopolies, an expansion of welfare services, the equalization of London rates and the taxation of site values. From the 1920s Labour took over the causes of the Progressives.[25]

For all later LCC elections in London, and indeed for those to the boards of guardians and borough councils, Morrison drafted the election programmes and manifestoes. His method was to take the programme of the previous election, together with subsequent conference resolutions, scrutinize them thoroughly, drop anything now outdated or of not sufficient electoral appeal and add items now more relevant and attractive. He then submitted his draft to the Executive which after consultation always approved it with only minor alterations.

Thus even before joining the council Morrison had shown himself to be a dominating figure. He influenced the activities of the LCC Labour Party as Secretary of the LLP, and attended the party meetings of LCC Labour members 'as a silent witness of their proceedings'.[26] He had watched closely over the LCC, mastering its powers and procedures, and digesting its reports and minutes, from which he culled material for his circulars. Morrison did not go into the LCC fresh and ignorant. In many respects he was more knowledgeable than the members already there. The Labour party on the LCC in 1922 was a puny group under the leadership of Harry Gosling.* Before the First War Gosling had welded together into a Labour party on the council the handful of trade unionists who had managed to get elected, normally in association with the Progressives.[27] By 1922 the party included, besides eight trade union officials, one political agent, two secretaries, a doctor, a compositor, a railwayman and two housewives. Gosling's leadership was in no way dynamic. Morrison was annoyed by his lack of attention to agenda papers and committee minutes, which caused him, thought Morrison, to miss a great deal and to let the majority escape unscathed. Morrison called his style leading from a back seat.[28] Another LCC councillor of the day, later Morrison's chief critic, recalled: 'If young ones made fierce speeches and had rows, Gosling at the end in a soft sweet speech, which was always listened to, smoothed things over. This didn't suit Herbert at this time. He was a

* Gosling was a member of the LCC from 1898 to 1925. In 1893 he was General Secretary of the Amalgamated Society of Watermen and Lightermen of the River Thames, in 1910 President of the National Transport Workers' Federation and in 1921 President of the Transport and General Workers' Union.

revolutionary and a radical; he wanted to municipalize everything. Herbert said: "I think we're badly led, what about it?" Herbert was always intriguing against Gosling."[29]

Between 1922 and 1925 Morrison sat on a large number of LCC committees, which gave him an insight into its multifarious responsibilities.* He was a most frequent attender; indeed his record of attendance at LCC meetings was the most regular of all members.† His devotion is even more striking when it is recalled that he was, during this period, a member of the Hackney borough council and in 1924 an MP. The one committee to which he was most attentive was General Purposes, where he could keep an eye on the activities of all committees whose minutes and reports passed through it before being submitted to the council.

Morrison speedily rose to the top of the Labour party at the LCC, becoming Chief Whip in 1923, responsible for maintaining contact with all members: a position which was an extension of his role as Secretary of the LLP.‡ As whip he served first Gosling and, when Gosling was replaced as leader during his time as Minister of Transport in 1924, Alderman Emil Davies. With indefatigable work Morrison held the party together and wielded tremendous influence, displaying tact, patience and judgment. He showed debating skill, administrative ability and general capacity for leadership.[30] Davies felt that Morrison should be the leader in name as well as in reality, and so in 1925 he stood down and nominated Morrison at the party meeting. Morrison was chosen by a unanimous decision.[31] 1925 was an important year for Labour at the LCC. In the March elections it had returned thirty-five councillors to the council; together with four aldermen Labour now had more members than the Progressives who had only six councillors and three aldermen. Thus Labour replaced the Liberals as the official opposition on the LCC. Against it was arrayed the huge majority of Municipal Reformers, eighty-three councillors and thirteen aldermen.

Morrison asserted his supremacy immediately with a dazzling performance. On 5 May the LCC met to consider the estimates of the various committees for the year ahead.[32] The session began at 2.30 p.m. and did not end until twenty-one hours later. He had so organized the Labour members that they were able to keep the debate going. The party had tabled twenty-four amendments on which they pegged speech after speech of criticism of the majority and of advocacy for their own proposals. The speakers were all primed, their roles rehearsed and their timing perfect. His mastery over LCC pro-

* He was a member at one time or another in the period 1922–5 of the following committees: General Purposes, Parliamentary, Housing and Local Government, Theatres and Music Halls, Town Planning, Education and London Electricity Supply.

† From March 1922 to December 1924 out of 93 possible council meetings he was present at 89 and he voted in 243 divisions out of a possible 286. He was present at 158 committee meetings out of 208, and 26 sub-committee meetings out of 47. (Details from LCC reports.)

‡ He was also whip of the Labour members on the Metropolitan Water Board and the Joint Electricity Authority.

cedure enabled him to defeat the majority's efforts to close down the debates. Morrison himself spoke at 5.30 a.m. urging that the LCC should own and operate petrol and trolley buses. *The Times* reported: 'Hour after hour passed with amendments of local interest, such as a request for consideration as to the provision of a bandstand in Bethnal Green Gardens, and division after division was forced.'[33] The quiet, tolerant reign of Gosling and Davies had gone; in its place was a thrustful and challenging leadership.

During his years of opposition on the LCC in the 1920s Morrison, as well as raising matters of interest to Hackney and Woolwich, championed his usual themes, notably municipal enterprise.[34] He urged the LCC to build houses itself and not to rely on contractors; he advocated that the LCC should operate a boat service on the Thames, a tourist agency and a theatre; he called on it to take over control of London's markets. Above all he urged municipal enterprise for London's transport. His ultimate objective was the unified ownership of all London transport by one local authority.[35]

He took a stand against various economies instituted by the majority, especially in education, housing and social welfare services, where he demanded higher standards and more expenditure. When the majority, in response to a government circular to reduce education spending, cut their estimates by £350,000, Morrison objected and replied to their claim that the service would not in fact be affected: 'if a cut of £350,000 was possible without affecting the efficiency or adequacy of the service, then it followed that the Council had been guilty of wasting £350,000 in previous years.'[36] He called for the building by the LCC of more houses, larger and of a better standard, speeding up slum clearance, rent reductions and greater security of tenure for tenants. He urged that in LCC tenements bath and washroom facilities should not have to be shared between three or four families, and that the LCC purchase compulsorily empty properties to make them available for the homeless, and he objected to the sale of council houses, which he said was evidence of the majority's 'passion for destructive "economy" '.[37]

He championed comprehensive town planning measures, notably the establishment of a 'green belt' around London, and the erection of new towns beyond it. His view of London, coming from a man renowned as a lover of London, strikes one at first as strange. To him, 'London is an absolute disgrace to civilization.'[38] It 'should never have been allowed to exist, and if it could be conveniently blown up it would be better for civilization. Ninety per cent of it is dull, dreary and miserable.' He objected to its chaos and sprawl. The further expansion of London in suburban dormitories led only to more congestion, and longer journeys to work. The solution was to establish satellite towns of about thirty thousand to fifty thousand in population. His vision was: 'conceive London as the sun with a whole series of planetary towns scattered round it at suitable points in the home counties. Each would receive strength from the mother city, each would have fresh air around it and in it, and each would lead an independent and self-contained existence.'

While within London itself he favoured redevelopment 'on garden city lines'.[39]

He championed the council's employees and their trade unions. Although not an advocate of a compulsory closed shop, he called for the posting up of notices advising employees to join their trade unions. He was eager to ensure that fair wages contracts were adhered to, and that council employees were given time off to stand as parliamentary candidates. Morrison's old puritanical streak was revealed when he objected to proposals for alcohol to be sold at dance and music halls[40] and for hotels and restaurants to have an extension of dancing time from 12 to 2 a.m. He attacked the latter measure because it 'pandered to a select parasitic class that a decent society would not tolerate'. Part of his objection to such a proposal was a concern for the staff at hotels and restaurants.[41] In 1928 the future film censor of Britain made clear his principles about film censorship, when the war film *Dawn* was refused a certificate by the British Board of Film Censors. The Foreign Secretary had claimed that its showing would cause bitterness between Germany and the United Kingdom. The LCC, however, on a non-party vote decided to allow the film to be shown, and Morrison was in favour. He argued first that it was important to show that the LCC was the final decision-maker on censorship and that there was a right of appeal to it from the Board. Secondly he stated 'the act of censorship was a grave act, justified only upon reasonably conclusive proof of the film being immoral or offensive to public decency'. Political expediency was no justification for censorship.[42]

Each year in May when the estimates were presented he organized marathon sittings. One in 1928 lasted sixteen hours from 2.30 p.m. to 6.12 a.m. when the party raised all the items they had advocated in their election campaign the previous March.[43] He was a master of the LCC's procedure, able to wring from every standing order the maximum advantage for Labour. One in particular he used frequently, whereby a member could move that a committee present a report to the council on a topic; thus he obtained a platform for his views, both when he put forward the motion and when the report was received. At every opportunity the Labour party at the LCC punched home its points with vigour, skill and humour.

On becoming leader of the Labour opposition in 1925 Morrison formalized the organization of the party. Each year there was an election for the leader, a seven-man policy committee and a Chief Whip.[44] Morrison sent a letter to new entrants, explaining how the Labour group operated, advising them to master the standing orders of the council and to tell the whip on what committees they wished to serve. He listed the facilities available at County Hall, and concluded 'on our efficiency, capacity and conduct during the next three years will depend the results of the 1928 election'.[45] The Labour members met each Tuesday at 1.30 p.m., one hour before the full council meeting.

The procedure was to hear a report from the policy committee and to go through the agenda of the council meeting, deciding the attitude of the party. Before each council committee meeting Labour members would huddle together to plan ahead. On each committee the Labour party had a 'shadow chairman'. Through personal contact with them and assiduous reading of committee documents Morrison had an over-all picture of the council's work and was alerted to weaknesses in the Tory majority or points on which controversy might arise.[46]

Morrison continued to serve on a wide range of committees* and to be a very regular attender.† He was most concerned that members should attend as regularly as himself. In the *London News* for June 1926 he observed that two members had been absent from council meetings, attending their wedding ceremonies. 'This practice of members of the LCC Labour Party getting married on Tuesdays without the sanction of the Party Whip is beyond a joke. Something will have to be done about it.' He even lectured women members that if they were going to have babies they should plan for them to be born in the recess.[47] Morrison was anxious that Labour should show itself fit to govern. He always urged the party at the LCC never to advocate anything which the party would not be able to implement if it were in power,[48] and he asked members not to ask questions of the majority unless they were to bring out something it had done which Labour would not do if in office.[49]

Sir Isaac Hayward‡ regarded Morrison as 'a natural leader with an uncanny judgment'. 'His leadership was accepted because he was always so fair minded. He never refused to listen to anyone's point of view and on any major issue he would consult a large number of people.' Lord Silkin§ noted that Morrison was 'a good speaker, good humoured and he could always argue very well'. George Strauss‖ described him as 'brilliant in debate, quick minded and quick witted. Often during a debate Labour speakers would make poor contributions because of their inexperience; then Herbert would wind up; he had mastered the arguments and could pull them all together. His approach was wise and humorous. He raised the morale of the party: a real leader.'

A leading member of the majority party, Lady Emmet of Amberley,¶ who was Chairman of the Housing Committee when Morrison was opposi-

---

* Between 1925 and 1930 he served on General Purposes, Finance, Improvements, London Electricity Supply, Parks, Parliamentary, Poor Law, Selection, Town Planning, Traffic, Highways, Public Assistance and Changes in London Local Government.

† Between March 1925 and December 1927 he attended 89 of 90 possible council meetings, voting in 230 out of a possible 241 divisions. He was present at 221 committee meetings out of a possible 280 and at 46 sub-committee meetings out of 55. From the Finance and General Purposes Committees he was able to watch over the whole gamut of council work. On the former he attended 22 out of its 31 meetings and of the latter he attended 79 out of 87.

‡ Member of the LCC 1928–65.

§ Member of the LCC 1925–46.

‖ Member of the LCC 1925–46.

¶ Member of the LCC 1925–34.

tion leader, found him 'most agreeable; he was straightforward and honest, a man who would never break a bargain and was very good in negotiation. He was able and disciplined, a good mixer, who had the knack of being able to get people together.' She said that Morrison used to tease the majority; he would speak with a quizzical look on his face and pull the majority's leg. Members stressed the significance of humour in Morrison's speeches. It was 'impish not waspish'; 'the arrows were sharp but not poisoned'.[50] The Chairman of the LLP, T. E. Naylor, wrote: 'No man on the Council was more feared by the Party in power, no man more popular with them "out of hours".'[51]

At Hackney Morrison had recognized that the electoral system did not inevitably throw up as members of local councils those most fitted to discharge the responsibilities of local government, and when he first became a member of the LCC he could see that the quality of the majority of Labour members was not such as to inspire confidence that they could be chairmen of committees. Therefore he set himself the task of recruiting to the LCC people with the necessary talents. There is a strikingly similar pattern to the ways in which those members of the LCC who were in the 1930s to fill the chairmanships under Morrison's leadership were drawn into the council in the 1920s. Morrison would spot people whose qualities he admired. He would urge them to come into local government, arguing that the party needed their service. Once they had agreed, he would, as Secretary of the London Labour Party, circulate their names as potential candidates to local parties. Informally he would suggest to the leaders of Labour strongholds that they should adopt a particular person. Usually Morrison's advice was sufficient, but if objections were raised then he would offer a grant from the LLP towards election expenses. In a brief time his protégés found themselves elected. He also brought on to the council as aldermen people with some experience or skill in which the party was deficient, such as accountants, lawyers and doctors. Thus Morrison gathered around him at the LCC an exceptionally able group of people, loyal to him, for they knew they owed their seats to him.

The choice of the first Labour alderman in 1919 had some significant repercussions. A. E. Davies was a City Financier and a close political friend of Morrison's. Morrison invited him to stand and urged his claims, and he was duly selected. This decision probably was the origin of Attlee's dislike of Morrison. Attlee said that Morrison had approached him to sound out whether he would be prepared to be an alderman. Attlee was keen and agreed, yet the next he heard was that Davies had been chosen. Never did he make any further efforts to have anything to do with the LCC. In Attlee's eyes Morrison had condemned himself as not being straight. This incident stuck vividly in Attlee's mind to the end of his life.[52]

Morrison's concern for his protégés was not limited to infiltrating them into the council: he encouraged them to specialize on particular topics and to speak in debates. He inspired them to persist. In this informal way Morrison gathered his closest colleagues on the LCC. Even after he had given up the leadership in 1940, his influence was still present, since the next leaders, Latham and Hayward, had both been his protégés. The Morrisonian style lasted to the very end of the LCC in 1965.

Morrison's leadership was not totally unchallenged from within his own party. Although he had been unanimously adopted leader in 1925, he was faced in 1926 with a rival, Susan Lawrence,* who won only six votes against his eighteen. But in 1927, 1928 and 1929 at the start of each county council year he was unanimously adopted.[53] Susan Lawrence was highly emotional and urged a more extremist policy than Morrison, typified in her remark, 'I don't preach the Class War, I live it.'[54] She was a focus for the few who had some grievance against Morrison. A more serious opponent was Cecil Manning, the Chief Whip from 1925 to 1929. He was a full-time political organizer at Camberwell, who felt that Morrison was neglecting the interests of the working class with his appeal to the middle class. Manning said: 'Herbert used to annoy people by claiming that Labour people weren't good enough and by seeking what he called quality and the intelligentsia.'[55] He complained that 'Herbert liked rich young men. He was a magnet for them.' However, Manning had a reputation of not being absolutely dependable.[56] Although Miss Lawrence and Manning had a handful of followers, they were unable to topple him. His detractors could only snipe from the sidelines.

Morrison was clearly the leader of the Labour opposition at the LCC. He led a team, most of whose leading figures he had recruited and encouraged, and to whom he had allocated spheres of interest. On any issue he took up, he had thoroughly mastered the facts and arguments, and in debate would propound his views in a direct, humorous and forceful style which harried the majority. He was no dictator. He put his views vigorously, but only after wide consultation. Decisions on policy were left in the end for the party meeting, although such was Morrison's pre-eminence that he always got his way.

* Member of the LCC 1910–28.

Chapter 8

On a Wider Stage

Morrison attended his first Labour Party conference in 1917 as a delegate of the ILP. He was silent, but in the following year he spoke on party organization. He opposed the suggestion of the National Executive Committee that they have discretion to accept the affiliation to the party of professional associations. He feared that the admittance of many new societies would turn the party into a gathering of very small and unrepresentative groups, and he was anxious lest they let in people who ought to be active members of their appropriate trade unions.[1] He was defeated. With his first speech at a Labour Party conference he had revealed his first love, party organization. On this topic he was to make most of his conference speeches in the 1920s and acquire a reputation as a specialist.

In the following year, 1919, he made his second speech – a bitter attack on the performance of the Parliamentary Labour Party. It had been feeble in trying to secure a democratic peace; it had not been vigorous in seeking the release of conscientious objectors, or in opposing the starving of women and children through blockade. Nor had it opposed forcefully the war against Russia. He appealed for the reference back of the report of the PLP to show that 'they demanded vigorous, straightforward, and energetic politics'. His proposal was lost.[2] At the next conference in 1920 he mounted another diatribe against the Parliamentary Party.[3]

In his first speeches at Labour Party conferences Morrison, who was later to be a pillar of the party establishment and scourge of its critics, was vociferously hostile to the Parliamentary Party and displayed no awareness of the limitations that restricted responsible leadership. His attacks may have been a shrewd way of making a name for himself; he may have been simply immature, for it is quite common for the erstwhile outsider and radical critic to develop into an insider, moderator and defender; he may have been conducting a deliberate campaign against Clynes' leadership of the Parliamentary Party, which was performing feebly, on behalf of MacDonald, Morrison's political hero. Morrison's strictures ceased once MacDonald returned as leader in 1922, and from that point the Parliamentary Party also greatly improved its performance.

At the early conferences Morrison was the spokesman of the local parties. In three successive years 1920, 1921 and 1922, Morrison urged that the local Labour parties be given the status within the constitution of the Labour Party which they deserved. The existing position was that local Labour parties were allowed to nominate candidates for five places on the National Executive Committee but the voting for these places was by the conference as a whole, so that the block votes of the trade unions determined who would represent the outnumbered local parties. Morrison proposed that local Labour parties alone should vote for their own nominees: 'the right of self-determination' as he called it in 1920. But he was voted down: 1,597,000 votes to 1,211,000.[4] At conference in the next year he argued that 'the whole power and electoral strength of the Labour Party depended in the last resort upon the character and the initiative and strength of the organization in the constituencies of the country'. Again his motion was lost: 2,913,000 to 591,000.[5] In 1922 he spoke again for 'self-determination'. It seemed that the party believed in it for Egypt, India and Ireland, but not for the party itself. He pointed out that the great feature of the growth of the party recently was the development of organization in the constituencies, and yet still the selection of local party representatives to the NEC was the subject of bartering between the trade unions. But once again he was beaten: 2,688,000 votes to 954,000.[6] Morrison, after three successive attempts, dropped the issue until the 1930s, convinced that the trade unions were not prepared to yield. In one sense his campaign had been valuable. It had persuaded the trade union leaders that they needed on the NEC genuine spokesmen of local parties. It was clear to them that there was no one better than the man who had revealed himself as their leading advocate and was himself the Secretary of the largest local Labour party.[7] In 1920 Morrison on his first attempt was elected to the NEC. He came bottom of the five elected, with 767,000 votes, just beating Emanuel Shinwell with 694,000. Top was George Lansbury with 2,112,000. In the next year he was not elected, but in 1922 came third with 1,926,000 votes to Lansbury in first place with 3,012,000. Morrison was to be elected to the NEC for the next thirty-three years with hardly a break. In a brief space of time Morrison had made a reputation. He was not contained by the boundaries of London, but was admitted to the governing body of the national party. This achievement was remarkable for one so young. In 1920 he was just thirty-one, the youngest member of the NEC, and introduced as 'the baby of the party'.

Morrison's election to the NEC in 1920 sealed his breach with the ILP. In that same year he was defeated in the elections for the ILP's National Administrative Council. He gave up his Chairmanship of the London and Southern Counties Divisional Council and never again appeared as a delegate at an ILP conference. His commitment now was to the Labour Party.

Morrison's attendance record at NEC meetings throughout the 1920s was so high, at eighty-eight per cent, as to rank him one of its most regular members. His assiduity was rewarded in 1927 when he was elected by the NEC to be its Vice-Chairman for the year 1927–8,[8] and thus in the following election year to be the party's Chairman. Even before he had been a minister and before he had led the party to victory on the LCC, he had been Chairman of the Labour Party: he was more than just a figure of London local politics.

On the NEC in the 1920s his main contributions were about party publicity and organization. On policy-making his involvement appears slight, at least until 1925. Then he began to sit on a number of sub-committees, often joint with the TUC, covering a variety of policy issues: unemployment, land reform, emigration, family allowances and the nationalization of mines. There is no evidence, however, that he decisively shaped the outcome of the deliberations. More importantly he was a member of a sub-committee set up in 1927 to prepare the draft manifesto for the next general election, which subsequently emerged as *Labour and the Nation*,[9] and he presided over the NEC meetings in March 1929 which went through the manifesto in its final stages.

On election to the NEC in 1920 he became a member of its Literature and Publicity Sub-Committee. He quickly made a mark, submitting poster designs and scrutinizing estimates. In his first year he achieved a minor success when the NEC agreed to print as a party leaflet for the November municipal elections a collection of quotations culled by Morrison from the press disposing of the allegation that Labour control of local councils was responsible for rising rates.[10] On the NEC Morrison advocated the need for party literature to be attractive to ordinary people. In 1924 he called for 'simple literature which would make the technical side of the Electricity and Mining problems easily understandable',[11] and he urged 'an immediate Publicity and Organizing Campaign in support of the Government and in opposition to the other Parties in readiness for the next General Election'.[12] He did not always have his way. In 1927 he had suggested that an article of his in *Socialist Review* be printed as a party pamphlet, but the NEC refused, stating that, although 'excellent for London it was not of sufficient general application to be published as a pamphlet'.[13]

He became a member of the Organization Sub-Committee in 1923. He sat on committees which handled relations between the Labour Party and the ILP and the Co-operative Movement, and he became a member of the National Joint Council, the body for liaison between the party and the TUC. Morrison was sometimes called upon to visit local parties where some dispute had arisen which required adjudication by head office. From this central position Morrison acquired considerable knowledge about the party machine, its internal procedures and its external relations with a variety of associated organizations.

As a stickler for constitutional rules Morrison came into conflict with Sir Oswald Mosley on at least two occasions in the 1920s when the Organization

Sub-Committee and the NEC had to reprimand the baronet. In June 1925 Mosley had to appear before the NEC to explain why he had withdrawn as a candidate at the Forest of Dean immediately after he had been selected. It was most improper for a candidate to refuse to be adopted after having gone forward. Mosley explained that he had withdrawn because the whole Labour movement in Birmingham, and in particular in the Ladywood constituency which he had represented as an MP, had protested against his move to another area.[14]

A more serious irregularity occurred in the following year, which embittered relations between Mosley and Morrison. The sitting Labour member at Smethwick, J. E. Davison, suddenly announced his retirement and at once Mosley was adopted unanimously by the local party. The first that the NEC heard of the affair was an item in the local press announcing Davison's departure and on the same day a letter from the Executive of the local party to say they would recommend Mosley to the full meeting of the party on the following day. Mosley and the local party had had discussions without any consultation with the Midland District Organizer of the party or head office which, under the rules of the party, was entitled to select a candidate at a by-election. The NEC considered this episode frequently in late 1926 and early 1927, determined that proper procedures should be adhered to,[15] and it is hinted that Morrison wanted Mosley to be refused endorsement.[16] The compromise was that a special conference of the affiliated organizations would be called, and if the individual selected agreed to abide by the constitution of the Labour Party then the NEC would accept the choice. The conference was duly held. Mosley was the only nomination, the NEC endorsed him and in the by-election he won. Mosley felt slighted by the NEC and said that he had no confidence in the head office and had no intention of working with them or communicating with them. The NEC set up a small committee to review with Mosley the whole situation. By March the affair had blown over. It was said that after 'interesting and friendly talks' the 'best of relations' were established, and Mosley agreed to work through head office.[17] Morrison's sense of procedural propriety had been outraged by Mosley's disdain for the party's constitution.[18]

Morrison also served on the Local Government Advisory Committee, together with the co-opted Clement Attlee who was not a member of the NEC. This small body of three, which included Grant Mackenzie of the party's research staff who acted as its secretary, was sometimes in the 1920s chaired by Attlee or Morrison, the first instance of them working together in the Labour Party nationally. The purpose of the committee was to advise the NEC and the staff of the party about matters of interest to Labour councillors and candidates. It considered publicity items for local elections, themes for the conferences, and which Acts should be reported on in memoranda for councillors. Morrison's presence on it is a sign that in the 1920s he was regarded as a leading specialist on local government matters within the party.

Grant Mackenzie found Morrison a likeable, genuine, straightforward and honest man. On the other hand quite a different person was revealed to Lord Henderson, then Willie Henderson, press officer at head office, and the son of the Secretary, Arthur Henderson. He found Morrison a man consumed with ambition, ruthlessly cruel, and very rough with people: an arch intriguer.

Once he was on the NEC Morrison's speeches at conferences were less frequent, covered a wider range of topics and were never critical of the leadership. Some were to persuade delegates that socialism could not be built in a day. This involved him in opposing many superficially attractive proposals and in arguing that conference should not seek to lay down detailed policy for a Labour government. He argued against proposals for levying surtax,[19] for raising the school leaving age to sixteen,[20] and he criticized James Maxton who wanted day-to-day guidance as to what he should do as an MP: 'Well, I hope the Whips will give it to him – (laughter) – and when the Whips have given it to him I hope he will do what the Whips tell him. (Renewed laughter.) If he does not do what the Whips tell him, I hope the Parliamentary Party will deal with him.'[21] Morrison 'laid Maxton out with a verve that delighted the Conference' and 'was already marked out as one of the keenest debaters'.[22]

At the end of the decade, therefore, Morrison was a very different performer at party conference from what he had been at the beginning. The former radical critic of the PLP had become the prudent defender of the party establishment, and he had become a figure of national standing, known far beyond London. In 1925 Morrison came top of the poll for the NEC; in 1928 and 1929 he came second to Lansbury, and in front of Sir Oswald Mosley and Hugh Dalton.

Morrison's most important contribution to the Labour Party in the 1920s was to help keep it out of the clutches of the Communist Party. He pursued communists with such implacable intensity that by 1928 he was renowned as 'our chief witchfinder'.[23] He was proud that: 'In Great Britain I was the man who did the most fighting to prevent the Communists from capturing the British Labour Party.'[24]

Morrison's argument was that communists owed their loyalty to the Communist Party and not to the Labour Party whose principles and methods were very different. The communists' quest for dictatorship, their taste for direct action, revolution and civil war, and their attachment to an armed uprising were not compatible with Labour's objective of peaceful social transformation. If communists sought election to Parliament, it was not for constructive reforms but as part of their agitation to break down the system. 'The Communist . . . like the militarist, is working not for constructive social reorganization but merely for a "bloody mess" in the hope that he can seize power in the middle of it.' Their real purpose in trying to join the Labour Party was not to work with it but 'to get inside and play hell', indeed to sabotage it, by conducting campaigns against non-communists.[25] He said: 'The Labour Movement in London is going to be run by London and not by

Moscow.'[26] Morrison's loathing of communists showed itself even against those with whom he had once been friendly but whom he now suspected of deviation. Walter Southgate was the secretary of the Hackney branch of the National Union of Clerks of which Morrison was a member. Some communists who had joined the branch discovered that Morrison was in arrears with his dues and publicized his forgetfulness as a betrayal of the working class. Southgate approached Morrison one night after a meeting and mentioned the money which was owing. Southgate was in no way criticizing Morrison, indeed his intention was to settle the unpleasant business as quietly as possible. Morrison snapped at him: 'Have you too joined the communists? I'll send you a cheque.' 'There was vinegar in his answer and manner', and from then on he treated Southgate with coldness.[27]

So strong was Morrison's belief in democracy that he felt that kid gloves should not be used against people opposed to democracy.[28] Morrison wrote: 'All our experience in London goes to show that the only way with the Communists is to take the offensive, and not be on the defensive with them.'[29] Because of his vigour there was no fusion between Labour and communist forces in London. Even before the Labour Party's national conference had come out firmly against the communists, Morrison in London had rejected their overtures. Following the conference of the Communist Party in 1920 it applied to be affiliated to the Labour Party. The Executive of the LLP in September 1920 unanimously turned it down.[30] The communists then organized meetings of their members and sought to persuade delegates to the LLP annual conference to vote for affiliation. However their request was again thrown out. Morrison pointed out that the refusal of the request for affiliation followed the views of the party's National Executive Committee and of the Parliamentary Committee of the TUC, although neither of the two organizations had yet been instructed to take such a line by their annual conferences. The London Labour Party's annual conference was the first broadly based group within the party to reject communist affiliation. In 1921 the Labour Party's annual conference rejected communist affiliation, by 4,115,000 to 224,000 votes and in the following year reaffirmed this decision by 3,086,000 to 261,000 votes.[31]

The communists now turned to pushing their members to join the Labour Party as individual members, to acquire official positions, and to be selected as delegates and as candidates at elections. Their effect at local party meetings in London was disruptive. They prolonged sessions until only they and their sympathizers remained and then carried resolutions critical of Morrison. Many loyalists, unable to tolerate the interminable meetings and incessant harangues, left, and local party membership fell. Morrison felt that the Labour Party was going to pieces, and so he mounted throughout the 1920s his offensive to clear out of the Labour Party any communist or fellow-traveller.[32] It was a difficult task since the communists had their allies widely scattered within the Labour movement and amongst its leadership. But Morrison persisted.

He drew the logical conclusion from the rejection of the Communist Party's application for affiliation that communists were not eligible to be individual members, delegates or candidates.[33] He sought to exclude communists, therefore, from all positions within the LLP. But at the NEC his line was at first not accepted. In October 1923 the Organization Sub-Committee of the NEC advised that communists 'should be accepted as candidates, as delegates, as affiliated members, and as individual members'. Morrison moved another motion, which was lost by ten votes to seven, that nothing should prejudice the right of the local Labour parties to refuse endorsement, credentials or membership to any person whose acceptance of the party constitution and principles was not considered to be bona fide. He then was successful in moving that when the NEC issued its report it would make reference to the powers already possessed by parties to impose discipline on their members and to protect the constitution and policy of the national party.[34] Thus the Labour Party had it both ways. The communists were not excluded, yet Morrison was free to exclude them in London. The NEC shifted slightly in Morrison's direction in 1924, when it voted to reaffirm its rejection of communist affiliation and, by nine votes to six, not to allow them to be candidates, but it still allowed them to be individual members and delegates. Only four votes could be mustered to exclude them altogether. Lansbury voted for there to be no barrier against them at all.[35] At the conference of 1924 Morrison pointed out that the communists wanted to get inside the Labour Party, to put 'sand into the machine', and he reminded delegates how the communists had run a candidate against MacDonald in the East Woolwich by-election and against himself too: so much for those who were supposed to champion anti-capitalist unity. In the final voting the rejection of affiliation was carried by 3,185,000 to 193,000 votes, the rejection of communists as candidates by 2,456,000 to 654,000 and a motion to reject them as individual members by 1,804,000 to 1,540,000.[36] Morrison wrote in *Forward* about the screams from communists who were no longer to be allowed to stand as Labour candidates: 'How difficult it is to understand the ethical and moral basis of people who will move heaven and earth to become the candidates of a party whose policy, in the view of the International to which they are responsible, is an entire and continuous betrayal of working-class interests!'[37]

Back in London he circulated all sections of the LLP with the decisions of the conference and stressed that the Executive would ensure that no communists would stand as Labour candidates.[38] Morrison now wanted more clarity about the position of communists as members of the Labour Party. The LLP annual conference at its 1924 session clearly rejected communists as individual members, but there was doubt about the status of affiliated members from trade unions. The communist sympathizers on the NEC stonewalled. They defeated, ten votes to nine, a motion by Morrison that no communist could be a member of the Labour Party, and that the resolution of the 1924 conference should be circulated to all affiliated bodies with the warning that if the resolution was disobeyed the organization would be disaffiliated. Instead it was decided to collect further information.[39] Morrison was almost despairing at the 'indefinite attitude of the Party'; he urged it to get off the fence, to stop 'letting down . . . the people who want to uphold the Party constitution'. 'Far better would it be to let the Communist Party affiliate and allow their people in with full rights, bag and baggage, than to continue the present policy of wobble, wobble, wobble!'[40]

At the 1925 conference the position became more satisfactory for Morrison. Communist affiliation to the Labour Party was again rejected; no communist was to be a Labour candidate, no communist was eligible to be a member of the Labour Party, and trade unions affiliated to the Labour Party were asked to refrain from choosing communists as delegates to the Labour Party. Following the conference Morrison was able to carry a motion at the NEC that the conference decisions of 1924 and 1925 should be circulated to all affiliated bodies.[41]

Enforcement of the policy was a problem. In London the Executive vetoed nominations of communists to the Executive, to the annual conference and as LCC candidates, but it had little control over the choices of local parties for borough or boards of guardians elections or over the choices of individual trade union branches.[42] In a 'stern letter' to secretaries of borough Labour parties Morrison pointed out that to choose communists would be an act of disloyalty.[43] When some persisted, he organized the disaffiliation of the offending parties and established new ones of loyalists. He replied to those who complained about his imposing a too tight discipline that disaffiliations were taken only as a last resort.

Morrison was ever watchful to spot anything which suggested that the Labour Party was not adamantly opposed to communists. At an NEC meeting in October 1925 he protested about distortions in the press which claimed that Labour's attitude to communists was weakening.[44] So angry was he that he had sent to the erring editors of the *Daily Express* and the *Daily Chronicle* solicitor's letters demanding withdrawal of the slur.[45] He was quick to pounce on Labour members for collaborating with communists, by speaking at their demonstrations or by writing in their journals. George Lansbury and William Lawther were criticized by Morrison for such disloyalty.[46] Morrison came up against this pair over disaffiliating parties who admitted communists as members, since they opposed disaffiliation.[47] He attacked unions which nominated communists as delegates to local parties. When some trade unions nominated as delegates to the party conference communists who were standing against official Labour candidates in elections, Morrison persuaded the NEC to debar them.[48]

In 1925 and 1926 the communists launched a major offensive against Morrison. They so disrupted the LLP annual conference in November 1925 that a second session had to be held in December. Morrison warned the party of communist tactics, and showed that they had formed a 'left wing movement for London' to penetrate the LLP.[49] He produced letters from the headquarters of the Communist Party to their local party committees, advising them how to organize groups within local Labour parties in order to gain a majority of delegates at the LLP conferences.[50] Morrison was himself not above using the techniques of the communists. He planted his own reliable members inside their organizations and whenever someone offered to defect to the Labour Party he asked him to remain and supply information. In this way he could learn about their plans and their supporters, and he could acquire their documents. His foreknowledge of communist plans enabled him to make some dazzling displays at LLP conferences. He knew in advance the questions he would be asked, and he knew where the individual communists were scattered throughout the hall. As soon as the first question was put, he would snap back his answer and then turn to each communist and give replies to the questions they were going to ask. He did it so humorously with a twinkle in his eye that the communists were knocked off balance.[51]

Morrison was proud of his ability to handle the communists. At a big meeting in the 1920s at the Crystal Palace, when microphones were first being used, Ramsay MacDonald faced a barrage from communist hecklers. Morrison whispered to MacDonald, but the microphone sent his words round the hall: 'Leave 'em to me. I'll deal with 'em.'[52] On another occasion MacDonald had received a quiet reception and Morrison thanked him for his splendid speech. 'I am glad that everything went peacefully. It is not because attempts at trouble were not made behind the scenes. Certain of the known troublesome elements were denied admission by the scrutineers at the gates whilst a few groups who were suspect inside found as not altogether welcome companions a couple of our stewards who were strong dockers or other hefty proletarians.'[53]

The communists developed other tactics. A familiar one was to organize activities, like demonstrations, or to form committees, to draw Labour members away from Labour party work into collaboration with communists on communist-led bodies. Lansbury frequently fell for this approach.[54] In 1928 the communists as part of a world-wide change of line began an open offensive against democratic socialists. In London they ran candidates against official Labour candidates for the LCC, boards of guardians and borough elections. In some cases they stood openly as communists, elsewhere they masqueraded as Labour representatives, the nominees of disaffiliated local parties.[55] Morrison was furious, for he had to spend a great deal of time dissociating the Labour Party from such candidates, since the opposition were claiming that Labour and communist were identical. He felt that the only result of their intrusion was to help the capitalist parties,[56] as in Bethnal Green where the communists had a strong hold over the Labour movement. Morrison deplored the borough council naming a new housing estate 'Lenin Estate',[57] and he was angry when the communist councillors by voting for their own nominee to be Mayor let in a Conservative in a three-cornered fight.[58]

Then came the borough elections. Morrison wrote afterwards: 'At Bethnal Green, where a peculiarly virulent brand of Communism had flourished for some years, the inevitable happened, and every Labour seat was lost – a clean sweep being made by the Liberal Party. There is a flavour of irony in the fact that in fighting against the so-called "Liberalizing" of the Labour Party the Bethnal Green Communists succeeded in so completely Liberalizing their own Borough.'[59] Any pretence that they desired a united front of the left was shattered.[60] By 1928 Morrison felt that Labour was clear of communist internal trouble; they were now a 'wash-out'.

Morrison often noted the similarities between communism and fascism, and loathed the latter as much as the former. When refusing to attend an LCC reception for the Prefect of Rome, he said that we who have condemned the violence of the Communist Party could not welcome one who represented the fascist dictatorship. 'He who interferes with the impartiality and independence of the judicature or the supremacy of Parliament and elected municipalities is an enemy of freedom, whether his language is of the left or the right. . . . The callous shedding of blood and the triumph of passion and hate over reason are dreadful things.'[61] He saw communists and fascists as really collaborators; each stimulated the growth of the other. 'The only people who can make the Fascists a danger are the Communists, whilst the only people who might make the Communist Party a body of substance are the Fascists and people of similar outlook.'[62] He warned the Communist Party of the consequences of their preaching of violence, for it produced 'a movement of corresponding political ethics and tactics more or less allied to the Tory party, . . . which may usurp police functions and those of the armed forces'.[63] Fascists and communists championed violence and civil war as means whereby through chaos their small clique could come to power. They did not believe in democratic or parliamentary institutions, using them only to further their destructive agitation, while 'the Labour Party believes that progress to Socialism can only be securely based upon popular understanding and popular consent expressed in a growing measure of electoral support for the representatives of Labour. We desire Socialism by consent, whereas the Communists desire dictatorship by imposition.'[64]

In 1924 Morrison made his first appearance in Parliament as MP for South Hackney during the period of the first Labour government. After the First World War Morrison had regarded work on a local council as more important than playing the parliamentary game. In local government Labour was in control in many boroughs, while in the House of Commons Labour seemed condemned to many years in opposition. His reasoning was that 'until Labour has shown its capacity in the field of municipal statesmanship it is questionable whether the electorate generally will be anxious to send our candidates to Westminster'.[65]

By 1922 his attitude had changed. He was asked to stand as a parliamentary candidate for South Hackney which contained the largest concentration of the poorest people in the borough. A by-election was imminent following the sentencing of the former MP, Horatio Bottomley, to seven years' penal servitude for embezzlement. The popular Independent member had so indulged his constituency that it was notorious as a bought division. Morrison put the matter before the Executive of the LLP.[66] Many had suggested he should stand but he had 'steadily declined . . . firstly because I had no immediate desire to take up a Parliamentary candidature, and secondly because there appeared to be no prospect of securing the necessary finances'. Now the finances had been found, yet he was still reluctant. Arthur Henderson and the National Agent were urging him on, but his main anxiety was about the effect his parliamentary activities would have on his work as Secretary of the LLP. He pointed out that now that Windle and Miss Somers had taken over much of the work of party organization he could concentrate more on policy, publicity and research and could keep a general watch on the administration. He could, if elected, do his necessary reading and writing at the House of Commons, and his knowledge of London municipal matters could be of use to the London Labour movement in Parliament. The tenor of his letter suggested that he thought he should go into Parliament, but he wanted the approval of the Executive. Of the seventeen members, fourteen replied, twelve in favour and two doubtful.

However, Morrison then told the Executive that he was not going forward.[67] It seems that Morrison's enemies in the South Hackney party had gained the upper hand and Morrison withdrew to avoid an open rebuff. The candidate selected was an ex-Liberal and Fabian, Holford Knight, KC. During the campaign Morrison was noticeably absent, for most of the time on holiday in Switzerland. Knight lost by only seventy-two votes in a straight fight with a Conservative: 9,118 votes against 9,046, a creditable performance considering that, as the National Agent reported to the NEC of the Labour Party, there was 'not a shred of effective organization in the Division', only a few names and addresses; and in any case Labour had never fought it before and 'evidences of the corrupt methods were abundant'.[68]

In the autumn of 1923 an opportunity at South Hackney loomed again when Knight gave up his candidature. The anti-Morrison forces advocated the claims of E. C. Fairchild[69] whom Morrison had narrowly defeated in 1915 for the Secretaryship of the LLP, while his own supporters strongly pressed his case. Again Morrison sought guidance from the Executive of the LLP.[70] He claimed to be still not anxious to enter Parliament, but it had been put to him that 'I should be useful to the Parliamentary Party. . . . There is the other consideration that it is of advantage to enter Parliamentary work fairly young in life and that the most likely of the London constituencies are gradually being fixed up with candidates so that suitable opportunities may not come later on.' On the Executive a majority again felt he should go forward.[71]

He went ahead, and with the election campaign almost upon them the South Hackney Labour Party adopted him at the end of November. In later years Morrison recalled that he had not at the time wanted to be an MP, and was persuaded only by the persistence of Windle.[72] A close friend of Windle's confirmed the importance of his influence, yet also gave an interesting version of Windle's motives. It was not so much that he saw the great role Morrison could play on the parliamentary stage as that by diverting Morrison's interests to Parliament he could reduce Morrison's interference in his own work of organization in London.[73]

The contest was three cornered. Against Morrison were arrayed the sitting Conservative, Captain Erskine-Bolst and the Liberal contender, Captain Garro-Jones; the issue between them was Protection or Free Trade. To Morrison this was a 'barren quarrel . . . a poisonous red herring drawn across the path of the common people by monopolist profiteers with a view to preventing the application of Labour's constructive policy'.[74]

The main themes of Morrison's campaign were to denigrate 'profiteers' and to claim that Labour's policy would solve unemployment. He advocated the capital levy, 'a scientifically graduated levy on accumulated fortunes of over £5,000', and was startled to find it fiercely opposed in the worst slum of the constituency by the very poor who felt that what people had saved they should keep. He outlined Labour's plans for tackling unemployment: large-scale public works, such as anti-pollution measures on the River Lee, minimum wages and hours, industrial reorganization and education, adequate maintenance for the unemployed and generally the treatment of unemployment as a national and not a local problem.[75]

Some of Morrison's meetings were rowdy; hecklers jeered at the 'conchie' and contrasted his cowardice with the martial qualities of the two Captains.[76] Morrison bore this with quiet dignity; in Hackney he was always most reticent about his wartime experiences and said not a word, even to fellow objectors.[77] He also was careful never to attack Horatio Bottomley whose reputation was still high in the slums where he had distributed his, and other people's, largesse so lavishly. Morrison ostentatiously declared that 'you will not hear one word from me in criticism of your former Member. He is in a place from which he cannot answer and the Labour Party does not believe in hitting a man when he is down.'[78] These words 'fetched the roof off', and he won goodwill as news of his speech spread.

The result, much to Morrison's surprise, was his victory with a majority of 2,821.* Despite the intervention of the Liberal candidate Morrison gained three hundred votes compared with the last general election and pushed Labour's share of the vote up by three per cent, which was slightly better than

* Hackney South,

1922		1923	
Conservative	14,017	Labour	9,578
Labour	9,276	Liberal	6,757
		Conservative	6,047

the rise of one per cent in the United Kingdom as a whole, but not as good as Labour's ten per cent increase over London.[79] From the count at the Kings Head he was carried shoulder high to the Town Hall. 'When the great crowd realized who it was, a great roar of cheering went up, and the cordon of police had their work cut out to keep the excitement under reasonable control, seeing that so many wanted to break through and shake hands with South Hackney's first Labour MP.'[80] Morrison's assessment of his victory was cool. He realized how flimsy was his success. He pointed out at his victory rally that his opponents had received more votes than he, that the next fight would be harder, and that the main task was to improve party organization.[81]

In 1923 he was thirty-five. Years later he looked back and mused 'I should like to be thirty-five and live for ever. That's the ideal age. A man usually dies before he can finish his job. That is sad.'[82] During the campaign his wife Margaret had been at Morrison's side more frequently than before. At a victory social he made one of his rare public references to her. He said he much appreciated her presence during the fight.

'Owing to the train services, he rarely got home except to sleep, and the danger now was that he might not get home for that.
– 'Poor old Herbert' – someone cried.
'No, no! It's "Poor old Margaret!" because I am concerned with the loneliness of the vigil which Labour men's wives have to keep. But I warned her on several occasions before I married her. We had no formal contract about it, but it was a condition of marriage that if she married an agitator she was asking for trouble, and I am afraid she has got it.'[83]

At this point of time, in the middle of December 1923, Morrison ruled out the possibility that Labour might in fact form a government. 'We don't ask for the responsibility of government until we have the power. We shall go on educating the people in the constituencies and perfecting our organization until we have the strength, and the electors the wisdom, to return a triumphant Labour majority to Parliament.'[84] However, MacDonald, following the Liberal failure to support a Baldwin administration, decided to form a minority government, convinced that it was important to allay fears that Labour was unfit to govern. As the administration was being formed Morrison's views altered and he was very disappointed when rumours that he was being considered for a position in the government turned out to be groundless. A place was found for Clement Atlee, as Under-Secretary at the War Office. Once again he was slightly ahead of Morrison. In 1919 Atlee was Mayor of Stepney, one year before Morrison at Hackney, and in 1922 he was returned as MP for Limehouse, nearly two years before Morrison.

In January Morrison organized a most successful victory celebration at the Royal Albert Hall. Speakers included MacDonald, Clynes, Thomas and Margaret Bondfield, but many present felt that the outstanding speech was made by Morrison. His description of Labour's rise to power was heightened by brilliant stage-management. He had carefully scattered throughout the hall contingents of party members from those London constituencies won by Labour. As he mentioned each seat which Labour had won, a contingent rose. The audience felt it was most dramatic as Morrison demonstrated the onward march of Labour. William Lawther remarked that Morrison's was 'a most moving performance, I could never forget it'. A miner from Durham turned to Lawther and said 'That's the fella who can do things.'[85]

Morrison's first few months in the Commons were a disappointment. He was reported in the Hackney press as saying 'Parliament is a very funny place, and the more I see of it the more I admire the Hackney Borough Council'.[86] Later he explained: 'the local government man did not know where he was for a month or two'; he claimed that: 'the object of the House of Commons was not to get things done at all; it was to prevent things being done, and the whole procedure was designed to make the process as difficult as possible.'[87] But he soon mastered the intricacies of parliamentary procedure. He was appointed to a Standing Committee which tackled the Rent Restriction Bill and a bill to give the franchise to females at twenty-one.[88] After a few months he was getting used to the Commons. He knew how to attract publicity to himself. It was noted that he wore a 'wonderful panama hat', the only one seen in the House of Commons that summer.[89]

He had been used to running his own show at the London Labour Party and on the Hackney council. Now he was a mere back-bencher and, what was worse, on the government side, unable freely to vent criticisms against the government. He found most ministers 'fatally aloof' from their supporters. In particular he felt that MacDonald and Snowden did not attend party meetings enough to explain their policies, and to listen to the anxieties of the ordinary MPs. Morrison recalled that the back-benchers 'found the whole situation trying at times'.[90]

Morrison's initial discomfort in the House was exacerbated by a disastrous maiden speech: the worst since Disraeli's, he heard a Tory member declare.[91] He was asked to speak by the whips, during a lull in the debate on the King's Speech, in favour of the Labour motion of censure on the Baldwin government which had not yet been brought down. Morrison was unprepared and, impromptu, produced a rambling, somewhat incoherent speech, devoid of memorable phrases and full of abuse of Liberals and Tories.[92] He was off his home ground and flopped badly. Austin Hopkinson, the Conservative who followed him, contemptuously opened 'There is a very pleasant convention in this House by which, when an hon. Member makes his maiden speech, the hon. Member who gets up next should congratulate him in set terms. I forget what those set terms are, therefore he may take the usual conventional compliment as paid.'[93] Morrison was downcast and the memory of his poor performance rankled.[94]

After this unsettling début Morrison limited himself to tackling topics mainly affecting London local authorities. He used Question Time to complain about the polluted state of the River Lee[95] and to condemn the Hackney council.[96] He sought leave to introduce a bill to prohibit the demolition of houses and the change of their use from residential to commercial purposes without the approval of the local authority.[97]

When he won the opportunity to introduce a bill, he promoted one very dear to his heart, the Labour Party's Local Authorities Enabling Bill for which he had argued in a pamphlet of 1921, *The Citizen's Charter*. The bill would allow local authorities to escape the limitations imposed on them by the legal requirement that they could perform only those functions for which they had clear and specific statutory authority. Thus local authorities would be granted a general competence to carry out a wide range of activities, making them almost equal in legal powers to a private company. To Morrison's opponents the bill offered a free hand for socialism, the municipalization of everything.[98] In reply he said that it did not allow 'universal irresponsible trading, in reckless competition with private enterprise'. What was undertaken had to be in the public interest, and provision was made for the Board of Trade to ensure that safeguards were complied with.

He was quick to spot in bills any attack on the rights of local authorities. For instance in a clause of the Central London and Metropolitan District Railway Companies Bill private enterprise was allowed to tunnel under the property of local authorities without paying compensation, whereas compensation was payable if the tunnel was under private property. This was typical, said Morrison, of the way 'private monopoly rides roughshod over the rights of ratepayers, while always willing to pay tribute to the interests of private concerns'.[99]

Any proposal which limited the powers of local authorities in London raised his hackles. He so bitterly opposed the government's London Traffic Bill that he voted on the second reading against his own party. He criticized the government for taking over a Tory bill which conferred on the Minister of Transport what he regarded as essentially municipal powers – including the regulation of omnibuses in London, their numbers and routes. He said that 'he did not care what Government was in power or what Parliamentary party was in the majority, he would fight the Whitehall officials every time for the right of London to govern itself'.[100] He said that 'if he had been expelled from the Parliamentary Labour Party, he would have opposed it because he regarded the Bill as nothing short of treachery to the people of London'.[101] On any matter affecting London Morrison could be guaranteed to have scrutinized the consequences thoroughly and to have briefed the London Labour MPs. He was quick to protest at any attempts to prevent the London Labour MPs from having their say; he said 'in regard to Bills affecting London, I think we have a right to be heard'.[102] He had no formal authority over his colleagues, but from his sheer ability and drive, detailed mastery of complicated problems and grasp of parliamentary procedure he created a united group.[103]

His final speech in the Commons of 1924 was during the censure debate on the Attorney General for withdrawing the prosecution against J. R. Campbell for an issue of the *Worker's Weekly*, the official paper of the Communist Party, which invited the military to refuse to participate in action against strikers or in a war. Against the proposal for a select committee to inquire into the withdrawal of the charge Morrison said it was wrong for politicians to sit on an inquiry into a judicial officer and his judicial decisions. He also claimed that the offending article would not get very far amongst the troops, since Campbell had little influence; his purpose was not to spread sedition but to embarrass the Labour Party. He criticized the Conservatives for making party advantage out of a judicial issue and noted how communists and Conservatives were once again helping each other to damage the Labour Party.[104] At the conclusion of this debate the government was defeated and MacDonald resigned. The Labour government was over.

In the 1924 election at Hackney Morrison faced a single opponent, Garro-Jones. The Conservative candidate had withdrawn, leaving the Liberal a clear run against Morrison, which proved, he argued, that Conservatives and Liberals had been carrying on a sham fight to deceive the people.[105] His prediction that the fight would be harder than in 1923 came true. He paraded a black cat with a red bow as a good luck omen.[106]

His address to the electorate proclaimed him as the 'Labour' candidate; the term 'socialist' was absent. And on his election leaflets even 'Labour' did not appear; he described himself as 'The Man who Fights Clean'! His appeal had eight points. 1 *Peace.* He commended MacDonald's efforts to achieve world peace, including the Russian treaty, which was not to help bolshevism which he and the Labour Party opposed but to promote peace and to relieve unemployment, since a loan was to assist the Russians to buy the products of British labour. He also praised Labour's strong support for the League of Nations. 2 *Housing.* He welcomed the new Housing Act, the prevention of profiteering in building materials and the continuation and improvement of the Rent Restriction Act. 3 *Unemployment.* 'constructive policy of national development and the restoration of international trade. A scientific policy in preventing unemployment, proper maintenance for those without employment.' 4 *National Finance.* He commended Snowden's 'sound financial policy' and looked forward to further reorganization, including the taxation of land values, safeguarding the old age pensioners, and benefits for widowed mothers. There was no mention of the capital levy. 5 *Profiteering.* 'Prevention of profiteering and exploitation by rings, trusts and monopolies.' 6 *Ex-servicemen.* They were urged 'to stand shoulder to shoulder with all the workers in the labour movement', while he would strive for justice in war pensions. 7 *Electricity*. He promised to continue to work to extend 'the Hackney policy of public ownership, which means cheaper electricity for British industry and British agriculture, and much wider facilities with a view to lightening the labour of the British housewife'. 8 *The Franchise*. 'Full adult suffrage. Extension of the franchise to women on the same terms that it is or may be granted to men.'

In his *Autobiography*[107] Morrison claims that he began the election campaign with great optimism, but the publication of the 'Zinoviev Letter' was bitterly disillusioning, especially as it showed MacDonald as a negative figure. Morrison eagerly awaited a strong lead from MacDonald but he failed to take a clear line. However, in order to quieten anxieties raised by the letter, Morrison wrote to local parties in London urging them to make use of the incident for Labour by inserting the following notice in their local papers. 'Beware of last minute untruths. Ramsay MacDonald's firm note to the Soviet Government *PROVES* that Labour can be relied upon sternly to uphold British interests and the constitutional position of the Army and Navy.'[108] Although he was asked no questions about it at meetings, and his canvassers reported no noticeable apprehension on the doorstep, he sensed that the electorate, especially the women, were troubled about the 'bloody Bolsheviks' as Labour was portrayed. He found meetings subdued; even the children did not sing the doggerel 'Vote, vote, vote for Herbert Morrison' with the gusto of 1923. On polling day voting was brisk in the morning and quiet in the evening, normally Labour's best time.

The result was for Morrison a not unexpected defeat.* The opposition, divided in 1923, had combined forces and pushed him out. But his performance was creditable. He had increased Labour votes by 2,073, a rise of four per cent, which was better than Labour's two per cent rise in the country as a whole and three per cent rise over London, and it was far better than Labour's result in the two Poplar constituencies where the Labour vote fell by two per cent and seven per cent.[109] His reaction was to attack Garro-Jones as a member of 'an insignificant party' for issuing 'lying literature' which was personally abusive. He complained that the Tories had told the people in 1922 to vote Coalition, in 1923 Conservative, and in 1924 Liberal. 'Am I not entitled to hope that at the next election they will tell their followers to vote Labour?'[110] Garro-Jones advised Morrison: 'stop whining'.[111]

During the 1920s Morrison went abroad as a Labour delegate to international conferences. He attended international labour and socialist congresses in Geneva and Brussels.[112] Such visits were so fleeting that he could have seen little of the countries or their inhabitants. He probably met only the delegates at the conferences and was limited in his range of contacts since he

---

* Hackney South, 1924 Liberal 13,415
                    Labour 11,651.

spoke no foreign language. He again tried to learn French, and possibly German, from a course of gramophone records. However, since he so rarely had the time to listen with any concentration, he failed to master another tongue.

These conference trips made little impact on Morrison. They prompted no speech nor article, whereas some visits he made abroad under the auspices of the Workers' Travel Association* certainly impressed him. The first was in August 1927 when he led a group of thirty to Germany for eight days to study municipal government in Rhineland towns. They toured many departments of the local authorities and listened to lectures from officials. Morrison was thrilled by the scope of German municipal enterprise.[113] He was especially excited by Cologne's Home Refuse Organization and he described in great detail its operations from the collection of the refuse to its disposal.[114] In 1928 he led a similar group to study Viennese municipal government. They visited Vienna's town hall, laundry, baths, flats, library, markets and gas works. Here again Morrison was captivated by 'its modern utilization of waste products'.[115] In the following year he returned to Vienna and added Berlin and Prague to the itinerary, concentrating this time on the organization of transport services.[116]

Morrison's insights into these nations were limited by his inability to notice anything not related to his campaigns for municipal enterprise. He saw the German cities as examples of socialism in practice. Vienna was the city 'Where Socialist Dreams Come True'.[117] The narrowness of his response to foreign countries startled some of his colleagues. Dr Alfred Salter wrote of an occasion during a visit abroad with Morrison at this time. 'Most of us were entranced with a particularly beautiful view of snowy peaks, sombre forests and shining cascades. Morrison could not understand our ecstasies. His only thought was of the waste of water power, and how many millions of volts or watts of electricity could be manufactured if the cataract were harnessed to a turbine.'[118]

Morrison acted as a leader of these groups on behalf of the WTA. The Secretary of the WTA, Ernest Wimble, was eager to develop a two-way traffic of Labour groups between Britain and other European countries, and so he wanted as leaders of the groups prominent Labour figures who would make useful contacts abroad with trade unions and socialist organizations. Morrison was Wimble's choice as the ideal leader of a group. His efficiency at organizing ensured that all ran smoothly, and his jovial personality kept the groups together as happy bands.[119]

Wimble's other activity at the WTA was to pioneer cut-rate package holidays. Morrison made use of these facilities, probably receiving reductions in charges for his services to the WTA. The WTA arranged all his family holidays, to Switzerland and to his favourite, the south of France. Here he found what he wanted for a relaxing fortnight: a comfortable hotel, the chance

* Cited later as WTA.

to bask in the sun, to swim in the warm sea, and friends with whom he could gossip and enjoy a sing-song.

Morrison made a number of speeches and wrote occasionally on foreign policy. At party conference in 1925, for instance, he advocated independence for Egypt and opposed its military occupation by Britain. If our concern was to protect the Suez Canal, it was better to have Egypt friendly and not antagonistic, therefore it should be governed by its own elected representatives; but he opposed recognition of Egyptian suzerainty over Sudan as replacing one form of imperialism with another.[120] Compared with his contributions on domestic issues, his interventions on foreign issues were sparse, and he showed no signs of original thinking or wide reading. He followed the party line and one can guess that his views were shaped by pamphlets published by the party and by articles in Labour journals.

After the war he displayed an unfashionable sympathy for the Germans. In August 1919 he protested against harsh reparations and deplored particularly the removal of milch cows. He urged the dispatch of more aid to relieve famine and the sending of surplus Army medical stores to hospitals where disease was rife.[121] The Treaty of Versailles was a *bête noire*. The French occupation of the Ruhr in 1923 aroused his anger. He assailed the French action as 'capitalist aggression and military tyranny'. He demanded the withdrawal from Germany of all the armies of occupation and advocated that the question of reparations should be left to a tribunal on which Germany would have equal representation.[122] In 1929, when he addressed the Labour Party conference as Chairman, he welcomed Labour's efforts to end war debts and its withdrawal of the occupation of the Rhineland.[123] His view was that Germany was the victim of an oppressive peace treaty whose provisions had to be eased, and that Germany should as soon as possible be brought back as a full member of the concert of nations.

The other country whose interests he supported in the early 1920s was the Soviet Union. After the war it seemed a gallant country struggling manfully against the intervention of foreign powers seeking to restore the Tsarist regime. At the Labour Party conference of 1919 Morrison pleaded for industrial action to stop intervention which he depicted as a crusade against the international socialist movement. He urged that the Soviets should be left free 'to settle for themselves the forms of government which they wish to adopt and which should then be recognized by the other governments'.[124]

Morrison's hostility to war deepened in the course of the 1920s. He identified war as being peculiarly capitalist. 'So long as the capitalist politicians are in power, and until secret diplomacy and private armament manufacture are altogether finished, there is no security against war.'[125] In 1926 Morrison spoke at the Royal Albert Hall to an audience of nine thousand on behalf of the Great War Resistance Demonstration, to drum up support for Arthur Ponsonby's Peace Letter Campaign. Its purpose was to secure from individuals a signed declaration that 'We, the undersigned, convinced that all disputes between nations are capable of settlement either by diplomatic negotiations or by some form of International Arbitration, hereby solemnly declare that we refuse to support or render war service to any Government which resorts to arms'.[126] Morrison appealed to the crowd to let the government know that 'you are finished with war, and that you will take no part in it, either collectively or individually'. Never again would Morrison be such an outright pacifist, and never in the future would he refer to his profession of the pacifist cause in the mid-twenties. In place of war as a means of settling international disputes Morrison called for international arbitration; he was a keen champion of the League of Nations.[127] In June 1929 the front page of *London News* carried a report of an interview between Morrison and the well-known actress and pacifist, Sybil Thorndike. Both clearly saw eye to eye on international affairs and felt that Britain could take a lead in achieving world disarmament by reducing her own armaments. In the 1920s unilateral disarmament was Morrison's policy.

His total opposition to war was to be shaken in the 1930s when he belatedly recognized that only force would deter or defeat those who would use force as an instrument of policy. It took a long time for this lesson to sink in, largely because Morrison was so appalled by the consequences of war. Abhorrence of violence linked his views on defence, foreign and domestic politics. It was the basis for his hatred of communists, fascists, and revolutionaries generally who did not abide by constitutional procedures. The alternative to such procedures was revolution and chaos, and the only victor, tyranny.

Chapter 9

Metropolitan and Public Utility Problems

In the 1920s Morrison became the Labour Party's expert on London government, and on transport and electricity. He made such a name for himself in the field of transport that it was no surprise when MacDonald appointed him Minister of Transport in 1929.

Morrison was keen to reform radically the system of London's government. He was the architect, and main advocate during the 1920s, of the proposals of the London Labour Party, which were submitted to the Royal Commission on London Government in 1922.[1] His interest in reform waned in the thirties, when the Labour Party took control at County Hall, and remained quiescent while he was in national government. In the fifties and sixties his interest revived, but he became a fierce opponent of the reforms he had championed in the 1920s.

London government in the 1920s was a complex administrative mixture. Apart from different types of directly elected local authorities there were numerous indirectly elected special boards and joint authorities as well as ministers themselves and the occasional committee to advise them. Boundaries were not uniform, jurisdictions overlapped, antagonisms were rife, and London was fragmented. There was no authority, directly elected, responsible for London as a whole. The largest authority, the London County Council, covered only that part of London built up to the last third of the nineteenth century. Morrison's tidy mind was appalled.

Margaret Cole recalled that Morrison hated like poison any idea of separate functional authorities or indirect representation. 'One could hardly say to Morrison "Metropolitan Water Board" without producing an explosion.'[2] 'Hole and Corner Boards'[3] he dubbed them, dealing with public property, employing public servants, providing public services, paid out of the public purse, yet 'answerable to no one but themselves'.[4]* They were undemocratic:

* e.g. Metropolitan Water Board, Metropolitan Asylums Board, Thames and Lee Conservancy Boards, London and Home Counties Joint Electricity Authority and Port of London Authority.

not directly responsible to the people and conducting their operations wholly or partly in secret, far from the scrutiny of the electorate who were apathetic in the face of such bewildering complexity. They were uneconomical: chief officers and staff were duplicated, resources were wasted, and related services were conducted separately. They were unenterprising: they exhibited 'too much joint and not enough authority', for their members too often regarded themselves as ambassadors from the body which had nominated them. Thus progress could be only at the pace of the most reactionary members who tended to think not so much of the needs of a service or London as of their own particular interest.

The City of London Corporation, which controlled the markets of Smithfield and Billingsgate, was another long-standing target of Morrison's hostility. As early as 1917 he asked 'is it not time London faced up to the pretentious buffoonery of the City of London Corporation and wiped it off the municipal map? The pioneer of civic liberty, the City, is now a square mile of entrenched reaction, the home of the devilry of modern finance and that journalistic abortion, the stunt press. The City is an administrative anachronism, and in our scheme of London Government we must consider 20th century needs as well as 10th century history.'[5] In Morrison's reformed system of London government there was no place for the City. He was also vehemently hostile to the administration of essentially local services by central departments or ministerial nominees. For instance the Metropolitan Police Force was a particular bogy, controlled by a Commissioner appointed by the Home Office.[6] Morrison's objective was 'home rule' for London: an end to its status as a 'municipal crown colony'. London was 'entitled to as much civic dignity and self-government as are the great provincial cities. We are not content to be the Cinderella of the municipal world.'[7] His plan was for a two-tier system of local government.[8] At the top would be a London Regional Authority, covering not just the built-up area but the rural area around and dependent on London. This countryside would be a mainly agricultural belt to stop the sprawl of London, and beyond which the new authority would build 'satellite towns' to accommodate London's growing population and mitigate her housing problems. Morrison was never precise about the actual area the top body should cover. It was usually an area with a radius of about twenty-five miles from Charing Cross. It was to be responsible for functions of a large-scale nature: regional planning; large housing and slum clearance schemes; electricity generation; transport, including tramways, omnibuses, local railways, the underground, taxis and char-a-bancs, traffic control and main highways; the Port of London; water; main drainage; river conservancy; police; fire protection; wholesale markets; asylums; the large poor law institutions; large hospitals and sanatoriums; higher education and teacher training. It would also be empowered 'to do such things and to undertake such works as may seem to the Regional Council advisable and in the interests of the area'. The Council, of a size of between 100 and 150 members, would consist of representatives directly elected on the basis of one or two from each parliamentary constituency. And as befitted a great corporation it would have a Lord Mayor, Sheriff and Aldermen, and the members would be paid so as to bring their status equal to that of MPs.

Beneath this huge authority would be a bottom tier of existing boroughs and districts, empowered to merge if they wished, for the more local and personal services. They would be responsible, amongst other things, for rating valuation and assessment, local electricity distribution, town planning, local highways, small housing and clearance schemes, local markets, local hospitals and clinics, care of children, elementary education, health and sanitary services and any other powers granted to them by the top-tier authority. Morrison recognized that London could not, like Birmingham or Manchester, have the single-tier, all-purpose county borough. The reason was that historically London was 'an aggregation of thirty or more towns, so that the Metropolis is one in a certain sense, but it is also thirty or more, and it is very necessary to recognize the separate identity of the localities as well as to realize the need for examining the problem of London as a whole'.[9]

Morrison's role in devising and propagating this policy was central. He wrote the first drafts of the party's policy statements and resolutions on London government reform, while very few changes were made by the party's committees. He wrote the memorandum for the Royal Commission and appeared before it as the London Labour Party's witness. During the 1924 Labour government after the Cabinet had decided to set in motion consideration of reform of London government, Morrison, who had pressed this issue on them, drew up a plan of action for Labour Members of Parliament from Greater London.[20] He was eagle-eyed to spot any shortcomings of an *ad hoc* body or central department. For instance, after the severe flooding of the Thames in January 1928, which killed fourteen and made thousands homeless, he pressed for a Greater London Authority to have control of all drainage, flood protection and river conservancy functions.[11] However, by the end of the 1920s he seems to have realized that the major transformation he was advocating was unlikely to be fulfilled in the foreseeable future. His growing awareness of this fact can be seen in the development of his ideas on a subject which was perhaps closest to his heart – London transport.

Morrison's first writings on London's transport problems were contained in a pamphlet of 1916, *The People's Roads*, originally published in the *Daily Herald*. He complained about the 'outrageously unfair competition' which the trams of London, operated by the LCC, faced from privately run omnibuses. The buses used the roads freely, paying no rates yet inflicting 'wear and tear' on the surface, while the local authorities were burdened with the cost of the upkeep of the roads, and their tramways paid rates on their track and contributed to street improvements. Further, the buses damaged the tram tracks, which in turn entailed higher expenditure by the LCC. The buses could go where they liked, selecting the most profitable routes, while the trams were limited, and any extension of their routes had to run the gauntlet of opposition and veto from the metropolitan boroughs. The LCC, however, had no powers to operate buses. The answer was 'the municipalization of the entire London passenger traffic'. Co-ordination, rationalization, equalization of burdens, could all be achieved by common public ownership and control.[12]

This policy remained Morrison's throughout the 1920s. The first objective was to create a new regional authority with the power to own and operate all transport facilities in London. As Morrison told the Select Committee on Transport (Metropolitan Area) in July 1919, it should be responsible for steamboats, tramways, buses, taxis, the underground and London railways. He told the Committee that 'in view of its importance this authority should not be one of the semi-secret "Boards" of which London already has too many'.[13] Morrison was also afraid that a specialist transport authority would be unable to co-ordinate the planning of transport services with related services, like housing, town planning, drainage, amenities and road maintenance.[14] The answer to London's transport problem was thus intimately linked to local government reform.

In the 1920s various bodies provided transport services in London. In addition to the LCC trams, eight local authorities within Greater London had tramway undertakings. The suburban railway lines, following a consolidation of 1919, were operated by the four main line private railway companies, the London and North-Eastern Railway, the London, Midland and Scottish Railway, the Southern Railway and the Great Western Railway. Most of the underground system had been merged into the 'Underground Combine' of Lord Ashfield, formerly Sir Albert Stanley, a President of the Board of Trade in Lloyd George's wartime coalition. The largest underground concern outside his control was the Metropolitan Railway Company which also had extensive overground lines. Ashfield was also the head of the London General Omnibus Company which had consolidated many small bus enterprises, and he controlled most of the other buses, trams, and trolley buses in outer London. Ashfield dominated the London transport scene.[15] In a dynamic manner he had devised a series of amalgamations. His objective was to unify all London transport under his private control. His targets were those elements beyond his reach, particularly the LCC trams. His main opponent was Morrison who also wanted unification of London's transport, but under public not private control. He felt that such a monopoly should be owned and controlled by a public agency, to serve the interests of the public, and not left to a private business serving the interests of a few shareholders. The politics of London transport in the 1920s was very much a duel between these two ambitious men.

In the early 1920s and especially in 1923–4 a new phenomenon arose in London transport: the small independent bus company, often financed by the motor manufacturers, who indulged in cut-throat competition not only against the LCC trams but also against Ashfield's bus company. They picked out the most profitable routes and raced back and forth, with vehicles frequently poorly maintained and unsafe. Unemployed men were glad of work as conductors and drivers at wage rates much below those of the Combine. The fares of the 'pirates' too were lower. These 'pirates' worried Ashfield. He was proud of providing a public service, even running buses on unprofitable routes and subsidizing them from profitable ones. The 'pirates' undercut the more responsible concern.

Ashfield wanted a 'protected monopoly', and the Conservative government in 1923 instituted a scheme to achieve this. Control over London transport, and particularly regulation of bus companies and their routes, would be vested in the Minister of Transport, advised by a committee of representatives from local authorities and the private companies. In this way Ashfield thought the activities of the 'pirates' would be restricted and order would ensue. The Ministry drafted the necessary bill.

Morrison was aghast and he mounted a campaign of opposition, drafting memoranda for the Executive of the London Labour Party[16] and the National Executive Committee.[17] Both accepted Morrison's line completely. He argued that this scheme, by transferring municipal functions to the central state, was 'a further interference with the rights of local self-government'. The advisory committee was a hotch-potch, likely to be totally ineffectual, and was yet another joint body to complicate the jigsaw of London's administration. Further, the scheme protected Ashfield from competition. Morrison devised a symbol for his campaign: an LCC tram menaced by the grabbing hand of the Combine.

Morrison now recognized that reform of local government was unlikely following the report in 1923 of the Royal Commission on London Government, which split three ways.[18] He informed the Executive of the London Labour Party that the establishment of a Greater London Authority was 'postponed indefinitely', and that if they stuck to the old policy they would lose public sympathy. The public were concerned about transport and the problem was how to meet this anxiety. It was essential to retain the principle of 'municipal control even if it is not control by an authority directly elected by the people'. Therefore as a purely interim measure he proposed a joint committee of ten: five from the LCC, two from the metropolitan boroughs, and three from local authorities in Greater London to regulate bus routes, to give observations to parliamentary committees on tramway bills, to supervise dates of road repairs and to advise the Minister about road improvement grants. His policy was adopted by the national and the London Labour parties.[19]

Before the government could proceed, the 1923 general election was held, which resulted in a Labour government; the new Minister of Transport, Harry Gosling, former Labour leader of the LCC, was expected to be sympathetic to the London Labour Party's position. In fact he commended the Conservative bill, with only slight amendments, to the Commons. The bill created the London and Home Counties Traffic Advisory Committee, composed of members selected by ministers, by local authorities, by private transport companies and by the trade unions, and conferred on the Minister of Transport the power, after consulting the Committee, to regulate bus services. He could prohibit or restrict the number of buses and limit the number of journeys to be made by the buses.

Why had the Labour Minister, and a London MP at that, gone so totally against the policy of the London Labour Party? Gosling had let himself be persuaded by his departmental officials to go ahead with a bill that had already been drafted; and since the Conservatives had wanted it when in office they were likely to support it in opposition and thus the bill would have an easy passage through Parliament. Also the influence of Ernest Bevin, the General Secretary of the Transport and General Workers' Union, was decisive. Like Ashfield, Bevin had built his union empire by a series of amalgamations, taking over in the process the Watermen's and Lightermen's Union which was Gosling's union. In return Gosling was made President of the TGWU. He was very much under the spell of the dominating Bevin.[20] It is said that when MacDonald was forming his government his first thought for Minister of Transport was in fact Morrison, but Bevin, realizing that he would not get his way with Morrison, urged on MacDonald the claims of Gosling.[21] Bevin disliked Morrison's plan for London transport and is likely to have persuaded Gosling to do what he rather than Morrison wanted. Another significant point is that Bevin and Ashfield, both tycoons, found they could work together. Bevin also felt that his transport workers would have a better deal from Ashfield than from Morrison; after all, Ashfield's bus workers were paid more than the LCC tram workers. Indeed the immediate cause for the Labour government's adoption of the Conservative bill lay in Bevin's claim for wage increases for London's tram workers. The employers argued that they could not afford them because of competition from the 'pirates'. Bevin in March 1924 brought the tram workers and busmen out on strike, and threatened to bring the tube services to a halt. To avert a collapse of London's transport services a hurried compromise was concocted. The government promised to promote the London Traffic Bill, thus crushing the 'pirates', and the employers were then able to offer an increase in wages. The strike was called off.[22]

The Labour government was not enthusiastic about the bill, but the problem was urgent. Gosling told the Cabinet: 'I do not think that the control of London traffic should be made to wait on the realization of the Labour Party's policy for the government of London as a whole.'[23] The Cabinet agreed that the situation was desperate, 'owing to the present congestion of traffic, the forthcoming Empire Exhibition, and to considerations affecting the earnings of tramway employees'.[24] The bill was 'a stop-gap measure of an experimental character pending the passing of more comprehensive legislation'.[25] To allay Morrison's opposition the Cabinet agreed to give the municipal representatives on the Advisory Committee a majority. There was also to be no place statutorily reserved for the Combine, although the Minister would be able to appoint 'persons connected with traffic interests'.[26]

At the bill's second reading in the House of Commons Morrison spoke in opposition and said that for the first time he would vote against the government, deliberately and with a clear conscience.[27] He would not vote 'against the interests of London and in favour of the interests of one of the most insidious financial corporations that this London of ours is cursed with'. He saw the bill as a victory for Ashfield who 'fought for this monopoly year in and year out'. He objected to the minister exercising powers rightly belonging to local government. 'I would prefer local government any day to Whitehall government.' He felt that London's status was now that of a 'Crown Colony', and he objected to London questions being controlled by MPs from Scotland, Wales or Lancashire. He criticized the Advisory Committee for being composed of representatives of interests and for being 'officered, staffed, appointed and controlled even to its procedure and the number of its quorum – all these things can be done only with the approval of the Minister of State. It will be advised by the Minister's officials as to how it should advise the Minister.' The bill was accepted by 211 votes to 112, and nine Labour MPs voted against, including Morrison and the Chairman of the London Labour Party, Naylor.[28]

In the battle over the bill Morrison came into conflict with Bevin. The bone of contention was the composition of Morrison's proposed joint authority. Morrison advocated that it should consist solely of representatives of local authorities. Bevin urged that it have at least one member of his union and one from Ashfield's Combine. Morrison argued that the representatives of the local authorities were not representing interests, but the public, and if representation was conceded to the union and the Combine, other interests would rightfully claim membership, like the cab proprietors.[29] 'An authority including interests does not attract me', said Morrison, and 'I do not like the principle of interests controlling themselves'.[30] The public interest came first.

This is the first recorded occasion that Bevin and Morrison clashed, and is the origin of the antipathy between them.[31] Up to this point they had worked together harmoniously. Now Bevin felt suspicious of Morrison and began to regard him as hostile to trade union demands. Bevin, for all his vision, saw political problems in narrow trade union terms. His criterion was to find solutions to benefit his union, whereas Morrison looked to the wider public interest and championed elected representatives of the public against sectional groups which included 'the somewhat sectional industrialism of Mr Bevin'.[32] By standing up to Bevin, Morrison earned his everlasting hatred. Bevin was a spiteful man who looked on opposition in very personal terms. For the rest of his life Bevin was to pursue Morrison with venom.

After 1924 Ashfield swallowed up many of the independent bus operators and girded himself for his major coup, the acquisition of the LCC tramways. Amalgamation of London's passenger services had been advocated by many official reports on London transport since 1863. Following the strike in March 1924 a government inquiry urged co-ordination. To examine such proposals was an obvious responsibility of the new Traffic Advisory Committee. In July 1927 it issued its conclusions in the Blue Report, 'A Scheme for the Co-ordination of Passenger Transport Facilities in the London Traffic Area'. It recommended a common fund of receipts and common management of the buses, tubes and trams, whilst retaining the existing patterns of ownership. Morrison again opposed, and was particularly angry that the three trade union members of the Committee had signed it. Indeed he criticized John Cliff, Assistant General Secretary of the TGWU, as being a powerful influence behind the report.[33] Morrison's view was that, although competition was condemned, the Committee failed to reach the logical conclusion of public ownership and control. A multiplicity of separate private ownerships would remain; a board of managerial technicians would be responsible to private owners; and by the scheme the LCC trams would be handed over to Ashfield's monopoly. The scheme was a ruse through which Ashfield could control the trams.[34] What was needed was, in default of a Greater London Authority, a special traffic authority representative of local authorities in London to absorb the powers of the minister and his Advisory Committee and to take over the various private undertakings.

The proposals of the Advisory Committee pleased Ashfield, who in the middle of 1926 met the leaders of the Municipal Reform majority of the LCC. Both sides were in agreement. These talks were not reported to any committee of the council and the Labour Party came to know of them only in December 1926,[35] when under Morrison's initiative a joint committee was set up of representatives from the LLP Executive, the LCC Labour Party, the London Labour MPs and the Executive of the Parliamentary Labour Party. Morrison was secretary, and consequently the drafter of all its memoranda. This committee was to co-ordinate Labour opposition to any take-over of the trams by Ashfield.

The Combine and the LCC sought ministerial blessing for their agreement. Having a large legislative programme the government was unwilling to promote extra legislation unless it was non-controversial. Morrison, however, promised to 'utilize every legitimate means to defeat it'. The Combine and the LCC decided to proceed by private legislation, which would require two bills, one relating to the powers of the LCC and the other to the Combine. By the autumn of 1928 the bills were ready. They enabled the Combine and the LCC to adopt the scheme of co-ordination, establishing a joint management structure and a common pool of receipts but retaining the separate ownerships. 'Common theft' was Morrison's description of it, 'a capitalist counter-offensive against public property'. When the proposals came before the LCC,

Morrison led his party in the fight of its life. He managed to prolong the two council meetings of November and December into the early hours of the morning. The November meeting lasted until just after 6 a.m., witnessed thirty divisions and heard nearly 150 speeches. Labour members had been carefully organized, rest periods had been arranged for some groups while others were committed to sitting in the Chamber, and speakers were marshalled in relays. 'Not a mistake in tactics was made.'[36] Morrison's inspiration enabled his followers to carry on through the wearisome hours of the early morning. His humour and cajolery convinced them that they were enjoying something of a game, but it had a serious intent, for it brought wide publicity to the Labour case, although the Municipal Reform majority held firm.[37]

Morrison mobilized all the resources of the London Labour Party against the bills.[38] Never before had Morrison's creation been involved in such a massive enterprise. Its theme was 'For co-ordination and public ownership' and its symbol was the familiar Combine's hand grasping for a tramcar. Demonstrations were held in central London and in the suburbs, addressed by Morrison or speakers he organized. All MPs, peers and LCC members were circulated with Labour's case, and Labour councillors in local authorities outside London were asked to protest against the bills; to assist them Morrison enclosed draft resolutions for their local parties and councils. Branches of trade unions and local parties affiliated to the London Labour Party were urged to protest to their MPs and the LCC. A huge petition was arranged. Thousands of protesting postcards were issued to the public for posting to MPs and LCC members. Posters, leaflets, window bills, designed and drafted by Morrison, proclaimed 'Hands off Our Trams'. He composed a shower of press statements, wrote numerous articles, and published a special issue of *London News* devoted to the fight. He gathered together his arguments in a pamphlet, *The London Traffic Fraud*, subsidized from the special fund which he had established, and Ramsay MacDonald contributed the foreword.

Morrison briefed the Parliamentary Labour Party; in February 1929 the second reading was taken and with the support of the Conservative government the bills passed, 161 votes to 107. Then occurred a most crucial period of delay, from 19 March to 19 April, while the bills were before the select committee. 'Valuable aid at this stage ... was given by the Labour Metropolitan Borough Councils, who jointly petitioned and appeared against the Bills, and were ably represented by Mr Stafford Cripps.'[39] He so delayed the proceedings that the bills received their third reading just before Parliament was dissolved. The Chairman of Ways and Means ruled that another third reading would have to be taken in the new House of Commons. The May 1929 general election returned a Labour government and the Prime Minister, MacDonald, appointed as Minister of Transport Herbert Morrison. The leading officials at the ministry gathered in the room of Sir Cyril Hurcomb, the Permanent Secretary, and urged the importance of carrying on with the bills which embodied a workable scheme. Hurcomb took out from the drawer of his desk a copy of *The London Traffic Fraud* and said, pointing at MacDonald's name: 'This man has appointed this man [pointing at the author's name] Minister of Transport.'[40] The bills were dead. 'And so London's tramways were rescued from the grip of private monopoly which, a few weeks before, had seemed to be their inevitable fate.'[41] But the problem of co-ordinating London transport remained. Morrison himself by 1929 was not dogmatic: in *The London Traffic Fraud*, as 'a possible alternative', he suggested that 'we are not unwilling to accept a fusion of municipal and private interests on the basis of a joint company with a predominance of municipal capital and directors'.[42] This was a far cry from Morrison's earlier position and indeed the rhetoric of his campaign. Such flexibility augured well for an agreement between Ashfield and Morrison.

The battles over the shape of London transport in the 1920s brought Morrison into close contact not only with Ernest Bevin but also with Stafford Cripps. Morrison had first met Cripps when they had both appeared before the Railway Rates Tribunal. Morrison had then asked him to come out publicly for Labour. The dusty reply was: 'I am more interested in the Church.' Morrison felt strongly that men of Cripps' intellectual calibre should be in the party, and experience of Cripps' handling of the metropolitan boroughs' case encouraged him to try again. In April 1929 he wrote to Cripps' father, Lord Parmoor: 'For some time I have been wondering if there is any possibility of your son, Stafford Cripps, joining the Labour Party. I have been watching his legal work with interest and admiration. Our people admired his splendid work on the London Traffic (Co-ordination) Bills.' Parmoor suggested that Morrison deal direct with Cripps and so he immediately wrote. This time Cripps joined.[43] Morrison next persuaded the West Woolwich Labour party, his own local party, to adopt Cripps as its candidate.[44] Although Cripps was not successful in the 1929 election, Morrison's hand could be detected again in arranging for Cripps to find a safe seat in 1930 so that the Labour government could use his legal expertise as Solicitor General.[45]

In addition to London transport the other subject on which Morrison was recognized as an expert was electricity. To him Hackney's undertaking was one of the crowning achievements of municipal socialism, and he frequently showed that municipal electricity undertakings were more efficient, enterprising and economical than private companies. In London in the early 1920s about seventy different bodies generated and distributed electricity, including local authorities, private undertakings, railway companies, tramway operators and factories producing it for their own use. As with London transport this multiplicity of small units required co-ordination, especially on the generating side. Morrison's first solution was to allocate electricity generation to a new London Regional Authority. Distribution, which needed smaller areas, would be in the hands of local authorities. When it became clear that radical reform of London's local government was not likely to be achieved in the near future, Morrison advocated that generation be the responsibility of a Joint Electricity Authority composed of municipal representatives, or at least of a majority of municipal representatives. But by the end of the 1920s he came to see that even the areas of the joint authorities were not large enough, and that generation and main line transmission required a national organization.[46]

In 1923 the Electricity Commissioners, appointed under an Act of 1919 to help achieve co-ordination of generation and supply, had completed discussions with the London electricity companies and local authorities about the establishment of a Joint Electricity Authority for the generation of electricity in London and the Home Counties. Up to then the companies had been obstructive, but now they gave way in return for concessions which Morrison found unacceptable. Under the proposed scheme they would still enjoy substantial administrative and financial independence, thus frustrating unification within a single authority. They would also be able to amalgamate and to levy higher prices, and to pay out higher dividends, which Morrison regarded as increasing excessively their profits at the expense of the consumer. Finally, whereas previously by an Act of 1888 the local authorities would have been able to purchase the companies in 1931, it was intended to extend this date to 1971. Morrison felt that such measures would facilitate the formation of a private trust, a veritable 'electricity octopus'.[47] As with London transport a monopoly was required, and a monopoly had to be publicly owned and controlled to serve the public interest and not privately operated for the benefit of a few shareholders.

Morrison was prepared to accept the establishment of the Joint Authority, because municipal representatives composed a majority of its members, but he opposed the powers to be conferred on the private companies. Legislation was needed to bring the changes into effect, and two groups of companies duly promoted private bills in the House of Lords. Two other companies also promoted bills to extend their areas of operations. Four bills were thus the target of Morrison's opposition. The bills passed rapidly through the Lords but in the Commons they were blocked, largely as a result of Morrison's agitation. The Executive of the London Labour Party had given him 'full power' to bring about the rejection of the bills. He skilfully organized the London Labour MPs, priming them with arguments and arranging for a series of delaying amendments. He mobilized the rest of the Parliamentary Labour Party with memoranda about the capitalist plot embedded in the bills.[48] So successful were his tactics that the companies agreed to bring the date of purchase forward from 1971 to 1941.

MacDonald, keen to placate Morrison, urged the minister, Gosling: 'I shall be glad if you will do everything that is possible to reach agreement with our London friends on the matter.'[49] But the Cabinet decided to 'support the London Electricity Bills which have already been passed by the House of

Lords, since their enactment would obviate delays in carrying out schemes in relief of unemployment'.[50] To appease Morrison a promise was made to introduce general legislation on electricity. However, the government fell before this could be done, or the bills passed.

In the next Parliament the bills were introduced again, with 1971 as the date for purchase. Morrison, now out of Parliament, continued to spur Labour MPs to reject the iniquitous bills which handed the metropolis over to 'incompetent profiteers'.[51] Despite his valiant efforts, the bills were passed in February 1925. Morrison threatened 'we shall rise again and when we rise we will deal with the unscrupulous wirepullers of electrical capitalism in no uncertain way'.[52] When the London Joint Authority was established he urged Labour local authorities to use it to the full; he even accepted appointment on the Authority. During his time of membership, from 1925-9, he scrutinized the activities of the private companies, exposing situations where, he alleged, they were obtaining advantages at the expense of municipal undertakings.[53]

The next stage in the development of electricity organization was the Conservative government's Electricity Supply Bill of 1926, which established the Central Electricity Board to be responsible at a national level for generating stations and the main transmission lines. To Morrison it was a step in the right direction; he objected, however, to the board itself, complaining that it was a body of businessmen, and yet another agency imposed on an already complex pattern.[54]*

Another major London problem occupied much of Morrison's time in the 1920s: what to do about Waterloo Bridge? Over a decade of 'indecision'[55] began in October 1923 when the first signs appeared that all was not well with the bridge. Pier No. 5 from the north side began to subside and the adjacent arches to sag. An immediate injection of cement into the foundations was not enough to stop further deterioration. The chief engineer of the LCC reported that 'the effective life of the foundations of the bridge is coming to an end'.[56] As an interim measure the bridge was closed, two arches were shored up with timber, and near by a temporary bridge was erected, thus allowing the old bridge to be reopened in July 1924 for a reduced amount of traffic. For over ten years committees and sub-committees galore were to argue interminably back and forth about what was to be done.

At one extreme were the preservationists, determined to protect what they regarded as Rennie's architectural masterpiece of 1816. At the other were those, concerned with the inadequacy of London's bridges to cope with ever-growing traffic, who argued that the bridge should be reconstructed to meet modern conditions or else that an entirely new bridge be built. In between were the compromisers, ever hopeful that a solution would emerge which would

---

* The Minister appointed the board after consulting a number of municipal, industrial and commercial interests.

allow the old bridge to remain in its splendour and yet London's traffic to flow speedily across the Thames. From the start Morrison put traffic needs first. Although anxious to preserve the architectural beauties of London, he felt that the existing bridge was inadequate for London's traffic. What was required was a bridge wider than the existing three-laned one, able to take both general traffic and the LCC trams: six lanes in all. Also the existing six arches had to be widened into five so as to facilitate the navigation of the river.[57] The construction of such a bridge, he argued, would enable British architects to produce 'a triumph of their craft'.[58] He opposed the view that 'all the decent architects died a hundred years ago'.[59]

The council resolved in April 1924 to reconstruct and widen the bridge whilst preserving in the new bridge the 'character and identity of the existing structure'. But how to do so was the problem. Committees and sub-committees of the council wrestled with the issue, considering reports from their officials and outside bodies. They were bombarded with letters and delegations from the conflicting interests. They veered one way and then another. In February 1925 Morrison appealed: 'There must be finality some time',[60] and in November he complained that the council and its committees 'wobbled all over the show'.[61] In February the council resolved to reconstruct Waterloo Bridge with not more than five arches and wide enough for six lanes of traffic. For the rest of 1925 delay followed delay as the Bridges Sub-Committee of the Improvements Committee sought further advice. The Ministry of Transport expressed readiness to co-operate in producing a scheme. The London Traffic Advisory Committee favoured a six-lane bridge. But a conference of preservationist societies[62] urged that a simple underpinning of the existing bridge would suffice. Their report was savaged by the council's valuer and chief engineer for inaccurate traffic statistics and inadequate knowledge, and it was alleged that their proposal was dangerous. The chairman of the Sub-Committee did his best to wriggle out of the council's resolution; he obtained adjournments of meetings, sought consultations on a four-lane bridge on the existing piers and managed to delay proceedings until advice had been taken from Sir Edwin Lutyens, the distinguished architect. Labour members were consistently voted down. Lutyens reported that radical reconstruction was needed. Simply widening the traffic capacity of the existing bridge by corbelling out footpaths on either side would mutilate the architectural proportions; widening had to accompany heightening. Labour members were insistent that there was no alternative to taking down the existing bridge and building a new one. The river users protested against the six arches and called for five at most. The Committee were hopelessly divided and reported their differences to the council, which resolved that steps be taken *'forthwith'* to implement the resolution of February. The chairman of the Sub-Committee resigned.

At the start of 1926 it looked as if action was imminent. The LCC organized a competition for the design of the new bridge, and included in the annual money bill an estimate of capital expenditure for it. Opponents mounted an attack in Parliament to strike out this item. Morrison protested at Parliament interfering with a responsibility of the LCC, and he urged those Labour preservationists who were tempted to oppose the bill that to do so would set a precedent for Conservative MPs to strike out of a Labour LCC bill projects of capital expenditure.[63]

Then the government struck a blow. The Prime Minister appointed a Royal Commission on Cross River Traffic in June 1926, which meant that the competition, demolition and rebuilding were deferred. Morrison was furious. The LCC had been inquiring into these problems for two years and were responsible for bridges across the Thames, yet they had not even been consulted on the appointment of the Royal Commission.[64] The Commission's report further angered Morrison. It advocated that the old bridge be simply reconditioned, and widened only slightly to four lanes by corbelling out the footways. However, closely linked with this patching up was a proposal for a totally new bridge at Charing Cross, a double-decked combined road and rail bridge. A new bridge at Charing Cross had been frequently discussed in the 1920s and was generally accepted as desirable, but was left on one side as too expensive. However, it now had the blessing of a Royal Commission, which recommended government grants to the LCC of seventy-five per cent for work on the bridge. The Royal Commission seemed to have produced an acceptable compromise, maintaining the old bridge with only slight alteration, keeping its six arches for instance, while catering for London's traffic needs through the new Charing Cross Bridge.

The Prime Minister announced the government's acceptance of these proposals in March 1927. Then followed tedious discussions between the LCC, the Ministry of Transport, and the Southern Railway Company. During these negotiations the idea of a double-decked bridge was dropped in favour of removing Charing Cross Station to the south bank and thus having the Charing Cross Bridge for road traffic only. On and on the engineers conferred about technicalities, as well as the accountants about compensation for the railway company. In 1928 at last all seemed to be going smoothly. The preservationist societies accepted the new ideas, and the Southern Railway agreed to move to a site on the south bank, although it was proving difficult over the terms of compensation. The ministry felt so confident that they urged the LCC in October 1928 to undertake widening Waterloo Bridge immediately. But the LCC were reluctant, until the Charing Cross scheme was really settled, despite the alarms of the chief engineer about the stability of the temporary bridge. By the time that Morrison became Minister of Transport in 1929 agreement with the railway company was in sight and plans for the new Charing Cross Bridge were at a very advanced stage. Morrison and the majority of the LCC Labour Party supported the Charing Cross scheme. As minister it was expected that Morrison would resolve all the difficulties over the bridge and that speedy action would soon follow.

For ten years Morrison had paid close attention to electricity and transport, mainly in the context of London. Both were the responsibility of the Minister of Transport, and this ministry was also responsible for dealing with Waterloo Bridge. If ever a man appeared to have groomed himself for this job it was Morrison, for he was acknowledged as the leading Labour specialist in these matters. The main drawback was that his gaze had been confined to London. As minister he would have to take a broader view. In 1929 he stepped onto the national stage.

Chapter 10

Minister of Transport, 1929-1931

The general election of May 1929 returned Labour as the biggest single party in the House of Commons, with 287 MPs. The Conservatives had 260 and the Liberals 59. In London Labour achieved its best performance, winning 36 seats. One of these successes was in Hackney South where Morrison defeated Conservative, Liberal and Communist opponents, with a clear majority even over their combined votes.* Morrison increased Labour's share of the vote by nearly five per cent which was better than the two per cent rise for all London and slightly better than the national rise of four per cent. Labour's London campaign had been directed from the headquarters of the LLP. Morrison issued the usual reams of advice and propaganda. He had drawn up the manifesto for London. Its two top items were London transport and London electricity. The national issue to which he gave prominence was unemployment, pointing out that Lloyd George's policy was borrowed without acknowledgement from Labour, indeed from schemes propounded by Morrison himself at the Gairloch hotel in 1921. 'Clear out the old parties' was his general message.[1]

When Ramsay MacDonald formed his administration, it was no surprise that Morrison was his choice as Minister of Transport. Of MacDonald Morrison wrote:

It was not easy to understand how his brain worked. I had the feeling, although I knew him quite well, that he didn't particularly want one to know exactly how his thought processes were moving along; that is to say, he had a number of things that he wished to keep to himself and not to impart. . . . Therefore it was not easy for his colleagues always to know how his mind

* H. Morrison   15,590
  Sir Tresham Lever (Conservative) 8,222
  Miss M. J. Gibbon (Liberal)   6,302
  J. T. Murphy (Communist)   331

was working and what conclusions he had really reached about matters which were under private discussion with him personally.

This put a strain on ministers, and MacDonald got rather bad-tempered, assuming that conspiracies were hatching. When hard pressed in the House he seemed uncertain of his line and sometimes evasive, with the result that he was mistrusted. 'His great hindrance was his inability to revel in the atmosphere of Westminster. He once, after a heavy attack by Sir Kingsley Wood, shocked me by saying savagely, "Herbert, I hate this place." '[2] Morrison also criticized the government for failure to manage its own back-benchers effectively. Ministers did not come regularly to party meetings.[3]

Morrison was critical over the lack of machinery to co-ordinate the work of the various departments.[4] A Home Affairs Committee considered the technical merits of individual bills, and there were a few *ad hoc* committees for issues as they arose. The result was that 'Ministers would put in their requests for the inclusion of Bills in the King's Speech, and a nice competitive scramble and argument would proceed round the Cabinet table'. The final legislative programme was thus somewhat 'accidental and fortuitous'. Morrison condemned MacDonald for taking 'little or no interest in shaping the legislative programme'. But he praised MacDonald's handling of the Cabinet: 'business-like, expeditious, and capable in the smoothing out of conflicts', but not so good at reaching clear decisions.[5]

Morrison was annoyed that he was not a member of the Cabinet, and he was soon pressing MacDonald to take him in. A difficulty had arisen when Morrison was about to start discussions with the interests affected by the reorganization of London transport. The Prime Minister and the Lord Privy Seal met Lord Ashfield without informing Morrison. He was furious and wrote to MacDonald, complaining 'in no petty or personal spirit' that his position with those he had to deal with would be very difficult 'if I am not given the fullest opportunities of being present when matters within my responsibility come up or are dealt with'. He feared that 'other parties are tempted to feel that when difficulties are reached the Minister can easily be over-ruled'. He pointed out that his ministry was among the most important departments. 'Public attention – as you have seen from constant references in the Press – is constantly upon questions relating to this department's work, viz – roads, traffic, railways, electricity, docks, harbours and canals . . . . I hesitate to raise the point, but I conceive that these difficulties largely arise, not so much from want of consideration, as from the fact that for some years the Minister of Transport has not been in the Cabinet', with the result that the ministry was looked on as 'a very second-rate affair'.

'I like to be an enthusiast in my work and not to experience these occasional set-backs and depressions. I should, therefore, be obliged if you would give serious consideration to increasing the status of the Minister in the direction indicated, but please do not feel unduly hurried in coming to a decision.' He concluded: 'You and I have been such good friends for a number of years that I feel I can send you this letter without being misunderstood. We get little chance for the old friendly talks these days, but if you find time for a rather more leisurely talk please let me know.'[6]

MacDonald replied at once, 'My dear Morrison', and said that 'in some respects I am sorry you wrote it'. He explained that he had wanted Ashfield's views 'in candid confidence', and 'only under the conditions of informality and old friendship was it possible. A. would not have talked in the presence of others as he did, and I wanted no reserve.' He said that 'I have secured A.'s assistance and the road is clear for the carrying out of the work.' As for Morrison's request to join the Cabinet: 'I spent much time considering the composition of the Cabinet at the beginning and after balancing everything up I came to the conclusions which you now see. For the time being it will have to stand. When, and if, changes are made it will have to be after an examination of the whole position, as any change in one respect will only lead to difficulties which I must try and avoid.'[7]

As a minister Morrison was a success, acknowledged by colleagues and opponents. Sir Austen Chamberlain wrote that in August 1931 the government had lost its bloom and that Morrison was 'the only minister who comes out of it with enhanced reputation'.[8] J. H. Thomas described Morrison as an 'outstanding success', displaying 'drive, energy, capacity and public spirit'.[9] Beatrice Webb thought him 'the only outstanding Minister'.[10] The Chairman of the Press Gallery called him 'by far the most useful and most practical' of Ministers of Transport since that office came into being in 1919. 'He had breathed life into the dry bones of a Ministry which but a few years ago was threatened with extinction.'[11] The *News Chronicle* saw him as 'the most tactful and best-humoured member of the Government ... always "put up" when the situation required delicate and careful handling'.[12] As an administrator he was favourably compared with Joseph Chamberlain, Winston Churchill and Lord Haldane. No wonder that both J. H. Thomas and Hugh Dalton mused that Morrison might one day reside at No. 10 Downing Street.[13]

He was regarded as a first-class minister above all by those who worked with him closest: his civil servants.[14] His Permanent Secretary, Sir Cyril Hurcomb, a man of such formidable reputation that, when civil servants went before him, they called it being 'Sir Hurcombsized', said that Morrison had a natural gift for administration and was a first-class administrator, who instinctively took a sound view. 'He was always concerned to see that plans were practicable.' Hurcomb said that there was never any conflict between Morrison and the civil service: 'He saw that civil servants must play a part in formulating policy and that they should not be restricted just to carrying it out, although the final decision would be the Minister's.' Hurcomb said that if he disagreed with any of Morrison's views he never left him in any doubt but wrote out his opinions. Morrison liked this, since it forced him to consider his position and to make a reply. They would discuss, argue, but in the end reach agreement. Hurcomb said that Morrison was not suspicious of civil servants, and he never had a moment's difficulty with him. 'He was very straight. One was left in no doubt about his position.' S. S. Wilson, Hurcomb's private secretary while Morrison was minister, said: 'One got answers from him quickly. There was no hold-up or bottleneck of papers on his desk. There was a general air of efficiency around the place.' Aubrey Clark, Morrison's principal private secretary from 1930 to 1931, said that Herbert was very assiduous and read all his documents. 'He always had a good grasp of the material. He got the point and knew what it was all about. And he had a decisive turn of mind.' Hurcomb himself said that Morrison was 'very quick on the uptake. I never had to tell him anything twice.' Reginald Hill, a senior civil servant in charge of the problem of London transport, described Morrison as 'ready to learn; he quickly grasped points, and was ready to listen to my arguments. His mind was not closed. He was not an educated person; one could hardly be unconscious of that. He was intelligent but not cultured. He had a practical intelligence – the practical was more important to him than the theoretical. He trusted his civil servants. From the start, he didn't hector or bully as some would do. He was never impatient and never lost his temper.' George Stedman, Morrison's principal private secretary at the ministry in 1929 and 1930, said that of twenty ministers he had served Morrison came in the top rank. 'He had just the right views about the relationship between the minister and a civil servant. He saw, which was quite different from some of his colleagues, that civil servants want to help ministers and not to obstruct them. He was good because he made policy decisively and clearly and then left it to the civil servants to carry it out. They knew that he would back them up as long as they didn't do anything foolish that made him look foolish.'

Stedman would arrange for Morrison each day the papers coming up from the department. If Herbert agreed, the department went ahead. If Herbert expressed doubt, Stedman would put the department's case. If Herbert still did not agree, and sometimes he didn't, he would say, 'Well, I'll see so and so.' Or Stedman would say, 'I think you ought to see so and so', who was responsible for that particular piece of work. Usually, however, Herbert naturally saw Hurcomb. They would talk and out of that discussion would emerge the decision. 'It was a perfect set-up. Herbert was a good listener, extremely patient; one could say anything one liked to him on any topic. He expected you to put your views to him. He didn't simply accept the views of civil servants, he always went into them to satisfy himself; he would never brush you aside.' Stedman thought that 'Morrison had a well-disciplined mind. It didn't jump quickly, but it moved in an orderly progression.' He never played off one civil servant against another secretly. If civil servants disagreed he would let them argue their case amongst themselves in his presence.

The most important day of the week was when he had to answer questions in the House. Herbert would be in early from 9.30 to 10.00 a.m. and he would go through them and make alterations and consult his advisers so that everything would be ready for 2.30 p.m. Hurcomb recalled that Morrison did not need much briefing, often just a chat as they walked to the House. 'Morrison didn't need to think out in any elaborate way what he was going to say.' Hurcomb admired Morrison's handling of deputations. He was always very good at dealing with people and had a 'Sunny Jim' approach. He showed them that he appreciated their point of view, and that he wanted to be fair, even though he didn't agree with them. Stedman said of such confrontations: 'He was courteous even if he disagreed or was going to disagree later. He would listen very well and show that he was listening by interposing a question to take the problem a little deeper. If he disagreed he would say clearly that he was sorry but he couldn't accept that, and he would give a reasoned explanation. On any issue Herbert was aware of the interests involved and how they would react. And if he was in doubt, he would seek out people to advise him.'

Hurcomb admired the way Morrison operated at lunches and dinners. 'He wasn't excessively jovial but made use of these occasions very effectively to win over people.' Stedman recalled: 'he was natural, but upheld the dignity of the office. He had a feeling for what was proper for a Minister of the Crown.'

The praise of civil servants for Morrison was because he was just the sort of minister they liked, primarily an efficient administrator. This laid him open to the accusation of being bureaucratic and the spokesman of civil servants. Dr Alfred Salter, who had seen him at close quarters for a long time at the LLP and was an MP in the 1929–31 Parliament, wrote: 'He is a born administrator, and this tends to make him bureaucratic and opinionated. . . . He cannot tolerate inefficiency or slackness. Everything must be up to parade-ground standard, not merely on the occasion of inspections, but at all times. He conceives the multitudinous phases of municipal and public life as aspects of an organizing problem, to be examined intellectually and dealt with as abstract matters of official routine. He thus tends to eliminate the "human touch" from government and to substitute the efficient civil servant for the less efficient councillor or public representative. For this reason he believes in centralization, and instinctively he gravitates more and more in the direction of bureaucracy. . . . With all his innate strength and force he is far too much in the hands of his permanent officials – as is the way with dictators, though he would doubtless deny this most strenuously.'[15] Sir Oswald Mosley described him as 'a narrow, rigid, vain little bureaucrat, devoid of vision and incapable of movement beyond his office stool'.[16] Thus the same man and the same characteristics appeared quite different to different observers depending on their point of view.

Morrison was assisted by three other politicians who served as his parliamentary secretaries, Earl Russell, Arthur Ponsonby[17] and John Parkinson. They performed routine chores, although Earl Russell piloted the Road Traffic Bill through the Lords and answered questions there on behalf of the minister.[18] Morrison was also helped by George Strauss whom he chose as his parliamentary private secretary. Strauss had been Morrison's 'lieutenant' at the LCC, and on election to Parliament in 1929 became Morrison's 'personal assistant' at the ministry. Strauss recalled: 'he was really helpful, as if he was training me to become a minister myself.'[19]

Morrison's success at the ministry was due not simply to his own capabilities. He was helped by the nature of the work and by the particular opportunities that came his way—though admittedly he exploited them to the full. He was responsible for two bills which he guided through Parliament. Much of the first, the Road Traffic Act, had been drawn up by the previous administration or was based on the proposals of a Royal Commission, and simply awaited a minister able to win parliamentary time. Although it contained some controversial provisions, it was not a measure which set party against party. The bill slid through, yet its controversial aspects enabled Morrison to appear a skilful and tough fighter. Similarly the London Passenger Transport Bill did not provoke bitter party opposition. It was a clever blend of features which appealed both to 'socialists' and 'capitalists'. Thus while the government generally seemed to flounder and other ministers were unable to get their bills through intact, Morrison won a considerable reputation.

Being an MP and a minister were not Morrison's only responsibilities. Between 1929 and 1931 he kept a close watch over the London Labour Party, remained an active member of the Labour Party's National Executive Committee and frequently attended meetings of the LCC and its committees. At the LLP Morrison became Honorary Secretary, and Donald Daines Acting Secretary. The Chairman and Treasurer of the LLP felt that it was important to retain an option on Morrison's services and so not to fill his post permanently. In any case the uncertainty of the national political situation meant that Morrison might be away for only a brief period. Daines handled the routine, while Morrison, 'available for consultation and advice', intervened or was brought in for more important matters, and he retained possession of the party's car.[20]

One might have thought that Morrison would have been very much in the background of the LLP while a minister, especially given the tone of his valediction: 'Nobody is indispensable, for when we die we must be replaced and the work carried on.' He appealed to party workers to 'keep the flag flying' and said 'I remain one of the crowd'. He asked members not to look up to him as a minister but to greet him as Herbert.[21] However, he did not recede from view. He attended most Executive meetings, and came to the headquarters two or three times a week, or else Daines chatted to him at the ministry or in the Commons. Morrison wrote the party manifesto for the 1931 LCC elections, and a statement on public assistance policy. He retained a close scrutiny over the selection of LCC candidates and handled any business that might give rise to controversy. For instance in 1929 the LLP and the ILP squabbled over the LLP's refusal to allow the ILP's journal, *New Leader*, to be on sale at an LLP meeting. Morrison dealt with all the correspondence. He replied to the ILP's complaint that he would allow only the *Daily Herald* and *London News* to be on sale: if he admitted more, sales of *London News* would fall; he criticized the *New Leader* for not boosting LLP meetings or generally helping the LLP, and he noticed that only one ILP branch sold *London News*.[22] Another matter to which Morrison devoted his attention was the organization of the LLP, contributing memoranda about reforms, for instance the abolition of borough parties and their replacement by the LLP as a single borough party for London. He never let Daines take over anything other than low-level items.

He retained his links with the LCC, although he gave up being leader of the LCC Labour Party. He wrote to members: 'So the time has come when I must cease to move among you as your chosen leader . . . I am available for consultations when desired, but you must stand on your own feet. . . .'[23] He attended almost all the party meetings and not just as a silent member. In March 1931 the minutes of the LCC Labour Party record that he 'suggested that a scheme should be put up for the development of the East End of London'.[24] He maintained good attendance at council and committee meetings, and even spoke at a few council meetings in his first few months as minister. In 1930 he took the chair at conferences of LCC Labour members to consider the new arrangements for health and public assistance following the 1929 Act which abolished boards of guardians and transferred their responsibilities to the LCC and the boroughs. Morrison's involvement seems not to have embarrassed the two men who took his place while he was at the ministry. Both Cecil Manning, leader from 1929 to 1930, and Lewis Silkin, leader from 1930, said that he did not interfere. They would frequently talk to him, and relations were harmonious.

On the party's NEC Morrison continued his activities. He was Chairman in 1928–9, attending twenty-one of twenty-two meetings from October 1928 to September 1929; in 1930 and 1931 although his attendance was slightly down it was one of the highest. He retained his active membership of NEC sub-committees dealing with party organization, election preparation, research and publicity, party discipline and relations with the ILP, the Cooperative Party, and the General Council of the TUC. He even served again on the International Affairs sub-committee.

His greatest constructive contribution to the NEC between 1929 and 1931 was producing model standing orders to govern relationships between Labour representatives on local authorities and local Labour parties. During the 1920s many provincial towns witnessed wrangling between local Labour parties and elected Labour councillors. The former complained that the latter were not following party policy, and sought to instruct them how to vote and to discipline them if they deviated. The councillors claimed that as elected representatives they should decide on the implementation of party policy free from dictation by outsiders.[25] Party headquarters was besieged with requests for help to resolve such difficulties. In March 1930, after a particularly virulent outbreak of dissension at Liverpool, Morrison persuaded the NEC to authorize the drafting of standing orders to regulate the relationship. A small sub-committee including Morrison was set up.[26] It asked the larger Labour parties for their views, consulted local members and headquarters staff, and examined standing orders adopted in a number of areas. Morrison wrote the preliminary drafts. His intention was that the rules should be purely procedural; a municipal programme was for local parties to decide. In August the NEC approved the final Morrison draft, with only one dissenting, and it was decided that Morrison should commend his standing orders to the party conference at Llandudno in October 1930.[27]

The standing orders were simply model rules to guide local parties. They embodied the procedures of the LLP; Morrison generalized the arrangements that he had devised for London. They outlined the organization and functions of the group of Labour members on a council: the full group meeting, the policy committee and the officers. The most crucial sections dealt with relations between the councillors and the local party. Election policy was to be determined by the local party, but the carrying out of that policy on the council was the responsibility of the group. It could not be dictated to by the local party. For liaison between the two, three representatives of the local party were to attend group meetings, able to speak and give advice, but not to vote. At the conference Morrison rejected the claims of local parties who wanted to go through the agenda of a council meeting and bind their councillors to vote in a certain way: 'They could not possibly run Local Government on the basis of Councils being marionettes, whose actions ought to be decided in detail from outside.'[28] He said he had seen a Labour majority wiped out as a result of such irresponsible methods. So well did he present his case that the standing orders were adopted. They remain to this day the basis for Labour organization on local authorities and were substantially adopted by Conservative local associations from the 1940s.

In a pragmatic way Morrison had worked out for the LLP procedural arrangements, strictly in the British constitutional tradition, which enabled a Labour party to carry out a reforming programme. They worked well in London, and he then transplanted them beyond the capital. Similarly he was to take the 'public corporation', which was evolved for handling London transport, and transform it into the means for socializing other industries. He did not pluck ideas out of the air, but devised procedures to suit particular circumstances, then out of this experience applied them more generally.

Morrison's thoughts developed gradually, building layer upon layer from successive experiences. Practice was the proving ground, and doctrinaire ideas counted for little. The objective of it all remained constant – a search for tidiness.

Between 1929 and 1931 Morrison undertook a vast range of activities. He toured all over Britain, officiating at a variety of functions. In one week in January 1931 he travelled from London to Hull and returned, then went to Glasgow and Lanarkshire.[29] As a party spokesman he visited more parts of the country than before, making himself known to an ever wider circle of party members. In the spring of 1931 he spoke at mass meetings from the West Riding of Yorkshire down to Hastings.[30] The national politician had emerged.

The first bill for which Morrison was responsible was, as he said, 'a great charter for the ordered use of the King's Highway'.[31] It consisted of five parts. In part one motor vehicles were divided into seven categories and, to drive the different types, licences were to be required, with higher age limits for the heavier vehicles. Certain physical defects would disqualify drivers from obtaining licences, and minimum standards for the construction and equipment of vehicles were to be laid down. Also in this part was the abolition of the speed limit of twenty miles per hour for light, but not for heavy, motor vehicles. Tougher penalties were imposed for dangerous driving; speed trials on highways were prohibited and motor cycles were to have only one pillion rider. In this part, too, were laid down the maximum hours to be worked by the drivers of lorries and buses. Among the miscellaneous provisions were powers for the minister to inquire directly into accidents, and increased penalties for taking a car without authority. Part two introduced compulsory third party insurance. Part three introduced the Highway Code and increased the powers of local authorities to close roads, designate one-way streets, set up roundabouts and road signs, and take over toll roads and bridges. Part four, on the licensing of buses and coaches, abolished the licensing responsibilities of 1,298 local authorities and in their place put ministerially appointed Traffic Commissioners covering twelve areas. They would have wide powers of regulation, issuing licences only for vehicles which met their safety requirements, ensuring that fares were reasonable and even deciding on routes and the timing of services. Part five enabled local authorities already possessing the power to run trams, to operate omnibuses after the approval of the Commissioners, as private companies could, without the burden of applying to Parliament for a private bill.

The bill had its first reading on 28 November 1929 in the House of Lords and an unopposed second reading in the Commons on 18 February 1930, when Morrison introduced its 103 clauses in a speech of one and a quarter hours.[32] Even Conservatives praised it as a lucid and witty exposition. The way in which Morrison commended the bill to the Commons was quite different from his speech before the Labour Party conference later in the year.[33] Before Parliament he argued in terms of efficient administration. The bill was a practical way of dealing with certain abuses; its approach was common sense, agreed by reasonable men of all parties, impartial inquiries and the various interests concerned. Before the conference the bill was presented as an instalment of socialism. It extended public ownership, protected the work-people and converted a competitive industry into a co-ordinated service. He claimed that the bill fitted *Labour and the Nation* (Labour's 1929 electoral programme) 'to the last comma'; they were modernizing each industry in turn and giving to each social objectives.

Although the bill empowered local authorities to operate buses and to regulate traffic, it removed their powers of licensing public service vehicles. Morrison had hoped to make counties and county boroughs licensing authorties, but their areas were too small and there was too much friction between them. He was bitterly opposed, as ever, to joint authorities, and so, since the need was for a national policy, he decided on centrally-appointed Commissioners. Even when telling conference that the bill was a 'substantial municipal socialist triumph', he warned local authorities that in running bus services they would have to co-operate with each other and even with private companies: 'If they try to keep motor transport on a parish pump basis, then municipal enterprise will be destroyed.'[34]

Morrison stressed that he had consulted closely with the interest groups involved, notably the trade unions. The biographer of Ernest Bevin noted that this bill, 'one of the most substantial achievements of the second Labour Government', incorporated many of the points put by the Transport and General Workers' Union, yet it did not go as far as Bevin wished.[35] In his first bill Morrison came up against Bevin over the provision for the minister to fix the maximum hours to be worked by drivers. Morrison said that although it was the job of trade unions and the employers to settle hours, he would fix those hours beyond which it would be dangerous to go. He was not acting as an arbitrator; his concern was the public safety. To placate Bevin, he said that he was anxious to have elasticity in the regulations, and so he could vary them on application from a joint body of employers and trade unions. Once again Morrison championed the public interest against Bevin's concern with trade union rights.

A major public controversy was caused over the abolition of the speed limit for cars. Morrison explained that if a limit of twenty miles per hour was preserved the police would have to tolerate many breaches of the law and, if enforced, congestion would be greater. If they fixed a limit of thirty, thirty-five or forty miles per hour, they would suggest that it was reasonable to go at that speed, but any speed could be dangerous in certain circumstances. He wanted the speed limit maintained for heavy vehicles, since their weight, and therefore their momentum in a crash, was greater, and at high speeds they damaged the road surface. Dangerous driving was the enemy, and to combat that he proposed increased penalties and strict enforcement by squads of mobile police.[36] He hoped, through the Highway Code, to develop in the road user a social conscience. He broadcast to the nation that the Highway Code was the most 'cheerful' document which ever came out of a department. 'It is based on the belief that people want to do the right thing provided they clearly understand that everybody will say that they are not nice people if they do not do it . . . some day all laws may be like that, but not yet.'[37]

The speed limit split all parties. Morrison argued that the whips should not be put on. MacDonald at first feared that a free vote would weaken the authority of the government. In the end he accepted Morrison's view that a decision on the speed limit was not a party matter, and a free vote ended the speed limit. Morrison's advocacy of this cause annoyed the pedestrians' associations who were furious at his assertion that many accidents were caused by dangerous pedestrians. In May 1930 he appeared at Central Hall to address a meeting of the Pedestrians' Association. At the outset he was barracked. Calmly he said 'I have come here to express my views and if I stay here, I am going to express my views. If I am not allowed to I shall return whence I came. That's all.'[38] He put his arguments, attacked reckless walkers, said he hoped he would not have to impose penalties on them and claimed that in the bill he had done much to help pedestrians. At the end he was cheered: a typical example of Morrison's winning ways with initially hostile audiences. In consultations over the bill Morrison had to deal with a wide range of groups: the motoring organizations, the insurance companies, the manufacturers, the medical professions, the road hauliers, the trade unions and the local authorities, who were all impressed by his non-doctrinaire approach.[39] So great an impact did he make that the Secretary of the National Safety First Association suggested that the new mobile police should be called 'Berties'.[40]

Another row blew up over the provision to enable local authorities to run buses. The House of Lords struck out the enabling clauses. Morrison was determined to fight: 'The Lords are in a fair way to raise once more the issue of the Peers versus the people.'[41] The provisions were reintroduced in the Commons as part of a private member's bill, which Morrison championed in an impressive speech.[42] The Commons voted in favour of the bill, and its provisions, slightly altered, were inserted back into Morrison's Road Traffic Bill at its committee stage. Thus local authorities were put on the same standing as private companies: able to apply to the Traffic Commissioners to operate bus services, without having to promote private bills.

Morrison set great store by the Traffic Commissioners, who were intended to be his agents in achieving national co-ordination of passenger transport. They were instruments of socialism, designed to 'prevent cut-throat competition', to ensure that vehicles were safe, that services were reliable, that prosperous and unremunerative routes were shared, that fares were reasonable, and that the wages and conditions of transport workers, drivers and conductors were fair.[43]

One feature of this bill reflected Morrison's view of the proper role of legislation in an increasingly collectivist state. He argued that a statute should lay down broad guidelines and empower ministers to issue regulations to fill in these principles, submitted later to Parliament for approval. An Act itself should not be weighed down with a mass of detail. His bill authorized the minister to make a vast number of regulations, about standards of motor construction, speed limits, motoring offences, and licensing. This was a model that Morrison was to advocate when a minister in the 1940s.

In piloting his bill through Parliament Morrison came up against the delays of parliamentary procedures. It had to run the gauntlet at the committee stage of 1,246 amendments. He experienced about four months of irritating obstruction. One Conservative said: 'My dear Morrison, it's not your Bill we're obstructing. It is the one that is coming on next before this Standing Committee that we are trying to hold up.' (A government bill on consumer protection.) 'This experience was one of the reasons why I was determined to reform the procedure of the House of Commons.'[44]

Morrison's handling of the bill was a personal triumph. At the third reading he received warm congratulations, even from the opposition.[45] The leading Conservative spokesman, Colonel Ashley, called the bill a 'model of legislation', and thanked Morrison for the 'tactful way in which he has put his Bill through'. In shepherding the longest measure of the session through the parliamentary process Morrison showed himself to be a formidable minister. His next bill posed greater problems.

While minister, Morrison did not give up all hope of reforming London government. He wrote a memorandum advocating a radical reform of local government in Greater London,[46] and pressed his proposals on Arthur Greenwood, the Minister of Health, then responsible for local government reform.[47] However, it was difficult for a minority government to undertake such a major measure fraught with controversy, and so Morrison devoted himself to setting up a body to run London transport.

The accession of Morrison as Minister of Transport dismayed Lord Ashfield. However, Hurcomb was able to reassure him that Morrison was a man in whom they could have the utmost confidence to devise an acceptable plan and carry it through. Morrison's first task at the ministry was to make it clear that the previous schemes were finished.[48] He used to reminisce that he told the civil servants: 'Sorry boys, you have wasted your time. London Transport is going to be a public monopoly.'[49] Hurcomb warned Morrison that the Cabinet might not support his rejection of the old plan. 'I'll resign' was Morrison's retort.[50] So worried was Morrison that he wrote to MacDonald just before the crucial Cabinet meeting, reminding him of a talk they had had before he had appointed him minister: 'in the end you agreed that in all the circumstances it was inevitable that they [the private bills] would be rejected.'[51] Morrison sent a memorandum to the Cabinet recommending that the old scheme be not revived. He personally had been strongly opposed; the issue had been prominent at the general election in London, when many of the advocates of the proposals were defeated. Labour MPs before the election had contested the bills hotly and the Liberals had given no support. If they had a third reading now 'there would be a revolt in our own ranks'. He suggested early talks with Lord Ashfield to try to persuade him to withdraw; if, however, he pressed the government to decide, he was to be told that the decision would be adverse.[52] The Cabinet accepted Morrison's recommendation.[53]

Ashfield felt that the two private bills were steps in the right direction and feared that if they were jettisoned nothing would happen in the future. Morrison posed the alternatives: either the bills had to be withdrawn or they would be negatived.[54] They were not withdrawn and so on 17 July 1929 Morrison advised their rejection at the third reading.[55] A vote of 295 to 172 killed them.

In 1929 Morrison knew what he opposed, the so-called fraud by which a private combine would run London's transport, but he had no constructive scheme to put in its place. Vaguely he wanted a public transport system, yet he had not worked out its form of organization. Hurcomb remembered that on taking office Morrison 'was very fluid over the means to be adopted. He realized that there were more ways of organizing administration than the departmental or local governmental.' He had not thought out the size of the transport area nor how to link up the main-line railways into the public system in London.[56]

By September the department had reached broad conclusions and submitted their proposals to the Cabinet. In his memorandum Morrison outlined the courses open. Firstly they could simply strengthen public control over the various private companies; secondly they could follow the approach of the two private bills and have a common fund and management whilst retaining private ownership; or thirdly, as Morrison favoured, they could 'assert at once the principle of public ownership' and 'transfer to some new joint authority, board or commission the ownership and operation of all the existing undertakings both private and municipal'. As to the precise form of the board Morrison was vague. He pointed out that the LLP wanted a Greater London Authority to run transport, amongst other services, but that until that body was instituted, a joint municipal authority was desired. However, he wrote, although under any scheme local authorities had to have full rights to make representations, 'their direct presence on the governing body might involve a cumbersome administration. I should therefore prefer to contemplate the establishment of a body more on the lines of the Central Electricity Board, or the British Broadcasting Corporation, with a somewhat similar relationship to the Minister of Transport and Parliament.'[57] Thus the former advocate of municipal enterprise was moving towards the concept of the public corporation, a shift which arose from discussions with his civil servants at the ministry in July, August and September 1929. Although the idea of the 'public corporation', or something like it, had been discussed in socialist circles before Morrison became Minister of Transport, there is no evidence that he was in any way influenced by such proposals.[58]

The Cabinet decided to set up a small committee to look into the problem, with Morrison as chairman.[59] Morrison and his department wrote the memoranda and recommendations which the other members accepted.[60] After three meetings they reported to the Cabinet in a memorandum of 7 November.[61] It first advised that the area of the authority should extend over a radius of twenty-five miles from Charing Cross, the so-called London Traffic Area of 1924. It listed five undertakings to be brought in: the railways, omnibuses and tramways of Ashfield's Combine; the Metropolitan Railway of Lord Aberconway; the tramways of the LCC and other local authorities; the suburban parts of the main-line railway companies; and the omnibuses of other private companies. It noted two major difficulties. Firstly, it was hard to sever the connection between the suburban and other services of the railway companies and bring the former into a system of common management; they would probably have to seek working agreements, and some kind of pool for financial receipts between the suburban services and the new authority. Secondly, the Metropolitan Railway Company was likely to prove difficult, since, although its network was an integral part of London's transport system, it felt it was more a main-line company since its operations extended beyond London.

Full public control was the objective, either by outright acquisition by the public authority or its purchase of a controlling interest. Then the memorandum examined the status of the new authority. It assumed that the creation of a Greater London local authority 'is unlikely in the immediate future', but suggested that 'if and when such an authority is created, it may be found expedient to merge any *ad hoc* traffic authority in it'. It then considered three forms. First: a joint municipal authority, which was rejected: to be fully representative it would be too large; a system of indirect election was not fully accountable and democratic, and rarely attracted the best municipal ability; its conduct of business would be formal, with debates which would cause delays and hinder the efficient 'business direction' of London transport. Second: a body representative of various interests, which was also rejected, as not producing men with the calibre to run the highly technical and sensitive business of passenger transport. Third: 'In the interests of efficient operation, we favour the third alternative, namely, a small board of business men of proved capacity. We have in mind a body somewhat similar to the Central Electricity Board, which is appointed by the Ministers, and consists of a Chairman and seven members selected after consultation with interests representing Local Government, Electricity, Commerce, Industry, Transport, Agriculture and Labour, but we should prefer to avoid any such scheme of representation as is thus indicated, and also any statutory obligation to consult with particular interests. We suggest that the Board should consist of not more than seven members appointed by the Minister of Transport. The Chairman and Vice-Chairman at least should be appointed on a full-time basis, and should be paid salaries substantial enough to command men of the highest business ability and experience. We realize, however, that it may be necessary to provide among the other members of the Board for some representation of public interests including those of Local Government.' There also had to be some machinery for the public expression of views about levels of charges for services and the provision of new facilities. 'Some supervision should be exercised by the Minister of Transport over large matters of policy and the financial arrangements of the Board, e.g. by sanction of new borrowings, prescription of the form of accounts, etc.' The Morrisonian public corporation was almost born. Morrison's role in shaping this concept was important. He wrote notes over the reports of his officials,[62] and scrawled in the margins, not just changing the phraseology but adding substantial arguments.[63]

An expanded London Traffic Advisory Committee of representatives from local government and the trade unions, with a majority of local government nominees, was proposed to channel the views of the public to the board and to the minister about facilities and services generally. Disputes about fares were to be handled by the Railway Rates Tribunal. Morrison was adamant that the minister should not be responsible for fares, which he wanted decided by an independent, judicial body which would not act on political criteria, especially just before elections.

Morrison was called to the Cabinet on 14 November 1929. He was congratulated for his work and his conclusions were approved. He was given authority to negotiate with the interests involved, and he was empowered, as he requested, to select, after consulting the Chancellor of the Exchequer, an eminent accountant to advise him on the complex financial aspects.[64]

Morrison wanted no public statement of his objectives for fear that a premature announcement would disrupt negotiations. However, on 1 December, W. H. Stevenson, editor of the *Daily Herald*, telephoned Morrison with a slightly inaccurate outline of his proposals. Morrison was flabbergasted and asked Stevenson to wait twenty-four hours to avoid embarrassing him. He consulted MacDonald and Snowden on the morning of 2 December and it was agreed that Morrison should make a statement in the House of Commons that day. Harry Gosling asked a planted question to which Morrison replied, outlining the approach of the government, stressing that they had come down for a simple system of public ownership, and were exploring the whole matter with the interests, and with the help of an accountant.[65] The editor of the *Daily Herald* wrote to Morrison: 'You have robbed us of an exclusive splash which was the result of many inquiries in the provinces, in London and in Berlin. I submit that this is not fair to us or helpful to you. No public man can run the risk of earning the disapproval of journalists, which will always tell against him in the long run.'[66] Morrison did not forget.

The long haul of working out the details of the bill began in earnest. The main items were the financial arrangements and the devising of means to bring the various undertakings into the new set-up. Most of the negotiations were handled by civil servants, the more important by the junior ministers, particularly Ponsonby, and the most important by Morrison himself. He kept a general overview of the progress of the discussions and normally dealt with the heads of the various undertakings involved.

One interest Morrison never appeased. The Transport and General Workers' Union, and particularly its leader Bevin, were highly critical of Morrison's plans.[67] The bone of contention was the composition of the board. Bevin felt that Morrison was neglecting the workers in the transport industry. Bevin wanted representatives of the trade unions to be members of the board, or at least for them to be consulted before the minister made his appointments. Morrison rejected both, arguing that the minister should have a free hand to select members, simply on their ability. His opposition to representation by interests was grounded on the same principles as his objection to joint municipal control. Such members of a board would think in terms of their own organization or area, and not have regard solely to the public interest. He said that if one group was granted representation, others would clamour for the same right, justifiably, and in the end 'labour' would be in a minority. He also feared that a board of interests would not be efficient. He told a reporter from *The Times*: 'By businessmen he meant men of a business turn of mind, which might include such people as Trade Union bodies as well as men of business experience in the ordinary sense of the word.'[68] He intended all along to appoint people associated with trade unions and local government. He called the proposals for guaranteed labour representation 'undignified and humiliating': as if trade unionists could not be appointed without an Act saying so. It presumed their inferiority.

Bevin, feeling that Morrison had rebuffed him, appealed to the Prime Minister, and gained two concessions: more labour representatives were added to the Traffic Advisory Committee and the qualifications for board membership were slightly altered from 'persons who have had wide experience and have shown capacity in industry, commerce or finance, or in the conduct of public affairs', to 'persons who have had wide experience, and have shown capacity in transport, industrial, commercial or financial matters or in the conduct of public affairs'.[69] Bevin was far from satisfied: 'It is in our view positively the worst form of public control.'[70] He resented Morrison's treatment of him, acting more like a capitalist minister than a friend of the unions.[71] Bevin expected deferential treatment, and yet Morrison handled him like any other interest and, worst of all, resisted him. Morrison turned his clash with Bevin to a slight political advantage, for he was able to show that Labour leaders were not 'the slavish instruments of the Trades Union leaders catering for that industry'.[72]

If he failed with the Transport and General Workers' Union, he succeeded with Ashfield. Morrison came to admire Ashfield and had him in mind to be the chairman of the new board. To nationalize Lord Ashfield was his objective. Morrison had a high regard for his efficiency, his spirit of public service and his friendly relations with the unions.[73] Ashfield was 'a nuisance to a socialist agitator', and was, as Ashfield himself told Morrison, 'the worst enemy my shareholders ever had'.[74] Ashfield took a kind of 'ministerial' view of London transport, concerning himself with policy, high finance and external relations with other bodies. He became a devotee of the public corporation and had a stiff fight in commending it to his companies who were reluctant to be taken over by the state. He persuaded them that they were getting a good bargain. Ashfield agreed to be nationalized in return for more than adequate financial terms for the shareholders.[75] Morrison recalled that the final deal with Ashfield was arranged after hard bargaining on three Saturday afternoons at the ministry. At the last one, they began at three and ended at midnight. Then Morrison, Hurcomb and McLintock (the accountant), who had not eaten during the whole session, went to Lyons in the Strand for a meal. They realized that they had had to pay a high price, but they felt that the terms were realistic and they had got the essentials.[76]

Dealing with Ashfield alone was a formidable task, but dealing with him together with his deputy, Frank Pick, was even tougher.[77] Pick was the master of detail, and surveyed the day-to-day management of the Combine. He had a quick capacious mind that readily absorbed the details of services, engineering, technology, architecture, and the trivia of staff administration. Ashfield used Pick as his forward attack, putting in an extreme claim; later Ashfield would intervene with a more moderate suggestion, appearing conciliatory, although putting forward what he had originally wanted. Those facing him eagerly grasped his offer. Morrison found Pick prickly, but was so impressed with his ability that he advised that he be appointed to the new board as deputy to Ashfield. Pick was nationalized too.

A difficult task for Morrison was to persuade the Labour Party to accept the 'public corporation'. He told the Labour Party conference in 1930 that his proposals were a measure of socialism, with the public taking over enterprises from private ownership.[78] George Strauss wrote that London transport was 'the first great industry which had been transferred from private to public ownership in modern times'.[79] The public corporation was the logical extension of Morrison's previous attitude to socialism, which he had always stressed had to stand the tests of being both ethically and economically sound. In the public corporation he reconciled the two. It was a device of socialism and a sound business proposition. He was also influenced by the desire to win as much support as he could from the Conservatives, and particularly from the Liberals. The Labour government's very existence, since it had no over-all majority, largely depended on the Liberal Party. All ministers were bound by an arrangement to consult the Liberal leaders before introducing legislation in Parliament, although some were more scrupulous about this than others,

F

and MacDonald occasionally had to remind his Cabinet about the convention.[80] Morrison took great pains to court the Liberals. In October 1930 he wrote to Lloyd George: 'I have all along kept in touch with Mr Percy Harris and Major Nathan as the Liberal Members of Parliament for London, so that they might have whatever information I could give.' He said that final plans would soon emerge and 'the Prime Minister thinks it would be useful before this happens that I should have a talk with you, or one of your parliamentary colleagues, in order that you may know our mind'.[81] Morrison claimed that in choosing the public corporation he was influenced by the Liberals' manifesto, *Britain's Industrial Future* which came down for a system of national boards for various industries and services.[82] His bill had Liberal support.

Morrison made efforts to win over the Conservatives. His stress on sound business was calculated to appeal to them. In the Commons Morrison teased the Conservatives. They had pioneered measures of nationalization: the telephones, London's water supply, the British Broadcasting Corporation and the Central Electricity Board; indeed, the latter was the closest model for his London Transport Board. 'Is the Tory party, in its desire for privilege, taking the position that it and it alone is entitled to introduce socialistic legislation? ... We reject this monopoly of Socialism. We demand that even a minority Government in this House, Socialist Government as it is, shall have its right to introduce its little share of socialistic legislation.'[83]

The main Conservative criticism was that the minister's powers were excessive and would turn the board into his puppet. In reply he stressed that to pack the board with political friends would defy statutory directions and would discredit the minister. He emphasized the independence of the board: 'No Board will allow the minister to dictate how they are to discharge their duties. Any minister who tried would be a fool, and would be asking for trouble. . . . The Board must feel itself directly responsible to the public for the success of the undertaking and their own reputations must be bound up in that success.' He admitted that the board would be likely to discuss problems informally with the minister, but it was not bound to do so. He felt that the relationships between a minister and a board would evolve in a 'respectful' common-sense way.[84] If a ticklish question of policy arose, the minister and the board would have a friendly talk; not, however, for the board to receive instructions, but so that both sides could understand the problem, 'and mutually consult, and agree as to what is the best thing to do'.[85]

Morrison came under fire from some on the left of the Labour Party for being too kind to the shareholders of the companies taken over. He was, however, adamant that their property would not be confiscated. Compensation was necessary; even share-owners had to be treated fairly. He admitted that in a fully socialized community such economic parasites, living off rent, interest and profit, would have to go. But that problem would be solved through the tax system, not at the point of socialization. He said it would be unfair to confiscate the property of the transport share-owners, just because they were first to be taken over. He also feared that such an action would provoke alarm amongst other shareholders; industry might be dislocated, managers and technicians leave and even a revolutionary situation arise. Compensation was vital; the question was how much and in what form. His formula for assessing the value of shares was the 'net maintainable reasonable revenue', after taking care of charges for, say, depreciation. He advocated this approach since it took account of the 'net revenue', the earning capacity, of the enterprise, which was more appropriate than basing calculations on capital expenditure, which could be wasteful and unproductive, or on the value of the assets, which was complex to discover. Having assessed the present earning capacity (over the previous three years in his bill), the next stage was to discover if that could be maintained in the future, allowing reasonable profits.

The form of compensation could be in three forms: first, cash, which he did not favour, since it would be very expensive at the start, and involve huge speculative loans; second, redeemable state-guaranteed bonds, which he also disliked since it would create a class of state-guaranteed rentiers, subsidized by the state if the industry did badly (they had a guaranteed interest and principal without the risk of ordinary investment); third, redeemable stock without voting rights, with interest paid only if a surplus was made. If the board did badly there would be no recourse to taxes to make up deficits, instead the Receiver would be put in after three years' non-payment. He was most concerned that the corporation should not feel that it always had the Treasury behind it. In order to redeem the stock he wanted a sum of money put aside for a sinking fund, so that a fixed number of years could be set for repaying the loan and redeeming the stock. In all these complexities Morrison relied on his financial advisers, but the crucial point was that the public corporation was to pay its way without any subsidies from central or local government.[86]

In the summer of 1930 Morrison mounted a campaign to obtain parliamentary time for his proposals. He wanted included in the King's Speech in October 1930 an undertaking to introduce his bill. He wrote a memorandum for the Cabinet, seeking an assurance that time would be found in the next session.[87] The Cabinet decided that it was impossible to give this undertaking 'having regard to the difficulties which have been experienced in carrying out the Government's programme for the present Session of Parliament . . . and the considerable list of important bills to be introduced during the next'.[88] Not daunted Morrison tried again in July,[89] pointing out that Ashfield and Aberconway had begun negotiations to merge their companies, which if successful would mean that the public would have to pay a larger price for acquiring the private undertakings. Before the Cabinet meeting Morrison wrote to some ministers seeking their support: 'We shall indeed be in a very difficult position with our own supporters in London and generally on the merits of the case if having brought about the failure of one attempted solution we fail to proceed ourselves with our own plan.'[90] The Cabinet, although sympathetic, found it impossible to give the decision he asked for until it had reviewed the major bills that were to be introduced in the forthcoming session. It decided to ask the Committee on Home Affairs to consider Morrison's case and it asked Morrison to proceed with the negotiations without any necessity for announcing the bill in the King's Speech.[91] Morrison tried again when he announced that negotiations were under way.[92] But the Cabinet in exasperation stated that there must be 'no lack of clearness that the Cabinet cannot commit themselves to a Government Bill next session'.[93] Persistence wins, and the next time he tried, in September, he succeeded. Before the Cabinet met, Morrison had warned the Prime Minister that Ashfield feared that if he delayed any longer he would miss the chance of the merger with the Metropolitan, so he had to go ahead unless the government intended to bring out its bill. And if the merger went ahead, it would 'put prices up against us and forestall some of the economies which should come to the new public authority'. Morrison wrote that it was urgent to include the bill for the coming session, 'quite apart from the political advantages of including a definite Socialist bill in our legislation and saving London Labour MPs, candidates and myself personally from what would otherwise be a serious situation'.[94]

In September Morrison circulated to Cabinet members a memorandum calling for their support.[95] '[Our] own policy is in principle similar to that outlined in the Liberal Yellow Book, and in view of the urgency of the matter it is doubtful whether the Conservative Opposition would be in a position to make a real fight against our proposals. 'I feel very strongly that it would be beneficial to the spirit of our own party if a socialist measure of this character were brought forward, especially as we have not yet been able to bring forward any definite socialist legislation.'

The Cabinet decided that the bill was to be included in the category of 'other essential bills', and was to be mentioned in the King's Speech. However the date of its introduction and the question of parliamentary time were to be left open until negotiations were more advanced.[96] By March 1931 the negotiations were finished except for the financial transactions. On the Committee on Home Affairs Morrison fought to introduce his bill at once, even though the Committee had had only a preliminary discussion about the bill.[97] At the Cabinet meeting on 4 March 1931 MacDonald showed his irritation at Morrison's speed.[98] Morrison replied that the bill had been circulated to the Cabinet with the minimum notice required. It was decided that the bill should go to the Treasury at the earliest possible moment, that the Home Affairs Committee should give 'very careful consideration' to it and that Morrison should continue his negotiations.[99] The Committee on Home Affairs examined the bill on 6 March, and the Treasury on 9 March. The Treasury wanted the bill postponed because the financial transactions had not been concluded.[100] On 10 March Morrison again knocked on the Cabinet's door for the final go-ahead. Only a few minor points of disagreement remained, some drafting changes were required, and the main outstanding question was about finance. Morrison pressed that the bill be not postponed until he had reached agreement on the financial terms. MacDonald stressed that there was 'very limited time available for legislation before the Easter recess'. The Cabinet decided to back Morrison.[101] The bill was introduced and had a successful second reading on 23 March.

Morrison had stormed the Cabinet. By perseverance, shrewd arguments and agile timing he had pressed his bill on a hesitant Cabinet and a reluctant Prime Minister. His reward was not just that parliamentary time was found for his bill. MacDonald wrote to him on 19 March inviting him to join the Cabinet.[102] MacDonald may have been irritated at Morrison's persistence, but he recognized his talent. Outside the Cabinet Morrison had been responsible for two major bills and had gained a reputation higher than that of many Cabinet members. Thus Morrison's wish was granted. Any strain in the relationship between the two disappeared. MacDonald wrote to Morrison after his speech in the Commons on the second reading, expressing regret at not being present; 'I have been told, however, what a first-rate speech you made. I am glad you have given your Bill a good send off. I send you my hearty congratulations.'[103] Morrison's speech also earned the congratulations of the Conservatives.[104]

The high spot of Morrison's handling of the bill in Parliament was at its committee stage. Since the bill was neither a public nor a private bill, but a hybrid bill, that is a public bill which affects the rights of a particular person or group of persons, its committee stage was taken before a joint committee of the Commons and Lords. It heard counsel from the interests involved and put questions to witnesses who could be cross-examined by counsel from the other parties. Only three of the ten members were Labour;* here the bill could have been sunk or mutilated.

On 10 June the chairman, the Earl of Lytton, made a remarkable statement. The committee wanted to ask some questions about the policy behind the bill; they felt it was inappropriate to call a civil servant and asked for the minister to appear. There seemed to be no precedent for calling a Cabinet minister as a witness before such a committee. Since Morrison was then at a Cabinet meeting the committee adjourned until he could be approached. The opponents of the bill hoped that Morrison would be such a flop, tripped up by the learned counsel, that the bill would be killed. Morrison, game as ever, agreed to appear and at 2 p.m., with hardly any time for preparation, turned up. For the rest of the day and the next day too, Morrison was examined by counsel for the various interests and by members of the committee. It was a gruelling time.

Those who witnessed Morrison's performance were filled with admiration. . Hurcomb, who knew that some members of the committee wanted 'to twist Morrison's tail', said he was 'brilliant'.[105] One counsel yielded the right to

* Five Conservatives, three Labour, and two Liberals.

cross-examine Morrison: 'Do you think I am a fool? That fellow was doing too well.'[106]

Morrison showed that he knew every facet of the bill, and could defend it vigorously in a moderate manner. As he was pressed harder he never became ruffled. His roughest handling was over the Metropolitan Railway Company which was still resisting; a tricky question was put:

> Q: Supposing the Committee did accede to the submission of the Metropolitan Railway on those lines – supposing that – would you drop the Bill, or go on with it?
>
> ——I am not quite sure that that is a question that ought to be put to me – not sure that I ought to be put into the position of anticipating what I would do in the eventuality of the Committee coming to a certain decision. ... I do not think it is fair to the Committee or myself that I should anticipate a deadlock between the Committee and myself.

The maestro of cunning knew how to appeal to different audiences. Before Labour colleagues, the bill was the only socialist measure of the government; before Liberals it was a plank in their own platform; before Tories it was a business proposition. He realized that the opponents of the bill expected him to wave the Red Flag, but he never used the world 'socialism' once during his day and a half before the committee.

In July, after thirty-five days, the bill emerged from the committee substantially unchanged. Only the power of the new authority to manufacture the bodies of motor vehicles had been expunged. Morrison reported to the Cabinet that the decision of the committee was extremely favourable to the bill, and he still hoped to get the power to manufacture put back.[107] That the bill came out to unscathed is a tribute to Morrison. Alone he had beaten the most eminent critics.

Morrison hoped for a speedy conclusion to his bill. His plan was for three full days to be provided for its final stages between 20 October and 6 November 1931. Before he could proceed, the Labour government was engulfed by the economic crisis and in August it collapsed. Once again at the very last minute a carefully worked out scheme to reform London transport seemed doomed to oblivion.

Electricity was another responsibility of the Ministry of Transport. Morrison urged electricity undertakings to expand and proclaimed that he had an all-electric house.[108] The gas companies complained about his propaganda and called on him to hold the balance between gas and electricity.[109] His passion for electricity brought him into conflict with certain amenity groups who protested about the erection of pylons over the Sussex Downs. If cables were put underground the cost would be nine times greater than overhead, and the dampness of the soil might damage their functioning. He wanted electricity readily available, especially to rural areas, and so he supported the pylons. On aesthetic grounds Morrison had no objections: 'They have a majesty and dignity of their own, and the cables stretching between them over the country-side give one a sense of power, in the service of the people, marching over many miles of country.'[110]

Morrison sought to promote electricity through the electrification of railways. In September 1929 he appointed Lord Weir to chair a committee to inquire into the economic, financial and amenity aspects of an extensive programme of electrification. It came down in favour, since the environment would be improved with cleaner air, services would be speedier and operating costs would be reduced.[111] In July 1931 the Cabinet referred the issue to a Cabinet Committee.[112] However, no progress was made because of the financial crisis. At a Cabinet meeting later in July the Prime Minister said that they had to avoid giving the impression that the government was seriously considering electrification since it would have a bad effect on the national financial position.[113] Another of Morrison's hopes was dashed by the crisis.

The fall of the Labour government in August 1931 also prevented Morrison from achieving his next measure of 'socialization', of electricity supply and distribution. Early on taking office he had called for public ownership to run this public utility under proper business management.[114] He set up a commit-tee under Sir John Snell, chairman of the Electricity Commissioners, to look into the organization of electricity distribution. Supply and distribution were in the hands of a number of local authorities and private companies. Their areas were inappropriate to the needs of modern technical developments, their tariffs varied, the quality and enterprise of the different managements also varied, and in rural and sparsely populated areas supply was costly, inadequate or even non-existent. Snell's report advocated regional under-takings, with the private companies absorbing local authority concerns if the former were dominant in a region and vice versa. The civil servants advised Morrison that it was a sound proposition, and in view of the parliamentary situation the best he could get through. Morrison rejected this advice. He could stomach neither expansion by the private undertakings nor their take-over of local authority enterprises. His preference was for a series of public boards appointed by the minister responsible for distribution and, although subject to a central board for co-ordination, supervision and the generation of electricity. Morrison presented a memorandum to the Cabinet in July 1931, outlining his proposals. He pointed out that in order for legislation to be achieved in the existing Parliament it would have to be formulated for intro-duction in the next session. The Cabinet referred the topic to a Cabinet Committee.[115] The government collapsed in the following month, and another of Morrison's schemes was aborted.

As Minister of Transport Morrison was a key figure in the continuing saga of Waterloo Bridge. When he took office negotiations were proceeding between the LCC, the ministry and the Southern Railway Company about the removal of Charing Cross Station to the south bank and the construction of a road bridge in place of the existing railway bridge. It was hoped that this project would prevent the demolition of Waterloo Bridge.

By August agreement was reached and it seemed that action would soon follow. Morrison offered the LCC a grant of seventy-five per cent of the net cost of the new bridge and of the work on Waterloo Bridge, and he urged the LCC to begin its reconstruction in the coming winter. The LCC transformed the Charing Cross proposals into a parliamentary bill. Criticism, however, was mounted against the scheme by some architects, town planners and amenity groups. They appealed to Morrison to persuade the LCC to withdraw the bill. He refused: the LCC and the ministry had worked together on the plan and had taken the best advice about its traffic, engineering, valuation and architectural aspects. It was the best practicable one in the circumstances. Morrison informed the Cabinet 'that it is this scheme ... or nothing, and that if this scheme fails, Waterloo Bridge will in all likelihood come down and the present railway bridge at Charing Cross will continue to disfigure London for another generation'.[116]

In February 1930 he commended the bill to the House and pointed out that if it was rejected then the LCC would demolish Waterloo Bridge.[117] The bill obtained its second reading, 230 votes to 67, and was sent to committee. Here disaster struck. The committee felt that the Charing Cross Station should be moved to another site from the one proposed. The proponents of the bill resisted. The committee then rejected the bill. Morrison, supported by the Cabinet,[118] was prepared to take unprecedented action and back the LCC if it decided to ask for a recommittal. The LCC, however, was reluctant and set up an advisory committee to produce within nine months a new scheme for a bridge at Charing Cross. On the committee were to be representatives from most of the bodies which had objected to the earlier plan. Morrison expressed concern at the delay: he could not see that any new bill, embodying the new scheme, would receive the royal assent until the summer of 1932. In the meantime the LCC would not undertake any work on Waterloo Bridge until the Charing Cross scheme was finalized.

In March 1931 the advisory committee reported its failure to produce an agreed scheme. The LCC then wavered between two plans, and asked Morrison whether he would support one or the other and confirm his previous offer of a seventy-five per cent grant for both bridges. At the Cabinet Morrison urged this course. He was, however, over-ruled. It was pointed out that the financial position of the country had deteriorated since the first offer had been made; the Road Fund was threatened with a serious deficit over the next five years; such grants were normally made only where unemployment could be relieved; and doubt was expressed as to whether the bill would get through Parliament since the schemes had not got overwhelming support. It was agreed that

Morrison should intimate to the LCC that the government would not express any views until the LCC had adopted a scheme.[119] Morrison told the LCC that he could give no firm commitment to support a particular scheme and that he must seriously consider such a very large expenditure at this time of difficulty. The LCC then decided on one of the schemes, and Morrison tried again at the Cabinet. He pointed out that the LCC would go ahead provided it got a seventy-five per cent grant. He feared that a refusal would mean missing an opportunity to proceed with a great improvement and he pointed out another consequence of refusal: 'the odium that may attach to the Government if Waterloo Bridge is pulled down as a result of the refusal of the Government to support the scheme.' It was in vain: 'The Chancellor of the Exchequer informed the Cabinet that the economic situation was so serious that there could be no question at present of incurring any Government expenditure on Charing Cross Bridge.' The Cabinet accepted the view of the Chancellor of the Exchequer.[120]

Morrison announced the decision. The Charing Cross scheme was dead, and the LCC stated that it would now have to demolish Waterloo Bridge and build a new one to take six lanes of traffic.[121] Morrison had failed to solve the problem. So much time and effort had been wasted. It was 'a spectacle of timidity, indecision, and surrender to self-appointed expert bodies'.[122] He blamed the architects, whose 'persistent wrangling and disputation' had prevented the achievement of any agreed proposals.[123]

Morrison said of his time at the ministry: 'I thoroughly enjoyed those two-and-a-quarter years. It was a nice post. The work was clean, constructive, with plenty of opportunities for enterprise and initiative; and one had many contacts with fresh minds in the transport world, with the trade associations and a great need to watch public reactions to one's policies and proposals – which made it all the more interesting. So this period at the Ministry of Transport was a valuable Ministerial apprenticeship. I had a good deal of freedom and opportunity to stand upon my own feet.'[124] Above all he was pleased with his work to reform London transport: 'He is a fortunate Minister who is called upon to deal with a big problem to which he has given close attention over a period of years.'[125] No longer was he just concocting formulas, but was in a practical way producing something.

He admitted his debt to his civil servants, and remained ever after a fervent champion of the British administrative class. He was delighted to find 'with what conscientiousness civil servants discharged their duties'.[126] Lansbury from his experience at the Office of Works took away a totally different view of civil servants. He felt they were not loyal to ministers and tried to sabotage socialist policies.[127] Similar allegations were made in the 1930s by Harold Laski and Stafford Cripps. Morrison challenged these accusations from his experience in local government and at the ministry. 'I cannot remember a case where civil servants or municipal officers appeared to be running the show when it was not the fault of the politicians.'[128] Morrison wrote to Hurcomb to thank him and his colleagues for 'VAST and loyal assistance'.[129] His admiration for his civil servants was reciprocated.

Chapter 11

The 1931 Crisis

The main plank of Labour's 1929 election programme was that it could cure unemployment. Less than two months after the election Morrison proclaimed: 'the settling of the unemployment question is going to be the first job of this Government.'[1] The story of the government's dismal failure and eventual collapse has been told by Dr R. Skidelsky.[2] An admirer of Lloyd George and Sir Oswald Mosley, he is scornful of Labour's attempts to grapple with the economic crisis. Incomprehension and incompetence seem to typify the Labour leaders. They had mouthed slogans about socialism for years without any firm proposals to implement it, and when they found themselves in office they became the prisoners of economic orthodoxy, pursuing irrelevant policies. Unemployment seemed to rise inexorably, from nearly one and a half million in the middle of 1929, to two and a half million by the end of 1930 and to 2,800,000 in July 1931.

It is important to rescue Morrison from the general obloquy and particularly from the venom of Mosley who singled him out as particularly obstructive to his schemes of national recovery through gigantic road works. Morrison's arguments were not the blind response of an incompetent or the stock replies of the idle or ignorant or conservative. Morrison's achievements at the Ministry of Transport show that he was an energetic minister who fought vigorously for policies he believed in. More money was spent on roads while he was minister than in any previous administration. Dr Skidelsky's accusation that Labour had no idea how to implement 'socialism' was untrue as far as Morrison was concerned. He was actually 'socializing' an industry, London transport; he was preparing to do the same to electricity, and through his Road Traffic Act was so reorganizing road transport services that they could easily be socialized when Labour had a majority in the Commons. Morrison championed the public corporation as the administrative institution through which 'socialization' could take place. But such socialization measures could not have an immediate impact on unemployment.

Morrison argued that road construction, and public works generally, could help mitigate, but not eradicate, unemployment. The exceptionally high unemployment encountered by the Labour government was in no way its responsibility. Three main causes existed: the capitalist system, the world depression, and a burdensome war debt settlement. Unemployment was an inescapable element of the capitalist system, or rather lack of system. Cycles of booms and slumps would occur as long as production was for profit and not organized to serve communal ends.[3] The creation of a socialist society, on a world-wide scale, was the only answer. The crash on Wall Street, similar crises in Austria and Germany, the world slump in prices, political troubles in China and India, all helped to disrupt world trade and cut Britain's share of the export market. Such an international dislocation, unforeseen in the election of May 1929, meant that the British government alone was unable to solve the problem in the short term, 'or even materially to mitigate the problem'.[4] Only a stabilization of political conditions in the world and a resumption of world trade at a high level were the answers. Protection was no panacea, since worse unemployment had struck Germany, the USA, Australia and Canada, which had erected tariff barriers. Britain had a special problem. Her productive industry carried a burden of too many and too high debt charges, both repayment and interest charges, especially on war debts. The post-war settlement had been a blunder, to be retrieved only by a capital levy whose proceeds would reduce the debt. Road works, therefore, could at best be only palliatives, and even then without immediate results because of delays in getting work to start. Morrison castigated those who advocated a short-cut cure as either fools or humbugs.

Morrison felt that Lloyd George and Mosley exaggerated the economic benefits from road-building projects. He was not just a mouthpiece of civil servants on this point, although he listened attentively to the Chief Engineer, Sir Henry Maybury, who underestimated traffic needs, was sceptical about whether a big programme could be implemented and doubted if any major advantages would follow. But Morrison cannot be accused of neglecting road construction. He nagged at Snowden and the Treasury to allocate him more expenditure, and he achieved a greater measure of success than previous ministers. Unlike the Conservatives, who had looked at road expenditure only one year at a time, Morrison in July 1929 produced an estimate of accepted expenditure for five years. The initial amount allowed was £37½ million, composed of £9½ million for trunk roads and £28 million for ordinary roads. Dissatisfied, Morrison agitated for an increase of £7½ million in the trunk road programme and of £9 million for ordinary roads. For months Morrison and Snowden wrangled.[5] In March 1930 Snowden agreed to shift £4 million from ordinary to trunk roads, keeping the total intact. Morrison persisted. In May he complained to the Prime Minister and begged his support against Snowden, increasing his claims. In June, after MacDonald backed Morrison, Snowden had granted many of Morrison's demands. Thus

Morrison managed to increase the allocation to trunk roads from the original £9½ million to £21 million: no mean success.[6]

Road building was not a function of central government, but of local authorities, assisted by central grants. To encourage them to build more, Morrison raised their grants, from fifty per cent to sixty-three per cent for ordinary roads, and from seventy-five per cent to ninety per cent for trunk roads. He also sought to reduce obstacles which caused delays. A long time was taken between the approval of a project and the start of actual work on the land. Particularly protracted were the procedures for designating and acquiring land. To ensure that people were not unfairly deprived of their property, ample opportunities were provided for them to object. Morrison urged a simplification of the procedures and the granting of more speedy compulsory purchase powers for local authorities. Some slight improvements were made, but still it took a long time to prepare a road scheme and to acquire the land.[7]

Because of such difficulties Mosley and others felt that road building should be undertaken by a national agency. As the champion of local government Morrison opposed an erosion of its powers, even resisting the advocates of hundred per cent grants to local authorities for road building, which he argued would destroy local responsibility. Only by making a financial contribution could local authorities have a voice in the road programmes and an interest in ensuring that the work was executed economically. He condemned those local authorities who asked for hundred per cent grants as trying to blackmail the state by saying that they would act only if they received subsidies.[8] Morrison warned his colleagues against even mentioning 'national schemes' for fear that some local authorities would 'hang back, in the hope that the Government itself will start work in the locality, in default of action by the Councils, and find the whole cost'.[9] He also feared that if a minister became responsible he would be bombarded with questions from MPs about stretches of road, which would clog up question time in the House. He predicted that local authorities would put up a stiff fight against a national body directing significant numbers of the unemployed from other localities into their areas to build roads, especially as the local authority would have had no say in the matter. He refused to scrap local authorities and replace them by 'State dictators'.[10]

Morrison argued that roads should be judged not just as a means of providing work but as contributing to a general transport network. Responsible for the whole transport system he had to balance roads, railways, canals and ships.[11] He attacked the Mosley and Lloyd George schemes to raise huge national loans for road building as an irresponsible illusion; the money would be spent with little benefit and yet a big burden would be laid on productive industry. He wrote to J. H. Thomas, the Lord Privy Seal: 'It is true that I refuse to be reckless in expenditure and to become the vistim [sic] of road obsession unless the Cabinet tells me to do so. Spending Ministers, it mees

[sic] to me, have as much duty to have proper regard to economy as Labour undrestands [sic] it as the Chancellor of the Exchequer himself.'[12]

Morrison also opposed Mosley's proposal for administrative reform: to put Mosley as an overlord over other departmental ministers. Having had experience of working with Mosley, particularly on the Cabinet Committee on National Schemes, Morrison was aghast: 'I often found his face looking fierce and unpleasant, especially when he was not getting his own way.'[13] On one occasion Mosley began to cross-examine Morrison about his ministry. Morrison seethed and 'felt something of the superiority of the aristocrat in his attitude in relation to myself as a working class Minister'. He said: 'if the Chancellor of the Duchy of Lancaster sought information from me as a colleague I would do my best to supply him with all the information he wanted, but if he was going to adopt an attitude of superiority, if he was going to be like an aggressive Counsel in Court severely cross-examining and attacking a hostile witness and treating me as such, well then, so far as I was concerned, he could go to the Devil.'[14] Morrison feared that under Mosley's plan 'action would be slower and friction increased'. Eternal argument would be the consequence.[15] He flailed the Mosley Memorandum and its signatories, noting that some had come over from the Tory protectionists and still had a certain amount of true blue blood in their veins: 'In due course they would be brought back to earth to find more appropriate political associates.'[16] 'They were either temperamental aristocrats [Bevan?] or had been reared in upper class society and had become accustomed to giving orders purely because their personal wealth or social position enabled them to do so.' [Strachey?] On Mosley's proposal for a Cabinet of only five Morrison felt 'that in his heart Sir Oswald Mosley regarded this as being four too many'.[17]

Morrison defended the government's record on unemployment.[18] Compared with the previous Conservative administration of 'drift, makeshift and muddle', Labour had been resourceful, spending more money, undertaking more schemes and putting more men to work. The government was taking the right steps to ensure that once the world crisis was over Britain would be ready to take full advantage of the opportunities available. The government was seeking to make each industry more efficient through reorganization; coal, road transport, housing and agriculture were the subjects of bills, while inquiries were investigating cotton, iron, steel and electricity. Public works schemes were being undertaken to provide a firm foundation for industry: roads, railways, docks, water, gas, electricity, land drainage and reclamation. To encourage world trade Labour's foreign policy was to seek peace and bring about a stabilization of trading; and to stimulate exports, trade commissions were hunting out markets.

Such activities Morrison defended as likely to 'bear results far more beneficial to the nation and the unemployed in due time than the adoption of panicky measures based on an indiscriminate distribution of public funds – which is certainly not a Socialist doctrine – and the harum scarum putting in hand of works irrespective of lasting economic advantage to the country as a whole'.[19]

Morrison had to fight on two fronts. Against the Treasury he sought more money for road programmes. He argued that this expenditure was not for relief work but for genuine traffic needs. Because of the increase in cars more roads would be needed and, if money were not spent now, more would have to be spent later.[20] He admitted that 'he could not demonstrate directly to the Treasury that the whole of the expenditure would increase the productive power of the nation. He could only contend that taking a long view the roads were required for more efficient transport.'[21] Snowden was a wall of resistance, even seeking to cut off certain grants in 1931. If Snowden's policy was followed, Morrison wrote, 'we shall be accused of restricting employment although the situation in that respect is more serious than at any time since we took office'.[22] The rigid force of reaction in the Labour government of 1929–31 was not Morrison but Snowden. On the other front Morrison had to contend with Mosley who complained that the road programme was 'really not good enough from one of the Departments on which the Government must chiefly rely for the advancement of work plans'. He criticized Morrison for not recognizing that roads were the most modern means of transport and for spending on the railways (an outmoded method of travel) money which ought to have gone on roads. He castigated Morrison for adhering to a fiscal theory that 'is a hoary relic of the last century', namely, that the nation saved money if the Treasury contribution to schemes was low and the local authority share high.[23] Morrison was caught between Snowden and Mosley.

The unemployed provided the issue over which the Cabinet was finally to be fatally split.[24] The crisis began on 1 August 1931 with the publication of the report of the Committee on National Expenditure, chaired by Sir George May. This committee of bankers and financial experts, set up in March 1931 to examine demands for retrenchment in government expenditure, rebuked the government for causing ruinous inflation, predicted a budget deficit of £120 million and advocated major cuts in public expenditure, including £67 million off payments to the unemployed. At the July Cabinet meeting before the recess there had been no mention of any difficulties and ministers dispersed for their holidays, Morrison to the south of France. Following publication of the report the Bank of England started to lose gold. Holders of sterling looked to the government for cuts in expenditure to balance the budget. Snowden telegraphed MacDonald to call a meeting of the Cabinet economy committee, and he instructed the heads of departments to prepare a list of economies, based on May's recommendations. Ministers were hurriedly called back. Morrison received his telegram and set off. By the time he got back the lists of cuts had been prepared, and ministers were asked by the Treasury to decide 'whether reductions to a maximum figure next year are best effected by carrying out the recommendations of the May Committee, or whether other methods can be suggested as alternatives'. Thus the 'maximum' reduction appeared to be accepted without any Cabinet decision. Morrison spotted this and asked for 'some preliminary decision from my colleagues on the main issue of reversing the policy of stimulating ... employment'. The Cabinet economy committee agreed on cuts of £78 million.[25] Then followed in Morrison's word 'miserable' Cabinet meetings;[26] the first on 19 August[27] agreed to economies totalling £56 million; Morrison's Road Fund expenditure was reduced by £7,800,000 and he warned the Cabinet that this meant a reversal of policy with regard to important road schemes.

The issue which divided the Cabinet was a ten per cent cut in unemployment benefit, a sum of £12 million, demanded by the Opposition and bankers as a symbol of the government's determination to stop inflation and opposed by the trade unions and many in the Labour Party as a symbol of the government's determination to defend the working class. By the Cabinet meeting of 22 August, following two others on the 20th and 21st,[28] it was clear that economies of £56 million were not enough to satisfy the Opposition and the bankers Snowden urged an extra £20 million in cuts, largely made up of the cut in unemployment benefit. The Cabinet refused; Snowden and Thomas recorded their dissent. The Prime Minister was authorized to see if the Opposition would accept an extra £20 million without any government commitment to specific reductions.

They adjourned at 12.10 p.m. and resumed at 2.30 p.m.[29] when MacDonald reported that the Tory and Liberal leaders would accept the figure if it proved acceptable to the financial authorities in Paris and New York. The Cabinet would not agree to the figure being a firm commitment, but decided to sound out the opinion of bankers in New York. On the 23rd at 7 p.m. the Cabinet resumed to hear the reply which did not arrive until 9.10 p.m. It was ambiguous but was interpreted to mean that New York was in favour if the Bank of England and the City supported a total cut of £76 million. MacDonald said that the City had assured him of their support for £76 million and the Opposition had pledged theirs.[30]

MacDonald had up till now kept his Cabinet together by avoiding a final decision on unemployment benefit. He made his final appeal: the country was suffering from lack of confidence abroad. There was, as yet, no panic at home, but the Prime Minister warned the Cabinet of the calamitous nature of the consequences which would immediately and inevitably follow from a financial panic and a flight from the pound. No one could be blind to the very great political difficulties in which the giving effect to the proposals as a whole would involve the government. But when the immediate crisis was over and before Parliament met, it would be possible to give the Labour Party that full explanation of the circumstances which had rendered it necessary for the government to formulate such a drastic scheme, which could not be given at the moment. The only alternative was a reduction not of ten per cent; but of at least twenty per cent; and he could not believe that the Labour Party would reject the proposals when they knew the true facts of the position: he was confident, indeed, that a majority of that party would accept them. A scheme which inflicted reductions and burdens in almost every other direction but made no appreciable cut in unemployment insurance benefit, would alienate much support and lose the party their moral prestige which was one of their greatest assets. In conclusion, the Prime Minister said that it must be admitted that the proposals as a whole represented the negation of everything that the Labour Party stood for, and yet he was absolutely satisfied that it was necessary in the national interest to implement them if the country was to be secured. He then pointed out that, if on this question there were any important resignations, the government as a whole must resign. Each member expressed his view. Morrison was in favour and was part of a majority of eleven,[31] but 'while a majority of the Cabinet favoured the inclusion in the economy proposals of the 10 per cent reduction in unemployment insurance benefit, the adoption of this as part and parcel of the scheme would involve the resignation of certain Ministers from the Government'. They must have been the minority of nine.[32]

The Cabinet placed their resignations in the hands of MacDonald, who told them that he would go immediately to the King and advise him to hold a conference with Baldwin and Samuel* the next day. He left at 10 p.m. and returned at 10.40 p.m. to say that he had told the King they could not agree and it was impossible for them to continue in office as a united Cabinet. The audience between the King and the party leaders was fixed for 10 a.m. the next day.

The Cabinet gathered for its last session at noon.[33] The Prime Minister announced the results of the meeting with the King. The financial situation had deteriorated. The King had asked him, Baldwin and Samuel to take upon their shoulders the burden of carrying on the government. MacDonald said that he 'had not failed to present the case against his participation in the proposed Administration, but in view of the gravity of the situation he had felt that there was no other course open to him than to assist in the formation of a National Government on a comprehensive basis for the purpose of meeting the present emergency'. There would be a small Cabinet, of twelve, which would not exist 'for a period longer than was necessary to dispose of the emergency, and when that purpose was achieved the political parties would resume their respective positions. The Administration would not be a Coalition Government in the usual sense of the term, but a Government of co-operation for this one purpose.' A general election would follow at the end of the emergency period and there would be no coupons, pacts, or other party arrangements. He would try to avoid by-election contests in the emergency but, if they had to take place, the leaders could send messages to their party candidates. While he held office, there would be no party legislation, but he would carry into law measures on which there was substantial agreement, and he mentioned Morrison's London

* Acting as Liberal leader during Lloyd George's illness.

Transport Bill. Economies would be on the lines of those submitted to the bankers, including the ten per cent cut in unemployment benefit.

After he had spoken the Lord Chancellor moved, and the Cabinet accepted, that it 'placed on record their warm appreciation of the great kindness, consideration and courtesy invariably shown by the Prime Minister when presiding over their meetings and conducting the business of the Cabinet'. The final decision was that MacDonald should place the resignation of the government in the hands of the King that afternoon.

Morrison's attitude to the formation of the National Government in August 1931 presents a puzzle. Morrison's own version is that from the outset he opposed it, indeed was the first minister to express his hostility, and rejected MacDonald's overtures to join. However, a persistent rumour of the thirties was that he was sympathetic to MacDonald and had asked to be a member of his new administration, but was turned down.

In his *Autobiography* Morrison relates that when MacDonald announced to the Cabinet that he had accepted the King's request to form a National Government: 'We were all shocked, and those of us who had no intention of going along with MacDonald felt that we had been badly let down.' 'The 1931 Betrayal' was how Morrison headed this section.[34]* He continued: 'Perhaps because I was the youngest member of the cabinet I was the first to get my breath and find my voice. "Prime Minister," I said, "I think you are wrong." He seemed to be shocked and turned round to me and snapped, "You think I'm wrong!" "I do," I replied, "Moreover, you will find it easier to get into this combination than to get out of it." '[35] Morrison told a similar story to Harold Nicolson, adding that he said to MacDonald, 'And I for one am not coming with you.'[36] After the meeting Morrison lunched with Mary Agnes Hamilton, and said that 'to him [Morrison], as to nobody else, a direct personal appeal had been made'.[37] And she concluded that he was 'one of the few ministers to whom MacDonald appealed to stay'.[38]

In his draft autobiography Morrison illustrated what he thought was MacDonald's desire to have him in the government: 'MacDonald telephoned me and asked me who I thought might make a Minister of Transport who would be friendly to the progress of the Bill, which he desired to save. I think he was hoping that I would say that I would be willing to undertake the task; but, of course, I was not. He said that if he was to help me I would have to help him. I gave him such advice as I could as to possible people outside the Labour Party who might make a suitable Minister, but, as far as I could tell, he didn't really seem interested in this. Although he didn't ask me to accept the office I feel pretty certain that that was what he was seeking; but, as I never had the slightest intention of joining the National Government, this was an unthinkable proposition as far as I was concerned.' In response to the

* 'A blunder at the best and a betrayal at the worst.'

phone call Morrison wrote to MacDonald a list of Liberals and Conservatives in favour of the bill. His tone was friendly and he concluded, 'I *personally* wd do what I cd to smooth the passage. All kind regards.'[39] MacDonald sent an amicable reply, adding that he [MacDonald] would soon have the credit for saving the party.[40] Morrison replied, again in a warm fashion: 'My dear PM . . . I know how you are feeling and I am very sorry about it all. We *all* have our difficulties. . . . So glad you are getting a weekend.'[41] The MacDonald and the Morrison papers show that there was no breach between them immediately after the last Cabinet meeting, and that MacDonald was not begging him to join nor Morrison begging to be admitted.

Other than Morrison himself the only source for the view that Morrison was asked to join the National Government was J. H. Thomas. In 1931 Thomas met Leah Manning and asked her to take a junior post at the Board of Education. He told her that Morrison was joining the government as Minister of Transport. Thomas seemed to be acting as a kind of recruiting officer for MacDonald.[42] Soon after her confrontation with Thomas, Leah Manning met Morrison. She asked him if an offer had been made. 'Of course', he said. His attitude was that if an offer had been made to someone as lowly as Leah Manning then it was obvious that one had been made to him.[43]

The press of the period suggests that Morrison was not absolutely firm against the National Government at least until the late afternoon of 25 August. In the morning papers of that date were stories that Morrison was likely to join MacDonald. *The Times* reported that Morrison 'is believed to be a loyal supporter of Mr MacDonald', and the *Daily Herald* noted that he 'may also be included in the new Ministry'. The evening papers of the same date quashed the rumour. The *Star* stated that Morrison 'to-day authorized the statement that there has never been any question of his joining the new Government', and the *Evening Standard* carried a similar disavowal. On the following morning the *Daily Herald* said that 'he has never been asked to take office in the new Government, nor has he ever been considered in that connection'. The *Manchester Guardian* claimed that 'there had never been any question of his joining the National Government' and the *Daily Telegraph* observed that Morrison's name was to be added to 'the list of ex-Ministers who have definitely announced that they will not enter the Ministry'.

If he had been so firm then, it is odd that totally different views of his attitude were so current.* One is led to suspect that he was not telling the

---

* Sheer confusion might be an explanation, as can be shown from an odd episode at Hackney. In the *Hackney Gazette* for 26 August appeared a report that Morrison had 'made the following statement to a "Gazette" representative yesterday: "I am seeking to be Minister of Transport. There is not, and never was, any question of my joining a National Government." ' In the next issue (28 August) the muddle was explained. 'As the result of an indistinct telephone conversation it was reported in Wednesday's "Gazette" that Mr Herbert Morrison, PC, JP, LCC, the Member for South Hackney, had stated, "I am seeking to be Minister of Transport." What he actually did say was, "I am ceasing to be Minister of Transport." '

truth about his first reaction. Indeed F. George Kay, who 'ghosted' Morrison's *Autobiography*, claims that Morrison told him that 'he had at first wanted to join MacDonald and had asked to be taken in. He admired MacDonald tremendously and saw that the Labour Party was likely to be smashed for a generation and he did not want to go down in the débâcle.' But he told Kay: 'There is no point now in saying so.' That he asked to join is supported by evidence from people close to MacDonald. His son, Malcolm, wrote in 1966: 'a few mornings after the formation of the National Government'* he met Morrison walking across Westminster Bridge. 'He told me that during the last days of the Labour Government's life my father had been "magnificent", that his policy through the crisis had been very wise, and that his persuasiveness in Cabinet had nearly succeeded in preventing the minority from deflecting the team from its proper course. But in the end "the timidity" of certain Ministers about defending the cuts in unemployment pay had won the day. Then Morrison told me that he had wished to join the National Government, and had offered to do so, but that my father at once urged him to abandon this inclination, saying that whereas Snowden, Thomas and he himself were elders whose time of leadership was nearly over, Morrison was one of the ablest of the younger national leaders whose influence through many more years would be invaluable to the Labour Party. So that junior statesman changed his mind and joined the opposition.'[44]

MacDonald's other son, Alistair, supports this version. Just after his father had been asked to form the government Alistair came across him in No. 10 Downing Street on the phone to Morrison. MacDonald was saying, 'I've told you before, don't join me. This is a very temporary period, an artificial situation of emergency. It will soon blow over. Stay out of the government. If you do come in, you'll do yourself no good politically. Bide your time and wait. I'm an old man but I'm doing what I think is right, what I've got to do. You're much younger. Wait. Wait until the balance comes back.' Alistair MacDonald said that he gathered from his father that Herbert wanted to join.[45] The Prime Minister's personal secretary, Rose Rosenberg, the former sweetheart of Morrison, told her sister Kate that after the final Cabinet meeting Morrison said to MacDonald that he was with him, but MacDonald told him to think it over, to stay with the party and not to ruin his career.[46] Emanuel Shinwell said that he had heard from 'good sources' that Morrison had wanted to remain but MacDonald had rejected him. Shinwell recalled driving in a car with Morrison from Transport House, when Morrison expressed the view that in six months' time MacDonald would be shown to be right.[47] The story that Morrison had requested to join and had been told to stay out was also put about by Clement Davies† who claimed to have had a talk to Morrison soon after the fall of the Cabinet.[48] Morrison strenuously

---

* Malcolm MacDonald said it was 'two to three days after the National Government was formed'. Interview.

† A Liberal MP, later the leader.

denied his assertions: 'I can only say that your belief does not stand up to reason as it would have been very silly in view of what I had already said to MacDonald.'[49]

There are a number of sources who show that MacDonald told Morrison not to join the National Government, although they never indicate whether this statement was in reply to a request from Morrison. At the very least it can be said that MacDonald would not have expressed such views to someone who was clearly opposed to the National Government. The Earl of Swinton wrote that MacDonald had told him that Morrison had been 'a little uncertain' whether to stay with the official Labour Party or to follow him. MacDonald said to Morrison: 'The bulk of the Labour people will go against me, and you will have a great future in the Labour Party. You would be better not to join me.'[50] The *Daily Mail* of 28 August 1931 described the scene at the end of the Cabinet meeting. MacDonald shook hands with Morrison and said: 'I would not ask you to join us. We older men are risking our whole future. You are a young man, still with a great work to do for the movement. I would not ask you to jeopardize your future as we are jeopardizing ours.'* A similar story was committed to his diary by George Strauss who talked to Morrison on the afternoon of 25 August. In the entry for that date Strauss wrote that MacDonald told Morrison, 'he would not ask him to join the Cabinet as doing so would ruin his political career. Morrison was young, he was old. He did not mind committing political suicide. Actually Morrison would not have joined the Cabinet if he had been invited to do so and he was pleased not to have to refuse an invitation from MacDonald.'[51]

Morrison was torn by conflicting loyalties: on the one hand to MacDonald whom he personally admired and whose policies he felt were in the national interest, and to his London Passenger Transport Bill, for which he had worked so hard and which was at its final stages; and on the other hand to the Labour Party and the trade union movement which was the basis of the party.[52] Lady Allen of Hurtwood recalled that Morrison and her husband, Clifford Allen, 'talked endlessly about it. Herbert was anxious to get the right conclusion and so he put forward different courses of action and weighed up the different consequences.'[53] On the night before MacDonald went to the palace Dick Windle, the National Agent, and Morrison had sat up into the early hours of the morning 'debating the pros and cons'.[54] On the following night, after it had been publicly announced that MacDonald was forming a National Government, Mrs Goodrich, a former sweetheart of Morrison's, got in touch with Morrison at the House. They walked a long time together through the corridors and over Westminster and Hungerford Bridges. He was 'frightfully upset' and showed that it had been a big blow. He expressed his admiration of MacDonald; she left with the impression that MacDonald had asked

---

* One may ask why MacDonald said all this if Morrison had indicated vigorously that he would not join.

him to join and that he had refused.[55] Quite a different impression was left on Mrs Penna, the daughter of William Morgan, the former circulation manager of the *Daily Citizen*. She said that on the night of MacDonald's resignation (probably after leaving Mrs Goodrich) Morrison turned up and said 'Can you give a cup of tea to a poor Cabinet Minister out of a job?' He never said a bad word against MacDonald and tried to excuse him. She felt that Morrison was disappointed at not being asked to join and that he would have done so if he had been asked.[56] Thus Morrison managed to convey to Mrs Penna a totally different impression from that left on Mrs Goodrich a little earlier and from that to be left on Strauss the next day. That he could make people have such divergent opinions in such a brief time suggests that his own mind was not made up. He was arguing within himself and putting to people he met different views, seeking something to tip him one way or the other. Guy Eden, a reporter on the *News Chronicle*, met Morrison outside the Ministry of Transport, leaning on a lamp-post, almost dazed. He said that MacDonald was to form a National Government. 'Guy, I simply do not know what I am to do. Shall I go over or stay with the party?' 'You must decide', replied Eden. 'I wish I knew', said Morrison. He was very confused and sought help and arguments. 'He was on the very edge of going in.'[57]

The most intriguing explanation of what went on between MacDonald and Morrison is presented by MacDonald's daughter, Ishbel, who was extremely close to her father and was also a shrewd observer of Morrison under whom she served at the LCC. She met Morrison on 9 September 1931 walking over Westminster Bridge. In her diary she wrote that he had told her that 'he was in favour of the Labour Government tackling the crisis but could not support Daddy in forming a National Government (anyway he confessed he had not been asked to remain at his post)'[58]: a different tale from that which he had told her brother a few days earlier on the very same bridge. Her view as to what had taken place has a ring of psychological authenticity. She says that on the break-up of the Labour government her father really wanted Herbert and the other younger members to join him in the National Government, but was too proud to admit to them that he needed them. When he saw them he put the case that they should stay with the party. He was hoping that they would press to join him. At the Cabinet meeting Morrison vaguely expressed his support for MacDonald, not openly asking for a job; to which MacDonald replied with the arguments for staying out, which Morrison took at face value and did not then try to rebut.[59] Then followed some hours of agonized internal arguing, when he asked MacDonald what he should do. MacDonald again put the previous arguments. There was considerable fencing between the two, with MacDonald only half-heartedly putting the arguments against Morrison joining and Morrison expressing his anxiety and hoping for a clear request to join. Neither really said to the other what he meant. This explanation fits in with the guesses of Morrison's chief cronies at the LLP and LCC: he had hesitated; his first reaction was to go with MacDonald, and he would have gone if MacDonald had made a clear request; when no call came and the hostility of the party solidified, Morrison followed the party.[60]

One might speculate as to MacDonald's motives in telling his obviously able minister not to join him, and making similar statements to other junior ministers. During those early few days, before the party and the trade unions had mounted their onslaught, MacDonald believed that the National Government would be brief: to carry out the financial economies and restore confidence.[61] After about six weeks it would resign and the old party politics be restored. During the period of the National Government it would be important for it to command the full support of the House of Commons, including the Labour Party. Therefore he wanted Morrison and other Labour ministers who had backed his line to remain active inside the Labour Party to persuade it to support the very measures they had urged when in government. Their presence would also help MacDonald return to the fold. For his own survival in the Labour Party he wanted support to counteract his enemies. He did not betray the party; he still felt himself Labour and did not leave the party. His error was that he did not make this view clear to the people he wanted as allies, and so they did not fight vigorously against his opponents who turned the party against him. The rift widened and the party expelled him. Foreign confidence became harder to obtain, the financial crisis deepened and the National Government had to last longer than MacDonald had intended. He became a prisoner of the Tories because the Labour Party had cut off his escape route. MacDonald may also have been utterly confused in a baffling and unprecedented situation. However, one must conclude that he took in only former colleagues who made forceful requests to join him, and that Morrison conveyed only ambiguity and hesitancy. Between the end of the Cabinet meeting on Monday 24 August and Morrison's last visit to the Ministry of Transport on the afternoon of Tuesday 25 August he let it be known to MacDonald, on more than one occasion, that he supported him, but obscured tentative probings with much speculation about the consequences. Hence MacDonald continued to put to him the reasons why he should stay out. By the time that Morrison had his talk to Strauss at the ministry he had accepted that he would not be joining.

On Wednesday 26 August the Executive of the Parliamentary Labour Party, the National Executive Committee and the General Council of the Trades Union Congress met together to discuss the situation.[62] Three ex-ministers spoke: Lansbury, Clynes and Morrison. The first two probably expressed outright hostility to MacDonald, while Morrison was more favourable, although guarded. What Morrison said is unknown. However in the *Daily Mail* of 28 August Morrison is reported as saying that he was not likely to lose his personal admiration for MacDonald nor his belief that his action showed exceptional political courage. By the evening of the 26th the Executives had decided to oppose. They adjourned until the next day when a further session drew up a joint manifesto: *Labour's Call to the Nation.*

Now Morrison put about the story that at the final Cabinet meeting on 24 August he had 'indicated that he would not join the National Government'.[63] Nevertheless during the first week of September he was still sympathetic to MacDonald. On 3 September he wrote to Clifford Allen, 'I still find it difficult to believe that Mac will lead the other group against us in an election.'[64] On 7 September at Hackney he attacked the Tories for pressing the Labour Cabinet to do what a united Labour Cabinet could not do. He said that the crisis was caused by the anti-British propaganda of the Tory patriots. He then expressed his first public criticism of the National Government itself: 'I never liked Labour leaders being in the wartime coalitions, though they had Labour's official approval; I cannot like Labour Ministers being in this Government where they have neither the official, nor the unofficial approval of the Labour Movement.' Then he expressed his 'high regard' for MacDonald and Snowden, and hoped 'none would forget in five minutes their great life's work for Labour and Socialism – work which would endure and be remembered when many lesser lights were forgotten'. He could respect their courage and believe in their sincerity. But what they were doing was wrong. 'It was a wrong to themselves; a wrong to international Socialism; and, in the long run, a wrong to the country.'[65]

About this time rumours that he had asked to join became so embarrassing that he made a statement that they were untrue. On 18 September at Hackney he said that: 'I thought my right course was not to be associated with the Government, and I decided without any hesitation to take the consequences.'

Morrison's behaviour in early September presents another puzzle. Dalton in his diary reveals that Morrison did not stand for election to the Executive Committee of the Parliamentary Labour Party.[66] Many former colleagues did, and it is clear from the list of those successful that Morrison would have stood a good chance of election. Why did he not come forward? Here is a mystery that still awaits explanation.

Even at the end of September Morrison, although condemning the government, and especially the Tories, always praised MacDonald personally. He slammed the Tories for their negative economy and social stagnation and for urging an immediate election. Their 'game was to use the Prime Minister as a figure-head in a great electoral offensive against Labour and Socialism'. But he believed that their greatest mistake was 'in thinking that by flattery and cajolery they could persuade the Prime Minister, whose long political life had been devoted to building up a powerful Labour and Socialist opinion, to become the temporary leader in the country of what would in effect be the Tory forces against those organizations of Labour, Socialism, Trade Unionism, and Co-operation, with which he had lived and with which history ought to identify him'.[67]

The shattering blow to Morrison came when MacDonald bowed to the Tories' pressure for an election and led them into battle. Clifford Allen told Ishbel MacDonald that 'Bert M' was 'rather intransigent, chiefly about the forcing of the Election'.[68] At Hackney for the first time he assailed Mac-Donald: 'I am driven against my will to regard Mr MacDonald as the Leader of an anti-Labour Coalition which, despite his pledges, is fixing up pacts and coupons against Labour.'[69] 'I can understand everything the Prime Minister has done up to the point of him allowing himself to be made the tool of the Tories in this crooked election.' He denounced MacDonald's electoral manifesto: 'how is it that not a syllable of Socialism appears in his manifesto?'[70] It was 'drafted on the basis that he must hide every Socialist principle for which in the past he had declared. . . . How was it that he submitted without protest to the denunciations of the late Socialist Government, of which he was Prime Minister and for whose policy until the break-up he was primarily responsible?'[71] MacDonald's 'betrayal' lay not so much in forming the National Government as in leading it against the Labour Party. In the LLP office Morrison turned the photograph of Ramsay MacDonald to face the wall.[72]

The decision to expel MacDonald was made on 28 September by the NEC, which declared that MPs, candidates and members supporting the new government cease to be members of the Labour Party. Only one vote was cast against the motion. It is not too fanciful to guess that it could have been Morrison's, since on this same day Morrison was reported as saying that MacDonald would never lead the Tories in an election against Labour. The NEC on 5 October then specified to the Seaham Labour Party that MacDonald 'by his own action, has ceased to be a member of the Party'.

In November 1931 the General Council of the TUC stated that it did not want MacDonald, Snowden or Thomas to return to the Party,[73] and in the early months of 1932 it looked as if some trade union leaders were hoping to purge the Labour Party of others who, they felt, ought to have followed MacDonald. The Chairman of the TUC had urged the party to keep its eyes open for careerists and stated that if any of the betrayers were taken back the trade unions would have to review their position as financiers of the party. Morrison criticized their spreading of suspicion and deprecated their demand to dominate the party to the exclusion of those who specialized in politics.[74]

Morrison remained on friendly terms, in private, with both Ishbel and Malcolm MacDonald, but as regards his relationship with Ramsay Mac-Donald there is some doubt. Malcolm said that Morrison, unlike some of his colleagues, did not 'cut' his father but managed to maintain 'cordial' relations. But Ishbel recalls that there was no contact afterwards. The LCC Labour Party in 1933 refused to attend an LCC luncheon for MacDonald.[75] Morrison remained on friendly terms with Clifford Allen, a supporter of MacDonald, but he kept his visits to Allen's house shrouded in secrecy.[76] Later in the 1930s Morrison sometimes referred to MacDonald, but never in such denunciatory terms as some of his colleagues. In 1935 he said, 'It is almost cruelty to animals to say anything about the Prime Minister. .... It is a tragedy for a man who has had a great life. We do not forget what he has done in our movement, but the present is an awful last chapter. It is a tragedy that he has got mixed up with this collection of oddities.'[77]

Section IV: Time to Reflect

Chapter 12

Morrison the Man

Being a minister changed Morrison's private life. With his increased salary he bought a new house, within a mile of the old one, but larger and with garage space: a four-bedroomed semi-detached at 55 Archery Road, still within the boundaries of his beloved Eltham and closer to the railway station. He was to live here for the next thirty years, proud of his middle-class home which symbolized the sort of person he identified with and wanted to win to the Labour cause. When he became a minister the family felt rich, but realizing that it would last for only a short time, they still had to be careful; the only extras purchased were new furniture.[1]

While at the ministry Morrison gave up being a vegetarian, non-smoker and teetotaller. A cigarette drooped from his lips almost continually except when he could obtain a cigar, and he acquired a taste for whisky. No longer lean and ascetic, he turned podgy. Dr Salter was aghast: 'Many of the people with whom you mix at present – as indeed others also – will say you are more human now that you have given up your non-smoking and total abstinence and other puritanical ways. Don't forget what you owe to the stern self-control you practised in the past, and don't fall into the laxer ways of the conventional milieu in which you now find yourself.'[2] The change was noticed at Hackney. When questioned about it, he replied: 'circumstances alter cases' or 'I've got more bloody sense now'.[3]

He met people with a different style of life from his own; new opportunities and temptations were opened to him, and he found he enjoyed the new delights, often the perquisites of office. He probably calculated that his previous habits inhibited his career; advancement required him to be more convivial. Beatrice Webb complained in 1936: 'he eats, drinks and smokes too lavishly, works his mind too hard and his body too little for continued fitness.'[4]*

* He disparaged really high living: 'the golf-course, week-end, race-course, country mansion, habitual hob-nobbing gets you into a way of life that is not good for Labour leaders. ... The Labour leader must remain the captain of his soul – and his soul must remain a proletarian soul.' (*Forward*, 13 June 1936.)

Morrison in the 1930s was short and stocky. He walked with great heavy strides, a 'hunch of the shoulder and sidewise tilt of the head'. He was bouncy and perky, yet clumsy. He was shaggy-haired with a quiff thrown back off his bulging forehead. His bad eye was always half shut which enhanced 'his cockney quizzicality' and 'adds to the Sam Weller impression'.[5] An observer in the Commons wrote: 'One feels one is joining him in a piece of documentary research as he bends over his notes and peers at his manuscript with his head and glasses held at a crooked angle.'[6] He was easily caricatured by cartoonists with a few deft strokes: a baggy suit, horn-rimmed glasses and a quiff.

An interesting description of Morrison came from the leading British phrenologist, Mr Robert Jenkins, who was also a Municipal Reform councillor at the LCC. Morrison was fascinated by phrenology, always recalling that his involvement in politics began with the advice of a phrenologist. He knew of Jenkins' high reputation from reports of his lectures, and occasionally he asked Jenkins to give him views about their colleagues on the LCC. In the mid-1930s Jenkins went to have tea in Morrison's LCC office. There was a group of Morrison's lieutenants in the room. Over tea he talked about phrenology and answered their questions. Morrison asked for a delineation. Jenkins felt Morrison's head, and said it showed that he had great mental powers of organization, of balance, of seeing causes and effects, of making nice comparisons, of being thorough, tidy, detailed and practical. He had a big, very disciplined brain. He had a weakness: he was much too cautious, but he also had energy, drive, destructiveness, ruthlessness; and these two tendencies, caution and aggression, fought each other and at times cancelled each other out. His greatest weakness, however, was that he lacked self-esteem, and so needed to call attention to himself and win approval. This 'approbation tendency' showed in that he never forgot people who had let him down or hurt him. He was also not a good judge of people. At this point Morrison pulled him up, was very rude and said the session was over: the first and the last time that Jenkins 'read Morrison's bumps'.[7]

Mrs Morrison rarely emerged into public view in the 1930s. While her husband was Minister of Transport she refused about nine out of ten invitations and came to functions only when she really had to, as when he opened a bridge at Letchworth – a kind of homecoming for her.[8] Later she would turn up to receptions at the LCC or sit in the gallery at the House of Commons, looking lonely and nervous. Morrison gave the impression to some that his wife was not interested in politics or his career and that he was disappointed that she had not worked harder to conquer her stammer.[9] To others he admitted that she had a wretched life. He was out all day, he would come home tired, and she would want to talk about what had happened; he didn't and was rough on her. He also confessed that one politician in the house was enough.[10] Close friends claimed that she followed politics and was a vigorous champion of her husband.[11] No one saw any evidence that the marriage was at breaking point, although Morrison was noticeably undemonstrative, and neglected her at public functions. When he had a ticket for a theatre or a concert – very rarely – he would ask a family friend to take her out.[12]

Morrison's daughter, Mary, recalled that the home was spartan; her parents seemed inhibited and uncommunicative. Her father was rarely at home. He left early in the morning and returned around midnight – if at all. At weekends, if he was there, he would get up late and read the papers. After lunch he would work on his official papers. He read very slowly and was not to be disturbed. If she said anything, he went 'Hmmm'. Sometimes she was able to persuade him to take her out; and if she ever asked for money, she would never hear the end of it. She knew that there were certain topics she must avoid – sex for instance, since it would embarrass her parents. Mrs Morrison was very lonely. She had no friends in the area. Morrison had told the family that they had to be careful what they said to the neighbours. He trusted no one. They never entertained. Mrs Morrison spent much of her time keeping the house clean, and her incessant dusting got on Morrison's nerves. Sometimes Mary heard her father return at night and her mother go downstairs. There would be shouting and her mother would break down sobbing. The marriage was odd; they were so completely different. Mrs Morrison was a shy simple soul, interested in handicrafts, weaving, gardening, music and dancing. Morrison was totally absorbed in politics. Beatrice Webb met the Morrison family in 1932, and wrote in her diary: 'His little wife is unaffected and dutiful and busies herself with household affairs and her child's education – she stammers badly and is insignificant in looks. . . . They live in a small suburban house, without a servant and are wholly untouched by London Society or any kind of servile snobbishness.'[13]

A party member said to Mrs Morrison in the 1930s that he hoped to see Herbert Prime Minister one day. She managed to get out the retort: 'I hope I never live to see the day.' She feared that the ordeal would be too much for her.[14] In the 1930s her health collapsed and she suffered a nervous breakdown. Lady Cripps befriended her and the two became close, despite bitter rows between their husbands. Lady Cripps said that Mrs Morrison had struggled to keep up with her husband but, while he was robust, she was delicate, and broke under the strain. Relaxing with the Cripps family she recovered, and Morrison spared her more of his time, but only briefly. He was soon immersed in politics again.[15]

Mary was alienated from her father at an early age. Her eighth birthday coincided with the general election of 1929, and Morrison had asked the voters of Hackney to put the cross opposite his name as 'Many Happy Returns for Mary'. She, however, rebuked him for bringing her name into his 'beastly politics'.[16] She could not communicate easily with her mother, while her father, disappointed that she had not shone at school, and annoyed that she did not support him actively in his political career and was generally ungrateful for all that he had bestowed on her, had little time for her.

Her main thought was to escape from this oppressive home. She acquired secretarial qualifications and in 1940 got engaged to, and in April 1941 married, an accountant in the civil service, the son of Morrison's colleague, Tom Williams, then Parliamentary Secretary at the Ministry of Agriculture. At least she pleased Morrison by marrying into a Labour MP's family.[17]

Morrison found the warmth he desired elsewhere, at the homes of party workers in Hackney or Woolwich, with friends of his early days or colleagues at the LCC,[18] or with his sister Edith at Brighton to whom he would pour out his troubles about his 'icicle' of a wife.[19] In these cosy homes he was treated like a favourite son. Invariably the women there were buxom and noisy, unlike Mrs Morrison who disliked them intensely.[20]

His private secretary, Miss Ethel Donald, also mothered him. 'She was always there, near him, watching him, shepherding him, seeing that he was where he ought to be at the right time.'[21] She was a formidable figure on whom Morrison depended. When he lived at County Hall during the international crises of 1938 to 1940 she moved in too, so as to be ready for any emergency. She also held parties in her Park Lane flat for Morrison. She was a paragon of a confidential private secretary.[22]

Morrison probably never had sexual relations with his wife from the early 1920s. Although some of his enemies claimed that he was frequently unfaithful, no firm evidence can be produced.[23] Indeed he so feared that a scandal would damage his political career that it is likely that he avoided *affaires*.[24] Even when out for an innocent meal with a female he was fearful lest gossip should link their names.[25] He was ultra-cautious, admitting to one lady that he never put anything intimate onto a piece of paper.[26] He was flirtatious, and was known to let his hands roam around girls, once receiving a slap across the face at a party conference.[27]

Outside the family Morrison was a genial companion, fun to be with, light-hearted, bubbling with anecdotes and a master of cheeky banter. He had no side; his attitude was the cockney, 'I'm as good as anybody.'[28] The more fastidious found him vulgar and uncouth. Unaware of the sensibilities of others, he would eat peas off a knife at banquets, and puff cigar smoke in a closed car; gruff in his requests for service he rarely uttered a thank-you.[29]

He was as unconcerned as ever about dress. In sharp contrast to the order in which he kept his political affairs, his clothes were untidy: his suits were torn, buttons came off and papers bulged in his pockets. A row of pens poked out of his top jacket pocket.[30] When chided about his sloppiness, he retorted: 'I always look on time spent in making myself look nice – that is, in cleaning my boots, brushing my clothes and having my hair cut, as loss of useful time which could otherwise have been spent in the service of the Labour Government. It is only the goading and stimulating encouragement that I get from Mrs Morrison that makes me look at all presentable.'[31] The clothes he wore were often inappropriate. His plus-fours were frowned on in the House of Commons and at lobby lunches. His formal dress was obviously hired, and eyebrows were raised when he turned up at the LCC in a violet knitted jumper over a waistcoat.[32]

His lack of concern for his appearance upset some people in another way. 'On one occasion he came to a meeting of the Council's most important committee – the General Purposes Committee – without his dentures, persisted in speaking at the meeting and seemed quite unaware of what other members may have thought.'[33] His teeth gave him trouble. He had frequent extractions and many sets of dentures, but he could never find one to fit with ease. His ill-fitting teeth caused him to whistle; over the radio his 's' sounds were sibilant. He even went to a school of broadcasting to improve his delivery.[34] The final straw came in 1939, when his favourite dentist was called up for service; he decided to have all his remaining teeth removed and a new set of dentures made. He feared that otherwise he might have to go through the war without teeth.[35] He was rarely ill in the 1930s; occasionally he had to have his ears syringed, and his feet at times gave him pain.

He had the reputation for meanness, even amongst his closest colleagues who would excuse him as being careful. He rarely paid for another's drink, never gave hospitality and constantly complained that he had little money.[36] His income in the 1930s is unclear. In 1940 it was calculated at about £1,500 a year.[37] The LLP paid him a salary of £500 as Secretary. From 1935 he also received £400 as an MP. When in 1937 this was raised to £600 Morrison submitted a query to the LLP Executive as to whether it wanted to reduce his salary. He pointed out that he had received £500 since the late 1920s and that in 1935 he gave his constituency party £150 and, each year after, £100 towards the provision of an agent, and 'I make contributions towards special efforts and local events from time to time'. The Executive decided to take no action.[38] Morrison's salaries totalled £1,100, and he could very well have made £400 extra from journalism, if not more.

He had a powerful urge for political activity and for domination. He was always bustling, stressing that he had to get on with some job in hand. He seemed bent on some perpetual errand.[39] Ritchie Calder commented: 'His inordinate capacity for work, regardless not only of appearances, but of meal times or of long hours, was responsible for the remark, "Herbert Morrison is Quins!" '[40] A reporter interviewing Morrison said it was 'like trying to drink a glass of beer in an express train dining saloon. You get a mouthful here and there between the shocks created by high speed travel. . . . The interview proceeds in 5 to 10 word sentences between phone calls, secretaries' importunities and visitors coming and going.'[41] 'Relax,' said Morrison, 'I don't know the word.'[42]

He was all work.[43] On a Fabian hike at lunch time 'he brought out the latest Labour Party pamphlets and inquired if the young folks had read them. Tea time found him discussing the LCC Agenda.'[44] At a restaurant near Transport House Morrison was spotted: 'Apparently he regards eating during business hours as an irksome necessity, for he employed practically all the time in dictating correspondence and part of a speech to his secretary.'[45] Even on a car journey he would bury his head in some paper, and always his reading matter was about politics.[46]

Lord Francis-Williams wrote: 'Politics is the air he breathes, the food he eats, the blood in his veins. He feels the movements of political life in his finger tips'; he was the absolute politician, with a 'sixth sense of politics'; 'politics is for him the only reality', 'a medium of expression', 'a way of life'. life'. 'He expressed the wholeness of himself in political action.'[47] He had no hobbies and played no sport. He lived for politics.

Many observers felt that this devotion was because of his restless ambition.[48] He would retort, however: 'My ambition is to do the job I am doing as well as I can, and if another job comes, to do that also. It is to do things, not to be something, that is the worthier ambition.'[49]* In whatever organization he was he had to be the predominant influence. A constant attender and intervener, he was always busily concocting schemes. But he was no autocrat. After wide consultation he would form a conclusion and urge it on his followers. He appeared an autocrat because he was so successful at cajoling support. He took political decisions quickly and never worried over them later. But he was agonizingly indecisive over personal matters – should he or should he not take a particular post was the sort of question that tortured him.

He cannot be dubbed either boss or compromiser. They are simply terms of abuse from those who disliked his particular policy at a particular time. If it went too far, he was a boss; if not far enough, he was a compromiser. He gave a lead, which made opponents dislike him, and he showed courage in standing up to vociferous minorities.[50] His political mind was as 'flexible and adroit as a conjuror's box of tricks',[51] but it was not imaginative. It was a 'pigeon-hole' or 'card index' mind, neat, well-ordered and balanced. He said: 'If I were asked to say what is my supreme purpose in public life, the answer would, I think, be the achievement of tidiness.'[52] Socialism was a way of clearing up muddles. His passion for tidiness was the secret of his success as an administrator and organizer. The impairment to his vision necessitated his taking pains to make his world ordered, so he could make his way through it with ease. With one eye he probed deeply, concentrating on detail and sorting items into neat patterns. The broad sweep was beyond his capacity. The physical disability was also psychic, mental and temperamental.

His concern was with the practical and the efficient. He appealed to common sense and acted the plain blunt man. He was a practical idealist, anxious not just to talk about socialism but to implement it.[53] This kind of approach lacked any spiritual appeal. He wanted his audiences to think, not cheer.[54] No spellbinder, he overlooked 'the hunger of a modern democracy for colour,

* Morrison saw the play *Yellow Sands* by E. and A. Phillpotts (1926) and proclaimed of its intense and dedicated socialist hero, Joe Varwell: 'I'm that remarkable fellow.' He really felt the character was modelled on himself. (Interview, C. A. G. Manning.)

audacity, the clash of drama'.[55] Beatrice Webb wrote: 'What he lacks and lacks completely is any kind of personal magnetism or charm. He is the antithesis of the Artist in politics and is emphatically the plain man and very plain at that.'[56]

His speeches were direct and powerful, full of facts and arguments, but without ornament. He quickly got *en rapport* with his audiences, yet when an assault was needed Morrison did not shirk: 'He is the master of the almost brutal frontal attack, but he also has a shrewd humour which he sometimes brings into play with devastating effect.' His style was cosy and chatty, with patter like a cockney music-hall comedian. His voice was at times squeaky and sibilant, but his arguments and timing were impressive.[57]

Those close to Morrison said that his brain was high powered, able quickly to spot the essential points of any document or discussion. His thought was well ordered; his memory was excellent and he enjoyed tackling a knotty problem. But he was limited. Compared with most politicians of his eminence there were huge gaps in his knowledge and in his cultural experience. He sometimes relaxed with a thriller, visiting the cinema occasionally for a cowboy or gangster film, or the theatre for a musical or a revue. Whenever this inadequacy was mentioned he would blush and go on the defensive, expressing pride in his humble origins and parading lists of the tomes he had read as a teenager. He wished he had been to university. He loved to go to Oxford in the late 1930s and enjoyed the atmosphere of All Souls.[58] Richard Crossman was horrified when he first met Morrison in the luxury of the rooms of A. L. Rowse, sipping port and exclaiming, 'Ah! this is the life. I want to ensure that everyone has a chance to take part in it.'[59] If he could not find time to catch up on the learning he had missed, then he would rely on others who had some specialized knowledge. Morrison had great respect for experts and professionals, and he had the ability to generate amongst them a team spirit and loyalty to him. He collected around him an entourage who were sure that he would be Prime Minister in time. With Herbert they felt they were at the centre of affairs.[60] He listened to their advice attentively; he questioned and argued, and mastered complex issues, fusing together a variety of contributions into a political programme. In the 1930s there is no sign in Morrison of any prejudice against well-educated people. His close colleagues were political friends. It is doubtful if they were really personal friends. He may have been a jovial companion, amusing his cronies with banter in return for hospitality and loyal service, but to none did he ever open his heart. Even in personal relations politics came first.

He was a 'pure politician', a rare breed at that time.[61] He won fame as a party organizer and in local government, which made it hard for influential sections of the party to identify with him. He was not an active trade unionist, and his political outlook was so suspicious of the sectional interests of trade unions that their leaders could not trust him. But neither could the middle-class intellectuals. Although he had intellectual pretensions, he seemed crude.

G

He was unique. The LLP was the only local Labour party in Britain rich enough to provide an organization which enabled its full-time Secretary to pursue a political career outside the party office.

He calculated that Labour could not win solely with an appeal to the working class. The middle class had to be brought under Labour's wing. Morrison was very much the spokesman of his own class. He represented the suburbs, where lived the clerk, the minor civil servant, the municipal employee, the technician, the laboratory assistant, the elementary school teacher, the commercial traveller, the small tradesman and shopkeeper and the office executive. Morrison realized their significance as a new force in politics, totally different from the middle class of the nineteenth century. In alliance with the working class they could overturn the 'established' classes and create 'a well-ordered, well-run society in which neither accident of birth nor occupation determines the status of the individual, but only the efficiency of his contribution to the social whole'.[62]

Although to his finger-tips a political animal, he had a most rigid set of principles for all his public conduct. He was the champion of 'cleanness' in politics. He would come down with a heavy hand on anyone who did not show the same scrupulous regard for propriety, and he would have nothing to do with a false prospectus. Declarations of intention had to mean no more than their inherent powers of fulfilment. He was a supremely honest man.

The overriding characteristic of Morrison was his itch to exercise power.[63] Beatrice Webb observed: 'he *hates* being in the wilderness'.[64] In his early twenties he was Secretary of the South-West London ILP Federation and Chairman of his local branch of the National Union of Clerks. At twenty-seven he was Secretary of the LLP at thirty-two Mayor of Hackney and a year later leader of the Hackney Borough Council; in his thirties he was the youngest member of the Labour Party's NEC, and at thirty-seven the leader of the Labour Party on the LCC. At thirty-two he was an MP, at forty-one a minister and at forty-three the youngest Cabinet minister.

A psychological explanation of this drive for political activity is necessarily complex. The loss of his eye and the consequent taunts of children of his own age drove him into introspection, to self-containment, and stimulated him to assert himself. His small stature also provoked him to win attention. With a policeman as a father he was used to authority and its exercise, and the tense relationship with his father drove him to show how well he could do. The failure of his marriage and the repression of his sexual instincts were further spurs. The limitations of his childhood background and environment, his meagre schooling and early dead-end jobs were a dismal setting from which this intelligent and able young man wished to escape, and yet at the same time they contained much that was dear to him, personified by the mother he worshipped and the sister who took her place. He did not turn his back on his environment, but sought to transform it so that succeeding generations would not have to suffer similar deprivations. As a sensitive observer he was appalled by conditions in south London at the turn of the century, and he found the answer in a substitute religion, socialism, which he first stumbled upon after the phrenologist had given him self-respect and a feeling that with exertion he could make something of himself.

He had good luck. He was the right man at the right place at the right time, and he grasped each opportunity as it arose, winning a reputation that helped him on to the next level. Active in the south London ILP as an organizer he slipped in as Secretary of the LLP on Knee's sudden death. Because he happened to live in Hackney in 1920 he was made Mayor on the sudden death of the previous occupant. He won such glowing praise in the council that he became Hackney's MP and ultimately a minister; he was so successful at the LLP that he moved on to the LCC where again he excelled, and on to the higher echelons of the Labour Party nationally. One job seemed to lead to another.

Chapter 13

Changing Gear, 1931-1933

At all elections in 1931 Labour suffered severe set-backs. In March in the LCC elections Labour had a net loss of seven seats. Its 214,256 votes, well below those polled in 1925, produced 35 members, the exact number of LCC Labour seats in 1925. In the London metropolitan borough elections in November the 459 Labour councillors were reduced to 257, two below the number in 1922, while Labour votes were down to 198,069, only 12,000 more than in 1919. The bitterest blow came at the October general election. Labour's 36 MPs in London shrank to five, and their votes fell by 220,000 to 562,483, which was 30,000 less than their total in 1924.[1] At Hackney South Morrison faced a single opponent, Miss Marjorie Graves, a Conservative. The battle was described as 'one of the most polite and gentle in the country',[2] with the debate mainly about the record of the Labour government and the merits of protection. Miss Graves won with 15,920 votes against Morrison's 12,827. Labour's share of the vote fell in Hackney by 6·5 per cent which was close to the fall nationally of 6 per cent, but less than the drop over London of 10 per cent. Once again Labour under Morrison had performed a little better in Hackney than elsewhere in London.

At the LLP a post-mortem was conducted. Morrison said that he had been prepared for a set-back, but not such a terrific sweep: it was a 'massacre'.[3] He put it down to six factors: the mendacious campaign of the Tory press, especially its story that Labour would endanger post office savings; intimidation from employers; the Tory promise to end unemployment through tariffs; the preferential treatment accorded the government in broadcasting; widespread combinations of Tories and Liberals; and the inadequacy of Labour canvassing.[4] He emphasized 'the confusion arising from our late leaders denouncing our policy as Bolshevism run mad'. Middle-class voters, in particular, who had previously voted Labour on the reputations of Mac-Donald and Snowden, had now voted against Labour.[5] He had stressed in his campaign that he was a free trader, hoping that Liberals, who had no candidate in Hackney, would swing to him.[6] His final assessment, however, was that Liberals and Conservatives had combined against Labour.

He was no longer an MP or a minister, nor was he a member of a borough council. Although he was now back as full-time Secretary of the LLP he did not resume such detailed control as he had in the 1920s. He left more to Donald Daines, the Assistant Secretary, retaining for himself control over policy and broad organizational issues, intervening only in exceptional cases. A new London District Officer, Hinley Atkinson, replaced Dick Windle in 1929. He was a Yorkshireman who had made an excellent reputation as an agent at Birmingham. In the LLP he proved himself a masterly organizer, a wizard at stimulating local parties and running election campaigns. Morrison trusted him, and in turn Atkinson was his devoted servant, to such an extent that some felt that Atkinson was more Morrisonian than Morrison. He waged war against communists and disrupters within local parties and ensured that only reliable candidates were selected. He was tactful in settling disputes within local parties, where he always championed the Morrison line. Morrison could leave the LLP to his dependable colleagues. Also, since in 1931 both parliamentary and local elections had been held, none were expected in 1932 or 1933. Thus Morrison was freed from the pressure of preparing for immediate campaigns.

During these years also he was not absorbed by the LCC. Although he was an alderman, he was not the leader of the Labour opposition. When he left the government in 1931, he expected to resume his leadership of the Labour Party at County Hall. Cecil Manning had been chosen leader in 1929 on the understanding that he would step down when Morrison gave up being a minister. However, Manning withdrew from the leadership in 1930, after an undistinguished year, and was replaced by Lewis Silkin who was party to no such agreement and saw no reason to retire. Tension grew until February 1932 when at a party meeting Silkin was confirmed leader with fifteen votes, while Morrison received fourteen; one ballot paper was returned blank.[7] Morrison was not prepared to serve as Silkin's deputy, and so Charles Latham was selected unanimously. Morrison was just a back-bencher. Lord Silkin recalled that he would have yielded if Morrison had had the grace to ask him. 'Instead he got Latham and Hayward to agitate against me in the party. They finally nominated him against me. I won and Herbert was very aggrieved.' Hayward claimed that Silkin had originally been chosen 'simply to keep the seat warm for Herbert. But when Herbert came back, Silkin argued that Herbert should not trot backward and forward across the river.' Some members felt that he would not be able to pick up from where he left off, after over two years out of touch with the LCC and its detailed operations. It was felt that he had to make up his mind if he was to be an LCC figure or a national politician. Some said that he was now a Parliament man: 'We felt he just couldn't come back when he wanted. He was transient; we were continuous.' In any case his attitude of regarding the leadership as his by right was widely resented. 'The vote was to teach him a lesson.' There was also much sympathy for Silkin who had carried the burden in difficult times.[8] After this defeat Morrison was not much in evidence at County Hall. Silkin's reputation, however, dwindled. He was not a forceful speaker, and members felt that Morrison would have scored more often against the majority. As the election year of 1934 came closer they became increasingly restive. Latham and Hayward told Silkin that Labour could not win under him, that they needed Morrison back in the saddle, and that Morrison would be run against him again and this time was likely to win. Silkin yielded. At the party meeting in February 1933 he proposed Morrison for the leadership, which was unanimously accepted; Silkin became deputy leader and Hayward Chief Whip.[9]

Morrison's behaviour over the leadership of the LCC Labour Party reveals characteristics which were to be repeated later in respect to the leadership of the Parliamentary Labour Party. He regarded the leadership as his. To achieve it he relied on trusty cronies to agitate on his behalf. He stayed sufficiently in the background so that he could say that he had not sought the position. When he was defeated, he became petulant. If rejected for the top job, he would accept no other. In 1932 he would not be deputy to Silkin, in 1935 he would not be deputy to Attlee, and in 1955 he would not be deputy to Gaitskell.*

From the winter of 1931 to the spring of 1933 Morrison had time to speculate and write about policy. His output increased: newspaper articles, pamphlets and an influential book. As a member of the Labour Party's National Executive Committee he threw himself whole-heartedly into the work of the Policy sub-committee and drafted key memoranda and reports. More and more he was known as a national figure, in demand for party meetings in the provinces. As a minister he had won a reputation as an efficient administrator; in 1932 and 1933 he made a reputation as a thinker. He became almost a socialist intellectual, and won the admiration of men like Harold Laski, Kingsley Martin, A. L. Rowse, Douglas Jay, Hugh Gaitskell, Hugh Dalton and Evan Durbin. He attracted such eminent supporters because he combined a grasp of socialist theory with a concern for practicalities. He appeared to have found a way to make socialism work.

At the beginning of 1932 he wrote six articles for Labour journals under the heading of 'The Case for Socialism Re-stated'.[10] Although crudely expressed and naïve, they were the basis for later more elaborate and elegant lectures and pamphlets.[11]

His first thinking in October 1931 was that 'Labour must move to the Left in the true sense of the term – to the real Socialist Left. Not the spurious left policy of handing out public money under the impression that we are achieving a redistribution of wealth under the capitalist system. That is one of the illusions of reformism.' He argued that under capitalist economic conditions

---

* He was deputy to Attlee from 1945 to 1955, but that was not immediately after his own defeat at a ballot.

there was a limit to social reform and to state cash disbursements. The need was for some hard thought about reorganizing industry on a socialist basis. 'The brain and manual workers – including the technical and managerial classes – must be organized for the mutual service of the Commonwealth and not merely to collar the crumbs from the rich man's table.'[12]

He characterized capitalism as production for profit without any social purpose. The system was unplanned. The alternative was socialism, which meant 'the public, collective ownership of the means of producing and distributing wealth; the management of the great economic undertakings efficiently in the interests of society as a whole; the planned and ordered use of our economic resources for common ends.'[13] All land had to be owned by the community so that its use could be decided 'from the viewpoint of social well-being'. He was prepared to allow individuals to own their own houses on long leases, although they would 'have to conform to the general plan of estate development in the interest of amenity'. In industry 'wasteful competition' had to be eliminated, for instance in transport, where all forms would be brought under a National Transport Corporation. Similar corporations would run 'the other great industries vital to the economic life of the nation'. He envisaged above them all a General Economic Advisory Council. Representatives of all industries, together with representatives of the consumers, the trade unions and the state, would meet from time to time in a great National Economic Council with possibly the President of the Board of Trade in the chair. They would examine the trade and industry of the community as a whole and make wide surveys of economic policy; but clearly the responsibility for the wider aspects of economic and industrial policy would be vested in the government and Parliament, leaving the actual management of the industries to those appointed on behalf of the community.

There was no single socialist form of administration; local services could be run by municipalities; those 'of a domestic or of an individual character' by co-operative associations; those of a governmental or routine nature by state departments; but 'those industries which are commercial in character and which require rapid, day-to-day decisions of an important character to be taken, and which must be ready on-the-spot, to meet the present or anticipated requirements of other industries or the general public, will in all probability be run by bodies which have come to be known as Public Corporations'. For each industry there would be a small board of management, appointed by the minister on the basis of qualities needed for the work to be done. The members would have 'competent business heads', and not all would be full time; 'it might be best for them to have contact with other phases of economic and social life'. Once appointed the board would be responsible for the management of the industry, subject to any checks set out in the statute. It would select its own staff. It would present an annual report on its activities. Questions could be put to ministers in Parliament, where also discussions on the work of the boards could take place. 'But Parliament would not run the industries. . . . Ministers would not run such industries but would only have certain specific powers where the general public was involved.' It was a 'business proposition for the community'.

He predicted that unemployment would be abolished; 'but everybody will be expected to work. Society will be entitled to say to a person who could work but will not work, "neither shall he eat".' People would no longer be 'the creatures of the economic power of the employer and the landlord. . . . Just as we have already achieved a wide measure of political emancipation, so Socialism will secure for us an enormous measure of economic emancipation.' 'Releasing us from a low down scramble for bread and butter, Socialism will free the mind and the soul for individual development.' Morrison's socialism was moralistic, indeed religious. He wrote: 'the good Socialist works with religious zeal for the redemption of mankind from the evils of poverty and ignorance. . . . He is conscious of the beauty of the ideal . . . he works on . . . for the deliverance of the human spirit from the enslavement of material things.'[14]

One problem about his Utopia often taxed Morrison: who was to do the 'dirty work'? His answer in the 1930s was the same: 'To a large extent the answer is, Nobody. Machinery [and electric power[15]] will do most of it, as it is doing much of it now. If some of it must be done by human beings, we will either have volunteers or it will be compulsory for limited periods. In any case, the people who do . . . [it] . . . will be held in esteem and will be properly paid.'

His themes run through his first book, *Socialisation and Transport*, published in 1933. Here he told the story of how he conceived the public corporation for London transport. It is a *tour de force* of description and prescription, which revealed Morrison as a major socialist theorist. The book was well received, except at Hackney where the Tory council banned it from their public libraries as 'not of sufficient interest'.[16]

The test for measuring the success of a future Labour government was 'how much private capitalist property organized and conducted for profit has been transferred . . . to the ownership of the community to be organized and directed for public service and for public ends'.[17] He had a time-table in mind: 'The vision of one Minister alone socializing two big industries in one year pleases me enormously; and it is a possibility.'[18]

Morrison was intent on giving his socialist theories practical application. Throughout the 1930s he played a major role in reshaping the policies of the Labour Party, so that when it won a majority it would have ready a well-thought-out and constructive programme. Following the 1931 defeat the National Executive Committee of the Labour Party set out to review future policy. It established a Policy sub-committee, on which served Morrison and Hugh Dalton. Attlee was not a member.[19] Dalton recalled that when he attended this committee he realized that 'Herbert and I must work in harmony',[20] and he noted that over the next twenty years the two of them had the most continuous membership and did most work.[21] The Policy sub-committee was divided into various groups to study particular topics. Here discussions were held with co-opted experts; memoranda were drafted and shaped into policy reports. After approval by the sub-committee and the full NEC, they were submitted to conference for commendation as party policy. In this way Labour policies of the 1930s were produced on transport, electricity, banking, agriculture and coal. Morrison was well pleased with the outcome which showed that the party 'is prepared to face the details and problems of policy as well as affirming broad principles'.[22]

Morrison gave most of his attention to the Re-organization of Industry Group, which had its first meeting in March 1932, when he was asked to prepare memoranda on transport and electricity supply.[23] He worked devotedly.[24] His reports were examined, amended only slightly on verbal points, and approved by the Group, the Policy sub-committee and the NEC which decided to submit them to the annual party conference where Morrison was to move their adoption as party policy. The Morrisonian programme laid emphasis on co-ordination by amalgamating numerous small enterprises, both private and municipal, into national organizations, wholly owned by the public without private shareholders. Morrison translated the form of his London Passenger Transport Board into a National Transport Board and a National Electricity Board.

He insisted on the principle which he had enunciated when Minister of Transport: that board members should be selected solely on account of their capacity. This stand brought him into collision with Ernest Bevin who wanted trade unions to have the right to nominate members. At the annual party conference of 1931 Harold Clay, an official of the TGWU and a member of the LLP's Executive and later its chairman, had criticized Morrison's London Passenger Transport Bill for failing to provide for industrial labour on the board. Morrison produced his usual objections and concluded: 'I hate disagreeing with the Transport Workers' Union, even on this narrow point', and he agreed to submit the question to an inquiry by the General Council of the TUC and the NEC.[25] Morrison and Dalton attended the sessions of the Economic Committee of the TUC in 1931 and 1932 when this topic was under discussion. Bevin circulated members with his criticisms but was in a minority of one as the General Council adopted Morrison's line.[26] The NEC held firm too, despite a letter from John Cliff of the TGWU calling for 'workers' participation'.[27]

Morrison and Clay resumed their debate at the 1932 party conference where Morrison spoke on behalf of his reports on Transport and Electricity.[28] Clay called for board members to be appointed only after consultation with the unions concerned in the particular industries. Workers had to be in the places of power; they were needed to humanize the boards; the stratification of industrial society had to be broken down. Morrison's plan simply perpetuated bosses in the form of an uncontrolled bureaucracy. The unions were divided: the Footplate men backed Clay, while the Railway Clerks and the NUR opposed him. Emanuel Shinwell advised further consultation. Morrison agreed. Since there was a division of opinion in the conference, in the TUC, and in the transport unions, he was prepared to have more consultations. Bevin agreed also to withdraw his amendment; he told delegates that he had taken up his position of hostility to the Morrison view because trade unions in the past had not been fully consulted and, when consulted, as over the appointment of the Traffic Commissioners, were not listened to. He felt he had had a more sympathetic hearing from the Port of London Authority, composed of interests, than from Morrison as a minister.[29]

Despite this dispute the unions continued to return Morrison to the party's National Executive Committee. In both 1932 and 1933 he won third place in the ballot, and in 1934 he came top with over two million votes, beating Dalton, Attlee (making his first appearance on the NEC), and Sir Stafford Cripps.

After the 1932 conference the NEC reconsidered the Morrison line. Lansbury, leader of the party and still Morrison's opponent, urged the NEC to defer Morrison's reports in view of the considerable opposition to the public corporation. Morrison stood firm and carried the NEC with only Lansbury dissenting.[30] This victory was a marked success for Morrison and for the NEC over the Parliamentary Party, between whom there had been for some time a struggle for influence. Lansbury, Cripps and Attlee, as the executive of the PLP, had launched, in a surprise move at a weekly PLP meeting, a call for immediate nationalization of the banks, land, transport, power, coal, iron and steel, and insurance, the abolition of the House of Lords and a drastic revision of parliamentary procedures to speed up government business. Against them were Morrison and Dalton, in favour of a more gradualist approach. Morrison criticized the parliamentary leadership: their 'revolutionary proposals will destroy all hope of the party securing a parliamentary majority'.[31]

Bevin's view that trade unionists should sit on the boards of the public corporations was pressed at joint meetings of the NEC's Policy sub-committee and the TUC's Economic Committee.[32] A formula was devised whereby the boards were to be composed of competent people and would normally include persons from the trade union movement. It was admitted that trade unions should have a place in the direction of the publicly owned industries and therefore would have the right to nominate persons for appointment to the board by the minister. He would have the final choice and not be obliged to follow the unions' advice. There was to be no statutory representation of trade unionists: only the right of consultation before appointment was granted.[33]

The scene was set for the 1933 party conference where it was hoped the Morrison line, agreed now with Bevin, would be accepted. However, Charles Dukes of the General and Municipal Workers moved a resolution for statutory membership on the boards for trade unions. Morrison was silent. Bevin now spoke against Dukes, expressing the fear that a statutory right could become a statutory limitation. The conference passed the resolution by 1,223,000 votes to 1,083,000.[34] Clearly the unions were divided. The approaches of both Bevin and Morrison were rejected. Morrison was not unduly worried. He merely let the whole issue lie quiet. He lost the skirmish in 1932 and 1933, but won the battle in the long term.

Morrison had another tussle with some vocal elements in the Labour Party about another aspect of his programme of socialization. At the 1934 party conference Cripps's Socialist League submitted a series of resolutions calling for the immediate measures of nationalization urged by Lansbury, Cripps and Attlee in 1932 without compensation for those deprived of their property. Morrison pointed out that politicians always had to 'consider what we can persuade the country to accept', and what they would not accept was 'confiscation'. He observed that 'the workers in some ways are more concerned about their little investments than some of the capitalists are about theirs'. He also argued that it was unfair to take over some industries and not pay for them, while leaving other capitalists free to make profits. The policy of the Socialist League was a recipe for industrial dislocation, which, amongst other things, would alienate the managers and technicians whom he was so keen to win for Labour. Compensation was an essential concomitant of public acquisition. Further it was not physically practicable to socialize all industries at the same time. Morrison defeated Cripps's resolution by 2,118,000 votes to 149,000. The conference, like Morrison, clearly thought that 'socialism in our time' was 'romantic nonsense'.[35]

Morrison's view on the composition of the boards of public corporations brought him into conflict with some sections of the Conservative Party. A group, led by Winston Churchill,[36] was fiercely hostile to the London Passenger Transport Bill, and put pressure on the National Government to drop it. The Prime Minister was in favour of the bill, as was the new Minister of Transport, P. J. Pybus. But the Minister decided to make amendments to placate opposition inside his party.[37] In place of ministerial appointment was substituted 'appointing trustees': five individuals, the Chairman of the LCC, the President of the Law Society, the Chairman of the Committee of London Clearing Banks, the President of the Institute of Chartered Accountants and the Chairman of the London Traffic Advisory Committee, who would choose the board of the transport authority. Morrison fulminated against this 'thoroughly bad proposal. It is essential that there should be public accountability for the composition of the Board.'[38] Now there was no responsibility to Parliament. Such selection by interests would open the door to 'log-rolling, jobbery and back-stairs influence'.[39]

Soon after the London Passenger Transport Board came into operation his criticism gave way to praise. The appointing trustees selected members of the board, 'as I intended',[40] with Lord Ashfield as Chairman and Frank Pick as his deputy; the other members were John Cliff, Assistant Secretary of the TGWU, one each from the LCC and the Surrey County Council and one from the London Traffic Advisory Committee: the redoubtable Sir Henry May-bury.[41] And as the board embarked on major developments, such as tube extensions, the substitution of trolley buses for trams, improvement of junctions between tubes and suburban lines and electrification of suburban lines, Morrison gleefully pointed out that he had been responsible for setting up the organization which made such developments possible.[42]

Throughout the 1930s Morrison was the leading advocate of the public corporation, to which he was as committed as in the 1920s he had been to local authorities. To those who chided him for his shift of loyalties he pointed out that for large trading undertakings the tendency was 'for their technical and administrative requirements to burst the bonds of municipal boundaries and municipal methods of organization'. Their interminable committee sessions did not allow enterprise to flourish, and councillors and officials were just not expert enough.[43]

Morrison is sometimes regarded as a man who had scant interest in ideas. However, he sought to restate socialism to meet the conditions of the 1930s. He also sought to make party members more interested in socialist theory so that they could educate the public in its fundamental principles. He said: 'Do let us remember that the degree to which any future Labour Government can socialize industry, the speed with which we can establish the Socialist State, is going to depend on the degree of Socialist understanding among the electorate of our country.'[44] The interlude of theorizing was brief. During 1933 Morrison increasingly turned his attention to the forthcoming elections to the London County Council.

Chapter 14

Leader of the London County Council, 1934-1940

Morrison was proud of the LCC, 'the greatest municipal authority in the world', resembling in many ways the government of a state rather than of a city. Covering an area of 117 square miles and a population of four and a half million, it had a budget of £40 million a year. He felt it was 'the greatest single unit of executive administration to be found anywhere'.[1] Of County Hall he said it was 'beautiful and inspiring',[2] and of his colleagues, they were 'the finest band of lieutenants' he could ever have desired.[3] As leader of the LCC from 1934 to 1940 he was tremendously happy, because he was constructing something, and he could see what was being built. He was acknowledged a success, even by his opponents. In later years he would wish he was back at the LCC.[4] So attached was he to the LCC that he 'resented criticism of it as criticism of himself'[5] and could not bear to think of its abolition. He was a fierce opponent of the London Government Act of 1963 which brought about the destruction of the LCC. His last years were filled with sadness at its approaching demise. His own life span was almost that of the LCC: 1888 to 1965 for Morrison, 1889 to 1965 for the LCC. The man and the institution were strangely one.

Most of Morrison's time between 1934 and 1940 was spent at County Hall, which was his real headquarters, not the LLP office where he only briefly popped in to see that all was well. During the international crises of the late 1930s he often slept at the LCC to be on the spot for any emergency. He had a camp-bed in his room, tucked away behind a screen. He padded the corridors of County Hall in his pyjamas. The press made much of this devotion to duty, and noted parcels of laundry being taken to his room.[6] He was in his LCC office every day when he was not away from London, and he read the reams of paper that flowed around the LCC. 'I wish I'd got two brains,' he told an official, 'for all the reading I've got to do.'[7]

In 1934 Morrison and his leading colleagues expected to increase their numbers, but not to win a majority. Preparations for the election had begun as soon as the previous election in 1931 was over. Local parties were urged to select able candidates, with time to devote to the LCC, not just local worthies or party members of long standing.[8] The Executive of the LLP set up study groups on housing, health, education and public assistance, and their reports were the basis for policy statements. From headquarters streamed out a flow of circulars giving advice on routine party work, legal and administrative problems, and policy and its presentation. Morrison drafted the manifesto which was approved by a joint meeting of the Executives of the LLP and of the LCC Labour Party. It was a model of generalization. Its message was that it was time, after twenty-seven years of the Municipal Reformers, for a change. A speeding up of programmes was promised, but without waste or fraud. Labour refused to accept the amount of the rates as the final test of good municipal administration. Municipal Reformers practised false economy which meant in the long run even heavier expenditure. Labour's main slogan was 'Let Labour Rule and London Flourish'. Others were 'Let us Get on with the Job', 'A Healthy London', 'For the Children's Sake', 'A Decent Treatment for the Poor' and 'Show Your Disgust'. Considerable aid was given by the *Daily Herald*, *Daily News*, the *Star* and *Reynold's News* which put Morrison's arguments to the fore. Against them the Beaverbrook papers thundered. Together with the Rothermere Press they started a campaign against the Co-op, urging the LCC not to allow the Co-op to tender for contracts. Morrison came out for no discrimination. In return the Co-op shops were filled with Labour propaganda.[9] Morrison held conferences for candidates to discuss housing, education, health, public assistance and finance. It was the most efficient campaign the LLP had ever waged. Morrison, Daines and Atkinson were well pleased at the performance of the machine. After the poll was over they sat at headquarters waiting for the results to be phoned in. Around midnight it was announced that Labour had won all six seats in Hackney. Morrison now knew that Labour had won, since Hackney was the average London borough. He had feared a deadlock with the balance held by the Liberals.[10] Labour polled 341,390 votes, the highest ever gained by any party in an LCC election. Its share of the vote was 51 per cent; the Municipal Reformers mustered 45 per cent, the Progressives three per cent and the Communists one per cent.[11] Labour had 69 councillors, 34 more than in 1931. With 11 aldermen Labour had a total of 80 members, a majority of 16, over the 55 Municipal Reform councillors and nine aldermen. They had lost 28 seats, and the Progressives (Liberals) had lost all their six members.

Beatrice Webb opened her diary entry for 14 March: 'Labour wins London: Herbert Morrison is the organizer of victory – a long pull and a hard pull lasting twenty years – the final victory doing endless credit to his doggedness, skill and masterfulness. He is a Fabian of Fabians; a direct disciple of Sidney

Webb's. . . . [He is] the very quintessence of Fabianism in policy and outlook.'

The Tories were thunderstruck, and Labour all over the country, and indeed socialists abroad, were heartened. After 1931 Labour had looked shattered. Yet within three years Labour had taken over the capital of Britain. James Griffiths was chairing a miners' conference in South Wales when the results were announced. They sang 'Cwm Rhondda' and 'everyone thought it was manna from Heaven'.[12] The victory also raised Morrison's standing as the man who could deliver the votes. He was looked on more and more as a potential leader of the party.

On his first appearance in the council chamber after the triumph, he 'smiled the smile of the modest victor, adjusted the red carnation in his buttonhole, smoothed his rebellious hair. Perhaps his speech seemed the best because it was the only one that was really audible.'[13] He did not gloat: 'I want the Party in London to enter upon the great and glorious responsibilities of governing the capital city not in the spirit of mafficking or khaki politics, but in a spirit of conscientious devotion to the public well-being and to the cause of the people.'[14]

From the moment of the 1934 success, 1937 was imprinted on his mind. That election would be far more crucial than 1934. It would be the test of whether Labour had been a successful administration. Winning in 1937 was his objective.

At the first party meeting after the election Morrison was unanimously chosen leader, a post he was to keep without challenge until he joined the Churchill government in May 1940. Rarely has a political leader commanded such loyalty. Many members of the LCC in this period attest to the good spirit of the Labour party. They were thrilled to be governing London, and were aware that all eyes were upon them and that opponents would be keen to spot blunders.[15] Morrison's supremacy was confirmed by his successes. Whatever he touched seemed to his advantage. Those members of the LCC who were also MPs contrasted the atmosphere of intrigue against the parliamentary leader in the Commons with the spirit of harmony inside the party at the LCC. All the top members admitted that he was the best man for the job. They had been brought onto the LCC by Morrison who had encouraged them. Their dependence on him enabled him to keep together a highly competent team.

At the first party meeting, too, the post of deputy was abolished. Instead there was an informal collective leadership.[16] A clue to its identity appears in the minutes of this meeting, where it is stated that Morrison had selected the chairmen and vice-chairmen of all committees after consulting Silkin, Hayward and Latham.[17] These three plus Morrison constituted what Morrison called 'the Presidium'. The day after the election results were declared these four met at a restaurant for lunch. Besides taking the most pressing decisions they made a compact to talk over major and controversial matters amongst themselves in private. But in public and before the rest of the party they would present a united front. This 'quadrumvirate' was the political leadership of the LCC between 1934 and 1940: a group of friends who could handle together delicate topics without fear of one letting the rest down. They practised arguments on each other and chewed over the consequences of taking certain courses of action. Their meetings could be anywhere: a gathering in Morrison's room or a huddle in a corridor, even a bunch of phone conversations. Never did their unity break. From the raised dais at the party meeting they surveyed the other members who invariably followed their guidance.[18]

Morrison was allowed as leader to attend meetings of all committees, but only occasionally would he sit in, when some tricky problem was under discussion. There were, however, two committees at which he was a most regular attender: General Purposes and Finance. Through these committees Morrison could keep his eye on what the other committees were doing. The only 'operational' committee which he attended with any regularity was the Town Planning Committee between 1934 and 1936, when he was involved in the establishment of a green belt around London.

Morrison allocated the members of the Presidium to key chairmanships. Charles Latham was Chairman of Finance, dubbed 'the iron Chancellor' for his strict scrutiny over the estimates of the other committees.[19] 'He tried to cut you down and put the brake on', said the former Chairman of the Parks Committee.[20] Dr Charles Brook, then Chairman of the Blind Committee, recalled that he and his chief officer would appear before Latham's committee and his officials. Latham would submit the chairman to 'a terribly tough' series of questions, forcing him to justify his claims for expenditure. The chairman emerged 'very subdued'.[21] Morrison, conscious of his lack of financial expertise, relied heavily on Latham.[22] Council officials admitted that Latham was 'very astute'.[23] A trade unionist recalled putting a case to Morrison and Latham for increased wages. Morrison thanked him for putting the case so well. Latham slipped Morrison a piece of paper, at which he glanced and then said, 'but the facts are – the number of men involved is so and so, their pay is such and such', and the claim was turned down.[24]

Isaac Hayward was Morrison's Chief Whip. His was a crucial responsibility, as Morrison's eyes and ears and strong arm. Hayward's job was to feel the party's pulse, to relay members' views to Morrison and to cajole members to follow the agreed line.[25] Morrison also used Hayward as a troubleshooter. In 1934 he was Chairman of the Public Assistance Committee, where a firm but deft hand was required to make the administration of relief more humane and yet not over generous'

Another key appointment was the chairmanship of the Highways Committee which was responsible for Waterloo Bridge. Here Morrison installed his former parliamentary private secretary, George Strauss. On the Hospitals Committee Morrison appointed Somerville Hastings, a distinguished surgeon, who was respected both by the medical staff of the LCC and by the Tory doctors on the council. To Silkin was allocated the chairmanship of the Housing Committee. Morrison felt that Labour would be judged at the next election on how well it had fulfilled its pledge to increase slum clearance and house building. For this major task he felt a senior figure was vital. Silkin's appointment was a surprise even to Silkin who had never taken much interest in housing. Previously he had specialized in hospitals and expected the Health Committee. There was a member who seemed to have a claim to the Housing Committee. Richard Coppock, Secretary of the National Federation of Building Trades Operatives, had been brought to the LCC as an alderman because of his knowledge of housing, and he wanted the chairmanship. Morrison rejected him. He argued that if Coppock was appointed, opponents would allege that he was a tool of trade unions in the building trades.[26] Morrison's concern to avoid suspicion that vested interests were controlling the LCC is again seen in the case of the Establishment Committee which dealt with the staff of the LCC. He asked Dr Esther Rickards to be chairman. She said: 'I know nothing about staff or trade unions.' 'Ah!', he replied, 'but you've no axe to grind.'[27]

Morrison was keen to use the talents of women. In addition to Dr Rickards he appointed as chairmen Mrs E. M. Lowe to Education and Miss Agnes Dawson to General Purposes. He loved to appoint women to positions which they had never held before, like Mrs Helen Bentwich to the Fire Brigade Committee, much to the consternation of the fire officers who felt such a committee was not suitable for a female, and Lady Nathan to the Metropolitan Water Board, 'to stir that lot up'.[28] He appointed his chairmen after consulting his Presidium and then submitted his list to the full party meeting which always approved his choice. He dismissed them at will, too, and on some occasions there was a tearful scene outside his room.

Morrison is often called the boss of the LCC in the 1930s, but the unanimous verdict of all the surviving committee chairmen was that he was not dictatorial, that he left them and their committees a very extensive discretion and never interfered in their responsibilities.[29] They would talk things over with Morrison if they were contemplating new proposals or new expenditure, or if a matter was arising which would cause trouble from the opposition, from their own party or from interests outside the council. They would go to Morrison even before putting the matter before their own committees. Morrison would listen attentively, asking an occasional question, then he would say what he would do. Morrison would also ask a chairman to see him, if he was worried, and ask how a particular problem had arisen. If he had any ideas of his own, he would invite the chairmen for a chat to see their reactions, probing the value and drawbacks of particular proposals. One chairman said, 'Even if he disagreed you never felt upset. You felt better for having listened to his views, because he had such good judgment.' But there was one thing a chairman had not to do: take a matter to Morrison that they had already discussed. 'He would refuse to look at it, saying, I never boil my cabbage twice.'[30]

Lord Latham recalled that Morrison 'gave the chairmen of committees freedom to develop their own plans and their own personalities'. Dr Rickards said that one could put any view to him and he would discuss it. Even back-benchers had the same experience. Lady Nathan recalled: 'He always took notice of what you said to him and he didn't stamp on you at the start.'[31] His style was different from later leaders. People who served under Morrison and then under Latham (1940–7) and Hayward (1947–65) were clear that Morrison 'led with a much looser rein', and was 'less bossy'.[32]

He could be remote to back-benchers who had incurred his displeasure. He excluded from office Cecil Manning and Santo Jeger because they opposed him and because he didn't trust them.[33] Reginald Stamp and Maurice Orbach felt that Morrison was inaccessible. They could not get hold of him at lunch or in the corridors, and when they tried to beard him in his room they found 'a dragon at the door' in his secretary Miss Donald.* A few members who were disgruntled said that left-wingers felt left out, with little to do except support the leadership. They could raise questions at the party meeting, but if hostile, were frowned on.[34] The dominant impression, however, was of general acceptance of the leadership.

Mary Agnes Hamilton wrote that the weekly party meeting was 'an exhibit of democratic leadership in action'. Issues of policy were frankly stated and a lead was given. Discussion was real and the final decision was a genuine corporate affair.[35] The Policy Committee, composed of the chairmen, was a steering committee for the party meeting. It met every Monday for two to three hours to consider all new policy proposals.[36] At this stage members would have before them papers from the officials of the committee concerned and memoranda from the chairman and the members of the party on that committee. The matter would be thrashed out and a decision reached. This conclusion would be conveyed to the next meeting of the full party. The LCC met at 2.30 p.m. every Tuesday. One hour before, the party group of members met to go over the agenda and take final decisions on the party line. There was not time to go into detail, and its normal practice was to accept the recommendations of the Policy Committee. After all, each major item had been considered by the officials, the council committee, the party group on that committee, the Policy Committee and probably by Morrison with his Presidium and in informal conversation with his chairmen. Morrison's concern for the Policy Committee and the party meeting was such that he seems never to have missed a meeting of either. Measures just sailed through. In a racy style Morrison pushed home his points of common sense. Although he put his arguments quickly and succinctly, he was no steam-roller. Members

---

* Miss Donald was Morrison's personal secretary, paid by the LLP. She sat in the ante-room to Morrison's room at the LCC. Morrison also had a secretary provided by the LCC for work of a 'non-party' character. Miss Donald served the party meetings and the whips, and handled Morrison's engagements. Her expenditure was separate from that of the LCC; even her postage was accounted for by the LLP.

would say what they wanted, and yet Morrison always won. He was so close to the party that he never put anything forward likely to be defeated.[37]

As well as being strategically placed at the centre of a network of relationships with the elected members, Morrison had a similar web of contacts with the permanent officials. Their view of him was the same as that of his officials at the Hackney borough council and the Ministry of Transport. 'He had a wonderful and marvellous way with officials. You had to consult him if anything cropped up that was likely to cause a rumpus. He read and thoroughly mastered all his documents in great detail. He knew the facts and the practical situation. He wasn't aloof and he would work with officials at all levels. He drove you hard, but you felt that his zeal inspired you and he was very appreciative of work that was well done.' Morrison would argue with officials on both policy and detail. He was always ready to change any preconceived views when he was faced by the facts and yet he did not just fall in with the officials' views; he was at times prepared to stand against them and say, 'that is my decision'.[38]

One of the first things he did as leader, on the morning after Labour had won in 1934, was to call the chief officials together for a conference. Here he spoke about their role and their relationships to him and to the other elected members. He said that their advice was required, and that he would always listen. He wanted from them a discussion of the pros and cons of various courses of action, with at the end definite recommendations. He wanted to know what they thought, not what they might think he would want to hear. In turn Morrison told his members: 'Always listen to the officials before you decide anything.'[39] He urged officials to be positive. He told Sir Howard Roberts in respect of legal advice: 'I don't want to know why I can't do this. Tell me how I can.'

With one official Morrison had a specially close relationship, the Clerk, Sir George Gater, who acted as his chief adviser, performing the same kind of functions as Dr Tee at Hackney and Sir Cyril Hurcomb at the Ministry of Transport.[40] Educated at Winchester, the former Chief Education Officer of the LCC began his service as Clerk at the same time as Morrison became leader in 1934, and he remained until 1939 when he entered the civil service. Tall, dignified and urbane, 'as gentle as an archdeacon', he was deferential to Morrison.[41] Morrison wrote to Gater in 1937: 'You have contributed more than you know to my work here since 1934. It is [sic] has *been* a great comfort to open my mind and heart to you and *know* that my confidence would be respected. You are a very great administrator and a first class psychologist.'[42] In 1939 he wrote again: 'what success I have achieved in my work for the Council has been in no small measure due to your kindly and diplomatic tact.'[43] Gater was devoted to Morrison, admiring his drive, buoyancy, and general capacity. Their relationship was happy. So dependent was Morrison on Gater, that some nicknamed him 'Mr Gater-Morrison'.[44]

Gater provided clerks to all the committees and so was in contact with all that the council did. From the officials' side he was able to keep an eye on all the council's responsibilities to complement Morrison's similar view over the politicians. Morrison also saw reports and papers in draft or proof form – officials' memoranda, committee reports and committee agenda – which enabled him to hold something up, to call in people for consultation and to intervene at an early stage before a policy had hardened.[45] He also learned what was amiss through his postbag. He was able to pick out significant complaints and bring them to the attention of the appropriate chairman or official. He culled the press for complaints, and took up grievances brought to him by trusted members of the party. He would gather officials and chairmen in his room to discuss controversial topics. He appeared mischievous as he pitted one against the other. He was a catalyst, sparking off a debate which would result in a constructive conclusion.[46]

Morrison was proud of Labour's achievements for the LCC staff. Salary cuts imposed during the period of economy after 1931 were done away with, and increases in pay, and better conditions, were granted. He was strict that all negotiations should be with appropriate trade unions. He treated union officials fairly but firmly. He did not impose a closed shop. Instead notices were prominently displayed, advising staff of the advantages of joining trade unions. Employees of contractors for the LCC were given improved conditions through new standing orders. Under Labour the staff of the LCC grew to meet new demands and to provide extended services. They were proud to work for an authority which won such a high reputation. Officials admitted that there was a difference between the period of Labour rule and what had gone before. No longer was keeping the rate down top priority. They had greater freedom to go ahead with projects and develop their services.[47]

Morrison was anxious that officials and members of the LCC should behave to each other in the proper way, which he spelled out to the two sides in meetings with them. 'He feared that the Labour people would be cowed by their inferiority, socially or educationally, to the officials, or else they'd go to the other extreme and be too bossy.'[48] Members were not to fraternize with the officials. They were told not to shake hands at County Hall, nor to address each other by their first names, nor to accept their hospitality. All contact was to be at the LCC. He pointed out to the officials that Labour people, if offered hospitality, would be unable to afford to repay it and would be embarrassed. These rules did not imply, Morrison said, any personal unfriendliness. Both sides had always to be courteous.[49] Morrison was alert to stop practices that could upset the relationship between an official and a member. Their lunch tables were kept separate.[50] Members had to pay for any meals provided by an LCC institution which they were inspecting, to eradicate the abuse of free food and flowing drink provided by some of the old boards of guardians. And at an LCC Labour Party meeting in 1935 Morrison 'reported that attention had been drawn to a practice of securing money subscriptions among committee members for presents to retiring officers and that whilst the sentiment behind such actions is understood and appreciated it is felt that the practice is undesirable'. It was stopped.[51] Above all members had to be free from the least suspicion of personal interest in making appointments or promotions. He warned the officials to report to him any lobbying for promotion or appointment; the candidate would be automatically disqualified. Soon after this lecture was given a vacancy occurred in the Engineer's department. The man with the best paper qualifications was the son of a Labour member who went to the head of the department to put his son's case. The head reported it to Herbert, who met his Presidium, and then ordered the rejection of the son.[52] Morrison was acutely sensitive to the accusation that Labour would use its patronage to advance the interests of its supporters. He was determined that no scandal should besmirch Labour's reputation: 'the only thing for which I would preserve capital punishment would be jobbery, bribery, and corruption in public services or robbery from public funds.'[53]

Morrison was the enemy of special interests which might make a member blind to his public duty. He advised members to stay beyond an arm's length from contractors who provided services to the council.[54] He disliked Labour members on the LCC being members of their borough council, since he felt they would look only at the interests of their borough and not at the welfare of London as a whole,[55] and he insisted that members should not tell their trade unions of committee business before it appeared in the council's public agenda.[56] The only reward for a member was a sense of public service, and perhaps the pride of seeing his name publicized. He urged officials when preparing reports for the press to have the correct initials and designations of the members. 'It is important to get them right. It is, after all, all we get.'[57] Morrison's scrupulous attitude earned him the praise of the opposition. 'Many may differ from Herbert Morrison politically but all admire his integrity and honesty.'[58] Morrison ensured that, as Labour won majorities in local government, it was not identified with the spoils system.

Morrison's success at the LCC also depended on his capacity to run rings around the opposition. They regarded him as formidable.[59] His condescending humour was annoying and no one on the opposition side had his agility in debate. They just could not answer his brilliant repartee, nor trip him up. His mastery of standing orders was such that he could manipulate the council's procedures to their disadvantage. He could disarm opposition by sheer effrontery. In 1935 he advised the LCC not to give a grant to the Kent and Essex County Councils for the building of a road tunnel under the Thames from Dartford to Purfleet. The Municipal Reformers complained that as Minister of Transport Morrison had urged the council to make the grant. He replied: 'As leader of the council I repudiate entirely the former Labour Minister of Transport, and reserve the right in the future to repudiate the present leader of the London County Council if my public responsibilities in another position require it.'[60] He continued 'if he went through life assuming that in every public office he held he had always to say exactly what he had said before he would "get in a mess" '.[61] In a speech to the miners of Blyth in 1935 he said:

> The only trouble with the Tories on the council is that we cannot get them to fight enough.
>
> You have heard of the fellow who was dead and would not lie down. There are people who are alive and won't stand up in opposition to us.
>
> It is becoming pathetic. They have an inferiority complex. They have come to such a pass that now and again I have offered to help them draft the amendment and give them my aid in discharging their function in opposition.[62]

He would 'leg-pull' the opposition; with his head on one side, his quiff poking up, a quizzical look on his face, and his finger wagging at the opposition, he would say, 'you naughty boys'. He was like 'a cheeky Cockney sparrow with a perky sense of fun'.[63]

Often Latham, or Charles Gibson, was put up to speak first, to make the opposition angry with denunciations. Finally Morrison would sum up in a conciliatory manner to soothe the opposition and yet never give anything substantial away. His performance raised the morale of the Labour benches, and yet cooled down the opposition so that the policies got through easily, while the press gave the meeting publicity, because there had been a row. Up to the time Morrison spoke the meeting was tense, passions were alight, but with a few witticisms he broke the tension. The younger Municipal Reform members were ashamed of their own leadership, which one member described as 'very weak, a lot of silly old boys with safe seats', and another as 'complacent, die-hard stick-in-the-muds'.[64] To some extent the battle between Labour and Municipal Reform was one between comparative youth and age. While the Municipal Reform leaders were men in their sixties, the Labour leaders were in their forties.[65] In private Morrison got on well with opposition members. When the opposition went on a deputation to him, he put them at ease and listened carefully, showing that he fully understood their position and sometimes he accepted a proposal. Although he rarely made a major concession he left them feeling that they had had a fair crack of the whip.[66]

The decision-making process at the LCC was so complex that it is impossible to attribute to any one person responsibility for a particular decision. Everything was considered by such a variety of people that one can describe the process only as 'teamwork'. Morrison's role, however, as captain of the team was crucial. Sir Isaac Hayward summed it up: 'On any major issue he would consult a large number of people, the officials, the chairman of the committee, experts, and he had an uncanny judgment. He would spot if something was not quite right.'[67] Morrison made the LCC a byword for efficient and honest government.

Morrison's objective was to make the LCC an exhibition of Labour's capacity to govern.[68] He contrasted the speed of decision-making under Labour with the vacillation of the Municipal Reform years. They had talked for ten years about Waterloo Bridge; Labour began demolition in ten weeks. A green belt around London had been discussed for ten years; Labour produced a scheme within one. In the first year of office Morrison announced each month a batch of decisions so that 'London soon realized that the new majority was a Party of action and decision'.[69] Speedily Labour drew up three-year programmes for the major functions, housing, town planning, health, education, even parks. Morrison characterized the Municipal Reform period as one of uncertainty, confusion, indecision and negation. He described the Municipal Reformers as Mr Dilly, Mr Dally and Mr Can't, whose slogan was 'Something Saved and Nothing Done'. Labour's characteristics were vigour, decision, efficiency, business-like administration: creative, progressive and public spirited. Obstacles which had impeded the Municipal Reformers seemed to melt away. Labour was prepared to spend more, to employ more staff, to develop services, to plan and to act quickly. He presented Labour as the party which cared, especially for children. It had idealism and regarded County Hall as the servant of the people of London, an instrument of social service, its work 'holy work',[70] to evolve 'a new and nobler city'. Even opponents reckoned that he was 'the man who did more to refashion the face of the City since Sir Christopher Wren'.[71]

Morrison gave most prominence in his propaganda to housing. Labour was waging an offensive against slums. There were more clearance areas and compulsory purchase orders; new sites were found for building. The opposition attacked Morrison for the deliberate injection of LCC housing into previous Tory strongholds. The standard of the houses was improved; they were larger and had more facilities, and Labour scrapped the Municipal Reform tenement where three families shared one bathroom. Rents were reduced for tenants coming from the slums, who often found the increased rents difficult to bear when they were rehoused. New houses and flats were built more quickly. More capital expenditure was incurred on the LCC housing programme.*

Symbolic of Labour's determination was to be a new estate on the Hackney Marshes. To make a significant impact on the slums of the East End it was necessary to have a site where considerable numbers could be rehoused, preferably in the vicinity of the former homes of the tenants who did not relish a move to distant parts. In 1935 after scouring the map Morrison suggested that only one area was possible, the Hackney Marshes. He proposed to take a

* See Tables (e), (f), (g), (h) for statistics of LCC expenditure on various services.

thirty-acre site out of 340 acres and build accommodation for about eight thousand people. The land selected was somewhat detached from the rest of the Marshes. It was not used for organized games, only casual games, and an occasional fair was held there. Lord Rothermere gave Morrison his whole-hearted support for a measure that would bring improved living conditions to the East Enders. Even the Tory minister approved. However the reaction in Hackney was hostile. In 1922 Morrison had led a successful opposition to a Municipal Reform scheme to take thirty-seven and a half acres from the Marshes to build a factory. Now he faced a bitter campaign, in which were involved many of his former allies, who protested at the violation of land which had been granted as open space in perpetuity.[72] Morrison offered to substitute as open space a fifty-acre site at Chigwell, five miles away, and he mounted an onslaught on the preservationists for obstructing an improvement in the living conditions of the slum dwellers. He said that those who stood in his way would be pushed out of the way. 'The Dictator of Hackney' was how he was dubbed.[73] 'I will not surrender' was his retort.[74]

The preservationists took the issue to court where the judge upheld their contention. The minister could not allow the LCC to take over the space which had been made open for perpetuity by a private Act. The only way to undo that Act was by another. Morrison now prepared to draft a private bill for that purpose: 'If I knew that the promotion of the Bill meant certain defeat for this Labour majority at the next council election, I am so convinced of my duty to the people of the East End that I would do it.'[75] However, a compromise was at hand, worked out by the Hon. Arthur Villiers who offered to sell to the LCC a twenty-and-a-half-acre site, adjoining the Marshes, on which houses could be built. Morrison accepted, although the price was higher than the LCC would have had to pay for his first choice.[76] The Hackney Marsh remained intact, the LCC got its site for the slum dwellers, but Morrison had failed to build his monument on the Marshes.

More money was spent on public health and welfare services, especially on the hospitals, which were modernized and re-equipped. More staff were employed, at higher salaries and with better conditions. Patients had a better deal; their diets were improved; wirelesses were installed, and their contributions for the residential treatment of tuberculosis ended. Mental patients were allowed a fortnight's holiday by the sea. Visitors to hospital inmates could have their fares paid. Morrison was proud of the LCC hospitals. He even complained to the BBC whenever an LCC hospital was mentioned on the radio without the initials LCC being prefixed.[77] Labour extended midwifery services and made free ambulances available by day and night for all maternity cases. Improvements in services for the blind stimulated the following electoral doggerel.

> For twenty seven continuous years
> With frosty eyes and tight shut ears
> The Tories spurned the poor Blinds' plea

To be considered humanly.
And then when Labour won the day
To show the world a better way
With ears alert and kindlier faces
It wiped away the old bad traces
That Bumbledom had still retained
And those that sat in darkness gained.[78]

New schools were built and old ones rebuilt; more was spent on their furniture, books and apparatus. More attention was given to playing fields. More staff were employed, at better conditions, to reduce the size of classes. Special schools were improved, with more aids for the handicapped; more nursery schools were set up. There was an improvement in the medical treatment of school children; more health inspections and more milk were provided. Some 'Tory Shylockisms', the result of economy cuts, were abolished: prizes were restored, more county scholarships introduced, while children in residential schools had an increase in pocket money, in educational visits, and a camp holiday each year. Technical and commercial educational establishments were further developed.

Morrison paid considerable attention to public assistance. His aim was to administer the service without any of the harshness of the old Poor Law, but there was to be no encouragement of layabouts. The barrack-like mixed workhouses were broken up, and the old, the sick, the blind, children and expectant mothers were treated separately, instead of all together in institutions for paupers. The LCC restored a coal allowance and eased the conditions for the receipt of relief. But the LCC, argued Morrison, had a right to know if an individual really needed help, and assistance was not fixed higher than what could be earned by a man when employed. At training centres the hours were reduced, and married men were required to attend only in exceptional circumstances. He was keen on training for the able bodied, to fit men for jobs, and it was to be punitive if the man was a shirker.[79]

One particular reform in the administration of public assistance was close to Morrison's heart. Under the Municipal Reformers applicants for relief had to appear before investigating committees of councillors and co-opted members. Morrison, in the face of some opposition inside the Labour party and from council officials, decided to abolish these committees which numbered about 120. In their place, full-time adjudicating officers were to interview the applicants and take the decisions. They had to report to twenty area committees, to whom they could refer difficult cases and to whom the applicants could appeal. Morrison wanted to streamline the administration of relief and to help the applicant by having his case dealt with by a professional in privacy. Morrison was keen to abolish the investigating committees because he felt that enough people of the right quality could not be found to serve on them.[80] The cutting down of lay participation in the administration of public assistance laid him open to the charge of being bureaucratic. He pointed out that elected members decided major policy, heard appeals and could deal with difficult cases. His vindication came when the new scheme got under way and very few appeals were made against the decisions of the officers.[81]

Services were allowed to develop at a faster pace. New headquarters and appliances were provided for the fire brigade. New main drainage schemes were proceeded with. More major highways and bridge improvements were undertaken. A great change came over the LCC parks. Victoria Park in the East End was transformed with a wide range of facilities, and other parks acquired more baths, sun-bathing sections, gymnasia, refreshment places, playgrounds, paddling pools, athletic grounds and bowling greens. Mixed bathing was allowed; during one hot summer in the 1930s the Chairman of the Parks Committee had suggested keeping the baths open till midnight. Morrison opposed: 'They'll be fucking one another.'[82] He was proud of the amenities for children, especially the entertainment during school holidays, when comedians, conjurers and story-tellers kept the children enthralled. Special children's lavatories were built to lessen the chance of indecent assault; and specially designed saucer-shaped paddling pools, to help parents to spot their children, were installed.

Cadet corps for military training were banned from LCC schools. He felt it wrong to inculcate militaristic values into the young. The 'cult of violence' had to be curbed and 'love for liberty and humanity' rekindled. In any case the corps were an unwarrantable interference with the liberty of the young.[83] He stopped school visits to military displays such as the Hendon pageant and the Aldershot tattoo.[84] Empire Day was renamed Commonwealth Day so that it should no longer be an occasion for implanting feelings of militarism, jingoism and racial superiority,[85] and Armistice Day was renamed Armistice and Peace Day to encourage attitudes favourable to the settlement of international disputes by arbitration and the League of Nations.[86] Municipal Reformers condemned him for lack of patriotism, while some of his own party wanted him to go further and have May Day a school holiday. But he refused to close the schools for a party political celebration.[87]

On gaining a majority at County Hall Morrison was able to introduce a reform he had long dreamed of: a green belt ringing London to stop its sprawl. In January 1935 a simple and practical scheme was introduced. Over three years the LCC would provide a sum of £2 million as grants to local authorities around London, for them to buy land which they were to own and administer and on which no building was to take place.[88] The outer local authorities began to buy and 'sterilize' suitable land. Morrison was proud of the first attempt since the days of Queen Elizabeth to stop the expansion of London. One publicity venture over the green belt almost misfired. He was photographed pointing to a notice at a gate near Denham, which said 'Private'. The caption was that with a green belt such areas would be open for the public to enjoy.[89] However, officials at the LCC were shocked since the notice had been erected by the Middlesex County Council on its acquisition of the land under the green belt grants. Morrison was nervous for weeks lest the error be uncovered.[90]

A happier foray into public relations was Morrison's flight over London. He proclaimed the 'area' a 'ghastly muddle',[91] and instituted a town planning scheme over the whole of London. But the LCC was seriously impeded by high compensation to be paid to people forbidden to develop their land. The LCC introduced a new code of building regulations, of such complexity that Morrison at a party meeting exclaimed to the chairman of the committee: 'Well I hope *you* understand them.'[92] He had a vision of a vast improvement of the south bank of the River Thames, between Waterloo and Westminster Bridges. He looked forward to the days when 'this dreary stretch may be cleaned up and a river terrace and open space laid out'.[93] Under Morrison's leadership the first steps were taken to acquire land on the south bank. Although critics might damn him for lack of aesthetic sensibilities, the man who instituted London's green belt, comprehensive town planning, the development of the south bank, and was responsible for the new Waterloo Bridge, was no ignorant vandal.

Morrison as Minister of Transport had refused grants to the LCC for the construction of a new crossing of the Thames at Charing Cross. The economic difficulties of the Labour government had blighted hopes of building this new bridge, to carry a north–south artery through London, without damage to Rennie's Waterloo Bridge. In 1931 the Chief Engineer reported, once again, that the old bridge should come down forthwith and a new one be erected. The new Conservative minister in February 1932 agreed to give a sixty per cent grant towards the enterprise and the council decided to go ahead. Clauses to enable the LCC to borrow money for the expenditure were put into the LCC's annual money bill. An eminent architect, Sir Giles Gilbert Scott, was commissioned for the new bridge and his plans were submitted in May 1932. Then disaster struck. The Commons rejected the clauses in the money bill for borrowing for the demolition of the old bridge and the building of a new one. The minister then announced that he could not possibly give a grant to the LCC for a purpose which the House of Commons disapproved. He asked the LCC to submit estimates for reconditioning the old bridge on its existing basis or else for widening it from two lanes to four. At this point Morrison put forward his own scheme to solve the difficulty: 'I should urge the Council to find the money out of the rates, thereby avoiding the necessity for asking Parliament to sanction a loan.' He calculated the cost at a penny rate for five years.[94]

The council told the government that it was in favour of a totally new bridge. The minister, however, said that he would give a sixty per cent grant only for a reconditioning or widening of the old one. The council expressed its disapproval, yet decided to follow the minister in view of the offer of the grant. The cost of reconditioning the old bridge and widening it to four lanes was about £685,000. Morrison called it a scandalous waste of public money on a third- and fourth-rate structure, totally inadequate for road and river traffic.* His was the only voice raised against the plan in the council when it was debated.[95] Designs for the scheme were submitted and the selection committee was about to choose, when the election was held which returned Labour with a majority.

The previous policy was now scrapped. The old bridge was to come down and a new one erected. The minister said he would make no grant against the wishes of Parliament and he would not urge Parliament to reconsider.[96] Clauses empowering the LCC to borrow were put once again into the annual money bill, which the House of Commons again deleted in May 1934. Morrison was not daunted. 'London is going to have a new bridge'[97] was his message. 'I am making no threats, but we intend to have this problem settled once and for all.'[98] The LCC decided to finance the enterprise out of revenue from the rates. The cost would be £1,295,000. The decision was taken to demolish the bridge.

In June 1934 Morrison and Strauss, followed by photographers and press men, put on heavy leather gloves and pulled on the chains of a hand hoist. 'Slowly the slab of granite rose from the bridge, and as it did so a piece about a foot long and six inches wide crashed to the pavement within an inch of Mr Morrison's foot.'[99] The *Morning Post* raged against Morrison's vandalism.[100] Morrison said: 'The bridge was not of such great importance or social significance, but it was symbolical that Labour was capable of decision, that the machinery of democratic public administration would work if the men and women in charge were determined that it should work.'[101]

In October 1934 a design by Sir Giles Gilbert Scott for a new bridge was approved and the council applied to the minister for a grant. In the money bill for 1935 the clauses for borrowing were again put forward, and for the third time rejected. In 1936 the LCC again put the clauses for borrowing into the money bill, and this time, with a greater Labour contingent after the 1935 general election, succeeded. The House sanctioned the clauses, despite fierce Conservative attacks on Morrison for flouting the authority of Parliament. The minister refused to make a grant, claiming that the vote in the Commons was just about enabling the LCC to borrow. The LCC had defied Parliament and he could not aid such action by a grant.[102] By the start of 1937 the old bridge had almost gone and work was soon to begin on the new. The minister again refused a grant, despite a deputation from all parties at the LCC complaining that the refusal was unfair to London ratepayers.[103]

By October 1937 all the formalities for starting work on the new bridge were completed and the order to commence was given. Once again a request for a grant was made and this time the government changed its mind. Now

* The Port of London Authority had objected to the proposal as a menace to river navigation.

there was a new minister, Leslie Burgin, more amenable than Pybus, Stanley and Hore-Belisha in the past, and the Labour victory in the 1937 LCC elections was a confirmation of the popularity of Morrison's stand. Also in 1937, for the second time, the House of Commons had approved the borrowing clauses in the LCC money bill. Morrison saw that time was ripe for a settlement, and he cunningly prepared a bargaining position. The LCC slowed down highways improvements on the ground that, without a grant for the bridge, the ratepayers of London were having to concentrate on that effort Burgin sent for Morrison and wanted to know why the improvements were not going on at the usual pace.[104]

'Well,' I said, 'we have got a lot of other things to spend money on, and we can't do too much. We have to pay for this Waterloo Bridge because you haven't given us any grant.' 'But,' he said, 'what can I do? How could I persuade the Cabinet to give you a grant?' 'Well,' I said, 'I should say this – "Prime Minister, this London County Council is a terrible body. They defied Parliament, they defied the Government. . . . But there will have to be a new bridge, and I would like to have a voice in what sort of bridge it is going to be. If there is no grant, they can do exactly what they like. I would like to give them sixty per cent towards the new bridge, but, Sir, not a penny, not a brass farthing, towards that wicked act of vandalism in destroying the late bridge." '

The Minister followed Morrison's advice, and told his Cabinet colleagues that co-operation between the government and the LCC was essential to solve London's traffic problems.[105] He wanted 'a general appeasement with the London County Council. . . . Comparing the position with that which faces us over German negotiations, he said that the settlement of the Waterloo Bridge took the place in these negotiations that the Colonies took in those with Germany. He could not accomplish anything important in transport in London without a settlement as regards the bridge.' The Cabinet noted that Morrison was prepared to meet them half way and was 'not unsatisfactory' over Air Raid Precautions. The Prime Minister, Chamberlain, said it 'would be very wrong and bad tactics' to continue the fight. At last the Cabinet agreed to offer a grant of £400,000 towards the building of the new bridge.[106] The grant was announced in the Commons on 22 December 1937.[107] The Christmas Box for London was welcomed by the papers. The controversy was over – after fourteen years.

Morrison summed up the significance of the issue. 'This great battle of Waterloo, as I see it, was really a battle between government and wobble, between purpose and lack of purpose in public administration. 'I have no personal quarrel with the men who wanted to preserve the old Bridge, but they were mistaking a bridge for a monument. After all, the function of a bridge in Central London is to get people and traffic from one side of the river to the other as quickly as may be.'[108] He reserved special scorn for the architects whose disputations had stimulated the politicians to oppose him.[109] He said of them, 'I can never understand the assumption common among architects that the only architects capable of doing a job well are dead.'[110] In the end the new Waterloo Bridge was the finest in London, Morrison's monument, which he wished had been called 'Morrison Bridge', after its real progenitor.[111]

As war drew closer Morrison devoted more time to civil defence as chairman of the committee responsible for the defence of London. He so thoroughly mastered the details of the service that he became the leading expert in the country, and the Association of Municipal Corporations and the County Councils Association asked him to represent them in negotiations with the government. The general feeling was that in air raids London would be the main target and would soon suffer mass casualties. Morrison's work was to secure the very survival of London. He had to build from scratch services to protect the people of London. Forces of firemen and ambulance drivers were organized. Schemes of evacuation of children, expectant mothers and the blind were worked out. The operation was on a huge scale. Morrison claimed, however, that despite great efforts in civil defence (or rather ARP, air raid precautions, as it was then called) there had been no holding back of other services. 'The clearance of the slums is still going ahead', hospitals were being developed and the midwifery services expanded.[112] But it did mean that such services were not expanded as fast as they would have been if the LCC had not had to build up its protective services.

More than most socialists Morrison displayed a sense of proportion about public spending. The public purse was not bottomless. In his first year of office the rate was increased by 10½d in the pound to a total of seven shillings, to make up, he alleged, for the neglect of the previous administration. He had never made promises of rate reductions; indeed his pledges about developing services meant higher expenditure which the electors had voted for. In the next year the rise was limited to threepence-halfpenny, so that by the end of the first term of three years the rate was in fact only a penny more than in 1931.[113] Morrison and Latham saw that Labour had to rebut accusations of financial irresponsibility which so bedevilled Labour's record, especially after 1931. The voters were ratepayers, and that meant deference to their views. Morrison could not proceed as fast as he or enthusiasts for particular services desired.

The Municipal Reformers, goaded on by the Beaverbrook Press, complained that London was badly governed by 'a pinchbeck Napoleon'.[114] They depicted Morrison as strident, with a gift for apt slogans, slick publicity and well-posed photographs,[115] a leadership of 'unfulfilled promises and glib propaganda'.[116] Labour's rule was extravagant as evidenced by the increase in the rates and growing capital indebtedness. Whatever improvements in services had taken place had been planned before 1934 by the Municipal Reformers but had been delayed by the socialist-induced economic crisis of 1931 which the Conservatives had had to put right. Most of the credit Morrison gained for developing services ought to have gone to the National Government whose guardianship of the country's finances was so sound that extra grants and low interest rates had benefited the LCC and helped it to stride forward. Further, Labour's rate of housebuilding was lower than that of the 1920s and Labour had failed to do what it had promised in hospitals, schools, medical care and nursery schools, where the Municipal Reformers promised to do better.

Was London under Morrison governed well or badly? Tables (e) to (h) in the appendices present key financial statistics of the LCC in the 1930s. They support Morrison's rhetoric. From 1930 to 1934 council expenditure was declining. After 1934 it increased significantly, which, having regard to a static population and static prices, meant higher standards of provision. Major increases took place in the rate expenditure of the council on main services, notably housing, and in the capital expenditure of the council, again notably on housing. These conclusions are supported by the increase in debt charges in a period of static interest rates and by the increase in the rates levied on a fairly stationary rateable value. After 1938 the threat, and ultimately the arrival, of war had an impact on expenditure, reducing the rate of increase in some cases and pushing it up in others. The conclusions to be drawn from the tables are that the LCC under Morrison's leadership expanded its services in the ways in which he promised. London was well governed.[117]

Morrison played a major role in shaping the LCC's image. Under Labour the LCC held numerous exhibitions to publicize its work; posters and advertisements declared its responsibilities; and County Hall was floodlit.[118] Before Morrison press relations had been a part-time responsibility of the library, whose attitude was to keep the press at bay and to give out as little information as possible. Morrison brought reporters down from the press gallery, where acoustics were bad, into the body of the council chamber.[119] A publicity department was created with a separate officer and his instructions were to give the press every assistance. When they wanted to go down the sewers Morrison ordered that it be done, much to the annoyance of the chief official who did not want pressmen poking in his sewers.[120] 'Herbert's attitude was to give the press a good show about the things they wanted and in return they would give you a good show when you wanted it.'[121] He issued press hand-outs and held press conferences, where he introduced sherry, not tea.

Preston Benson, a journalist who covered the LCC in the 1930s for the *Star* said: 'Herbert was accessible to all journalists and they liked him. He was straightforward and trustworthy. He would give you a lot off the record and yet he would never lead you up the garden path. He used to feed journalists with news more than any other politician.' If Morrison wanted an item to appear in all the papers, and yet it was not big enough to announce at a press conference, he would contact Benson and give him the story which Benson would then put in the diary column in the *Star* that evening. The news editors of other papers would see it and would send their reporters out after it, so that it would appear next morning in all their papers. This was Morrison's technique of breaking the story. He sought pressmen's advice. He created news, and knew how to present it in a way the press could use, with quotable catch-phrases. The *Star* was of particular importance to Morrison since it was the only London evening paper at all sympathetic: 'Herbert's anchor.'[122]

Some officials felt he was over-sensitive to the press. Presentation sometimes became more important than content, and he would judge an official's memorandum by its usefulness for reporters.[123] Some felt his concern for publicity to be a sign of personal vanity. 'He took,' said Sir Allen Daley, 'a childlike pleasure in a cutting that was favourable, though he could not easily brush off an adverse one.' He loved being photographed, and he so revelled in cartoons, especially Low's, which showed him as a mighty giant, that he hung them on the walls of his room in County Hall. Morrison was a master of personal publicity. He held a press conference in November 1936 on housing policy. Silkin talked about the LCC housing plans, while Morrison sat at a large desk. 'But on the feet which he twiddled underneath the desk Mr Morrison wore no shoes, only grey socks. . . . He rose still shoeless, and padded cat-like around the room.' The *Evening Standard* even produced a verse for the occasion.[124]

> When Hist'ry treats of Herbert's fame,
> No matter if it lauds or mocks,
> One matchless record he can claim –
> *He governed London in his socks.*

His concern for personal publicity was calculated. Morrison depended on professional advertisers and public relations men to advise him on how best to promote the LCC and the work of the Labour Party there. In June 1934 Morrison formed an unofficial group of Labour sympathizers to help him on publicity work. Not only did they advise on the LLP's election material, but they guided him in the day-to-day presentation of LCC activities.[125] When the LCC civil defence service began, recruitment was slow. Morrison called in an advertising agency which arranged a demonstration of the Auxiliary Fire Service at County Hall. He appeared at a window of County Hall, got on a ladder and climbed down to a fire appliance from where he addressed the crowd; the press was full of photographs of Morrison at various points on the ladder.[126] The experts advised an emphasis on personal publicity, and it certainly paid off. Morrison and the LCC became synonymous. He became the best-known figure in local government in Britain. No local leader, before or since, gained such a national reputation for his work in a local authority.

The vindication of Morrison came at the polls in 1937. Of all the election campaigns fought by the LLP that of 1937 was its finest achievement: the most professional campaign ever fought in Britain. In 1935 Morrison had urged local parties to select good candidates, to build up their funds and to get their organizations in order. He saw the value of public relations methods, and made use of George Wansbrough. Wansbrough, an old Etonian and graduate of King's College, Cambridge, had been introduced to Morrison in the early 1930s by Dalton. Although a wealthy businessman, Wansbrough despaired of the Tories and admired Morrison's practical efficiency. They became close allies and Morrison persuaded the West Woolwich Labour Party to adopt him as prospective parliamentary candidate. A friend of Wansbrough's was Robert Fraser, then of the London Press Exchange and later Director-General of the Independent Television Authority. They talked about the coming election and both agreed that 'good publicity' was essential. Fraser said that at the Exchange he had the ideal man to take charge of Morrison's publicity, Clem Leslie, who had achieved fame as the creator for the gas industry of 'Mr Therm'. Wansbrough introduced Leslie to Morrison,[127] and they immediately became very attached to each other. Leslie recruited a team of advertisers, public relations men and journalists, sympathetic to Labour, who gave their services free. Leslie was chairman of the group, and they devised all the Labour publicity material. 'We were responsible for the strategy of the publicity, the writing, the layout and some of the ideas. Herbert was a good client. He didn't interfere. He told us the message and I could see that housing offered a good theme.'[128]

The team felt that the Labour Party had to be personalized in Morrison. The Executive of the LLP was asked to approve, and it agreed to 'the name of Mr Morrison being given prominence in the election for publicity purposes'.[129] A typical poster was of Morrison with his arms around a little boy and girl, and modern LCC flats in the background. They devised such slogans as 'Labour Puts Human Happiness First', 'Let Labour Finish the Job', 'Labour Gets Things Done', 'Let Labour Build the New London'. Better homes for children, healthier children, better-educated children were the constant images, linked always to Morrison. The team devised an advertisement for the Tory press: a dialogue between two reasonable Tories. It concluded that they would vote Labour this time: 'That chap Morrison's a leader – he and his people have got a bit of life and colour into the running of London; housing and schools and hospitals and the Green Belt all on the move. They've made us remember we've *got* a government of our own.' – 'True enough. They're doing a good job. I'm fair-minded. I'll give them a chance to finish it.'[130]

The publicity team was kept apart from the normal machinery of the LLP. It was very 'hush-hush'. Morrison realized that it would provoke opposition from inside the party, which looked askance at such 'capitalist' techniques. Joan Bourne, then women's organizer at the LLP, was 'nauseated' at the personification of the Labour Party at the same time as the party was fighting the 'Führer' principle on the Continent.[131] But Morrison always trusted the

H

professional. Lord Calder, then Ritchie Calder, wrote that 'part of his success can be traced to his knowledge of how to win over and handle experts. . . . He galvanized them into enthusiasm by his example and by his appreciation.'[132]

All possible sources of funds were tapped. The TGWU and the NUGMW each gave a thousand pounds; Latham and George Wansbrough sought out rich individuals for donations. Wansbrough himself gave five hundred pounds and he persuaded George Strauss to give the same amount.[133] Over eight thousand five hundred pounds were raised which was seven times more than for any previous election. Nearly three thousand pounds of the total were raised from anonymous contributors.[134] Morrison was in the thick of the action, overseeing the whole campaign, drafting the manifesto, writing articles, giving speeches, being interviewed and photographed, and delivering a twenty-minute radio appeal.[135]

The Municipal Reformers were knocked off balance. On the one hand they claimed Labour was extravagant, and on the other that Labour had broken its promises and had not achieved as much as they would have done. They alleged that Morrison was unpatriotic, served communist interests and was a warmonger for urging intervention in the Spanish Civil War. Even the Crown was dragged in by the 'loyal' party whose leader declared: 'I have no hesitation in saying that the most profound and serious effect would be produced throughout the country and Empire and on foreign opinion if, in Coronation year, the capital of the Empire returns Socialists to control the greatest administrative body in the world.'[136]

On polling day Morrison wrote to the Clerk of the LCC: 'Today is like waiting for the return of the jury and wondering whether it is thumbs up or thumbs down.'[137] The result was what Morrison wanted. Whereas the Municipal Reformers increased their vote to a record 402,723, Labour shot even further ahead with 446,116, fifty-one per cent of the vote, gaining six seats from the opposition. The poll of 43·4 per cent was the highest since the war. At the end of the day the 75 Labour councillors and eight aldermen had a majority of 30. In 1934 the majority had been 16. Morrison had done it again.[138] 'I believe we can rule London for ever,' he declared. 'So, when you meet the man who says it "can't be done", pat him on the back, give him a cheery smile, and say, "Gertcher!" '[139]

Chapter 15

The Party Politician

Morrison wrote: 'Electoral victories are not enough. The size, the quality and the idealism of the Labour Party are no less important than winning elections. The Labour Party does not exist merely to return candidates to Parliament and to the local authorities. It exists also to create a new social life, a more educated democracy, and an always improving type of youth, of manhood and womanhood.'[1] He said that he would sooner fight an election 'on a clear constructive policy of Socialism and fail to win fifty seats that I could have won by playing with superficial politics. . . .'[2]

Morrison, as Secretary of the LLP, continued to give the same assiduous devotion to the Executive as in the 1920s, attending all its meetings except one between 1931 and 1940. But he was not so involved in the minutiae. Donald Daines ran the office, and carried out the chores that had once been his, such as organizing conferences, distributing circulars, contacting affiliated organizations and collecting funds. Election work was in the hands of Hinley Atkinson who kept an eye on local parties and straightened out their difficulties.[3] Also at the head office was the women's organizer, Miss Annie Somers, who remained until 1936 when she was replaced by Miss Joan Bourne. Miss Bourne observed that the officials of the LLP were a collection of physical freaks: Morrison had only one eye, Daines was plagued with asthma, Atkinson was crippled in his hip and the chief clerk, Miss Atkins, had a bad heart.[4] Despite their handicaps Morrison was confident that the routine of the LLP would be carried on smoothly, so that he could play a major role elsewhere.

The finances of the LLP, after a shaky start in the early 1930s when the party was in deficit, picked up, until by 1940 Morrison left it with a total of £6,835 4s 8½d. The membership figures fell to their lowest of the decade in 1931–2, 208,793, but by 1939 had risen to 255,520.[5]

One potential source of money eluded Morrison's grasp in the 1930s: the London Co-operative Society. Although the Royal Arsenal Co-operative Society, based at loyal Woolwich, remained a firm supporter, the LCS refused, despite repeated requests, to affiliate to either the LLP or the party nationally. In the 1930s Morrison was a member of the National Joint Committee of the NEC and the Co-op which tried to work out an agreement. Morrison sought full affiliation, but the LCS wanted to stay separate, using its political funds for its own Co-operative Party and its candidates, even going so far as to want its MPs not to accept the standing orders of the Parliamentary Labour Party. The Co-op claimed that its support of the Labour Party in election campaigns and with its literature was sufficient. Morrison, however, feared that in Parliament a group of ten to twenty Co-op MPs would have a future Labour government at their mercy; they could not be a state within a state, maintaining their own organization and policy. Assistance was not enough; they had to foot the bill. But the Co-op objected to being 'a milch cow to be milked on behalf of the LLP'. Morrison wanted access to the seventeen thousand pounds spent by the LCS for political purposes. He proposed for the LCS the same status within the Labour Party as the trade unions, with special machinery established for the party and the Co-op to discuss trading questions which were of concern to the Co-op. It, however, wanted only a joint committee to co-ordinate the activities of two separate organizations.

When negotiations failed, Morrison plotted a 'putsch'. He organized conferences of party members to press local Co-ops to affiliate and he circulated a memorandum of his views as ammunition for members to use at Co-op meetings. It was in vain. Labour members did not turn up in force, the Communist Party remained in control of some local Co-ops, and the LCS protested against Morrison's 'underhand' methods. Although he might point out that he was an enthusiastic supporter of the Co-op and had defended it against attacks in the Beaverbrook Press, and against Neville Chamberlain's attempt to tax the Co-op dividend, Morrison was never able to persuade the LCS to affiliate.[6]

Relations between the LLP and the national Labour Party during the 1930s were harmonious, except for a brief period after 1931 when Transport House, as part of its economy measures, reduced by a hundred pounds its annual payment to the LLP. The LLP's Treasurer protested about 'dictatorial termination of a financial arrangement'.[7] The cuts were restored in the later 1930s as the financial situation improved. Otherwise nothing disturbed the congenial relationship; largely because the LLP was so successful, and because Atkinson, the London District Organizer, was trusted by both Morrison and head office, Morrison on the NEC was always able to defend the LLP against detractors.

On the Executive of the LLP Morrison remained the dominating figure. At LLP conferences, too, he was the outstanding performer. They were quiet in the 1930s; only on civil defence was there opposition to Morrison of any significance.[8] Disloyal elements had been cleared out and Atkinson kept a close watch on the local situations. Another reason for the calm was pride in the successes of the LLP and its record at the LCC. Morrison allowed conference to act as a safety valve, where members could complain that the LCC was neglecting some service. Instead of slapping them down, Morrison persuaded the conference to remit their resolutions to the LCC for consideration. Their resolutions were sent to the appropriate chairmen of committees who would reply with reasoned comments. These would be considered by the Policy Committee of the LCC Labour Party, which would report to the Executive of the LLP which in turn would report to the proposer of the original motion. It took about four months for the process to complete its course, by which time the intensity of feeling had subsided and new issues had arisen.

A potential for conflict existed between the Executive of the LLP and the LCC Labour Party. But there was not even any tension.[9] Policies were drawn up by joint committees, there was frequent consultation and, above all, the same key people served on both the LCC and the Executive. Morrison guided the former as leader and the latter as Secretary. On the Executive were all the members of his LCC 'Presidium', who were also, like Morrison, the most regular attenders. Other leading LCC members served on the Executive, like Somerville Hastings, Esther Rickards, Agnes Dawson and Freda Corbet. In all, ten members of the Executive, nearly half and all the most important ones, were on the LCC. Thus when conference motions were considered, the same people were approving what they themselves had decided on earlier occasions. Through this overlapping membership Morrison and his LCC lieutenants were able to control the LLP. They ruled by persuasion.[10] The appearance of dominance arose from the acceptability of their proposals.

Morrison continued the educational activities of the LLP. In the 1930s he instituted an annual series of lectures. In 1933 the title was 'Planning London for Socialism', and in 1936 'Building the New London'. Others covered fascism, communism and socialism, the history of the development of the Labour movement, and examinations of current problems. Morrison used academic sympathizers, often from the LSE, to draw up these courses, provide study notes and bibliographies, and deliver the lectures. He had a list of 107 experts prepared to talk. Included was a lecturer, Hugh Gaitskell, who in 1938 was specializing in foreign affairs, finance and economic questions.[11]

The LLP organized weekend and summer schools, at which Morrison spoke, often on local government or on ideologies. He tried to establish reading and study circles, where members would read and discuss a text. The LLP organized speakers' classes, and Morrison urged members to sit in the public galleries of local councils to learn about public administration. He drew on experts to help shape party policy; in 1933 he established research groups on housing under Latham, public health under Silkin and education under Professor Tawney, whose reports formed the basis of Labour policy at the LCC elections of 1934.

The recreational and cultural activities sponsored by the LLP still existed in the 1930s, but Morrison grew more sceptical. The LLP Sports Association, although by the mid-thirties covering ten sports, including netball,[1] rambling and table tennis, as well as the staple football, and although enrolling four thousand members in seventy-five local sections, complained each year of 'poor support'.[12] In 1938 Morrison advised winding it up; he felt it diverted energies from political work. Its organization cost money and staff for an uncertain return and it was 'undesirable for members of the Labour Movement to segregate themselves from the rest of the community, because friendly and social contact between Socialists and other people tends to break down prejudices against the Party, and to make possible a respect for Socialists and the extension of Socialist thought'.[13]

The LLP choral union fell on hard times. In 1932 only seven local choirs existed, too few to tour Europe, and the audience at the annual festival was sparse. In 1934 Morrison pleaded with local parties. 'Let us help to brighten your meetings and social functions', and a course for conductors was organized.[14] He explained, 'we must not only work our way to Socialism, but, with joy in our hearts, we must sing in the course of the journey'.[15] But he soon felt it was time to stop, especially as the choral union became a 'vehicle for ultra-left propaganda'.[16] Political work had to come first and the LLP could not afford a full-time organizer to look after the union. The party had to 'get down out of the clouds'.[17]

One of the most important roles of the LLP was as co-ordinator of local Labour parties in London, especially after Labour gains in the borough elections of November 1934 and 1937, which pushed the number of elected Labour councillors up from 257 in 1931 to 729 in 1934 and 778 in 1937, controlling 15 councils in 1934 and 17 in 1937. Morrison felt that it was crucial that they should not pursue differing policies. In 1934 he reconstituted the consultative machinery that had been somewhat dormant from the middle 1920s: the Municipal Consultative Committee, containing represent-atives from the local parties and groups, called at various times to discuss common problems and to evolve a common view. Morrison also organized 'municipal conferences' and 'departmental consultations' to discuss par-ticular policies. He had hoped that such gatherings would be at regular intervals. By 1936, however, he came to the sad conclusion that they should be called only when the occasion warranted, since regular conventions could not be sustained through lack of demand and time.[18] He found them successful only when some controversy arose which needed either a protest against some government iniquity, or to settle squabbles within the LLP.

He advised local parties always to examine the financial and administrative consequences of any policy before it was adopted and to have no truck with favouritism in appointments. In 1934 the famous lecture he had delivered to the members and officials at the LCC was transformed into the 'Memorandum for the Guidance of Labour Borough Aldermen and Councillors', issued to all Labour representatives, even long after Morrison had left the Secretaryship.[19]

Another pet subject was the relationship between the local party and the council group. He had already embodied his views and LCC practice in the Labour Party model standing orders, adopted by conference in 1930. They were twice revised, only slightly, by conferences in 1936 and 1939, when the main controversy was whether local parties should instruct council groups. Morrison condemned as undemocratic situations where the group was made 'the creature' of the local Labour party, where the council agenda was picked over by the local party or trades council and orders were issued to councillors about how to vote.[20] He advised local parties not to neglect party work once they had obtained a council majority, since the party's strength would determine whether another majority would be obtained.[21] He also advised councils with huge, sometimes hundred per cent, Labour majorities to appoint as aldermen members from the opposing parties. He found councils without an opposition appalling, and called on Stepney, Poplar and Bermondsey to create such an opposition, hoping, in vain, that Tory strongholds like Chelsea, Westminster, Holborn and Hampstead would bring Labour representatives onto their councils.[22] His passion for clean government indicates that he was far removed from the legendary Tammany boss with which he was so often compared.

Dissatisfaction with Morrison flared up in the summer of 1937, when some members tried to organize an association of constituency Labour parties in London to pronounce on national and international policies. The object was to bypass machinery controlled by Morrison and to take up a different line from him on civil defence and the Popular Front. The LLP condemned this unauthorized organization. Morrison pointed out that party machinery was complicated enough without an extra layer; it was also totally unnecessary since the LLP held frequent conferences for consultation, and organized demonstrations on national and international policies. He noted that the proposed association was unrepresentative of the Labour movement since it excluded the trade unions and the Co-ops. It fizzled out.[23]

Morrison kept in touch with local parties through personal contact, through Atkinson who constantly toured the areas, through the Executive, and through scrutiny of the press and his postbag. In turn, Morrison continued to issue from the LLP office a flow of circulars. By 1940 he had issued almost 240 *Municipal Circulars*, and countless other 'notes' or letters. The *London News* flourished, with net monthly sales around 5,500. It provided Morrison with an authoritative platform. As its editor he could play at being a journalist, although Daines did most of the work, while he kept an eye on it and wrote regular articles. Morrison tapped the skills of journalists friendly to him to help bring out the editions, to devise the layout for instance, and to put the copy together.[24] A constant stream of material flowed into and out of the LLP offices. Even the Tories had to admit that: 'The Labour Party now has what must be the finest publicity organization ever known in municipal politics.'[25] The occasional demonstration still had its place, but Morrison felt it served little purpose except to prevent communists from running the show; it won no votes, probably alienated some, and did not improve party organization.

Morrison continued to value the Women's Section of the LLP. By 1935 there were eighty-six local sections in London, and the LLP, through the Women's Advisory Committee and Conference maintained a full programme of meetings and weekend and summer schools. The League of Youth, which Morrison had hoped would provide a similar outlet for young people, proved a big disappointment. In 1935 it had fifty-five local sections, but in the late 1930s became increasingly dominated by Popular Fronters and communists, and in 1939 it was disbanded.

The main objective of the LLP was to win elections. Campaigns similar to those for the LCC elections of 1934 and 1937 were mounted for the borough elections, but not on the same scale. Preliminary conferences were held for party workers on publicity, party organization and electoral preparation, and candidates met to discuss policy. Morrison himself wrote the manifestoes after consultation with leading party members, and the Executive made only slight amendments. During the borough elections of 1934 Morrison and Beaverbrook held a slanging match. The press lord mounted an offensive against Labour, and Morrison criticized him for usurping the functions of political parties. 'Lord Beaverbrook ought to get his wings cut, and he will get them cut if I ever get the chance to do it.'[26] Beaverbrook replied that 'Mr Morrison is like a presentation clock. He is very handsome, but he is never quite right.'[27]

The campaign of November 1937 was the greatest effort ever made in borough elections by the LLP. More money was spent and more material issued than before, and Morrison sought the advice of Clem Leslie and his team of professional publicity men. The emphasis was on health, housing and municipal facilities: clearing out slums, saving sick babies, and providing public baths, parks and libraries, which the Tories were too mean to consider. The motto was that Labour put human happiness first, while at the same time not indulging in wild extravagance. The slogans proclaimed 'Let Labour Save the Mothers and Children', 'Let Labour Build a Better London', and 'Throw out the Tory Skinflints'. Labour made striking gains in both 1934 and 1937, the best in its history.

Parliamentary elections also engaged the LLP. For the general election of 1935 the office provided speakers for 390 meetings, issued 500,000 newssheets and numerous posters, election notes and circulars. It played a crucial role in by-elections of the 1930s, achieving nine Labour gains, the most notable at East Fulham in 1933. Atkinson had considerable power as London District Organizer in promoting candidates for adoption by local parties. Although the choice was theirs, he could suggest people they should look at. Atkinson and Morrison worked together to ensure that sound candidates were selected. Once in the 1930s, at Putney, their operations were exposed. Here, the adopted candidate was the actor Miles Mander. In 1934 he wrote a book in which he advised his son to sow wild oats. Morrison was worried that this rather risqué piece would alienate the religious voter.[28] The NEC withdrew its endorsement of Mander.[29] The Putney party reluctantly accepted, except for one ward party which had to be suspended. The *Daily Express* said that Morrison 'has nothing to learn from Stalin . . . when it comes to liquidating an oppositionist centre'.[30]

Just before the outbreak of war Morrison was awaiting the general election of 1940. Electoral preparations were put in hand, and *London News* acclaimed, 'Hail Victory'.[31] The war, however, delayed the election for five more years.

During the period 1919–39 the LLP gradually increased its support. First it obtained victory in the solidly working class areas and then penetrated constituencies of the lower middle class. As the 1930s progressed Labour seemed to be creeping up the social scale. Morrison's appeal to the middle class was paying off. However, the bulk of Labour support still came from working class areas. In London 'it seems likely that by 1935 Labour had gained a small footing among the lower and middle sections of the middle class, was much stronger but still far from solid among the skilled manual class, and had a good majority among the poor unskilled class'.[32] Morrison's courting of the middle class was more successful in attracting as elected members people from professional, business and commercial occupations than in winning their votes *en masse*.

Morrison was a leading figure in the Labour Party nationally, on its NEC and at conference. From his days as Minister of Transport he had gone around the country more and more. By the end of the 1930s he must have visited every county and major town in Britain. He consolidated his popularity with constituency parties by championing a measure which he had first urged in the early 1920s: the right of the constituency parties alone to vote for their own representatives on the NEC. In 1937 he commended this proposal strongly, appealing to the unions to give way. As a result the rules were revised, and in the elections for the NEC Morrison came top of the poll for the constituency party section. During the 1930s Morrison never fell below third place, and he came top in three years, 1934, 1936 and 1937. This result indicates that he was highly regarded both by the constituency parties and by the trade unions who had determined the vote before 1937. The unions may have been suspicious of Morrison, but they recognized that he commanded considerable support in the party and could not be excluded from the leadership. He was clearly a figure of national eminence, ahead of Attlee in 1934 and 1935.

Morrison continued to attend the NEC as frequently as he had in the 1920s; in 1939 and 1940 he was rarely absent.[33] Dalton wrote in his diary: 'Morrison is important in the EC, intellectually able but aggressive, and a pedantic stickler for procedural precision and party discipline.'[34] During the 1930s Morrison was a member at one time or another of many of the sub-committees of the NEC: Organization, Research and Publicity, Policy, Elections, and International Affairs. He sat, as a representative of the NEC, on the Economic Committee of the TUC's General Council and on the committee which handled the party's relations with the Co-operative Movement. Most importantly he was the NEC's representative on the National Joint Council of Labour (after 1934 the National Council of Labour), where the party, trade unions and Co-op conferred. This council was far more important as a policy-making body in the 1930s than before, since it brought the leading trade union figures, like Bevin and Citrine, together with the politicians. It was the supreme institution of the Labour movement.[35] Morrison was especially good on policy documents. He would draft sections and comment in detail on other drafts. The minutes of the NEC and the NCL do not enable one to disentangle the contributions of individuals. But Lord Citrine said that he played a big policy role; 'he did his work and was very active.'[36]

Morrison served on the Local Government and Social Services Group, acting as chairman in 1932. He was responsible for drafting proposals for local government reform, which entailed a single-tier system of county borough or unitary authorities with only advisory committees below.[37] His memorandum was sent to a number of local Labour parties whose comments were so adverse that it was shelved.[38] In 1936 the party decided to establish, as Morrison had long wanted, a Local Government Department to co-ordinate the work of parties on local authorities. Like the LLP it was to provide information, guidance, electoral assistance and literature. He was frequently a member of teams sent to investigate controversies inside local parties, and he gave considerable attention to publicity and electoral preparations. Shinwell judged him, after Arthur Henderson, 'the finest campaign manager the Labour Party ever had'.[39]

He looked forward intensely to the general election of 1940, when he hoped to repeat his successes in London. In 1939 he told the party's Campaign Committee, of which he was chairman, that the party needed a programme of measures that could be achieved within the lifetime of a single Parliament, not just a manifesto of propaganda and long-term aims. And this programme had to appeal to the new rising middle class.[40] He called for a fund of ten thousand pounds, he avidly scrutinized the lists of aspiring candidates to exclude the unsound, and he urged a national survey to spot marginal seats. His efforts for 1940 came to nothing at the time, but he laid the foundations for victory in 1945.

In the 1930s Morrison was a prominent performer at party conferences, making three to four major speeches at each conference, covering a wide range of topics. He was simple, straightforward, easily understood, chatty, with a teasing humour; facts and figures were fully marshalled behind common-sense arguments. He swayed people who had come to conference to vote against him. He was at his best in a critical debate when he was up against stiff opposition and superficially attractive arguments. He was put up by the NEC to defend the most unpopular positions. But then he hammered opposition into the ground. Morrison was a star performer, whose speeches, 'full of meat', were talked about after the session. Alongside Morrison, Attlee cut a poor figure.[41]

In the 1930s Morrison set his eye on the leadership of the party, making an open bid for it in 1935. Back in August 1931 no one guessed that Attlee would one day win that prize. Luck helped, for in the general election of 1931, while Morrison, Greenwood, Dalton and Henderson were defeated, Lansbury and Attlee were returned to the House. Lansbury became leader, and Attlee, as the next most senior figure left in the Commons, became his deputy. Although Greenwood was returned at a by-election in Wakefield in April 1932,[42] Morrison remained a prospective candidate at Hackney and was not returned until the 1935 general election. If he had come back earlier he might have defeated Attlee in 1935.[43]

No offer of a safe seat was made to Morrison; no one gave up a seat to let him in and Hinley Atkinson said that Morrison never approached him to switch from Hackney, which looked winnable in normal circumstances. His caution prevented him from getting back to the Commons at the most amazing by-election of the period, that at East Fulham. Hinley Atkinson estimated that Labour could win it. He wrote to Morrison, who was on a tour of Russia at the time, suggesting that he let his name go forward.[44] Morrison and Charles Latham, who was also on the tour, conferred. Morrison could not believe that it could be won. East Fulham had been Conservative since 1918, and even if it was won at a by-election, when people's hostility against the government was at its height, it could very well be lost at the general election. Latham said: 'Herbert was always thinking ahead, not just for the next year but for many years into the future.' Morrison refused, as did Dalton whom Atkinson next approached.[45] In the end John Wilmot gave up his candidature at Lewisham East and won the seat, converting a Conservative majority in 1931 of 14,521 into a Labour majority of 4,840. Morrison had made no error. He would have got back to the Commons in the blaze of favourable publicity, but in 1935 he would probably have been defeated.

The election of 1935 in Hackney was quiet, compared with the rowdyism of the 1920s. His main opponent, again Miss Marjorie Graves, played fair and there was no personal slanging. Local Tories stressed Morrison's attempt to despoil Hackney Marshes and made much in Jewish quarters of the LCC decision to purchase pencils for its schools from a German firm. The Labour Party claimed that Morrison's policy over the Marshes was 'an action of supreme political courage' and in the Jewish area alleged that local fascists were in league with the Tories. Local issues seemed to be to the fore. The *Manchester Guardian* and *The Times* felt that Morrison's prospects were doubtful, and the *Morning Post* found evidence of positive hostility to Morrison. Although Miss Graves had called a halt to electioneering on Remembrance Day, Morrison put up a poster which read:

> Election Crosses
> Not Wooden Crosses
> Vote Labour and no more war.

'This inopportune slogan has lost Mr Morrison more votes than anything else he has done.... Protest meetings were held ... wives and mothers addressed angry groups.... His refusal to answer questionnaires and his condemnations of questioners at public meetings as "paid hecklers" have given him a name for high-handedness.'[46] Meetings were not enthusiastically attended and the canvassers of both parties reported an unusual proportion of doubtfuls: about a third.[47] But the result was a tremendous victory for Morrison.* He pushed Labour's share of the vote up by fifteen per cent, double the rise over London and over the whole country.

Morrison called his relationship with South Hackney, 'a real bond of fellowship'.[48] Local party members felt he was an excellent MP. He left the agent to deal with minor details and followed his advice. He was ready to meet any constituent and give help. He would turn up at any party meeting. 'He never missed a chance to appear' and after the meeting he always got a piece about it in the press. He paid great attention to the women. 'He was very good at talking to the old dears, telling them that they were the backbone of the party.'[49] Morrison used the columns of the local party's monthly paper, the *South Hackney Citizen*, to inform members of his views and activities.[50] He mixed affably, but was not one to go into public houses and drink with the boys. He preferred to have a snack at the homes of party members.

In the House of Commons Morrison, as a front-bencher, was not a questioner of ministers about problems of his constituency, nor was he for ever raising 'constituency points' in debates. Complaints from his constituency were handed to the agent who dealt with them or passed them to representatives on either the borough council or the LCC.[51] Morrison was not a constant attender at the House. After his failure to be elected leader of the Labour Party in 1935, he gave more time to running the LCC than to the Commons. The press felt that when he did perform, he was not up to his usual standard. In his first speech after re-election, in the debate on the Address, his first point was to reply to Tory leaflets about the LCC contract for pencils with a German firm.[52] However, his speeches in the House between 1935 and 1940 were comprehensive, touching not just London, but broader domestic and foreign issues. If his name went up on the Commons' indicators, MPs

---

* Labour   15,830
  Conservative 10,876. See Table (a).

would come into the chamber, for they knew that he would never bore them.[53]

He spoke for bills promoted by the LCC and used statistics from the LCC to show how government proposals were likely to damage its interests.[54] As a representative from London's East End he brought to the notice of the House the Jew-baiting activities of the fascists in 1936.[55] He acted as a spokesman for local government, often briefed by the local authority associations, to protest about government measures that adversely affected their interests.[56] He kept an eye on his old department, the Ministry of Transport, protesting at the Treasury's attempts to control the Road Fund,[57] and welcoming the bill which made trunk roads a national responsibility.[58] In 1938 he was sceptical about certain road safety measures recently introduced, such as tests for drivers, the resumption of speed limits, and the erection of 'Belisha beacons' at unsuitable sites.[59] He was the protector of the motorist, claiming that the 'cyclist and the pedestrian should also be considered as the root cause of road accidents'.[60] He felt very oppressed as a motorist: 'I am in mortal fear lest I get collared myself. Life is a little difficult for the driver, what with keeping his eye on beacons, traffic signals and his speedometer, and now and again looking ahead to see if there is anything there.'[61] Driving must have been a nightmare for Morrison with just one eye; it certainly was for his passengers.[62]

In debates on industry he championed public ownership.[63] Labour, he claimed, were the true patriots, since they wanted the nation to be the master of its own resources.[64] He showed interest in other issues which foreshadowed his responsibilities in future ministerial posts. He urged that the BBC should not be an organ of propaganda, even in retaliation to provocative broadcasts from abroad or in wartime. It should disseminate information about Britain's public achievements, even the views of the Opposition.[65] He was an early champion of television: 'an amazing invention' with 'enormous possibilities'. He sought to extend the television service over greater parts of Britain and, with cheaper prices for sets, over a wider range of the population.[66] He spoke on libertarian issues: on the Emergency Powers legislation in 1939 he expressed anxiety about the sweeping discretion conferred on ministers, notably in censorship and in the imposition of a curfew. He stood out against controlling opinion and advised that pacifists be allowed to speak freely.[67]

The most impressive speeches of Morrison in the House were five on Air Raid Precautions and civil defence.[68] Briefed by his LCC officials and the local authority associations, and with first-hand experience at the LCC, he displayed a mastery over broad policy issues and a grasp of financial and technical details that made him a force to be reckoned with; he revealed his credentials to be Minister of Home Security. Morrison's speeches on home affairs thus ranged over a variety of topics. He was not, however, uninterested in foreign affairs. Between 1936 and 1939 he made major speeches in the Commons about British foreign policy in relation to Germany, Italy, Russia,

Spain, the League of Nations, the USA and Palestine. Morrison's performances in the House of Commons between 1935 and 1940 confirmed the impression he had made as Minister of Transport that he was now a national politician of the front rank.

Chapter 16

Enemies on the Right and on the Left

In the 1930s Morrison devoted a considerable amount of time to fighting fascists and communists. In the summer of 1934 he became alarmed about fascist violence at meetings in London. He denounced the savagery displayed by the fascist stewards and compared their methods with those of fascists in Germany and Italy.[1] He organized a conference of the London Labour movement in September, attended by 1,200 delegates. Morrison drafted the resolutions of the conference and a memorandum on Labour's attitude to fascism. His analysis was that fascism arose in three circumstances: when a country was in a state of economic depression; when parliamentary and governmental institutions were weak, indecisive in action, badly led, or new and inexperienced; and when a strong Communist Party provoked a counter-attack. But fascism itself involved 'an iron dictatorship' and was 'no remedy for our economic troubles'.

He laid stress on socialist education, particularly among the middle classes, who 'must not be neglected by Labour if they are to be saved from the clutches of reaction'. He warned members that to over-react would only publicize the fascists and encourage their spread. Toughness, not hysteria, would prevent their growth. He felt that the British people responded to appeals to reason; indeed the fascists were weak because of the 'irrational and theatrical' character of their appeal. The solution was 'by constructive propaganda and education, to create a Socialist public opinion', and to convince the people that 'democratic institutions are capable of decisive and effective action'. The conference adopted Morrison's line. One resolution stated: 'Realizing that forms of military drilling and organization, with the object of upsetting constitutional government, are proceeding, it condemns the Government's failure to deal with such attempts to bring about the militarization of politics.'[2]

Nothing appears to have been done to follow up the conference, largely because the fascists quietened down. However, in 1936 they reappeared with more ferocity. Their activities were concentrated in the East End of London, where their Jew-baiting propaganda, demonstrations and marches found a ready response amongst some people who lived cheek by jowl with Jewish neighbours. Into the LLP headquarters came reports of a build-up of tension. The fascists claimed in the back streets of Stepney that if the Jews were 'got rid of', unemployment, bad housing and low wages would be remedied, as in Germany. Animosities were aroused on one side and acute terror on the other. Windows were smashed, slogans daubed on walls, Jewish shops attacked, razor blades embedded in potatoes and apples; groups of youths fought, and individuals were assaulted. The communists organized counter-demonstrations. Escalation of violence looked certain.[3]

As the Labour Party conference met at Edinburgh in October 1936 more disturbances flared up, and Morrison brought forward an emergency resolution condemning the violence of the previous day. The situation, if left to go on, meant that 'the East End of London was to be made the battleground of organized Fascism and organized Communism'.[4] He criticized the government for not banning the particular fascist march that had led to disorder. He demanded government action against fascist incitement to civil and racial strife, their parades and militarized politics. Banning the marches did not raise the issue of free speech, since they were designed to stimulate disorder. He also called for an inquiry into the organization and finances of the fascists. The conference was unanimously behind Morrison.[5]

Back in London he called together a meeting of Labour elected representatives from the East End. They agreed to send a deputation to the Home Secretary to explain the seriousness of the situation and to demand action. Morrison led the deputation on 20 October.[6] He submitted three specific recommendations: that all military uniforms and quasi-military training by political parties should be prohibited; that the Minister and the police chiefs should have power to 'divert or deal with processions and street demonstrations that are of such a character that they are likely to lead to civil disorder or racial strife'; 'That the police practice of taking records of speeches made at meetings with a view to possible legal proceedings – a practice which has been common with regard to Socialist and Communist meetings – should also be applied to Fascist meetings.' The government brought forward the Public Order Bill which enacted much of what Morrison wanted, including the banning of uniforms and drilling, and the control of parades.

Morrison organized the anti-fascist campaign of the LLP. He set up an East London Advisory Committee, comprising the chairmen and secretaries of the local Labour parties in the areas affected, the leaders of the borough councils, the Executive of the LLP and three officials of the London Trades Council. This body was responsible for guiding local parties before they took any anti-fascist action. Some, however, disappointed at Morrison's apparently wary attitude, ignored him and arranged counter-demonstrations. They wanted some immediate and dramatic action, and to co-operate with the communists or their anti-fascist 'front' organizations. Morrison instructed local parties to desist, since the fascists thrived on the subsequent disorder.[7]

He organized a series of six indoor public meetings on 'Socialism, Peace and Democracy' and spoke at five. Three LLP leaflets were issued, entitled *British Liberty Is Worth Saving, British Women: Don't Lose Your Rights* and *Fascism Hates Trade Unions*.[8] This educational campaign dismayed those who wanted more vigorous action. Morrison retorted: 'It really is no good getting excited about Fascist activity in East London, having meetings and consultations, pressing the Executive to act, and then failing to carry through the vitally necessary educational campaign.'[9] He was disappointed that his efforts to spread knowledge were not adequately supported.[10] Many Labour members in the East End who were in the thick of the disturbances found Morrison's lectures and leaflets laughable. Their vision was confined to their own area, while Morrison considered the wider repercussions. He disliked 'direct action' and feared that if Labour members became too enthusiastic for such tactics they would not be content with constitutional procedures; and he wanted to keep clear of the communists.

The fascists made Morrison a target for their abuse. In March 1939 at the Hackney Town Hall nearly two hundred hecklers were ejected, and in the uproar fireworks were exploded and bad eggs thrown. Speakers were drowned by the singing of fascist marching songs and there were cries of 'Mosley'. A youth jumped up, screaming at Morrison and shaking his fist. 'Out with him, officer,' said Mr Morrison. 'Out with him. We pay a police rate and we will get free speech. Don't let him protest. The police don't let them do it in Germany.' He reflected after the hall had been cleared: 'These unfortunate people, like criminals, are the product of a decaying system. It is sad that these boys, through economic reasons, should be forced to become the instruments of a foreign government.'[11]

In the East End Morrison's policy drove many left-wingers into the arms of the communists who appeared ready to act decisively against fascism. In certain parts of the East End Morrison was hated by many active in the Labour movement. They had fought him since the early 1920s, over the plight of the unemployed, Poplarism, the relationship of the Labour and Communist Parties and about the proper role of elected members in local government. Morrison despised the malpractices of some of the East End borough councils; he felt their members sub-standard, so much so that Morrison's chairmen of LCC committees rarely represented East End constituencies.[12] He thought they looked after the interests of their boroughs to the detriment of the whole of London. Although Morrison had loyal parties in the East End, there was always a vocal group antagonistic to him. It is ironical that Morrison, who so personified to the rest of Britain 'the cockney', faced his bitterest opponents from cockneyland itself. No wonder that some felt he was more a south Londoner than an East Ender.[13]

The communists regarded him as their main enemy and they disrupted his speeches. At Poplar he spat back: 'Some of you would prefer a Tory Government. We know our enemies. I have come across this coalition of Conservatives and Communists before. Tories have a very warm place in their hearts for Communists and so have the Communists for the Tories,'[14] and at Deptford he had to be escorted from a hall by fifty policemen: 'All was orderly until the chairman called on Mr Morrison.' He was on his feet for three-quarters of an hour making repeated efforts to deliver his speech, but they howled him down and the meeting was abandoned in pandemonium.[15] In 1935 at the May Day rally in Hyde Park as soon as Morrison started speaking the communists started hooting. Eight policemen escorted him to a taxi amidst catcalls. Shouts of 'Judas' and 'What about Morrison's dictatorship' clashed with 'Good old Herbert', and the 'Internationale' competed with 'For He's a Jolly Good Fellow'.[16]

From 1933 the communists sought to associate with the Labour Party, no longer in their eyes 'social fascists', to present a United Front against fascism. From 1937 a wider combination was also suggested, containing Liberals and even Tories who were prepared to resist fascism in a Popular Front. The communists also organized *ad hoc* alliances for particular causes where sympathizers could collaborate. In March 1933 the Communist Party and the ILP wrote to the LLP and the London Trades Council seeking to join with them in a United Front. Morrison wrote a memorandum for the Executive, pointing out that the Labour and Socialist International advised them to have no truck with such proposals and that the National Joint Council of the TUC and the Labour Party agreed. He warned local parties not to associate with the communists and their front organizations: the first of many such letters.[17]

Morrison showed that the communist line was to serve the interests of the USSR. Now that Stalin felt that Nazi Germany was a menace he sought an alliance with social democratic parties. For years Russia had denounced the League of Nations as a capitalist conspiracy, but then joined it and sought collective security agreements when the Nazi threat grew. After the Nazi-Soviet pact of August 1939 Morrison concluded that 'British Labour cannot do business with a political party which cannot call its soul its own'.[18] The Russian invasion of Finland infuriated him and he turned on Labour people who tried to justify the aggression for trying to 'whitewash something that is obviously and shamefully immoral'.[19] Stalin showed himself a Tsarist imperialist, a betrayer of the Russian revolution; and the British Communist Party was revealed as 'the mere tool of an imperialist foreign government associated with the Nazis'.[20]

In the early 1930s Morrison had expressed some warm feelings towards the Soviet Union, which were periodically publicized by the Beaverbrook Press to suggest that Morrison was not a patriot. He admired the original Russian revolution and had sympathy for the economic collectivism of the Soviet Union. When Russia had supported collective security through the League of

Nations he had urged the National Government to collaborate, although he opposed any collaboration with the Communist Party at home. He argued, with frequent and copious illustration from communist writers, that the communist call for co-operation had ulterior motives. It was just 'a tactical manoeuvre', to enable the Communist Party to infiltrate and eventually destroy the Labour Party, leaving as leader of the Labour movement the highly disciplined Communist Party.[21] He urged members not to fritter away their energies on front organizations. He became an expert about these bodies, writing in 1933 a party pamphlet, *The Communist Solar System*, where he described the various bodies designed to disintegrate Labour and to assert communist leadership. He noted that they 'come and they go and, like burglars, when they are found out they sail under a new name'.[22] He persuaded the party to draw up a list of 'proscribed' bodies, membership of which was incompatible with membership of the Labour Party, and at the NEC he regularly brought it up to date.

Morrison also had to handle what he called 'the running mate' of the Communist Party, the ILP. In 1932 it had decided to disaffiliate from the Labour Party after a stormy few years of controversy. Morrison was saddened at the departure of the party to which he had once belonged, but it had become so 'bent on mischief' and so damaging to the Labour Party that it was best for it to go. He had hoped that, after the Labour Party had reformed its constitution in 1918 to become a fully equipped political party with individual members, the ILP would transform itself into a socialist propaganda organ, 'pure and simple'. However, it began to duplicate the work of the Labour Party, concocting different policies. Overlap and friction increased. In Parliament ILP members wanted to be responsible to the ILP and not accept decisions of the PLP; they attacked Labour Party leaders and policies, and criticized the Labour government of 1929–31. They became 'a party within a party'. Morrison doubted whether the ILP was really socialist in 1932. It seemed to care more about doling out cash benefits than 'out and out Socialism'.[23] He said: 'I would sooner have an honest Communist than one who has not the courage of his convictions.'[24]

At the conference of 1934 he mounted an attack on Harold Laski, Ellen Wilkinson (both of whom were later to be his warm champions) and Lord Marley for activities in the proscribed organization, the Relief Committee for the Victims of German and Austrian Fascism. He exposed its connections with the Comintern and explained that its objective was not philanthropy but the creation of confusion in the Labour movement. Disciplinary action had to be taken against both ordinary and more elevated members who associated with communists on public platforms or sent circulars to local parties. He called the trio 'unduly innocent', used by the communists for their own ends, and suggested that they needed rescuing. They had a choice: either to leave the Committee or the party. The conference backed Morrison, despite an emotional outburst from Aneurin Bevan.[25] The Left Book Club frequently incurred Morrison's strictures, as 'the cleverest "innocents' club" yet devised by the Communists',[26] and Morrison condemned it for seeking to control local Labour parties and to organize elections to the NEC.[27]

Morrison tried to persuade people with an inclination towards the communists of the error of their ways, especially if he thought they were otherwise valuable Labour members. Clem Leslie and his wife had Morrison to dinner one night and expressed their support for a Popular Front. 'He wiped the floor with us and converted us. He was really persuasive.'[28] With others, however, he sometimes failed. In the 1930s Ted Willis had organized a coup at the Labour League of Youth, which swept off its National Committee such rightists as George Brown and Alice Bacon. The League clamoured for co-operation with the communists. In an attempt to patch up a reconciliation Morrison asked Willis to the LLP office. Over a cup of tea Morrison said that 'no door in our great party is closed to you, Ted, as long as you are a democrat, and that is up to you'.[29] Two other leftists, Maurice Orbach and D. N. Pritt, claim that Morrison tried to tame them. Orbach said that he could have been Morrison's 'golden boy' at the LCC if he had toed the line, and Pritt claimed that he was offered the post of Solicitor General in a future Labour government if he dropped 'all this left-wing nonsense'.[30] When Morrison felt that an individual had gone over to the communists, he did not let previous personal friendship diminish his hostility. His childhood sweetheart Nellie Harslett was in the 1930s, as Mrs E. Goodrich, Chairman of the Wandsworth Trades Council. She co-operated with the communists in a fund to send an ambulance to Spain. When Morrison learned of this venture, he became 'cold and indifferent'. However, at the time of the Russian invasion of Finland his attitude changed again overnight after she had put forward a motion for the LLP conference condemning Russian aggression.[31] Involvement, however innocent and well meaning, in a 'front organization' was enough to damn in Morrison's eyes even a friend, let alone an opponent of long standing. The most significant of Morrison's confrontations with old colleagues was in 1937 when he clashed with one of his chief lieutenants at the LCC, George Strauss.

The disagreement stemmed from Morrison's declarations that Labour and communists should have no compacts in elections.[32] This attitude was maintained when the communists suggested a United Front for the LCC elections of 1937, to stimulate enthusiasm among activists and to attract more votes. Morrison pointed out that the LLP had shown that it could stand on its own feet. 'That is why it is powerful.'[33] It also seemed odd for the communists to want to join with the LLP in view of their previous bitter attacks on Morrison's administration at the LCC, for being a bad employer, for paying mean scales of relief in public assistance and for operating a training centre which they called a 'slave camp'.[34]

The communists were up to all kinds of tricks to show their eagerness to join forces. They inquired if the Labour Party had any posters they could put up at Communist Party meetings; they sent their election material to Labour committee rooms to be distributed with Labour literature.[35] They claimed to use information from Labour pamphlets for their propaganda. Harry Pollitt, the communist leader, wrote to Morrison: 'I have great pleasure in sending you copies of the material that we are issuing in connection with the LCC elections. It's good to be alive these days.' Morrison replied: '. . . it is perhaps well that we should place on record that the publications you enclosed with your letter have been issued without our desire or authority . . . I am glad that you find it good to be alive. I gather that the Tories also find it good that you are alive.'[36] Strauss disobeyed the LLP ruling and publicly welcomed communist assistance, signing the United Front manifesto and joining the Unity Committee. The Tories and the Beaverbrook Press gleefully alleged that Labour and communists were in harness. Morrison was 'Mr Pollitt's Kerensky'. Strauss (identified as 'a Jew of German extraction'[37]) was openly co-operating and 'has been Mr Morrison's political protégé for many years, and is now his right-hand man at County Hall'.[38] The *Sunday Express* went so far as to state that Morrison and Pollitt 'are directing the campaign to keep the Socialists in power at County Hall'.[39] Morrison was so furious that Beaverbrook reporters were refused admittance to press conferences.[40]

After the Labour victory Morrison removed Strauss from the LCC chairmanship of the Highways Committee and the vice-chairmanship of Finance, despite his contribution of five hundred pounds to the election fund. The party meeting supported this decision. Strauss accused Morrison of attempting 'to dragoon everyone into goose-stepping behind the leaders'.[41] He claimed that the communists had contributed to the Labour victory. They did 'an immense amount of canvassing, envelope addressing and other election donkey-work in the Labour Party offices' and, he claimed, in those areas where there was co-operation the results were better than where communist help was rejected.[42]

Morrison now felt compelled to make a public statement. In private he had been distressed at the rift between himself and a former close colleague. He said that he had a high regard for Strauss's competence; he had been an efficient chairman but, if Strauss remained chairman, it would be said that Morrison's assurances that there was no link between the Labour and Communist Parties were given in bad faith. Since Strauss had defied the party, 'he really ought not to be surprised and indignant about having to pay the price of not holding high public office on behalf of the party'.[43]

Dissension over the communists also brought Morrison up against the Labour League of Youth. Morrison saw the League's functions as primarily educative and recreational. He felt that as an integral section of the Labour Party it should not be independent, with its own national conference, committee and secretary.[44] What he most opposed was that the League should debate and issue resolutions on policy. He feared that the League would become a battleground for contestants seeking to control the League as a 'voice of youth'.[45] The LLP Executive argued about this issue in 1933. A motion was proposed to allow the League to debate and resolve upon party policy. Five were in favour, and seven against, but the chairman, Harold Clay, excluded Morrison's vote on the ground that the Secretary could not vote, then gave his own vote in favour, thus producing a tie, which he resolved by his casting affirmative vote. Morrison wrote an angry memorandum stating that the Secretary was meant to be a full member of the Executive with the right to vote, and that in the past he had always done so, for instance over the 'Communist difficulties'.[46]

Most members of the League looked on him as a reactionary. Ted Willis typified the left-wing Popular Fronter. He explained: 'Herbert could not see why young people were on the left. He had no sympathy or understanding for the young people's revolutionary feeling. As a pragmatist who thought logically he felt that the antics of the young people were a waste of time and indeed spoiled the image of the Labour Party. He felt that the League of Youth was an unnecessary irritation and that young people should be active within the Labour Party. Herbert simply couldn't see the thought processes of the young.'[47]

People like Willis came to play a dominating role in the League, arranging 'unconstitutional' conferences, fixing elections to wipe out the 'loyalists', and passing resolutions at variance with party policy. In 1939 the NEC ordered its disbandment. It was simply not worth the time, money, effort and trouble to keep it in being. The LLP in turn brought an end to its youth organization.[48]

Nineteen thirty-nine was a crucial year in the battle against the forces urging alliance with the communists. The NEC and the bulk of the party felt that as a general election approached the ranks of the party should close. However the leading champions of the Popular Front intensified their activities. Cripps submitted to the NEC a memorandum advocating that Labour should join forces with all opponents of the National Government, even in certain constituencies allowing Liberals and communists a clear run against a government candidate. The NEC rejected the memorandum.[49] Then Cripps circulated it widely within the party and outside. Morrison at the NEC moved a successful motion that the Organization sub-committee should examine the matter and report to the NEC, that the report should be sent to Cripps for him to make observations, and that the NEC should consult Cripps.[50] The sub-committee, on which Morrison sat, condemned Cripps's campaigns to change the direction of the party and its leadership. The NEC endorsed the report and asked Cripps to reaffirm his loyalty to the Labour Party and to withdraw his memorandum by a circular to those to whom it had been addressed. Cripps refused, and was told that he would be excluded from the party.[51] He asked for a chance to state his case at the annual conference, and the NEC referred the request to the Conference Arrangements Committee.[52]

A number of other members of the party had signed Cripps's memorandum and had been asked to dissociate themselves from it. Four refused: Aneurin

Bevan, George Strauss, Robert Bruce and E. P. Young. The NEC in March 1939 threatened that if they did not withdraw from their campaign within seven days they would be expelled. Morrison had not wanted this letter sent. He proposed a softer course of action (which was defeated: ten votes to thirteen) to inform them that their replies were unsatisfactory, and that the NEC should report to conference that it would exclude those who declined to give undertakings to cease participating in such organized campaigns. He wanted them to be asked once again to stop their activities in view of the grave international situation and the need for unity.[53] Morrison was not thirsting for expulsion. As Susan Lawrence reported to Beatrice Webb, he was urging 'that the other MPs should not be expelled, and that an attempt should be made to bring Stafford back'.[54] His colleagues overruled this plea for delay. The National Agent informed the recalcitrant members of the decision of the NEC. Their 'unpardonable disloyalty' consisted of:

(a) The persistent propagation by self-appointed Groups of programmes and policies diametrically opposed to those of the Labour Party.
(b) The organization of a widespread public campaign in association with and supported by political parties ineligible for affiliation to the Labour Party.
(c) The use of personal wealth to communicate wholesale with affiliated organizations.
(d) The creation of machinery with staffs and offices throughout the country for the purpose of undermining the integrity of the Party and the authority of the Annual Party Conference.
(e) The persistent making of speeches and writing of articles which are abusive of the Party, its principles and policy.

The NEC could not permit such agitation by a permanent opposition within the party 'and at the same time gather strength to fight for power'. Since the individuals would not withdraw from the Popular Front campaign, they were 'hereby excluded from the Party'.[55]

Once the NEC had reached the decision to expel, Morrison no longer campaigned for toleration. In reply to a protest from Beatrice Webb, Morrison wrote that the expulsion of Cripps was inevitable, because of his 'fairly persistent organized activities within the Party to weaken its effectiveness for reasonable unity'.[56] At the party conference Morrison defended the NEC's decision and won a handsome majority.[57]

Morrison is often described as a harsh disciplinarian, but over Cripps he was cautious. He played for time, hoping that an accommodation might be made. Although Morrison had been instrumental in getting Cripps into the party, they had engaged in many public confrontations throughout the decade. For example, in 1934 Morrison took Cripps to task for his statement that a Labour government would face 'a first rate financial crisis' on taking office. 'To assume or to blazon forth to the world' such a view was 'suicidal tactics'.

It presented the Tories with the war cry: 'A vote for Labour is a vote for a first rate financial crisis.' 'It may be good melodrama, but it is not fighting politics.'[58] Despite such public rows they, and their wives, remained in private quite close. In 1937 Morrison wrote to Cripps: 'No one has regretted more than I the difficulties which have risen between yourself and the Party.' He was anxious to retain Cripps's 'valuable and decisive influence'.[59]

In the summer of 1939 the expellees sought to be readmitted to the party. Morrison now was not keen to take them back. His motion at the NEC for the rejection of Cripps's request was defeated by thirteen votes to twelve.[60] Instead the Organization sub-committee surveyed the situation and drew up a set of undertakings for the expellees to sign.[61] By the end of the year Bevan had agreed, and in February 1940 so had Strauss, promising to refrain from campaigns in opposition to the declared policy of the party and to accept the constitution, programme, principles and policy of the party without reservation.[62] Cripps, however, refused.[63] But he remained on reasonable terms with Morrison.

In the 1920s Morrison had played a prominent part in removing communists from the Labour Party and in frustrating their attempts to infiltrate it or link with it. In the 1930s he was still the party's leading anti-communist. At the NEC he constantly took a tough line, and at almost every party conference he made a major speech against the communists and their collaborators. It would have been all too easy for delegates to have fallen for the superficially attractive slogans of the Popular Fronters. The force of Morrison's speeches, the clarity of his arguments, their solid logic, his grasp of the facts and his power to convince kept the party on the path of sanity.[64] Morrison played a considerable part in preserving the integrity of the Labour Party in the 1930s. He enabled it to enter the war as a self-confident and self-reliant political organization.

Chapter 17

Frustrated Ambitions

'I can truthfully say that I have never sought advancement or power, preferring to leave things to circumstance and the Party.'[1] Thus Morrison mused on his career in his *Autobiography*. He frequently voiced this refrain, deploring careerists. 'I think I can claim that I am not an ambitious person. This may be a defect of character which has deprived me of the material benefits of life.'[2] Others, however, saw Morrison as 'consumed with ambition' and 'a constant intriguer'.[3]

He never sought well-paid jobs in private enterprise, and rejected in the 1930s two remunerative offers made just after he had left the government: the executive chairmanship of the British Electrical Development Association with a salary of five thousand pounds per annum and an executive post with the Metropolitan Gas Company with a salary of his choice.[4] He wished to stay in politics, 'his true and only professional love'.[5] He told Mary Agnes Hamilton: 'It's better for me to live more or less as the comrades do; I might get out of touch – or they might feel I have got out of touch.'[6]

In the early 1930s Morrison very much wanted to be Secretary of the Labour Party nationally.[7] Since 1915 he had been Secretary of the largest local party in the country, and an exceedingly successful one, and since 1920 he had served on the NEC and so knew the intricacies of organization at party headquarters. As early as September 1930 there were rumours that Arthur Henderson, the National Secretery since 1912, wished to resign.[8] However, in 1932 and 1933 Henderson still remained because, wrote Tom Jones in his diary, he could not find an appropriate successor. Morrison 'is the most suitable but is suspected of being too friendly to Macdonald' [sic].[9]

The NEC grew increasingly restive at Henderson's neglect of his office as he travelled abroad and was immersed in the Disarmament Conference. Dalton wrote in his diary review for 1934 that Henderson was most reluctant to retire and in the end was forced out by pressure from the NEC.[10] In May 1934 he told the NEC of his intention to resign. The timing was a blow to

Morrison who, just two months before, had become leader of the LCC. Henderson was opposed to Morrison, because 'the Parliamentary Labour party must decide policy between the annual conferences, because they inevitably *will* do so when parliament is sitting. Therefore it is no good having a powerful man like Herbert Morrison who would be wasted if he were not allowed to dominate the Party; also, Morrison ought to stay leader of the LCC and make a success of it.'[11] Henderson supported Middleton, 'the time-long assistant secretary', hoping that his son, Willie Henderson, would become assistant and eventually succeed Middleton.[12] Morrison apparently tried to obtain Henderson's backing but received 'no sign of support at all'.[13] The other candidate was Arthur Greenwood.

Up to the annual conference in October Morrison was hopeful. He was not prepared to give up the leadership of the LCC which he felt he could combine with the Secretaryship. What finally blocked his cause was the opposition of some trade unionists, particularly Ernest Bevin, who felt that if the Secretary was also an MP the influence of the parliamentary party on the Labour Party would be too strong, and that the party should follow the principle of 'one man one job'.[14] Greenwood was not prepared to give up being an MP, nor would Morrison renounce his parliamentary ambitions. The NEC devised a compromise, whereby the Secretary could be an MP but would have to resign the Secretaryship on taking a place in government. This proposal was defeated at the conference by 1,449,000 votes to 841,000.[15] When the conference vote was announced, Morrison was 'white, stiff-lipped and sick to the gills'.[16] He and Greenwood then withdrew.[17] The short list of six names was put before the NEC in November and two ballots were held; finally a unanimous vote selected Middleton.[18] But to the *Morning Post* on the basis of his speeches at the party conference, Morrison was 'the present dictator of the Party . . . and he will continue as such, no matter who succeeds Mr Henderson as Secretary'.[19] Morrison did not give up hope of one day acquiring the Secretaryship, and he maintained an undercurrent of criticism against Middleton for inefficiency.[20]

Far more importantly Morrison regarded himself as a serious candidate for the Labour leadership. From the start of 1934 speculation about the future leader began in earnest. The 'possibles' were Arthur Greenwood, Sir Stafford Cripps and Major Attlee, 'the temporary leader of the Opposition',[21] who took over when Lansbury was ill. But Morrison was the favourite;[22] after his vigorous conference speeches in 1934 *Time and Tide* saw him as 'now its leader by right of conquest'.[23] Lansbury probably hoped to hand over to Cripps, yet Morrison's best speech at the 1934 conference was a witty denunciation of Cripps which put him out of the running.[24] Morrison was at the top of the poll of members of the NEC. The *Sunday Express*, predicting he would be leader, said: 'He has had a run of success.

He led the Socialists to victory in the LCC elections last March. He progresed triumphantly through the conference at Southport.'[25] It was, however, occasionally pointed out that he was out of favour with the trade unions[26] and that 'it was Mr Bevin who cracked the whip and cowed the delegates'.[27]

Up to the conference of 1935 Morrison still remained in front. He toured the country, speaking at numerous party meetings; his press articles increased and he forged an alliance with Tom Johnston who ran *Forward,* so that each week on its front page appeared an article by Morrison.[28] He looked like 'the rising hope of the Labour Party, one might almost say, its only hope'.[29] At the conference Morrison sought to soften his image, and win over those who thought him 'grim and truculent when in the saddle'.[30] In the debate on the use of sanctions against Italy for her invasion of Abyssinia, Lansbury had stated his pacifist case and Bevin had brutally savaged him. Morrison summed up for the Executive with a masterpiece of fudging designed to get the maximum vote and to please everyone. Kingsley Martin had supplied Morrison with a memorandum which formed the basis of the speech.[31] Unconditional support of sanctions would encourage the government merely to justify armaments; Labour's acceptance of sanctions was based on support of the Covenant of the League of Nations which meant not only restraint of the aggressor but also disarmament, international instead of imperial control of the colonies, revision of treaties, sharing markets and redistributing raw materials. The speech had phrases for all shades of opinion, bar the extremes. And he went out of his way to be kind to Lansbury. Morrison felt that his task was to try to pull the conference and the party together. He paid tribute to Lansbury's great services, and appealed for tolerance for minority views within the party. As Lansbury left the platform Morrison shook his hand and said: 'Stand by your beliefs, George', a kindness Lansbury never forgot.[32] The Executive received a huge majority.[33] Lansbury retired from the leadership.

Morrison may well have believed what he said. After all he had been a kind of pacifist himself. On international affairs he was much closer to Lansbury than to Bevin. But this speech, in the context of the fight for the party leadership, was a bid for support from those quarters which had been most opposed to him, the so-called left around Lansbury. Morrison appeared more tolerant than the heartless Bevin who knew at once what Morrison was up to. After the speech, as Morrison was receiving a big ovation, Bevin complained to Isaac Hayward, 'I say all the nasty things, while others get the credit', and he told the reporter, Trevor Evans: 'There are too many namby-pambies about. Even Morrison was trying to soft pedal, but no doubt he has his own reasons', suggesting he was thinking of the leadership.[34] At the National Council of Labour Bevin made his anger plain to Morrison: 'it was a raw deal for him, when he had defended the Executive policy, for an Executive spokesman to be over-kind to George Lansbury and the pacifist minority'.[35] Morrison did not relent, but wrote a public defence of his action.

I have had entrusted to me a full share of the task of enforcing standards of Party loyalty and discipline in certain directions. Increasingly I have regarded this task as a necessary duty rather than a pleasure.... On the present issue, and with the present minority, the majority must, I think, reflect and consider before it operates a universal and mechanical discipline. Universal and mechanical discipline, irrespective of the subject matter and the nature of the minority, would destroy the very soul of the Labour Party. Provided they express their personal views with due consideration to the legitimate interest of the Movement, I personally will be no party to treading brutally on their political necks.[36]

Morrison was now so obviously the real leader of the Labour Party that it was important to get him into the House. A by-election pending at Farnworth seemed a timely opportunity.[37] Lansbury retired, however, before Morrison could be adopted, and Attlee, as deputy, took over. Almost at once the general election was upon them. Morrison played a prominent part in the campaign, speaking over the whole country, broadcasting twice on radio, including the final appeal, and writing many articles for the press. He wrote in the *Daily Herald* a series of twenty-one lengthy articles entitled 'What Every Voter Should Know', which covered all aspects of Labour policy. He prophesied: 'If they entered the fight with the necessary confidence and aggression [two qualities not noticeable in Attlee] it was quite possible for them to win a Parliamentary majority.'[38] The *News Chronicle* noted that the campaign 'is being dominated by one man – Herbert Morrison'.[39] On radio he was a 'distinct success'.[40] Beatrice Webb wrote that his speech 'was overwhelmingly the best – alike in subject matter, arrangement, voice and manner'. Morrison 'stands out as the one and only successful leader'.[41]

Although Labour improved significantly on 1931, returning 154 MPs as against 52, Morrison argued that it was not good enough. In 1929 Labour had won 288, and he had thought between two hundred and 240 was now possible. In an implied criticism of Attlee he wrote: 'Since 1931 we have not yet evolved a clear leadership. . . . Most of us had hoped to win more seats. . . . That was particularly so when we had succeeded in maintaining the essential unity of the Party. . . . We ought to have done better. Look at the "certainties" we have failed to win.... Was our appeal wide enough and constructively concrete enough?'[42] Now that Morrison was back in the House, he felt poised to snatch the leadership.

A group covering a wide range of views within the party supported Morrison: the intellectuals of the right who wanted a strong leader; those who felt that Herbert, as a local boy who had made good, would give the party a figurehead it badly needed; and the practical party men who wanted to see a social programme planned and rammed home as he had done as leader of the LCC.[43]

Attlee noted that Morrison had the support of the 'intelligentsia and the Press'.[44] Francis Williams, then editor of the *Daily Herald*, looked on him as the modern man, not bound by old ideas. He attracted the young, the moderates, the middle class, and the intellectuals who admired him as the theorist of applied socialism.[45] A. L. Rowse, then a Labour candidate in Cornwall, said: 'His victory at the LCC and the success of his administration were a pivot of hope. He did a first-class job, top hole. He offered constructive and responsible government which was very appealing to the younger generation.'[46] Douglas Jay, Hugh Gaitskell and Evan Durbin, protégés of Dalton, 'were all supporters of Herbert, because he was active, popular, sensible and had achieved electoral success on the LCC'.[47]

Philip Noel-Baker was in favour of Morrison: 'because he was the ablest and best speaker and had a wide range covering not only domestic but foreign policy too'. He liked Morrison's support for collective security through the League of Nations and his condemnation of armaments,[48] which also attracted Kingsley Martin, editor of the *New Statesman*, who backed him as being 'dynamic, open to ideas, keen to argue and above all keen that the party should succeed and win'. Martin 'thought him the best available leader for the Labour Party. . . . He had far more drive than anyone else in the Party except Bevin . . . though Morrison built his leadership on a kind of democratic cajolery which was very different from Bevin's autocratic bullying.'[49] He explained that some of the left of the party supported Morrison because they felt they could have a dialogue with him. He would listen to their case and give a reasoned reply. He was interested in ideas; and, as Tawney told Martin, he was in reality more radical than he sounded. This would also explain Laski's support.[50] D. N. Pritt, almost a communist, voted for Morrison, because of his 'drive and capacity'.[51] And Cripps was for Morrison whom he called 'by far the ablest and soundest man in the labour movement'.[52]

Hugh Dalton was Morrison's campaign manager. In May 1935, when Dalton was lunching with Charles Latham, the latter said that he and Morrison should get together and discuss the future. Dalton replied that Morrison always seemed to wear armour when they talked, as if he feared that Dalton was a rival.[53] It was not until the autumn that Dalton made overtures to Morrison. Mary Agnes Hamilton, acting as Dalton's spokesman, told Morrison at the 1935 Brighton conference that he was 'not after the leadership and preferred Morrison to have it. 'She said that a remarkable warmth at once began to develop. Previously he had been tepid.' Dalton invited Morrison and his wife to his country cottage in Wiltshire for the weekend of 5–6 October. Dalton took Morrison for a walk, and between Dudmore and Woodend said: 'I am not consciously a candidate for the leadership; I am not going after it. This doesn't mean that, if, at some later stage, there was a strong demand that I should take it, I should necessarily refuse. But I have other desires. I feel, though it isn't a job one would hold out glad hands for in the present state of the world, that I could do the FO better than anyone else in the Party; if the external world was quiet, perhaps I could do something big on the Home Front.[54] But, as for the leadership, I think it should go to someone who has *not* had exceptional opportunities', which in his autobiography Dalton amplified as, 'to a man of working class origin, who had not been to a public school or a university'.[55] Dalton said that Cripps 'has now cooked his goose'. Attlee was 'very small', and Greenwood 'has hurt his mind by drinking'. He said he preferred Morrison. 'He is a good deal taken aback, I think. He says little. "Thank you ... I think there *is* something to be said for the leader being a proletarian. I don't let my mind dwell on it much for if one is disappointed, one may become bitter ... with the available material, the natural place for you would, I should think, be either the FO or the Treasury." So the ice is broken.'[56] Dalton then bustled here and there, booming out his entreaties. His stock opening was to describe the choice as between a nonentity, a drunkard and Herbert.[57]

As the newly elected MPs gathered in London, lobbying began. The most vigorous campaigner was Hugh Dalton. On 16 November Morrison, at Dalton's request, went to his flat and pored over the list of new Labour MPs. Dalton wrote in his diary, 'It seems hopeful. If Clynes doesn't run, Attlee is the most dangerous' on the grounds of 'sentiment and inertia'. Morrison suggested 'if Clynes will move [me], that will practically settle it'. On the 18th Dalton visited Clynes and had a long discussion. Clynes felt: 'it should go to a younger man. . . . Not Attlee at all.' At sixty-seven Clynes felt unable to undertake it himself. He preferred Herbert and gave Dalton authority to say so. He would not, however, promise to nominate him, but wanted time to think it over. Clynes pointed out that Dalton was the first to speak to him about it. 'I say to myself that all the rest have been bloody slow.'

Over the next few days Dalton canvassed. On 20 November he held a dinner party at his flat, ostensibly for four new MPs to meet Konni Zilliacus. Later about ten others joined them. The leadership issue came up and 'we were nearly all for H.M.'[58] 'The host and other speakers emphasized the advantages of Mr Morrison's election.' Plans were made to enlist support for his claims, but no pledges were extracted.[59] On 23 November the Beaverbrook Press carried stories of the meeting. 'It aroused indignation among supporters of Mr Attlee and Mr Arthur Greenwood. An Anti-Morrison movement began at once. It was urged that Mr Morrison has a full-time job in leading the LCC and that he could not effectively combine with it the leadership of the Parliamentary Party.'[60] Morrison rang up Dalton '(a daily occurrence now) slightly bothered about the degree of press. But I persuaded him that the least said by either of us the better.' On Tuesday, 26 November, Dalton went early to the Commons, 'to do a final canvass for H.M. Attlee running round with a slightly nervous grin, eagerly greeting everyone. Grenfell with him. I find a great disinclination to *move* H.M. Clynes has evidently run back into neutrality, some of his union favouring Greenwood. He is a little coward.'[61]

The Parliamentary Labour Party and the National Executive met at 11.30 a.m. in Committee Room No. 14 of the House of Commons with Attlee in the chair.[62] Shinwell first moved that nominations and voting be taken at a later date, but could muster only three votes. Clynes was then asked if he would accept nomination, and declined. Greenwood was nominated, then Attlee and finally Morrison.[63] Then an MP,[64] by arrangement with Dalton, asked a question which, ironically, damaged Morrison: Would the candidates, if elected, give their full time to the job? Attlee replied: 'If I am elected, I shall carry on as before.' Greenwood said 'yes' and Morrison launched forth 'rather heavily and at too great length'. The gist was that he put himself in the hands of the party. If they thought he should give up the leadership at County Hall, he would. If they thought some accommodation could be found, at least till the next LCC elections, he would fall in with that. He was sure that some convenient arrangement could be made. His statement was not well received. He seemed evasive. 'It's not fair' and 'very slick' were shouted.

Then followed balloting. Attlee received 58 votes, Morrison 44, and Greenwood 33. An MP called out: 'Fancy putting up a new member for the Leadership.' The second ballot then took place at which Attlee received 88 and Morrison 48. Greenwood and Morrison then proposed Attlee who was acclaimed unanimously. Nominations were invited for the Deputy Chairmanship. After Greenwood had been nominated, Morrison was, 'but declined to stand', saying he was too busy with the LCC. Greenwood was chosen unanimously. A week later at the next session, elections for the Executive of the PLP were held. Morrison tied with Tom Johnston in third place with 100 votes, following Clynes with 114 and Dalton with 104.[65] Morrison was at least regarded as part of the leadership.

There are many explanations for Morrison's failure. The so-called left of the party could hardly have supported Morrison with enthusiasm. For nearly twenty years he had hammered them at conferences. His concern for gradualism, constitutional procedures, financial responsibility and appeals to the middle class, together with his scorn for communists, United Fronts, Socialist Leagues and 'socialism in our time', struck no sympathetic chords in them. Despite his tolerance for Lansbury, the ex-pacifist was an advocate of civil defence, urging co-operation with the government over air raid precautions. His obsession with the public corporation seemed to bolster up capitalism through bureaucracy. They distrusted his eagerness to reassure businessmen, as well as his emphasis on compensation for property taken over by the state.[66] Morrison seemed an 'arch-reactionary'.[67]

Morrison was also defeated by the loyalty that many MPs had for Attlee, especially those of the 'rump' Parliament of 1931 to 1935. Attlee had been deputy to Lansbury since 1931 and had often acted as leader in his absence. His colleagues felt that he had been an able parliamentarian, who had done 'a damn good job',[68] standing up gallantly against the massive majority of the National Government. Attlee himself was 'pretty sure of the support of the majority of my colleagues in the last House'.[69] As temporary leader after Lansbury's retirement, Attlee had led the party in a general election which increased their number by over a hundred. It seemed an act of ingratitude to deprive him of the leadership after he had done so well. Morrison, absent from the Commons since 1931, seemed an interloper. Indeed Attlee had greater parliamentary experience. A member continuously since 1922, he had devoted himself to Parliament. But Morrison had been an MP only in 1924 and in 1929–31: on the first occasion as a mere back-bencher though on the second as a minister. His experience of Parliament was limited, but the party was choosing a *parliamentary* leader above all.

In his *Autobiography* Morrison laid much of the responsibility for his defeat onto a group of Labour MPs who were Freemasons,[70] alleging that at the New Welcome Lodge meeting three days before the election support for Greenwood had been arranged. This lodge was formed in the early 1930s by the Secretary of the Parliamentary Labour Party, Scott Lindsay, who was a most influential figure in the PLP of the early 1930s. The Deputy Chief Whip of this period said that the Chief Whip, Charles Edwards, was 'politically a dud and the work of the Whip had fallen to Lindsay who ran the show. He knew more than anyone about the procedures of Parliament and he was tremendously able.'[71] He drew up lists of Labour members to serve on committees or to go on delegations and allocated speakers for debates. Labour MPs in the Parliament of 1931–5 realized that if they wanted to make a reputation they had to keep in with Lindsay, and he acquired around him a clique. He was a convivial fellow who liked to drink and treat his comrades. They would meet regularly, when the House was sitting, at 6 p.m. in the bar. Greenwood was the most senior in the bunch, most of whom were working class trade unionists from the provinces, somewhat out of their depth in the Commons but grateful to Lindsay for his guidance and hospitality. Some of these were in the New Welcome Lodge, of which Lindsay was Secretary. In April 1938 a party official[72] showed Hugh Dalton the three-year-old summons from Lindsay to members of the lodge for the special meeting held three days before the leadership election. On the back was a list of lodge members; it included sixteen Labour MPs, the most notable being Arthur Greenwood. Dalton learned that Morrison had seen the document. 'I have got a copy locked up in my drawer. Someone sent it to me a few days after the election.'[73] Scott Lindsay was the pivotal figure, and Greenwood the most senior Labour politician, in both groups. It was natural that he should be their choice for leader. Lindsay apparently told Dalton that Greenwood had told him that if elected leader he would see that Lindsay 'would never be out of control on important occasions'.[74] Lindsay and Morrison were at daggers drawn. Morrison thought him incompetent, and disliked his drinking habits, while Lindsay resented Morrison's, and anybody's, attempts, including those of the Whips' Office, to curb his influence. He was always 'gruff and off-hand' with Morrison. The pals of the Lindsay–Greenwood set voted for Greenwood on the first ballot and switched to Attlee on the second.[75]

There was a fear that Morrison would be too dominant. Powerful leaders could take the party in the wrong direction, as it was thought MacDonald had. What was wanted was a leader who would follow the party. Attlee fitted that bill, but Morrison was divisive; he enjoyed controversy. Attlee, however, shunned dissension. He sought to conciliate and unite. With Morrison the party would be rent by disagreements over policies, tactics and personnel.[76]

Morrison appeared too ambitious and, as the Earl of Swinton guessed, 'probably prejudiced his prospects by appearing a bit too much of the professional and the manipulator.'[77] He was not a good intriguer. 'All knew what he was up to. He could not dissemble.'[78] He seemed as artful as a wagon load of monkeys.[79] James Walker, MP for Motherwell, wrote satirical verse about Morrison:

> The man on whom the party leans,
> Who never says just what he means,
> Nor ever means just what he says,
> As skilfully with words he plays.[80]

Attlee by saying so little earned a reputation for rectitude. What also told against Morrison was the rumour that he had wavered, or worse, in 1931. This incident earned him 'eternal distrust'.[81] His loyalty was suspect.[82]

Morrison was also too closely identified with London. Only twenty-two Labour MPs were elected by London constituencies; the majority came from the provinces: the industrial regions of the Midlands, the North, Wales and Scotland, where anti-London feeling was strong. Although Attlee was a Londoner and sat for a London seat, he was never so intimately associated with London as Morrison. Many doubted if Morrison understood the problems of the provinces and the attitudes of the provincials. One lobby correspondent felt that the northern MPs regarded Morrison as 'too clever by half', a slick Cockney who was not to be trusted, a view held also by Bevin, a provincial from the south-west.[83] With Morrison as leader it was feared that London would receive undue attention. David Kirkwood wrote: 'It is a pity he is so much caged there.'[84]

There is a conflict of views as to whether he was out of touch with the rest of the country. Sir William Lawther pointed out that Morrison was always very popular at the Durham miners' gala, and Sara Barker and Alice Bacon recalled him holding audiences of Yorkshiremen spellbound. Jean Mann wrote that Morrison reminded her of 'a Scots Granny', with his 'wisdom and sound common sense'. He may have sung 'Maybe it's because I'm a Londoner'

I

in Scotland's loveliest scenery, but: 'He kept the common touch.'[85] On the other hand Lord Bowles recalled a disastrous speech at Preston when Morrison talked about the achievements of the LCC to the annoyance of the Lancastrians. Hinley Atkinson agreed that Morrison knew little about the country outside London and often asked him how such and such a policy would go down in the North or the Midlands. Sir Isaac Hayward felt that there was a gap between Herbert and MPs from outside London: 'He didn't fully appreciate the attitudes of provincials who would say of Herbert, "Who is this fella? We're as good as he is." They were big men in their own areas and couldn't see why Herbert should be deferred to. Herbert didn't really understand this sort of feeling, although I told him about it often enough.'[86] At the first ballot it was guessed that Greenwood had the bulk of the votes from the provincials who had not been in the 1931–5 Parliament; at the second ballot they switched to Attlee.

Morrison would not give a clear undertaking to relinquish the leadership of the LCC. The principle of 'one man one job', which had cost him the party Secretaryship, also damaged his chances for the leadership. The very position which had made his reputation as a vote-winner and administrator stopped him from acquiring the party leadership. In Parliament he would be in opposition, for five years probably, without executive responsibilities. To give up running the nation's capital was too great a sacrifice.

Many trade unionist MPs did not support Morrison. The rows over the composition of the public corporations, his uneasiness about the strike weapon, his championship of the constituency parties, his concentration on the middle class vote, his ideological and theoretical pretensions, and above all the fact that although claiming a working class origin he was clearly not of the blood-brotherhood of the trade unionists, served to alienate the trade union element among the PLP. His knowledge of and sympathy for the trade union movement were in question.[87] At party conferences Morrison did not sit drinking beer with the trade union delegations, but was with the more intellectual types. He liked to surround himself with people who had ideas, not trade union men. He felt he knew their experience and wanted people about him who were socially and intellectually superior to himself.[88] Bevin was determined that Morrison should not be leader. 'No general instructions were issued by him but ways were there to make Bevin's influence felt among the trade union MPs.'[89]

The clash between Bevin and Morrison was more than personal. Attlee wrote that Bevin 'thought mainly in terms of, so to speak, internal organization – the organization of a body bound together by the same single interest', while Morrison 'had much more experience of government, of genuinely public affairs, of handling things so that enemies as well as supporters could live together with a sense of benefit'.[90] Francis Williams saw the clash as between Bevin's economic socialism and Morrison's parliamentary socialism: 'between the industrial leader who thought of Parliamentary power as one stage in the transfer and dispersal of that power which his experience taught him to regard as the most fundamental, economic power, and the political leader who thought of social change as something to be brought about primarily by legislative act.'[91] Between the two a collision was inevitable, and it was made even more fierce by the pathological hatred of Bevin for Morrison.[92] Sir Isaac Hayward told Morrison that if he and Bevin could be allies they could rule the country, Morrison replied, 'It's not my fault, I've tried.'[93] MPs, aware of this antipathy, knew that Bevin would not co-operate easily under Morrison's leadership. The two wings of the Labour movement, political and industrial, seemed likely to be united more under Attlee. Of the three candidates, Morrison was the one with a background closest to the working class, yet the trade union members preferred a public school, very bourgeois, leader.

The feeling of the PLP was that Attlee should be leader and that Morrison should be deputy. If Attlee failed them, they could move Morrison up, but he had first to serve them in Parliament. Morrison's refusal to accept nomination for the deputy leadership was a blunder. If he had taken it, he would have been in an excellent position to supplant Attlee later. As it was, 'he did himself a great damage and lost much respect'.[94]

The choice of Attlee was a blow for Morrison's supporters. Dalton was very upset: 'A wretched, disheartening result! And a little mouse shall lead them,' he wrote in his diary.[95] Hugh Gaitskell, Douglas Jay and Evan Durbin heard the result together and were thoroughly depressed. Labour's chances of winning power seemed far distant.[96] Beatrice Webb was annoyed at the choice of the 'irreproachable but colourless ... somewhat diminutive and meaningless figure' of Attlee.[97] Morrison was shocked, and it rankled for ever.[98] The party had shown it was not ready to govern. He was better occupied at the LCC.[99] Mrs Morrison told Lady Gater that Morrison 'was crushed and faced the wall for a week'.[100]

Morrison's anger with the supporters of Greenwood was revealed in an article in *Forward* immediately after the decision.[101] Ostensibly an open letter of advice to new Labour MPs, it was a deadly attack on Greenwood: 'Parliament is almost the easiest place in which to become a chronic drinker. . . . A speech in the House becomes "impossible" without a stimulant.' His scorn for Attlee appeared in a journalist's account of an interview with Morrison in November 1935. 'One of the things he dislikes most intensely is hesitation among political leaders, especially of his own party . . . Political cowardice is crime No. 1 in his calendar.'[102] When Beatrice Webb suggested that Attlee was only a stop-gap, 'he observed sadly, that the Members of the PLP were "sentimental" and having once made a man leader, would stick to him!'[103]

Between 1935 and 1940 Attlee's leadership never seemed secure. There were rumbles of dissatisfaction, but no overt action to lever him out. The two most favoured as his successors were Greenwood and Morrison who was most often mentioned as the likely leader and in the thick of the plotting. It seemed as if his clique of adherents, MPs and journalists, lost no opportunity to discredit his rivals and to propound his advantages. Morrison always claimed no knowledge of such activities,[104] and it is possible that his friends were promoting his cause without his authority. If he had been inspiring their activities, he failed to give them the support they needed to clinch his challenge. Too involved at the LCC, he had not the time to lounge around the bars and the tea-room and the corridors. He was not a frequent attender or speaker at debates. When he made an impressive speech, he was pointed out as Attlee's main rival. When his speech was poor, his decline was assumed. He was no dud, since he was regularly returned to the Executive of the PLP in either first or second place. But he was not a regular attender at its sessions. He was not close to Attlee. Attlee's personal assistant of these years, Peter Thurtle, wrote: 'The surprising fact is that, looking back, I find that I do not remember Morrison as a member of the leadership team of the Parliamentary Labour Party in the way that I remember such less well-known figures as Tom Williams, George Hall, Dalton, Noel-Baker and others. With all these I had almost daily contact but not with Morrison.'[105] But he never withdrew so completely as to put himself out of the race.

In November 1936 Morrison came top of the poll for the PLP Executive, a triumph ascribed by the *Sunday Express* to his superb performance at the Edinburgh party conference. It also noted that Dalton, although coming second, was in a stronger position, 'for Morrison has bitter and unforgiving enemies among the Trade Union leaders who support Dalton, while Dalton has few foes among the parliamentary party who support Morrison'.[106] The Labour success at the LCC elections of March 1937 was a fillip for Morrison. Even Attlee praised him: 'Mr Morrison has shown what he can do in ruling a great city. In the future he will show what he can do in ruling a great country.'[107] A. L. Rowse wrote almost a manifesto for Morrison, claiming that his was 'the authentic voice of the party'.[108]

By 1938, however, Attlee was still in the saddle and Morrison's fortunes seemed low. In January the *Daily Telegraph* noted that Morrison 'speaks comparatively infrequently nowadays in the House',[109] and in July the *Sunday Express* commented, 'The biggest failure in the ranks of Labour is Mr Herbert Morrison. He is way down. He does not attend the House of Commons enough. As a result he is ill at ease when he speaks there.'[110] Dalton was no longer a champion of Morrison who had disappointed him by his lack of growth, and by growing in the wrong direction.[111] Morrison told Beatrice Webb that he 'preferred to occupy himself with directing the great municipal government of London rather than waste his energies intriguing at Westminster'.[112]

Morrison's friends were keen to press his claims. William Nield, a party official, told Dalton that 'little Laski had been suggesting to H.M. that Attlee's leadership was intolerable, equally Greenwood's Deputy Leadership. His suggestion was that H.M. should be Leader and Cripps Deputy. Cripps apparently was present when this suggestion was made.'[113] Nield himself urged Morrison 'to concentrate much more on the House and to earn the right to the Leadership. He thinks that pressure by him and others is having effect.'[114] Morrison's star was rising; his 'closest friends scurry around the lobbies at Westminster, there and here, fro and to, staking out his claim for the reversion of Labour leadership. Their propaganda is meeting with some success. But the trade unions are scared of Morrison.'[115] By June 1939 it seemed that there was an 'immense and far-tentacled intrigue' to impose Morrison. Ellen Wilkinson in *Time and Tide* and the *Sunday Referee* praised Morrison when Attlee was taken ill, and hoped he would be leader soon. Francis Williams in the *Daily Herald* wrote that Morrison had a commanding position in the public eye through his courageous and imaginative leadership in London.[116] These articles were raised at a meeting of the PLP on 14 June. Morrison said: 'He had had nothing to do with inspiring the article [of Ellen Wilkinson]. He had not seen it beforehand. If he had seen it, he would have advised that it should not be published.'[117] After the party had decided for Attlee in 1935, he had loyally co-operated with him. If a vote of confidence in Attlee were put to a vote he would vote for it, and if a vote of censure on Ellen Wilkinson were pressed he would abstain. Dalton noted, 'I was conscious of a certain hostility in the atmosphere while he was speaking, though he was heard quite silently.'[118] The vote of confidence in Attlee was carried *nem. con.* and the proposal to condemn Ellen Wilkinson was dropped. The affair blew over, but Morrison's reputation had been damaged. He guessed that he could not win with the existing composition of the PLP.[119] It was better to wait for the imminent general election. With a new batch of MPs, he would be more strongly supported. By detaching himself somewhat over the last four years from Attlee and Greenwood he could avoid blame for an electoral set-back and yet by occasional interventions maintain his credentials for the top position. His devotees kept up their pressure, exploiting scepticism about the performances of Attlee and Greenwood. He was treading along the edge of a precipice: to one side was a too close involvement in the existing leadership; to the other was disloyalty. The results were that many felt he was not backing the leadership as he should, while his supporters were disappointed at his failure to grab the leadership from Attlee. He seemed to want it handed to him.

After the start of the war the comrades of the PLP did not rally around their leader. In the autumn of 1939 Morrison appeared involved in what looked like a bid for the leadership, following the enhancement of his reputation as organizer of the evacuation of over half a million children from London at the start of September. Attlee had been ill since Whitsun, and his deputy, Greenwood, was in charge and had made a good showing. He was preferred by MPs, said the *Sunday Express*, to Attlee, but 'many predict that he [Herbert Morrison] will be one of the big political figures thrown up to a pinnacle by the volcano of this war'.[120] Trevor Evans of the *Daily Express* was doubtful, because Morrison had annoyed so many trade union bosses.[121] Attlee returned in October and was 'obviously ineffective and much below even his normal par'. Dalton hoped that Greenwood would challenge Attlee, so that 'once we loosened the earth and got the Leadership moving, it would be much easier to bring Morrison in later in place of Greenwood, if, as was indeed possible, the latter did not wear well'.[122] Before Dalton could start plotting in earnest, Alfred Edwards, a Labour back-bencher, wrote to Dalton, Attlee, Morrison and Greenwood, urging them to let their names go forward so that the PLP should not be deprived of its right to vote for its leader.[123] Morrison sent copies of his reply to Dalton, Attlee and Greenwood. He accepted the decision of 1935 'with good grace', but he reserved the right 'to accept nomination at an appropriate time, particularly after a General Election'. However, he would be 'no party to raising the matter during Mr Attlee's illness'. He felt that since 'the health of Mr Attlee is still in the process of recovery it would not be a kindly or generous action for the leadership to be contested this year'. He concluded: 'I do not propose to accept nomination at this time, although I should have to reconsider this if a contest were forced from another quarter.'[124]

When the PLP met for the new parliamentary session on 15 November there were four nominations for leader: Attlee, Greenwood, Morrison and Dalton. Greenwood announced that he would withdraw to maintain unity. Morrison and Dalton followed suit, and so Attlee was returned unopposed.[125] Morrison read to the PLP a copy of the letter he had sent to Edwards.[126] The affair annoyed many MPs who felt that some intrigue had been afoot. Dalton and Morrison lost about twenty votes when elections for the parliamentary Executive took place a week later. Morrison was not pleased with Dalton for deserting to Greenwood. Dalton tried to patch up his relations with Morrison through a note complimenting him on his Commons speech of 6 December: 'the way of earth shifters is hard in this political allotment and I am not attracted to do any more digging at present. Yours, with undiminished regard.'[127] Back at the LLP office, as Morrison went through his press cuttings, he came across an article urging Attlee to exercise his leadership 'with more vigour and greater vision'. Morrison underlined 'more vigour' and 'greater vision'.

A major obstacle to his ambitions was the continued suspicion of the trade unions and Bevin. Between 1935 and 1940 some brushes between Morrison and the unions kept alive the distrust that had smouldered for so long. In the autumn of 1937 Morrison vigorously attacked some trade union leaders, including Will Lawther of the mine-workers, for saying that Labour MPs sponsored by trade unions should obey the instructions of their union: 'The Parliamentary Party will, I am sure, always give special and sympathetic consideration to the views of the TUC, but if the country comes to regard the Parliamentary Labour Party as a mere robot, controlled and instructed from outside, the country will not like it; and the country will be right. Many of us would not wish to be MPs under such conditions of public irresponsibility.'[128] Morrison told Beatrice Webb that 'he feared an eventual split between the TUC organization trying to make the best of capitalism and the labour party attempting to supersede capitalism by socialism'.[129] She noted that he wanted 'to prevent the trade unions being the dominant influence in the L.P. He scents "workers' control": taking the fictitious form of a conspiracy of the organized workers with the capitalists, to exploit the rest of the community.'[130] The vendetta between Bevin and Morrison continued. Bevin proclaimed a more vigorous armaments programme than Morrison who still adhered to hopes of disarmament and collective security through the League. In any case Bevin felt that the Labour Party devoted too much attention to foreign affairs, and that included Morrison who was a constant speaker and writer on the subject. In March 1939 Bevin wrote to Attlee complaining that too much time was spent on foreign affairs. 'Matters of domestic policy should receive more attention.'[131] What further enraged Bevin were the rumours of plots insti-gated by Morrison against Attlee.

Another burden that Morrison had to bear in the late 1930s was that he was often named for inclusion in a Coalition or genuinely National Govern-ment. Politicians and journalists spun webs of fantasy, concocting coalition governments to include the best men from all parties. Viscount Weir of East-wood in 1934 described Morrison as 'his favourite Labour politician' and would have had him in a government of sanity with Ramsay MacDonald.[132] In 1935 David Keir, political correspondent of the *News Chronicle*, construc-ted his ideal Cabinet, with Lloyd George as PM, Winston Churchill as Mini-ster of Defence, and Morrison as Chancellor of the Exchequer, the only Labour figure in a six-man Cabinet.[133] In May and June 1935 rumours sped up and down Fleet Street that Morrison was to replace Walter Runciman at the Board of Trade.[134] Morrison strenuously denied it.[135] The Morrison involved was W. S. Morrison, but such was Herbert Morrison's prominence, and ac-ceptability to his opponents, that he was naturally thought of by the pundits.[136] In 1936 Tom Jones heard talk of a 'genuine' National Government – with Morrison included,[137] and Harold Macmillan urged the creation of a great new Centre Party, led by Morrison, left of centre, 'a fusion of all that is best in the Left and the Right'.[138] Beverley Baxter in 1937 made a similar call, for a Democratic Party formed from a merger of the Labour and Liberal parties; the leader would not be Attlee. 'Herbert Morrison will be the Man of Des-tiny. . . .' 'Mr Morrison is neither an intellectual nor a revolutionary, nor a Tory in Socialist's clothing. He is definitely an administrative and courageous leader of the moderate Left.'[139] 'Romantic nonsense' was Morrison's des-cription of the article.[140]

In 1938 there were attempts to get Morrison to join forces with the anti-Chamberlain Tories. Dalton recalled that Kingsley Martin, after Hitler's march into Vienna, proposed such an alliance and that Morrison showed great interest, although it never materialized.[141] A more serious effort was made after Munich by Macmillan who hoped to forge an alliance between the Labour Party and Churchill, Duff Cooper and himself. Cripps liked the idea and saw it as an opportunity to shunt Attlee out of the Labour leadership, replacing him by Morrison. Dalton tackled Morrison who was cautious: 'Yes, it might be quite interesting.' Later that same evening, however, he told Dalton, 'Don't hurry it.' The meeting never took place, largely because of Eden's refusal to participate.[142] Morrison toyed gingerly with the idea of a common cause with the anti-Chamberlain Tories. He walked around Eltham with George Wansbrough discussing the arguments for and against. Although tempted, he was aware of the difficulties from within his own party; it would be hard to carry it into an alliance with men whom it had been attacking so vigorously.[143] That Morrison was so acceptable to those outside the Labour Party suggested that he was not so committed to the party as some of his colleagues, and it reactivated the rumour of his support for MacDonald and the National Government in 1931.[144] It cast doubts on his loyalty and helped keep him out of the leadership.

Chapter 18

Foreign Affairs in the 1930s

In the 1930s Morrison was not wholly occupied with domestic issues. Foreign affairs were the subject of many of his articles and speeches. On deputations to the government and in the Commons he was frequently Labour's spokesman. He travelled abroad widely, holidaying in the south of France, attending socialist congresses in France and Belgium, lecturing at Geneva and Paris and visiting the USSR, the USA and Palestine. Despite such a broadening of his horizon, his views on foreign affairs were superficial. He was not a fluent speaker of another language, nor did he read foreign literature. He was not knowledgeable about the history and culture of other countries and he never studied in any depth problems of international policy. He simply had not the time to make himself a specialist. He formed his views of foreign policy without the detailed analysis he gave to home policies, tending to accept the conventional line of the party, which fitted neatly into the set of attitudes he had acquired before 1914. He saw international relations in simple terms: international rivalries were the result of economic competition; the League of Nations would settle differences between nations; and collective security without national rearmament would deter aggressors. He never examined the basis of such general statements, nor their implications, nor their practical application.

Although most of his views on foreign policy were common to most Labour members of the time,[1] some of them were distinctive. Because of visits to the USA and Palestine, not only was he more sympathetic to the USA than most of his colleagues, but he was also an ardent Zionist. He was the first member of the party establishment to urge intervention in Spain to assist the government against Franco. On British rearmament he took an uncharacteristic view. He backed the policy of opposing arms estimates (and conscription), which could easily be justified in terms of the party's traditions and tactics and appealed strongly to Labour activists, but was incomprehensible to the ordinary floating and probably Labour voters, and made it impossible to get a serious hearing for Labour's strong case against the government's general handling of foreign policy. On this topic he was more oriented to the party activists than to the electorate: an odd posture for Morrison. Nevertheless he forcefully advocated and was personally heavily involved in co-operating with the government over civil defence, a policy which the party activists opposed. Here, however, Morrison's experience of local government weaned him from a simply emotional response. The woolliness and inconsistencies of many of Morrison's views on foreign policy arose because he lacked the knowledge, and the time to acquire the knowledge, needed for making informal judgments.

Morrison's view of international politics was at one with his view of domestic politics. The objective was the same: tidiness. He complained: 'The world is in a shocking muddle, and if the muddle continues a terrible disaster within a few years will be the inevitable result.' As socialism was the solution to muddle at home, so 'world socialism' was necessary to end chaos in foreign affairs.[2] The cause of disorder was economic. The origins of war lay in economic rivalry between nations. Capitalism was the main incentive to war.[3] Hitler's urge for territorial expansion was greed for Rumanian oil, Ukrainian grain and the riches of the British Empire.[4] Even Chamberlain's policy was reducible to class terms, for the Tories sympathized with Hitler, Mussolini, Franco and the ruling clique in Japan as class allies against governments of the left.[5]

The answer to the world's problems lay in collective action to stop the cutting of throats economically.[6] But the government never followed this course. Morrison predicted during the 1930s that its drifting, dodging trouble and failing to stand up to the dictators in a scheme of collective security, would stimulate more demands, since they were convinced that they could get their way by threat of violence. The rest of the world, tired of British inaction, would leave Britain in isolation as trouble came nearer to 'our doorstep'. In the end, Britain would stand alone.[7] Morrison put the blame for this disastrous policy on to Chamberlain, Hoare, Simon, Halifax, Eden and Baldwin. The last was a weakling who would have made an 'excellent Mayor of Bewdley'.[8] Chamberlain, 'Britain's Public Enemy No. 1', even while Chancellor of the Exchequer, was more positive; he led, while Baldwin drifted, but he was 'pro-Fascist in his foreign policy'.[9] Hoare was condemned for the Hoare–Laval pact, which damaged Britain's reputation as a world power as well as the authority of the League.[10] Sir John Simon, the 'tragic and dangerous failure', undid the work for disarmament of Arthur Henderson and let Japan walk away with Manchuria through not mobilizing the League.[11] Eden, claimed Morrison, was 'worth his weight in gold as a shop walker in one of the West End stores',[12] and had 'long since been broken in by the old gang'.[13] Lord Halifax, on his appointment to the Foreign Office, was Chamberlain's 'messenger boy', and out of touch with popular feeling.[14] Morrison's contempt for the government was intense, as was their contempt for the Labour Party. There was no basis for co-operation.

Morrison argued that much of the blame for the troubles of the 1930s could be put on the mistakes of the allies after the First War. Germany had been economically punished and had genuine grievances. The Tories in the 1920s were harsh to the democratic republican Germany to whose downfall they contributed by perpetuating economic muddle, and then in the 1930s were sympathetic to the Nazis who cheated over disarmament. The Tories bore a heavy responsibility both for Hitler's accession to power and for his successes. Yet, despite Morrison's objections to the Treaty of Versailles, he felt it was no justification for Hitler's methods.[15]

To remedy the injustice of the peace treaties Morrison advocated action through the League of Nations. Against the government's conception of the League as 'a mere debating assembly and a filing office', Morrison proposed an active institution which settled disputes and curbed aggression, an 'incipient super-Government of the world'.[16] Within the framework of the League's Charter he called for regional arrangements whereby groups of nations would come together to settle their disputes and to set up collective security measures. He looked forward to an all-European treaty of 'non-aggression, arbitration and mutual assistance'. He proposed that all colonial territories should be vested in the League which would then under a mandate system hand them to specified nations for their administration into nationhood, without exploitation.[17] He was not for giving up the British Empire; he was proud of the British colonial record: 'I hope I am not a "Jingo", but I feel that perhaps the British are the most considerate Colonial administrators of any Government in the world.' Nations would retain their territories, but under League supervision.[18]

The League of Nations was to solve problems, not to bolster up an existing situation.[19] Any country, even Germany, with a grievance should take it to the League and accept arbitration. If member countries resorted to war, then the other nations were to resist the aggressor with collective economic, financial and military sanctions. It was necessary for the peaceful nations to organize a 'Peace Bloc'.[20] He did not feel that force would be needed, since the potential aggressor would be deterred from actual aggression by the threat of collective action and, if that failed, then financial and economic sanctions would bring him to his senses without any need for war.[21]

To make his peace block credible, arms were essential. He did not oppose armaments; he wanted them not for national purposes but to preserve international peace. Each nation would contribute arms to the peace-keeping organization, and the amount would depend on the strength of the potential aggressors. It might indeed be more than the Tory government were in fact planning.[22] Morrison complained that the British government was not prepared to put its weight behind the League and collective security. Instead it preserved a 'pre-war militarist outlook', remaining in isolation.[23] It 'cold-shouldered' the League.

In 1936 he put forward his case in a widely reported speech at the Institute of International Relations at Geneva.[24] Champions of the League like Philip Noel-Baker, Kingsley Martin and Konni Zilliacus who corresponded with Morrison voluminously on League matters,[25] regarded him as one of the leading advocates of the League and collective security in Britain. In 1938 he organized, as Chairman of the Labour Party's Campaign Committee, a nation-wide 'Peace and Security Campaign', to draw together the peaceful states under the banner of the League.

Morrison wanted the USA actively involved in the League of Nations and a system of collective security. More than any other leading Labour politician in the 1930s he was an admirer of the USA. As early as 1929 he had written: 'We wait in patience for the development of an American political, social and international consciousness which shall yet make its great contribution to the progress of mankind.'[26] His first view of America was based mainly on the didactically socialist novels of Upton Sinclair whose volumes he reviewed enthusiastically in *London News*. Sinclair in 1941 looked on Morrison as 'an old friend', who 'was in my home three or four years ago'.[27] He was the only fiction writer whose works Morrison regularly read, and he urged his daughter to read them.[28]

His view was also shaped by three visits he made to the States. In 1936 he was there from 8 April to 16 May, in 1937 from 24 March to 3 May, and in 1938 from 25 March to 20 April. In all he covered about fifty thousand miles. He described the visits as 'strenuous': a round of public meetings, luncheons for educational purposes, speeches at trade union suppers, radio talks, interviews with newspaper men and personal consultations.[29] As he first sailed into New York he was 'subdued' by the skyline, and later shaken by the police escort and the reporters who mobbed him.[30] He was impressed by the menus at restaurants which detailed the nutritional value of the fare.[31] In 1937 he visited Hollywood and talked with Paul Muni on the set of *The Life of Emile Zola* at Warner Brothers.[32] In Los Angeles he suffered his most embarrassing experience. He thought he was to lecture on socialism. As he began the audience appeared dumbfounded. The organization had mixed up the speakers; he was down as talking on Palestine.[33]

His visits seemed to confirm what Sinclair described. He was horrified by the tenements and the slums;[34] he found the economic struggle 'grim and sordid', unemployment higher than in Britain, and the unemployed suffering worse.[35] He reckoned that Britain was far superior in housing, slum clearance and city transportation.[36] He said he would 'sooner clear out of public life than run the "spoils system" '.[37] The man with the reputation of a Tammany boss said, 'I should not make a good American politician.'[38] He calculated that America was 'about 50 to 100 years behind Britain in social legislation', about fifty years behind in housing and about thirty years on labour questions.[39] He was struck by the 'conservatism' of the USA; on the first visit even the New Deal failed to impress him: 'Essentially it is a system of capitalism which has adopted and adapted some Socialist ideas.'[40] After his first trip, as he landed, he said, 'I'm glad to be back. When I saw England again I thought what a wonderful country it is. There is something so sound about it all.'[41]

The initiative for his visits came from a small group of social democrats. In December 1934 he received a letter of invitation from A. Cahan, editor of the *Jewish Daily Forward*: 'You would find a most enthusiastic welcome in centers like New York, Chicago, Detroit, Pittsburgh, Philadelphia or Boston. I am speaking on behalf of those Socialists who are consistent Social Democrats and admirers of the English Labour Party. We are anti-communist one hundred per cent. We have no use for such branches of Bolshevism as are typified by the ILP and certain members of the Socialist League. It is our desire and ambition to give the United States a chance to see and hear a living specimen of your wonderful movement. I need not tell you that your name is well known here and that you have many admirers among the sober minded Socialists in the United States.'[42] For his third visit, of 1938, he was invited by some left groups, eager to set up a new party, in New York City. There was little Morrison could do to help. The socialist movement was small and divided; trade unions were split between industrial and craft unions, and most of organized labour supported Roosevelt.[43] He did his best, talking to little bands of the faithful about Labour Party organization and policy, and 'how we won in London'.[44] He appeared before a Senate committee to explain the LCC's housing system[45] and spoke before the New York City Council about the LCC.[46] He met prominent American personalities like the trade unionist John L. Lewis, and Secretary of State Cordell Hull,[47] and President Roosevelt.

On Roosevelt's election Morrison was disparaging; he had been elected simply by 'bad trade and unemployment'. There would be no fundamental change in the economic situation. By 1936 he wanted to meet him, and wrote to Eden, the Foreign Secretary, to see if an interview could be arranged, and his passage through Customs eased.[48] But no meeting took place. He felt that Roosevelt in the face of unemployment was 'moving'. 'I know not where. I am not sure that he knows where. But he is breaking down the old aloofness of the State to the condition-of-the-people question.'[49] In 1937 he had a talk of one and a half hours with Roosevelt and was captivated. He described him as 'one of the finest men he had ever met'.[50] In 1938 they had another session together, and Morrison came away saying that the 'buoyant and charming'

President was 'the most human politician I've ever met'.[51] He found him 'an extremely capable man – human, anxious to do everything possible to give the people a better time and more security. He is not a Socialist. He is a Liberal, and believes in private capital. Within those limitations he is trying to do a good job. He has the support of organized Labour, but at the moment he has also the rather bitter enmity of the Capitalist classes. He is a great admirer of the LCC.'[52] A year later he declaimed: 'One statesman who can best speak the mind of the British people today is not to be found among the British Ministers at all, but is the head of a foreign state, namely the President of the United States. It is a thousand pities that among our Ministers we have no one who approaches President Roosevelt for drive, rallying power and idealism.'[53] Morrison continually urged America to involve itself in world affairs: to take this world by the scruff of the neck and make it behave itself.[54] For his efforts the Hearst press dubbed him a communist: a 'peripatetic Piccadilly propagandist'.[55]

Although at home Morrison was an unyielding opponent of co-operation with the Communist Party, in foreign policy he preached collaboration with the Soviet Union. He saw it in the 1930s as 'a genuine power for peace and a genuine friend nowadays of the League of Nations'.[56] He admitted that he did not admire its internal regime, nor those of Poland, Greece or Rumania, but: 'These considerations must be set aside, the real test being whether countries will co-operate in a genuine fashion in the promotion of a peaceful and prosperous world.'[57]

His outlook on Russia was greatly shaped by a fortnight he spent with the Workers' Travel Association, touring the country in August 1933. He wrote his impressions in six articles in the *Daily Herald*.[58] He noted the lack of democracy, tight political control, excessive police powers, censorship and all-pervading propaganda; people would not talk freely with him, and the lack of freedom of expression impoverished intellectual life.[59] He pointed out, however, that whereas fascists in Germany and Italy had destroyed parliamentary democracy, in Russia there had been none for the communists to destroy. If he were faced with the choice between fascism and communism, he would choose the latter, since, although both were political dictatorships, the point of the latter was the emancipation of the people from the exploitation of capitalism and landlordism.[60] He admired the system of public ownership and planning, which had cured unemployment and had raised the standard of living, which, he noted, although an improvement over Tsarist days, was much lower than in the West.[61] He saw no sign of either economic or political collapse, but he felt that there was too much political control over industry.[62]

He found little similarity between the attitudes of Russian communists and the Communist Party of Great Britain. The former appeared practical, cautious, believing in gradual development; they did not accept workers' control, and distributed social benefits according to the means of the recipients.

He noted that they had thrown over the materialist conception of history and now adhered to the doctrine of 'great men', as shown by their adoration of Lenin and Stalin.

He expressed his admiration for the Soviet experiment in an uncharacteristic outburst: 'The decisiveness, "the finality", and the sweeping character of the Bolshevik revolution appeals enormously to one's liking of big things, to one's sense of romance, and to one's desire to "smash this sorry scheme of things entire".' However, a more radical revolution would be achieved in Britain by other means, for 'if we are able, with an informed Socialist electorate behind us, with the support of a working class and middle class which understand the great purpose of Socialism, and which is prepared to work and sacrifice for its establishment, to achieve the great change peacefully and with deliberate construction, I think it will be better, more certain, and in all likelihood more swift.'[63]

He judged that Russia's foreign policy had changed since the 1920s. It no longer acted as leader of a world revolution. Its predominant consideration was 'the political and economic well-being of Russia',[64] which dictated that it join the League of Nations and co-operate in a scheme of collective security. It wanted peace to complete its economic adventure.[65] He castigated the British government for rejecting collaboration with Russia, and he urged closer economic relations.[66] But the government would not trust Russia. British obduracy, alleged Morrison, caused the fall of the Foreign Minister, Litvinov, who was genuinely for peace, and the rise of Molotov[67] who concluded in August 1939 the Nazi–Soviet pact, 'the blackest treachery conceivable against peace and freedom'.[68] When Russia attacked Finland in late 1939, Morrison was horrified. He urged military aid for Finland, which provoked cries of 'hands off the Soviet Union' from the British Communist Party. He did not allow the Soviet aggression to be used as a pretext for justifying a peace with Hitler aimed against the Soviet Union.[69]

Morrison may have been in the 1930s starry-eyed about Russia, eager to trust its promises and over confident of its competence to carry them out. His idea of collective security, including Russia, might have deterred German aggression. But the British government never put Russia's intentions to the test.

Of all the countries visited by Morrison in the 1930s, Palestine made the deepest impression. His journey there in 1935 converted him to Zionism. He recalled it as 'one of the most inspiring experiences I have had'.[70] He was taken to Palestine by Dov Hos, a representative of the Histadrut, the Jewish trade union movement, which sought to win British Labour to the Jewish view of Palestine. With Morrison he succeeded. They liked each other from the start; both were practical, common-sensical able men.[71] Even before their meeting Morrison was favourably inclined to Jews. The Jewish Socialist

Party in Britain, Poale Zion, had as early as 1920 affiliated to the Labour Party nationally and to the LLP. Some of the leading figures in the LLP and at the LCC were Jews, like Silkin, Strauss, Frankel, Lady Nathan, Mrs Bentwich and Dr Rickards, and at Hackney there was a considerable Jewish community.

In Palestine he saw 'Socialism on the highest level'.[72] He waxed so warm about the kibbutzim that Susan Lawrence exclaimed that she could not recognize the new Herbert Morrison. Normally tough and matter-of-fact, he now appeared sentimental and enthusiastic.[73] In the House of Commons he declared: 'I came back with a humble feeling that I should like to give up this business of House of Commons and politics and join them in the clean, healthy life that they are leading. . . . It is one of the most wonderful manifestations in the world.'[74]

His descriptions were lyrical. He wrote 'of the Jewish pioneers I saw at the Waters of Merom preparing for the reclamation of thousands of acres of marshy and swampy land in the midst of a malaria-infested country; of the workers at the phosphate works by the Dead Sea; of the men who have fashioned and who run the great electricity power works by the Jordan, generating electricity by water power for all Palestine with the exception of Jerusalem; and above all the workers on the Jewish collective agricultural colonies who have turned sand dunes into good agricultural land, and who are manifesting all the fine qualities of self-discipline so that they may experience the collective joy of collective economic achievement in the interests of that great national cause in which they believe.'[75] The young people he saw 'are surely among the most splendid human types to be found anywhere in the world', and the audiences he spoke to, including one of fifteen thousand, the largest he ever addressed,[76] were 'not unlike the best type of working-class political audience to be found in Durham, Northumberland and Scotland'; they were not effervescent, noisy and excitable, but cool, collected, weighing the words of the speaker. He expatiated that Palestine 'of all countries, not excluding Russia, had shown the greatest example of unselfish, co-operative and human effort'.[77]

Its 'socialist' aspect won him over. 'Here are colonies in which people are working on a voluntary co-operative basis, with no element of dictatorship or compulsion behind them. . . . They are doing it for no money wage at all. It is being done not as a mere capitalist exploiting business, but directly in association with and under the control of the great Jewish trade union organization, the Jewish Federation of Labour.' 'It is work typical of the finest of British colonizers in the history of our Empire. You cannot sneer at this kind of thing.'[78] 'It is a lesson to the whole world.'[79]

Morrison was one of the first Labour MPs to visit Palestine, and he was always ready to meet Jewish Labour leaders.[80] To a large extent Morrison was used by the Zionists. Their most daring exploit was later revealed by Colonel Rivlin, chief editor of the Israeli army's monthly magazine. Haganah, the

Jewish underground army, used to smuggle arms into the country through various people. When Herbert Morrison landed, unbeknown to him 'one suitcase full of weapons was brought in as belonging to him', to avoid Customs, and was collected by a terrorist, Katriel Katz.[81]

In the Commons Morrison championed the Jewish cause, treating the policy of the government towards the Arabs as one of appeasement.[82] He condemned it for not maintaining law and order, and for allowing Arab terrorists, incited by the Mufti whom he depicted as an agent of Mussolini and Hitler, to commit acts of violence against Jews. He blamed the disturbances of the 1930s on well-to-do Arab reactionaries who maintained a feudal tyranny. He argued that these landlords and politico-religious leaders were appeased by the government because their class interests coincided. He most deplored the restriction on Jewish immigration into Palestine, which damaged its economy, since the enterprise of the Jews made possible economic development, and indeed enabled a larger Arab population to exist in Palestine. Also the Balfour pledge of a Jewish national home in Palestine had to be honoured. The Jews, persecuted in Europe by the fascists, needed a place 'in which they can live as human beings, a place they can call their home, and one in which they can be masters of their own destiny'. He condemned making Palestine a permanent Arab state in which the Jews would be an insecure minority. He never put forward his own solution, but came close to the Zionist view of two states, one Arab and one Jew, with the latter a substantial one, taking into account the fact that the Arabs had obtained extensive territory after the First War in Syria, Iraq, Transjordan and Saudi Arabia. He hoped that Arab and Jew could live together. As early as 1929 he had said: 'No enduring divergence of interests exists between the Jewish and Arab working populations in Palestine.'[83]

From Hitler's accession to power Morrison maintained a barrage of abuse against him in *London News*, noting his persecution of socialists, trade unionists, co-operators and communists,[84] assaults on religious denominations,[85] and above all his venom towards Jews. As early as May 1933 *London News* carried extracts from *Mein Kampf* in which Hitler pursued his anti-Semitic theme.[86] Morrison said: 'Hitler and his mob are a disgrace not only to Germany but to the whole civilized world, for it is contemptible idiocy to persecute one race',[87] and he felt it indecent to assume that no Jew had a right to live in Germany:[88] 'I stand against tyranny in all forms and in all places, whether it is exercised against races, religions or political creeds constitutionally held.'[89] Morrison denounced any praise for fascism he spotted in the British press or on film news-reels.[90] Lloyd George was criticized for returning from Germany, 'apparently a half-baked Nazi';[91] Mussolini was as bad as Hitler: 'Who was guilty of political assassination? Who was responsible for the castor-oil exploits? Who is still torturing and maltreating his political prisoners? Who denies the right of the people of Italy to think and say what they like about Italian public affairs?'[92]

Morrison addressed numerous 'open letters' to the people of Germany and Italy, as fellow victims of a muddled world, urging them to throw off their brutal regimes and return to civilized standards.[93] 'Germany has not been encircled. Your Government has encircled itself.'[94] So optimistic was he of the effect of direct appeals that he constantly urged the British government and the BBC to broadcast in German and Italian information about Britain to the countries concerned.[95] His hope for a rebellion was one reason why he advocated a personal boycott of German goods and services, and why he opposed the granting of loans to Germany. These methods, he hoped, would weaken the Nazi regime and bring home to the people of Germany the disgust of the rest of the world.[96]

Labour support for the National government would have been possible as was shown in the autumn of 1935 when it opposed the Italian invasion of Abyssinia. Hoare's speech of loyalty to the League was welcomed by Morrison.[97] However, the Hoare–Laval pact dividing up Abyssinia convinced Labour of the government's untrustworthiness. The failure to apply oil sanctions against Italy also showed that the government had capitulated to Mussolini, fearing that, if he fell, a government of the left would take over. Morrison noted that the Tories intervened against the Russian revolution, but not against fascist revolutions. The government's initial protestations of loyalty to the League were simply window dressing for a general election, and to lull the world before yielding to Italy.[98]

Although the government was reluctant to enforce sanctions against dictatorships, it acted, Morrison noted, with alacrity to institute sanctions against the democratic, constitutionally elected government of Spain, when it was under attack from fascist rebels and invaded by fascist powers. Morrison 'was the first man of any section of the working-class movement in this country to advocate intervention'.[99] From the start of Franco's revolt in 1936 Morrison pleaded on behalf of the Spanish government.[100] Against him were arrayed Dalton and Bevin, who supported the British government's line of official neutrality, also the policy of the socialist Leon Blum and his government in France. Dalton recalled of Morrison: 'Often he seemed to stand alone.' He never made clear how far he wanted to carry intervention.[101] For Dalton it was but one more instance of Morrison's lack of judgment in foreign affairs. Morrison argued that a constitutionally elected government faced a revolt of generals who had broken their oath of fidelity. To him armies should always serve civil authority. Franco's actions were an affront to constitutionalism. He was also disgusted that Franco used Moors against his own people; 'What patriots! What Spaniards! What degenerates!'[102]

Morrison urged that the British government should aid the Spanish government. However, the French and the British governments decided on a policy of non-intervention: no war material was to go to the Spanish government. The leading organs of the Labour Party, the NEC, the Executive of the PLP and the General Council of the TUC, endorsed this policy, overruling Morrison's objections that non-intervention was 'humbug', a device to impose sanctions on the democratic government, while allowing the traitorous rebels to receive assistance.[103]

Others who took Morrison's view hoped that at the coming party conference in Edinburgh Morrison would speak out. However, 'Herbert sat with folded arms while his colleagues outlined their official view. Had he wanted to criticize and to express his personal views, it would have been necessary for him to have resigned, for the practice of the Labour Party is that Executive members attending the annual conference must voice the Party view. It is no secret now that at that time some of his friends thought it would have been better had he been more true to himself and less loyal to the Party. But what Herbert Morrison did then he would expect of others placed in a similar position. The tactics of Sir Stafford Cripps would never receive his blessing.'[104]

Vindication of Morrison's view came almost immediately after the close of the conference. Convincing evidence was presented that the fascists were breaking the non-intervention agreements. The party called on the government to restore to the Spanish government full commercial rights, including the purchase of munitions, but it would not urge the British government itself to export arms to Spain.[105] Throughout 1937 Morrison denounced 'non-intervention'. The fascists used the non-intervention committee to drag out discussions and then, having made an agreement, they broke it and there were more fruitless negotiations.[106] The British government tolerated fascist intervention and yet imposed sanctions and an arms embargo on the Spanish government.[107] The British government put its class outlook first, allowing a constitutional government to be crushed and the fascists to gain strategic positions in the Mediterranean, menacing Gibraltar, encircling France, imperilling the North African colonies and endangering our Mediterranean shipping and communications.[108] When the government concluded an Anglo–Italian agreement in 1938 Morrison was aghast: Britain condoned piracy in the Mediterranean, aggression against Abyssinia and Spain, and a fascist advance in the Mediterranean. It damaged the League of Nations which ought to have been mobilized to stop arms reaching the rebels and to help the Spanish government.[109] In Trafalgar Square Morrison called on the British government to let the Spanish government acquire arms.[110] But Franco, the 'satellite' of Hitler and Mussolini, defeated the constitutional government, and the British government decided to recognize the new regime.[111] Morrison protested in the Commons, accusing the government of supporting Franco all along. His one ray of hope was: 'There is no true permanence in his Government. I doubt very much whether that Government will last.'[112]

The government's policy towards Czechoslovakia was another illustration of its treachery which angered Morrison. His view was that Hitler had no rightful claim to any part of Czechoslovakia. The existing frontiers had lasted for nine hundred years; the so-called disputed areas, the Sudetenland, had never been German, and if the people of this area could not live together there should be 'an appropriate exchange of population without territorial change'. In a deputation to Chamberlain, Morrison urged the 'Sudeten Germans being free to go into the Reich and oppressed inhabitants of the Reich free to escape into CS from Hitler's rule'.[113] Morrison felt that the Germans in Czechoslovakia were simply creating trouble to force a concession. The answer was for Britain, France, and the USSR in alliance to tell Hitler: 'You must not do it.'[114] The Munich agreement infuriated Morrison. Chamberlain had brought the country to the brink of war and had dishonoured it, betraying the Czechs, weakening French morale and estranging the USSR and the USA. Germany had made strategic gains, and no longer was any frontier in Europe safe.[115] Morrison wrote an LLP pamphlet, *Why London Looked War in the Face*, a formidable diatribe against the government's failure to forge collective action against an aggressor.

On 19 October 1938 Dalton held a party for a number of leading Labour figures to discuss foreign policy after Munich and took notes on Morrison's contribution:[116]

We must reconsider the meaning of Collective Security. The elements may no longer be there. There may be nothing effective to collect. The USSR, like other dictatorships, often leaves one guessing. No public debate or free press to guide you. Events in France, splits, etc., in spite of much 'formal democracy', a lesson to all good democrats. You cannot make policy without the raw material of policy. League of Nations, etc., was a policy towards which we must work again, but we cannot get back quickly to old positions of strength. France is a potential ally with some strength but a potential liability with some weakness. British Government can be attacked on its foreign policy plus its arms and ARP incompetence. Concentrate arms and ARP policy primarily on defence. Lift up the status of ARP and spend a lot more money on it. Evacuation and shelter. Employment. Convince people that they will be substantially safe. This will strengthen you diplomatically and strategically against Hitler. Colonies. The question will be asked 'Will you fight for Tanganyika'? Think about it. With 100 per cent efficient national defence, even in some isolation owing to breakdown of League and Collective system, we should still be a great Power. Every dictatorship that goes to war gambles with its regime. Especially in war, dictatorships are eternally vulnerable through propaganda and discontent. Keep out of trouble as much as you can and make yourself as strong as you can for defence. Germany may have a run in South East Europe but will not make herself more popular thereby with non-German peoples. Keep friends studiously with USA, a queer blend of big business and idealistic sentiments. This country sees that the Government is both wrong and inefficient in its foreign policy, arms, ARP etc., but still doubts whether *we* are fit to run the show. New Zealand and the second LCC election show that public confidence can be gained by performance. We must be socialistically national in spirit. Germans have absorbed their unemployed. It is a scandal that we have two millions out of work when needed for ARP, arms, and necessaries of life.

Munich forced Morrison to reappraise his views on foreign and defence policies. He could now see that his old slogans about collective security and The League of Nations were empty.

Chapter 19

Defence and War

To Morrison arms were anathema, and disarmament the objective. When the National government began to rearm in 1935, expanding the air force in reply to German rearmament, Morrison was a leading Labour opponent. His case was that the country was embarking on a 'mad and wasteful armaments race', whose inevitable consequence was war. Indeed the government was neglecting the lesson of the origins of the First World War and was showing itself to be the party of militarism.[1] He objected to armaments for use only in the national interest. The alternative was collective security through the League of Nations, so that 'each nation requires less armaments to deal with potential aggressors'.[2] During the general election campaign of 1935 Morrison's message was: the Tory party was the party of war, while Labour was the party of peace.[3] The loss of the election did not make Morrison alter his view. In April 1936 he pointed out that the government 'are never short of money for the means of destruction. They are only short of money for the means of life.'[4]

As Hitler's menace grew, popular pressure for arms increased. The NEC in March 1936 discussed Citrine's proposal that the party should support rearmament providing the government promised that the arms would be used only through the League. At a joint meeting of the Executive of the PLP, the NEC and the General Council, Morrison said that such a pledge would not suffice, since he could not trust the government.[5] Divisions in the Labour leadership were sharp. Dalton was a protagonist for rearmament, and spoke for it at the 1936 party conference. Morrison, however, cut the ground from under his position in a speech which Bevin damned as one of the worst pieces of tight-rope walking he had ever seen. Morrison rejected both unilateral disarmament, the line of pacifists such as Lansbury, and unilateral rearmament, the government's policy. He supported armament by Britain only as part of the collective armament of the peaceful powers. He also warned the conference that decisions about whether to vote for or against the defence estimates in the Commons were not for the conference but for the PLP, which was in conflict with what Bevin appeared to be urging.[6] Morrison's view prevailed.[7] Rearmament was tolerated only as a contribution to a totality of international force. Dalton's case was blurred.

The next controversy was over the defence estimates. Dalton argued that the party should not vote against them, or else the public would think that it was not in favour of strengthening the country's defences. Morrison wanted to vote against. He was not prepared to give the government a blank cheque: 'I do not take the position that my country should be disarmed, but I say, "Arms – what for?" '[8] 'But against whom? Germany or Russia? Fascism or Socialism? For peace or for war? We do not know. And the Government flatly refuses to tell us.'[9] At the meeting of the PLP Morrison's line was backed by Attlee and Greenwood. Dalton spoke against them. In the end the PLP decided to abstain, by forty-five votes to thirty-nine.[10] Morrison followed loyally the decision, arguing that it 'was not very different from past policy, since it was a way of showing Labour's lack of confidence in the Government's foreign policy'.[11]

By the next party conference Dalton and Bevin had mobilized a vote in favour of rearmament. Morrison was silent. When the PLP came to consider the defence estimates in 1938, Dalton noted in his diary that Morrison, Shinwell and Johnston, 'all in the beaten minority last year, said that they thought that we could not chop and change from year to year and, having decided not to vote against last year, could not vote against next month. If we have broken the back of this folly I am well pleased.'[12]

This issue drove a wedge between Dalton and Morrison. Dalton had been a champion of Morrison whom he had seen as the future leader. But now Morrison was 'a disappointment to me on foreign affairs and arms policy'. Indeed, he seemed to have parted company with all sense of reality. Dalton's explanation was that: 'international affairs were, for him, a comparatively unknown field, and of arms he knew nothing, having been a conscientious objector in the First World War and never having mixed with military men.'[13] But Morrison had a case and argued it cleverly, convincing the conferences of 1935 and 1936. Without Morrison it is likely that the Labour Party might have split, following a sharp confrontation between the rearmers and the unilateral disarmers. Morrison bridged the gap and helped to wean the more pacifist elements to accept arms. He maintained party unity, a consequence of his attempt to have it both ways. The country, however, suffered. The government failed to rearm quickly enough, and used the excuse that Labour was opposed, a flimsy argument when the size of the huge government majority is considered, but one that gained widespread acceptance. If the government had supported schemes of collective security and had treated the League with more respect, Labour might have given enthusiastic support to rearmament, even urging larger programmes. As it was, the government forfeited Labour's trust through its evasions, wobblings and the impression it created of sympathizing with the dictators.

Morrison also resisted vigorously the introduction of conscription in 1939. He not only believed deeply in the importance of voluntary as against conscripted service, but also made great efforts to ensure that the voluntary principle worked in practice. In the late 1930s he made frequent appeals for volunteers for civil defence: air raid wardens, rescue teams, first aiders, police helpers, firemen and ambulance drivers.[14] In January 1939 he spoke at the Albert Hall, together with leading governmental and church figures, for more volunteers, essential to preserve free institutions.[15] The left, at the Labour conference later in 1939, called him Chamberlain's 'recruiting sergeant', a latter-day Horatio Bottomley. Morrison pointed out that he had never appealed for armed helpers, only for civil defence volunteers, and he easily won over the conference.[16] The NEC had agreed to support appeals for national service, as long as it was voluntary.[17] To Morrison a government which was standing up to fascist dictators must not copy totalitarian techniques of mobilizing the population. He attacked those who demanded conscription for ignoring 'the fact that people will make every effort for a just cause'.[18]

The Prime Minister had said, as late as March 1939, that there would be no conscription in peacetime. Then he changed his mind. Morrison and the Labour Party opposed this decision, even at this late stage, arguing that the voluntary system had not broken down. Conscription, they said, would not strengthen the country's defences. Rather it would dislocate the economy and introduce controversy when unity was essential.[19] The government majority held firm, and the PLP was able to achieve only a few amendments, for example higher pay for the conscripted militia and an undertaking that they would not be used to break strikes.[20] Within the Labour Party Morrison pursued a valiant battle against the left who wanted Labour to withdraw from civil defence work as a protest against the introduction of conscription. Morrison stood firm; they had their statutory duties to perform. He won the day against the defeatists.[21]

That Labour could not support conscription in the summer of 1939 is evidence of the government's failure to make itself trusted and of Labour's failure to appreciate reality. Labour could not entrust to the government, with its deplorable record, the power of conscription, despite Hitler's take-over of Czechoslovakia in March 1939 and his harassment of Poland. Although rearmament and conscription were now clearly aimed against Hitler, Morrison and the woolly left continued to mouth the old slogans. Opposition to conscription also reflected Morrison's passion for democratic institutions. His life was devoted to showing that democracy could be efficient, if rightly led.

A major battle won by Morrison in the late 1930s was to persuade the Labour Party to co-operate with the government over civil defence. He faced stiff opposition from many inside the party who felt that measures to protect the civil population would induce a 'war mentality', since people would feel protected against the enemy. Morrison also had to conduct a campaign against the government. He felt it indecisive in civil defence; he pointed out in-adequacies and delays. As leader of the LCC and chairman of its committee for civil defence, he was responsible for the defence of the area most vulner-able to air attacks. He so mastered the briefs from his officials, becoming the leading expert on civil defence outside central government, that the local authority associations asked him to be their spokesman in negotiations with the government.

The main features of his arguments were fixed as early as 1935, in response to a Home Office circular, requesting local authority co-operation for the protection of the civil population in case of aerial attack.[22] Morrison said that co-operation over civil defence implied no acceptance of the government's foreign policy or rearmament. Indeed the necessity for ARP (Air Raid Precautions) revealed the failure of the government's foreign policy. He had a duty to ensure that the sufferings of the civilian population, if bombed, were minimized: 'As long as it is possible for hostile air raids to take place upon my country or in London, it is a sacred obligation on my part to consider what can be done to succour children, women and men who might be in-jured.'[23] The whole cost of the extra duties put on local authorities for air raid precautions should be met by the government and not local authorities. Protection against air attack was a major responsibility of the national government.

The left in the Labour Party complained that he had decided party policy on this matter without sufficient consultation. He retorted that as leader he had a responsibility to lead. With his blessing officials at the LCC had had consultations on civil defence with civil servants at the Home Office, and he had promised H. J. Hodsall, the civil servant responsible for civil defence, 'that he will do his best to get co-operation not only in the London County Council but also as far as he can in the Metropolitan Boroughs.'[24] In the end he carried majorities on the LLP Executive and conference, and at the NEC and party conference nationally. At the LCC Labour Party he defeated opposition to ARP, which claimed it was 'wrong to delude the populace into imagining that adequate protection against air raids is possible'.[25] Morrison maintained that air raid precautions made him even more hateful of war, since its horrors were vividly brought home. He could not see that operating first aid schemes, and maintaining essential communications and services, would make anyone more warlike.

The government circular of July 1935, although indicating the work it wanted local authorities to undertake, made no mention of cost. The local authority associations decided not to enter into any commitments until the question of cost had been settled, and in December 1935 they asked the government to bear the full cost. The government was silent until February 1937 when the Home Office increased local authority fire-fighting responsibilities, but again nothing was said about cost. The associations advised that no capital expenditure be undertaken until that was settled. In July 1937, two years after the first circular, the government invited the associations to discuss the point at issue. Morrison was their spokesman. He demanded that the government bear the whole cost. The government offered to contribute fifty per cent, arguing that local authorities had to bear a proportion of the expenditure to have an interest in checking extravagance. After considerable argument the government undertook to be responsible wholly for certain items of central concern, like gas masks, and to pay grants ranging from sixty per cent to eighty-five per cent towards the remaining items, with the highest grant going to authorities whose expenditure was over the product of a penny rate. Morrison urged that the government pay ninety per cent if expenditure was over a penny rate and a hundred per cent if it was over a twopenny rate, but the government stuck firm. The associations, although dissatisfied, felt that Morrison had wrung from the government 'substantial concessions'.[26]

The LCC machine was put to the test at the Munich crisis. Morrison was 'at hand at County Hall for continuous consultation when swift decisions were necessary'.[27] The LCC was poised to evacuate twenty thousand teachers and 500,000 children, and had actually evacuated 3,100 defective children and 1,200 from nursery schools. Teams to repair drains and tackle dangerous structures were alerted, as were the firemen, ambulance and first aid workers, but because of Chamberlain's concessions they never had to spring into action. Morrison judged the performance of the LCC, 'a triumph of emergency organization',[28] but he was dismayed at the government's incompetence. In the Commons he flayed it with a speech of meticulous illustration.[29] Although people were ready to help, the government had failed to plan for their use; it had no plans for hospitals or first aid posts; there were not enough gas masks, steel helmets, fire-fighting appliances, stretchers and vehicles. Shelters were inadequate and Morrison feared that the public would panic in the scramble for a place. He urged a huge programme of shelter construction. He lashed the Home Office for inaction since 1931. To send instructions to Town Clerks in sealed envelopes, only to be opened in case of attack, was crass stupidity: they had to be prepared beforehand. He complained: 'the Government had no evacuation policy, and would not make use of the machinery for evacuating the children which the London County Council would have been proud to place at their disposal.' He battered the government over its lack of aerial defence installations around London. Some of his data was supplied by Basil Liddell Hart, the specialist on military matters, who had briefed the Labour leaders about the lack of preparations and had been particularly impressed by Morrison. Morrison wrote a letter to the Prime Minister along the lines suggested by Liddell Hart.[30] Dalton was also impressed with Morrison's efforts to 'hustle' the government over London's defences.[31]

In 1939 Morrison urged the government to produce a 'shelter' policy and to perfect the machinery for evacuation. He advocated not just blast and splinter-proof, but bomb-proof, shelters. He suggested that the unemployed, of which there were still far too many, and especially miners, should be set to build deep tunnels. The 'Anderson' shelter in the back garden was not effective enough, and most families had no back garden to hold a shelter. 'Deep shelters' were his goal, to avoid civilian panic.[32] Shelter policy was just as vital for the conduct of diplomacy as the army, navy or air force.[33] In the same year he managed to gain an important change in a Civil Defence Bill; at its committee stage he persuaded the government to accept an amendment that an owner of working class flats had to provide shelters if over half the occupiers demanded them.[34] Once again he tried to persuade the government to pay the whole cost of civil defence; yet again it was in vain.[35]

Morrison had made such a reputation on civil defence that in 1939 the government asked him to be the Regional Commissioner for London, in charge of civil defence and of all governmental activities if central administration broke down. Morrison refused the offer, as did Tom Johnston who was offered a similar post for Scotland. Johnston recalled that the reason for their rejection was that they feared that the government would commit another Munich; it was a protest against appeasement.[36]

Evacuation arrangements took up much of Morrison's time. LCC administrative staff and teachers were organized for moving out school children, the under-fives and their mothers, expectant mothers and the blind. In May he appealed on radio for those eligible to register so as to prevent gate-crashers when the time came.[37] Only a twenty-one per cent response was obtained, mainly because mothers were not prepared to be separated from their children.[38] His target was to complete the evacuation in four days. By the end of August all looked well: 'The machinery of evacuation was all ready to move directly the Government gave the order.'[39]

When the time came, the Morrisonian machine ran smoothly. Between 1 and 3 September, 607,635 individuals were moved.[40] Children gathered at their schools and were taken to railway stations and bus terminals. Morrison spent hours touring the schools and stations, wishing them good luck and a safe return to dear old London. He watched them put on trains for unknown destinations with military precision. At the end of the exercise he returned to County Hall and congratulated the police, the transport service and the education authorities, but he was disappointed. Out of one and a quarter millions originally registered for evacuation only about half turned up. Still, Morrison, as commander-in-chief of the operation, was widely praised for the success of evacuation. His flair for organization was plain for all to see. 'The biggest social experiment, I suppose, in history' was a success.[41] London's youngsters were scattered from Land's End to the Wash.

The main problem after the evacuation was with people not rushing from London but eager to return, as the expected rain of bombs never fell. Within six weeks seven per cent of the evacuees had returned and the rate of return shot up. By March 1940 a hundred thousand children had returned and he had to devise a new scheme of registration and organize a new programme of re-evacuation.

From the time of the evacuation until he joined the government in May 1940, Morrison lived at County Hall. Ritchie Calder described him: 'at work at his desk in his shirt sleeves, his tie still unknotted, his unruly cockscomb still undisciplined, and, alongside, his camp-bed just as he had tumbled out of it'.[42] His whole life was devoted to supervising the LCC in its mammoth enterprise of defending London. Previously his daily routine had been to rise at 7.30 a.m. and then to go first to the offices of the LLP, after which he went to County Hall, crossing the river in the evening to the Commons to finish the day before returning home about 1 a.m.[43] The *Star* reported on 1 November that he had hardly left his room for a week.[44]

On the outbreak of war the normal procedures of the LCC were suspended. Authority was in the hands of an Emergency Committee (the old ARP Committee transformed) chaired by Morrison and consisting of the leading men from both sides, six Labour and four Conservatives. Other committees no longer met, although full council meetings continued as well as full party meetings. Morrison kept in touch with the chairmen and vice-chairmen of the suspended committees, and ordinary members of the council still had access to chairmen and their chief officers. Morrison had powers to act on his own initiative if his emergency committee was unable to meet. In theory he was the dictator of London; in practice he continued widespread consultation.

Morrison was anxious that even in war democratic local government should be kept alive. He informed local party secretaries that in their boroughs the council and elected representatives should be 'supreme in the direction of policy, principles and finance'.[45] It was important to show that democracy was more efficient than dictatorship.[46] The LCC returned to its traditional mode of operation in the new year: committees were restored.[47]

During the early months of the war, although Morrison found that the government's handling of civil defence had much improved under the guidance of Sir John Anderson, Home Secretary from September 1939, he still criticized its indecision over shelters,[48] and just before he was taken into the government in May 1940 he urged once again that the government should bear the whole cost of civil defence. Yet again his appeal was rejected.[49]

Distrust of Chamberlain prevented the Labour Party from joining a coalition government in September 1939. At a session of the NEC and the Executive of the PLP Morrison moved the successful resolution that Labour should not accept an invitation to join the government.[50] He argued that there could be no '*political* co-operation with or support of a Government to which we are opposed on the normal fundamental essentials of public policy'.[51] Charles

Peake* reported to Sir Alexander Cadogan† that Morrison had told him that: 'An opposition was a functional necessity of the English Constitution and should not be dispensed with unless those who composed it could bring exceptional and valuable gifts to a Coalition Government. Frankly, this was not the case with the present Opposition and he doubted whether there were half-a-dozen members of it who could add anything in strength or decision to the present Government. Most of the Labour Front Bench, he said, were frightened of power and few were capable of drive unless they had a strong committee behind them.'[52] Still, he warned the government that if ministers who muddled the peace, muddle the war, they must go, and better men take their places.[53]

The war began inauspiciously for Morrison. A barrage balloon moored behind County Hall, the 'Herbert Morrison Special', failed to rise.[54] In October 1939 Morrison became a weekly contributor to the *Daily Mirror* which took his name into more homes than ever before. His first article asked why the war was worth fighting; for international order, security, and fair play was his answer.[55] Between September 1939 and January 1940 he created the impression of a responsible backer of the government, offering criticism only of a constructive kind, urging greater efforts in civil defence, a deep shelter policy, and more planning in mobilizing resources.[56] When commenting on the resignation of Hore-Belisha in January 1940, he reserved his spleen for the ex-minister rather than for the government.[57] In December 1939 Morrison told Charles Peake: 'if the war continued as it had begun he thought the Prime Minister would see it through in his present office and he doubted whether there was a better man.'[58]

His support of the war brought criticism from the communists who accused him of making a truce with Chamberlain.[59] Morrison, indeed, had the good fortune of being allegedly on the death lists of both the fascists and the communists.[60] He campaigned for Labour candidates in by-elections at Southwark in February 1940 and at North Battersea in April 1940, where the communist 'stop-the-war' candidates ran. He denounced the hypocrisy of the communists for wanting to stop the war against the Nazis, but not the Russian war against Finland.[61] He called them a contemptible body of servile instruments of a foreign government. Their victory would be met with rejoicing by the German propaganda machine. When the votes were counted, Labour held its seats comfortably.

In the first few months of the war, Morrison feared that the LLP would collapse, as members' attention was diverted and financial contributions dried up. Evacuation, the black-out, extra night work, mobilization into the forces, had disrupted meetings, reduced membership and diminished party income. His power base was being eroded. He consulted his Executive. A special fund was established for maintaining the organization and local

* A member of the News Department of the Foreign Office.
† Permanent Under-Secretary at the Foreign Office.

parties in financial trouble. He circularized party secretaries that the party should maintain vigorously its organization and activities. He wanted it 'ready to take the field at the end of the war to secure a future democratic triumph for Labour and Socialist principles'.[62]

He tried to find a useful role for the LLP that would attract attention and win public confidence. As in the First World War he organized a 'London Workers War Vigilantes Committee', consisting of five representatives each from the LLP, the London Trades Council and the Co-operative Movement, for joint action on domestic problems, particularly to expose profiteering and increased food prices. They protested that rail charges were increased without any hearing of objections, and they called on the government to alleviate a shortage of coal which was causing considerable misery in London.[63]

In January 1940 Morrison organized the LLP's first social gathering since the outbreak of war, to celebrate its silver jubilee. The invitation cards proclaimed 'Fancy dress optional . . . dancers must wear dancing shoes', and a Morrison circular stated, 'the blackout should not seriously deter anybody from attending, for the moon will be up on January 20th'. It was almost like old times. One difference was that the Executive no longer met at the LLP offices. It gathered at Morrison's room at County Hall or at a committee room at the Commons, depending on Morrison's convenience. The records were taken to Daines's house from which much of the office work was done. Headquarters was kept open for only part of each day, and the annual conference was postponed. The prospect for the LLP looked bleak. The organization that Morrison had built up from his bed-sitting rooms in the First World War looked as if it would revert to a similar shoe-string basis in the Second.

In February 1940 Morrison's attitude to the government changed. He became more aggressive, complaining of lack of energy in waging the war.[64] He called for 'direction, decision and drive'.[65] Articles in the *Daily Mirror*[66] and the *Daily Herald*[67] punched home his criticisms. In March 1940 he made a slashing attack in the Commons on the Ministry of Supply for incompetence and lassitude, alleging malpractices, probably corruption, in the awarding of government contracts, whereby intermediaries, in return for a commission, were used to secure orders. The results were, he alleged, that the agents made substantial gains, prices were pushed up and contracts were awarded to bad firms. He named the individuals, firms and contracts concerned.[68] His revelations gained considerable press coverage. Morrison realized that this speech was significant. He had asked Clem Leslie to listen to it from the public gallery.[69] Morrison recalled it 'had an electrifying effect on the House, and undoubtedly damaged the reputation of the government in general and Burgin [the Minister] in particular. It may be that it was because of this speech that the first office I held in Churchill's government was that of Minister of Supply, though I certainly had not any such thing in mind when the speech was made.'[70]

In March and April his militancy increased. He called for less 'gentility' to neutrals. If Norway failed to stand up to Nazi intimidation, it should be treated as an enemy.[71] He urged attacks on German ships in Norway's waters. Later he claimed that Churchill encouraged him to keep up this pressure, probably to assist Churchill's position with his colleagues.[72] He said that we could not go on permitting neutrals unwittingly to help a Nazi victory. They had to come off the shaky fence on which they were so dangerously perched.[73]

When at last the government took action, its expedition to Norway collapsed, and Morrison composed for the *Daily Mirror* 'the most bitter indictment' he had ever written, headlined, 'I Say Get Out'.[74] 'We look like being defeated if the Ministerial leadership of the nation remains as at present constituted. . . . Their semi-isolationist foreign policy left us with fewer and fewer friends. . . . It is the higher direction of the Government that is failing . . . mentally and psychologically unfitted for the mighty task to which the nation has set itself.' He condemned their Norway expedition as too late and ill-prepared; intelligence surveys were neglected, and the Germans had been informed of our intentions. These accusations he had made also the night before in the House of Commons in a speech which was probably the most momentous of his life.[75]

When Morrison spoke in the adjournment debate on 8 May 1940 he felt 'that the country was at the crossroads, and the great personal issues involved, combined to make it an unforgettable moment of history'.[76] On the second day of the debate, about the failure of the mission to Norway, Morrison opened and stated that the Labour Party would divide the House at the end of the debate, a rare occurrence on a motion to adjourn. He expanded his attack on the Norwegian venture into a general condemnation of the government's conduct of the war. He singled out for censure the Secretary of State for Air, Sir Samuel Hoare; the Chancellor of the Exchequer, Sir John Simon; and the Prime Minister. Neville Chamberlain was so staggered by Morrison's speech and the decision to divide the House that, immediately Morrison had sat down, he intervened with an unprecedented appeal to his friends to support him – 'and I have friends in the House'. However, too many of them abstained or voted with the Labour Party for his government to carry on.[77] When the nation was in most difficult straits, a bold speech by Morrison contributed forcefully to pull the government down.[78]

There is as much confusion about Morrison's behaviour in May 1940 as in August 1931. We are still not able to unravel precisely what role he played either in the events leading up to the PLP's decision to force a division on the motion to adjourn on 8 May, or in the events which led to his joining the Churchill administration as Minister of Supply on 12 May. Morrison's version was that, when the party came to discuss the debate, 'neither Attlee nor almost any member of the Labour Party Front Bench Committee had considered what to do on this important occasion. When the committee met on the day of the debate, I urged upon my colleagues that we should have a division. This seemed to come as a great and unconsidered surprise.'[79] His view was that the party should seek to defeat the government and be 'ready to take our share of responsibility as part of a very different government'.[80] Morrison's story is that he convinced the initially reluctant committee to follow his course. James Griffiths recalled: 'Herbert was the actual leader and he saw the chance to destroy the government. He saw that they could take a division at the end of an adjournment debate, thus turning it into a vote of censure. He was the man who had pressed for it in the Parliamentary Committee.'[81] Lord Francis-Williams, relying on Attlee's information, claimed that both Attlee and Morrison sought a division against Dalton's opposition.[82] Dalton agreed that he opposed, and that Morrison was for a division.[83] Attlee, however, in a letter to Laurence Thompson when the latter was writing his book, *1940*, claimed: 'I presided at the Party Meeting and I not Morrison proposed that we should call a vote against the Government. Morrison reluctantly [sic] agreed.'[84] Lord Williams of Barnburgh also wrote to Thompson, 'There is no doubt in my mind as to who moved the resolution, it was Attlee.'[85] What seems to have happened is that Morrison proposed it at the meeting of the Parliamentary Executive Committee, and later Attlee proposed it at the full meeting of the PLP. Thompson, however, on the basis of Attlee's letter devised a theory that Morrison was reluctant because he was engaged in conversations with leading Conservatives about reconstructing the government, including the taking in of himself as the spokesman of Labour. An official party vote against the government in the House put a stop to such moves. Hence, Thompson contends, it was ironical that Morrison had to announce the decision on 8 May which blocked his chances of joining a Coalition Cabinet.[86] But, if there was no reluctance by Morrison, Thompson's theory falls flat.

In order to show that not just the Labour Party but the nation was against Chamberlain, Morrison wanted Lloyd George, the energetic war leader of the First World War, to make a vigorous speech against the feeble leader of the Second. Morrison wrote: 'I sent messages to him through Megan Lloyd George, but for quite a time I could get no definite reply. Sometimes the answer was he would think about it. Sometimes it was that he did not feel like coming to the debate. I asked Megan to go back again and to impress upon him that this really was a vital occasion, and asked her to beg him on my behalf to come into the debate and make a really vigorous attack on the government which was needed in the interests of the country and the prosecution of the war.'[87] James Griffiths recalled: 'Herbert asked me to try and get Lloyd George along. He had tried but failed. He also asked me to get Lloyd George to speak from the Labour front bench, not from the Liberal box.' Griffiths at this time was Secretary of the Welsh Group of MPs, of which

Megan was Chairman. Griffiths went to her and she complained that she had been trying to get through to Lloyd George, but his secretary, Miss Stevenson, was blocking her way. Eventually they succeeded. Lloyd George sat on the front bench next to Griffiths. They spoke together in Welsh. 'Lloyd George was hesitant about speaking and I said that there would be great disappointment if he didn't speak; they are waiting for you and looking to you. I played on Lloyd George's vanity, knowing that he would like to do down Chamberlain.'[88]

In his *Autobiography*,[89] Morrison wrote that on the day after the fateful division on the adjournment debate Chamberlain asked Attlee and Greenwood to join a reconstructed government under him as Prime Minister. 'After Attlee had informed the rest of us on the committee about this he reported to Chamberlain that we were unwilling to enter a government under him as prime minister, that there would have to be a new prime minister of vigour and, in our judgment, capable of leadership of the whole nation in the war.' After Chamberlain made fruitless efforts to patch up an administration, he decided to resign and Churchill was sent for. Churchill had conversations with Attlee and Greenwood, and invited Labour to join his government.[90] Churchill mentioned Morrison as one 'whose services in high office were immediately required', and so offered him the Ministry of Supply. Morrison recalled that: 'Friends advised me to accept in the national interest, and so I agreed. Anyway, if I may say so, I have not been one to evade responsibility.'[91]

Events were not so simple. Following the division on 8 May Chamberlain invited Attlee and Greenwood for a discussion, which took place at 6.15 p.m. on 9 May.[92] With Chamberlain were Halifax and Churchill. Attlee recalled: 'N.C. pressed us strongly to join his government and was vigorously supported by Winston.'[93] Attlee said: 'I am bound to tell you, P.M., that in my view our Party will not serve under you, nor does the country want you.'[94] On being asked if the party would serve under another, Attlee replied that 'in my opinion they would but that I should have to put it to the Party'.[95] On the morning of the next day, 10 May, following the German invasion of Holland and Belgium, Chamberlain phoned Attlee again to ask about changes in the government. He and Greenwood merely issued a vague statement:[96] 'The Party, in view of the latest series of abominable aggressions by Hitler, while firmly convinced that a drastic reconstruction of the Government is vital and urgent in order to win the war, re-affirms its determination to do its utmost to achieve victory. It calls on all its members to devote all their energies to this end.'

The Labour Party leaders were gathering at Bournemouth for the party conference, starting on 13 May, but Morrison decided not to go. He recalled: 'I had a struggle in my own mind as to whether to attend the conference or not. Naturally, I wanted to, but I was the Leader of the London County Council and chairman of its General Purposes and Civil Defence committee.

K

So far as we knew to the contrary, bombs might drop on London at any moment and many expected they would. I decided, therefore, to remain in London with my people. I did so after I had consulted Attlee, who character-istically left it to me.'[97]

At the NEC meeting at the Highcliffe Hotel, Bournemouth, on 10 May, a letter from Morrison was read: as leader of the LCC, it was imperative for him not to absent himself from London at this crisis, and in any case Attlee was aware of his views regarding the situation. Attlee put two questions to the NEC. Will the Labour Party serve under Chamberlain? Will they serve under someone else?[98] After considerable debate the NEC resolved that Labour was prepared to take its share of the responsibility as a full partner in a new government, under a new prime minister. Attlee and Greenwood were to return to London to discuss the implications of the decision with the Prime Minister.[99]

At about 5.00 p.m., before they left, they received a phone call from Chamberlain's private secretary, inquiring if Labour could yet answer the two questions. Attlee recalled: 'I phone [sic] the reply No to the first Yes to the second. The other was unspecified,'[100] and he read out the NEC's resolu-tion. This decision dislodged Chamberlain. At about 6.00 p.m. he tendered his resignation to the King, and after about half an hour Churchill went to the Palace and was asked to form a government. Attlee and Greenwood arrived back in London and were met at Waterloo by a junior minister at the Ad-miralty and Maurice Webb, who told them that Chamberlain had resigned and that Churchill wanted to see them at the Admiralty.[101] Maurice Webb recounts that news of this was brought to Morrison at County Hall by a journalist friend [himself?] who woke him at 1.30 a.m. Morrison in pyjamas and dressing-gown received the news casually as a letter from a postman. His first thoughts were about the position of the Labour Party; what had happened, on what basis was it going into the government, what was its programme, had Churchill a blank cheque? With so many questions in his mind he now decided to go to Bournemouth to find out what had been arranged.[102]

Morrison was at the NEC meeting which gathered at twelve noon on Saturday 11 May in Bournemouth. Attlee and Greenwood were absent. Dalton reported that Chamberlain had resigned and Churchill was to form a government, and that the Labour leaders would meet him later. At 2.00 p.m. Dalton reported that he had phoned Attlee but had no news. At 5.00 p.m. it was announced that the new Prime Minister had formed a War Cabinet of five, including Chamberlain, Attlee and Greenwood.[103] Morrison muttered to Grant Mackenzie: 'These aren't the right people to represent the party.'[104] Dalton recalled: 'Morrison was rather awkward. He said that this didn't sound like a Government which would stand up any better than the last one, and that it would not impress the public. He was inclined, he said, to stay outside.'[105] The NEC instructed Dalton to tell Attlee that it felt that it was of great importance that members associated with the industrial side of the movement should be included. At 6.00 p.m. Dalton reported that Attlee, over the phone, had said that Churchill had intimated that he was very anxious that several of the industrial leaders not now in Parliament should be given office. By seventeen votes to one, the NEC finally agreed that Labour should join the coalition.[106] On Sunday 12 May the NEC met at 10.30 a.m. with Attlee present. He said that Churchill had stated that he would invite Bevin to join the government; the NEC agreed to find him a parliamentary seat.[107] At 4.00 p.m. the NEC, the Executive of the PLP and the General Council of the TUC gathered and approved all that had happened.[108] Morrison was not present at any of the meetings on the twelfth. He had attended only those on the eleventh. Indeed, he played little part in the events leading up to the new coalition. Attlee, Greenwood and Dalton were the active ones. Morrison most likely disagreed with the arrangements that were made. Probably he had hoped for a different coalition, with a more prominent role for himself.

Morrison's May Day (5 May 1940) message had included a sentence: 'I am going to reserve the right to get rid of Chamberlain as soon as I jolly well can.' On 6 May, the day before the start of the adjournment debate, Halifax's diary noted a meeting with Morrison, probably about Labour joining a coalition.[109] In the *Daily Mail* of 6 May a letter from Cripps (signed by 'a British Politician') was published, suggesting a new government, under Halifax as Prime Minister, with an inner Cabinet of Churchill, Lloyd George, Eden and Morrison who was to be the principal Labour representative.[110] Another combination floating about was that Lloyd George should be Premier, Churchill the Deputy and Minister of Defence, with Morrison in charge of Home Affairs as a Minister without Portfolio.[111] So confident was Morrison that he would soon be in a government under Halifax as Prime Minister, that on 8 May after the adjournment debate he told R. A. Butler that the idea of Labour joining the government was 'coming along well'.[112]

The Labour leaders' choice for a successor to Chamberlain was Halifax. Morrison told Peake that if Chamberlain went then Labour 'would welcome the Foreign Secretary in that capacity'. As for Churchill, Morrison said that Labour 'feared the prospect of the First Lord succeeding as Prime Minister'.[113] He was distrusted for his reactionary views on India, his previous hostility to Labour and his generally extremist and erratic past. Attlee and Dalton both wanted Halifax, and the NEC never expressed a view as to whom it wished to succeed Chamberlain. The Labour Party's decision not to join the government under Chamberlain was the crucial event which brought Chamberlain down, but Labour did not force in Churchill. Attlee and Greenwood found that Churchill was the Prime Minister when they returned to London from Bournemouth. They accepted his offer and made no effort to substitute Halifax.[114] Morrison probably expected that Halifax would form a government and would call him to a Cabinet position. This would explain why

Morrison remained in London on 10 May while the NEC met at Bournemouth. He was waiting for a call which never came.

It would also explain his annoyance when he was offered the Ministry of Supply. Dalton claims to have suggested to Attlee that Morrison should go to Supply where his 'energy and gift of organization' were needed to tackle the 'mess'. Morrison expressed the wish to be in the War Cabinet without a department. Dalton recalled that 'several of us urged him, in the national interest, to take Supply if he was offered it'.[115] Morrison told a somewhat different story to the LLP. Churchill 'asked me, in the urgent interests of the country, to accept the office of Minister of Supply'.[116] 'I searched my own mind and conscience very closely and decided it was my duty, not only to the Party but to the country to render what service I could.'[117] Later in the war he recalled the interview with Churchill: 'It was the most discouraging interview I have ever had. Mr Churchill said "I don't offer you cheerfulness, I don't offer you good fortune, I don't offer you quick success. I offer you nothing but tears and blood and sweat and toil." There was nothing very attractive about any one of the four. Nevertheless Mr Churchill did it in a way that, although it was the most cheerless invitation to a life of anxiety and stress and trouble, you just felt you would have been a worm if you had said No, and that is just as he meant it to be.'[118] He was lumbered with a post which he admitted was hardly one to run after.[119]

He took his leave of the LLP. The arrangements of 1929–31 were repeated. Daines became Acting Secretary with an extra £75 a year, while Morrison was granted leave of absence without pay. Miss Donald was to accompany him. The Executive also decided that Morrison's 'offer to be available in a consultative capacity be accepted and he be accorded the right of entry to the Party office, the Executive Committee and the Party Conference'.[120]

Although Morrison remained an alderman of the LCC, he yielded his leadership to Charles Latham. In a farewell speech to the LCC he said how exceedingly happy he had been, and that he now made a sad transition. He moved from work which involved 'the construction and building up of human life', to 'making the instruments of war'. Still, they were for the 'defence of civilization, human dignity and human liberty'.

PART TWO
1940–1965

Chapter 20

Supply, and the Blitz Begins, May–October 1940

When Morrison moved across the river to his new offices at the Ministry of Supply, overlooking the embankment, he found his predecessor, Burgin, clearing out his papers. Burgin said: 'You don't deserve the job to be handed over to you all in order after the way you treated me. But you are a lucky chap and are inheriting a fine machine.'[1] Morrison knew that in fact all was far from well in the department. He took off his jacket and set about launching an emergency armaments drive. The department worked through Whitsun without taking a holiday, and throughout the summer of 1940 he was to be seen working around the clock in his shirt-sleeves, his hair an untidy mop, often chewing a cigarette, projecting an encouraging image of pep and drive.[2]

The problems facing Morrison were daunting. Britain's army was too small and ill-equipped, yet measures to expand it and improve its armaments clashed with demands from the RAF, which had first priority on military supplies. Within weeks of Morrison's taking office the existing army was smashed and stripped of weapons on the Continent. There was virtually nothing left in the quartermasters' cupboards to rearm the quarter of a million survivors from Dunkirk. 'It is difficult to believe that Hitler would have stayed his hand in June', wrote Morrison in a memorandum to the War Cabinet, 'had he known the nakedness of the land.'[3] The subsequent battle in Britain's skies led to still heavier demands from the RAF and also exposed woeful deficiencies in the anti-aircraft defences. Pressures from all sides for more munitions were enormous and the resources available were pitifully small. Shortages of raw materials, especially of steel, drop forgings and castings, created numerous industrial bottle-necks. Morrison was besieged by other departments, and especially by Beaverbrook at Aircraft Production, in the desperate scramble for supplies. Even when the materials were available, there were infuriating delays while the military chiefs made up their minds what design of tank or anti-aircraft gun they most wanted.[4]

Morrison's first concern was to strengthen his departmental team. His Permanent Secretary, Sir Arthur Robinson, though a respected Whitehall figure, was not dynamic enough for the critical situation facing them, and so Morrison brought in Sir George Gater, the former Clerk at the LCC, as joint secretary. He appointed his old friend, and adviser, Clem Leslie, as Director of Public Relations and brought into the Ministry a number of men with experience of working in industry. He set up a new Tank Board to try to get agreement on what were the basic tank requirements of the army, and re-organized the section dealing with the critical shortage of machine tools.[5]

Morrison made his first speech as Minister of Supply on 20 May. He said: 'The peace and civilization of the whole world depend on the effort we make now to produce arms and win the war . . . If we waste a minute at the desk or bench we sacrifice a life . . . Everything that I can do to extend the scope of the arms drive and to enable you to work to the utmost advantage I will do, and I will try to do it in the spirit that I commend to you – the spirit of duty, determination and comradeship . . . work at war speed.'[6] He followed this two days later with a broadcast to the nation on similar lines. 'The Depart-ment of State, which I control,' he warned, 'will – it must – demand from the civil population a harder and sterner way of life than we have been used to. In peace you may have become accustomed to think of profits, and of business as usual; or of the safeguarding of sectional privileges. In war . . . we shall permit no private vested interest to stand in the way of the nation's need.'[7] Next day the King signed the first ministerial order under the Emergency Powers Defence Act authorizing Morrison to take control of factories needed to produce munitions and equipment and also to prescribe the hours of work, the labour employed, and the price of goods.

The United States was the largest single source of stocks of machine tools, weapons and other military goods, and Morrison was especially worried at the initial lack of American support for the British war effort. He pressed the Prime Minister to intervene personally to win American sympathy. Churchill would not be drawn: 'I am sure that only events will serve to turn opinion in America . . . I cannot consume my limited life and strength in the task you seek to set me. Forgive me for appearing unresponsive, but I must keep my first efforts for the war.'[8]

An important part of Morrison's job at Supply was to improve morale in industry and to mobilize the community for the war effort. He had to follow up, in a much more mundane way, the great morale-raising impact of Chur-chill's speeches to the nation. He visited munitions factories, sometimes accompanied by King George VI, and on the shop floor talked to the men who were producing the guns and tanks. He also launched a series of propaganda campaigns, guided by Leslie's expert hand, which projected Morrison's image as one of the dynamic new ministers who were finally getting the war effort moving under Churchill's inspiring leadership. In June he launched a new series of plays on the BBC called the 'Victory Drive' which dramatized situa-tions in munitions and aircraft factories under titles such as *Go To It* and *Marching On*. He was particularly adept at using snappy slogans – 'Go to it',

'Keep at it' – which were quickly taken up and used as greetings to Morrison when he visited factories.

His most successful publicity campaign was to salvage waste materials suitable for re-use in war production. At first he relied on voluntary community effort inspired by massive publicity, but he later compelled local authorities to undertake salvage collection.[9] Broadcasting his plan for a National Salvage Campaign he announced a new slogan – 'Up Housewives and at 'em', and threatened to punish local authorities which were slack.[10] Shortly afterwards, he appointed Robert Morrison, MP for North Tottenham (a borough with a good reputation for refuse collection), as National Controller of Salvage.[11] In August he opened a salvage exhibition at Charing Cross Station, boasting that salvage recovered in July was double that in June, and he announced two new slogans: 'Scrap for Victory' and 'Your old iron will win the war'.[12]

As a publicist, Morrison was undoubtedly a success at Supply. He also reorganized the department, strengthened its staff, instilled it with a sense of urgency, and eliminated the air of graft and petty corruption which had hung around the Ministry and the private contractors working for it.[13] Within four months of taking office Morrison was able to report to the War Cabinet that 'the special and considerable deficiencies in arms and ammunition, created by the losses on the Continent, have been made good to an appreciable extent'.[14] Much of the improvement was due to increased production planned before he took over and to special help from the United States, but Morrison had also made a quick impact. Some of the ministers who dealt directly with him were impressed. 'From my point of view at the War Office', recalled Lord Avon, 'Herbert delivered the goods.'[15] Beaverbrook praised 'his efficiency and competence'.[16] Even so, doubts existed about the adequacy of his Ministry. The scramble for raw materials and labour led to constant conflict in the Cabinet,[17] with Morrison caught in the cross-fire between Beaverbrook and Bevin.* This inter-departmental squabbling grew worse and by the end of September Churchill had decided on a major reconstruction and asked Beaverbrook to take over at Supply and co-ordinate all war production.[18] Morrison had not been a failure; he had thrown himself into the job with his usual breezy enthusiasm and certainly re-invigorated the department. Given much more time he might well have learned and improved. But he was certainly far from the ideal Minister of Supply,[19] having no experience of industrial or military affairs. The Prime Minister was not, however, harsh on Morrison in moving him on. Churchill had in mind a job which was ideally suited to his experience and talents.

Churchill's decision to promote Morrison to Home Secretary, at the beginning of October 1940, can be understood only within the context of the blitz which had by then been battering London for the past month. Previously the capital had been spared from heavy bombing. The Germans had concentrated

* Bevin was Minister of Labour.

their attacks on destroying Britain's air defences as a prelude to invasion. In late August, however, the RAF bombed Berlin and Hitler then announced that he would wreak revenge on British cities.

On the afternoon of Saturday, 7 September 1940, large formations of German planes blackened the clear autumn sky over London. Their bombs set the East End alight and they returned in waves over the virtually un-defended city throughout the night. When the all-clear sounded at dawn about a thousand people had been killed and the fires could be seen raging from miles around. The blitz continued for the next fifty-seven successive nights, with some day raids as well, and was not halted until May 1941, by which time twenty thousand citizens had been killed and some seventy thousand wounded.[20]

The first few nights of bombing made a shattering impact, especially on the East End. People wandered individually and in family groups in the streets looking for shelter. Many had lost all their life's possessions. Some carried their salvaged belongings in sad bundles or stacked on old perambulators or handcarts. There was little public transport and often the gas and electricity had been cut off. A spontaneous and chaotic evacuation from London took place, with large numbers sleeping in the open in Epping Forest and thousands occupying the Chislehurst caves. The bombed-out who stayed in London sought haven either in local authority rest centres or in deep shelters, which they tried to turn into substitute homes below ground. The rest centres, usually in schools, had totally inadequate facilities to cope with the dazed, dirty and bewildered people who flooded into them. The shelter situation was even worse and blew up into a major crisis for Churchill and the government during September.

Government shelter policy, directed by Sir John Anderson as Home Sec-retary, had concentrated on providing two kinds of shelter: domestic shelters (known as 'Andersons') which were basically trenches dug in the garden and roofed over, and street brick shelters to protect people caught in the streets during bombing. Each was designed for brief occupation during a short raid. Some deep shelters were also provided, but not many because they were the most expensive to construct and the least favoured by governments which feared the development of a defeatist 'deep shelter mentality' among the people. Once the blitz began, however, Londoners desperately sought for deep shelter, apparently safe, away from the noise, where they could stretch out during the nights of ceaseless bombing, for which the Andersons, which were cramped and prone to flooding, and the street shelters, which were uncomfortable and vulnerable to direct hits, were not designed.

There were too few deep shelters to cope with the masses of frightened Londoners, and those that existed, having no facilities for family occupation, rapidly became sordid. There were no bunks for sleeping and often not even seats. Open buckets were used as latrines, and there were no adequate washing facilities. Prostitutes paraded and drunks staggered among the sheltering families. The noise and the stench became unbearable. The most notorious was the so-called Tilbury shelter, part of the Liverpool Street goods station off the Commercial Road. People queued all day to enter and police were used to control the stampede when the gates were opened at 4.30 in the afternoon. Up to fifteen thousand people slept there each night, often lying on top of the food boxes stored in the goods yard. The floor became covered in faeces and urine, which spread into sleepers' blankets and covered the shoes of those standing up. There were only two taps to serve this mass of people and the only medical services were provided by one Jewish doctor and three Jewish nurses who worked for nothing and brought their own medicines.[21]

Londoners sought alternative havens beneath the earth. The underground railway stations were the most appropriate. The government at first instructed London Transport not to allow the tubes to be used as shelters, but people simply went down them and stayed there and nobody could throw them out. The Central Line extension from Liverpool Street through Bethnal Green to Stratford and Leytonstone was particularly popular, having been tunnelled but not yet electrified, and it became one long worm of sleepers during the blitz. By the end of September 1940, it was estimated that nearly two hundred thousand people were sleeping in the London tubes each night without organized facilities.

Revulsion about the shelter situation boiled up in London during September. There were reports of growing bitterness among ordinary Londoners and that the King and Queen had been booed on a visit to the East End.[22] Morale in the blitzed areas was in danger of cracking. The widely-held view of London resisting the blitz with fortitude and calm and carrying on business as usual is in some respects far from the truth. In certain parts of the capital, mainly in the East End where the devastation was so terrible and so sustained, there was an almost total collapse of the fabric of social life. Public services failed and the people blamed 'them' for the appalling conditions. 'It was more than bricks and mortar that collapsed in West Ham', wrote a contemporary Fabian Society observer, 'it was a local ordering of society which was found hopelessly wanting, was as weak and badly constructed as the single brick walls that fell down at the blast.'[23] Communists quickly moved in to exploit the discontent. They launched a national campaign for better shelter provision. They secured election as unofficial wardens or marshals in the shelters and took the opportunity not only to fan the flames of discontent but also to press their propaganda against the government's conduct of the war and in favour of a negotiated peace with Germany.[24] Britain may not have been quite on the threshold of its St Petersburg revolution, as George Orwell was currently suggesting in his private diary,[25] but clearly the situation was very serious. London was now the front line of Britain's battle with Germany: if its morale cracked the war would be lost.

Churchill had to act. It was not a matter of specific policy reforms. Remedies for most of the shelter problems were already being initiated by the minister responsible, Sir John Anderson. But these would inevitably take time to fructify. Something more dramatic was needed, more symbolic and comprehensible to the ordinary Londoner. This was achieved by the removal of the austere and impersonal Anderson and his replacement by the one politician above all identified with the people of London, who had devoted most of his life to advancing the welfare of London, and whose knowledge of its problems and its citizens, whose contacts with the local authorities dealing directly with the consequences of the blitz, were unequalled. The radical journalist, Hannen Swaffer, later claimed that he finally inspired Morrison's promotion, urging Beaverbrook to tell Churchill at the beginning of October that 'cockneydom was on the verge of revolt', that the communists were about to march on Whitehall, and that Morrison must be put in charge of the blitz because 'he is the only man that Londoners trust . . . if London runs, the war will be lost'.[26]

Whatever source inspired it, the logic and sense of the move was overwhelming. It was one of Churchill's most felicitous reshuffles, with both Anderson and Morrison proving superbly successful at their new tasks.*

* Anderson became Lord President of the Council.

Chapter 21

The Home Office and Home Security: Dealing with the Blitz

Morrison's promotion to Home Secretary and Minister of Home Security brought greater responsibilities than anything he had previously undertaken, encompassing two major departments. As Home Secretary he was by tradition the senior Secretary of State, covering the general fields of law, order, citizenship and civil liberties, and was also the 'residuary legatee' of the government. The police came under his supervision and this task gave him particular pleasure in view of his father's career as a policeman. A few weeks after taking office he paid a formal visit to Scotland Yard – the first Home Secretary to do so.[1] After the war when he became Lord President he retained the use of a police car, instead of the usual Whitehall Humber saloon, as a sign of his affection for the force.

The Ministry of Home Security was a much more recent creation. After Munich, Chamberlain assigned the field of civil defence to Sir John Anderson, then Lord Privy Seal, with the commitment to make it a separate ministry attached to the Home Secretary should war break out: in 1939 Anderson switched to the Home Office and retained the responsibility.[2] Involving all civil defence against air attack, the job in the blitz was even more onerous than the Home Office. Under Home Security were placed responsibility for air raid wardens, the fire-fighting services, first aid, rescue and decontamination squads, for such facilities as shelters and all civil defence equipment, and for arrangements concerning air raid warnings and the black-out. The Ministry of Home Security could not of course act as an isolated unit in the field of civil defence. Many departments were involved before, during and after an air attack: The Ministry of Transport with traffic control and road and rail repairs, the Ministry of Health with casualties, the Ministry of Food with supplies of food, and the military with the disposal of unexploded bombs. Morrison as Minister of Home Security had the central task of co-ordinating these activities, which he performed primarily through his chairmanship of the Cabinet Civil Defence Committee.

In his two departments there was some overlapping of function. The police and the fire service were used by both departments, though the former were officially under the Home Office and the latter under Home Security. The Home Secretary was responsible for administering the large number of emergency defence regulations passed at the beginning of the war, many of which concerned Home Security matters. This overlapping of function was reflected in some joint staffing and was made easier by sharing the same building at the lower end of Whitehall. Organizationally, however, the two departments were separate, and for Morrison it meant a double responsibility and an enormous range of policy problems passing through his hands. By 1945 his headquarters staff contained some 1,500 under the Home Office, roughly four thousand under Home Security, and about 1,300 common to both, quite apart from those in the regional offices.

Thirteen regional commissioners and their staffs, whose organization was modelled on the government's contingency plans to deal with the 1926 General Strike, were crucial agents in the conduct of Morrison's functions at Home Security. They had been established primarily as representatives of the King's government in their respective self-sufficient regions should the state disintegrate under German invasion. Fortunately, lacking that necessity, they concentrated on their subsidiary role of supervising civil defence operations at the regional level. They became important links in the chain of civil defence command, starting in Morrison's war room in a Whitehall basement, from where he could communicate with all the regional offices, which in turn remained in contact with local ARP controllers. By this means every twelve hours local information about damage and casualties was transmitted to Morrison's war room, where a comprehensive national picture was built up which he could then report to the Cabinet. Equally, when a particular locality was subject to intensive bombing, extra civil defence assistance was mobilized from a wide area, and usually the regional commissioners moved in to help the stunned local authorities get services moving again. In Stepney, where the local authority proved very unsatisfactory, Morrison took away their powers and put the borough completely in the hands of commissioners.[3]

In dealing with the blitz crisis Morrison was fortunate in that – as a contrast to when he took over Supply – he found his new ministry running efficiently. Broad planning for civil defence had begun seriously in the mid-thirties and the central and regional machinery had clicked smoothly into operation at the outbreak of war. Immense, new and often unpredicted problems had arisen with the blitz, but the department was already energetically pursuing solutions to them. Morrison never disguised the debt that he and the country owed to his predecessor Anderson and was always generous about him. He described him as 'one of the great public servants of our time' and pointed out that the glaring deficiencies which undoubtedly existed in October 1940 were in no way Anderson's fault.[4] Even so he felt it necessary to strengthen his predecessor's official team with staff of his own choosing. He brought Gater from

Supply to act as joint secretary with (and soon to replace) Sir Thomas Gardiner at Home Security. He also brought Clem Leslie to continue handling his public relations, and the inevitable Miss Donald for his Labour Party affairs.[5] Firebrace, the former Chief Fire Officer at the LCC, was introduced to add weight to the fire defence team.[6] Morrison made full and constructive use of his junior ministers, making a clear allocation of duties among them and leaving them scope for a good deal of personal initiative. Ellen Wilkinson took direct responsibility for shelters and was put in charge of a new standing committee on shelter policy. She threw herself energetically and emotionally into this task and quickly became a devoted admirer of her chief, leaving many with the, probably mistaken, impression that she was Morrison's mistress.[7] William Mabane, the other parliamentary secretary at Home Security, was given more general civil defence functions, while Oswald Peake, the able junior minister at the Home Office, handled legal and technical matters.[8]

Morrison went to great trouble to strengthen the regional commissions, often with people he had met and come to respect in his local government days.[9] He took the opportunity to redress the political balance among the commissioners, resisting Churchill's efforts to push in his party nominees and trying to make appointments of able Labour supporters.[10] Arthur Bottomley, Charles Key, Jack Lawson, George Lindgren, Hector McNeil, Percy Morris and Sir Hartley Shawcross were some among Morrison's regional appointments who either already were or were later to become prominent in the Labour Party.* Morrison appreciated as well as any Conservative the value and importance of patronage in serious party politics, but he insisted that the recipients have the ability and qualifications for the job. From the beginning at the Home Office Morrison was building up the network of associates who hitched their futures to his political star – the 'travelling circus' which became a familiar part of Morrison's operations in Whitehall and Westminster over the next decade.

Morrison's promotion to the Home Office was announced on Thursday, 3 October 1940. Early next morning he went into the office to take command and then attended a Cabinet at noon.[11] In the afternoon, after visiting Buckingham Palace to kiss hands on receiving the seals of office from the monarch, he began a tour of deep shelters in south London. An air raid started while he was inspecting the Southwark tube station and his question-and-answer sessions with shelterers and with accompanying journalists were conducted against a background of deafening ack-ack barrage.[12] The following day he went to the East End with Admiral Evans, the peppery London commissioner who had accompanied Scott through a different kind of blizzard to the South Pole thirty years earlier, and bombs fell close to the official party. Morrison ordered the opening of Bethnal Green tube station as a deep shelter – to be

---

* Others were W. Quin, O. G. Willey, C. R. Keene, W. Astbury and H. Medland, Deputy Commissioners in the Scottish, North East, North Midland, South Eastern and South Western Regions respectively.

the scene of a disaster which shook his career three years later – and then moved west to see the dreadful conditions in the notorious Tilbury extension.[13]

During these first few days Morrison was striving to establish an image of vigour and purpose in dealing with shelters, the overriding problem facing him. He worked on this night and day, fitting in his office paper-work and a constant stream of meetings and visitors between his inspections of the bombed areas.[14] Londoners looked to Morrison to protect them from the blitz nightmare; to fail them in this would have incalculably damaging consequences, personally and on a much wider political level. On the day he took over, the *Daily Herald* published prominently an open letter to Morrison from Ritchie Calder, one of the most influential radical journalists then reporting the blitz. Calder wrote:

> Dear Herbert Morrison,
> When I heard that you had been appointed Home Secretary I went home and slept soundly ... I have heard the bitter rumblings. I have seen men and women, these tough London workers of whom you and I are proud, whose homes have gone but whose courage is unbroken by the Nazi bombers, goaded by neglect and seething with resentment and furious reproach. THEY LOOK TO YOU ... Much of the breakdown which has occurred in the last month could have been foreseen and avoided; or having arisen could have been mastered by anyone who understood the human problem of the Londoners and the complications of local government ... you have a task as great as your abilities. Go to it, Herbert.[15]

Big things, near miracles, were obviously expected of Morrison. The day after Calder's letter he issued a public statement 'to my well-loved fellow citizens of London and of all the other great cities, towns and districts on which the enemy is waging his reckless war. In these times, under such an assault, no man can promise you safety. . . . But what can be done to ward off danger, to lessen hardship, and to organize some measure of rest and decent living for those of you who suffer directly, I am determined to do. . . . Give me a little time, a reasonable chance, and I will be ready to answer to you for my efforts.'[16] It was the right tone, the personal touch. The following week in Parliament he already had to begin to answer in a two-day adjournment debate devoted to Britain's air raid defences. Morrison was welcomed from all sides in his new ministerial role, though many of those who wished him well thought he had an impossibly heavy task on his hands and were savage in their criticisms of the civil defence facilities he had inherited.[17]

Some of the worst deficiencies, at least in relation to shelter provision, were already in process of remedy before Morrison took over.[18] Local authorities were asked to construct more deep public shelters (without altering the main policy emphasis on domestic shelters), to provide better amenities in them, bunks, lighting, heating, drinking water, sanitation and first aid, and also to provide more staff to control the crowds in large shelters. Finally, two days before Anderson left Home Security, the central government conceded greater grants to local authorities for the costs of building and equipping shelters.

Even with these reforms of detail, the government's shelter strategy when Morrison took over remained based on the dispersal of the population in 'Anderson' and street shelters, which provided the maximum cover for the minimum cost and avoided corroding the national will with the dreaded 'deep shelter mentality'. Morrison accepted that, whatever the other arguments, there simply was not enough steel and cement available to change to a policy of massive construction of deep shelters.[19] He did, however, work from the beginning to convert the Cabinet from its opposition to the principle of deep shelters. On 30 October he told the War Cabinet that it was essential to counter communist agitation on the deep shelter issue but that he could not do so adequately 'if he adopted a wholly negative attitude towards the provision of deep shelters'.[20] Despite the objection by some ministers that a more positive approach would be to concede that the previous policy was wrong, Morrison secured agreement to announce immediately a programme of tunnel construction to shelter another hundred thousand people in London, and a lesser number in the provinces.[21] These new tunnels in the event contributed little to protecting people from bombs. They were not completed until after the main blitz was over and were mainly used later as billets for allied troops in the massive build-up prior to the Normandy invasion. But the reversal of policy towards deep shelters announced in Morrison's broadcast of 3 November was important as a morale booster, a sign to the public that a new minister was in business and the wishes of ordinary Londoners would now be more respected. He was also able to report in his broadcast more immediate improvements to facilities in existing shelters and the tubes. A ticket system of entry and the allocation of bunks to regular occupants were introduced and ensured orderly occupation and a regular community in each shelter. From late October permanent canteen facilities began to be established in the large shelters and mobile canteens visited smaller ones. Chemical lavatories, ventilation, lighting and running water steadily became more common as local authorities implemented the instructions and badgering from Morrison's ministry. In some cases, night classes, film shows and various forms of organized entertainment were provided. Just before Christmas Morrison was able to boast that since he came to office over 200,000 bunks had been installed. 'The worst of the over-crowding in the big shelters is now a thing of the past' he claimed.[22] By the spring of 1941 most Londoners sheltering underground were sleeping in reasonably civilized dormitories. 'What is most striking,' wrote Orwell in his diary, 'is the cleanly, normal domesticated air that everything now has. Especially the young married couples, the sort of homely, cautious type that would probably be buying their houses from a building society, tucked up together under pink counterpanes. And the large families one sees here and there, father, mother and several children, all laid out in a row like rabbits on a slab. They all seem so peacefully asleep in the bright lamplight. The children lying on their backs, with their little pink cheeks like wax dolls, and all fast asleep.'[23] Morrison's first and most urgent problem had at least been brought under control.

He had also by the spring of 1941 filled the remaining gap in Britain's shelter provision – protection for those people, usually the majority, who did not go outside to an Anderson shelter or a street shelter or a deep public shelter, but simply stayed indoors throughout the night's bombing. The original inspiration of the indoor shelter which later became known as the 'Morrison' is still unclear. Morrison in his autobiography claims that he first decided on the principle and then forced the department's engineers and scientists to produce a design within twenty-four hours by threatening to lock them up in a room until they agreed.[24] Certainly Morrison was made aware of the need for an indoor shelter on his early visits to the blitzed parts of London and the provinces. However, when John Baker of the Home Security Research Experiment Division was asked to design an indoor shelter he was told that Churchill himself was the source of the idea and had actually submitted a rough sketch (on an old envelope) of a shelter with a pointed arch roof.[25] Baker, one of the world's best structural engineers, ignored Churchill's gothic inclinations and designed a flat-topped shelter with a steel frame and wire-mesh sides. Being ductile it did not shatter like bricks but bent and absorbed shock energy from an explosion. It was big enough for two adults and two children to sleep in, could support a collapsed house on top of it, and was easy to produce and to erect. Meanwhile the engineering department of the ministry had constructed an arched shelter as Churchill suggested and the two models were taken to 10 Downing Street on New Year's Day 1941 and placed in a room adjoining the main hall. Morrison arrived early for the demonstration and Baker described to him the basis of his design. 'I only had ten minutes to explain it,' recalled Baker, 'but when Churchill came into the room and first looked approvingly at the arched shelter, whilst actually sitting on top of mine, Morrison went on to explain the principles of mine as well as I could myself.'[26] Churchill at first approved both designs but the department eventually decided in favour of the flat top because it was simpler to manufacture and to erect. In January the Cabinet authorized an initial production order of 400,000 'steel table shelters'.[27] By the end of March some were available to the London public. The press had already carried the story that 'Mr Herbert Morrison himself invented the new indoor shelter'[28] and by April, under Leslie's inspiration, it was being described in departmental papers and official instruction booklets as 'the Morrison shelter'.[29] Morrison was not, for a time at least, deceived by his own publicity. He wrote generously to Baker in 1943 congratulating him on his appointment to a chair at Cambridge and adding that 'if the shelter that has become associated with my name were the only result of your work the country would have had cause to be grateful to you'.[30] Fifteen years later, when Baker met Morrison in a Cambridge pub and reminded the ageing politician of his shelter creation, Morrison 'went silent, blinked rather bewilderedly, and said "but I thought I designed it" '.[31]

While Morrison was dealing with the special problems of deep and indoor shelters, much broader questions had arisen concerning air raid defence. The 'Home Front' as organized in 1939–40 was not always proving adequate to the unprecedented pressures put upon it. From November 1940 the German *Luftwaffe* began to spread its assault into the provinces, often to places previously considered immune from – and therefore unprepared for – aerial attack. A rapid succession of devastating raids was launched on Coventry, Birmingham, Bristol, Sheffield, Portsmouth, and Southampton. Before the winter was over Exeter, Cardiff, Plymouth, Swansea, Belfast, Liverpool, Hull, Manchester and Clydeside had joined the list of shattered cities. Morrison grew very worried that morale would crumble in the regions as it had begun to crack earlier in London, and he and his junior ministers made frequent visits to the blitzed areas around the country.[32] As late as May 1941 he was still apparently worried: 'the people cannot stand this intensive bombing indefinitely', he warned the Cabinet civil defence committee, 'sooner or later the morale of other towns will go even as Plymouth's has gone.'[33]

He was completing one of his earliest provincial tours, to Bristol, Cardiff and then to the West Midlands in mid-November, when the most dramatically destructive single raid of the war hit Coventry. Morrison and his wife were staying the night of 14 November near by at Himley Hall with Lord Dudley, the regional commissioner. His secretary, Austin Strutt, Clem Leslie and Sir John Hodsall, the inspector general of civil defence, were also in the party. They were beginning a champagne supper when they heard the first waves of German planes bombing in the distance. They went outside and could see flames already lighting the clear sky over Coventry.[34] In the next eleven hours of ceaseless attack five hundred tons of explosive and thirty thousand incendiaries completely destroyed the city's historic centre. The regional plans to provide outside assistance for any locality under attack worked well in terms of getting civil defence workers and equipment to Coventry, but once there they took a terrible battering. Some of the outside brigades also found they could not function when they reached the burning streets, either because of lack of water or because their equipment did not fit the water pipes. Local mortuaries could not accommodate all the dead, which included many civil defence workers. A senior regional officer in a secret official report immediately after the raid likened its effect to that of 'an earthquake'.[35]

Morrison travelled to Coventry on the morning after the holocaust. Beaverbrook, who was concerned with the damage to the city's crucial aircraft production factories, and the Minister of Health, Ernest Brown, joined him for part of the time. They had a very difficult meeting with the Mayor, the Town Clerk and the chairman of the city council's emergency committee. The Mayor offered Morrison a glass of whisky, apologizing that there was no water to go with it. The Chief Fire Officer, Brakes, sat there still unwashed and unshaven and finally fell asleep in the meeting.[36] The local officials complained that there had been no fighter or anti-aircraft defences and that the German planes had been allowed to fly over the city for hour after hour while they systematically destroyed it. Air defences were not Morrison's concern and until the development of radar and night fighters in 1941 there was little anybody could do about stopping the Germans. He was troubled by the many questions they raised about civil defence and listened to their claims that it should be made compulsory and even constitute an exemption from military service.[37]

Coventry was so stunned that at first Morrison found an almost total lack of will or desire to get the town moving again. It was pervaded by an air of defeatism. Morrison moved in vigorously. 'He gave orders right and left', telling the army GOC to bring in the Pioneer Corps to clear the damage, activating Brown on health problems, instructing the staff of the regional commission on how to reorganize the town.[38] Morrison, the city boss, was on his home ground – a municipality had come to a halt, he knew how to get it moving again. He was assisted, as often on these blitz visits, by the arrival of the King on the Saturday, the sixteenth, touring the still smoking remnants of the city and trying to raise the morale of its shocked populace.

The Cabinet, to which Morrison reported every few days on air raid damage and casualties,[39] was upset by the publicity given to the destruction of Coventry. Existing censorship policy was to delay reports of raids for several days and then in general not to release the names of localities bombed in order not to give the Germans information on the results of their raids. Ministers, and especially Eden, were angry with the details about Coventry broadcast by the BBC and instructed Morrison, together with Duff Cooper, the Minister of Information, to 'report what changes, if any, were necessary in the constitution and management of the BBC in order to ensure its effective control by His Majesty's Government'.[40] In due course two 'advisers' were appointed to maintain liaison between the BBC and the Ministry of Information. Morrison was not happy with the repressive instincts of his colleagues, who were also at this time beginning to turn on the press with a very heavy hand.[41] He defended the publicity over Coventry and acidly pointed out that 'the enemy must be aware that they had in fact bombed Coventry'.[42]

Morrison had returned to Whitehall from his traumatic provincial tour convinced that radical measures were essential if civil defence was not to collapse under the pressure of the German air assault. The demands of the Coventry officials were similar to those put to him earlier in the bombed towns of the west country and they recurred when he visited Southampton and Portsmouth early in December, finding each town physically and morally shattered. At Southampton a large part of the population had quit the city in a chaotic exodus and the civil defence services had virtually collapsed.[43] He quickly set his departmental machinery to reorganize civil defence in the light of recent experience.[44] This was typical of Morrison's approach to government: to visit the problem on the ground and talk to people who actually suffered from it and dealt with it; to consult officials and get in reports and views; and finally to synthesize experience and recommendations into new policies.[45]

Morrison worked at the Ministry throughout the Christmas of 1940, eating his Christmas dinner in the office and sleeping on his camp bed in the bomb-proof basement shelter at night.[46] Final confirmation of the need for still more radical reforms in civil defence came with the great fire raid on the City of London on the Sunday night of 29–30 December, when the fires raged out of control throughout the deserted financial district. By then he was in a position to make his first proposals to Cabinet* – for compulsory recruitment to civil defence and to enable men liable for military service to be taken into full-time civil defence work instead. Morrison also told the Cabinet on New Year's Eve that the press outcry about the failure to cope with the fires was justified and he secured approval from his colleagues for his suggested remedy, to introduce compulsory fire-watching.[47] 'We must raise a big new army of fire-watchers,' he said in a newspaper interview, 'a watcher on the roof of every building.'[48] The new fire-watching scheme was still to be primarily voluntary, but where there was a shortage of volunteers the local authority, through the regional commissioners, was empowered to enrol street fire-watching parties and compel participation. Fire-watching patrols were required for all business premises. In a New Year's Eve broadcast, Morrison explained that no fire brigade could be expected to deal with mass incendiary raids without large community assistance. The compulsory principle was being introduced because 'some of you lately, in more cities than one, have failed your country. This must never happen again . . . every group of houses and business premises must have its fire party. Fall in the Fire Bomb Fighters!'[49] In another broadcast later in January he again adopted this schoolmasterly tone with its blunt reference to slacking. He would never have resorted to compulsion, he asserted, were 'all the people patriotic and courageous enough'.[50] By the end of the month his scheme was in operation, securing a dramatic increase in recruitment.[51]

The speed and success with which Morrison had introduced fire-watching was acclaimed in the press.[52] He soon ran into serious trouble, however, with the trade unions. They complained at not having been consulted and objected especially to workers being required to protect their employers' premises without remuneration, which they saw as unpaid overtime. Protests arose from individual unions and at the NEC throughout the spring and summer. Large numbers of workers throughout the country refused to obey the order.[53] At the TUC in Edinburgh in September there was a barrage of criticism of Morrison, but by then he had trimmed to the storm and had made concessions in advance to the General Council,[54] which was able to announce that there

---

* These were implemented in the National Service Act of April 1941 – although in practice few people were conscripted or opted for civil defence work under the Act since alternative demands for manpower grew more pressing after the summer of 1941.

would be some financial compensation and that employers would have to provide sleeping and sanitary facilities for fire-watchers.[55] From this point on, however, there was not a great deal for the vast army of fire-watchers to do since, apart from during the 'little blitz' of 1944, German fire-raids became infrequent. The scheme therefore became something of a white elephant, involving an enormous and expensive administrative apparatus.[56] But Morrison had prepared the means to deal with any renewal of mass incendiary bombing; it is no criticism of his scheme, but a cause for relief, that it largely stood by unneeded.

Morrison now turned to the largest single task of administrative reform he executed in the war – the reorganization of the fire services. Like his other civil defence measures it was characterized by a move away from the voluntary principle to compulsion and away from the local authority base to a national organization.

Britain's fire services at the beginning of the war were composed of two elements, the nucleus of professionals and the large voluntary element of auxiliaries mobilized as part of civil defence. They were organized into brigades based on local authority areas, of which there were 1,668 in all, having a wide variety of standards in men and equipment. Even before the blitz began, the Home Office under Anderson had shown concern at potential defects in the fire services; these worries were more than justified by experience under air attack. Morrison's provincial tours in late 1940 and his visits to Manchester and Merseyside in February 1941 and to Clydeside in April brought home the urgency and widespread extent of the problem. He had partly dealt with the incendiary threat through fire-watching, and the shortage of manpower through compulsory recruitment. But the fundamental weakness of fire-fighting organization under a multiplicity of local authorities, with varied standards of technique, training and equipment, and each too small to provide the major service necessary in the emergency of a mass raid, was trickier to handle. From the end of 1940 Home Office memoranda were raising the question whether the fire services could any longer be left in local authority hands;[57] by April the departmental view was moving towards amalgamation of the local brigades, even to the point of nationalization. Morrison claimed in his autobiography that he had been convinced of the need for nationalization even earlier, since his visit to Coventry in November 1940.[58] This exaggerates the speed of his conversion. He was loath to surrender the local authority base and was afraid of offending the local authorities by taking the service away from them. One of his favourite sayings at this time was: 'the fire services are the brightest jewel in the local authorities' crown.'[59] He at first considered a degree of lower-tier amalgamation well short of nationalization and was not finally convinced that there was no alternative to the extreme policy until April 1941. Late in that month London suffered its heaviest raids so far, with more than two thousand fires burning over a wide area. Most dramatic of all, Plymouth was destroyed and the morale of its citizens broken in five nights of massive attack which exposed the complete inadequacy of its fire and other civil defence services.[60] At midnight on 28–9 April 1941, coinciding with the culmination of Plymouth's destruction, Morrison summoned a conference of his officials. Their discussions were punctuated by the reverberation of exploding bombs. Whitehall was illuminated by the bluish-white light of incendiaries. Morrison decided to nationalize.[61] He secured Cabinet approval on 8 May[62] and rapidly began a round of conferences to explain his intentions to the regional commissioners and the local authorities – promising the latter to return the fire services to them after the war, which he did.* Some, such as Glasgow, objected bitterly, but he railroaded the plan through, informing the Commons of his proposals on Tuesday 14 May and a week later pushing through all its stages the Fire Services (Emergency Provisions) Act, which authorized him to bring in the nationalized service by ministerial regulations. There was little opposition from MPs who a week earlier had seen London again burning beyond the control of the battered and disorganized fire services. The *Luftwaffe* finally converted most people, like Morrison, away from 'the local principle'.

Morrison gave his department a time limit of three months to carry out the revolution in fire service organization. It involved not only transferring control from the local authorities to the Home Office, but also setting up in detail a completely new fire service hierarchy. At the pinnacle was the national headquarters established in an underground fortress in Westminster; it was self-contained, could continue for three weeks without outside supplies, and survived a flying-bomb explosion thirty yards from its entrance in July 1944. The eleven regions, themselves subdivided into 'fire forces', were the working units for control and administration. The pace of work and progress in Morrison's ministry during this reorganization was remarkable. Every item had to be decided, complex details of ranks, promotion procedures, uniforms, discipline, training and conditions of service, as well as arrangements for new communications systems, purchasing and accounting systems, and the actual buildings in which to house them. Selecting the right men to command the new fire forces was a major task in which Morrison took special interest.[63] By July most officers were appointed and ready to take over and, although some forces still lacked a proper headquarters, the Treasury was able formally to assume financial control.

Morrison's nationalization of the fire service was an unqualified success. It became possible to plan fire cover for the whole country and to ensure a co-ordinated command structure in any area of operations. It also brought into

---

* The Fire Service Act of 1947 passed the fire services back to 157 county and county borough authorities. This was a major reduction in fragmentation compared to pre-war. Many of the wartime improvements in standards and conditions of service were also retained. The resulting combination of the best features of Morrison's nationalization with a good deal of local responsibility was very much in the Morrisonian style of politics and administration.

existence a single promotion ladder and the standardization of training, qualifications and equipment, with a consequential improvement in technical competence which proved of permanent benefit. At the peak of its strength in 1943 the new National Fire Service employed 343,000 full- and part-time firemen and firewomen. The speed with which it was established and the smooth way in which the new organization functioned were a tribute to Morrison's ministerial skill and to the high calibre and dedication of his Home Office staff. The pace of change was actually too much for them in one area – the department simply forgot to lay many of the new fire service regulations before Parliament. This grave omission came to light in 1944 and Morrison, ever the constitutionalist, was deeply upset, going before the Commons 'in a white sheet' to confess his error, and quickly pushing through an indemnity bill to legalize retrospectively all action taken since 1941.[64]

By the summer of 1941 Morrison had completed his reorganization of Britain's home defence forces. He now had time to apply the finishing touches. He took a close interest in getting good uniforms for his troops, employing outside designers to produce smart styles, including optional trousers for the ladies, which he insisted were essential protection against the cold winter nights. He ordered an official fashion parade in June 1941 and took Miss Donald along to give an independent feminine opinion. He also pressed for the issue of gold and blue badges because they were bright and cheery.[65] This concern to cheer up the people recurred frequently, leading him to argue for shorter black-out hours in the summer and also to change the original name of ARP – which he felt was dull and pre-war – to the more positive title of Civil Defence. Morrison could watch with pride a great civil defence parade in Hyde Park that July. Grizzled veterans of the previous war, the breasts of their new dark blue uniforms bristling with medals and ribbons, marched alongside youths too young for military service, in step to the bands of the metropolitan police and the London fire brigades. Churchill's reference from the rostrum to 'the courageous and resourceful leadership of Mr Herbert Morrison' was received with loud cheers.[66]

Chapter 22

Civil Liberties: Newspapers, Aliens and Mosley

As Home Secretary Morrison was responsible for law and order and civil liberties. National security in war required serious limitations on normal individual freedoms, constraints imposed through the long list of emergency defence regulations. In consequence a number of very delicate issues arose which tested his political skills – and liberal principles – to the full. His involvement in the censorship of the press and with the internment of Britons and aliens suspected of disloyalty were issues of particular difficulty which provoked serious political storms.

It was only Morrison's third day at the Home Office when Churchill raised in the War Cabinet the need for stiffer press censorship. He referred to an alleged subversive propaganda campaign in the *Sunday Pictorial* and the *Daily Mirror* criticizing members of the government and questioning the competence of certain generals. Churchill claimed that there was 'more behind these articles than disgruntlement or frayed nerves. They stood for something more dangerous and sinister, namely an attempt to bring about a situation in which the country would be ready for surrender and peace.'[1] Morrison asked for more time to consider the matter, but warned his colleagues of the dangers of taking a course of rash suppression of opinion. His instinctive attitude to the press was permissive. In the Commons debate on the emergency regulations in 1939 he had warned that 'to seek powers whereby you can suppress truth . . . will be doing a harm and not good . . . after all the British people are not sheep . . . they are capable of forming their own judgment in the light of debate and discussion.'[2] This was still his view, in which he was fully supported by his Permanent Secretary, Sir Alexander Maxwell. Morrison submitted a memorandum to the Cabinet on 9 October pointing out the difference between criticism which was loyal, and constructive in intention, as in this case, and that which was fundamentally disloyal and designed to undermine morale. He supported a proposal first suggested by Beaverbrook that representations should be made to the Newspaper Proprietors' Association, but not in any sense as an ultimatum. Churchill reacted angrily to the moderate approach but

Morrison firmly defended it and in the end the Cabinet supported him, agreeing that Beaverbrook and Attlee should privately see the newspaper proprietors. Morrison was instructed to investigate the ownership of the two newspapers and to consider adapting the existing defence regulations* to apply to cases such as this.[3] He was able to report in due course that Churchill's naïve suspicions of sinister political interests controlling the *Mirror* and *Pictorial* were unfounded, and Attlee that the editors of the two newspapers had promised to behave.[4] The Cabinet agreed to let the matter rest for the time being, though Churchill continued to snipe privately at the two radical journals.[5] The government's hostility was by now focused on much easier prey.

The communist *Daily Worker* had already been warned in July 1940 that some of its writings were in contravention of defence regulation 2D. Since Russia became Nazi Germany's ally in August 1939 the Communist Party in Britain had waged a campaign of disruption in industry and propaganda through the *Daily Worker* to undermine the national war effort. Pursuing an official policy of 'revolutionary defeatism' the paper canvassed public support for a negotiated peace with Hitler and supported communist candidates contesting by-elections on this 'stop-the-war' ticket. In late 1940 the party sponsored and the *Worker* advertised a series of 'People's Conventions' to promote a negotiated peace. Any government concerned to maintain national morale and unity in the darkest days of the blitz was bound to be disturbed. Morrison brought the matter before Cabinet at the end of December[6] and in mid-January they approved his proposal to suppress the *Worker* under 2D. On Tuesday 21 January the police moved into the newspaper's offices in London and Glasgow. There were no incidents or resistance and the proceedings were conducted in an atmosphere of courtesy on both sides. Another offending journal, *The Week*, edited by Claud Cockburn, was taken over at the same time.

These were the most 'oppressive' censoring acts executed by Morrison at the Home Office, but he had no qualms. 'The suppression of the *Daily Worker*,' he wrote later, 'was not, of course, an attack on freedom . . . the slavish obedience to the Moscow line was a negation of freedom of the printed word. There was evidence that the paper was fomenting unofficial strikes and disputes. The articles in it were insidious enough to cause direct damage to the war effort . . . Not unexpectedly there was no protest from Russia about the closing down of the *Daily Worker*. The Soviet Union always admires bold and firm action.'[7] The parliamentary party voted overwhelmingly to endorse Morrison's decision, as did the NEC, though in the Commons, Aneurin Bevan moved a motion of qualified protest because the newspaper had not been allowed to state its case, and he received the support of half a dozen left-wing colleagues.[8] The ban on the *Worker* was not for any specific period of time.

---

* Defence Regulation 2D, which came closest to being appropriate, as it stood defined the offence of 'systematic publication of matter calculated to foment opposition to the prosecution of the war to a successful issue'.

After Hitler invaded Russia, however, British communists suddenly became enthusiastic supporters of the national war effort and agitation began to permit their newspaper to publish again.[9] Morrison at first resisted, but in August 1942, after pressure at party conference and the NEC, and with the prospect of censure at the coming TUC, he submitted and lifted the ban.[10]

While the *Worker* was silenced, the Prime Minister had returned to the attack against the *Mirror* and the *Sunday Pictorial*. In October 1941 the *Pictorial* published an editorial accusing Westminster politicians of 'letting the people down' and concluding that Churchill ought to pack off many of them, including half of his ministers, 'for a permanent rest-cure'.[11] Churchill immediately demanded that the Home Secretary should suppress the *Pictorial*. At Cabinet Morrison was instructed to report back on whether the offending editorial was in breach of existing defence regulations 2D or 2C, and if not, to devise a new regulation which would cover such writings. He was also asked to investigate whether the editor concerned, Mr Stuart Campbell, was guilty of breach of privilege.[12] Morrison rapidly secured answers to these questions – all negative and ungratifying to the Prime Minister's repressive instincts.[13] His memorandum to the War Cabinet concluded with the classic liberal position, which he and his departmental advisers firmly held, that 'the democratic principle of freedom for expression of opinion means taking the risk that harmful opinions may be propagated'. The Cabinet accepted Morrison's argument and decided to take no further action for the time being.[14]

Morrison had again, as in the autumn of 1940, in the secret confines of the Cabinet, defended the freedom of the press against Churchill. Early in 1942, however, the issue of press censorship arose more acutely and publicly. This coincided with the nadir of the nation's fortunes in the war. Defeats in the Middle and the Far East, culminating in the humiliating surrender of Singapore, provoked a growing chorus of criticism of Churchill's administration. The *Daily Mirror* went back onto the attack, criticizing the higher echelons of the armed services and calling for drastic changes in the government. On 6 March 1942 it published a cartoon by Zec portraying a merchant seaman floating in oily wreckage on the ocean with a caption beneath referring to the recent price rise for petrol of one penny a gallon – seeming to imply that the lives of seamen were being sacrificed simply to increase petrol profits.

Churchill leaped in again demanding a clamp-down on the press. Morrison this time shared a little more of his colleagues' irritation with the paper, but he still took a more tolerant line, arguing in a memorandum to the special committee on press censorship that suppression was neither desirable nor practicable. He was being strongly advised by the perceptive Leslie that the *Mirror* criticisms simply reflected real and widespread disenchantment with the government and that it would be very imprudent to hit out at the mouth-piece for genuine popular feeling.

By 18 March the Law Officers had advised that the offending articles and cartoon appearing in the *Daily Mirror* in March were infringements of regulation 2D and the government could suppress the paper if it so wished. The Cabinet, however, decided to give one more chance to the newspaper and to follow Morrison's more moderate approach of appealing to the good sense and voluntary co-operation of those running the *Mirror*.[15] Next morning Morrison summoned to his room at the Home Office the *Mirror*'s editor, C. E. Thomas, and its deputy chairman, Guy Bartholomew. He deplored the recent tone of their paper as certain to make readers feel that the war was not worth the fighting and the sacrifice. He went on to explain the force of regulation 2D, pointing out that it could be invoked now on the evidence existing against them. But he offered them one more chance of good behaviour. They could make public the substance of this discussion. He went across to the Commons to make an official statement on the issue in response to a private member's question (which had in fact been drafted and planted by the department).[16]

A week later there was a full debate on the freedom of the press. Bevan led the criticism with a stinging personal attack on Morrison,[17] referring embarrassingly to his articles in the *Mirror* in 1939–40 denouncing the Chamberlain administration. Others expressed genuine concern that even in war the basic principles of a free press should not be undermined. The majority of MPs were however firmly behind Morrison, and there was no division.[18] The press, understandably, was least happy with him. *The Times, Manchester Guardian, News Chronicle*, and even Labour's *Daily Herald* objected at his threat to use defence regulation 2D in future. The National Council for Civil Liberties also expressed grave concern and organized a mass protest meeting in London in April.[19] It was not a happy experience for Morrison, to be pilloried as an enemy of civil liberties when he had fought so long behind the scenes to protect the freedom of the press.

In the middle of the *Daily Mirror* episode, Morrison became embroiled in another public controversy, which concluded with his sacking from office the distinguished mandarin who had headed the British civil service throughout the inter-war period. This incident originated on Wednesday 11 March 1942 when fifteen firemen from the North West Region of Morrison's new National Fire Service went from Bolton to Dumfries to play against the Scottish Region in a fire service football competition.[20] The Lancashire men triumphed by fourteen goals to four, but regrettably had travelled the 278-mile round journey on regional fire engines using official petrol allocated for fire service operations. Still more unforgivably, the deputy regional commissioner, Colonel Blatherwick, who had a reputation for taking a cavalier attitude to the perquisites of office, had also travelled to the match, using his superior's official car and chauffeur while the regional commissioner was on duty in London.

Morrison learned within hours of this expedition[21] and was not amused. He sent for Blatherwick on the Friday and severely reprimanded him.[22] Blather-wick immediately resigned and demanded a board of inquiry into his case – which was refused. As far as Morrison was concerned, that was that; he quickly found an able Labour supporter, R. S. Chorley, to replace the aggressively right-wing Blatherwick. A week later, however, the matter was reopened in public when Sir Warren Fisher, who for twenty years until 1939 had been Permanent Secretary at the Treasury, wrote a letter to the *Manchester Guardian* denouncing Morrison savagely for his treatment of Blather-wick. Fisher concluded: 'if a single (and far from fatal) mistake of judgment is to be handled with such Prussianism by a Minister of the Crown (in England) what should be the fate of ministers for countless and most serious mistakes by them?'[23] What gave this attack its special flavour was that Fisher was a special commissioner in the London Region, initially appointed by and still effectively holding office under Morrison's own Ministry of Home Security. Morrison responded quickly but moderately, pointing out that Fisher had made 'a public attack upon the minister under whom you are serving. As you know, such action is not in accordance with the traditions and practice of a public servant . . .' He asked whether there existed 'the degree of confidence between us that is essential to proper working'. Fisher replied snootily: 'a man who has upheld standards and traditions during twenty years headship of the civil service does not require schooling on such a subject from anyone in public life.' The arrogant implication that a Whitehall mandarin was not accountable to a mere Labour minister probably sealed Fisher's fate. Morrison wrote back asking for his resignation. But Fisher refused to accede to what he called 'this extraordinary behaviour' and Morrison was forced to write again terminating Fisher's employment as from that day. This vitriolic exchange of letters was then published in full in the press, certainly to Morrison's benefit.[24]

The firemen's expedition was a molehill of error which became mountain-ously inflated by the main protagonists. Fisher, by his arrogance, left the minister little choice between sacking him and swallowing humiliation.[25] Morrison was particularly touchy about the misuse of public petrol in the weeks after the Zec cartoon. He was at this time under great political pressure and, like the government as a whole, was likely to get jumpy and to over-react to further stresses. Dalton saw Morrison at a meeting of the Lord President's Committee on 3 April and reported him 'quite silent and seemed rather under the weather, perhaps as a result of his rows first with the *Daily Mirror* and then with Warren Fisher'.[26]

Morrison's duties most directly relating to individual liberties concerned conscientious objectors and people detained for security reasons under the Defence Regulations. The issue of conscientious objectors arose in respect of both military service and (after the 1941 National Service Act) of civil defence duties, since each was compulsory by law.[27] The primary responsibility lay with Bevin at the Ministry of Labour, but Morrison was closely involved through his civil defence ministry and because as Home Secretary he was responsible for the courts and prisons where many conscientious objectors ended up. It became a standard practice for people to prove the sincerity of their claim to be conscientious objectors by their willingness to serve imprisonment rather than accede to a call-up medical. Morrison's intervention was required when questions arose about the treatment of conscientious objectors in prison, or of disparity between sentences, or when a pardon was requested for somebody who had already served sentences for refusing a medical but had still not been accepted as 'sincere' by the relevant tribunal. Such petitioners often made reference to Morrison's own objection to the previous war and he was clearly placed in an embarrassing position. Morrison argued in Whitehall in favour of more lenient treatment of conscientious objectors, often conflicting with Bevin, who wanted savage prison sentences. The bill as drafted, setting a maximum penalty of twelve months in most cases, with no minimum, and defining the situation and rights of conscientious objectors more fully than ever before, reflected some at least of the efforts of Morrison and his advisers.[28]

Under the Defence Regulations the Home Secretary was empowered to restrict the activities of, or detain, any person who he had cause to believe threatened to act in a manner prejudicial to the public safety or defence of the realm. It was not the original intention that the key regulation affecting British citizens, 18B, which was added shortly after the war started, should be used to detain more than a few persons, though the related aliens order was bound to be more widely applied. The collapse of the western front in the spring of 1940 and the near-hysteria in Britain about the role of the 'fifth column' of indigenous traitors led, however, to radical extensions in the scope of the 18B regulations. These revisions in May 1940 authorized the detention of members of organizations which were subject to foreign influence or whose leaders had associations or sympathies with governments at war with Britain. The largest and most overt body of native candidates for 'fifth column' activities in Britain was the British Union of Fascists, which continued to publish propaganda sympathetic to Hitler and deriding our national war effort. In late May 1940 the BUF leader, Sir Oswald Mosley, and 379 of his followers were arrested and detained under the emergency regulations.

By the time Morrison took over as Home Secretary in October, the detentions, both of aliens from countries at war with Britain and of British subjects attached to disloyal political groups, had reached their peak. Morrison's job was to decide not who to detain but who to retain and who to release. It was the kind of quasi-judicial function at which he was particularly adept and from the beginning he pursued a policy of greater liberality, arguing to the Cabinet in November that 'we could now afford to take a rather less stringent line'.[29] At first he was mainly concerned with alien detainees, a large number of whom were not only innocent of fascist attachments but were themselves tragic victims of Nazi tyranny in Europe. To alleviate their situation Morrison immediately decided to free those eminent in the arts and sciences, college students and others who had been resident in Britain for at least twenty years. Any willing to join the Auxiliary Pioneer Corps were already being released, and by December Morrison had freed some eight thousand aliens, nearly a third of those in detention, and in the years ahead there was a steady stream of further releases. He also arranged for most of those still detained to be transferred from prisons to more suitable internment camps, mainly in the Isle of Man, and in due course to segregate the hard core of fascist bullies who for a time terrorized the other inmates. His most important reform was to allow detainees to appeal to special tribunals to prove their sympathy for the allied cause. Virtually all the detainees appealed and Morrison spent an enormous amount of time reading the tribunal reports, or listening to them read by his secretary as he travelled around the country with the curtains drawn in his official car.[30] Friends of the detained refugees who raised their cases with Morrison found him sympathetic and quick to act in restoring their freedom.[31]

From the end of 1940 Morrison's attention moved increasingly to the British citizens in detention under regulation 18B.[32] The House of Commons was naturally sensitive on this issue, not only in its traditional role as protector of constitutional rights and civil liberties, but also because one of its members, Captain Ramsay, had been detained under 18B. Morrison's critics were in no sense fascist sympathizers but they were concerned that people had been imprisoned by ministerial edict without trial. Morrison was always worried by any accusations of illiberalism and in his first year he reduced the number of detained British fascists by over half.[33] Even so, an amendment was put down criticizing him in November 1941, and in July 1942 his critics carried their protest to a lobby vote.[34] He continued to release the British fascists and by the end of 1943 the number detained was down to 266. Then Morrison suffered a major political storm about 18B – though not, ironically, about his alleged illiberalism, but because of his decision to release the most notorious detainee under that regulation, Sir Oswald Mosley.

Mosley had been in Holloway Prison with his wife since their arrest in 1940.[35] Pressures began to build up for his release in 1943, originating according to Morrison from 'Mosley's class friends and political sympathisers'.[36] Concern was expressed about Mosley's health, since he suffered from recurrent phlebitis and had also lost a good deal of weight. His friends asserted that he would not survive another winter in prison, but the prison doctors at first could see no evidence for this alarmist view. The matter came to a head in October 1943 when Churchill himself raised Mosley's case. Morrison found no basis for action on the existing evidence, but called in outside medical advice from Lord Dawson of Penn. Following further examinations, which showed worsening of the phlebitis, the prison doctors suddenly agreed that there was a risk of complications developing; they changed their previous advice and now recommended release.

Morrison faced a serious dilemma. To free Britain's leading fascist and sympathizer with Hitler would certainly incur odium, especially among Labour supporters. Yet not to release him was now apparently to risk Mosley dying in prison, without trial, and so becoming a martyr for his squalid gang.[37] After the latest medical reports, Mosley's death in prison would seem to be Morrison's direct responsibility; he would find great difficulty in explaining this away, especially after Churchill's recent initiative to protect Mosley. Morrison decided provisionally to recommend a temporary release and then secured Cabinet approval (despite Bevin's strong and widely publicized opposition) for permanent release on very stringent conditions,[38] which amounted virtually to house arrest.*

The announcement of Mosley's release on 17 November 1943 heralded the biggest storm of Morrison's wartime career. Sackloads of letters of protest arrived at the Home Office.[39] Reports flooded in of hostile public reaction throughout the country. Mass meetings of protest took place, especially in factories on war production, and deputations of workers marched into Whitehall. The Communist Party was predictably extremely active in organizing these protests, but indignation was felt throughout the Labour movement. The executive committee of the Transport and General Workers' Union passed a resolution that they heard the news 'with alarm and dismay ... regarding this as a grave reflection and an insult to the people in the fighting services ... there is no justification whatever for the release'.[40] Other trade unions† publicly joined the transport workers in their protest. On 23 November Durham miners resolved to call on their national federation to strike if Mosley was not put promptly back in jail.[41]

Morrison made his official statement of explanation to the Commons on the twenty-third. Outside a crowd of some two thousand demonstrators clashed with the police and later moved to Caxton Hall to hold a protest meeting. The House was packed and listened to Morrison in virtual silence, then giving him a big ovation at the end. Press observers saw it as 'a great personal triumph' and described it as 'Mr Morrison's day'.[42] It was generally felt that the electricity had been taken out of the issue.[43]

Greater trouble in fact lay ahead, for Morrison was faced by the mass disapproval of the organized Labour movement, which was more serious than a few thousand militants in Parliament Square. Shortly after his Commons statement the National Council of Labour issued a statement that it 'dissociates itself from the action of the Government' and would remit the matter for further action to its constituent bodies – the TUC, the NEC and the Administrative Committee of the parliamentary party.[44] Next day the General

---

* The Mosleys, after brief residence with a friend and then at a Cotswold inn, spent the rest of the war quietly and under close police surveillance in a house they bought at Crux Easton near Newbury. (Sir Oswald Mosley, *My Life* (1968), pp. 412–13, 416.)

† Including the railwaymen, the engineers, the mineworkers, the firemen, the General and Municipal workers, the distributive workers and the Civil Service Clerical workers.

Council of the TUC wholeheartedly endorsed the NCL decision and virtually every speaker was extremely blunt in his criticisms of Morrison's decision which was repeatedly described as a major blunder.[45] The NEC, meeting on the twenty-fourth, passed a resolution regretting Morrison's decision.[46] Morrison had now been censured by two of the three most important bodies in the Labour movement. Next day he faced the third, the parliamentary party. Opinion was reported to be moving against him, especially among trade union MPs.[47] Morrison vigorously defended his action to the party meeting, pointing out that the Defence Regulations must be administered on a judicial basis and it would be quite wrong to allow political considerations to enter, as his critics were suggesting. An official resolution along these lines, broadly supporting Morrison, was passed, but only after a critical amendment had been narrowly defeated by fifty-one to forty-three.[48]

A full day was set aside to debate the Mosley issue in Parliament on 1 December. Press comment in the days before the debate reflected the extent to which Morrison was seen to be in the middle of a political crisis. The *Daily Herald* said it 'would be sorry to see him discredited in his own party for a lapse of judgment which in his heart of hearts he probably regrets. The Labour Party cannot in fact do without him. He stands head and shoulders above all other Labour leaders; and when in due course the Party secedes from the Coalition to fight its own political battles, it will need his leadership and personality if it is to make any real impression on the mind of the electorate ... if the Labour Party were to demote him and put him on the shelf or in any way to deny his future place, it would be making a disastrous mistake.'[49] Hannen Swaffer wrote along similar lines that 'it would be almost a disaster to the working class cause if his decision over Mosley ended the career of Morrison, the ablest and most outspoken of all the Socialist leaders.'[50]

In the debate Morrison faced a critical amendment regretting 'the decision of Your Majesty's advisers to release Sir Oswald Mosley, which is calculated to retard the war effort and lead to misunderstandings at home and abroad.' Among its signatories, although the Labour Party was officially supporting him, were three of Morrison's fellow members on the party's Administrative Committee.[51] Morrison treated the crowded chamber to more emotion than was usual in his style, together with some typical humour and sharp debating thrusts. He was momentarily in trouble when Sydney Silverman intervened to claim he had seen all the medical reports and that none of them contained anything serious until 9 November when, he alleged, high level intervention persuaded the doctors to change their opinions. Silverman then called upon him to publish the evidence. Morrison angrily refused and quickly moved on without attempting to disprove Silverman's allegations.[52] Observers agreed that Morrison had put up a fine parliamentary performance,[53] and the amendment was defeated by 327 to 62. The *Evening Standard* asserted that 'Mr Morrison's authority over Parliament is second only to that wielded by the Prime Minister'.[54] But he cannot have been completely happy. Barely half of

L

the parliamentary party supported him. Among the fifty-one Labour dissidents were six of his thirteen colleagues on the Administrative Committee.[55] The storm took a little longer to blow out. When he spoke at Wembley Town Hall shortly afterwards, he was constantly heckled and had to threaten 'either you listen or I will wind up'.[56] Just before Christmas, however, the TUC, the NCL and the NEC decided to drop their campaigns to have Mosley re-interned.[57] Organized opposition from the main wings of the Labour movement now ceased.

Whatever doubts may persist about the medical advice on Mosley – and that gentleman's survival into a healthy old age can hardly diminish them – Morrison's conduct of the case can only be held to his credit. He followed the experts' advice and stood by his decision undeterred by the inevitable storm of criticism, mainly from his own natural supporters. It was characteristic of his political life that he was left carrying the can of unpopularity. In an odd masochistic way Morrison rather enjoyed this role of not bending to popular clamour, especially if he could dress it up with a little self-righteousness.

On the Mosley issue – as on press censorship, on the release of alien internees and on conscientious objection – the Home Office under Morrison was a liberal influence in government. Basic liberties were not lost sight of under the exigencies of mobilization for total war. Morrison deserves great credit for this. He was often schoolmasterish in style but he was not politically an authoritarian. When asked about his achievements at the Home Office he proudly claimed: 'We have maintained in this country a high degree of civil liberty. There have been no state actions which could be described as persecutions of people or bodies because they held certain opinions. We have kept for ourselves a high standard of free speech. No country in the world has a higher standard of civil liberty.'[58] He resisted the constant public pressure to suppress eccentric bodies, such as the Jehovah's Witnesses, and told other departments to reduce their requests for more defence regulations since 'there is a limit to how far you can push people around'.[59] He owed much to the humane influence of his capable Permanent Secretary, Sir Alexander Maxwell, who gently but firmly kept Morrison and the department committed to the liberal principles in which he so passionately believed.[60]

Chapter 23

Into the War Cabinet

Morrison by 1942 had his Whitehall responsibilities comfortably under control. German air attacks continued, but only spasmodically. There was a rash of heavy bombing of cathedral towns in the spring of 1942, but then for the next two years little more than tip-and-run raids, mainly on coastal towns. Morrison's huge civil defence army coped easily with the relatively light demands placed upon it. Such underemployment of national resources could not be tolerated for long, however, especially as shortage of manpower increasingly became the main problem confronting the government's war effort. Drastic switches of full-time civil defence personnel into war production were proposed from 1941 onwards. Morrison bargained hard in Cabinet and in committee to maintain the strength of his forces against any future blitz emergency, but he had to accept that the immediate demands of the war offensive deserved greater priority than those of civil defence.[1] He replaced some of them with men and women compulsorily directed into part-time civil defence – provoking considerable public concern about the moral welfare of the ladies on night duty.[2] Despite this supplementation of part-timers, the decline in his civil defence establishment accelerated from 1942 until the end of the war; the fire-watching regulations themselves, though mounting in volume, were actually operated with decreasing stringency.

Even when the air attacks were light in the middle of the war Morrison continued his regular visits to the regional defence forces. He made major tours to the Midlands in 1941, 1942 and 1944, to the North West in 1941 and 1943, to Yorkshire in 1942 and 1944, to the North East in 1941, 1942 and 1944, to Wales in 1941 and 1942, and to Scotland in 1941 and 1943. Looking at his peregrinations throughout the kingdom, it is difficult to understand the persistence of his reputation as a person who rarely set foot north of Watford.

One delicate responsibility which Morrison took most seriously was Northern Ireland, involving him both from the point of civil defence and because it came under the constitutional supervision of the Home Office. He visited it each year. He started with instinctive prejudices against the Unionists, but changed his opinions after direct contact with the situation.[3] He was impressed by the passionate loyalty of the Ulster Protestants and deeply angered by the neutralism of some of the northern Catholic Irish, who were even rumoured to leak military information to the German embassy in Dublin. Shortly after returning from Belfast in July 1943 he addressed the Thirty Club in London, with the Stormont Prime Minister, Sir Basil Brooke, as guest of honour.[4] Morrison praised the loyalty of Ulster as 'almost aggressive in its nature' and went on to suggest that the differing relationship between Britain and the two parts of Ireland during the war was 'bound to have a permanently modifying effect on many people's opinions in this country'. He went on to regret that southern Ireland 'should have stood aside neutral and indifferent to this . . . fateful struggle in the history of all mankind'. This speech created considerable furore, provoking a sharp riposte from De Valera, the Irish Prime Minister, in which (not for the first time) he blamed England for partition. Morrison's Irish preferences were now firmly changed. He no longer seemed concerned with the lack of social justice or political democracy in the six counties. After the war, he continued to keep a protective eye on Ulster's interests in the Labour Cabinet.[5]

The Home Office brought Morrison a host of routine problems and miscellaneous policy decisions, ranging from horse-racing to prostitution, from regulating cinemas to capital punishment and the ban on ringing church bells. He was also concerned in a wide range of public appointments – in the Church, and especially recorders, stipendiary and metropolitan magistrates. With some of these peripheral issues, and especially those in the areas of social morality and personal behaviour, he was temperamentally far from at home. Morrison was always happier dealing with institutions or broad policies in a political context than with individual behaviour in a social or moral context. He was not at ease with something like the scandal in 1944 over conditions at LCC remand homes for delinquent children. It took a lot of pressure to make him believe that 'do-gooders', such as Basil Henriques, J. A. Watson and Lady Allen of Hurtwood, had a case against the LCC and his Home Office. His instinct was to trust his bureaucratic machine. Even when he conceded a judicial inquiry, he insisted that it be in private and never allowed the evidence to be published.[6]

He was even less happy with some of the social problems which arose from the wartime disruption of the family structure and the disintegration of established patterns of morality and behaviour. The large concentrations of troops with time on their hands and, in the case of American forces, with money to spend, led to a good deal of loose living. Bands of female camp-followers grew, and the widespread prostitution, illegitimacy and venereal disease increasingly concerned the Home Office from 1942 onwards. There was little a Whitehall department could do but it was certainly an area in which someone as prudish and puritanical as Morrison did not want to get too involved.[7]

The regulation of cinemas and theatres raised questions of morality which he did not relish. Shortly after he took over as Home Secretary the cinema industry had asked for amendments to the 1932 Sunday Entertainment Act which would give them freedom to open on Sundays without local authority approval. (At this time only about half of Britain's population had access to cinemas on Sundays.) The theatrical organizations also asked for permission to open on Sundays. Morrison decided to test the opposition, inviting the Lord's Day Observance Society and the Imperial Alliance for the Defence of Sunday to the Home Office, where they pointed out the extreme risk of alienating the Almighty at this crucial point in the war. Against this threat of divine wrath Morrison had to set the immediate risk of upsetting Ernest Bevin, who sought greater leisure facilities for workers on Sundays and insisted on the abolition of all sabbath restrictions on cinemas and theatres. Morrison was reluctant to offend the local authorities as well as the guardians of morality and he urged a compromise: war workers would have special rights of admission for Sunday cinemas, and theatres would open as well providing the local authorities approved. Bevin refused to give way and the dispute was taken to full Cabinet, which supported Morrison.[8]

The revised regulations were laid before Parliament in April, strongly supported by Morrison who concluded that they would 'help to keep people cheerful and happy'.[9] The whips were not put on, since the issue seemed more appropriate for a free vote,[10] and Morrison was beaten by 144 to 136. It was a painful political failure. He had failed to deliver the reforms the entertainment industry wanted, he had upset the religious fanatics, and he had clashed with the unforgiving Bevin, to no ultimate purpose. He genuinely wanted a more cheerful life for people, but not at this political price.

Capital punishment interested him much more. As Home Secretary it was his duty to decide whether to recommend royal pardons for murderers sentenced to death. His personal instincts were tough and punitive; at this time he definitely believed in 'an eye for an eye'.[11] He did not appear disturbed by the obscene brutality of the execution process itself – indeed he once even expressed a desire to see a woman hanged.[12] He suffered few worries about the possibility of irrevocable judicial errors, inclining as always to trust the competence of the administrative machine. He showed little interest in more modern psychological approaches to criminal behaviour. Motivation for murder did not seem to concern him – though he did confess that he would be tempted to pardon any man who chopped off the head of a nagging wife.[13] Despite these primitive instincts, Morrison viewed each capital punishment case that came before him dispassionately and with great care. One of his great ministerial qualities was his detachment where quasi-judicial decisions were concerned. He looked closely at extenuating circumstances which might justify a pardon. He was encouraged in this by his humanitarian Permanent

Secretary, Maxwell, who was a strong believer in the abolition of capital punishment and influenced the department towards greater liberalism on this as on other issues. One important reform they introduced was to establish a general, though not rigid, rule to recommend reprieve if the murderer was under nineteen years of age. It was applied controversially in 1945 in the notorious case of the murder of a London taxi-driver by an American soldier and his Welsh girl friend. Morrison firmly pressed the case for pardoning the girl, who had been only eighteen at the time of the crime. The reprieve outraged the Americans, who saw discrimination in the decision to hang only the American soldier. The American ambassador, Winant, visited the Home Office to protest, but Morrison insisted that the rule on reprieving youths be applied.[14]

Morrison was immensely successful and personally very happy as Home Secretary. The job suited him: the judicial approach, the need to take decisions on broad principles of equity in a political context, the close liaison with local authorities and the similarity of some of the departmental tasks with those involved in running a municipality. He inspired great admiration and loyalty from his civil servants. He listened well, mastered his briefs, argued, and then took his own clear decisions. 'He is one of my heroes,' observed a later head of the Home Office who had worked in Morrison's private office as a young man. 'He was such a lively and interesting person and had a most original mind. He came in and stirred up the place in a most agreeable way. I've never seen anyone so impose their stamp on a department. After Anderson, who for all his outstanding qualities was so unapproachable, this lively cockney who would talk to you about all his problems was very refreshing.'[15] Morrison's friendliness, his directness and lack of side, the common touch, appealed to most people working with him and was absolutely appropriate for the essentially democratic conditions of war. Only Morrison could interview the Metropolitan Police Commissioner, Sir Philip Game, with his shoes off and large holes gaping in the toes and heels of his socks.[16] Yet such earthiness and the general bantering *bonhomie* he maintained with his officials never became over-familiarity. He remained 'always the Minister'.[17] The civil servants respected him because he was superbly successful at delivering the political goods for them and because he also understood the problems and needs of the administrative machine. He used his advisers constructively, throwing provocative ideas and questions at them, encouraging them to put opposing views to his own for the sake of the argument, and then finally making up his own mind – and he always took responsibility for the decision himself. 'Morrison always carried the can,' said his wartime private secretary, 'that's why he always had loyal civil servants. Once you had his trust, he stood by you totally.'[18]

His working week was heavy and diverse. He started in the office at about 10.00 a.m., looking first at the press and then dealing with urgent departmental business. Most of the rest of the morning was occupied with meetings: the Cabinet, Cabinet committees, the PLP and its Administrative Committee, the NEC and numerous departmental conferences.* He often took along correspondence and papers to read or sign unobtrusively in these meetings. Parliament fortunately met only three days a week in the war, and where possible Morrison delegated parliamentary business to his junior ministers, but he had to be in the Commons for Questions on Thursdays and for all important legislation emanating from the department. Because his days were so full of meetings – and the Cabinet frequently met until late in the evening – he was forced to do the bulk of his paper-work at night. He often read in bed until three and even four in the morning. As a good professional, he insisted on being properly prepared for the next day's business, though it meant going for months on end with very little sleep.

One aspect of his approach which was a revelation to his officials was his concern and skill at press relations, which he handled in close consultation with Leslie.[19] He called frequent press conferences and made a point of providing the maximum information compatible with national security, knowing that if he was generally honest with journalists they would be less likely to believe or print rumours to his discredit.[20] He took care to give the press advance copies of major speeches or at least of those passages which he thought of most significance. He was also careful to time his speeches and announcements according to the deadlines of the newspaper and radio reporters. He understood news and used it to his advantage. He always had a summary of the morning's press on his desk when he came into the office after breakfast. 'The corridors of the Home Office are paved with dynamite,' he used to say, and he expected the press to alert him when something might be about to explode in his face.[21]

Morrison enjoyed virtually no family life during the war. Margaret went to the west country, to Dawlish, to escape the blitz, and he rarely had time to visit her there.[22] She occasionally travelled to London to see him, to celebrate her birthday over a meal together or, in 1941, for the marriage of their daughter, Mary. They went on holiday together to the Lake District in 1943, but Morrison never really relaxed and enjoyed himself with her. One glorious day they went for a walk by Windermere and before long Morrison sat down on a tree trunk and started to read a sheaf of papers on workmen's compensation, telling Margaret to walk on with their companion, Chorley.[23] He took her with him on a few of his regional tours, staying with Lord Dudley in the Midlands and with Lord Rosebery in Scotland; but she was never at ease on official occasions or in high society. For most of the war they were apart and even when together the relations between them seemed to the outsider to be curiously remote.

---

* As an example of this burden of committee meetings, in 1944 alone he had 176 meetings of the Cabinet, 80 of the reconstruction committee, 59 of the Lord President's committee, 40 of the legislation committee, 28 of the civil defence committee and 22 of the machinery of government committee. There were also other special ministerial committees and all his party committees. (Pimlott memorandum, 26 July 1945, copy in Morrison papers.)

Effectively without a home of his own in London, Morrison led a strange nomadic life from 1940 to 1945. In the week he slept either in the basement of the Home Office, where he had his own bedroom and bathroom, or at the Howard Hotel in Norfolk Street. Sometimes he went to Miss Donald's flat at 55 Park Lane for a meal or a party. At weekends he usually went to the country, ringing the changes on a wide circle of friends: Ellen Wilkinson in Buckinghamshire, the Frasers in Bedfordshire, Lady Rhondda in Surrey, Lady Allen at nearby Hurtwood, or the Wilmots in Norfolk. It was in most cases the lady of the country house who was his close friend. He often arrived with little prior warning, his official police car and cavalcade of escorts sweeping in to impress the local villagers. He would take work with him, and a flow of fresh boxes arrived over the weekend. He spent most Sunday mornings in bed reading his papers. But when not working he was able to relax and obviously enjoyed his country visits enormously. His hostesses found him no trouble at all, easy to look after, willing to mix in with the family, and especially happy with any small children. 'He was the easiest and most pleasant of guests', recalled one of them, 'always merry, we never saw him melancholy or bitter. It is a mystery to reconcile the kind, simple Morrison who stayed with us in the war with the picture of the man ten years later.'[24] He was just a friend, happy to join in any party or sing-song, and he never discussed his work. He was considerate about the difficulties of feeding guests in the war, and generally took along either gifts of food and drink or his food coupons carefully cut out to cover the meals he would consume. He liked the warmth of friendly families and the company of cosy women. He became human on these visits. Certainly he was not a countryman who needed to commune with nature after a week in the city. It is doubtful if he actually noticed the countryside. On one visit to Lady Allen he asked to go horse-riding. He mounted and remained precariously balanced on the moving animal, with his arms stretched out straight sideways and his legs stretched rigidly down. For his hostess, as no doubt for the Home Secretary, 'it was a frightening experience' and there is no evidence that he repeated it or sampled many other country activities.[25]

In November 1942 Morrison was rewarded for his ministerial success by promotion to the War Cabinet. Cripps had proved a sad failure as Leader of the Commons and left the Cabinet after repeatedly clashing with Churchill over the management of the war.[26] Churchill needed to replace him with another Labour minister in order to maintain the party balance in the coalition. Morrison's national prestige guaranteed him the place. He was also helped in Churchill's eyes by a series of stirring speeches he had made during the previous weeks. All were on a similar theme of defending Britain's war effort and chiding her critics abroad – especially in the United States where there had been vociferous complaints about Britain's military contribution and about her imperial role in India, which had annoyed the Prime Minister. On 29 October, in a speech in Hackney glowing with patriotic fervour, Morrison reminded our American allies that Britain entered the war on 'a question of principle and of our pledged word. We were not pushed into it either by words or by the bayonet of an enemy in our back.' Clem Leslie had written most of the speech but the telling phrase about the bayonet in America's rear, which so pleased Churchill, was put in by Morrison himself.[27] Two days later he made a similar speech in Cardiff and again returned to the theme in a direct broadcast to the United States on 18 November, four days before his promotion.[28] He said that 'for the British this has always been a people's war. . . . They intend that the world after the war shall be as free as goodwill and good intelligence can make it from the threat of poverty, insecurity, aggression and more war. They are tough and they are not fools. If those things are what you want, then you and we are the right sort of allies.'[29]

This was exactly the kind of punchy, patriotic stuff Churchill liked to hear. The following weekend he summoned Morrison to Chequers. Morrison arrived about noon on the Sunday and found the Prime Minister in bed, surrounded by a litter of official papers. Churchill switched on the radio at news time for the announcement of Cripps's resignation. He then invited Morrison to step into the vacancy in the War Cabinet.[30]

Morrison's promotion was received with widespread public and press acclaim. From the right, the *Daily Express* said that 'by firmness in the right place, by energy and honesty of purpose he has won immense approval. His active brain will be a source of strength in the direction of the war.'[31] From the left, *Reynolds News*, which had often criticized him on particular policies in the past, still praised him for never having lost sight of 'the relationship of socialism to the war . . . Mr Morrison is about the best administrator we have discovered in this country since Lord Haldane's time.'[32] Beaverbrook wrote privately: 'Churchill apart, you are today by far the biggest figure in the country.'[33]

Morrison's star was shining. Elevation to the War Cabinet did not really make all that difference to his working life – he had previously attended many War Cabinet and committee meetings, since Home Office and Home Security business was often on the agenda. This promotion was a reflection of his prestige, public recognition by the Prime Minister of his great success as a minister. Despite the patriotism and combativeness they had in common, Morrison was not in fact Churchill's kind of man, but the Prime Minister had progressively come round to acknowledge his ability. Churchill told one trade union leader that he considered Morrison's mind the best of all the Labour ministers in the government.[34] He wrote warm personal letters to Morrison in 1940 and in 1942 congratulating him on speeches he had made.[35] In late 1941 Beaverbrook wrote to praise Morrison for the excellent way he had presented his case to Cabinet: 'the best argument I have heard in my eighteen months of ministerial service ... you grow in power every day.'

Beaverbrook added: 'I spoke with the Prime Minister after the Cabinet. I understood him to take the same view as I hold.'[36] Morrison's relationship with Churchill later went through rougher passages. They clashed particularly sharply over how to prepare for and deal with the flying bomb threat.[37] Somehow Morrison's style grated on the Prime Minister.[38] He was never made one of the favoured inner circle who drank at 10 Downing Street after midnight.

With his party colleague, Bevin, there was no *modus vivendi*. Bevin's dislike for Morrison had by the war 'hardened into an immovable prejudice . . . Morrison was the politician personified and in Bevin's vocabulary this was sufficient condemnation by itself.'[39] Around the oval War Cabinet table Morrison usually sat on Eden's right, opposite Churchill and Attlee. Bevin sat on Eden's left and embarrassed him and other colleagues by the stream of sneers and jibes he muttered when Morrison spoke. These offensive taunts must have been deeply hurtful to Morrison, but he ignored them and never stooped to retaliation.[40]

When Morrison joined the War Cabinet the Beveridge report on social security was the main domestic item on its agenda.[41] The public reacted with great enthusiasm to this blueprint for a better Britain. The government, however, was cooler. The Treasury under Kingsley Wood argued strongly that the nation could not afford Beveridge and that the coalition must not commit any post-war government to such massive public expenditure. Conservative politicians protested against conceding radical and permanent social changes under the temporary pressures of war. Churchill himself seemed quite negative on the proposals. Morrison took a much more sympathetic approach and was, as Dalton noted at the time, 'the best friend of his [Beveridge] old plan in the Cabinet'.[42] Closely advised by Leslie, he drew up a paper setting out a series of statistical counter-assumptions to the Treasury's case that Britain could not afford Beveridge.[43]

To accept the Treasury's pessimism, he argued, 'would be a surrender to idiocy in advance. I need not point out to my colleagues that the great majority of the public is looking forward expectantly to the adoption of something substantially like the Beveridge Plan. . . . The social benefits of the Beveridge Plan are very great. And to remove the plague spots of extreme poverty . . . will react most favourably upon the economic health and soundness of our society. Indeed, it is arguable that the adoption of a social minimum as a first charge upon the national income is a measure that would be justified on practical as well as humanitarian grounds, whether the trend of income was up or down, and whatever the post-war future might hold for us . . . this boon of social security which has good claims to an absolute priority among all the aims of home policy, represents a financial burden which we should be able to bear, except on a number of very gloomy assumptions. I can see no need to make or act upon such assumptions. I should certainly not like to have to expound and defend them to a nation bearing the full burden

Herbert Morrison, aged 5, in 1893.

Herbert Morrison, aged 12, in 1900.

Herbert Morrison, aged 22, in 1910.

Campaigning in the early 1920s.

HERBERT·MORRISON
"Carried?"

"Myself when young...."

Morrison in his twenties,
his dead eye exposed.

Above right Morrison as
Chairman of the Brixton
ILP in 1911 as drawn by the
artist Willy Pogany.

Right Morrison in the late
1920s.

Performing as Mayor of
Hackney, 1921, aged 33.
Left Minister of Transport,
1930.

At the Labour Party
Conference in Brighton
in 1929, when Morrison
was Chairman. His wife
and Arthur Henderson
are on the bench to his
right.
Left Morrison at his desk
at County Hall in the
1930s.

At the May Day Parade
in Hyde Park, 1939.

Below With Aneurin
Bevan at the Labour
Party Conference at
Norwich, 1937.

Bottom right Dancing
with his wife on holiday
in the Isle of Wight, the
first Christmas of the
War, 1939.

Inspecting blitz
damage as Minister of
Home Security, 1944.
Right Morrison joins
an exercise of his new
National Fire
Service, 1942.

Dancing with Barbara Castle at the 1945 Party Conference at Blackpool.

Below The 1945 election campaign: Morrison speaking for Dr S. Jeger, candidate for St Pancras S.E.

With the Prime Minister, Clement Attlee, and Foreign Secretary, Ernest Bevin, in the garden of 10 Downing Street, August 1945.

Below The burdens mount up, 1947.
Below right Leaving Hammersmith Hospital after his thrombosis, 1947.

Outside 11 Downing Street, going to the
first Cabinet after devaluation of the pound,
September 1949.
Below Talking to Bevin and Hugh Dalton at
the Labour Party Conference at Margate,
1950.

Carried away by Attlee's oratory at the
Labour Party Conference at
Scarborough, 1951

Left As Foreign Secretary Morrison
leaves a commemorative service at
St Paul's with Winston Churchill and
Anthony Eden, 1951.

Helping in the 1959
election.
Below Still interested
in the future.

The new life peer at home with his second wife, 1959.
Below On the job as Film Censor in the early 1960s.

of total war.[44] Morrison wanted the government to commit itself immediately to the broad principles of the plan. He argued this again in Cabinet in February 1943[45] and in a private meeting with the Prime Minister at Downing Street, but Churchill dug in his heels, arguing that no commitment even in principle could be made until after a post-war election. Morrison's comment was that in this case Labour had better begin to prepare for the election now.[46]

In the Commons debate on Beveridge, starting on 16 February, Anderson opened for the government and his negative approach created a disastrous impression on Labour and progressive opinion.[47] Fears that the government did not really intend to do anything about post-war reform deepened, and support mounted for a Labour amendment critical of the government's motion. At stormy meetings of the parliamentary party on 17 and 18 February, Morrison and Attlee tried to cool the atmosphere and Bevin, who anyway disagreed with some of the Beveridge proposals,[48] tried 'bullying and threatening' the back-benchers not to vote against the government.[49] Morrison was placed in a terrible dilemma when pushed into the firing line to wind up for the government on 18 February. He had to defend a negative policy which he had fought in vain in Cabinet to make more positive. He was not happy with the responsibility[50] but he set about making a professional job of it, by stressing those parts of Beveridge – sixteen of the twenty-three recommendations – which the government did accept.[51] Morrison spoke for an hour, his hair disordered, the dispatch box covered in papers.[52] His spirited performance was received with almost universal praise.[53] Some disgruntled Labour and Tory members were swung by him away from supporting the critical amendment.[54] Even so there were 119 in the minority, the biggest rebellion against the Churchill government in the war. It could easily have been worse without Morrison's contribution. He relaxed the atmosphere and defused what threatened to be a major political crisis. According to James Griffiths it was 'the best debating speech Morrison ever made'.[55] Dalton described it at the time as 'a grand speech. I am quite sure that if this had been made on the first day there would have been no crisis at all.'[56]

Morrison had to pay a political price for his parliamentary triumph. His skill in defending the government looked to the left wing in the Labour movement like doing the dirty work of the Conservatives in opposing social reforms. As in the clash with the *Daily Mirror* in 1942, and in a different way over Mosley's release later in 1943, Morrison was put up to oppose strong sentiments in his own party in defence of positions mainly established by the Conservatives, and especially by Churchill. He found himself in similar situations over the Old Age Pensions Bill in May 1943 and to some extent with the Workmen's Compensation Bill in October. As a professional trouble-shooter he did what was required of him, did it well, and even seemed to enjoy doing it, now as later under Attlee. He could face a storm of hostility without giving way to the temptation to let the Opposition know that he had some personal sympathy with their position. But he paid a price in offending a growing number on Labour's left – people whose votes went against him when he was narrowly defeated later in the year in the contest for the treasurership of the party.[57]

A fortnight after his parliamentary triumph in the Beveridge debate, Morrison found a more complex, more protracted and certainly more tragic crisis on his hands. Widespread fears of large-scale German retaliation for the recent massive RAF raids on Berlin led to increased occupation of London's deep shelters at the beginning of March 1943. At a quarter past eight on the evening of 3 March the air-raid sirens wailed in Bethnal Green. People ran from their homes, from pubs and cinemas to the tube station, which was the largest deep shelter in that part of London, and had been the first tube station which Morrison agreed should be opened as a public shelter.[58] Ventilation and other facilities had since been constructed, with bunks for some five thousand people, but the shelter still had only one entrance, down two flights of stone steps with a landing and a sharp turn half-way down.

Shortly after the air-raid warning sounded, an anti-aircraft battery a quarter of a mile away fired off a salvo of rockets at the approaching German planes. The sharp and unfamiliar noise of these new rockets alarmed the people in the streets. The crowds approaching the entrance to the shelter hurried forward causing a sudden and severe pressure on the backs of those already descending. At the moment of pressure a woman carrying a baby stumbled down the bottom steps of the first flight and the man next to her also fell. In a few seconds a mass of bodies pressed and were pressed on top of those below and became an immovable and interlaced heap. Those at the bottom were pinned against the wall of the landing that faced them where the stairs turned, so they could not fall further but were simply crushed by the weight of avalanching bodies. One survivor told the subsequent coroner's inquest how after the woman in front of her fell 'we all seemed to fall. I think Mr Stedman took the baby out of my arms. Other people fell on top of me. I was there about three hours in the actual pile. All the time I could see my five children.'[59]

The tunnel and steps filled from the floor to the ceiling with bodies, in such a tangled and complex mass that the casualties could not easily be removed, even from below, for a very long time and the steps were not finally cleared until twenty minutes to midnight. The final casualty figures showed 173 dead, of whom 84 were women and 62 small children, and 62 injured. Curiously, subsequent medical examination showed virtually no bone fractures in the bodies. All the victims were suffocated and the medical evidence indicated that the cause of death was steady and intense compression which simply prevented breathing. Death was within seconds of the fall. Some at the bottom of the pile, especially children, inexplicably escaped; others at the top, although with less weight upon them, died.

Within twenty-four hours Morrison had decided to set up an independent inquiry into the tragedy and had selected the chairman: Lawrence Dunne, a respected metropolitan magistrate.* More controversially, he also decided that the inquiry should be in private because of fear that publicity of the full horror might demoralize the British public and encourage the Germans to intensify such air raids. This created great dissatisfaction in the East End where there was a protest demonstration demanding an open inquiry.[60] Morrison left the question of whether to publish the inquiry's full findings until he had the full report before him, but he promised Parliament that its conclusions would be published, subject to any security considerations.[61]

The Dunne Commission report was in Morrison's hands by the end of March. It set out various defects in the structure, lighting and supervision of the shelter entrance and rebuked both the regional commissioners and the Bethnal Green local authority for not properly inspecting and improving it. Morrison quickly instructed that the regional officers responsible for the oversight should be formally reprimanded. The report was also read to the Bethnal Green emergency committee, under injunctions of secrecy. Despite the passing strictures upon them, however, the councillors appeared to emerge relatively unscathed, for the real weight of Mr Dunne's conclusions assigned the overwhelming cause of the tragedy not to the minor structural faults in the shelter entrance but to the behaviour of the people approaching it. He concluded that the disaster was caused by a number of people losing their self-control at a particularly unfortunate place and time, and that forethought in structural design or better supervision could not have safeguarded against the disorderly confusion, amounting almost to panic, which prevailed on the evening of 3 March.

It was Morrison's original intention to publish an edited summary of Dunne's conclusions as a White Paper. However, he decided on security grounds against publication and simply to make a short oral statement to the Commons, with no reference at all to the near panic among the people concerned.[62] This he did. But the whole business then took a most embarrassing twist. Bitter resentment at the decision not to publish led to protest demonstrations in Bethnal Green. A pressure group was formed – the Shelter Victims Committee – which asserted that the whole affair had been hushed up by Morrison from the beginning in order to cover up the negligence of the Bethnall Green council. The committee began to collect money to finance legal proceedings against the council, claiming compensation for the victims and their next of kin. Over two hundred claims for damages waited on the conclusion of the test case which was heard – in private, on the government's insistence, and without any reference to the Dunne report – in July 1944. Mr Justice Singleton found against the council, concluding that the clear cause of death was unsafe steps, poor lighting and inadequate supervision at the shelter entrance, and awarding damages totalling £1,550. Bethnal Green appealed, but again lost. Furthermore, the Master of the Rolls, Lord Greene, devoted part of his judgment to a strong attack on Morrison for insisting that

* Dunne was made Chief Metropolitan Magistrate in 1948.

the case be held *in camera*. He said that 'the fact was perfectly well known before ever this trial opened that there was no panic' and this was above all a case 'where evidence could be given in open court'. He described the Home Office's arguments for holding it in private as 'of the flimsiest description'.[63]

The situation Morrison now faced was bizarre. Two law cases had been decided about the disaster without the sitting judges ever being aware of Dunne's conclusion that the prime responsibility lay with a loss of control tantamount to panic among the people entering the shelter and not with the shelter structure. Bethnal Green faced ruinous financial penalties for negligence from which it had already secretly been partly exonerated. Morrison himself had been publicly censured by the Master of the Rolls for acting upon 'flimsy' evidence of panic, when he knew there was substantial evidence which he could not reveal.

Some sanity had to be restored. After hectic discussions in Whitehall over Christmas and into the new year of 1945, Morrison decided to publish the Dunne report. A full statement was made to the Commons on 19 January 1945 explaining the background to the affair.[64] He decided that Bethnal Green must be fully compensated for all legal costs and damages.[65]

Morrison concluded his term as Home Secretary as he began, dealing with an aerial bombardment of London. The weapons of destruction raining from the sky were, however, now more terrifying and difficult to repulse. Since 1942 the Chiefs of Staff had been aware that the Germans were developing long-range rockets to launch against Britain.[66] The Prime Minister and Morrison were warned in the spring of 1943 and the Ministry of Home Security began to prepare against the threat, building up reserves of Morrison shelters and devising evacuation schemes. By the autumn of 1943 British intelligence informed the government of a second variety of missile, the pilotless aircraft, and Morrison now began to get very alarmed.[67] His department calculated frightening figures for possible casualties, running to a hundred thousand dead and a quarter of a million injured per month. He began to press for a halt to the run-down in civil defence forces and urged that more manpower and resources be diverted to shelter construction.[68] Churchill, however, was strongly influenced by the scepticism of Lindemann, his scientific adviser, about the rocket threat and would not agree to divert substantial resources away from the invasion build-up.

The first pilotless planes – which were soon, on Morrison's suggestion, designated 'flying bombs'[69] – fell in Chiswick and in Epping on the night of 12–13 June 1944, a week after the allied invasion of France. In the next three months over five thousand flying bombs struck Britain, mainly in south London and especially in Croydon and Lewisham, which suffered as badly as in the worst days of the 1940–41 blitz. The flying bombs posed different problems from that earlier blitz. The raids were now less prolonged in time and more scattered and unpredictable in direction. There was more surface damage to buildings and more street casualties, but fewer fires, less damage to gas and other service mains, and less danger to civil defence personnel who normally operated after and not during an attack. The chief administrative problem lay in finding an appropriate warning system, which would protect people without bringing the whole of London to a halt at the approach of one flying bomb which might fall in a playing field in Peckham. Churchill demanded a more localized warning. This proved difficult, since the target locality was unpredictable, so Morrison was instructed to reduce the amount of general warning given. He was very reluctant and was later upset when there occurred incidents with terrible casualties and complaints that little or no warning had been given.[70] He was also annoyed at a plan to deceive the Germans by feeding them false information indicating that their missiles were over-shooting London. This deception was intended to lead them to shorten their range and so make the missiles fall short in the open country of southern England. The scheme had some success, but also resulted in Morrison's south London receiving some of the battering intended for the smarter central areas and he angrily protested at this.[71] Civilian morale was not good after five years of war and Morrison was often on the receiving end of public anger and loud abuse when he visited the victims of flying bomb attacks.[72]

The flying bombs were smaller and less destructive than originally feared and Morrison's depleted civil defence forces could probably have coped with them adequately, especially as the RAF and the anti-aircraft gunners grew increasingly proficient at shooting them down over the sea or over open countryside. More worrying was the imminent threat of silent and unseen rockets against which there was no defence. In a memorandum to the Cabinet at the end of June 1944, Morrison expressed his fears that civilian morale would break: 'I have a high degree of faith in the Londoners and the people of the small towns of southern England. But . . . there is a limit, and the limit will come.'[73] He pressed for heavier air attacks on the launching sites. He secured Cabinet agreement to a radical reappraisal of civil defence plans, including the decision to stimulate a massive evacuation, of industry as well as people, from the capital.[74] Meanwhile hundreds of thousands of Londoners left for the safety of the country of their own volition. Then curiously the air of crisis in Whitehall seemed to pass. As the allied armies broke out from Normandy to advance rapidly across France and into the Low Countries, the Chiefs of Staff grew optimistic and advised that the rocket threat was receding. Morrison, previously the most agitated in his concern, was convinced at the beginning of September that there was little now to worry about. He told the Cabinet that there was 'increasing unlikelihood' of rocket attacks and that the flying bomb assault would shortly cease; he therefore recommended that they discontinue the recently agreed evacuation schemes.[75] He made a well-publicized speech claiming that the battle for London was now over and that the brave city had finally beaten Hitler.[76]

The timing of these statements was most unfortunate. People who had spontaneously evacuated in the summer began to pour back into the capital. The evening after his speech the first German rocket struck a residential street in London and the missiles continued to fall in the days ahead, though the public was not informed for some time and the string of explosions led to puzzlement.[77] By the end of the year over five hundred rockets had hit London, and this terrifying bombardment continued virtually until Germany surrendered. Morrison's earlier fears about the missile threat to the capital, and especially south of the river where he lived and which bore the brunt of the attack, had proved justified. It was a terrible experience, made tolerable only by the daily improving prospects of an end to the war. London remains the only city in the world to have suffered sustained attack from long range missiles, the symbolic hardware of modern warfare. Morrison and his department were kept working frantically at the problems of civil defence right to the end of his period in office, just as he had to deal with them on the very first day he took over in October 1940.

As German military resistance crumbled in the spring of 1945 Morrison was able to enjoy winding up some of the paraphernalia and restrictions of war, ending the black-out and then the dim-out, lighting up London again, stopping fire-watching, dismantling the civil defence services and the regional commissions. One of his last ministerial actions was to go to the Channel Islands immediately after their liberation – the only part of the the monarch's home territories to suffer German occupation. He sailed from Portsmouth on 13 May aboard the destroyer HMS *Impulsive*, together with a small party of officials. They reached Guernsey on the fourteenth, spent the day there, and then sailed to Jersey, where he addressed the States Parliament and spoke to an enthusiastic crowd in the main square. He visited the Gestapo Headquarters, the German fortifications, and watched the embarkation of the surrendered garrison. He was in great form, enjoying every moment of his visit. He was relieved to find that the break of five years had not weakened the Islands' ties with Britain.* He was happy to discover and report that there was little evidence of collaboration and that, at least until the last few months, when food supplies ran out and everyone was starving, the Germans had behaved well towards the local population.[78] He returned to the mainland on the *Impulsive* and set off that weekend for the Labour Party conference at Blackpool, which was to see the coalition brought to an end.

The Ministry of Home Security was wound up and its remaining functions transferred back to the Home Office at the end of May. By then Morrison had returned to opposition, preparing for the coming general election and the

* The Channel Islands are not part of the United Kingdom, but are dependencies of the Crown, with their own systems of law and administration, and enjoying a large measure of domestic autonomy. Morrison's official relationship was both as a member of the Privy Council and as the Minister acting as the channel of communication between the Islands, the Crown and His Majesty's Government.

exciting politics of post-war Britain. He had been Home Secretary longer than anyone else in this century and he left the office with a satisfying and justified sense of a difficult job well done. He always looked back nostalgically on the Home Office, like the LCC, as a time of happiness for him. At a departmental dinner given in his honour towards the end of his term he spoke with feeling of his great admiration for those who worked with him, for their efficiency and their humanity, for the way in which even under the pressures of the war's darkest days they never lost sight of the liberal principles which are at the heart of the British political system. This admiration was mutual. In reply his Permanent Secretary, Maxwell, said that Morrison reminded him of Alan Breck in *Kidnapped* who immediately after a savage fight on board ship remarked 'And O, man, Am I no' a bonny fighter?' That he certainly was.[79]

Chapter 24

Labour Politics, Post-War Reconstruction and the 1945 Election

Throughout the war, despite his heavy ministerial commitments, Morrison continued his diverse political work for the Labour Party. In the parliamentary party he was a ministerial member of the Administrative Committee, the group elected to provide a link between back-benchers and ministers in the coalition government. In London politics he had resigned from the leadership of the LCC* and handed over to Donald Daines as Acting Secretary of the London Labour Party, but he never lost touch with either body. At County Hall he maintained close relations with his successors as leader, Charles Latham and Isaac Hayward. He never interfered in LCC business, but members were still conscious of his intangible influence.[1] At the London Party headquarters, Morrison had access to the machine when he wanted.[2] He remained on the executive committee and slipped across Westminster Bridge to attend its meetings when the business seemed important. He was especially worried by the decline in London membership and the threatened collapse of Labour's metropolitan organization. By 1942 membership had dropped to only a third of the figure at the outbreak of war and there remained only six full-time constituency agents compared with thirty-one in 1939. Morrison addressed executive meetings on this problem and helped to organize special conferences of London parties to discuss improving party organization.[3] He never lost sight of the need to keep Labour's electoral machine in London in good shape for the post-war election.

The main centre of Morrison's multifarious party activities in the war was undoubtedly the National Executive Committee. He attended most meetings of the full NEC as well as several of its sub-committees – the War Emergency committee (until it was abolished in 1942), the Policy committee, which prepared policy statements for annual conference, the Elections committee, which discussed the selection and endorsement of candidates, the committee on reconstruction plans, which was set up in 1941 to discuss Labour's post-

* He remained an alderman till 1945.

war plans, and the International committee, which he joined in July 1942.[4] He found the burden on his time and energy very taxing and at one point in June 1941 he asked to be allowed off the key Policy committee, but he was pressed to continue.[5] He was now perhaps the most influential single member on the NEC. 'He did a tremendous job there,' recalled one colleague, 'taking it very seriously despite all his other responsibilities.'[6] He was a leading spokesman for the executive at each year's conference. In 1942, when the left wing attacked the leadership for maintaining the electoral truce, Morrison led the counter-attack from the platform.[7] His forthright criticisms of those who wanted to pull out of the coalition drew wide praise. 'Attlee did not shine at the Conference,' wrote one political commentator. 'Morrison did. Right or wrong, he is a brave man. And it is courage that in the last resort our democracy respects.'[8] Churchill sent him personal congratulations for 'the spirited manner in which you faced our critics at the Labour Conference and recalled the main body of the Party to its duty. You showed great courage in all this, and I am sure the Labour Movement will appreciate what you did as much as I do.'[9]

By this time Morrison was also making a striking impact in the Labour Party and in the wider community by his concern with the problems he anticipated and described as arising in post-war Britain. Through a series of inspired and widely publicized speeches he turned people's minds forward to the purpose and fruits of victory: to what kind of social, economic and political reconstruction was required in Britain. This was a quality that was wholly missing from Winston Churchill's approach to the war. To Churchill it was a big fight which had to be won on the battlefield. But many people, especially on the radical side of politics in Britain, though not only there, felt the need for clarification and commitment on what are normally called 'war aims'. They wanted to know why they were fighting and making such sacrifices. They knew the military objective: to defeat Hitler's Germany. They also wanted political incentives. Churchill, both from party political necessity and from personal inclination, would give no lead in planning the post-war world – as became clear at the time of the Beveridge debate. He then circulated a Cabinet memorandum beginning: 'A dangerous optimism is growing up about the conditions it will be possible to establish here after the war. . . . The question steals across the mind whether we are not committing our 45 million people to tasks beyond their compass. . . . While not disheartening our people by dwelling on the dark side of things, Ministers should, in my view, be careful not to raise false hopes as was done last time by speeches about "Homes for Heroes". . . . It is for this reason of not wishing to deceive the people by false hopes and airy visions of Utopia and Eldorado that I have refrained so far from making promises about the future. We must all do our best and we shall do it much better if we are not hampered by a cloud of pledges and promises which arise out of the hopeful and genial side of man's nature and are not brought into relation with the hard facts of life.'[10] Most other Conservatives would not move where Churchill feared to tread: many were anyway opposed to any alteration in the *status quo* during the war. On the Labour side Attlee, despite his worthy virtues, was not the kind of personality who inspired the mass of the people with visions of a bright new world. Indeed, as he grew older the Labour leader became more and more skilful at managing his volcanic colleagues, but appeared less and less interested in the policies and ideals which agitated them. Ernest Bevin certainly had the stature of a national leader and did share much of Morrison's concern for reforming the social order in Britain. But he was personally much closer to Churchill and responded to his appeals not to rock the coalition boat. Bevin was also highly suspicious of Morrison's motives and viewed his campaign on post-war reconstruction as just another manoeuvre to replace Attlee as leader.[11] Apart from these, Bevan and the small group on Labour's left, the Tory Reform Committee on the right, and later on the new Commonwealth Party each exercised valuable pressure towards social reform; but none of them had substantial influence inside the political system. So the task of guiding the aspirations of the British people in general, and the Labour Party in particular, beyond the current military obsessions towards the building of a better society after the war fell mainly to Herbert Morrison.

He undoubtedly saw the opportunity to improve his political standing and above all to strengthen his claims to the leadership of the Labour Party. It was a marvellous chance to shed the 'municipal' image and emerge as a national figure. But it would be a crude and over-cynical simplification of Morrison's complex character to conclude that this was his only motive. Morrison did care deeply and sincerely that the post-war world should contain less injustice and greater social democracy.[12] He saw the war as a great opportunity to make such progress and believed that under no circumstances should the people fight and make sacrifices without social, economic and political rewards. He put his position convincingly in a newspaper interview in the new year of 1943. 'The fighting will not cease because the soldier lays down his arms and returns to mufti. . . . The one fatal thing would be to relax and go back to superficial pleasantries. To think the battle was to give us the freedom of the West End . . . the switching on of the lights of the world will be an enjoyable experience – but no more than a symbol. You ask me what we can do now with a political truce, with reform and reconstruction held up until our full energies can be devoted to them. I think so far as is consistent with our war-winning efforts that this should be a period of education, of getting ready to exercise full intelligence and understanding, to read and study all points of view.'[13] All his life he had believed in planning and drafting policies in advance and in involving people in discussions about the basic issues which concerned their welfare. This is what he did throughout the war.

He began the 'period of education' on post-war problems remarkably early. On 11 December 1940, in the middle of the blitz, when invasion and defeat by Germany seemed only a matter of time, he spoke of the need for a more egalitarian post-war society, with better provision for welfare, health and social security to put an end to poverty. Next day the right-wing *Daily Mail* attacked him for this 'political speech'.[14] He returned to this theme on several occasions during 1941 and 1942.[15] He made his real impact, however, with a series of major speeches in the six months after he joined the War Cabinet late in 1942. By that autumn he was convinced that Britain would win the war.[16] He also had his department comfortably under control and ticking over smoothly. As Ellen Wilkinson told Dalton in October 1942, Morrison, 'having been deeply absorbed in his job until recently, is now feeling that he has got into running order, and is taking much more interest in wider questions, including post-war problems and the future of the Labour Party'.[17]

He launched his campaign at Swindon on 20 December 1942 and in fairly quick succession made important speeches at Newcastle on 10 January 1943, at Nottingham on 13 February and at the Guildhall in London on 24 February. He opened discussions on the main themes that were to recur in his pronouncements to the end of the war: the kind of economic, industrial and social organization that should be preserved or created in post-war Britain, including the nature of the inevitably close partnership between the state and industry; Britain's economic prospects and the need for international economic co-operation; and the kind of United Nations organization essential to preserve world peace.

At Swindon, with the Beveridge report in everyone's mind, he called on the nation to look beyond social security, which he described as 'at best nothing more than ambulance and salvage work; rescuing and patching up our social casualties. We cannot rouse ourselves and others with the slogan "minimum subsistence for all" . . . I believe that education is a better taskmaster than unemployment, leadership than want, faith than fear.' He went into some detail about continuing wartime control of industry in Labour's economic plans, but his main purpose was to raise the eyes of the people to broader horizons. 'Sound measures of law and administration are not enough,' he said. 'Our public policy as a whole will not be sound unless it is founded firmly upon a clear appreciation of values other than material ones. Efficient organization of industry is right, but not enough. We want better standards than . . . doing the best for oneself. We need to love our neighbour as ourselves, not merely in the sanctity of the home or in a circle of friends, but in the practical workaday world.'[18] His vision and concern were not limited to Britain. He devoted a good deal of his Newcastle speech to the place of the Commonwealth in the post-war world, seeing it as 'a great factor for stability and progress'. With specific reference to India he said she could 'have full self-government for the taking'.[19]

Clem Leslie was the main aid to Morrison in writing these speeches. Morrison would set out the broad theme that interested him, Leslie then wrote a speech around that theme, and finally Morrison would touch it up with some of his own phrases and flourishes.[20] Leslie also consulted individual experts for guidance on technical aspects of social or economic policy.[21] Their contributions helped another series of reconstruction speeches Morrison delivered in May 1943, when he focussed in greater detail than hitherto, especially on family problems, calling for a new 'charter of motherhood', for greater provision of nursery schools, for substantial children's allowances and for an urgent population policy at national level.[22]

It was appropriate that Morrison should play a leading role in the important debate on Labour's future policies at the annual party conference in London over Whitsun 1943. He had not only initiated and led discussion on post-war problems through his speeches to the nation at large. He had also been a prime mover in getting the party to formulate remedies for these problems within Labour's official machinery. Back in April 1941 Morrison had written formally to Middleton, the party Secretary, suggesting that the NEC should establish a special committee, including outside experts, to prepare economic and social policies for the post-war period.[23] Following this initiative the executive set up a new Central Committee on Reconstruction Problems, with Shinwell in the chair and Harold Laski as secretary.[24] Morrison was a member of the new committee and at its first meeting on 30 July 1941 proposed the setting up of a further special sub-committee on Social and Economic Transformation in Great Britain. This was adopted and he was made a member of that committee as well, along with Dalton, Shinwell, Laski, Wilmot and Harold Clay.[25] Through this committee machinery meeting regularly over the next two years the party formulated its policies for the future, with Greenwood and Laski preparing important draft policy papers in 1942 and Morrison himself contributing considerably to the 1943 draft document on 'The Labour Party and the Future'. At the NEC in March 1943 he called for the coming conference debate on this document to be 'lifted to the highest possible level'.[26]

The debate at conference was of above average standard and Morrison himself made an important winding-up speech outlining the nationalization intentions of a future Labour government: 'we must have the public ownership of the natural monopolies; we must have the public ownership of the common services, of industries like transport and mining, which are at the service of all other industries; we must have the socialization or the regulation of those restrictive monopolies of capitalism which themselves are based upon the economics of scarcity, and we must have control of the essential agency of the banking system, the Bank of England, that ought to become the agency of State policy and not the agent of private policy. I have been preaching these things in recent speeches,' he went on, 'and some of the newspapers upon the Right have been critical of them. That, in itself, is a sign that the battle is not far off . . . if we are to succeed in this task, we must equip ourselves mentally for its advocacy, for its exploitation. The Party organization must be overhauled from top to bottom nationally, locally as well, in order that it may be the great instrument capable of leading the British people on the right lines, capable of achieving as decisive a victory in this dangerous and difficult transition from war to peace, as triumphant, as victorious, about those problems, as, make no mistake, we are going to be triumphant at the expense of our enemies in the field.'[27]

Morrison sat down to a thunderous ovation.[28] It was a moment of triumph, the proper reward for the energy and vision he had devoted to post-war reconstruction in the past two years. He spoke, and was received, as an authentic national leader of the future. Before the conference a Tory MP wrote of him: 'Herbert Morrison has every right to look ahead and feel that the political summit is not beyond his endurance or his abilities. If he attains the Premiership at some distant date, we in the Tory Party will . . . know that we have in him a man of judgment, character, integrity and a man who in his own way deeply loves the country which gave him birth.'[29] The *Daily Express* concluded: 'The rise of Herbert Morrison is the outstanding political event of the last three years.'[30]

His triumph and pleasure at the 1943 conference proved, however, sadly brief. Next day, Tuesday 15 June, he suffered a painful political set-back. He had put up for the treasurership of the party – which involved retiring from the constituency section of the NEC – and he was defeated by Arthur Greenwood. He was suddenly off the executive altogether for the next year.

The previous party treasurer, George Latham, had died in the summer of 1942. In January 1943 the London Labour Party executive decided to nominate Morrison for the vacancy.[31] He was not present at the meeting but it is hard to imagine that he did not know of, or even help to inspire, the nomination. Success in this contest would give him a place *ex officio* on the NEC and would also demonstrate publicly his strength and popularity in the mass party. It was a logical though not an essential step towards establishing his claim to the leadership when Attlee went. However, in April a major obstacle appeared: the engineers' union nominated Greenwood, the party's deputy leader, for the treasurership. Greenwood was a serious contender, popular in the party and with strong union backing. A further complication arose shortly after when Glenvil Hall was nominated for the post by the mine-workers.

In the weeks before conference the various unions took their positions and it became clear that, despite energetic canvassing on his behalf by such friends as Ellen Wilkinson, Hugh Dalton, Sam Watson and George Ridley, Morrison ran the risk of defeat.[32] He had the backing of the General and Municipal Workers, the cotton workers, the railway clerks, the London printers and the Royal Arsenal Co-operative Society, but this was not enough. The railwaymen had joined the engineers in supporting Greenwood, and Bevin gleefully made sure that the vote of the transport workers went against Morrison.[33] With the miners and the steel workers behind Hall, there were not many union votes left for Morrison to pick up. On the eve of the conference, Dalton met Sam Watson and George Ridley and they did their sums. Morrison could not win – though it looked as if Greenwood would not have an over-all majority, and so they decided to try to get a second ballot, in the hope that the miners would swing to Morrison after the elimination of Hall.[34] A special meeting of the NEC was summoned, and Harold Laski and Sam Watson moved that a second ballot should be introduced, but the vote tied eleven to eleven and the chairman, A. J. Dobbs, gave his casting vote against.[35] Morrison, who with Greenwood had stayed away from this meeting, was very angry with the decision, seeing it as a deliberate attempt to shut him out of high office in the party. 'They know quite well what they are doing', he complained to Dalton.[36]

The ballot result announced to the conference on the Tuesday showed Greenwood had 1,253,000 votes to Morrison's 926,000 and Hall's 519,000. Had there been a second ballot – and had Sam Watson and Will Lawther of the miners' union been able to swing Hall's miners' votes to Morrison – then he could have won. It was not to be. The treasurership, a key office in the rise to party power of MacDonald, Henderson and later Gaitskell, eluded Morrison's grasp, at a time, ironically, when his standing in the country had never been higher. He took the defeat badly at first, asserting angrily that he would not stand for the executive again.[37] He soon resumed his normal cool composure and he was given a tremendous ovation when he went later to the rostrum to speak against more co-operation with the Communist Party. He thanked the audience, saying that this was probably his swan song as a spokesman for the executive (shouts of 'No!') and promised to behave himself.[38]

The reasons for Morrison's defeat were complex. It did not mean that the party thought he was not up to the job of treasurer. Labour's rank and file were at this time in a peculiarly volatile mood. After the Beveridge debate there was a widespread feeling that it was necessary to remind Labour ministers in the coalition of their socialist principles and their party roots. This was done not only by punishing Morrison but also by electing to the NEC this year such active critics of the coalition as Emanuel Shinwell, Harold Laski and John Parker. The trade unions also viewed Morrison's rapid political advance with some apprehension. Bevin was of course animated by a venomous hatred, but others had less personal reasons for opposing Morrison. They were worried, as the *Manchester Guardian* pointed out at the time, by any developments which 'might mean an escalation of the political side of the movement . . . they were going to have no more Hendersons and MacDonalds. They prefer the milder leadership of Attlee and Greenwood to the purposefulness of Mr Morrison.' Morrison had seemed to them impetuous and too openly ambitious in pushing himself forward as a national leader.[39] As Hannen Swaffer wrote: 'Labour strangely enough now fears the bold leadership it knows it wants. Morrison is both popular and unpopular for the same sort of reasons that kept Churchill out of power.'[40] There was widespread respect for Morrison and sympathy for him in defeat, but also a feeling that a check to his meteoric progress would not do this cocky cockney any harm. 'Mr Morrison is still young as Labour politicians go,' concluded the *Manchester Guardian*. 'The Labour Party has lost none of its estimation of him. It appreciates his gifts, but it requires more deliberate methods of moving. Mr Morrison has probably learned that it is not responsive to high pressure methods of salesmanship even if the goods to be put over are of the most excellent workmanship and novelty.'[41]

Shortly after his defeat Morrison addressed a meeting of the London Labour Party at the Holborn Hall. He was a star attraction. People queued over an hour to get in and the hall was packed. He referred briefly to the treasurership battle, reassuring them that 'there is no bitterness in me', but he quickly moved back onto his favourite broader themes of post-war reconstruction. He regretted that the debates at conference contained 'not enough which would attract the sympathetic interest of the young man in the Eighth Army or the young woman, his sister, doing a service job in our own country'. He said that 'what we need is to make the country realize that tinkering and patching with our social system is not good enough. The basic question is who will control industry.' He concluded that whatever happened politically and electorally the Labour Party must 'set out on a great campaign of public education in the realities of post-war policy. Let us do so. We politicians must do our duty conscientiously, efficiently in the public interest. But men and women in the street and in the services – you must do your duty as citizens too. The parliament and government will be of your making too. Take your part; prepare yourselves for the task of decision and selection when voting times come. Paradise will not be handed to you on a plate. It must be worked for, fought for, voted for. Go to it.'[42] This was Morrison at his best, bouncing back from temporary defeat and once again lifting high the banner for Labour's march towards post-war victory and government, taking 'all the decent people' with it, involving them in working together for the collective good. No other figure in the Labour movement at this time so symbolized this determination and optimism, this will to make sure that it was Labour which shaped Britain's post-war destiny.

Morrison's reconstruction speeches naturally upset many in the Conservative Party. In arguing for a socialist Britain in the near future he seemed to them to be bending the rules of coalition government. Churchill took him on one side in late 1943 and asked him to desist. Morrison refused to be deterred.[43] Now off Labour's NEC, he concentrated his efforts in the Cabinet and especially in the sub-committees on reconstruction and on reconstruction priorities, which were heavily involved in following up the Beveridge proposals. After the Commons vote on Beveridge he had told the Committee on Reconstruction Priorities that parliamentary support 'rests on the assumption that the Government does in fact mean business, that all reasonable speed will be used, and no false or undue caution evidenced'.[44] Churchill still tried to limit reconstruction planning, arguing that in the war they need plan only for the 'transition' period to peace, but Morrison insisted in Cabinet that acceptance of the Prime Minister's 'transition' principle should not preclude early consideration of longer-term objectives. He especially had in mind changes in the organization of industry, including nationalization, to guarantee high levels of employment.[45] He also pointed out that many of the plans being considered in the reconstruction committees had by late 1943 reached the stage where decisions in principle would have to be taken quickly; they could not wait until some distant 'transition' period. He cited the prime example of the proposed scheme for comprehensive social insurance and insisted that when it came before Parliament the government must be prepared to take an immediate decision and announce its position accordingly.[46]

His impatience to advance his ideas for a radical reorganization of industry led Morrison to clash even with his Labour colleagues in 1944. He drafted in October a memorandum advocating 'a great national plan of capital re-equipment and technical reorganization' and envisaging a major extension of public control. He intended to put it before the Cabinet but first, out of courtesy, circulated it to senior Labour ministers. As he wrote to Bevin: 'We miss many chances by failure to discuss a line of action beforehand. When the two of us (or three of us) happen to find ourselves of one mind . . . we really get somewhere . . . surely it isn't beyond our wit or will to make the necessary arrangements to keep together for the things that really matter?'[47] But Bevin was bluntly unsympathetic, implying in his response that Morrison was up to his tricks of playing for the leadership again. He wrote to Attlee about Morrison's industrial proposals in November: 'I myself am being forced to the conclusion that a country run by a series of London Transport Boards would be almost intolerable.'[48] Attlee produced a paper of his own and Morrison sat down with him, Bevin and Dalton at 11 Downing Street on 22 November. Bevin restated his opposition and did not seem keen on any radical reforms in the war. Dalton was more sympathetic but doubted, from his own ministerial experience, whether there was practical hope of achieving anything under the present coalition government.[49] Attlee as usual said little. Morrison stuck to his guns and reserved his freedom to act as he judged best despite their lack of support.[50]

Labour's 1944 conference had been scheduled to meet as usual in May, but just beforehand the government asked that it be postponed in order not to interfere with railway traffic, needed to build up for the imminent invasion of Europe.[51] The rockets crisis then added to the transportation problem and the party did not assemble until December.[52] Conference had before it several important issues, including British military intervention in Greece and the question of remaining within the coalition. For Labour's electoral future, the most important debate was on the NEC policy document, *Economic Controls, Public Ownership and Full Employment*. This reaffirmed the principle of public ownership and proposed taking control of the Bank of England, but otherwise contained no specific commitments to nationalize particular industries. Delegates were unhappy with this caution and a resolution was passed from the floor calling for 'the transfer to public ownership of the land, large-scale building, heavy industry, and all forms of banking, transport and fuel and power'.[53] This rank-and-file victory over the executive was not as momentous as is sometimes believed. Labour never did, in fact, nationalize land or building, and would certainly have nationalized fuel, power and transport anyway – Morrison, Bevin and the miners would see to that. But the resolution gave an extra impetus towards nationalization, if any were needed, and made it much more difficult to retreat from nationalization commitments (as Morrison found to his cost when trying to compromise over iron and steel in 1947).

Morrison was of course not on stage fighting the battle for the NEC. For the first time in years he sat among the ordinary delegates in the hall. As such he went to the rostrum to speak on workmen's compensation and was given a rousing reception.[54] He had, however, been renominated for the constituency section of the NEC and was comfortably re-elected, coming fourth behind Harold Laski, Emanuel Shinwell and Jim Griffiths, and just ahead of Aneurin Bevan. This perhaps compensated for his failure earlier in the year to get the succession to Jim Middleton as party secretary for his friend and protégé Maurice Webb, the lobby correspondent of the *Daily Herald*. As in Morrison's personal bid for the treasurership in the previous year, trade union opposition was again decisive. The trade unionists resented the way in which Morrison tried to fix support for Webb in advance. They instinctively preferred Morgan Phillips, as an ex-miner, to the middle-class Webb, but they also again felt that Morrison was trying to extend his influence too much over the party machine and he had to be checked.[55]

After his re-election to the NEC Morrison resumed his place on various sub-committees and it was through his chairmanship of the Policy committee and the newly established Campaign committee that he exercised such great influence on the party's preparations for the 1945 election. The Campaign committee* co-ordinated all the election services and funds, and arranged for the distribution of propaganda literature. It was a small, high-powered group – Morrison, Attlee, Dalton, Greenwood and Morgan Phillips – and according to Dalton they gave Morrison as chairman 'quite rightly plenty of elbow room'.[56]

The Policy committee had the job of preparing Labour's election manifesto. Morrison himself was responsible for the first draft, which he produced by the end of January and over the next two months the committee discussed and revised it. The document then went to the full NEC which approved it for presentation to conference, after which it became in due course the famous manifesto *Let us Face the Future*.[57] Morrison wrote later that his 'feelings in drafting the programme were inspired by one major factor: the changed nature of the electorate. I knew that victory would go to the Party which recognized and served this mature and thoughtful public. I do not believe there has been an occasion before when the men and women of Britain were facing their civic responsibilities so resolutely and intelligently.'[58] A commitment to nationalize iron and steel was firmly included in the programme –

* This was distinct from the Elections committee (of which he was also a member) which was mainly concerned with the selection and endorsement of candidates.

despite momentary wobbling by Morrison, who had to be hauled back in line by Dalton.[59] However, the nationalization of land, building and banking were not specifically mentioned, so the resolution at the 1944 conference was to some extent side-stepped.

Morrison launched this new policy programme to the public at a big press conference on 21 April 1945. The following weekend he went to Bath and to Bristol and delivered major speeches expounding and praising the document. At Bristol, where a mass meeting welcomed Sir Stafford Cripps back into the party, Morrison stressed that the proposed nationalizations were practical and undoctrinaire. 'The Labour Party offers a short-term programme of socialization of a limited number of industries and in each of these industries it rests its case on the practical facts of the situation.' He then went on to deal with each industry in turn: that coal should be nationalized to ensure greater investment and efficiency; that for electricity nationalization was a rational development since it was already a public utility; that transport should be taken over as a common public service. 'The doctrinaires,' he argued, 'are those who defended private ownership for its own sake, irrespective of our grave industrial problems, of historical developments, of public needs, or the needs of productive industry, and of the outlook and attitude of the mass of workers in the industries being socialized.'[60]

The policy document was put before conference at Blackpool in May and Morrison opened the debate. He reminded them that the whole nation was following their discussions with a coming general election in mind. 'The future of British industry, the ensuring of full employment, the control of financial and credit institutions, agriculture and housing,' he argued, 'these will be the essentials of this fight. Permanent social reform and security cannot be built on rotten economic foundations.' The only solution was to socialize industry in order to get a firm economic base for social reform. The vast Empress Ballroom at the Winter Gardens was crammed with delegates and they gave him a great ovation. It was 'a remarkable scene of enthusiasm . . . delegates cheered for minutes on end.'[61] The press was full of praise for his speech, for its punch and its bubbling humour. According to the *Daily Express* he was 'the present idol of the delegates and undoubted leader of the party today'.[62] They sensed that Labour was coming to the end of the dark tunnel it entered in 1931, that the light of victory lay ahead, and they knew that Morrison as much as anyone had led them towards it. He was in sparkling form throughout the conference, particularly enjoying, as always, the Mayor's Ball, where he stayed right till the end, dancing the last waltz with Ellen Wilkinson who was this year's conference chairman.[63]

Even before Labour's 1945 conference assembled, Churchill's great coalition government was, in the prevailing heated political atmosphere, coming to an end. Bevin had joined Morrison in making sharp attacks on Conservative attitudes and policies, which irritated their right-wing colleagues in the Cabinet.[64] The Tories themselves had begun denouncing Labour policy proposals and Churchill's speech to their conference in March 1945 implicitly accepted the imminent break-up of the coalition and the renewal of party warfare. As domestic legislation had increasingly absorbed the attention of politicians – since as far back as Beveridge in early 1943 – the doctrinal differences between the parties re-emerged. It could only be a matter of time. Morrison's own 'post-war' speeches and the policies being pushed by Labour ministers in the Cabinet reconstruction committees built up pressure on the loose patchwork of the coalition. 'Defeat knits together,' wrote one Tory Cabinet member, 'victory opens the seams.'[65]

Germany surrendered on 7–8 May 1945. After short speeches by the leaders of the political parties in the Commons, MPs adjourned to St Margaret's, Westminster, for a service of thanksgiving. Morrison was walking in the procession just behind Churchill when a police horse suddenly reared and plunged towards him and he had to jump for his life.[66] The euphoria and community of spirit in victory did not last long in Cabinet. With Germany beaten the last threads binding the parties were breaking. Churchill felt that the future of his government must be settled quickly, and certainly before Labour's conference began on 18 May. Attlee was away in San Francisco for the opening of the United Nations and so Bevin, who was acting in Attlee's absence, and Morrison, because he was on the NEC, went to see Churchill on 11 May to discuss the date of the general election.[67] Morrison strongly put the merits of October. This allowed a decent interval for preparation: the service vote would be organized by then and an accurate new register would be in force. Bevin supported him, indeed relations between the two Labour men were unusually amicable in these negotiations. But a clear difference of response emerged when Churchill proposed delaying the election and continuing the coalition until the defeat of Japan. Bevin was obviously attracted by the suggestion.[68] Morrison's own position had at one time seemed ambiguous. In 1943 and 1944 he had left some observers with the impression that he would co-operate in a post-war coalition.[69] From mid-1944, however, he asserted unequivocally in public and in private that the coalition should not go beyond the end of the war.[70] At one time he may have been unclear about whether the end of the war meant the end of the German or the Japanese war. Now he was firm that it meant hostilities with Germany – which were already terminated. He also believed that the election should not be sprung immediately but should be delayed three months or so. Each of these points had been specifically promised to the House of Commons by Churchill himself when moving the Prolongation of Parliament Bill only six months earlier.[71]

Morrison and Bevin, with the agreement of the NEC, told Churchill that 'Labour would be willing to remain in this Government until a date not involving another Prolongation of Parliament Bill which means roughly that the break would come some time this session.' Morrison telegraphed this information to Attlee in San Francisco, who replied agreeing with their line.[72] Attlee returned from San Francisco a few days later and took up the discussion with Churchill, who gave him a letter setting out a proposal to delay the election not just to the end of this session but for the unspecified period until the end of the war with Japan. The only alternative, he said, was an immediate dissolution and election. Attlee promised to get a decision from his colleagues at the party conference starting the coming weekend. He made no objection to the principle of continuing until the Japanese defeat and left Churchill – as he left Dalton – with the impression that these terms were acceptable to both himself and Bevin.[73]

Labour's NEC met in Blackpool in the Town Hall after tea on Sunday 20 May and discussed Churchill's letter. Attlee characteristically hedged his position on it, putting the arguments for and against continuing the coalition, though he still privately favoured the proposal.[74] Morrison, however, spoke up strongly against and virtually everyone present supported him.[75] The majority instructed Attlee to draft, with Morrison's help, a reply to Churchill stating Labour's unwillingness to prolong the coalition until the defeat of Japan and asking that the election be held in the autumn when the new register would be ready. Churchill replied that in view of Labour's attitude he would resign straight away and requested Labour ministers to place their offices at his disposal. Next day he went to the Palace, first to tender his government's resignation, and then both to agree to form a new caretaker administration and to obtain a dissolution of Parliament in three weeks' time for an election on 5 July. This rapid *démarche* meant that Morrison and his party colleagues never had the chance formally to withdraw from the coalition as they intended. When they returned to London the coalition was dead.[76]

At the end of the Blackpool conference Morrison flew to the Isle of Man for the weekend. He had some Home Office business to complete there, but he also took the opportunity to have an operation on his right foot by Sir Herbert Barker. His ankles often gave him great pain – a legacy from childhood – and he had flown to see Barker a year earlier. The treatment seemed to work: afterwards he said he 'felt like a schoolboy again'.[77] Back in London the following week he dropped into the Home Office to wind up his affairs and went to the Palace formally to hand over his seals of office to the monarch. He and the other retiring Labour ministers enjoyed farewell cocktails with Churchill at 10 Downing Street, on Monday 28 May. Next day the new caretaker government was in operation and Morrison was sitting with his colleagues on the opposition front bench for the first time in five years. There was an immediate return to the cut and thrust of party politics, with Morrison baiting Churchill at question time and the Prime Minister ticking off his late Home Secretary.[78]

Even though Parliament dragged on through the first two weeks of June 1945, for Morrison the election began immediately he moved into opposition. This was the moment for which he had so long prepared: intellectually through his reconstruction speeches, organizationally through his work on the NEC and the London Labour Party. He took an office in Transport House and ran the national campaign from there, working closely with George Shepherd, the national agent, with Willie Henderson, who was responsible for publicity, and with the Secretary, Morgan Phillips.[79] Earlier planning in the Campaign committee now bore fruit. They were able quickly to distribute one and a half million copies of *Let us Face the Future* and over a hundred thousand copies of pamphlets on the ministerial work of Morrison and Bevin in the coalition government. They kept a close eye on the press and Morrison himself published major propaganda articles at the beginning and at the end of the campaign.[80] When Churchill made his notorious broadcast on 4 June, alleging that no socialist system (including by implication a Labour government) 'could afford to allow free, sharp or violently worded expressions of public dissent – they would have to fall back on some form of gestapo', Morrison issued Labour's immediate reply, calmly demolishing this 'penny dreadful' politics point by point. 'It makes me sad and depressed,' confessed Morrison, 'that Winston Churchill should have allowed himself to be used at this tragically low level.'[81] He struck the right note from the beginning, as did Attlee in a subsequent broadcast, projecting Labour as the party which was fit to govern, and leaving Churchill looking irresponsible.

Morrison built a close relationship with the *Daily Mirror* during the campaign, healing any wounds left from their clash in 1942.[82] The *Mirror* gave telling support to Labour, and after one particularly helpful editorial Morrison telephoned Sydney Elliott, the political editor, to say he would like to get on better terms with the chairman, Guy Bartholomew. Elliott arranged a lunch at a private dining room in the Mayfair Hotel. Morrison bustled in, put his arm round Bartholomew and addressed him as 'you six-ribboned cherub', and the ice melted. From that point, Bartholomew became a firm friend and Morrison worked closely with the *Mirror*. He consulted Elliott about his own broadcasts and invited Zec, the cartoonist at the centre of the 1942 storm, to advise on Labour's posters. He took from the paper its brilliant election theme of 'vote for him', aimed at the women with menfolk abroad in the services.[83]

In addition to electioneering at national level, Morrison was heavily occupied with the campaign in London. He resumed his post as Secretary of the London Labour Party immediately on leaving the Home Office.[84] Above all, he had to fight and win his own new constituency, East Lewisham. There had been newspaper speculation that he might leave South Hackney since the summer of 1944.[85] Early in the new year of 1945 he summoned a press conference and announced that he had accepted an invitation from the East Lewisham Labour Party to apply for nomination as their candidate, with the approval of his executive in South Hackney. There were two other applicants – both trade union sponsored – but at the selection meeting on 10 February Morrison was comfortably elected with fifty-five out of the sixty-two votes cast on the first ballot.[86]

In his press statement in January Morrison said he had two motives in leaving South Hackney for East Lewisham. First he mentioned that Hackney was declining in population and would be subject to redistribution after the coming election. Second, and more important he argued, was that East Lewisham, which had never been won by Labour, was exactly the kind of white-collar constituency which the party must win if it was ever to become truly national in character. 'For many years,' he said, 'I have counselled the Socialist Party that if it is ever to secure an independent stable parliamentary majority, it must gain and keep the support not only of the politically conscious organized workers, but also of large numbers of professional, technical and administrative workers, of whom there are many in East Lewisham. It is because I have confidence in the reasoned appeal the Socialist Party can make to all sections of the community – manual workers and black coats alike – that I have decided to go to East Lewisham, if I am selected, emphasizing by this action my conviction that the soundest socialist appeal is that which is most universal in its scope.'[87]

There is no reason to question that this was a decisive, and very commendable, motive in Morrison's change of constituency.[88] Again and again in his speeches over the years he had stressed that the Labour Party must cease to be a sectional interest and must strive to represent 'all the useful people' in the community. The best way to demonstrate this publicly was for him to fight a constituency where the social composition of the electorate was a cross-section of the community. Because of this genuine desire to lead Labour's advance into white-collar England he turned down the offer of a completely safe seat at Deptford early in 1945.[89] It required courage to give up one safe seat and to spurn another on the eve of Labour probably forming a government. Certainly there is no evidence for the current rumour that he was running away from a contest with a communist candidate in Hackney – 'Morrison's retreat from Moscow' as one paper described it.[90] He always relished fighting communists, who irritated him by trying to disrupt his meetings. He was not running away from them but he would certainly be pleased to see the back of them.[91] There was little doubt that he would have won, as would any Labour candidate in Hackney in 1945.[92]

He did, however, have other reasons for changing his constituency. As he said in his press statement, the Hackney electorate was declining. Only 51,160 in 1939, it had now shrunk to probably half that size; whoever won it in 1945 would certainly have to find a new seat for the following election. The London Labour Party had done an analysis in 1943 on the future redistribution of metropolitan seats and had put Hackney top of the list of boroughs due for a reduction in parliamentary representation.[93] His time at South Hackney was therefore bound to be limited. Over and above this, however, he found the local party narrow in its interests, not stimulating enough for him intellectually, cramping his style and limiting the kind of speeches he could make there.[94] Some local activists resented that as a busy minister he had not been able to spend a great deal of time with them.[95] But he was definitely not unpopular and had always paid special attention to the women's section, the core of his loyal support.[96] Even had his constituency relations been perfect, however, he would have wanted to move. He wanted to deal with a wider public.

East Lewisham, close to his Eltham home, was a most attractive seat. The London Labour Party report, mentioned above, proposed giving the borough an extra seat at the next redistribution, thus making sitting MPs safer. The East Lewisham constituency itself had a large electorate of 79,000 in 1945, and the main population inflow since the previous election had been to two huge new council estates, the Dowton and the Bellingham. Once the new electoral register operated these would swell the Labour vote. The local constituency organization was in excellent shape considering the difficulties of war, having maintained a surprisingly high membership over the war years,[97] mainly due to the skill of its agent, Jim Raisin, one of the most capable organizers to work in the Labour Party. Even so, East Lewisham had never been won by Labour and had in 1935 a Tory majority of 6,449. Morrison could hardly claim to be putting his head in a Tory lions' den, but he was taking a risk. This move from Hackney to Lewisham, with its mixture of personal political calculation and genuine high principle, was typical of Morrisonian politics.

The four weeks of the 1945 election were an intensely busy and exciting time for Morrison. He was concurrently managing Labour's national campaign at Transport House, the London campaign at the Westminster Bridge Road headquarters, and fighting to win Lewisham. He also made heavy speaking tours in the provinces.[98] The broad pattern of his activities was to hold a meeting in his constituency each week-day evening and to fit in his organizational work, canvassing and visits to other London constituencies during the rest of the day. At the weekend he travelled far and wide: to Lancashire and North Wales on the weekend of 16 and 17 June, to Southampton and the South West on the twenty-third and twenty-fourth, and to the North East for the last weekend in June. Everywhere he was a major attraction. The public was in a serious mood and interested in politics. People wanted to hear the man who was most identified with Labour's programme of promised post-war reforms. One candidate for whom he spoke recalled that 'Morrison was the biggest man in the party'.[99] It was only appropriate that he was chosen to make Labour's final broadcast to the nation on 29 June. Morrison strode through the campaign like the real leader of the Labour Party and a future leader of his country.

During the last few days before the poll he remained in London. In his constituency Raisin had everything ticking over, though he refused to show his candidate the canvass returns in order not to encourage complacency.[100] Morrison started each day at the constituency headquarters in Brownhill Road. From there he went on his round of canvassing, speeches and meetings. He was driven everywhere in a twenty-four-horsepower Sunbeam Talbot saloon provided by the Royal Arsenal Co-operative Society. His lady driver

M

had previously worked with a private car hire firm. In that capacity, she collected Morrison from the Howard Hotel one day at the beginning of June; by the time they were crossing Waterloo Bridge he had offered her the job as his election chauffeuse, and within a couple of hours he had arranged it all. She found him enjoyable company and immensely considerate to work for, always making sure that she had somewhere to eat while he was at engagements. As they drove around he chatted away and told her stories of his childhood, once asking her to make a detour to the site of his old school. Another time they ran out of petrol while racing back to his constituency from a meeting in Edmonton. The near-by garages were closed but he showed no irritation. He simply chuckled and led her to the local fire station and borrowed eight gallons.[101]

His Lewisham campaign reached a colourful climax when Churchill visited the constituency on the very eve of poll, 4 July. Enormous crowds turned out to hear the great old man speak at Lewisham clock tower. Morrison provocatively directed his own canvassing cavalcade to drive near by.[102] In his speech Churchill described Morrison as 'cowardly' and 'un-British' for having blamed him for the flying bomb tragedy at Lewisham market place, when no warning had been given. 'Of all the colleagues I have lost,' he concluded, 'he is the one I am least sorry to see the last of. I hope that Lewisham will throw the intruder out. He only came here because he ran away from a communist.'[103] Morrison countered at his final meeting at Ladywell Baths, attacking Churchill afresh for allegedly banning warnings for lone flying bombs.[104] With the two wartime comrades and veterans of dealing with the blitz now touring 'bomb alley' denouncing one another, Morrison's 1945 election campaign came to a tumultuous close.

After polling day on Thursday 5 July there was a delay of three weeks before the count, a curious limbo period in which the nation had already made its decision on Britain's post-war government, but politicians of the respective parties did not know if the power was theirs. Morrison still had a little electioneering to do, visiting the North where wakes holidays had delayed the poll. Otherwise he was at last able to take a little rest. Margaret had returned from the west country and they began to get the house in Archery Road back into shape after the wartime neglect. The garden was terribly overgrown with grass and weeds, obscuring the Anderson shelter.[105] Morrison felt unable to predict the election result with any confidence. Earlier he had thought that it might prove very close between Labour and the Tories, and that the Liberals might hold the balance.[106] As the campaign progressed he could not help being struck by the tremendous optimism of local Labour Party workers, but he wrote that off as amateur enthusiasm.[107] Even a professional could only wait and hope till 26 July.*

---

* Attlee and Dalton each thought that Labour could win no more than 290 seats and so would not have a majority. (Attlee to Dalton, 13 July 1945. Dalton papers 1945.)

Chapter 25

Labour Into Power, July 1945

Morrison attended the count at East Lewisham on the morning of 26 July. His comfortable victory* in a seat considered marginal augured well for the national result. He then sped off to Transport House to join Attlee and other party leaders, listening as the results came in over the radio. Morrison, according to his own story,[1] was now fairly optimistic, though others sensed that he was unsure about the outcome.[2]

The first intimations of the impending massive victory for Labour came at twenty-five minutes past ten with the news that Harold Macmillan was beaten at Stockton-on-Tees. Before the day was out five members of the caretaker Cabinet and eight senior ministers of Cabinet rank had lost their seats. The national swing to Labour since 1935 averaged twelve per cent; in London it was seventeen per cent. Labour won 179 seats from the Conservatives and lost none to them. Seventy-nine constituencies, many of them the kind of middle-class suburban seats which Morrison had so long and so ardently wooed, were won for the first time. Labour had secured 393 seats and had a majority of 146 over all other parties and groups in the House.[3] There was to be a Labour government for the first time in fourteen years and for the first time in British political history it was to be a Labour government in full power, with a clear and overwhelming majority enabling it to carry out its great promised programme of reform.

Before the grand affairs of state could be tackled, however, a number of problems within the Labour Party remained to be settled. First was the question of the party leadership and hence, now, of the prime-ministership of the country. Morrison, Attlee, Bevin and the party Secretary, Morgan Phillips, gathered for informal talks in Bevin's room at Transport House during the afternoon of the twenty-sixth, while Laski and other members of the NEC were in the Secretary's room still listening to the results on the radio.[4] A message arrived from Winston Churchill conceding defeat and informing Attlee that he would go to the palace to resign at seven o'clock that

* Figures: Morrison 37,361; Pownall (Conservative) 22,142; Russell (Independent) 931.

evening. Churchill added that he would advise the King to send for Attlee to form the new government. At this point Morrison interposed and suggested that Attlee should not accept any such invitation from the monarch until after a meeting of the Parliamentary Labour Party had been held to elect its leader.* Morrison also, according to Attlee, 'expressed reluctance to serve under me as he thought the Party might want him as Prime Minister'.[5] Both Attlee and Bevin resisted Morrison's argument. During the discussion the telephone rang in an adjoining room and the caller, Sir Stafford Cripps, spoke to Morrison. According to Morrison when he returned to join his colleagues, Cripps supported his view.[6] But Bevin was quite adamant and, while Morrison was out of the room, had urged Attlee to go quickly to the palace and so settle the question once and for all. Attlee† probably needed little urging from his trade union friend and colleague. After taking late tea with his family at the Great Western Hotel, Paddington, he was driven by his wife to the palace in their little Austin car and there accepted the King's commission to try to form a Labour government.

Morrison's action on the afternoon of 26 July fitted in with his customary image as a conspirator and ambitious for power in the Labour Party. Certainly it irritated Bevin and confirmed once again his view that Morrison was a trickster who could not be trusted and who would play for personal power even on the day of the party's greatest triumph. According to Dalton, Bevin at one point telephoned Morrison angrily and warned him 'if you go on mucking about like this, you won't be in the bloody Government at all'.[7]

Bevin knew, as did most other people in the top ranks of the Labour Party and in the press, that for some time there had been moves to replace Attlee by Morrison as leader of the party. The main people publicly identified in this agitation were Maurice Webb and Ellen Wilkinson, both close friends and political associates of Morrison. Harold Laski, the chairman of the NEC and Professor of Political Science at the London School of Economics, had also campaigned to get Attlee out since 1942, hoping to replace him with either Morrison or Bevin.[8] Laski was well to the left of Morrison in the party, but there was considerable mutual respect between them.‡ Aneurin Bevan followed Cripps in assuming that there would be a leadership election before forming a government and personally preferred Morrison to Attlee.[9] The left

---

* Dalton suggests that Morrison had already, as had Laski, written Attlee a letter along these same lines. (H. Dalton, *The Fateful Years* (1957), p. 468.)

† Attlee refers to this episode in his draft (unpublished) autobiography: 'There was some little difficulty with Morrison who had some idea that he ought to be Prime Minister ... The idea was fantastic and certainly out of harmony with the feeling of the Party.' (Attlee papers, Vol. 1/17.)

‡ Morrison once rebuked a parliamentary colleague who was denouncing Laski as just an intellectual. 'There is a difference between intellectuals who rise *with* the Labour Movement and those who rise *on* it,' he pointed out. 'I object to those who rise on the movement. Laski rose with it.' (Interview, A. Lewis.) Morrison tried to get Laski a peerage later, though without success. (*Autobiography*, p. 238.)

felt that Attlee was 'lacking in punch'.[10] Others in the parliamentary party and trade union leaders outside conveyed to Morrison during 1944 and 1945 their preference for him as leader.* Laski and Ellen Wilkinson were openly canvassing for a leadership change at the Blackpool party conference in May 1945. Shortly afterwards Wilkinson approached Hugh Dalton privately to ask him to persuade Attlee to retire in favour of Morrison, but Dalton declined on the grounds that it was 'impossible to change now'.[11] Laski wrote directly to Attlee telling him bluntly to go and also asked Arthur Deakin to sound out Bevin on whether he would be willing to take over, but with equal lack of success in both endeavours.[12] The campaign received assistance (perhaps inspired) in the press. The *Evening Standard* in the middle of the election campaign carried a large profile of Morrison describing him as the 'most striking personal success' among Labour's younger generation. The article referred to Attlee disparagingly as a mere 'caretaker' and then went on to describe Morrison's outstanding qualities of honesty, incorruptibility and decision-making, all clearly in terms of his qualifications for the Labour leadership.[13]

In his *Autobiography* Morrison wrote blandly: 'I was disturbed to learn that moves had begun to propose me as Leader of the Party in place of Attlee. I promptly took steps to see that these activities stopped.'[14] It is difficult to believe, however, that he had not known all along of the campaign on his behalf or that he was so deeply shocked by it. Certainly the pressure against Attlee on behalf of Morrison did not cease even with electoral victory. That night, on Thursday, 26 July, the Labour Party held a great Victory Rally in Westminster Central Hall. Morrison, who arrived in his own little private car – and had his usual trouble trying to park it[15] – was in very high spirits. One observer wrote: 'I have never seen Mr Morrison happier than he was at the Westminster Central Hall rally. Beaming, sometimes boyish, always impish, he was good old Herbert even to those who had never before set eyes on him ... wiping the perspiration from his brow, he said, "It really is a great occasion, isn't it?" The Hall was packed with people standing at the sides, and at the back, and the whole audience joined in community singing – "John Brown's Body", "Three Blind Mice", all the great community songs.'[16] Not all, however, was innocent pleasure and collective joy. Even at this late stage Morrison and his friends were canvassing Labour Members of Parliament at the rally and urging them to support the demand, which Morrison had put to Attlee and Bevin that afternoon in Transport House, that the parliamentary party should have an opportunity for a free vote on the leadership. Morrison himself took to one side Jim Raisin and 'Puck' Boon who had helped with publicity in his constituency, and said: 'There is a chance I shall be offered

---

* Dalton reported the formation of a group of Labour MPs in 1944 to press for a change in the leadership, with a preference for Morrison. (Dalton diary, 18 October 1944, Vol. 31.) Other MPs and trade unionists used Raisin as an intermediary to urge Morrison himself to take the initiative in seizing the leadership. (Interview, J. Raisin.)

the premiership. I am not sure I am big enough to do it. What do you think ?'[17] He approached John Parker entering the gentlemen's lavatory and said 'we cannot have this man as our leader', but Parker, like Dalton, felt it was now too late to change.[18] Morrison also sent for George Isaacs, the president of his union, NATSOPA, and asked him to write a letter urging Attlee not to go to the palace yet but to wait until after the next day's party meeting.[19] A stop was put to these activities, at the rally at least, when Attlee arrived direct from the palace to announce from the platform that he had already accepted the King's invitation to form a government. The ringing cheers of approval that greeted this gave Attlee's action the stamp of the *fait accompli* which Bevin had intended when advising it in the afternoon.[20]

Morrison did not let the matter drop. On the next afternoon, Friday the twenty-seventh, there was a meeting at Transport House of the former Administrative Committee of the PLP, with Attlee, already Prime Minister, in the chair.* After Attlee had made an opening statement that it was urgent for him to establish at least a skeleton government to take over the administration while he and the Foreign Secretary were at Potsdam, Morrison intervened to raise the question of the leadership.[21] He referred to the decisions arrived at by the party in 1933 after the MacDonald débâcle and pointed out that these provided that certain formalities should be gone through in connection with the formation of a Labour government. The most immediately relevant of these provisions, he suggested, was that before any offer to form a government could be accepted, the Parliamentary Labour Party should first meet to elect its leader, either confirming the existing incumbent or selecting a new one.[22] Morrison was indeed constitutionally correct in reminding them that after 1931 the NEC had drawn up a long list of recommendations concerning what procedures should be followed when next Labour contemplated forming an administration. These covered the election of the executive committee of the parliamentary party, the selection of ministers, liaison with back-benchers etc., and they were overwhelmingly approved by the 1933 Hastings conference. The resolution definitely and specifically stated that the parliamentary party should meet to decide whether or not to form a government and that first it should consult the NEC and the General Council of the TUC. It did not, however – and this was where Morrison made a misinterpretation – say anything about electing the leader before he accepted the premiership. The original brief to the NEC in 1931 had seemed to ask for that, calling on them to examine the procedures 'with regard to the choice of Premier and Members of the Government'[23] but their subsequent report contained no reference to the 'choice of Premier'. It did insist on elections of a new executive committee for the parliamentary party as quickly as possible after the general election, and this could be interpreted as implying a leader-

* The Administrative Committee was set up in 1940 to provide liaison between back-benchers and Labour ministers in the Coalition. It contained the elected members of the Parliamentary Executive Committee, together with the officers of the party.

ship election before forming a government[24], but it did not specifically say so. In any case, the Administrative Committee did not seem very concerned to follow to the letter the strict procedures laid down in the very different circumstances of 1933. Attlee was now at least consulting them – though not the NEC and the TUC – and they authorized him to go ahead with the formation of his new government. The meeting which began at 3.00 p.m. was over in half an hour.[25]

Morrison hardly emerged from this episode with complete credit. He may have simply been trying to follow the party's constitution, but his interpretation of the 1933 rules was open to question, while his personal interest in provoking a leadership contest was embarrassingly obvious to all. Attlee, while clearly not very concerned with the 1933 decision, did not blatantly go against it, at least getting authorization from the Administrative Committee. He was anyway more concerned with the constitution of the country than of the party. 'If you are invited by the King to form a Government, you don't say you can't reply for forty-eight hours. You accept the Commission and you either bring it off successfully or you don't, and if you don't, you go back and say you can't and advise the King to send for someone else.'[26] It also seemed to Attlee and to many others at the time, and still seems now, somewhat ridiculous to suggest that a leader who had campaigned at the head of the party in the general election, and for whom a majority of the people had voted, should not then become Prime Minister but should be replaced by someone else whose candidature had not previously been declared and explained to the electorate. Had Labour lost, then the situation would have been different. A leadership contest would have been acceptable – and Morrison, as the dominant national figure in the party at this time, would probably have been elected.[27] But Labour won under Attlee's leadership and so Morrison's personal endeavours were doomed to defeat, as well as damaging him in the eyes of his colleagues. It was curious that he should have pursued this matter to the very end. Morrison was normally a man of immense common sense, practicality and acute awareness of what was and was not politically possible. In this episode he behaved strangely out of character. Interestingly, he also behaved oddly in 1935 and again in 1955 when the Labour leadership was more legitimately open to his grasp. Morrison spent much of his life dreaming of attaining the pinnacle of power in the Labour Party, but whenever he came within sight of it he appeared to dither and to lose some of his customary control, confidence and judgment. In his *Autobiography*, which is as unrevealing on these events as on many others, Morrison states that other people had pressed him to support the case for a forty-eight-hour delay and simply adds that this point was raised at the committee meeting.[28] He nowhere admits that he personally raised it. He gives the impression that he was not a wholehearted supporter of this argument. The clear implication of what he wrote is that other people were the real source of the agitation for a delay in order to hold a leadership election; and that he did not feel strongly about the question, supporting the case on the objective constitutional grounds that an earlier NEC had prescribed such an election, but quite convinced that there was no question that he or any other candidate would displace Attlee. It is, of course, possible that he was indeed, as he here suggests, merely acting as the spokesman for other people who did have good constitutional arguments on their side. He may have acted in this way, without commitment, without illusions, and without personal hopes. But it seems more likely that hindsight and the desire to play down his ambitions, which run throughout his memoirs, led him to claim retrospectively more detachment and clarity than was apparent at the time. It seems much more likely that in July 1945 Morrison was in an extremely confused state of mind, experiencing a mixture of motives, suffering concurrently from an ambitious urge to grab any opportunity to get the leadership, a sense of loyalty to friends and followers who had campaigned on his behalf, and a nagging awareness that a change of leadership at this point was simply not on.

Morrison went to see Attlee and the Chief Whip about his own position in the Labour Cabinet on the morning of 27 July; he apparently discussed his own ministerial appointment on the fairly firm assumption that Attlee would be the Prime Minister who disposed of offices. He first asked for the Foreign Office.[29]

Apart from any genuine interest in foreign affairs, Morrison in his bid for the foreign secretaryship was probably making some calculations about power relationships in the Cabinet. Traditionally, the two senior posts were the Foreign Office and the Treasury. The two senior Labour politicians in his and in most other people's minds, apart from Attlee, were Bevin and himself. Morrison was aware that he ought to have one or the other of these positions to preserve his status. A serious point against the Treasury was that it had been somewhat downgraded during the war; in 1945 the Foreign Office seemed of slightly higher political status. Morrison also knew that Bevin was particularly interested in taxation questions and was rather looking forward to taking on the Exchequer. He probably went to see Attlee having in mind that the most convenient arrangement to all concerned would be if he took the Foreign Office and Bevin went to the Exchequer, though he was certainly not adamant about this. Attlee, with his normal shrewd appreciation and ability to fit the best men to the most appropriate jobs, resisted Morrison's pressure. But he satisfied Morrison's concern about his position in the party hierarchy. When Morrison 'asked to be number two', Attlee recalled, 'I readily accepted'.[30]

When resisting Morrison's claim for the Foreign Office, Attlee suggested as an alternative that Morrison should take not the Treasury but the Lord Presidency of the Council, acting as a sort of overlord on the home front, together with the deputy prime ministership and the leadership of the House of Commons. Morrison at first refused, aware that a co-ordinating minister without portfolio is at a disadvantage in any confrontation with a great department of state. But the Chief Whip pressed him to take it, and he accepted.[31] At that point Attlee still apparently intended to send Bevin to the Exchequer and Dalton to the Foreign Office.* By the afternoon of the twenty-seventh, certainly by the end of the meeting of the Administrative Committee, Attlee had decided to reverse the responsibilities of Bevin and Dalton. Morrison claims in his *Autobiography*[32] that he was responsible for the switch, having given advice to that end to Attlee. There are several other claimants to the role of influencing Attlee's mind on these two positions.[33] Attlee has staked out his own modest but convincing, claim for having taken the decision himself. Bevin, whom he described as a 'tank', and who had made an excellent speech on foreign affairs at the 1945 conference, seemed better suited than Dalton to deal with the Russians. The bad relationship between Morrison and Bevin was another, and probably decisive, reason for Attlee to allocate them distinct spheres of operation. 'Ernie and Herbert didn't get on together,' he said, 'if you'd put both on the home front there might have been trouble.'[34]

This antipathy between the two Labour leaders undoubtedly originated from Bevin. A man of great and ranging vision in many ways, Bevin also had many mean qualities, and could descend to petty spite when dealing with people he did not like or trust. The distinguished and suffering company of his enemies over the years included Citrine and Beaverbrook as well as Morrison and many lesser trade unionists who had crossed his path. His distrust of these colleagues and former colleagues – like his unquestioning trust of others, such as Attlee – once held, was unshakeable and found endless forms of expression. The bad blood between him and Morrison certainly did not arise because the latter was in any way anti-trade union or was unacceptable to trade unionists. Morrison maintained long and good relations with many trade union leaders.[35] He did, however, often insist on taking a view wider than just the trade union interest, and this threw him frequently into conflict with Bevin. In such conflicts Morrison firmly stood his ground. Bevin did not appreciate such acts of resistance, not a familiar experience in the transport workers' union. He regarded people who disagreed with him over policy as carrying out a personal vendetta against him – his 'Corsican concept of public business' as one close observer described it.[36] He also resented the independent political bases – London, the Labour party machine and the parliamentary party – from which Morrison was able to make his stand against the big trade union boss.[37] Morrison's political reputation, with its overtones of sharp dexterity and even deviousness, aroused Bevin's hatred of all he suspected of trickiness. 'It was

---

* On 13 July, Attlee had written to Dalton: 'I understand from Ernest Bevin that he is not in the running [for the Foreign Office]. His ideas turn in another direction, and I agree with you that the Home Front is his sphere.' (Dalton papers.) Dalton had asked for the Foreign Office himself and advised Bevin to the Exchequer, and Bevin had personally asked for the Chancellorship on the twenty-sixth. (A. Bullock, *The Life and Times of Ernest Bevin*, Vol. II (1967), p. 393. Dalton diary, 16 May 1945, Vol. 32.)

an unreasoning hatred', recalled a journalist who knew both men well, 'he called Morrison a scheming little bastard. He thought there was a catch to everything he did.'[38] The events of the twenty-four hours after the election victory certainly strengthened this view of Morrison in Bevin's eyes. Soon after the new government was in office in 1945, Bevin sent for Francis Williams, the Prime Minister's adviser on public relations, and urged him to 'keep your eye on 'Erbert when I'm not 'ere, Francis. Let me know if he gets up to any of his tricks. I wouldn't trust the little bugger any further than I could throw him.'[39] Again, later, when there was a clash over whether the overseas information services should be under the Foreign Office or the Lord President's Office, Bevin told his PPS, Christopher Mayhew, to go along to the relevant committee meeting with Morrison and to 'look out for his tricks'.[40] Morrison never understood this unrelenting suspicion and dislike and hoped to make a reconciliation.[41] Mayhew, who was successively PPS to each of them after 1945, tried to build bridges but could make no progress with Bevin, who nurtured his hates and was as unwilling to surrender them as he was to give up members to another union.[42]

That Friday night Attlee issued his first list of appointments to constitute a 'skeleton government' which he had told the Administrative Committee must be formed prior to his departure with the Foreign Secretary to Potsdam. Apart from Morrison, Bevin and Dalton, Greenwood, Cripps and Jowitt made up the first phalanx of the new government. Next morning, Saturday, Churchill's caretaker government formally resigned and Morrison, together with the other newly appointed ministers, went to the palace to take their seals of office. They drove straight back from the palace to the Beaver Hall in the City for a meeting of the new Parliamentary Labour Party at eleven o'clock. Ellen Wilkinson was still agitating to replace Attlee with Morrison. The evening before she had gathered together at the Newcastle Station Hotel the newly-elected Labour MPs from the North East who were about to take the overnight train to London. She urged them to support a motion to elect Morrison as leader which she promised would be moved at next morning's party meeting.[43] At Beaver Hall she approached Edith Summerskill in the ladies' toilet and tried in vain to get her support.[44] Undeterred, she argued with Leah Manning at the meeting itself that Attlee must be replaced. 'He's no good. We must have Herbert.'[45] But Bevin was introduced to the excited meeting as the new Foreign Secretary and he took the opportunity promptly to move a vote of confidence in Attlee as leader of the party and the new Prime Minister. This was immediately seconded by Arthur Greenwood and supported by George Isaacs, representing the trade union MPs. It was carried by acclamation, thus finally burying in the triumphant unity of the party any last traces of rebellion against Attlee's leadership. Attlee then spoke, promising that he would proceed immediately to implement Labour's election manifesto.[46] He then left the meeting with Bevin to fly to Potsdam until 2 August. Before going he handed over the chair to Morrison, in this way establishing him publicly before the party as deputy leader. It was a moment full of irony and symbolism. Morrison, the perpetual claimant to the throne, the potential beneficiary from a succession of moves to displace Attlee, was left to run the meeting, the party, and the skeleton Cabinet. He had some of the realities of power, some of the trappings and the prestige, much of the responsibility, but not the satisfaction of the highest office. It was a scene and a situation that was to be repeated often in the years of government ahead. Morrison did much of the hard work, but while Attlee had Bevin loyally at his shoulder he could walk out, leaving his deputy in charge, confident that the ultimate power would lie with him.

Chapter 26

At Work as Lord President in the Labour Government

As the new Labour government settled down in the late summer of 1945 to deal with its tremendous programme, Herbert Morrison was personally faced with a remarkable range of tasks and offices. Without in any way belittling the tremendous stature of Ernest Bevin at the Foreign Office or the qualities of Attlee as Prime Minister, there is little doubt that Morrison was the most important single dynamo in the government's machine. The breadth of his responsibilities was perhaps unprecedented in modern government.

Morrison's most prestigious Cabinet task was to act as Attlee's deputy when the Prime Minister was away for any reason. He was not formally appointed to be deputy prime minister, a post of no constitutional legitimacy in Britain, but Attlee had assured him that he would be second in the Cabinet hierarchy. He took charge of the government when Attlee flew to Potsdam in July, and again when the Prime Minister visited Truman in Washington in November. Henceforward he automatically presided over the Cabinet in Attlee's absence.

Morrison's formal duties as Lord President of the Council were not very onerous.* He was responsible for the work of the Privy Council Office and presented the business to the King and Council when it met, which was not very frequently. The real and continuous burden of Morrison's work as a Cabinet minister lay in his role as the chief co-ordinating minister on the home front. He achieved this co-ordination through his chairmanship of the Lord

* The Lord President of the Council is one of the oldest offices of state which goes back to when the Privy Council was the King's main instrument of government. The office was created in 1497. An Act of Henry VIII laid down that the Lord President, together with the Lord Chancellor, the Treasurer and the Lord Privy Seal, should, if they were Peers, take their place among the highest members of the Peerage. The office continued as part of the nucleus of the emerging Cabinet in the seventeenth and eighteenth centuries. As a relic of this period, the Lord President must attend meetings of the Privy Council when he submits the various Orders in Council to the King for approval. He is also responsible for supervising the activities of various organizations which operate under royal charters, such as many schools and charitable foundations.

President's Committee, which contained most senior Cabinet ministers from domestic departments. It acted as a sort of preliminary Cabinet and clearing-house for domestic policy issues, from items of minor detail up to the broadest questions of national planning.*

The range of items coming before Morrison's full Lord President's Committee was quite remarkable. Its first meeting was on 19 August 1945. By September its agenda covered white fish, new towns, national parks, food supplies, house-building, the national fire service, coal nationalization and a memorial to the late President Roosevelt. In April 1946 it was discussing river boards, the film industry, a new institute of management and a proposed increase in railway fares. By the autumn they were faced by problems concerning metal prices, the disposal of war surplus goods, legal aid, relations between government and the universities, wages policy, agricultural policy, the scheduled economic survey, foreign exchange control, fruit and vegetable imports, and the proposals to introduce driving tests and abridged birth certificates. The whole spectrum of domestic government passed before Morrison's chair.

Morrison's responsibility to co-ordinate ministers as well as policies was essential to the efficient working of the government. Some ministers lacked experience in office and in Parliament; others were widely acknowledged to be of poor calibre and would turn to Morrison for guidance.[1] Morrison's PPS, who took notes at the meetings of the nationalizing ministers, recalled that 'Herbert held their hands; for example, Barnes asked Morrison what to do and how to do it . . . and that went for a lot of the nationalizing Ministers.'[2] All could benefit from Morrison's mastery of administrative and parliamentary procedure. A young law officer recalled that 'Morrison influenced me tremendously. He knew far more than I would ever know about the parliamentary reaction to political proposals . . . the Government of 1945 was to some extent working in the dark and Morrison's sane and experienced guiding hand was tremendously valuable.'[3]

In addition to general co-ordination in the domestic field, three particular jobs of great importance were placed under Morrison's responsibility in 1945–7: to co-ordinate national economic planning and development; to shape and co-ordinate the proposed measures of nationalization; and to plan the

* Attlee described its functions as similar to those carried out by the Lord President's Committee in the war, when it was left to run the home front while the Prime Minister and Cabinet ran the war. 'It deals authoritatively with the taking of decisions which do not need to come to full Cabinet, with settling inter-departmental differences prior to their coming to the Cabinet.' (Draft autobiography, Vol. 1/17.) This comparison with Anderson's full wartime committee, though helpful, is not precise. From 1945 the Prime Minister and the other senior Cabinet ministers were more interested in, and more likely to interfere in, domestic policy than had been the case in the war. In this sense, 'the Cabinet reasserted itself and this meant that the role of the Lord President's Committee was inevitably diminished.' (Johnstone Interview.) Bevin, Attlee and (until 1947) Greenwood had similar, but less extensive co-ordinating roles after 1945 in the fields of foreign affairs, defence and social services respectively.

timetable of Labour's whole programme of legislation over the next five years. Each of these was pursued through the growing network of Cabinet committees and sub-committees, which had been a feature of Churchill's wartime administration and was now further developed under Labour.[4]

The Lord President's Office itself was structured to deal with the policy areas covering the first two of these more concrete of Morrison's functions. One small but highly important section, under Max Nicholson, was concerned with economic co-ordination.* A man of mercurial intelligence, firing off ideas like a catherine-wheel, Nicholson had been a leading advocate of national planning before the war at the Political and Economic Planning research institute. His was the kind of fertile and radical mind which Morrison liked to work with and, selectively, to plunder. There was, however, a price to be paid. Nicholson was not considered 'sound' by the Treasury mandarins, who were irritated by his enthusiasms, his irreverence and his undisguised hostility towards them. This was to be one important problem in Morrison's future losing battle to maintain economic planning under his control.[5]

Nicholson was formally head of the Lord President's Office, with the rank of under-secretary. In practice, he shared responsibility with Alexander Johnstone, he taking economic planning and Johnstone handling the nationalization programme. In total number, even including the scientific secretariat added in 1947,[6] Morrison's department was small, but in calibre it was very high. Johnstone and Nicholson were intellectual heavyweights. John Pimlott, who had been Morrison's private secretary at the Home Office and Home Security since 1944, continued to run the private office with great ability and tact, assisted by a succession of bright young civil servants destined for higher places – D. O. Henley, G. R. Downes, David Stephens, William Murrie and Martin Flett. Morrison's four successive PPSs – Christopher Mayhew,† Patrick Gordon Walker, Stephen Taylor and Edward Shackleton – were of similarly high calibre, containing two future Cabinet ministers, one very able future junior minister, and a future university vice-chancellor. Morrison liked to give opportunities and experience to the bright young men in the party: he involved these PPSs in his work, showing them papers, asking their views, and getting them to write memoranda.[7] They were also, significantly, all middle-class intellectuals. Morrison always surrounded himself with people who had the qualities and education that he lacked.

---

* This economic planning position had originally been allocated to John Maud, but he rapidly moved on. Morrison then, typically, inquired in Labour Party circles for a recommendation of an economic adviser who was independent of the Treasury and did not share the Treasury's ignorance of and hostility towards planning. Nicholson, who was in Washington for the Ministry of Transport and about to leave the civil service, was suggested as fitting the bill. (Interview, M. Nicholson.)

† Mayhew was recommended by Attlee, a fellow old-Haileyburian. Morrison sent Ellen Wilkinson to inspect Mayhew before taking him on in August 1945. (Interview, C. Mayhew.)

Morrison's role as chief economic co-ordinator in the first two years of the post-war Labour Government has remained shadowy, both in his own and in other people's books describing this period. This is understandable. His job in this field was defined only in general terms. Most of his work was done in committees out of the public eye, and these were themselves often concerned with co-ordinating the work of other still more hidden inter-departmental committees. Such activities leave little public mark; they also tend to be complex and far from exciting when described in print. This economic function was, however, of considerable importance. The economic situation had rapidly moved into crisis within weeks of Labour taking office in July 1945. The sudden end to the Japanese war was in one sense an embarrassment: government planners had relied on a longer period between Germany's surrender and the complete return of peace to re-establish Britain's export markets. With the Japanese surrender came the end of American Lend-Lease aid, which had bridged our yawning balance of payments gap for some years of the war. Keynes saw Britain with three choices: what he called 'Starvation Corner', 'Temptation', and 'Justice'. Starvation corner was ignoring outside aid and living a life of economic isolation, planning and rationing as Soviet Russia did in the 1920s. Temptation was to take massive American loan assistance on their terms and live henceforward as an American subsidiary. Justice was the recognition by our allies – to whom we owed money – that it had been spent in their cause and therefore they ought to provide Britain with large loans without too many strings. During the early months that Morrison was Lord President, Keynes and his team were in the United States attempting to negotiate justice. They finally secured a loan, but hardly on terms that could be described as justice, and so Britain had to face its transition from war to peace in financial conditions likely seriously to cramp reconstruction at every turn.[8] Britain had to pay her allies a price for defending democracy short only of the price Germany paid for attacking it. It was a crisis that from the beginning clouded the prospect for making the kind of increases in public expenditure essential if Labour were to carry out its promised social revolution.

Morrison led a troika of ministers responsible for economic development and planning. He was personally in charge of what was termed the Central Planning of Economic Development, and the specific operation of physical controls, as well as co-ordinating the other ministers. Hugh Dalton ran financial and budgetary policy at a Treasury still depressed by its wartime downgrading, though fighting to re-establish its dominance in Whitehall.[9] Stafford Cripps was at the Board of Trade, junior in political status within the trio in 1945, but a voracious worker, building up close contacts with industry, and ambitious to extend his political domain.[10]

This team of economic ministers under Morrison hoped to carry out the party's election manifesto promise to 'Plan from the ground up, giving an appropriate place to constructive enterprise and private endeavour in the national plan.' The precise machinery for this promised planning, and any relevance of it to Labour's assumed socialist scheme, had never been established by the party: only the general statement of intent. Morrison himself was by inclination a devoted planner: whether at home, or in the LCC, or in Whitehall, he liked things ordered and he liked to do some of the ordering. But as he grew older, alienated by the depressing Russian example of full socialist planning, convinced that the British people would not support or accept the political revolution which it implied, and increasingly attached to the mixed economy and to *ad hoc* public interventions, the gulf between him and more dogmatic socialist planners widened. He was by this time basically a pragmatist, operating the government planning machine to maintain an ordered economy during the major transition from war to peace, to mitigate the inefficiencies and barbarities of capitalism, and above all to secure full employment.

Morrison did not create Labour's planning machinery, he inherited much of it from the war, when a succession of Lord Presidents – Neville Chamberlain, Sir John Anderson, and Attlee – had held over-all responsibility for this broad economic field.* In peace, the economic objectives were elevated among national priorities, with the commitment to high employment in the 1944 White Paper as a cornerstone. The existing planning machinery was quickly adapted for its enhanced post-war role. Edward Bridges in the Cabinet Office played a major role in this, in consultation with Morrison and especially, right from the beginning, with Cripps. Economic development and departmental co-ordination were to be achieved† – or at least attempted – through Morrison's Lord President's Committee, which was composed of most senior ministers. Much of the detailed work of economic planning was done, however, in the network of sub-committees of ministers or of civil servants which reported either to the Lord President's Committee or directly to the Cabinet.‡

Morrison was advised on macro-economic planning by the Official Steering Committee on Economic Development. By September 1945 it had already decided to draw up a national economic plan. This would involve forecasting the productive output and demand for materials and labour of individual

---

* By the end of the war the Ministry of Production was the chief co-ordinating ministry and, where industry was concerned, the Ministry of Supply and the Board of Trade did the work.

† The exception was overseas economic policy which was at first placed under a separate committee headed by the Prime Minister. This division and diffusion was later felt to be a weakness in the economic machinery and greater centralization was introduced in the reorganization of September 1947.

‡ The relevant committee was the Ministerial Economic Planning Committee, serviced by the Official Steering Committee on Economic Development, containing top civil servants from departments involved. These proved too large for effective action and the main work was done by a small 'nuclear group' of officials and another of ministers – Morrison, Dalton, Cripps and Isaacs (Minister of Labour).

industries as well as of the economy as a whole. Individual departments were asked to submit their particular needs and plans for the financial year 1946–7 and this initial stage was completed by December 1945. The national plan was to proceed in two stages: first would come an Economic Survey of resources, and then would follow discussions and decisions to adapt economic policy to meet national needs in the light of that detailed survey. The Economic Survey was built up from information requested from individual departments in October. The Steering group then gathered and assessed this economic intelligence, prepared forecasts and proposed plans. Servicing it were three working parties: on manpower capability, on investment capability and on trends in imports and exports. They produced the raw material information which was collated into a national balance sheet of manpower, national income and expenditure, and overseas payments and receipts. In this way gaps between demand and resources available were supposed to be revealed. From the autumn of 1946 Morrison was urging the Steering Committee to move towards longer-term planning, proposing that they should produce a five-year survey projecting the economy to 1950. He also pressed for the recruitment of more economists to strengthen his planning team.

When it came to implementing the broad economic strategy, the most important micro-economic function Morrison carried out related to the allocation of resources. He had taken over from the war a wide armoury of physical controls – over production, over manpower and over distribution of resources. Direct controls over most areas of industrial production were in practice abandoned after 1945 and manpower planning covered little more than demobilization. Controls over the allocation of essential raw materials, however, had to be maintained to keep some order of priority in markets disrupted by shortages of supply and the demobilization of the war economy.

His Lord President's Committee, and the other economic sub-committees, listened to the case for allocating raw materials to one industry or department rather than another, and then allocated the limited supplies accordingly among successful claimants. Building was also controlled, in theory at least, by Morrison through a system of building licences. It was not easy decision-making. It led him at times into fierce clashes with colleagues.[11] In some cases decisions were complicated by the fact that the amount of one resource available, such as steel, would depend on the previous allocation of another essential raw material, such as coal. They were faced, as Morrison said, 'with the reconciliation of the irreconcilable'.[12]

Morrison was proud of the job he did as economic co-ordinator. He claimed that Britain at this time 'was the first great nation to attempt to combine large-scale social and economic planning with a full measure of individual rights and liberty. Planning as it is taking shape in this country under our eyes, is something new and constructively revolutionary which will be regarded in times to come as a contribution to civilization as vital and distinctly British as parliamentary democracy under the rule of law.'[13]

Other commentators were then and subsequently a little more sceptical of Morrison's economic achievements. 'He is spreading a veneer of planning gospel over a vast deal of higgledy-piggledy departmental practice,' observed the *Financial Times*.[14] Officials who worked close to Morrison, and admired him, shared the general view that he was not really suited to his planning job: 'he did not move easily in the higher sphere of economics',[15] as one adviser put it.

Ministers do not, of course, have to be trained experts in their field. They need to master their subject sufficiently to ask the right questions, to listen to expert advice, and to have judgment and clarity in taking decisions based on that advice. Morrison in fact had all these requisite abilities. He was interested and keen on planning in principle.[16] He certainly worked tremendously hard at his economics. Nicholson recalled him taking home economic reports, reading them through the night, and next day asking pertinent questions based on a mastery of the broad detail as well as the general argument.[17] What he lacked was something deeper, a flair, a feel, and a developed instinct for economic decisions. His upbringing, his education and his work experience, apart from personal inclination, had left lacunae in his capabilities. These were exposed when he came to deal with industry at the Ministry of Supply in 1940, with economic planning after 1945* – and with foreign affairs a few years later. This failure to master the economic field might not have mattered too much if the institutional machinery had been well devised to bring out his virtues and cushion his failings. After all, most ministers are not wholly suited to most departments. The machinery was, however, too fractured, too diffuse, with too much advice, often conflicting, coming in from different directions. Morrison was supposed to co-ordinate, but the channels of advice and decision-making were too shadowy and rambling for him ever to get matters firmly in his hands. Had he possessed more knowledge and assurance in this field he might have imposed more order, but he did not have them. Equally important was the fact that the Treasury was not centrally involved in his economic planning empire. Economic planning simply could not work apart from the senior finance department. As the Treasury after 1945 gradually reasserted its traditional pre-eminence in Whitehall, tensions and jealousies built up between it and the Lord President's Office,† in which Morrison's little team, although distinguished and high powered, was bound to lose.[18]

Morrison's responsibility for co-ordinating Labour's nationalization programme was much more suited to his interests and talents than was his

---

* Clem Leslie noticed this weakness also at the Home Office in the war, when he briefed Morrison on economic questions coming before the War Cabinet. He 'had to push Herbert and pull him along in economic matters. He wasn't up to it.' (Interview, S. C. Leslie.)

† Nicholson claimed that 'even before 1947 the Treasury did its best to make sure that Morrison was only titular, not effective economic manager. Morrison was never allowed to carry out the role properly.' (Interview.)

economic brief. He worked through the important Socialization of Industry Committee, which he chaired, with Alex Johnstone as Secretary.* The ministers responsible for particular Acts of nationalization – Shinwell, Barnes, Wilmot, Winster, and, later, Gaitskell – submitted memoranda to Morrison's committee setting out their proposals for the organization, structure and finance of the new publicly-owned undertakings, together with suggestions for the basis of compensation, the powers of the relevant minister, opportunities and channels of complaint and influence for the consumer, the position of labour, pensions for workers, etc. The committee sifted these proposals, advised on them and reported to the Cabinet, after which the bills themselves were drafted and re-submitted to this committee, as well as to the Future Legislation Committee (again with Morrison in the chair), and finally, to the Cabinet.[19] Morrison took an active role and interest, not only in formal meetings but also through personal chats with ministers in private corners. Shinwell recalled Morrison often 'interfering' but conceded it was helpful interference because he 'was so well informed'.[20] Morrison, rather than the individual ministers, took the initiative in recruiting members for the new nationalized boards. He asked a trusted industrial journalist to approach Arthur Horner, the communist miners' leader, to drop his communist affiliations and join the new Coal Board. The journalist broached the subject to Horner at a dawn meeting. Horner, squatting like Buddha on his hotel bed drinking tea, replied, 'no, for two reasons. I couldn't face the contempt of my old comrades on the left and I would find intolerable the sceptical sneers of my new comrades in the Labour Party.' Horner knew the emissary was from Morrison and told him, 'you are the third in the last fortnight'.[21] Morrison sent another friend to approach Lord Reith to ask if he would take charge of either the nationalized gas or electricity industries. Reith turned them down on the grounds that neither would keep him fully stretched – though he would have considered the railways a more serious proposition had they come on offer.[22] In the transport field Morrison dominated the Minister, Barnes, and even himself fixed the salaries of members of the new nationalized boards.[23]

Morrison was not, of course, starting from scratch in planning Labour's nationalization programme. During the war especially, and in some cases before, there had been degrees of public intervention in the industries concerned. Parts of the electricity, gas, civil aviation and telecommunications industries were already in public hands. Committees of inquiry, either independent or departmental, had investigated the possible post-war restructuring of the coal, electricity, gas, telecommunications and iron and steel industries. For transport, perhaps the most complex of all, the wartime Minister, Reith, had drawn up a scheme for nationalization remarkably similar to that executed by Labour in 1947 and had gone some way towards 'drafting the necessary bill for a transport corporation'.[24] But usually previous

---

* There was a parallel committee of officials which prepared working papers for Morrison's ministerial committee. (Interview, D. Jay.)

thinking had stopped short of full nationalization. What Labour now did was firmly to grasp the nettle of public ownership. Having decided this principle, and put it before the electorate in 1945, the main problems then were to choose the best industrial structure and the best legislative timing. This was where Morrison's role was so important. Before the war he had developed the concept of the public corporation as the form of management best suited to large-scale public industry and this was the vehicle used after 1945. He was the acknowledged expert on nationalization. He more than any other single Labour leader was responsible for putting nationalization at the heart of Labour's programme. Through the Socialization of Industry Committee (and his Future Legislation Committee), he was in a key position to influence both the precise structure and the timing of the various nationalizations. He did not always win. While he was away ill in 1947 the transport nationalization proposals were altered against his wishes.* His own unsuccessful efforts to compromise short of full nationalization of iron and steel are also well known.[25] Morrison could not win all his battles.† He accepted his defeats gracefully, as a natural part of politics – at this stage of his life at least, if not later. Over all, his influence on Labour's socialization programme was very great indeed.

The need to impose a selective time-table on Labour's whole field of proposed legislation became rapidly evident in the summer of 1945. Every department was then submitting proposals for drafting and the parliamentary counsel were soon overwhelmed with half-finished bills. The head counsel, Sir Granville Ramm, drew Morrison's attention to the threatening crisis and they, together with William Murrie from the Cabinet Office, worked out a system of future programming. The existing Cabinet Legislation Committee, a small body composed primarily of the Law Officers, was mainly concerned with the detailed examination of drafts of current parliamentary bills and delegated legislation. The related but distinct task of shaping and timing Labour's whole five-year legislative programme and arbitrating among the ministers competing to secure one of the limited number of places for their pet departmental legislation required, as Morrison immediately saw, a separate and differently-composed committee. He established for this purpose the Future Legislation Committee, with himself in charge.[26] Its main brief was to implement Labour's manifesto, *Let us Face the Future*, within the lifetime of the 1945 Parliament. It sat down from the beginning to sort out priorities among the many promises and commitments and to spread the major and controversial legislative

* He wanted the big road and rail interests merged into one co-ordinated inland transport corporation. He also regretted the concessions to Co-operative Society pressure giving exemption from nationalization to 'C' licence holders. (*Autobiography*, pp. 258–9.)

† His unsuccessful efforts to influence the National Health Service in the direction of municipalization in 1946 is another example in the social field.

proposals over the five parliamentary sessions which it was assumed faced the Government. This was the kind of forward planning which Morrison believed in, had so often argued for, and at which he was so adept. 'Herbert played it like a game of racing demons. He would deal with thirty or forty bills . . . calling on each minister in turn to explain his bill, how long it was, how much time it needed – Herbert went at great speed. He did not waste words, he was most efficient, full of bustle, exhorting and wise-cracking.'[27]

It was partly on the work of this committee that Morrison based his not unjustifiable claim that 'the Labour Governments of 1945–51 organized their legislative programme and Parliamentary Business more thoroughly than any previous Administration . . . it demonstrated that Parliament could be a work-shop as well as discharging its necessary functions as a talking shop.'[28] The committee was small and excluded departmental ministers, any of whom might at some point have a vested interest in the time-tabling decisions that had to be taken. It heard the representations and arguments of the various ministers wishing to promote bills and, after questioning them, the members of the committee, which primarily meant Morrison, William White-ley as Chief Whip, and Lord Addison as Leader of the House of Lords, delib-erated and decided upon the order of the sessional legislative programme ahead. Some, as Morrison later described, 'we had to exclude from the con-siderations of the sessional programme, for lack of merit, or because there was just not time, whilst others we would include in the list for introduction if time would permit. In any case it was necessary to get into our minds a picture of the sessional time-table as it would be if all the requests were met and another picture or pictures of the situation after pruning had been engaged in.'[29] Then a document was prepared for the Cabinet's final decision. Having settled the next session's time-table, this committee would meet from time to time to receive progress reports and to consider possible revisions. Once the proposed bills had been time-tabled and drafted, these drafts were then sub-mitted to Greenwood's Legislation Committee. Morrison sat on this com-mittee as well from 1945, and he took over as chairman in 1947; from then on he supervised the whole field of government legislation in terms of both planning and detailed drafting.*

The most difficult problem which faced the Future Legislation Committee was that of constructing the programme for the first session, in 1945–6, since it was not initially clear which bills would be drafted in a satisfactory form and ready for Parliament at an early stage. The result was something of a hotch-potch, but in the circumstances not a bad start. Morrison pushed through

---

* It is some indication of the amount of work involved that between 1945 and 1950 these committees processed, prior to their passing into statute, 347 Acts of Parliament containing 8,640 pages of legislation. Many of these bills involved constant re-drafting and reviewing by the Legislation Committee – iron and steel nationalization went into twelve drafts, transport nationalization into twenty-one drafts, and the Town and Country Planning Act into twenty-three drafts. (H. Morrison, *Government and Parliament*, pp. 238–9, 241–2.)

immediately the Supplies and Services (Transition Powers) Bill which authorized various instruments of economic planning and control and which had
been substantially drafted under his supervision as Home Secretary during the
war. The Trade Union Bill was slipped in early, repealing the Trade Disputes
Act of 1927 which the Conservatives had passed in the aftermath of the
General Strike and which Labour had always promised to the trade union
movement would be an early reward for a Labour victory. The development
of the Welfare State was also quickly set under way with three great reforms
of the social services, the National Insurance Bill, the Industrial Injuries Bill,
and the National Health Service Bill. Coal was picked out for top priority
in the nationalization programme, though civil aviation, the Bank of England
and international telecommunications were also part of the first year's time-
table.* This left the other major measures promised in the election manifesto
to be spaced out over future sessions: electricity and transport nationalization
and town and country planning legislation were to come in 1946–7, with gas
and iron and steel nationalization to follow after that as the time-table
permitted.

Apart from his major Cabinet responsibilities – as co-ordinating minister on
the domestic front, and specifically for economic planning, for the nationalization programme and for the legislative programme – Morrison was put in
charge of a number of miscellaneous policy fields in 1945 and was also given
ad hoc tasks later as they cropped up, such as negotiating for extra American
food supplies and supervising the proposed Festival of Britain. He sat on the
Food Committee and was spokesman in Cabinet on agricultural matters.[30]
Morrison was also responsible for government communications policy,
covering press, radio, television and the domestic information services, in
which capacity he chaired the Cabinet Information Committee.

    This last job was close to Morrison's heart. He had many of the qualities
necessary to make a good journalist, with a sharp sense of how to present
news. As a minister he always went out of his way to be accessible and helpful
to newspapermen, and was always aware of the commercial pressures and
time constraints under which they worked. He gave them a lot of information
off the record. He trusted them and never misled them. Certainly he used them
for his own purposes, as do most politicians, but never by indiscretions or
misleading them with false information. He achieved the right balance,
managing the news without trying to manipulate the journalists. He probably
had more friendly contacts in Fleet Street – and made more effective use of
them – than any other contemporary politician. He especially liked to use the
Star, the radical London evening paper which over the years had played an
important role in building up Morrison's image as 'Mr London'. He courted

* In its first session Labour passed eighty-three Statutes containing 1,390 pages of legislation.

a succession of *Star* editors in the 1930s and 1940s: Edward Chattaway, Robin Cruikshank who continued in close touch with Morrison when he moved on to edit the *News Chronicle*, and Arthur Cranfield. In return for favourable treatment of himself he went out of his way to help the *Star* with early stories. He built up a whole network of journalist contacts who liked him, trusted him and whom he could use: Mellor, Francis Williams and Leslie Hunter on the *Herald*, Bartholomew on the *Mirror*, Trevor Evans on the *Express*. He often consulted them and took their professional advice on news presentation.[31] He was in advance of his time in his awareness that governments in the twentieth century must communicate to the people and that public relations had become an essential instrument of modern mass politics. He himself set an example, employing a close public relations adviser throughout his time in office, Leslie in the war and Boon afterwards. He fought long and hard and often with little help from his colleagues, including the Prime Minister, to present the Labour Government in the best possible light.

Morrison's concern with publicity did, however, sometimes give offence, even in Fleet Street itself, and it must be admitted that it did at times become almost unhealthily obsessive. His day began with the morning's press coverage. With the passing years he grew more touchy about press treatment of himself and if he felt he had suffered unfairness he would write or telephone to the offending newspaper to complain.[32] In June 1946 he foolishly upset the National Union of Journalists' chapel of the otherwise friendly *Daily Herald* by denouncing Percy Cudlipp for his treatment of Morrison's conference speech. This sensitivity was certainly one motive behind his support for setting up a Royal Commission to inquire into the press in October 1946.* Over the next two and a half years while the Commission sat he carefully built up files of clippings illustrating press misrepresentations and personally submitted some of the items as evidence.[33]

A final responsibility given to Morrison was for the scientific work of the government and he probably took it more seriously than any previous peacetime minister.[34] Soon after taking office he set up the Barlow Committee on Future Scientific Policy. It in turn recommended the formation of a Council

* The NUJ Conference in the spring of 1946 had passed a resolution demanding a press inquiry and a Labour back-bench motion was passed by 270 to 157 in the Commons in October. There were suspicions that Morrison and his friend Maurice Webb (who was on the National Executive of the NUJ and the chairman of the PLP) were actively involved in inspiring both initiatives. (See *Recorder*, 2 November 1946 and *Newspaper World*, 28 June 1948.) The Commission reported in June 1949 and Morrison welcomed it, especially its proposal for a Press Council. He also in the Commons debate in July pointed out that the press reception of the report had justified the need for such a Council by distorting and suppressing some of its conclusion that the press was often guilty of distortions and suppressions.

on Scientific Policy to advise the Lord President. Morrison established this new body under Sir Henry Tizard in January 1947. The existing scientific secretariat in the Cabinet Office was then transferred to his office. This secretariat serviced the new advisory council, other scientific committees, and · maintained liaison between the Lord President and the three research bodies under his domain: the Department of Scientific and Industrial Research, the Medical Research Council and the Agricultural Research Council. It also advised Morrison personally. Not all professional scientists were happy with Morrison's position in their fields. Some had hoped for a full Ministry of Science. Morrison's personal lack of expertise also occasionally gave offence. His speeches and technical mispronunciations at times provoked pained hilarity.[35] Certainly he was out of his depth in many areas of scientific research, as are most politicians and laymen. He relied very much on his professional advisers, and especially the passionate enthusiasms of Nicholson. Morrison's contribution, and it was not a minor one, was to rationalize the scientific machinery and to give scientific development the full backing of his own substantial political muscle. His success in establishing in 1949 the Nature Conservancy, one of the more golden bees in Nicholson's crowded bonnet, was an example of this collective contribution.[36]

This wide range of governmental activities placed a heavy work burden on Morrison's shoulders. The time and energy absorbed in Cabinet committees alone was very considerable. The Lord President's Committee met every Friday morning at 9.45 a.m. The Industrial sub-committee met on Monday mornings at 11.30. The Legislation Committee met on Tuesday mornings at 9.45, and the Defence Committee, of which he was a member, on Wednesdays at 3.45 p.m. The Socialization of Industry Committee and the Economic Steering Committee met frequently, the Committees on Information and on the Machinery of Government met less often. There was also, of course, the full Cabinet itself, which usually met twice a week, on Tuesday and Thursday mornings at eleven, and often at other times in crises or for unfinished business. The papers relating to these Cabinets – usually a dozen or so bulky folders – would reach Morrison's private office in Great George Street at around six on the Monday and Wednesday evenings and his officials would go through them to draw his attention to problems particularly relevant to him and to suggest helpful approaches or information. The box of papers would then be sent to Morrison, either at the Commons or at the Howard Hotel, by about nine in the evening, though because of his parliamentary and other responsibilities he could rarely begin to look at them till he climbed into bed, usually in the early hours of the morning. One Cabinet colleague recalled that he personally just could not cope with all the Cabinet papers and looked only at material concerning his own department. 'But next day it was clear that Herbert had mastered the lot, for in the Cabinet he was able to talk intelligently about every item. He must have had a master mind. Of course, as Lord President everything was his subject.'[37]

Morrison sat on one side of Attlee in Cabinet and Bevin on the other. Attlee usually took Morrison's view first and then went round the table to conclude with Bevin and then his own summing up. According to George Isaacs, Morrison, Bevin and Bevan 'contributed most' and there was often 'a triangle of fireworks' between them.[38] 'Morrison was undoubtedly a dominant figure in the Cabinet,' recalled Johnstone, who served for a period in the Cabinet Office. 'He intervened at the right time to make good contributions. He was obviously of prime ministerial calibre.'[39] Attlee himself conceded that Morrison was a good member of Cabinet: 'he talked only on what he knew about'.[40]

Attlee handled his senior colleagues gently, leaving them all to have their say, while he doodled in apparent boredom. He would then sum up concisely, announcing the consensus, without imposing his own views – if he had any.[41] Morrison's style, when he deputized in Cabinet or when chairing Cabinet committees, was strikingly different from Attlee's. He was more positive, even 'bossy', giving a lead, showing greater interest in and knowledge of the policy issues, trying to coax his colleagues towards a firm conclusion.[42] 'He was a pleasure to sit with,' recalled one fellow minister. 'He could shut up somebody who had nothing to say or could bring something valuable out of someone who was reticent. He could act as a catalyst bringing a committee to a decision.'[43] Morrison's greater interest and commitment, compared to Attlee, was to his credit, but the touch of the schoolmaster in him upset some of his colleagues. 'He did not stand fools as gladly as some,' observed Attlee, who had himself almost unparalleled experience in that field.[44]

As a departmental minister Morrison won the respect and admiration of the group of outstanding civil servants who worked with him at the Lord President's Office after the war, 'Morrison was the most *professional* minister I have ever worked for,' said Nicholson. 'He had no *amour propre* about his work. If officials pointed out that a speech was no good, he would tear it up. He told officials they must give him their honest views even if wholly in conflict with his own. But if he overruled them they must then go off and do what he decided ... Morrison, deep down, had a hankering to be a sort of civil service permanent secretary and was brilliant at understanding the way that administrators thought.'[45] Edward Bridges, the official Head of the Home Civil Service, who suffered some sharp clashes with Morrison between 1945 and 1947, agreed with Nicholson on this, if on little else, describing Morrison when Lord President as 'a very fine minister indeed ... His handling of departments and relations with civil servants were very good.'[46] Alex Johnstone, perhaps the most orthodox civil servant in Morrison's dynamic office, shared their admiration. 'Morrison was a very fast worker, prepared to take advice, and able to make up his mind quickly. He had that rare gift of being interested in the efficiency of the administrative machine. This made him a delight to work for as a civil servant . . . I felt that in the Lord President's Office we were part of a team. I look back to it as one of the happiest of my times in the civil service.'[47] Others in that brilliant team – Downes, Murrie, Henley, Stephens, Flett – shared this admiration.[48] Morrison was a civil servant's minister as well as a politician's politician.

Chapter 27

Managing Parliament and the Party

Morrison's work as a Cabinet minister was only one part of his triple function in 1945: he also had important parliamentary and party roles, each in the area of man-management and so particularly suited to his talents and character. As Leader of the House of Commons, he had overriding responsibility for carrying through the government's programme and also for guiding the House through its business procedure. He had wide, and potentially conflicting obligations – to the minister in charge of legislative proceedings on any particular day, to government supporters on the back benches, to the Opposition, to the House as a whole. The minister piloting legislation was naturally very important. Morrison would say, 'This is his big bill and his big moment and we must back him up as much as possible.' As when chairing a committee, he 'had this stage sense, of who was on the centre of the stage and who should be brought on; he was always thinking about this'.[1]

Morrison had the great virtue in this job of accessibility to anybody, however junior. 'He would settle in his room in the Commons and hold open court for MPs barging in with their troubles,' recalled one colleague.[2] They felt able to talk to Morrison 'because he always had time to talk. He was much less formal than Attlee. With Attlee one could only get a "Yes" or "No". Herbert would listen in a most open-minded way. He would discuss, encourage, give advice, and in fact he would *do* something.'[3] Wilfred Paling recalled how, when Postmaster-General, he was in difficulties with a bill and went to see Attlee. The Prime Minister immediately referred him to Morrison, who invited Paling to breakfast at the Howard Hotel, where they sorted it out satisfactorily. 'You could argue with him and discuss and fall out. Herbert could talk back in one's own language, in a working-class plain style. But Attlee would not answer back. You couldn't discuss things with him. . . . If anyone wanted plain talking, they would certainly go to Herbert and not to Attlee.'[4]

Despite the criticisms which the Conservatives occasionally made of Morrison in the heat of the moment, he was always deeply aware that the

Leader of the House is the guardian of the Opposition's legitimate rights as well as those of the government and that he must champion the interests of Parliament as a whole even against pressures from close ministerial colleagues. This was the delicate balance that Morrison had to maintain. On the one hand, together with the Chief Whip, William Whiteley, he was a partisan minister forcing through Parliament at high pressure a massive government programme of controversial reform. On the other hand, he was a servant of the whole House who had to remain sensitive to parliamentary feeling, able to distinguish genuine from bogus concern, and quick and flexible in providing the House with necessary opportunities to question and criticize the government.[5] His skill and humour in maintaining this balance was unquestioned and has been acknowledged by political opponents as well as by comrades. Sir Edward Fellowes, a most distinguished Clerk of the House of Commons, described Morrison as the best Leader he had seen in forty years' service in the House.* 'He had a feel for the House of Commons and seemed to know instinctively how it would react. He must have been born with the ability to manage people and to organize them.'[6]

The House of Commons has many feminine characteristics and its reactions to a minister or a Leader of the House reflect acute sensitivity about how that minister feels towards it. 'If one is to be effective in the House of Commons,' as Morrison later wrote, 'one must love the place. The House has an uncanny capacity for knowing who really likes it and who does not. The House will forgive much in a Minister if it likes him and if it knows he likes the House. . . . Nobody can play a great and enduring part in that Assembly unless he knows what he is talking about and is sincere; and a successful relationship cannot be achieved unless one respects and even loves the House. And for no Ministers is this more important than the Prime Minister and the Leader of the House of Commons.' He went on to quote Sir William Harcourt who, on taking farewell of the House of Commons as its Leader in 1895, stated: 'I would ask leave to say that for every man who has taken part in the noble conflicts of Parliamentary life, the chiefest ambition of all ambitions, whether in the majority or in the minority, must be to stand well with the House of Commons.' 'Those are my sentiments also,' Morrison added.[7] This ambition he achieved. His period as Leader of the House of Commons, particularly in the early years, together with his time as Leader of the LCC and as Home Secretary in the war, represents the third – and final – successful peak in Morrison's career.

From the beginning in 1945 Morrison saw that his job as Leader of the House would be made much easier by improvements in two areas: by speed-

---

* Fellowes placed Baldwin second and R. A. Butler third. Others to express admiration for Morrison in this role include Lord Avon, Lord Chandos, G. Isaacs and C. Johnson (interviews with the authors). Harold Macmillan and the former Conservative Chief Whip, James Stuart, have published similar views. (H. Macmillan, *Memoirs*, Vol. III (1969), pp. 54–5. J. Stuart, *Within the Fringe* (1967), p. 142.

ing up parliamentary procedure, and by organizing the Parliamentary Labour Party in such a way that the government's back-bench support was kept loyal and happy. The procedural changes were rapidly initiated. On the second day of the new Parliament, 16 August 1945, Morrison went to the House of Commons and moved that the government should take over all private members' time because of the needs of the heavy reconstruction programme. This produced the first division in this Parliament, a vote of 329 to 142 emphasizing the landslide nature of Labour's victory.[8] The following week Morrison moved the setting up of a select committee on parliamentary procedure to consider ways of making Parliament more efficient in the face of the massive legislative burden that lay ahead of it.[9]

Morrison himself gave evidence to the select committee, urging especially that the committee stage of bills should, when desired, be taken upstairs in small standing committees rather than on the floor of the whole House. Standing committees were, of course, already used for the committee stage of run-of-the-mill legislation, but it was the practice to keep major measures and politically controversial bills on the floor of the House. Morrison and the government now proposed that all bills should go to standing committee for their committee stage, except for certain finance bills and any bill of 'first class constitutional importance', such as the Parliament Act or the Statute of Westminster. The number of standing committees available for this purpose was increased and their membership reduced.[10] Morrison and the government also strove to alter the traditional casual attitude of MPs to standing committees: 'They must do something like a real day's work when required instead of just a few hours.'[11] Morrison was not just seeking to save time through the use of these committees. He wanted to change the whole attitude of the Commons to its working machinery. The conventional view saw Parliament as just a debating chamber, sometimes served on a rather unsystematic basis by a few committees. 'It was necessary,' he later wrote, 'to develop the doctrine and practice that the House should split up into committees to carry through bills. . . . Unless standing committees took this view any attempt to develop them into useful parts of the legislative process, instead of mere time savers, would break down . . . our practice of sending important and controversial bills upstairs did much to improve things. Members increasingly realized the importance and interest of the work. Indeed, often there was competition to get on to the committees.'[12] Morrison's experience in local government was clearly evident in his approach to this parliamentary reform.

Perhaps the most controversial change initiated in the early days of the government was the decision to use the guillotine in standing committees to accelerate progress there. This followed logically from the previous decision to send important bills, particularly controversial bills, to these committees. It was precisely this controversial legislation that was most vulnerable to obstruction and where the government might, therefore, need to resort to the guillotine to maintain progress in its programme. There was no alternative if the government wished to guarantee getting its programme through. In the event, the guillotine was used on only three bills during the six years of Labour government.* Morrison certainly disliked invoking it, which he realized 'can make a mockery of the legislative process'.[13] To redress the balance of power in Parliament a little, he argued that, since the opposition was potentially to be fettered by the guillotine procedure, it was important that in the committees they be treated with the utmost consideration. He said: 'The Opposition are entitled to somewhat more consideration than the majority. If the Committees will try to handle the matter in that style, and the Opposition will try to conduct themselves in committee style, I believe that, under this new era, we can build up Standing Committees that will work on business lines, leaving the rather more free-for-all controversies to the Report stage and the Third Reading on the Floor of the House.'[14] He wanted the committees to develop their own atmosphere and conventions, appropriate to the work they did.

The select committee made three reports, in October 1945, January 1946 and October 1946. Not all of the committee's detailed recommendations were accepted by the government, which, in turn, pressed certain modifications which the committee had not supported, but the procedural changes introduced were certainly useful in helping Morrison to organize and conduct the business of Parliament.† They appealed to him because they were modest, pragmatic examples of gradualist and evolutionary change.[15] The only political controversy arose concerning the definition of what was 'constitutionally important' in relation to bills which might, therefore, be retained in the Chamber of the House and not sent to standing committee. The Conservative Opposition, and particularly Anthony Eden, took the view that Labour's nationalization schemes were of constitutional significance. Morrison strongly rejected this view which he said was based upon an outdated assumption that anything which interfered with the free working of the capitalist system of production and distribution somehow involved revolutionary constitutional doctrine. 'An argument about how best a nation can get a living within the system of parliamentary democracy does not involve revolution in any way. It involves issues about which there may well be arguments. They are of real importance. But *ad hoc* bills on such matters hardly raise large constitutional issues.'[16]

---

* On the Town and Country Planning Bill and the Transport Nationalization Bill, both in 1946–7, and on the Iron and Steel Bill in 1948–9.

† Apart from this greater use of committees, and the application of the guillotine there, reforms were also introduced relating to the use of the Committee of Supply, and to shortening proceedings on the Budget resolutions and the Finance Bill. (*HC Debs*, Vol. 435, Cols 31, 32, Vol. 443, Cols 1549–61. H. Morrison, *Government and Parliament* (1964), pp. 207, 210–14, 216–18.)

When it came to his third broad role, managing the Parliamentary Labour Party, Morrison was faced in August 1945 by a worryingly large and unpredictable body. Of the 393 members, 263 were new to the House.[17] Many of these newcomers had not been active in the party before; their foibles and potential deviations remained to be tested.

It was important to establish a formal organization and procedures for regular meetings as rapidly as possible. Morrison and Attlee held discussions with the Secretary to the PLP, Carol Johnson, who played an important part in devising the machinery and procedures for the party, as well as in advising Morrison on day-to-day management. Johnson prepared a report and recommendations, which Morrison put to a meeting of the PLP on 22 August 1945.[18] Elections were to be held for a non-ministerial chairman and vice-chairman to hold office in the coming parliamentary session. This would give the party a legitimate existence and spokesmen separate from the government. At the next meeting, on 10 October, with Morrison again in the chair, he was able to declare Neil Maclean elected chairman and his friend, Maurice Webb, vice-chairman.

The parliamentary party met weekly on Wednesday mornings. Maclean (and later Maurice Webb) took the chair, but it was usually Morrison, as party manager, who was called upon to intervene or sum up on behalf of the government and deal with the points raised by back-benchers. 'He was most judicious in summing up,' recalled Carol Johnson, 'and always dealt with people's arguments seriously. He rarely lost his temper or treated opponents frivolously. He always argued and tried to convert them. Attlee was often not present . . . so it was more often Morrison than Attlee who actively bore the brunt of managing these full party meetings.'[19]

Managing the Parliamentary Labour Party was in some ways even more difficult and delicate than handling the whole House of Commons, since Labour members were more prone to internal argument and division when meeting separately as a party than when they functioned within the ideological and emotional discipline of the Commons' Chamber. The most important problems concerned communications between the Cabinet and its back-bench supporters, and the commitment of those supporters to the policy decisions of the government. Morrison's report to the party on 22 August, which was accepted, suggested solutions to both problems. It proposed to establish a formal Liaison Committee to facilitate communications, and to set up new policy groups to integrate back-benchers with the policy thinking of the government.

The new Liaison Committee was a valuable instrument in Morrison's work of managing the parliamentary party. Its job was to keep its collective ear close to the ground and detect at the earliest possible moment any rumblings of discontent brewing within the party. Back-benchers came to it with their complaints and Morrison then arranged for the relevant ministers to attend meetings to explain their policies or to deal with individual criticisms and dissatisfactions. The committee met regularly in Morrison's room in the House of Commons on Tuesday afternoons to prepare the business for the next morning's meeting of the full party, though it also assembled frequently to deal with sudden crises or other urgent matters as they arose.* Its meetings were harmonious, with Morrison the dominant figure.[20] 'He had this sixth sense,' commented the then party secretary, 'of spotting when trouble was coming and moving to meet it and head it off. He was always around the House and in close touch with people personally as well as through the Liaison Committee and through the PPSs and the whips. You could always nobble Herbert. He used to carry little strips of blank paper – ones normally used for taking messages in the telephone booths – and he would write down on these the points people raised with him and later would act upon them.'[21] His basic concern was to make sure that no gulf emerged between the government and its back-benchers, maintaining the firm parliamentary base from which the 1945 Labour government was able to launch such a major programme of reform. In the eyes of Harold Macmillan on the opposition benches, Morrison was 'the best party manager' he had known in his lifetime.[22]

The first business decision of the new Liaison Committee, at its initial meeting on 11 October 1945, was to set up the back-bench policy groups recommended at the earlier party meeting, and to appoint chairmen to them. In his *Autobiography* Morrison seems to claim all the credit for setting up these groups, stating that 'to make controversy and disagreement constructive I encouraged members to form themselves into groups concerned with topics of particular interest to them or in which they had special knowledge'.[23] This is slightly misleading since some policy and area groups had existed earlier for some time. Carol Johnson had been pressing for their extension.[24] There is no doubt, however, that Morrison was the main creative force in developing the back-bench policy groups on a systematic basis. He had clear motives. As Leader of the House and effective party manager he stood to gain most from the successful working of the group system. Happy back-benchers made less trouble. Their individual experience and expertise could also contribute to government legislation.† 'Without them,' concluded Morrison, 'the remarkably smooth procedure on complicated bills for socialization would not have happened.'[25]

These policy groups met with varying frequency, those concerned with foreign affairs, defence, or economic matters assembling most often. They summoned outside experts to talk to them, discussed policies among them-

---

* It was composed of the Party Chairman (first, Neil Maclean, succeeded a year later by Maurice Webb), the Vice-Chairman (Maurice Webb, succeeded in 1946 by W. Glenvil Hall), the Chief Whip (Whiteley), a non-ministerial Labour peer, and Morrison. Carol Johnson, secretary to the PLP, serviced the committee.

† For example, back-benchers contributed considerably to the drafting of the 1947 Agricultural Bill. The National Insurance legislation was another area to which back-benchers contributed. (Interview, G. Jeger.)

selves, and circulated papers and memoranda. When agitated about the government's actions or intentions in their policy sector, the group chairmen made representations to Morrison's Liaison Committee, and he made arrangements for the relevant minister or ministers to meet the back-bench group under the auspices of the Liaison Committee. By the end of October 1945 eleven groups had been set up, with their chairmen appointed.* Already policy disputes over old age pensions, Palestine, and the nationalization of civil aviation were being handled by the relevant groups and were testing their liaison role.[26] Some ministers, such as Dalton, welcomed them and tried to use their respective groups constructively. Bevin, on the other hand, resented any interference from the foreign affairs group and was never on good terms with it. Bevan also viewed his health group with characteristic disdain and was the subject of formal complaint from them to the Liaison Committee early in 1946 for refusing to discuss details of the proposed National Health Service.[27]

To some extent the groups could be viewed as a typical Morrisonian manoeuvre to keep the back-benchers busy, happy and quiet, by giving them the impression that they were occupied on important business, while the real task of policy formation went ahead undisrupted at ministerial level. As one popular newspaper observed: 'Some cynical humorists suggest that the plan is a brainwave of Palace of Westminster school-master Herbert Morrison and that the real purpose is to keep the parliamentary boys occupied and so out of mischief.'[28] But it would be wrong to be wholly cynical. Morrison did sincerely believe in involving as many members of Parliament as possible in the business of politics and, as in his efforts to develop the Commons standing committee system, in encouraging members to develop their own specializations and expertise. This would get the most out of the parliamentary talent available and, in turn, would raise the professional standards and reflect credit on the House of Commons which he loved.

With party discipline, where Morrison's reputation and image was that of the stern school-master, his approach to the parliamentary party in 1945 was in fact one of considerable flexibility. He recognized that 'with our big majority it would be a dull assembly if we overdid discipline. I told our MPs we don't want a gramophone record instead of a debate. I hope that there will be a good deal of free speech, even to the extent of disagreeing with Ministers, so long as it doesn't upset the apple cart.'[29] His view was that: 'Reasonable unity, discipline, and good comradeship are necessary, but I should not like what may be called 150 per cent discipline. That would mean parliamentary death.'[30] To some extent, of course, the flexibility and tolerance of Morrison's disciplinary approach, which can be illustrated and proven on numerous occasions of internal dispute during this government, arose from a shrewd appreciation based upon his own experience of the very real limits to the

---

* In the fields of Civil Aviation, Finance, Trade and Industry, Social Insurance, Local Government, Agriculture and Food, Education, Legal and Judicial, Shipping, Fuel and Power, and Fisheries. (Interview, C. Johnson.)

N

application of discipline on any parliamentary party. The Labour MPs were not servile lobby fodder and would have reacted mulishly to an insensitive or excessively heavy hand dealing with them. But quite apart from expediency, Morrison did believe in principle in running a happy and willing ship based as far as possible upon what he called 'that good fellowship and co-operation without which a parliamentary party whether or not in power cannot succeed'.[31]

It was in this spirit that Morrison himself decided early in the government to advise the suspension of the Labour Party's standing orders which governed the conduct of Labour MPs, and hence were the basis of possible disciplinary action. New standing orders had been under discussion at the end of 1945. At a special joint meeting of the Liaison Committee and the NEC it was agreed to reduce them from ten to three.[32] This joint meeting also accepted Morrison's suggestion – which he was careful to clear first with Attlee – that as an experiment these revised standing orders should be suspended until the end of the 1946–7 parliamentary session, when the question could be reviewed. Morrison then put the proposal, in the form of a recommendation from the Liaison Committee, to a full meeting of the parliamentary party at the end of January 1946, and got its approval by a large majority.[33] This experiment did not mean that all disciplinary weapons had been surrendered. The power of the parliamentary party to withdraw the whip on account of very serious things done or said by a member in the House remained – as did the power of the NEC to withdraw the support and label of the party as punishment for activities outside of Parliament. These were the sanctions which MPs really feared. What the suspension of standing orders did mean was that in the grey area of day-by-day dissensions which fell short of these ultimate sanctions, Morrison wanted the party to work out differences within the flexible relations of a team of human beings under his leadership rather than under a rigid framework of rules.

His energies and time were involved at all levels in managing the party: as Leader of the House maintaining a smoothly running majority, in the Liaison Committee, at tricky party meetings. On the NEC – where after 1945 he continued to chair the Policy committee and to sit on the International and the Elections committees, as well as regularly attending the monthly meetings of the full Executive – he was also concerned in any later stages of serious discipline. In fact, surprisingly few sanctions were applied during this Labour Government. Five members were expelled[34] – four of them because their activities appeared to place them spiritually closer to the Communist Party than to the Labour Party – but on the whole, the party was kept in line not by sanctions but by warnings, exhortations, appeals for unity, and by implied threats, or a combination of some or all of these, with Morrison normally playing the leading role. For example, in October 1945 Sydney Silverman had put down an early day motion criticizing the government's proposals on old age pensions and calling for an immediate increase. A hundred and sixty-nine

Labour MPs signed in support of the motion. It was discussed at a crowded two-hour meeting of the Parliamentary Labour Party on 16 October, the first of many such gatherings in this Parliament. Attlee did not attend and Morrison went along to act – successfully – as pacifier.[35] Dissent was taken further in December 1945 when Labour members actually went into the lobby against the government to oppose, first, the American Loan and, secondly, in the form of the Bretton Woods Bill, the monetary strings which the Americans attached to that Loan. The party's standing orders were still in operation at this time, but Morrison and the whips sensibly chose not to apply any discipline.* There were no more incidents of revolt in 1946 until the minor cases of cross-voting in the committee stage of the Civil Aviation Bill in August and then the much more serious rebellion over foreign affairs at the end of the year.[36] Given the many strains and tensions which existed in the parliamentary party during the 1945 Parliament – the permanent gulf between Marxist revolutionaries and evolutionary pragmatists, the frictions between individuals of differing types, such as the intellectuals and the working-class members, the difficulties arising from such a high proportion of the Labour MPs being new to the House and the parliamentary party – given these, then Morrison's period of party management was by any standards immensely successful.

This combination of management tasks which Attlee shrewdly assigned to Morrison in 1945, in Whitehall and in Westminster, was particularly suited to his talents and character. He was good in committee, a firm chairman, and interested in a wide range of policy issues. He worked well with officials and was an expert on the machinery of government necessary to process Labour's policies. He was well versed in the ways and procedures of Parliament, which institution he seemed to love with a depth of affection he almost never showed towards human beings. He was very skilled in the arts of manipulating his colleagues, sensing their deeper wishes and fears, ready to sweeten them a little, to lean on them a little, and always searching for the compromise which would carry people over a conflict. To Anthony Eden on the Conservative front bench, seeing him busily at work in almost every part of the Labour machine, Morrison was 'the linchpin of the post-war Labour Government . . . he was a formidable man'.[37]

Morrison's string of official duties allowed him a web of offices in central London and he buzzed from one to another during the ministerial day. His main base, as Lord President, was in the building stretching from the corner of

---

* Apparently Morrison felt that a demonstration of dissent might strengthen the hand of the government in negotiations with the Americans. He may also have noted that the rebels contained some of his friends, such as Richard Stokes and Stanley Evans.

Great George Street towards Horse Guards Parade,[38] with his desk looking across St James's Park towards the palace.* His small staff were in adjoining rooms. He had another important office, as deputy prime minister, around the corner at 11 Downing Street, immediately accessible to both the Prime Minister and the Chief Whip on either side. Up one floor of the wide, finely carved staircase, above the Chancellor of the Exchequer, was Morrison's flat. His personal office, once the drawing room, was long and high, red-carpeted, with two fireplaces, a large bookcase and a long dining table for Cabinet committees and other meetings which he chaired there. His desk was in the corner, near the window. Adjoining was his bedroom and another office in which Miss Donald worked. All of Morrison's official Labour Party business was executed through Miss Donald at 11 Downing Street, and a clear distinction was maintained between that and the departmental work of his civil servants in the Lord President's Office around the corner. In addition, he still had his office at the London Labour Party and he had a large room in the Palace of Westminster, from which he organized his work as Leader of the Commons and parliamentary party manager. He also maintained a suite of rooms at the Howard Hotel in Norfolk Street, which he used for private political negotiations, and where he often slept if kept late in town.[39]

Morrison worked ceaselessly – 'as hard a worker as I have ever come across', according to one of his senior advisers.[40] He moved from appointment to appointment, from office to office, from morning till well into the following night. His diary was always black with engagements for weeks in advance. One visitor to Miss Donald, seeking appointments, vividly recalled that she would show him Morrison's diary 'and for weeks on end it was completely full from morning till late at night and often impossible to fit anything in even for five to ten minutes. Nobody could grasp the terrible pressure on a leading Cabinet minister without seeing his diaries which are a vivid memory to me.'[41] Morrison was usually punctual for this vast list of appointments and was well able to switch from one subject to another from meeting to meeting. 'He liked to be well prepared, always did his homework and mastered the brief from his officials,' said Nicholson. 'Morrison was confronted by a vast range of problems and he worked hard to master them all but he rarely appeared hurried or harassed. I've rarely seen a minister who looked less harassed. . . . He was very good at putting his different hats on . . . he was a great roles man . . . his life was in compartments and he always kept the compartments completely apart.'[42] Put simply: 'Herbert clearly had a pigeon-hole mind.'[43] Little time, or even desire, remained for a personal hat, a separate compartment for private life. Morrison's life was work – in government, in Parliament and in the Labour Party.

* Oliver Lyttelton occupied this office until the election. Afterwards Lyttelton went back to collect a few personal things. He went into the lavatory 'and there was the dirtiest hairbrush I had ever seen in my life, beside a notice saying, "This is the property of the Lord President of the Council. Please do not touch." ' (Interview, Lord Chandos.)

Chapter 28

On the Treadmill, 1945-1946

Whatever the tensions and minor embarrassments about the party leadership in the immediate post-election period, the rest of the summer and autumn after the 1945 general election was a time of celebration and triumph for Morrison. Britain was at peace and wanted a better new world. Labour was at last in power and committed to build that new world. Morrison was at the heart of government and could begin to bring to fruition all that he had read about, dreamed about, talked about, thought and planned during his political lifetime. He exuded confidence and relished the excitement in the political atmosphere.

He went to the House of Commons for the election of the Speaker and the swearing in of new members at the beginning of August. They met in the Lords' Chamber* after lunch in a scene of confusion, crush and babbling excitement. One observer described how 'a great cheer goes up because Mr Herbert Morrison strolls in and sits down with all the nonchalance of attending a Hackney Borough Council'.[1] It was 2.45 in the afternoon. Churchill entered and sat on the other side of the chamber next to Eden and Butler and his supporters rose and sang 'For he's a jolly good fellow', followed by three cheers. In response some Labour MPs stood up and started to sing the 'Red Flag'. Others, including Morrison, looked a trifle embarrassed.[2] As yet it was not a proper House of Commons; the Speaker had not yet been elected and members had not taken their oaths. It was just a meeting of elected representatives with only the Sergeant-at-arms present. Morrison's sense of propriety, decorum and his respect for the traditions of the House would, however, make him feel that community singing was somehow not appropriate for the Palace of Westminster. It was rapidly brought to a halt and silence restored by the traditional three knocks on the door and Black Rod marching down the central aisle summoning the Commons to hear the Proclamation of the opening of the new Parliament. Morrison, who was substituting for the absent Attlee, rose and walked out with Churchill, who was still irritated with him

* The Commons' Chamber had been bombed and was still being rebuilt.

following their election clashes, and so there were none of the customary friendly exchanges.[3] Other political leaders followed behind in pairs but most members stayed behind and waited till they returned, when they re-elected Clifton Brown to the office of Speaker. Morrison then formally moved the adjournment of the House for a fortnight until the State Opening of Parliament.

On the eve of the State Opening the Labour Party held a huge celebration rally at the Seymour Hall in London. Among the two thousand guests were recently elected members, defeated candidates, party workers, wives and others who had contributed to the recent great victory. It was a moving occasion for a working-class party that had waited nearly forty years to reach this point on the threshold of power. Morrison addressed them and characteristically refused to be carried away by the emotions of the moment. Instead he coolly and realistically urged the party to begin from that moment to look forward to the next election and to plan and work for its victory.[4] Next day the King came to open the new Parliament. In the traditional procession to St Margaret's, Westminster Morrison walked behind the Speaker in his full robes in company with Churchill, Eden and Attlee, now back from Potsdam, all acknowledging the tremendous reception of the cheering crowds lining the routes.[5] That night was VJ night marking the final end of the war with Japan. Vast crowds packed central London dancing and singing in Piccadilly and Trafalgar Square and up and down Whitehall. Bonfires burned outside Buckingham Palace and in the parks. In the docks ships fired their rockets, fireworks flashed and glowed, St Paul's, the Houses of Parliament and much of the City were lit up by searchlights, a striking replica and reminder of when London was first alight in the war just five years earlier. Morrison, who at that earlier time was about to step into the national political limelight as Home Secretary, now stood as deputy prime minister on the flag-draped balcony of the Ministry of Health. Searchlights picked out himself, Bevin and Attlee as they stepped forward to acknowledge the crowd singing 'We want Clem'. Ten days later Morrison attended yet another Victory Rally, in his own Lewisham constituency. By now the party atmosphere and high jinks were coming to an end. Earlier in that week the United States had terminated the Lend–Lease supplies to Britain and the country faced 'an economic Dunkirk'. In Lewisham Morrison warned his party faithful that they would have to tighten their belts and that there lay ahead a long hard road which would take fully five years to cover if they wanted to complete their promised programme of reform.

Morrison spent the summer and autumn of 1945 preparing for that long road ahead: appointing staff, establishing committees, selecting legislation for the coming session.[6] The new Parliament was rapidly initiated into the accelerated tempo of life and work under a Labour administration. As the individual bills in the first year's programme were drafted in the departments and approved by Morrison's Future Legislation Committee they were put in quick succession before the House of Commons. The nationalization of the

Bank of England received its second reading by the end of October. Dalton's other measure, his first Budget, with its moves towards more progressive taxation, was ready at the same time. The Chancellor cleared its main proposals privately with Morrison, Attlee and Bevin before putting it to the Cabinet and Parliament.[7] By Christmas 1945 the Finance Bill was through all its stages, Bank nationalization was ready for the Lords and the big National Insurance Bill establishing much of Beveridge's Welfare State was before the Commons. Several departmental ministers had taken the opportunity to show their paces, with Dalton perhaps outstanding at this stage. Morrison was the essential common factor, in committee and in the Commons, advising, cajoling, time-tabling, and generally organizing Labour's legislative offensive.

Just before Christmas 1945 Morrison was able to get away for his first break from the heavy routine of Westminster and Whitehall. He went to the Midlands for a weekend, primarily to address a meeting of Labour supporters in local government, but he also slipped off on the Saturday afternoon to watch Nottingham Forest play Aston Villa.[8] The following Monday he set a seal on the London part of his career when he formally opened the new Waterloo Bridge. Morrison had performed the ceremonial opening rites when the bridge was partially opened to traffic in August 1942. It had in practice been fully open to traffic since November 1944. Then the war situation was critical, and the opening celebrations appropriately austere. This time there was a fanfare of four national fire-service trumpets at the opening. Coloured streamers hung between the lamp standards on the bridge. Afterwards Morrison gave a luncheon party at County Hall, with turkey, ham, Christmas pudding, wines and liqueurs on the menu, and a seven-inch cigar for everyone to finish with. Morrison made a witty and triumphant after-luncheon speech, periodically interrupted by the hootings of tugs in the fog on the Thames outside.[9]

The hectic parliamentary activity continued for Morrison when the House resumed in the New Year of 1946. He was immediately plunged into the Coal Nationalization Bill, where he wound up the second reading debate for the government, and in the Ministers of the Crown (Transfer of Functions) Bill where he moved the second reading. The stream of legislation followed its parliamentary course: the National Insurance Bill resumed in the first week of February, followed over the next eight weeks by the National Health Service Bill, the Housing Bill and the Civil Aviation Bill. Morrison also answered questions on an enormous range of issues: on Wales, taxation, broadcasting, prisoners of war, the costs of entertaining the forces, the wages of Bank of England typists, and the decision not to reopen the Liverpool Cotton Exchange. At the end of March he went to Leeds to deliver a speech on the subject of the government's first hundred days in office, in which he could claim with justice that they had done more than any previous government in a similar period of time.

The pressure of work imposed upon Parliament by Morrison drew forth many angry comments and complaints. The *Manchester Guardian* observed that: 'Mr Herbert Morrison is omnivorous for work himself and he is enormously enjoying the job of piling work upon the House of Commons.'[10] The Opposition in the Commons was not so obviously enjoying the process, repeatedly complaining that there was too little time for them to digest too much work. A Conservative back-bencher (Colonel Marlowe, MP for Brighton) referred to Morrison as 'the right honourable and totalitarian member', and was forced to withdraw by the Speaker, during the discussion on the following week's business at the end of January.[11] During all this extravagance Morrison was 'sitting with folded arms in grinning contemplation of his third waistcoat button'.[12] Morrison pressed on. He rushed through the repeal of the Trade Disputes Bill in five days, with only two days in committee, provoking complaints from Eden on the ruthless use of the closure.[13] White papers flowed from government departments. Still ahead of them in the summer lay a formidable list of outstanding business: the final stages of the Coal Bill and the National Insurance Bill, together with the National Health Service Bill, the proposed nationalization of telecommunications and civil aviation, and general debates on the iron and steel White Paper and on foreign affairs. Morrison's busy energy drew admiration, but he also upset a lot of people. Not only the opposition, whose motives for slowing down the government's programme were not all disinterested, but his own back-benchers resented his lash upon their backs, complaining especially when in the spring he extended the hour until which the House normally sat from 9.15 p.m. until 10.00 p.m.[14] One of his Cabinet colleagues noted in his diary in the summer that 'Morrison in particular must be checked for trying to interfere with everybody and everything'.[15]

The opposition quickly began to focus on Morrison as the personification of the Labour government and often referred to him in their speeches, which reflected their irritation but were not always wholly unfair. Harold Macmillan's description of him (made in the debate on coal nationalization) as 'the Lewisham Bantam' caught some of the flavour of Morrison's cocky and combative performance in the House and was taken up elsewhere in the press.[16] A younger Tory, Derek Walker-Smith, also characterized Morrison accurately towards the end of March when he described him as 'the Government's handyman'.[17] This is exactly what Morrison was, but it was a style that had its disadvantages, leading to inevitable haste and superficiality in dealing with this vast range of issues at such great speed. As Walker-Smith observed: 'Mr Morrison is a good speaker. The trouble is, however, that, speaking so much, he is a better speaker than most people on many things but not so good as some on anything.' The press also began to notice in May that his parliamentary speeches, though humorous, sometimes slipped into flippancy, back-chat and badinage.[18]

In May Morrison wound up an emergency debate on the government's decision to withdraw troops from Egypt, the first division on foreign affairs in this Parliament. Later in the month it was iron and steel nationalization, where he again wound up the debate on the White Paper and uncompromisingly insisted 'these are going to be public corporations, business concerns, they will buy the necessary brains and technical skill and give them their heads'.[19] Morrison also had to intervene in the national insurance debate in May to rescue the minister, James Griffiths, from savage attacks upon him by a group of left-wing back-benchers. The pace of life and pressure of work may have been beginning to tell on Morrison whose temper seemed unusually frayed. Spinning around on George Thomas, who was shouting from behind denouncing all means tests, he rasped back: 'It is all very well to throw that phrase across the Floor of the House, but if my Hon. Friend were sitting in the Cabinet or in Cabinet committees, he would have to face the actualities of the situation.'[20] Over a clause whereby after six months an unemployed man would have to make out a case for extending extra benefits above national assistance level, Morrison again clashed with his own back-benchers. Once more he turned his back on the opposition to shout at his own rank and file: 'I cannot believe that those of my Hon. Friends who have feelings on this matter ... are affirming the docrine that any citizen, even a working-class citizen, has the unconditional right to withdraw money from the State without question, query or justification.' Back-benchers shouted back at him 'Why not?' Morrison retorted angrily: 'Any Socialist who affirms that is affirming something contrary to the self-respecting and upright principles of socialism itself.' Not surprisingly the Tories were grinning throughout these exchanges at such early glimpses of rifts in Labour's ranks.[21]

Morrison was also very busy in his economic job in this first year of the new Labour government. Much of his work was with the massive agendas of his network of committees. Sometimes, however, he found time to get away from Westminster and Whitehall. He devoted a number of speeches up and down the country, and abroad, to educating the public on the facts of Britain's economic plight and needs. Early in September 1945, speaking at the opening of the Kensington Thanksgiving Week, he warned that 'we don't want a gay time around Eros in Piccadilly in the first two or three years and then a smash. If we want to achieve some sort of promised land in the future, we have got to hold ourselves in during the first period.'[22] The same theme of explaining Britain's economic and industrial problems and urging greater savings, exports and production, recurred in other speeches he wrote at this time.[23]

Early in the new year of 1946 Morrison's economic proselytizing took him on his first post-war transatlantic visit, an eight-day trip to Canada, and then to the United States. He sailed in the *Mauretania* on the night of 27–8 December 1945 and arrived at Halifax, Nova Scotia, on 2 January. The Canadian conservative press, and especially the *Montreal Gazette*, criticized him strongly for spending so much time with the Canadian socialists and alleged that he was meddling in Canadian politics. This was taken up by the Conservative press in Britain and blown up into a minor political storm. Morrison certainly went out of his way to strengthen ties with the Canadian labour movement, and at the end of his tour had private talks with the American Federation of Labor. These meetings reflected the respect in which Britain's new Labour Government and its leaders were held by other developing labour movements abroad. The bulk of his public activities and statements, however, was devoted not to partisan matters but to discussing and advancing Britain's economic interests and the need for both Canadian trade and Canadian aid.[24]

Later in his tour, when based in Toronto, Morrison made several references to Labour's nationalization plans. At a press conference on the ninth he listed iron and steel as one of the 'certain things Labour would nationalize in due course'.[25] Two days later he returned to the subject in a broadcast. Considering that he was three thousand miles from home in a country which was presumably not well informed on details of the British political and industrial situations, Morrison went into surprising detail about Labour's nationalization programme and the nature of the public corporation vehicle which it would use. His explanation was in no sense defensive, but he did go out of his way to reassure a North American audience devoted to capitalism and sensitive about communism by stating categorically that 'the great bulk of our industry will remain private industry and we shall not quarrel with it while it is private enterprise and not private unenterprise'. He also stressed that Labour would not be rigid or dogmatic about precise details of organization for the new nationalized industries.[26]

Morrison flew from Toronto to New York for the last lap of his hectic North American tour, and when he received British newspaper correspondents, after arriving on the morning of Friday 11 January, he was reported as still being in 'high spirits'. He went out of his way to praise the Canadians, the British monarchy and to defend the British Empire: 'We are friends of the jolly old Empire', he said, 'we are going to stick to it.' 'The Monarchy is a real factor among cementing influences between Britain and the Commonwealth. The Monarchy is a great institution.'[27] Morrison was energetically projecting to journalists and commentators an image of hustle and bustle. He took lunch that day with America's top radio commentators. In the evening he was guest of honour at a dinner of the American Council on Foreign Relations and made a speech about Britain's current situation. Next morning he visited the headquarters of the British Information Services, then took lunch with more New York newspaper editors and radio executives. He left for Washington in the afternoon and that evening made an important network broadcast to the United States and Canada. In it he described life in post-war Britain and justified its current austerity as necessary to build sound foundations for a better future.[28]

In the United States, as in Canada, the current negotiations for a large dollar loan to Britain dominated the tactics of Morrison's visit and his speeches. Addressing a luncheon given in his honour by the National Press Club in Washington, he declined to discuss the proposed American loan, but that was really what his speech was about. Meeting head-on the doubts of American bankers and politicians, who suspected that Britain was at best a bad financial risk and at worst actually turning to communism, Morrison went out of his way to stress that Britain was in very good spirits and really did believe in free trade and in paying her debts; he added that the Labour Government certainly would never dream of nationalizing industry purely from 'abstract Socialist theory, but for the fact that the industries concerned must be reorganized and placed at the efficient service of the country'. That same day, as he was certainly aware, Representative Dirksen, the influential Republican from Illinois, was urging Congress to hold up all proposed loans to foreigners and particularly to the British. Morrison, who had visited President Truman before lunch, stressed his bi-partisan role and appealed to American memories of wartime friendship by paying a warm tribute to Winston Churchill, who had just arrived in the United States for a winter holiday in Miami. This reference was warmly cheered.[29] That weekend the Washington correspondent of the *Sunday Times* wrote that 'Mr Morrison made a favourable impression here, not as a representative of the Labour Government, but as a spokesman for all the Commonwealth, which role he played tactfully and well'.[30] When Morrison arrived back by air at Northolt Airport, he was clearly very pleased with himself and with his visit. From the economic point of view, he had probably successfully achieved one main purpose in satisfying American financial and political opinion that the Labour Government in Britain was not raising its large dollar loan from America simply to pay for its nationalization programme. From his personal political point of view, his first major visit abroad had left most people who dealt with him with an impression of energy, vigour and competence; certainly nobody commented at this time that he was out of his depth either in handling foreigners abroad or in the specific economic field. As ever, he managed the press skilfully and received considerable and very favourable coverage.[31]

On his return his departmental responsibilities grew even heavier, since Sir Stafford Cripps went to India to lead a mission negotiating a political settlement, and while he was away Morrison officially acted as President of the Board of Trade. Despite this massive work load he still found time to go out into the provinces to speak at weekends. He had speaking engagements in Yorkshire in late March as part of the export drive and visited Birmingham in April to address Midland employers and trade unionists as part of the government's general production drive. The strain inevitably took its toll and on the earlier visit to Yorkshire Morrison fell ill and remained in bed for a couple of days in Bradford.[32] He addressed another similar conference of southern employers and trade unions in London in June, and at the end of the month made a major broadcast over the BBC network about the general economic situation, always returning to the themes of the need for economic planning, for manpower planning, and to give up consumption and put up with shortages in the short term in order to have prosperity, stability and more freedom later. The growing difficulties of labour shortage and wage inflation were also beginning to be reflected in his statements in the summer of 1946, coming as a surprise to many in the Labour movement and the general public who had assumed that the main problem after the war would be a trading slump and a return to pre-war unemployment.[33]

The looming crisis in world food supplies, with prospects of cuts in Britain's meagre rations, and fears of a major famine in some countries, absorbed more of Morrison's overstretched time and energy in the late spring of 1946. Britain was particularly concerned about the food supplies for two countries under its responsibility: the British Zone of Germany concentrated on the Ruhr industrial complex, and India. The Ruhr was not a major food producer and its inhabitants suffered during 1946 from increasing deprivation; there were fears of riots and a fresh upsurge of fascism. In India famine had long been endemic, but was now approaching disaster proportions, and Britain had no means of helping four hundred million starving people. These were not the only two countries afflicted; ex-President Hoover of the United States had just returned from a world tour estimating that twenty-seven nations held less than two months' food supplies. Over the longer term what was required was an adequate supra-national organization to deal internationally with food problems.* In the short term Britain simply needed more food, by whatever means.

The British Cabinet discussed the problem on 9 May 1946. They felt strongly that Britain was carrying too much of the burden already and was quite incapable of coping with the accelerating crisis. More than a little bitterness was expressed that Britain had for long put up with harsh rationing, with the prospect of more cuts to come, while the United States had great abundance, suffered no rationing and was showing reluctance to carry more of the burden. Morrison was instructed to go immediately to the United States and discuss a fairer sharing of that burden.[34]

The choice of Morrison was interesting. It partly arose from his general economic responsibilities, which extended to membership of the Cabinet Committee on Food. He was also Cabinet spokesman for agriculture and handled publicity on the food situation,† but it more reflected his role as an all-purpose handyman: as he said in his *Autobiography*, he went 'as a sort of watchdog for trouble'.[35] Significantly, Sir Ben Smith, the Minister of Food, a Labour stalwart but of not much political weight, did not go along. Before leaving London on the evening of 11 May, Morrison explained to the press that the absence of the Food Minister was because 'this is above a departmental matter'. He went on to explain: 'I am going on Prime Minister's level and I don't expect to have to consult the Cabinet much.'[36] Morrison let it be

---

* At the time the existing Combined Food Control Board was only temporary and the proposed Food and Agricultural Organization (FAO) was not yet fully working.

† Morrison was pressing Sir Ben Smith for more action from January 1946. (Morrison to Smith, memorandum 31 January 1946. Morrison papers.)

known to the press that he would put to President Truman a new Anglo-American plan for joint co-operation to end the world food shortage, including the proposal to release all British food stocks to Germany and India if the Americans would also release their stocks and guarantee future supply. Morrison emphasized the urgency and importance of his visit and indicated that he wanted no other appointments during his American visit, stating his belief that the political future of the whole democratic Western world depended on solving this food problem.[37]

Morrison flew off from Northolt in a silver Lancastrian, broke his journey at Gander in Newfoundland and was in Washington by ten in the morning on Sunday 12 May.[38] On arrival he made dramatic statements to the press. 'It is no use pretending that the battle against famine is not going against us. It is. Famine will soon be killing civilians and turning out future Fascists more quickly than Hitler and Mussolini ever managed to. . . .'[39] After paying an early courtesy visit to President Truman on his first evening in Washington, Morrison spent the next few days in consultation with his own officials at the British Embassy, and then in very tough negotiations with American government representatives. The real clash came on Wednesday, the fifteenth, with the American Secretary of Agriculture, Clinton Anderson. Prior to this meeting, Morrison had been advised by his officials to soft-pedal the British case, but apparently he overruled them and was determined to tell the Americans bluntly that he felt that the policy of treating Britain, Germany and India as one entity for food supplies was 'intolerable' and that he would insist they should be treated as separate items.[40] After the Wednesday meetings there were reports of violent disagreements between Morrison and the Americans. Morrison, characteristically using the mass media to carry his battle onto a popular level, made a coast-to-coast broadcast on the American radio networks. He outlined the grim world famine situation and took pleasure in pointing out that American pigs ate better than most human beings throughout the world: 'It must not be said that anywhere the hog troughs are full while the children's plates are empty.' He continued, not without a touch of melodrama, to assert that 'the forces of famine are breaking through across the Rhine, the Danube, the Ganges and the Yangtse. The forces of civilization are at this moment taking a worse beating than at any time since Pearl Harbour and the Battle of France.'[41] The echoes of Churchill at his most rhetorical, or perhaps of Ed Murrow, the American war-time correspondent in London, were not meant to be lost upon the American audience. But most American opinion was highly suspicious of Morrison's and Britain's intentions. They believed that Britain maintained large secret hoards of food and that the Labour government was trying to railroad the Americans into rationing and also to renew lend lease food aid to Britain in a new form. In reality, the grain supplies to the British Zone of Germany were now down to enough for only two weeks.[42]

Morrison's mission reached its conclusion in final talks with Anderson, joined by the Acting Secretary of State, Dean Acheson, on the afternoon of the sixteenth and in discussions with President Truman again the next morning, when an agreement was finally reached. In respect of the British Zone of Germany, the Americans explicitly acknowledged that it was part of the world food problem and not Britain's sole responsibility. In addition, the Americans agreed in principle to look at the question of treating the American and British Zones in Germany as a common food zone with equal food supplies. India was also accepted for treatment as a special famine case.[43] These appeared to be major negotiating achievements by Morrison, though in due course it was to emerge that the extent of America's commitment was more ambivalent than Morrison at first suggested. In return for these American concessions in principle, Morrison had been forced, mainly by the hard line of Clinton Anderson, to make very concrete and material concessions. He promised that Britain would give up claims on 200,000 tons of the precious wheat supplies due to her in September, a concession that made bread rationing in Britain in the near future almost a certainty.[44]

Morrison cabled to the Cabinet in London that in order to secure agreement it was necessary to give up the 200,000 tons of scheduled wheat supplies. The British ministers and officials dealing with the German crisis were reported to have received the news as 'something of a shock'.[45] Morrison, however, had been sent with a virtual free hand to negotiate and the Cabinet, which knew that it must get the German and Indian burdens shared with America, had little alternative other than to approve his actions. Immediately, the government began to prepare contingency plans for bread rationing and for the rate of flour extraction in bread-making to be increased to ninety-five per cent. The Tory Opposition and press gleefully exploited bread rationing (it was introduced on 27 June) as proof that Labour's policies had failed and the effect on public opinion was reflected in the swing to the losing Tory candidate, Edward Heath, at the Bexley by-election. At his American press conference on the seventeenth to announce the agreement, Morrison was clearly aware that he had gone to the limit in concessions. 'It will be a blow to my Government,' he said, 'but everybody has to do their best in this matter.' Morrison left Washington that day for New York and then went on to Ottawa for discussions with the Canadian Government on the food problem. He finally flew from Canada in a Lancastrian of Transport Command, arriving in London on the twenty-first.[46] It had been a difficult visit and Morrison could not have been wholly happy with the outcome. There was still more trouble to come.

Rumblings of the storm were heard when Morrison reported to the Commons on 23 May about the agreement. Churchill replied very critically for the Opposition, asserting that it was not clear to them what in fact had been gained in the negotiations, though the concession of 200,000 tons of future wheat allocation seemed to the Conservatives to be a very tangible and costly sacrifice.[47] Next day the matter blew up into an international crisis. An American government spokesman, reacting to a garbled version of Morrison's Commons statement, told a press conference quite bluntly that 'no commitments of the sort specified by Mr Morrison have been made by this Government'.[48] The British press was immediately full of reports of this conflict of interpretations concerning the recent agreement. For Morrison, the personal and political problem was the growing opinion that he had negotiated a bad bargain, in which Britain made concrete concessions for no specific return, and on which he appeared to have completely misled the House of Commons the day before.[49] The explanation was that on the American side there had been an inter-departmental squabble, with the War Department vetoing reference in the official communiqué to any specific commitments; in particular they were concerned that there should not be a reduction and diversion of food supplies currently going to Japan. Not for the first or last time British politicians and officials discovered that making a firm and clear agreement with the American government was like trying to shake hands with an octopus. But Morrison also shared some responsibility for the misunderstanding. The American agreement to help solve the food problem was really no more than a firm statement of intent; he gave the Commons the impression that it was a more concrete commitment. He wished to impress MPs by maximizing the extent of the American contribution and minimizing the British contribution. Yet this was bound to upset the Americans. The matter was finally cleared up and put to rest when Morrison made a further statement to the Commons at the end of May, explaining the misunderstanding and claiming that Washington had authorized him to confirm that his own earlier statement to the Commons did 'correctly represent the understanding reached in our discussions'.[50] Morrison was able to retire from the battlefield in reasonably good order. One of the permanent casualties was Sir Ben Smith, who resigned two days before the debate in pique at Morrison's Washington visit. He was succeeded by John Strachey. Smith was old at sixty-six, exhausted by responsibilities and recurring crises far beyond his capacity to handle, and Attlee anyway intended to sack him at the earliest opportunity.[51]

At Whitsun 1946 Parliament took a brief and well-earned rest. For Morrison and the Labour Party, however, the ceaseless political activity of their first year in office continued unabated. The party conference met at Bournemouth in the second week of June. It was the first assembly since their election victory and spirits were high. It was a great time for Morrison, bustling around the conference hall and the corridors and the side rooms of the hotels. People recognized and acknowledged the great role that he had played both in the election victory and in managing the government's programme since. Morrison was, as one respected observer described, 'the man who will dominate this Conference'.[52] He was the main speaker at the great mass rally on the eve of the formal conference opening. On the Wednesday he returned to an old theme and a recurring task, opposing a resolution from the engineering union and the Fire Brigades Union to admit communist affiliation to the

Labour Party, making what one correspondent described as 'the most bitter and trenchant speech of the Labour Party Conference'.[53] He savagely attacked the communists as potential spies, subordinating British to foreign interests. 'The Communist Party is not only a political party,' he said, 'it is a conspiracy.'[54] The motion to affiliate the communists was rejected overwhelmingly and Morrison then successfully moved an amendment to the Labour Party constitution to make it permanently impossible for other political organizations to affiliate.[55]

Morrison's next and main intervention was in a newer role, speaking for the first time at conference as the government's economic supremo introducing a debate on manpower and the economic situation. He described the economic planning machinery which he claimed was being rapidly developed and then pointed to the success of demobilizing the war economy into a position of peacetime full employment. 'Full employment has never been attempted as a policy in peace-time Britain. Indeed it has never yet been attempted by any country in the world with our form of democratic government and our standards of personal freedom,' he argued. 'This Government is going to attempt it.'[56] He received a tremendous reception, greater than that given to the Prime Minister or to Bevin when they spoke.[57] But conference was not all politics and, as usual, Morrison threw himself with great energy and pleasure into the social side. At the opening Party Ball he 'danced an eightsome reel with wild abandon. He pranced and swung, kicked his heels and emitted barbaric yawps with demonic delight.'[58]

Before returning to Westminster from the conference, Morrison made a pleasant diversionary visit to rural Norfolk. He addressed farmers about agricultural policy and food production, for which he acted as spokesman in the Cabinet. It might have seemed odd and out of character for this cockney, who was frequently alleged to know nothing of life outside of London. In fact, Morrison always went out of his way to cultivate the agricultural vote.[59] He knew that Labour had to build up and consolidate its strength in the countryside if it was to maintain itself as a majority governing party representing all sections of the country. At conference the National Executive Committee's statement on agricultural policy had been rejected and many delegates expressed the view that Labour was doing too little for the farm workers. Morrison now quickly went off to the heart of the farming country to try to repair the damage and reassure the farm workers and the farmers that, given time, Labour would not forget them.

The government ploughed on with its massive legislative programme throughout the summer. Still in the pipeline after Whitsun were the later stages of the Finance Bill, the National Health Service Bill, and the New Towns Bill, and the bills to nationalize civil aviation and cable and wireless.

Morrison's tight parliamentary schedule inevitably led to renewed friction in the House. MPs returned from the Whitsun recess to two successive all-night sittings on the committee stage of the Finance Bill; one of them was the longest since 1936.[60] Morrison publicly warned members not to be in too great a hurry to fix their holiday arrangements since he was still unable to give a firm date for the start of the summer recess.[61] By the middle of July he had organized the Parliamentary Labour Party into three groups which ran a shift system, with only two groups needed on all-night duty at any one time, to maintain a majority, allowing the third group home to sleep. 'We have conclusively demonstrated,' he told the Lewisham Co-operative Society at this time, 'that the old, leisurely and slow-moving method of the Mother of Parliaments was not necessary . . . it is the policy of the Labour Government to see that Parliament and the machinery of Government are the public spirited and efficient servants of the nation.'[62]

Commentators in the press continued throughout 1946 to refer to Morrison as a dictator in Parliament, though there was also admiration for his management technique – his humour in handling people and difficult situations, his skill in giving the impression that he was doing what Parliament wanted rather than vice versa, his mastery of parliamentary procedure and tactics. His exchanges with Churchill on Thursdays when discussing the following week's business aroused particular interest and amusement.[63] Morrison was usually announcing a heavy programme and a tight schedule. Churchill frequently intervened to protest against the speed of legislation, the sending of important bills upstairs to committee, and the fact that little or no time was left to debate other issues. Churchill's attendance in Parliament in 1946 and 1947, as later, was thin and erratic. The sharp and humorous exchanges with Morrison on Thursdays were among the few occasions when the great old war-horse could be relied upon to turn up and display his talents. Morrison normally parried Churchill's thrusts with wit and relish,* though he was absolutely firm in resisting any attempts to slow down the government's progress. Looking back on these exchanges later, Morrison recalled how after a while he began to feel it was getting beyond a joke, going on too often and too long. 'That was borne in upon me when the story went around that it began to be called the Children's Hour. I began to think that it was not quite consistent with Parliamentary dignity, and somehow we quietened off.'[64]

By early August 1946 Morrison had piloted seventy bills through Parliament, and another fourteen were to receive the Royal Assent before the end of the session in November. This parliamentary year was indeed the '*Annus Mirabilis*' and 'High Tide' of Dalton's memoirs. Popular support for Labour continued high, as did the interest in politics in general. Sales of Hansard soared. Newspapers were full of politics, alive again after the drabness of the party truce in war. 'Parliament was a living and dramatic spectacle, successfully challenging competition with all other forms of entertainment.'[65]

Exactly a year to the day after the State Opening of this new post-war

* Sir Edward Fellowes recalled that although Churchill occasionally lost his temper, Morrison never did. Fellowes believed that Churchill never entirely forgot and forgave their wartime disagreement over the Lewisham bomb incident. (Interview.)

Parliament, Morrison took his first serious holiday. He needed peace and quiet to rest after an exhilarating but exhausting twelve months. Southern Ireland seemed ideal and he flew with Margaret to Dublin on 15 August. They then travelled (in an official British police car, a twenty-seven-horsepower Humber) to Glengariff in County Cork. They stayed there for four weeks. He relaxed, read and walked. Inevitably, he became involved with the local community. On one occasion he took part in a local charity quiz, but failed because he could not answer the question about which English poet lived in County Cork (Edmund Spenser). With his holiday over, Morrison took the opportunity to do a little state business in Ireland. He went to Dublin and had talks with De Valera. Afterwards, he gave a press conference and was repeatedly questioned about partition, on which he tried to be non-committal. From Dublin he went to Belfast and stayed over the weekend as guest of the Governor-General of Northern Ireland, Lord Granville, at Government House, Hillsborough, renewing the friendly contacts he had made during the war on his frequent visits to Northern Ireland as Home Secretary.[66]

Back refreshed from Ireland, Morrison took the opportunity before the reopening of Parliament to get out into the provinces and renew his campaign to educate the public on the harsh economic facts of life. He spent the last two weekends of September 1946 addressing meetings in Scotland and in Manchester. On the Clyde he denied rumours that the government was softening in its socialist plans and would back down on some of its nationalization promises – he insisted that iron and steel would definitely be taken into public ownership in this Parliament. He did, however, admit that the economic problems facing them were formidable and pointed out that nationalization was no substitute for harder work and higher production. He went to the Cambridge University Union in mid-October to oppose a motion deprecating 'the increasing tendency of the state to interfere in economic affairs', and vigorously defended the Government's policies. It was a reflection both of the high current interest in politics in general and of the stature of Morrison personally that the attendance to hear him, with a thousand students packing the Union Hall and the doors locked against crowds of others trying to get in, was the highest since 1919.[67]

One subject which began to creep ominously into his speeches at this time, and was arising on the agenda of the Lord President's Committee, was the threatening coal crisis.[68] He expressed concern in public in his Manchester speech in September. He repeated his worries at a press conference in mid-October, called to review progress in the first year of the peace economy, and he grew more troubled as the winter deepened.[69] Morrison was acutely aware that a hard winter could precipitate a serious fuel crisis, with all that would imply for Labour's hopes of economic recovery. At the end of November he told a Leeds audience that 'our voice in world councils would be more effective if we had thirty million tons of coal in reserve than if we had a whole cluster of atomic bombs'.[70] Next day in Newcastle he warned a mass rally of miners that 'shortage of coal now threatens us with permanent austerity'. He closed by imploring the miners to step up production and not to let their Labour Government down.[71]

Dark clouds loomed also over the parliamentary party. During the first session, after 1945, Labour MPs had been wafted along on a wave of triumphant euphoria. The New Jerusalem was about to be built and there was a sense of pride in the party's leaders and confidence in their policies. By the second session the novelty and excitement were wearing off, the problems and the threats to Labour's hopes were growing. These doubts and uncertainties were reflected in growing rumblings within the parliamentary party. So far the old and permanent divisions between left and right, between revolutionaries and constitutionalists, between the dogmatists and the pragmatists, had not publicly reasserted themselves. There had been minor revolts in the lobbies, such as those on old age pensions and on the Civil Aviation Bill, but nothing of real significance. By November 1946 the mood was changing. On the thirteenth, members from both sides took four and a half hours to agree to Morrison's motion that the government should again monopolize all private members' time. In the end, the Chief Whip had to move the closure. Much more dramatic was the revolt on foreign policy. A month earlier twenty-one Labour back-benchers had written a private letter to Attlee calling on the government to abandon Bevin's foreign policy and to follow a more distinctly socialist line,* independent of both the United States and communist Russia. When they received a negative reply, the dissidents tabled an amendment to the Address advocating their 'third force' foreign policy and it immediately received fifty-seven signatures of support. The Parliamentary Labour Party met on 13 November, and after a stern lecture from Morrison about disloyalty, voted by a large majority condemning the rebels' actions and recommending them to withdraw their names from the amendment. They did not, however, obey. Some seventy deliberately abstained in the Commons vote and the number of signatories to the amendment increased to nearly a hundred.[72] Pressure now arose from an indignant right wing to discipline the rebels and to restore standing orders. Morrison steered a skilful middle course. He used the right-wing pressure to frighten the left, but in fact resisted it, refusing either to take disciplinary action or to reimpose standing orders. At the decisive meeting of the party on 28 November he moved a motion deploring organized minorities acting as caucuses contrary to party policy. It also, in urging that standing orders remain suspended, reasserted faith in running the party through 'good fellowship and cordial co-operation'. His views prevailed and his motion was passed nearly unanimously.[73] This had been the first major crisis of loyalty and threat to the unity of the government's supporters. Significantly, it was in the foreign affairs field, where most

* This reflected a rapid loss of confidence in Bevin's policy. On 27 March 1946, only six dissented from a motion at the PLP completely endorsing the government's foreign policy. (*Daily Herald*, 28 March 1946.)

of the future disciplinary problems were to arise. Morrison had handled it well, mixing school-masterly sternness with tactical flexibility. The numbers were anyway too great for discipline to be practical. Difficult days lay ahead and Morrison properly sensed that what was needed was to cool down tempers and not to create martyrs.

Section IX: The Watershed, 1947

Chapter 29

The First Setback

By 1947 Morrison had been in high office, except for a brief break in the summer of 1945, for nearly thirteen years. The last seven years were a time of continuing crisis involving the extraordinary pressures of war and of the immediate post-war period. During the war he had effectively run two separate large departments of state, subject to the constant alarms and emergencies of the bombing and then the rocket blitzes. After 1945 he was the most heavily burdened minister, supervising and co-ordinating Labour's massive programme. He had been active as deputy prime minister, member of the Cabinet, chairman and member of several Cabinet committees, head of the Lord President's Office, and Leader of the House of Commons. He frequently participated in debates. He managed the Parliamentary Labour Party at its formal meetings and in other ways behind the scenes through the Liaison Committee and the Whips' Office. He remained at the centre of power in the Labour Party at national level, through his influence on the NEC and its sub-committees. There he was actively engaged in policy decisions, in organizational decisions, and in questions of discipline. Locally he kept his foot in the door at the London Labour Party, often attending Executive Committee meetings, maintaining contact with the Acting Secretary, Daines, and frequently suggesting or even writing articles for the London Labour Party newspaper, the *London News*. He attended and was the star attraction at the London Labour Party's annual conference, at its May Day celebrations, and at other social functions. Morrison continued to tour the country, especially at weekends, making speeches about the economic situation. The Production and Prosperity Drives launched late in 1946 added to the claims on his time, since publicity and information in the economic field were his responsibility. He also attended many official functions and dinners in London, usually as a guest of honour. Occasionally, as at the gala reopening of the Royal Opera House, Covent Garden, in February 1946, he took Mrs Morrison; but normally he went alone in his official capacity.

In fact his life was an endless treadmill of work and official business. He ate, slept and lived on the job. He had little or no private life or relaxation and it is not clear he would have wanted any or would have enjoyed it. As he moved from workplace to workplace, he was always reading documents, carrying papers and taking the opportunity to discuss questions with people *en route*. He certainly was not 'a third-rate Tammany Hall Boss' as Nye Bevan once alleged, but he had many of the characteristics of the American hustler and operator, ceaselessly working, manoeuvring and manipulating. The physical pressure on a man no longer young was tremendous. At the end of such long and exhausting days, Morrison would normally take to bed with him his box of papers to read in preparation for the next day's business; it was one of his golden rules of politics that a successful man did his homework, and Morrison continued to obey it. He often, as a result, enjoyed little sleep. During the war at the Ministry of Supply he had managed to get to bed at about one or two in the morning and rose again at eight; at the Home Office he frequently did not retire until three or four a.m., to be up again at eight, and even this brief rest was liable to be broken by the noise and vibration of bombs exploding near by. After 1945 he was back in general to working till around two in the morning and then getting up at eight. He was fortunate in that he fell asleep easily and slept deeply. He also contrived to have a rest in his office in the afternoon whenever possible. But the constant pressure and the lack of sleep inevitably took their toll, and he succumbed to the strain with his first major illness in January 1947.

Morrison had taken little rest over Christmas and New Year 1946–7. Parliament continued its remorseless programme: in the week before Christmas Morrison wound up on the second reading of the massive Transport Nationalization Bill.[1] Crucial problems were piling up in the Cabinet: India, Palestine, and the coal crisis. Especially pressing were the 1947 Economic Survey and the draft White Paper containing the economic implications and conclusions of the Survey, which reached his desk just before Christmas. They were depressing reports, underlining the terrible difficulties facing the country in Morrison's field of responsibility. His many committees met right through until the eve of Christmas. He worked on his Cabinet and departmental papers throughout the holiday. Morrison, as Dalton wrote in his diary, 'is very bad at leaving things alone and stopping work'.[2]

His fifty-ninth birthday on 3 January made the occasion for a rare quiet evening at home with his wife. But he had spent the day working, interrupted only by the customary embarrassing exchange of congratulations with Attlee at 10 Downing Street.[3] He told the *Daily Herald*: 'I should like to be thirty-five and live for ever. That's the ideal age. A man usually dies before he can finish his job. That is sad. I know that there will be a legislative programme still and a lot of other things unfinished when I die. On the other hand I confidently hope that a good deal of the legislative programme will be law before I die . . . I have been lucky during my life in having had the opportunity to get things done.'[4] It was in character and in a way sad that Morrison saw life's great purpose in terms of an almost endless legislative programme. It is also interesting that he talked about dying as a possibility, since this did not normally enter his conversation. He was usually very aware that in order to continue to be assumed as the natural successor to the party leadership it was necessary to exhibit or admit no signs of physical decay.

The Cabinet work-load grew dramatically heavier in the early New Year.[5] Morrison was working particularly hard on the draft of the White Paper due to be published within a few weeks, containing the conclusions of the Economic Survey for 1947–8. The coal crisis impinged even more heavily on the Lord President's Committee. Morrison had also added to his near-term burdens by agreeing to visit district conferences of the Labour Party to address the faithful on current problems of foreign policy, on which the parliamentary rebellion in November and December had given strong warning of mounting discontent. The strain finally became too much. Morrison cracked.

On Friday evening, 10 January 1947, Morrison gave a small party for the Attlees on their Silver Wedding anniversary.[6] It was a nice gesture – though perhaps not without an element of political calculation in drawing attention to the party leader's advancing years. On the following Sunday morning, Morrison was taking a walk in Eltham Park near home when he 'felt a sharp pain in the calf of my left leg'.[7] There had been some symptoms the day before when both legs ached. The pain was quite severe and he was virtually unable to walk. He telephoned his doctor, Dr Maclellan of Harley Street, who found that a clot of blood had formed in the deep veins of the left calf and firmly advised him to go to bed and stay there until the condition had subsided completely.[8] At first Morrison did not take kindly to the advice, but he finally submitted and cancelled his appointments, including a scheduled visit to Cardiff the following weekend. But he continued working on his papers, sitting at home in his arm-chair at Eltham with his feet propped up.[9] The first news of his illness was given to the public on the following Thursday, 16 January, when an official statement was issued from the Cabinet Office stating: 'The Lord President is required to rest for a few days because of a superficial thrombosis in the calf of the left leg. He is able to carry on with his work but unable to attend meetings.' It was a hectic week in which the Cabinet met six times.[10] In Morrison's absence Dalton took over the Lord President's Committee, the Socialization of Industry Committee and responsibility for broad economic planning.[11] Arthur Greenwood took over the leadership of the Commons and also took Morrison's place in the chair of the Commons Committee on Privileges.

Morrison was still impatient to get back to work and was letting it be known that his indisposition was slight and his absence would be brief. It was assumed that he would be back in full harness by the reassembly of Parliament on Tuesday the twenty-first.[12] At the end of the week however, his condition dramatically deteriorated. He was awakened in the night with severe pains in the lower part of the chest on the right side. Maclellan was summoned the next morning and it was clear that a fragment of the blood clot had become detached from the calf and had travelled to the base of the right lung. This was serious and could be fatal. Maclellan stated that Morrison must go to hospital for special nursing. Morrison refused to go to a private clinic and insisted that it must be an LCC hospital. He was quickly admitted to Hammersmith Hospital, where he had a ground floor room to himself in complete privacy. Within hours of his arrival he was put on Heparin, a new drug which reduced the tendency of the blood to coagulate. This treatment, with a drug whose side effects were not then fully known, itself produced new dangerous complications. Soon Morrison's kidneys began to haemorrhage and he spat blood. The crisis occurred over the weekend when not all of the undoubtedly high-class hospital supervision was in immediate attendance, Maclellan, who was visiting Morrison as a friend but had no status in the hospital, intervened and took him off the treatment, personally dismantling the drip which was being used. Five days later the anti-coagulant treatment was resumed in a modified form. Morrison at first responded well and after making steady progress began to get up early in February. He was visited by the Prime Minister and by Bevin, and Winston Churchill sent him a bowl of spring flowers with good wishes.[13] Some of the time Morrison took the opportunity to read again his favourite Robbie Burns. Things were looking much brighter, though one black cloud appeared on 6 February when Ellen Wilkinson, who had long admired Morrison to the point of love, committed suicide. She had always suffered from ill health, especially asthma, and kept going on drugs. Her appointment as Minister of Education presented a burden which her frail frame could not carry. The news reached Miss Donald in the morning and she immediately telephoned Dr Maclellan, afraid that 'this could kill Herbert'. She asked Maclellan, a man of outstanding tact and sensitivity, to go to Hammersmith that afternoon and break the news gently. She then contacted the BBC and persuaded them not to broadcast news of the death on the one o'clock news so that Morrison would not hear it unprepared. When told, 'Morrison did not say anything, but he suddenly looked years older'.[14] Dalton also visited Morrison afterwards, and noted that he 'did not look at all well'.[15] It is unlikely that there had been an affair between Morrison and Ellen. She, like other women admirers, would no doubt have been willing, and there was no lack of opportunity, but Morrison was always obsessively cautious, afraid of any scandal which might damage his career. He did not send flowers to the funeral.[16] Years later, at the time of the Profumo affair, he remarked to his second wife that men in public life ambitious to reach the top had to be like Caesar's wife and ensure that nobody could point to signs of moral defect.[17] His definition of moral dereliction was narrow even by the prudish standards of the 1940s. 'He had a strong sense of what South London would disapprove of.'[18]

In mid-February, Morrison was almost ready to go home. But there was a sudden second attack of thrombosis with a further extension of the inflammation of the veins in the left leg. After forty-eight hours, again a portion of the clot became detached from the veins in the leg and travelled to the lungs, this time to the base of the left lung. The situation now became very serious indeed. According to his doctor, 'Mr Morrison's spirits, usually so resilient, sank to a low level'.[19] The famous Lord Horder was brought in, partly on the initiative of another medical friend of Morrison's, Dr Edmund Hambly.[20] Again the controversial question of using anti-coagulants arose among the swarm of physicians hovering around Morrison. On balance it was decided to use Heparin, but once more there was a return of kidney bleeding in a mild form and the drug was then discontinued. For a time his life hung in the balance. As he later wrote, 'not conscious of it at the time, I afterwards realized that I had drifted near to death and then back to life and recovery'.[21]

During February, while the condition of the lung slowly improved, Morrison was almost completely out of the news and there were virtually no references to him in the newspapers – the first time that he had suffered such privacy for many years. His department came to a standstill. 'The whole office went dead,' recalled one of his civil servants. 'We officials were just shadows of the minister. The Whitehall machine would not recognize us while the Emperor was away.'[22] Early in March Morrison was receiving visitors again. He read the daily newspapers and the Hornblower novels,[23] but was forbidden to work on government papers. When Emanuel Shinwell, in desperation, contacted Morrison about the fuel crisis, asking for advice and assistance, Morrison had to tell 'my good friend that I was very sorry; I was still in rather bad shape, and I was incapable of helping him, much as I would have liked to'.[24] Shinwell later firmly expressed the view that had Morrison been well enough to intervene he could have saved the government from much of the muddle it got into over the fuel situation.[25] Maurice Webb also visited Morrison in Hammersmith, keeping him in touch with moves in the party. But in the middle of Webb's report Morrison interrupted him and said 'Just shut up for a quarter of an hour'. He then switched on the radio to listen to the daily adventure series of *Dick Barton, Special Agent*. Afterwards Morrison spent some considerable time explaining to Webb the earlier adventures of Barton in the episodes leading up to that evening.[26] Lady Allen of Hurtwood had a similar experience when visiting Morrison in Hammersmith. Suddenly at 6.45 p.m. he told her to go because he wanted to hear *Dick Barton*.[27]

Morrison was completely out of national politics. While he was away others moved into his territory: on 10 March Cripps was put in charge of the government's publicity and information services and he substituted for Morrison in the big economic debate discussing the whole question of economic planning and resource budgeting. Cripps made a very good impression. There was periodic speculation in the press about who might be Morrison's successor: Chuter Ede's name was mentioned, as were Bevin and Cripps, though not Arthur Greenwood who was deputizing very inadequately as Leader of the House.[28]

Morrison's lung improved slowly and the inflammation in the veins in the legs subsided. He resumed consultations with his civil servants and began to read departmental papers. He left the hospital on 25 March, leaning on a walking stick and assisted by his wife.[29] The hospital had planned to discharge him the day before, but Morrison had objected because 'that's my wife's washing day'.[30]

The following week Morrison left Victoria in the Golden Arrow train to go to Paris and then to the south of France to recuperate. He arrived at Menton on Thursday 3 April and stepped off the train into glorious sunshine. The next day was not so good, wet and windy, but from the weekend onwards Morrison benefited from the fine Riviera sunshine. Staying with him at the Hôtel des Anglais were his wife and daughter, Dr and Mrs Maclellan, and Morrison's Scotland Yard detective, Leeson. It was a quiet family hotel, where Queen Victoria was said to have once stayed; a large picture of her dominated the lounge. Morrison had a big airy room overlooking the Mediterranean. He took all his meals in the hotel restaurant, from the window of which he could see the Italian frontier a quarter of a mile away. The charge for each member of the party was around twenty-five shillings per day. The hotel proprietor told an English newspaper reporter that this was below their normal charge, but Mr Morrison himself had insisted on paying only that much and he 'did not wish to argue that point'.[31]

Morrison lived a simple life of quiet routine while recuperating. He breakfasted at eight every morning, took a short walk before lunch, assisted by a stick and wearing an overcoat even in the sunshine, spent most afternoons reading on his balcony overlooking the sea, and then took another short walk in the evening before dinner at seven. He drank little, smoked an occasional pipe or cigar, and was in bed each night by ten o'clock.

Morrison did not see the Prime Minister before going abroad; he did not even inform him of the details of his proposed departure. Attlee raised this gently in a letter shortly after, suggesting that had he known, he would of course have called on Morrison to say good-bye. Morrison replied, with the politeness but slightly jagged edge which characterized their exchanges, 'sorry we missed, but as Press was well posted on my movements I thought No. 10 would know all particulars'.[32] Attlee kept in touch with Morrison about the proposed government reshuffle, which they had first discussed when Attlee visited him in Hammersmith Hospital. A number of problems had since arisen. Pethick Lawrence, at the India Office, had 'come to the end of his tether and can no more carry on'. Attlee had tried to persuade Wilfred Paling 'to go upstairs but he would not'. Attlee also felt that the government 'could do with an extra Minister without portfolio. I do not know', he added, perhaps considerately, 'whether you will be fit to carry all the heavy load you have been carrying and you might be glad to get some help.'[33]

Morrison replied urging Attlee to delay the reshuffle until after his return: 'a talk between you and I and Whiteley is so much more effective and useful.'

But he anyway pressed his views: 'We *can't* spare Cripps from Board of Trade'; for the Post Office, 'I would prefer one of our business or commercial back-benchers – there is lively creative work to be done at the Post Office'; he suggested Patrick Gordon Walker as Paymaster General, to help him with some economic and public relations chores; and 'by the way I doubt if an RC should go to the FO'. He was, however, more concerned with the urgent need for a radical reconstruction in the whole administration than with quibbling about particular details. He told Attlee bluntly 'We are carrying a fair amount of dead wood. The back-benchers know it and they are unhappy about it, though it is difficult for the most decent to raise their voices. They are not going to be satisfied with moving the draughts around the board – they want the dead wood moved *off* the board, and they are right.' He went on to urge Attlee to bring in youth and to insist on competence. 'We should search the back-benches for bright and promising people otherwise our political stock and the efficiency of the Government will fall. This is the big reason why we should wait for a talk with the Chief Whip: and when the new ones, like the old, are warned that they are on trial we should mean it, for too many regard office as a freehold and that leads to slackness in some cases.'[34]

Morrison was telling Attlee how to run the government, or, at least, how he would run it. It was typically Morrisonian. First, bring on the bright young men. He had always done that, in local and in national politics. The Labour Party was the stronger at all levels for the team of Morrison protégés. Then, insist on the highest standards of competence in government, as he had done at the LCC. He always resented the Labour image of good intentions and high principle achieving nothing because of inefficient execution. All government should be responsible, efficient and effective. Labour government should add idealism, but not at the expense of competence.

Despite Morrison's efforts at delay, which included writing to the Chief Whip,[35] the ministerial changes were made before his return from France. Attlee's letter informing Morrison of the details was surprisingly personal and chatty: 'I'm so glad to hear of your progress . . . The sunshine is cheering us up. It is perfect here this afternoon.' He went on to gossip about Churchill in decline. 'Poor old Winston gets deafer every day. He intervened twice this afternoon to ask why a motion had not been seconded, when the seconder had only just sat down, and why the government had not made a statement when Greenwood had just made it. It is really embarrassing. All good wishes. Yours ever, Clem.'[36]

The ministerial changes did not produce widespread satisfaction. Morrison later complained to Dalton that Attlee had been up to his old game again, merely 'moving all these people round like people on a chess board', even when it was 'obvious that some of them are complete failures and should be got rid of altogether'.[37]

At least Attlee had provided help for Morrison, making Marquand Paymaster General with a brief to assist on economic planning if required. But the deeper dissatisfactions – with the way in which the government as a whole, and the economic management as a whole, were being run from the very top – remained untouched, simmering away until the lid blew off in the summer. Then, as now in April, Morrison was to be consulted and yet not centrally involved, and was again to find himself overseas, dependent on Attlee's laconic letters, when the big reshuffle took place.

After a fortnight of this quiet routine at Menton, Morrison was looking and feeling considerably better. He even visited the Casino at San Remo and felt fit enough to dance briefly there.[38] He left Menton by car and was driven to Paris where he stayed a few days in the British Embassy, spending his time sightseeing or resting, and dining in the evenings with French politicians. He travelled back overnight by Golden Arrow to Victoria and was greeted at the station by friends and some constituents from Lewisham and by his Parliamentary Private Secretary, Gordon Walker. The Press reported him bronzed and looking well though noticeably thinner and walking stiffly.[39]

Morrison was very keen to let it be known that he was fully recovered and fit to resume office. He told the press that he would spend the weekend catching up on his papers and then 'Back to the office on Monday'.[40] He took time off on the Saturday afternoon to go with Gordon Walker to the Cup Final at Wembley where his local team, Charlton Athletic, won the Cup. He did not really understand football, as he willingly admitted, but it was clearly an excellent opportunity to establish himself with the wider public as being back and ready for duty. In fact he had great difficulty in climbing the stairs at the stadium and felt unwell during the game.[41] On the Monday he attended his first Cabinet and settled in again at his Downing Street office. Next day he returned to the House of Commons. Members had been carefully warned in advance that Morrison would enter the Chamber at three o'clock and 'There was therefore a suitable air of expectancy when he came in a few minutes after the hour'.[42] It was noted with pleasure how bronzed he was, and that his hair was still nicely tousled, if rather greyer. 'He was as perky, if not as cocky, as ever. For a moment he behaved like a new boy at school. He handled his Order Paper awkwardly. He seemed ill at ease – until the whole House cheered. And it was a sincere cheer. *They* knew the boss was back.'[43] Cheers came from all sides as he sat on the Treasury bench for the first time since before Christmas. As if regaining his touch slowly he took one single question, replying quietly, 'No Sir'. The temperature warmed up to a little nearer normal at business time on the Thursday, however, when Churchill welcomed him back and hoped 'the strain of his duties in the House will not be more than he can sustain – speaking in a physical and not a political sense'.[44] Morrison in return graciously granted Churchill's request for an extra hour and a half's discussion on the third reading of the controversial Transport Nationalization Bill on the following Monday.

The first real test of whether his political stamina was restored took place not in the House but in his constituency. One thousand five hundred of

Morrison's constituents attended the May Day Rally in Lewisham Town Hall and welcomed him back with resounding choruses of 'For he's a jolly good fellow'. Morrison's main purpose in attending was to make a presentation of an easy-chair to his former agent, Jim Raisin, who had now been appointed London District Organizer of the Labour Party. Morrison owed a great deal to the skilful organizing ability of Raisin, who had first worked with him years ago in Hackney, as indeed he was to owe much in the future to Raisin's wife, Mabel, who was taking over as agent in Lewisham. Each of the Raisins was very important to Morrison's political life. They maintained for him a secure and successful constituency base. Under their guidance the Lewisham party, in its various forms before and after boundary redistribution, achieved the highest membership in the country. They managed to combine efficiency and humanity in a quite brilliant way: under them the constituency party was both a remarkably effective vote-gathering machine and a lively social organization for constituents and party workers. In their view, Morrison was an ideal constituency member, always knowing when to participate in constituency affairs, and when to stay out and leave matters to the local activists. They were professionals and the local constituency machine reflected this.[45] Like a number of other people throughout Morrison's life, they devoted much time, energy and affection, including sacrifices, to working with him and for him. It is sad that towards the end they, like some others, felt betrayed, and that Morrison perhaps took them too much for granted.

Morrison looked well at the Lewisham rally and showed no strain from his recent illness.[46] He made a speech, the first since his return. He went straight back on to the economic theme which he had been hammering before his collapse. Admitting the existence of a major economic crisis, he stressed the need to press ahead with economic planning, with controls and more nationalization in order to achieve greater production and prosperity. Morrison was aware that Cripps was increasingly staking out his claim to the economic field and that he must re-establish his status there.

Morrison sensibly did not plunge back directly into the full official routine he had followed before his illness. Despite repeated assurances that he was back to complete fitness, he carefully shed some of his load. He resigned from the International sub-committee of the NEC and also from the chairmanship of the Committee of Privileges of the House of Commons. He rested in the afternoons on doctor's orders, and it was noted that he did not attend all-night sittings at the House.[47] More significantly, Morrison had finally given up the secretaryship of the London Labour Party, which he had held in one form or another since 1915. The move was not significant in terms of work or influence; Donald Daines had been in all respects but formal title the effective Secretary since Morrison went into government in 1940. As for influence, Morrison could continue to be a power behind the scenes in the London Labour Party whenever he wished to exercise his political weight and great reputation. But it was a break, emotional as well as political. Morrison's thirty-two years as Secretary of the London Labour Party spanned and symbolized much of his political working life. It was his first major political post and he was reluctant to give it up: for nine out of the past eighteen years Morrison had held high national office but he had never taken his name down from the secretaryship of the London party, leaving poor Daines in the unsatisfactory position of Acting Secretary, doing the work and loyally keeping Morrison informed, but never till now enjoying the real trappings and honour of the office. Morrison still saw the London Labour Party as his own organization. Come a general election and then, as in 1945, Morrison moved back into his chair and became the local election boss again. It was typical of the relationship that in 1945 the London party had bought a new car at a total cost of £418 for Morrison's use during the election campaign. With the campaign over and won, and Daines back doing the bread and butter work, the Executive Committee felt it was 'clear that the office in the absence of Mr Morrison had no special need of it'. Daines was told to sell the car. A month after, it was sold – to Morrison himself for £400.[48] By late 1946, with Morrison clearly due for a long period in central government, the dual secretaryship had become anomalous and Daines was appointed full Secretary. The Executive Committee showed its appreciation of Morrison's magnificent services to Labour in London by authorizing the purchase of a 'portable wireless set at a possible cost of £25 for presentation to Mr Morrison'. They also decided to give 'a modest form of dinner' in his honour. This was held at the House of Commons in December 1947. Past and present members of the executive were there, together with Attlee, Lewis Silkin and Charles Key from the government. Morrison could look back with genuine pride at what he had laboured to build. In this year, 1947, the membership of the London Labour Party rose to 285,000 and there were now more than one hundred Labour members on the LCC and over a thousand on the London borough councils.[49]

Speculation inevitably persisted about Morrison's health during the summer of 1947. Some later observers, looking back with the aid of hindsight, suggested that the illness had damaged Morrison permanently and was one explanation for his later poor performance as Foreign Secretary and in opposition afterwards.[50] In fact there is no serious evidence to support this view and quite a lot to the contrary. Morrison's doctor, who saw him regularly once a fortnight in Harley Street, asserted emphatically that the recovery from the thrombosis was complete. The only after-effects were that his leg remained badly swollen. He had regular massage and wore a surgical stocking for the next two years. His general health was good and his heart strong. His only continuing health problem concerned his feet, which were 'like bunches of onions'.[51] To celebrate his recovery the East Lewisham party took him on a delightful trip down the Thames on a Sunday in late June. The paddle steamer *Golden Eagle* was chartered and four hundred party members sailed to Southend for the day. Morrison and Margaret sat happily on deck in the sun. It was one of those informal party occasions at which Morrison un-buttoned and exuded jollity as he enjoyed himself among his own people.[52] Certainly to all appearances Morrison had resumed precisely where he left off when taken ill. At the Margate conference at Whitsun he made his usual address to an eve of conference rally and in mid-week he made the main speech on the economic situation, dealing primarily with manpower and the need for greater production.[53] In the House of Commons he also returned to find business as usual: he resumed charge of the massive legislative programme, with a great deal of business being rushed upstairs into committee, and the Tory opposition still complaining about a lack of time for proper debates.[54] The nationalization of electricity and of transport, the Agriculture Bill, the National Service Bill (which took forty hours including one all-night sitting) and the Town and Country Planning Bill were all loading the time-table. Town and country planning proved particularly contentious, not only because of the bill's content, but because of Morrison's and the government's efforts to rush it through. The bill itself covered a hundred pages and there were a further seventy-five pages of amendments, making a total of some four hundred amendments in all; this bill was pushed through in three days and many of the amendments were only in the hands of MPs a day before they were expected to discuss and vote on them. Morrison continued to handle the opposition in general, and their leader in particular, with skill and humour. After the old man returned in July from his own operation, Morrison went out of his way to cross the floor and shake Churchill's hand. Before announc-ing the following week's business Morrison said 'The Rt Hon. Gentleman has made a remarkable recovery and all the signs are that we shall have trouble from him very soon. We are delighted to see him back in his place.'[55]

If anything it was the rumblings from behind Morrison, rather than those from across the floor, which worried him and his colleagues in the government. The growing economic crisis, precipitated by the terrible winter of 1946–7 and the consequent fuel shortages, had finally shattered the euphoria that followed the 1945 electoral victory. Now the party was full of doubts and complaints. The real explosion was to come in August and September. But even in May and June Morrison was back to his management role, lecturing back-benchers at meetings of the Parliamentary Labour Party on their behaviour, and urging better discipline, while resisting pressure from some to restore standing orders. Sensing the need to change to a lower gear during the second half of the Parliament running up to the next election, he promised the parliamentary party on 4 June that there would not be such a heavy legis-lative programme in the following session, and in passing urged them to cultivate the middle classes.[56]

Chapter 30

The Storm

The storm which struck the Labour government in the high summer of 1947 arose directly from the mishandling of two major strands of policy: steel nationalization and economic planning. Morrison was intimately connected with both policies and he was thus to suffer considerable buffeting.

It will make for clarity to disentangle the two policy areas and describe them separately, but in reality the troubles with the economy and with steel ran together, each feeding the hysterical atmosphere of suspicion and recrimination within the party, and making rational and balanced decisions more and more difficult.

The nationalization of iron and steel was a highly emotional issue for many in the Labour movement. To those who had witnessed the cruelties and sufferings of the pre-war industry, nationalization was both a remedy for the workers and a revenge on the steel masters. But the party had no detailed blueprints for nationalization and little progress was made in the new Government's early days towards carrying out the 1945 election promise. Iron and steel were low on the list of priorities of Morrison's Future Legislation Committee, in line with both the 1944 TUC's chosen list of preferences and Morrison's personal inclinations.

The Ministry responsible, Supply, was at first wholly taken up with absorbing the former Ministry of Aircraft Production. It started to get to grips with the steel question early in 1946, setting up a new steel section under Frank Lee. It was at this time that the Supply Minister, John Wilmot, finally rejected the industry's own modernization plans as inadequate and decided to go for full nationalization. He submitted his proposals to Morrison's Economic Policy Committee in March 1946, but Morrison raised objections, fearing that the changes would disrupt steel production at a critical time for the national economy. The committee could not reach agreement and the proposal was passed on to the full Cabinet, where Morrison's objections, and Attlee's uncertainty, were overruled by the combined strength of Bevin, Dalton, Bevan and Cripps. A Cabinet committee was appointed to prepare plans for full nationalization.[1] In the meantime, Wilmot announced that he would set up a new Iron and Steel Board, replacing the existing Control Board, with the brief to collect information on the industry and advise on the process of nationalization. At this point, conflict with the employers came into the open and the British Iron and Steel Federation refused any further co-operation with the proposed board,[2] forcing Wilmot to compromise, and when the new board was finally appointed in September 1946, in return for the participation of the BISF he agreed to withdraw any mention of advice on nationalization from its terms of reference. Meanwhile, other agents of delay were at work: within the ministry, for instance, there was division over whether to nationalize completely or just to take a majority shareholding – which would secure control without involving a radical alteration in the structure of the industry.

When Morrison fell ill at the beginning of 1947 the process was still bogged down. Dalton took over the Lord President's Committee from him and tried to hurry things along. At the first Cabinet after Morrison's return from recuperating in the south of France, on Monday 28 April, ministers agreed to Wilmot's preliminary headings for a nationalization bill, and decided to proceed in the next, the 1947–8, session by a simple acquisition of shares, while retaining the names and forms of the existing individual companies. This looked like a final decision, but in fact the main political difficulties with steel now lay just ahead. The Cabinet verdict was, as Dalton described, 'only a majority decision ... and a wavering decision at that'.[3] Against – though mainly because they wanted to nationalize gas first, rather than because they shared Morrison's deeper doubts – were Attlee, Shinwell, Tom Williams, Greenwood, Jowitt and Addison. Attlee had been approached, while Morrison was in hospital in the spring, by the steel industry leaders. Sir Andrew Duncan and Ellis Hunter came to see him to argue against full nationalization. The Prime Minister was receptive, and when Morrison returned to add to the strong minority of Cabinet doubters, he received 'an agitated approach by the Prime Minister ... saying that he was quite sure we had made a mistake'.[4] Morrison, typically but probably foolishly, took on the responsibility for trying to produce a compromise between the government and the steel employers.

Morrison's action was an error of judgment, setting himself against most of the big men in the Cabinet. Yet his motives and reasons are fairly easy to understand. He undoubtedly agreed with Attlee. He had never been enthusiastic on full nationalization of iron and steel[5] – though later he was unusually angry at suggestions that he was 'against' steel nationalization. He claimed simply to have investigated the pros and cons.[6] Certainly he struck at least one colleague as being 'genuinely open-minded'.[7] As economic overlord, however, he was very receptive to the additional argument that precipitate nationalization would disrupt steel production at a time when Britain's economic future hung in the balance.[8] After the terrible winter, production was down, exports dragging, the trade balance increasingly unfavourable, and

o

the precious dollars of the American loan draining away. The pressures were mounting. Duncan had been on good terms with Morrison for some years and found him accessible and open to argument.[9] Morrison liked dealing with tycoons, such as Duncan, and in general they liked him, as Chandos said, 'because you got down to brass tacks with him'.[10] Morrison readily agreed with Attlee's request to lead the manoeuvres to compromise on iron and steel – against the wishes of his senior colleagues in the Cabinet and against the deeper sentiments of the party (though not of the steel union leadership, which had swung to Morrison's point of view). Morrison had a streak of rash courage within his otherwise cautious character. He often took an almost perverse delight in pursuing what he saw as 'realism' against the endemic dogma or woolly sentiment to which his party was prone. In this case it was very unwise, leaving himself politically exposed. Attlee was the main instigator; he shrewdly left Morrison to do the work and take the punishment if it went wrong.[11]

The Cabinet, never having been solid for nationalization, now backtracked and authorized Morrison to explore the possibilities and terms of a compromise with the steel masters.[12] Morrison then began discussions with Duncan. He was aided by Wilmot, some of whose departmental advisers supported a compromise. The discussions went on right through the summer of 1947. Morrison eventually clarified a hybrid scheme which was acceptable to Attlee and Wilmot. It involved public supervision of iron and steel but fell short of full nationalization. Under its proposals, the powers of the existing Iron and Steel Board to control the industry would be strengthened. The employers' administrative headquarters – Steel House – would be transferred to service the Board. The last and most (though not very) radical proposal was that the government should have reserve power to take over a unit of the industry, on the recommendation of the board, if it proved inefficient.[13]

Morrison had met the requirement of his brief. He had produced a compromise plan which was acceptable in broad terms to most of the steel bosses and to Lincoln Evans, general secretary of the steel union, was acceptable to himself and the Prime Minister, and which he believed he could sell to the party. The problem was still the Cabinet. Morrison put his plan to them in the midsummer of 1947. Discussions on it in late July and early August produced a crisis. Bevan, with a parade of anger and high principle strikingly similar to that exhibited in the Budget crisis of 1951, threatened on 31 July to resign if there was any compromise from full nationalization. The majority of the Cabinet agreed in rejecting Morrison's plan: but they dissented from Bevan's urgency and inclined to do nothing about steel in the coming session. This was the final decision of a long and exhausting Cabinet going on throughout the morning of 7 August. Morrison's scheme was firmly rejected and buried for ever.* The Cabinet reaffirmed its intention to introduce full nation-

* In his *Autobiography*, p. 296, Morrison mentions only three ministers against his plan, but Dalton, more convincingly, in a full diary record, claims that it was a clear majority.

alization, while expressing doubts whether it could be achieved in the coming session.[14]

This Cabinet decision was conveyed to a 'very hysterical and steamed up' parliamentary party meeting on the following Monday, 11 August.[15] After a discussion on the economic situation, led by Bevin and Attlee, Morrison was called to man the barricades on steel. A resolution was moved from the floor demanding full nationalization in the coming session. This was in line with a back-bencher's petition then going the rounds which had already acquired nearly two hundred signatures. Feelings in the party were obviously and openly against Morrison's position. He, as usual, did not waver under fire. He replied to his critics 'very ably',[16] conveying the government's decision to go ahead with nationalizing appropriate sections of the industry, but insisting that the timing must be left to the Cabinet. He appealed, unsuccessfully, for the motion from the floor to be withdrawn, but was rescued when 'the previous question' was moved and this scraped through on a vote of eighty-one to seventy-seven.[17]

For Morrison especially this was not a happy episode. He had suffered the odium of supporting the steel compromise without any compensating success for his plan. At the end, as so often, he was left holding the baby. When the steel compromise was finally put to the hostile Cabinet, it seemed wholly Morrison's responsibility. Attlee, never a believer in lost causes, barely spoke, later explaining that he did not support Morrison in Cabinet because 'it was not my job' to do so.[18] Wilmot, till then the minister in charge of steel, was virtually sacrificed to atone for the waverings of his Cabinet superiors. He was unlucky: being outside the Cabinet, he lacked the power to control the destiny of his ministry. Attlee sacked him in October and never found him another job in the government.[19]

This messy conclusion to the iron and steel episode coincided with the disastrous culmination of the economic crisis which had been brewing throughout 1947. Back in the new year, just before Morrison fell ill, his Ministerial Committee on Economic Planning (Morrison, Dalton, Cripps and Isaacs) had been sweating over the draft for its Economic Survey for 1947. At the heart of the problem was the acute manpower shortage: the manpower deficiency for the year was forecast to rise to over 600,000. The Committee drew up proposals for essential cuts in military personnel both from the fighting ranks and from supply. They also recommended postponement of the long-scheduled rise to fifteen in the school leaving age and the conscription of women to national service. This plan was put to the Cabinet on 16 January 1947. It was the first week of Morrison's illness, 'which,' wrote Dalton, 'as

(Diary, 8 August 1947, Vol. 35.) Lincoln Evans, the steel union leader, later claimed that Bevin was uncertain which line to take and that he, Evans, could have swung him to support Morrison's compromise had he not been abroad at a conference in Stockholm at the time of the crucial Cabinet meeting. (Interview, Sir Robert Shone.)

he was one of the joint authors of our plan, was very unfortunate and weakened our debating stiength'.[20] The Cabinet rejected all these proposals. According to the Chancellor, 'much of it was brushed aside . . . in an atmosphere of emotional impatience and intellectual levity'.[21] The service ministers had been particularly intransigent, led by Albert Alexander and backed by Attlee. Dalton, who took over Morrison's Cabinet committee chairmanships during his illness, was furious. He wrote to Attlee afterwards complaining, 'I was astonished at the blank wall I met, both from you and Albert', and warned him that 'we are, I am afraid, drifting, in a state of semi-animation, towards the rapids'.[22]

The economic situation continued to drift and deteriorate over the rest of the winter and spring, while Morrison was recuperating. The winter itself was of almost unprecedented severity and length. Coal supplies were frozen at the pitheads, while industry's stocks ran perilously low. In February, electricity supplies had to be cut and large sections of industry came to a halt. Unemployment briefly shot up to two million. Production sagged. Export losses were estimated at £200 million. The gold and dollar deficit, which had begun to rise in the last quarter of 1946, rocketed to $500 million in July, the month when sterling was finally made fully convertible according to the conditions of the 1946 American loan.[23] Other external factors, such as deflationary policies in the United States damaging British exports, added to the internal difficulties of over-full consumer demand and very high capital investment leading to inflationary shortages of labour and materials.

Given the world-wide famine of dollars, and that sterling was probably over-valued, it was surprising and culpable that Dalton and, especially, his financial advisers, made such inadequate preparations against the pressures which would inevitably arise when sterling was made convertible. Countries holding credit sterling balances with Britain naturally wanted to buy basic necessities, such as corn and coal, from America; for until now, they had lacked the dollars to do so. Sterling convertibility gave them an opportunity to use their sterling balances for dollar trade. It was the only European currency now freely convertible and there was bound to be a rush to switch.

The Treasury and the Bank of England had not, of course, been entirely negligent: convertibility was introduced in stages and mutually protective arrangements made with some creditors. Exchange controls were not completely ended. Most important, official forecasts had suggested that sterling could take the expected temporary strain providing the national targets for exports and for coal and steel production were met. But these forecasts were too optimistic. As the flight out of sterling began and gathered momentum daily, the Treasury and the Bank, like the Cabinet, seemed paralysed.[24] No approach was made to Washington to defer or rescind convertibility. The Cabinet ministers dithered and ducked from taking firm, if painful, measures. The most obvious orthodox remedy, hammered home at them weekly by the influential *Economist*, was deflation. But it would have to be savage to guarantee effectiveness, threatening to bring unemployment and, possibly, having to be accompanied by devaluation. The spectre of 1931 was too haunting for a Labour administration happily or quickly to contemplate such medicine – though it had to swallow much of it in stages over the next two years. As Morrison said in the Commons debate on 8 July: 'The Government didn't feel it right to impose shortly after the war . . . cuts of a scale which would require a drastic adjustment of our standard of living until it is perfectly clear and certain that this is the only course open to us.'[25] This humane, but self-defeating, reluctance to impose a harsher regime on the British people could not continue much longer.[26]

As the storm clouds gathered on the economic front, Labour's optimism, symbolized by the booming confidence of Dalton in his Budget speeches of 1945 and 1946, and the jauntiness of Morrison in his earlier speeches around the country, naturally evaporated. In this depressing climate, Morrison strove to re-establish his primacy in the economic team following his absence in the four months until May, during which time the Treasury had reasserted its influence against his department. He took over from Cripps the fortnightly press conference begun in March and devoted to educating the press and public on the economic situation. Cripps had made a strong impression in Morrison's absence, as he also did when introducing the Economic Survey to the Commons.[27] Journalists noted the change in style at the press conferences, from Cripps with the passionless technical skill of a surgeon in an operating theatre to the more pugnacious Morrison. Morrison also made these occasions, which were held in various government buildings and even in cinemas, more relaxed. Usually about 150 journalists attended. 'The whole thing is pleasantly informal. Everybody smokes. Morrison, seated between his experts, puffs his pipe, makes the official statement, then answers a shower of questions, often joking with the correspondents, most of whom he knows well.'[28] Although never really at home with masses of statistics or with complex economic analysis, Morrison was able to coast amicably through these meetings with long-familiar newspapermen. He mainly banged away at the well-worn themes of the need for more steel and for more coal and for less dollar imports.

He was also in the summer pushing ahead with building up his economic planning team. He announced the membership of the new National Planning Board early in July, explaining that its task was 'to advise His Majesty's Government on the best use of our economic resources, both for the realization of a long-term plan and for remedial measures against our immediate difficulties'. Morrison summoned the first meeting of the board before the end of the month, with Edwin Plowden, the new head of the economic planning staff, as its chairman.[29]

Morrison was scheming to bring back into his team his friend, Clem Leslie, as the Planning Board's chief public relations officer, and to get promotion for Max Nicholson, whose radical intelligence and non-establishment attitudes were seen in some quarters to be just as provocative as Leslie's proposed high salary. When Dalton saw Morrison shortly after he left hospital at the beginning of May, he noted that: 'He spent too much time this afternoon talking about his staff. He wants to get the inevitable Leslie back from Industrial Design to do his publicity and he wants Master Nicholson to be promoted. He said he thought he ought to have the rank of Permanent Secretary, but that he found Bridges "a bit sticky about this".'[30]

The difficulty was not only about Nicholson's status, but also where the new Planning Board, through its chief officer, was to be centred: in Morrison's own office or, as Bridges wanted, in the Cabinet Office. Morrison feared that if Plowden was based outside the Lord President's Office this would put his own economic advisers, and especially Nicholson, in an isolated and ambiguous position. For reasons of departmental bargaining power, he also wanted Nicholson on an equal status to the other top civil servants. With Nicholson at Permanent Secretary rank, Plowden in the office, and public relations in the experienced hands of Leslie, Morrison would have re-established, even strengthened his position in the economic hierarchy of Whitehall. Such centralization, combined with his own ministerial role as chairman of the relevant Cabinet committees, also made some sense in terms of efficient decision-taking, though it still left the Treasury fatally outside the process. But the civil service establishment was less happy. Morrison's henchmen were not 'sound' in conventional Whitehall terms – Nicholson and Leslie were both 'outsiders' in the career sense. As a team, working for the deputy prime minister, having high rank and financial status, they would represent a fortress of countervailing power to the Cabinet Office and Treasury. To the orthodox Whitehall machine it was desirable ultimately to eliminate them; in the short run, their threat could be minimized, for instance, by working to depress the status of Nicholson and to detach Plowden and Leslie altogether.* Demotion, fragmentation, isolation and ultimately elimination, were the stages by which the Lord President's independent economic powers were whittled away and the Treasury was re-established in its primacy.

Morrison's difficulties with his staff came to a head early in July. He clashed with Bridges on the fourth. Next day, Bridges wrote him what was, from a civil servant to a deputy prime minister, a remarkable warning. In a 'Personal and Private' letter, Bridges said he was deeply 'disturbed about what will happen if, as I gathered is your intention, you press your point of view ... I hope you will not think I am taking too much on myself if I say that all my instinct prompts me to urge on you, if I may say, that you should not press your point hard, if you find it meets with resistance.'[31]

Morrison replied in an even more frank tone, complaining of Bridges' lack of co-operation, of his hostility to Nicholson, of the efforts to subordinate him to the Treasury and to prevent the Lord President's Office from functioning as a team. Bridges had warned him not to press his case too hard. Morrison

* Plowden was attached to the Cabinet Office, Leslie to the Treasury.

now tried to make it clear that, while he was the economic boss, he would not allow questions of economic organization to be settled over his head. If he allowed this matter to go by default, it would reflect a serious weakening in the authority he had exercised before falling ill. Morrison made his points clearly and his position unequivocal:

Thank you for your note of the 5th inst. I am afraid I also was unhappy and disturbed – indeed, 1 have been from time to time during the period of my present office. . . .

I trust I am wrong, but I have a feeling that when you and I meet about my problems, you have a disposition to resist . . . I was no party to the effort to tuck the economic planners into the Cabinet Office and I conceive that it weakens my authority and tends towards an unhealthy 'separation' in the office. My office must be co-operative with the depts but also possess a proper degree of independence, even of the Treasury. I sometimes wonder whether you wish me to be over-dependent on the Treasury: but as you know I am always anxious to give the Treasury view full weight and have often supported the Chancellor in his difficulties. Another & more delicate point. I have a feeling you have it in for Nicholson & want to clip his wings. I could not submit to this – he's too valuable to waste. I shall always be grateful to you for urging his services on me, but if we don't let him have scope & the necessary authority in discussing matters with the Depts. he can't function. He has not sought & I would not permit him to cramp Plowden's position & rights. So far as I know they get on well together. For many months I have urged to you that he should be up-graded with no results except mysterious hints against him. He is an able & valued officer, he has my confidence, it wd. be foolish as well as unfair to restrict him to the verge of relative uselessness. Nor can I run my office as if it were a series of separate & unrelated pieces of machinery. I am worked hard enough without that. . . . Of course if higher authority wants the economic planners to be run as a separate organism, it could be transferred to the Paymaster-General, the M/ without Portfolio or the Lord Privy Seal. But if I am to carry this tricky task I cannot agree to the shaping of the organization being settled over my head.

Sorry to write like this but it is best that you & I should know our respective minds.[32]

Morrison was quite clear about the proper relationships between himself, civil servants and the Prime Minister, and as the minister responsible for economic planning he had the right to press his views about the appropriate staffing and machinery. The Prime Minister could overrule this, as he said. But he would not be deflected by official obstruction without arguing the matter out. This combination of moderate language, openness to argument, and a glimpse of steel should it come to a fight, was typical of what was best in Morrison's politics. Most civil servants who worked with him, including

Bridges, respected him for it. But this concern for staffing and salaries and status gave fuel to Morrison's critics. To them he seemed to be more worried about creating a caucus of old friends in his office than with the economic problems facing them. Morrison 'is just trying to collect a circle of old familiar faces; Government by crony,' wrote Dalton. It was unfair, especially coming from Dalton, who practised 'Government by crony' on a larger scale than anybody except Churchill, but it was being widely and damagingly said.[33]

Morrison's return to the driving seat in the economic troika was apparently underlined when he was chosen to open for the government in the big economic debate on 8 July. This was a critical parliamentary occasion, a week before sterling convertibility was resumed. It was also Morrison's first major speech in the Commons since his return from illness and it attracted much press and political attention. It was not a success. He properly emphasized the gravity of the nation's position, admitting that the gaps in production and exports had defeated the government. Without dramatic overseas aid – he referred here wistfully to wartime Lease-Lend from America – he saw no alternative to 'great readjustments' in 'our production and in our whole standard of living'.[34] It was a sad tale of failure, 'a sombre and sobering address – a grim speech in a glum House'. Morrison's presentation was flat. He read out his long, typewritten speech with little animation. At the end he slumped down dejectedly and then came under withering attack from the Conservatives opposite, while his own ranks sat dispiritedly quiet behind.[35] To the Tories, as to the Governor of the Bank of England and to some American spokesmen, the threatening economic collapse meant that Labour's ambitions for further nationalization must be abandoned. So in the world at large, as in the Cabinet and the Parliamentary Labour Party, this economic débâcle became interwoven with the saga of steel nationalization and Morrison's concurrent and equally unrewarding efforts there.

The Cabinet spent July and much of August, when it wasn't fighting about steel, coming to grips with the bleak economic outlook. Ever since January, Dalton, who has been excessively blamed for his role in the débâcle, had been trying to get his colleagues to accept a programme of expenditure cuts: in the armed services in Palestine, Egypt and Germany, and in imports, such as food and tobacco from the United States. Only Cripps, and he but passively, gave support. The other ministers, particularly Attlee, Bevin and Alexander, would not 'face the plain facts of arithmetic'.[36] But by the end of July Morrison had come out more openly and firmly in support of Dalton in Cabinet.[37] He had, of course, long been aware of – and had frequently expressed public concern at – the mounting economic problems. He was the minister who at each economic press conference publicized the latest list of depressing statistics on shortfalls in Britain's dollar reserves. But he had certainly not pursued the necessary remedies with his customary energy. Now at last, with the tidal waves of disaster bearing down upon them, with the attempts at sterling convertibility and at a compromise on steel crashing in failure, Morrison and his colleagues plunged into a desperate three weeks of crisis decisions, beginning with the Cabinet of 31 July and concluding with the Cabinet suspending convertibility on 17 August. The whole future of this Labour government, elected in triumph and high hopes only two years earlier, seemed at stake.

The pressures on Morrison, as on other senior ministers at this time, were tremendous.[38] Late at night on 30 July, Morrison, Bevin, Dalton and Cripps met with Attlee at 10 Downing Street, to prepare for the following day's crucial Cabinet on the economy and on steel. Edward Bridges and Wilfred Eady were there from the civil service top echelon. They had before them the Chancellor's Cabinet paper setting out the alternative economic measures open to the government. They had reached the point where decisions could no longer be delayed. Bevin 'who had obviously had a very good dinner . . . was at his worst'. After an hour of rambling and not always sober observations from the Foreign Secretary, Morrison walked angrily out of the meeting, muttering as he went that he had 'had enough of this drunken monologue'. Attlee showed 'no power of gripping and guiding the talk'. Dalton himself, now regularly taking benzedrine stimulants,[39] was again frustrated from making progress and the meeting broke up inconclusively, with Bevin lurching in his characteristic sailor's roll towards the door and inquiring 'where do we sleep tonight – in 'ere?'[40] It was all very human, but, even allowing for any characteristic exaggerations in Dalton's reportage, perhaps not a serious way to run a government in a crisis. To Morrison, apart from his normal hostility towards Bevin, the occasion must have seemed irresponsible, which was the worst and least forgivable form of government.

Next day, before the Cabinet, Dalton told Attlee that he would resign unless his measures were approved; Cripps, rather reluctantly, agreed to leave with him. The Cabinet was at the same time faced by Bevan's blunt threat of resignation if they accepted Morrison's compromise plan for the steel industry.[41] Labour was in appalling disarray. Morrison was at the heart of it, as author of the steel compromise and as 'the Minister in charge of the economic drive'.[42] After the Cabinet he summoned an emergency meeting with the TUC, on the eve of the August bank holiday, and begged that all export workers go on overtime. He also raised with the union leaders the explosive issues of wage policy and direction of labour.[43]

After the bank holiday, which Morrison spent working on the crisis, he piloted rapidly through the Commons the Supplies and Services Transitional Bill, giving the government emergency powers.[44] Next day Parliament adjourned, its mood soured by the bitter clashes of the last few weeks. The Conservatives at last began to scent recovery from their recent electoral rout. In August they took the lead in the Gallup poll for the first time since the war. Labour was depressed and demoralized, in proably its lowest spirits of the whole Parliament, a far cry from the triumphant pleasures of its first summer adjournment only a year before. As the parliamentary correspondent of the *Manchester Guardian* wrote: 'not since 1931 has Parliament broken up for a summer holiday with this sense of economic as distinct from foreign crisis threatening.'[45] For Labour the 1931 analogy was frightening.

The parliamentary adjournment did not mean rest for Morrison. He was left to hold the fort in a London heat-wave while the Prime Minister went on holiday to North Wales.[46] Within days the financial storm broke upon his head. The haemorrhage of Britain's dollar reserves had gathered pace in the weeks after convertibility, as overseas holders of sterling balances converted them into precious dollars. By the third week of August the dollar credits which Britain had obtained from the 1946 American and Canadian loans were three-quarters exhausted. The situation was out of hand. On his first weekend in control, 15–16 August, Morrison conducted frantic telephone calls with Attlee in Wales, with the Chancellor in his Wiltshire retreat, and with officials in Washington. An emergency Cabinet was summoned for the Sunday afternoon. Aircraft and cars were dispatched to remote parts of the kingdom to collect ministers from Inverness and from the Channel Islands, to bring Attlee back from remote Wales, Bevin from pretty Swanage, Dalton from West Leaze.[47] They met from 5.00 p.m. till just before 8.00 p.m. and took the basic decision to suspend convertibility. Morrison had a few minutes' conversation beforehand with Attlee and Dalton. He felt and expressed himself very strongly on the mishandling of the whole economic situation, particularly blaming the Treasury and the Bank of England for what he alleged was their inept advice.[48]

After the critical Cabinet of 17 August most ministers returned to their holiday retreats. A small nucleus among them – Bevin, Dalton, Cripps and Alexander – remained to assist Morrison, as acting Prime Minister, over the last hurdles of ending convertibility, which was finally arranged on Wednesday the twentieth.[49] During that day, amid hectic last-minute negotiations with Washington, Morrison took time off to hold his scheduled press conference on the economic situation. He put on a skilful performance, giving no inkling to the 250 journalists crowded into the Ministry of Food cinema at Montague House of the imminent crisis move.[50]

With convertibility suspended, and the most immediate threat to the currency reserves halted, the government turned to other longer-term measures of protection. The inner Cabinet of ministers remaining in Whitehall met throughout the following week, working on plans for increased exports, for more painful restraints on consumer spending and for cuts in the investment programme.[51] Morrison was effectively in charge of the government throughout this period of intensive activity, co-ordinating the formulation of the new measures and the inter-departmental discussions necessary to implement them.[52] By the time Attlee returned in early September, releasing Morrison to take his own holiday, the main ministerial and administrative work had been completed.

Morrison broadcast to the nation on the Saturday evening after the convertibility suspension, explaining the crisis and calling upon further reserves of Dunkirk spirit. He was still in good humour, always enjoying being in charge even when things went badly. The radical press continued to be kind to him. The *Star*, ever a friend, carried an article, perhaps inspired, reporting that after his broadcast 'within a few minutes of his leaving the microphone, Mr Morrison's office was receiving messages of congratulations'. The newspaper took the opportunity (lest any competitors for the leadership might hint that he was in no physical or mental shape to take power) to point out that despite his mammoth work-load, 'he is very fit and has completely recovered from his recent illness'.[53] The *Daily Herald* enthused similarly a few days later, describing how Morrison had been 'holding the fort in London and putting in an incredible amount of work, through the heat wave'.[54] Morrison certainly needed friends at this time, for a crisis was blowing up in the party, both about the leadership and about the direction of economic policy within the government.

In his *Autobiography* Morrison repeated the charge he made to Attlee before the Cabinet on the seventeenth, placing the responsibility for the 1947 economic crisis firmly at the door of 'the faulty administration at the Treasury for which Dalton must be held responsible as head of the Department'.[55] The evidence for Treasury inadequacy in 1947 and on many other occasions in Britain's post-war economic experience is too substantial to question. Dalton himself reports how he was assured by his advisers in July that convertibility had been discounted and would not put serious pressure on Britain's reserves. The former Chancellor later reached the considered opinion that 'it would be less of a disaster if the Foreign Office ran our Foreign Policy than if the Treasury and the Bank ran our Financial Policy.'[56] Even Cripps, whose later orthodoxy endeared him to his advisers, once asked his Treasury officials to leave a meeting of the powerful Economic Planning Committee and then told the Committee that he did 'not trust his own officials' because of their hostility to planning.[57]

The ministers who dithered throughout 1947 in Cabinet, avoiding difficult decisions, and thereby making more painful ones ultimately unavoidable, were also to blame. Bevin and Alexander resisted the service cuts to the end. Attlee never took a stand against these two, often supported them, and did not give the government a firm lead on this basic issue. Dalton was much less complacent than is generally believed and was concerned to implement urgent measures to control the gathering crisis;* but he sadly underestimated the extent to which convertibility would sweep away our reserves and made no contingency moves towards Washington to mitigate the convertibility obligation. Cripps was passive until too late. The responsibility and guilt were widely shared. The nation as a whole, impatient from the deprivations of war,

---

* For an impressive refutation of the conventional view that Dalton was also positively responsible for the current inflation through his policy of low interest rates, see the article 'Investigating a Legend', by 'an Economist' (C. A. R. Crosland) in *Tribune*, 11 February 1949.

was reluctant to face the necessary sacrifices of peace. But in the end Morrison himself must take the main blame. He was the economic chief. He sat in the Cabinet and in committee from May to July and offered nothing of relevance to the crisis. He was building his economic staff superstructure while the dollar foundations of the economy washed away. When, inevitably, the reappraisal of the nation's economic management happened, it was not surprising that some people would press for Morrison's to be one of the heads put on the block.

Chapter 31

The Putsch

The main source of political discontent with Morrison as chief economic minister was Stafford Cripps, although Attlee, Bevin and Dalton did not dissent from Cripps's general line of criticism.[1] As early as April Cripps was telling Dalton that Morrison was 'incapable of handling planning' and insisting that Bevin must take over. Cripps warned the Chancellor that 'unless we can get our planning done right, we shall be sunk'.[2] Cripps persisted in his criticism after Morrison returned from convalescence, and expressed to Dalton concern 'both as to [Morrison's] health and as to [his] capacity to tackle – or really to understand – this new Planning job'.[3] Dalton himself had noted, quite early in Morrison's tenure of the planning post, and before it became fashionable to say so, that he 'was a bit out of his depth on the technicalities'.[4] This certainly became the conventional wisdom in due course. Attlee, himself no master of the deeper economic technicalities, later wrote in his unpublished draft autobiography that 'Morrison's knowledge of these things tended to be secondhand'.[5]

As the government ran into more troubled waters, over steel and over convertibility, discontent within the Parliamentary Labour Party about its leadership grew more widespread and took a more sweeping line. Attlee became the target for feverish criticism. In late June back-benchers were discussing replacing Attlee by Bevin. Morrison, apparently, was not mentioned for the succession. Despite his, and friendly newspapermen's, efforts to spread the word about his boisterous good health, 'it was generally felt that Morrison was a sick man and could not do it'.[6]

On Saturday 26 July, Morrison went to speak at the Durham Miners' Gala. This invitation was always an honour and, despite the bad weather this year, an exciting occasion for any Labour politician. Morrison was generally well appreciated by the miners because of his homely style of speech.[7] This time he appealed to the miners to work a full five-day week, without absenteeism. He compared them to the fighter pilots of the Battle of Britain, with the fate of the nation in their hands. Afterwards, he went to lunch at the County

Hotel. Dalton, who was also speaking, sat next to Morrison and found him 'still fidgetting about the organization of his office and bothering to have Plowden in *his* office rather than in the Cabinet secretariat'.[8] He also thought him 'a little distant and difficult. He may suspect that moves are going on.'

The 'moves' continued after the gala, when Dalton drove back to London with Bevin. The Chancellor told Bevin that many people wanted him to be leader. Bevin in response openly criticized Attlee for his weakness and unwillingness to make up his mind. Of Morrison 'he said that he was no more use now, and was obviously a sick man'. But Bevin declined to participate in any moves to change the leadership.[9] Bevin was quite satisfied with Attlee, whom he frequently compared to Campbell-Bannerman – to him a model Prime Minister.[10]

For the next three weeks ministers were swamped in the convertibility crisis, but the movement against the leadership rumbled on. Cripps had not lost sight of the need for change – and perhaps the chance of advancement. Before the emergency Cabinet to suspend convertibility, on 17 August, Cripps went with Dalton to see Bevin privately at the Foreign Office, entering unobserved through the back door. Cripps 'made a tentative approach to Bevin "to take over", as Cripps put it'.[11] But the Foreign Secretary still resisted the blandishments of his fellow plotters. He said to his Parliamentary Private Secretary afterwards, 'Why should I do him out of a job? What's Clem ever done to me?'[12] The *Daily Mail* alone caught wind of what was going on and three days later carried a banner headline to the effect that Attlee was about to resign and be replaced by Bevin.[13] It was premature. The real putsch against Attlee did not get seriously under way for another three weeks.

On the morning of 5 September Cripps went to see Dalton with 'some very striking ideas'. He proposed that the two of them should approach Morrison to form a delegation to see Attlee and request him to retire in favour of Bevin. Cripps felt Attlee would have to agree. He suggested that a party meeting should then be called at which Morrison would formally propose Bevin for the leadership. The scheme clearly had its weak points – notably, the assumption that Morrison would carry a dagger on behalf of his enemy Bevin, who, as leader, would probably treat him far worse than Attlee did, and that Bevin would agree to a putsch on his behalf against his friend, Attlee. But Cripps was adamant. He was convinced that unless Attlee were removed, 'the Government, the Party, and the country were all sunk . . . no leadership, no grip, no decision'.[14] He told Dalton that he was considering resigning explicitly 'on the ground that Attlee was no use as Prime Minister in this crisis'. He thought Morrison could be persuaded to join in the pilgrimage to No. 10, and had arranged to have dinner with him that evening. His views on Morrison's incapacity as an economic planner, and the need to replace him as well, had grown, if anything, even more violent. Cripps claimed that the chief planner, Plowden, was in despair because he found the machinery for managing the economy unworkable and had come to tell Cripps he was thinking of resigning.[15] Clearly, Morrison's head, or at least his economic face, was due to join Attlee's on the block if Cripps had his way.

Morrison's potentially fatal supper with Cripps went, not surprisingly, a little less smoothly than the leading kingmaker anticipated. Morrison was too experienced a political fox to play the role allocated to him. After all, he was being expected to lead a coup which might fail, to the discredit of all participants, and which would be of no benefit whatsoever to him if it succeeded. Attlee was not a good friend, but his cool reserve was infinitely preferable to Bevin's almost pathological hatred and suspicion of him. Morrison, who had many ears to the ground on his behalf within the parliamentary party, cannot have been unaware that Cripps was gunning for his economic job as well. Few politicians can have been offered a less promising proposition than was put to Morrison at supper that evening. He was offered a hiding to nothing. It reflects on Cripps's political judgment that he ever thought Morrison, with all his political experience and shrewdness, would for a moment dream of co-operating. Over the dinner table, Morrison, predictably, agreed with Cripps's criticism of Attlee. Equally predictably, he dissented from the praise and suggested elevation of Bevin. He made it clear that he would not serve under Bevin, and bluntly accused Cripps of trying to put a pistol to his head. Morrison made it clear that if there was to be a change, *he* should be Prime Minister.[16]

Their final agreement was that Morrison would see Dalton next day, Saturday the sixth, at noon, in case he had second thoughts. Morrison was clearly shaken by these uncongenial developments. As on every other occasion, before and after, when the party leadership was at stake, he seemed to lose his composure and to lack dignity. Dalton reported, probably with a touch of characteristic malice and melodramatic exaggeration, that Morrison 'greeted me gruffly, almost in tears. Gradually as we talked he recovered his composure. But he had been very much shaken, both physically and in his pride.' Morrison revealed that he had been unable to sleep the previous night as the issue churned over in his mind. His pent-up bitterness and resentment towards Attlee poured out. The Prime Minister 'was no good now, and he had never *led* the Party, and he didn't know how to say thank you to those who did their best to help him.' He also attacked Bevin, describing him, with shrewd accuracy, as 'a strange mixture of genius and stupidity'. Even more to the point, Morrison said that he simply did not trust Bevin not to knife him in turn if Bevin took the leadership with himself as No. 2. Morrison was quite frank about his basic position – he 'wanted to be Prime Minister, not for any reason of vanity, but simply because he felt he could do the job better than anybody else'. He claimed that his health was now fully recovered and that 'statements to the contrary in the Press were inspired, this was a favourite trick of discrediting a man'. He did not agree that Bevin was the only candidate who could get trade union support for the government, but believed that he himself 'could do it just as well'. Whatever happened, Morrison took a characteristically constitutional position, as in July 1945, and also insisted that 'the Parliamentary Party must be treated fairly. They must not be presented with a *fait accompli*. It must be possible for nominations to be made at the decisive meeting, and a fair vote taken.' Morrison said that he would abide by the result and would be willing to serve under anyone, including Bevin – which was a shift from the view he put to Cripps at supper the previous evening. Towards the end of the meeting he apparently lapsed into nostalgia, saying how he sometimes longed to go back to the LCC, which was a 'quiet, decent and useful life'.[17] This nostalgia for County Hall recurs periodically in his speeches, usually when it became tough at Westminster. No doubt, Morrison hankered for the days when he was unquestioned political boss. But it also appears, here and elsewhere, that despite appearances to the contrary, really deep down he did not relish the savage in-fighting for power at the highest national level. Despite his ambition, his toughness, his reputation as a rough manipulator of the political machine, he never went for the highest political power with the cool, calculating ruthlessness or the appetite which his image might have suggested. Perhaps it was his lack of a public school education. Perhaps it was a profound lack of self-confidence. Perhaps it was a genuine distaste for the 'blood on the carpet' which political cannibalism in the upper reaches of British political parties usually involves. Something was lacking in Morrison at that level, perhaps not wholly to his discredit.

After these meetings with Morrison, Cripps and Dalton concluded that he was of no practical use to their conspiracy, and they must proceed without him. Morrison himself continued to brood over the weekend and on Monday 8 September wrote confidentially to Cripps setting out his reasons for rejecting Cripps's approach.[18] The most striking feature of this letter is that it is clearly written for the record, possibly with future biographers in mind. He wrote:

By hand.   11, Downing Street,
                                                              S.W.1.
                                                   8 September 1947.

My dear Stafford,
    Since our talk of Friday night last, I have given the most careful consideration to the proposal you then made after you had consulted Bevin and Dalton and which I gathered had their support, provided I agreed: namely that you, Dalton and I (not Bevin) should approach the Prime Minister early this week with a view to persuading him to resign his present office; that Bevin should become Prime Minister with our support (my own being regarded as vital) and directly responsible, with special overriding powers (I rather think you said 'almost dictatorial'), for economic affairs, you assisting him in this field; and that I should be Leader of the House of Commons and the holder of such departmental office as might be agreed, retaining my

present accepted status of Deputy Prime Minister; and that you hoped that Attlee would accept office in the new Government.

I told you that I was not disposed to agree, but that, at your request, I would think it over. This I have done. My decision is that I cannot be a party to the proposed arrangement.

First, it bears a remarkably close resemblance to predictions which have appeared in the Tory Press during recent weeks and might well arouse suspicions of intrigue (maybe unfounded) in the minds of members of the Party. I think the first I heard of the idea was in an article by the political correspondent of the 'Daily Mail'. I had no reason then to believe the story to be true and, with the authority of the Prime Minister, I caused it to be denied.

Second, until I reminded you of its rights, you seemed to forget that the Parliamentary Labour Party (if a vacancy arises) elects the Leader of the Party; upon my pointing this out you did say that of course the matter would have to go to the Party in Parliament. With respect, I do not think this attitude is good enough. The Party would, I think, feel that it had been presented with something like an accomplished fact, or a 'frame-up', and then asked for a merely formal ratification. Should a change in the leadership arise (which as things are involves a change in Prime Minister), the right of the Parliamentary Party to make nominations and, if need be, proceed to an election for the post must be preserved. This is altogether apart from the consideration that other members of the Cabinet may have views.

As I say, therefore, my conclusion is against the ideas you put to me. My view is that if and when Attlee resigns, the Parliamentary Party should have its rights maintained and that all accepting nomination should be willing loyally to serve (in any office mutually agreed naturally) under any Leader of the Party freely elected by our members in Parliament. I was defeated when I stood for the leadership in 1935, but I have given Attlee loyal co-operation ever since. So it should be with anybody else. If the issue of leadership arises, all must accept the risk of election or defeat in the spirit of good comradeship.

Please forgive the bad typing: it is my own!

Yours sincerely,

Herbert Morrison

P.S.: As you know I am due to go on leave on Wednesday, Sept. 10; and after working through August I can do with a break; if there *have* to be political difficulties added to our economic ones I should be grateful if they could await my return.[19]

The crude impression left by this letter is that the plot against Attlee had as its objective certain almost dictatorial powers, and that it was proposed without full respect to the constitutional rights of the parliamentary party and with the soiling connivance of the Tory press. Morrison's position is projected as loyalty to Attlee, as in the past, and strict adherence to party wishes. The postscript hints at other people's unpatriotic disloyalty in pursuing political jobbery at a time of great national economic crisis. There is no mention of Morrison's own strong doubts about Attlee's competence or, especially, about his clearly stated desire to take over himself. Morrison *had* declined to join in the putsch and he always did defend the rights of the parliamentary party. But his letter was clearly drafted to put his position in the best possible light; significantly it was one of the few letters of which he made a copy and he kept to the end of his life.

Cripps was not the shrewdest tactician in British politics at this time, but he immediately saw the purpose of Morrison's letter to him. The same day he replied confidentially in long-hand. He put on record that he had not claimed to have consulted Bevin and pointed out that Morrison 'agreed that the present PM ought to go and someone with more grip should take his place but you indicated that you thought you had the necessary qualifications'. He said he 'did not at all forget any rights of the Parliamentary Party but I thought that if there were substantial agreement as to what should happen there would be unlikely to be much difficulty. . . . I am sorry that we don't see eye to eye on this matter and whichever of our views is best for the country in this crisis I hope may prevail.'[20]

Cripps was apparently afraid that Morrison intended to publish his letter immediately any putsch took place. He told Dalton that his own letter, also ready for immediate publication, was meant to torpedo that tactic.[21] Morrison replied in turn on the same day acknowledging Cripps's letter and urging him, whatever happened, 'not to resign, at any rate at this stage. The country is in difficulties and needs the help of all of us, especially a man of such ability as yours. People might think you were running away at a moment of stress and taking the all too easy course of getting out. It is an awkward moment and I do think you should in any case leave it over for the time being. Resignation is sometimes the right course and produces good results – but not often; and it needs more concrete issues than exist at present.'[22]

When Dalton saw Morrison at tea-time on Tuesday, the ninth, the Chancellor found him 'much steadier than on Friday'. Morrison then reflected on Cripps's poor political judgment. He also looked forward to getting away for a holiday rest the next week. He told Dalton pointedly that he hoped 'not to be brought back for any political crisis'. Dalton was deliberately vague, but felt, perhaps unfairly in the circumstances, that 'it may ease the tension if Morrison is away for a month'.[23] The current tensions could after all hardly be attributed to the presence of Morrison.

That evening, of the ninth, the crisis of Labour's leadership came to a head and was resolved. Cripps went to see Attlee (who had returned from North Wales the previous night) after dinner. There was no delegation of ministers as originally planned. Nor did Cripps now propose to threaten resignation, though whether or not he was influenced by Morrison's (and Dalton's) advice is not clear. He put his proposals to Attlee. In the interests of the country, the government and the party, Bevin should take over as Prime Minister and as 'overlord' Minister of Production. Cripps had in reserve his proposed new Cabinet. Attlee would remain in the government as Chancellor of the Exchequer. Dalton would go to the Foreign Office. Morrison would become Lord Privy Seal, with his main responsibility as Leader of the Commons (clearly a demotion). Cripps would replace Morrison as Lord President.

Attlee knew his man. The Prime Minister was a master at allocating jobs – at moving the chessmen on the board, as Morrison often complained. Sometimes it was a question of what job a man would do supremely well, sometimes of what job would buy him off. With Cripps it was both. Attlee took no offence at Cripps's approach, but simply offered him the top economic post. Cripps, a man of overt integrity and well-exposed Christian principles, seems to have found that his previous overriding concern about the Prime Minister – that 'the Government, Party and country were all sunk' unless Attlee, who was 'no use', were removed – was now suddenly evaporated, with his own promotion. His innate sensitivity did at least lead him to pause when confronted by Attlee's masterly move. But after a discreet delay he conceded. One occasion for pause apparently had been a hitherto unrevealed sympathy for Morrison. Cripps told Dalton that he 'felt rather a dirty dog *vis-à-vis* Morrison. In effect, he would be pinching most of Morrison's job.' He also worried that Morrison might be misled into thinking 'that this had been a deep-laid plot against him from the start'.[24] Certainly Morrison might have found it hard to escape the suspicion that he had been under a sustained attack from the President of the Board of Trade since April. Morrison was now out. Cripps was in. He was the right man for the job. But only a high-minded and upper-class Christian from the moralizing and Marxist left of the socialist movement could get away with such blatant self-advancement. Morrison, with his reputation as an ambitious and unprincipled operator, would never dare to try.

It is interesting at this point to quote in its entirety Morrison's description of these events in his *Autobiography*. He recalled: 'I was told that Cripps wanted Bevin to be Prime Minister, and that Dalton agreed to this. Bevin, it was said – apparently wrongly – was ready to accept. I was asked what I would do. I have never felt up to indulging in high conspiracy and I refused to participate. Anyway, the conspiracy failed.'[25] For a combination of laconic accuracy with non-information, it could hardly have been improved on by that master of non-communication, Attlee himself.

At the time it must have seemed seriously worrying to Morrison that the plotters did not consider him to be Attlee's natural successor. After all, he was deputy prime minister. Much of the press and the rank and file in the party considered his succession to be both desirable and inevitable. The trade unions were not as big an obstacle as is often suggested; Morrison's practical politics appealed to the right-wing big battalions – as was seen when they rallied to him after he was ejected from the NEC in 1952. His real opponents were among his colleagues in the top positions of the Labour Cabinet.

Morrison went away for his much needed rest the day after Cripps's visit to Attlee in September. He flew to the Channel Islands with his wife. Police escorted them to Croydon Airport and patrolled the tarmac runway while his aircraft waited to take off. These special precautions were because of rumours of impending Jewish terrorism in the United Kingdom in protest against Bevin's Palestine policy.[26] Morrison, in view of his strong sympathy towards the Palestine Jews, and lack of it towards Bevin, would hardly have been an appropriate victim. He and Margaret stayed at a small hotel on Guernsey. They enjoyed the plentiful food after the rigours of English rationing. The weather was mixed – 'some days fine, some wet'. Morrison fished, went on a boat trip to the tiny island of Herm, read a couple of detective novels, carried around with him an impressive volume on parliamentary procedure and generally enjoyed himself. He caught up on some of his lost sleep; shortly after he arrived the hotel cancelled their regular dinner dance in consideration for their distinguished guest. He told Attlee that he was 'beginning to feel "unwound"'.[27] But he did not want it thought that he was an invalid: the *Daily Herald* dutifully reported that Morrison 'sends a message through a friend who met him there that he is having a fine time and feeling very fit indeed'.[28] Towards the end of his holiday he crossed the narrow water to Jersey and received further treatment to his foot from Sir Herbert Barker. Morrison and Margaret returned to Croydon on 5 October – a day earlier than planned, he told the press, 'because the Prime Minister wished to talk some things over with him'.[29]

Attlee had taken an extraordinarily long time reorganizing the administration while Morrison was away. He was apparently clear and firm at the very beginning. He agreed with Dalton on 10 September that Morrison 'is not a fit man in health and he cannot handle these planning problems anyhow'. He asked Cripps to co-ordinate economic affairs in Morrison's absence. But he then delayed while consulting widely before making the official changes which he had in mind.[30] In particular, he was being pressed by his Chief Whip, Whiteley, to think carefully before making radical changes. Whiteley was to some extent looking after Morrison's interests while his chief was away. He wrote to Guernsey early in Morrison's holiday to give him a private report on the latest negotiations between Cripps and Attlee. Morrison wrote back immediately and gratefully – though regretting that 'it's a bit rough to be involved in these anxieties (no fault of yours!) when one is trying to forget the less pleasant aspects of ministerial life'.

Morrison reassured Whiteley that 'the advice you gave the P. Minister to go warily about Cripps' proposal was right'. He had been thinking about the proposed new big Ministry of Production and was not convinced that it was sensible. As to his own position, Morrison said: 'I would not *necessarily* be difficult provided the conditions were right and I contrived to hold my chairmanships (with possible exception of Economic Planning Committee) and the Lord President's Committee was not made a farce.' He concluded: 'Should the idea of a special economic planning Minister (that's what it really is) prosper I should certainly wish to be consulted and the announcement would have to take care of my position and clear up the persistent fairy-tales about my health – I should have been stone dead in recent weeks if true!'[31] Morrison was not contemplating putting up much of a fight. He seemed reconciled to losing his policy responsibility. All he asked was to keep his chairmanships, to be consulted, and that the public announcement should not rub salt into his wounds. He gave Whiteley permission to show Attlee his letter, as well as sending the Prime Minister a postcard.

Ten days later Attlee wrote to him in Jersey. His letter was strikingly authoritative in tone and informative in detail. 'I have already discussed with you the members of the Government who ought to go,' he wrote. 'These are Greenwood, Westwood, Bellenger, Oliver, Leonard, Collick, Thomas and Burke. Perhaps also Inman and Nathan. I think that Shinwell and Wilmot require change. I should like to reduce the numbers in the Cabinet, but I don't think that I can do much at present as, although there are Departmental Ministers who in theory should not be in the Cabinet, the importance of their subjects at the present time, the need for adequate representation in the Cabinet of the TU element and of the younger generation make any drastic cutting down of numbers undesirable.' Turning to the economic matters specifically affecting Morrison, Attlee stated:

I propose to have now a single Economic Committee over which I should preside. Its members would be the Lord President, Foreign Secretary, Chancellor of the Exchequer, Minister for Economic Affairs, Lord Privy Seal and Minister of Labour. Its functions would be to take decisions within Cabinet policy on the working of the Economic plan which go beyond the scope of what can be decided by a single Minister. It should not be overburdened with documentation. With regard to your own work, you have had a very heavy task on the Home Front and with AG [Greenwood] retiring there is too much for one man, however efficient, especially when he is the second man in the Cabinet who, like the PM, must have time to think of matters of major policy.

You are at present Deputy PM, which means close attention to all phases of our work . . ., Leader of the House, a task which will not grow lighter as the Parliament grows older, Chief Liaison with the Parliamentary Party and with the Party organization, Head of the COI, Minister responsible for Science and for the formal work of the Lord President's office, Chairman of the Lord President's Committee and the Socialization Committee, in charge generally of Economic Affairs and economic planning and the Home Front. AG's retirement will mean that we want a new Chairman for the Legislation Committee and for the Social Services Committee, and it would be appropriate for you to take these. This is clearly too great a charge and I think that we require to separate off the co-ordination of the Economic Front from these other important functions. I propose, therefore, to make a Minister for Economic Affairs, whose job would be to co-ordinate our economic efforts both at home and abroad and to see to the carrying out of the economic plan under the general direction of the Committee detailed above. I propose that Cripps should fill this office. He would be empowered to give directions to the Production Ministers and to other Ministers where the economic plan impinges on their activities. I do not propose to create a new Ministry on the lines of the Ministry of Production. He would work with a small picked staff. Marquand, as Paymaster General, would work to him.

Relieving you of these functions would give you time for the House and the Party and for the whole of the non-economic side of the home front. Your membership of the Economic Committee would ensure that the claims of home consumer and of the social services were not unduly subjected to our export needs while you would, of course, make your contribution like the rest of us to the decisions and discussions of the Committee as to economic and financial policy.

I hope that you will agree that this is the best set up to meet our present circumstances.[32]

Attlee had met Morrison's reservations about a Ministry of Production by proposing to set up a Ministry of Economic Affairs instead. For the rest, he was crystal clear about taking responsibilities from Morrison and giving them, with strengthened power, to Cripps.

Morrison replied promptly and at great length. He began by complaining: 'I am sorry that once more – 3rd time – you feel you must decide on Government changes while I am away. It puts us both at a disadvantage. However I thank you for the fullness of your letter and will set down my own views.'

His strongest views, not surprisingly, were against Attlee's proposal to send Bevan to Supply, where he would take over the steel nationalization issue from Wilmot. 'I am doubtful about your proposal here as I am about the political judgment (at times) of the source from which it probably came. [i.e. Cripps][33] ... It is, I suggest, important not even to appear to reward intrigue and disloyalty or to appear to manifest fear.' Having thus rapped Attlee's knuckles for trying to buy off both the threatening resigners, Morrison restated his position on the steel issue. Of Bevan's suitability, he stated: 'I am not sure this job is up his street, able and brilliant as in many ways he is. Private industry has got to be brought along over the wide field concerned and – whatever happens – the iron and steel people have to be handled with decision *and* care if we are to get the output which is vital. In any case I think it essential that the socialization should not go forward next Session (an autumn Budget rules it out anyway, unless some other Bills go). I earnestly trust you will be firm about this.' Morrison's personal preference on steel continued to be for the compromise which he had negotiated and which the Cabinet rejected. 'For myself I would have done the forward deal with the industry and I think it's a tragedy we didn't. But if you put the colleague you mention there *and* his policy [full nationalization next session] it will be a smack in the eye for you, me and the TUC who have been helpful and would have been more helpful if my hands in advocacy had not been tied.' Bitterness clearly still rankled over the steel débâcle and what Morrison saw as Attlee's betrayal of him. Constructively, Morrison urged that Attlee send Bevan to the Ministry of Labour, and suggested G. Strauss for Supply. In the event, Attlee did stand firm on not nationalizing steel next session, and sent Strauss to Supply as Morrison advised. Bevan remained at Health, despite recurring dissatisfaction on his own part, and with his performance in the eyes of others; when he finally moved, however, it was to Labour, as Morrison suggested.

After commenting on Attlee's other proposed ministerial changes, Morrison turned to the central question of his own position. He agreed wholly with Attlee's proposal for a special Minister of Economic Affairs, recalling that he had himself suggested it to Attlee earlier. His concern was with the press treatment of his own position. 'I don't want to be bumped by the Press and should like the announcement to make clear (1) that I have recommended this course, and (2) that there is a change in that my own responsibility was that of a Cabinet Committee chairman and that present circumstances require something more in the line of a full-time executive Minister. . . . Please do not let it be thought that my health (which has stood a heavy test since my return and is good) is the reason. There has been malicious gossip, I fear, in this regard. . . . I would ask that the press announcement (could I see?) should make clear that my status as deputy Prime Minister is preserved and that I shall have duties to perform in charge of various Cabinet Committees.' Nowhere does Morrison protest – which would mean admit – that he has suffered a demotion, but his efforts to cover his flanks in the press reflect a deep awareness that he was exposed to disparaging comment.

For the record, Morrison set out his own future duties as he saw them: he would keep his original four Cabinet committees, absorb Greenwood's Social Services Committee as well as the Future Legislation Committee. He was giving up one major part of the Lord President's responsibilities, those in the economic sphere, to Cripps. It was a rationalization. Morrison now co-ordinated the entire home front in Cabinet committees except for economic questions, which were progressively being centralized into Cripps's single capable pair of hands. But it was also, from Morrison's point of view, a diminution of responsibility, which in politics means power. As he pointed out to Attlee, 'while the duties you list do look formidable, many of them do not take up much time'. Morrison did have in addition to ministerial duties his highly valued responsibilities for managing the Labour Party. 'Of course,' he wrote, 'I will continue to work closely with the Parliamentary Party and do what I can with Head Office – not that I can be held responsible for Transport House which has a Secretary who has views of his own, naturally. In any case, I would not wish to be publicized in a way which mixes up party management (as it is disparagingly called) with my ministerial functions.' He closed by pointing out that the letter 'touches on delicate personal matters' and requested it be shown to no one else except Whiteley.[34]

Morrison was being very reasonable. Other ministers with less political weight had refused to play ball with some of Attlee's attempted reshuffles. Bevan, in particular, was never easy to place. On this occasion Attlee did his best to persuade him to leave Health for Supply or the Board of Trade, but failed;[35] he had similar difficulties in 1950 and 1951. Shinwell was sticky about going to the War Office and Alexander and Wilmot at first refused to go to the Lords. With these lesser figures the Prime Minister suffered something of a trial of strength. Morrison, a bigger politician, suffering some demotion, could always be persuaded by reasonable argument. The reorganization made ;ense to him, as in the general interest. He tried to protect his public status but easily gave up some of his empire. He always liked to be thought of as reasonable and responsible. Perhaps he was also feeling weakened by failure and illness and insecure in his bargaining position. In fact, he was indispensable to the government at this time. But he never once tried to use this as a lever.

Attlee wrote again on the twenty-third, expressing pleasure at the broad agreement between them. He was taking account of Morrison's suggestions for the reshuffle. He added the sweetener that he had finally approved the promotion of Nicholson, for which Morrison had fought so hard and so long. He was also promoting Morrison's PPS, Patrick Gordon Walker.[36] Morrison replaced him as PPS by Dr Stephen Taylor, another bright young professional protégé for his stable of middle-class recruits.

Details of the economic changes were announced on 29 September and filled the headlines of the press next day. The official announcement from 10 Downing Street explained that: 'The present economic situation calls for much closer integration of internal and external economic policy and the Prime Minister now needs the assistance of a senior colleague who can give his undivided attention to our economic problems at home and abroad.' The new Central Economic Planning Staff, the Economic Information Unit and the Economic Section of the Cabinet Secretariat were put under Cripps, who would control not only the home economic front, but also overseas economic and trade policy (which had never been in Morrison's hands). The reference to Morrison simply stated that he would devote himself to being deputy prime minister and Leader of the Commons 'and will continue to exercise co-ordinating functions in other than economic matters. He will also take over the duties hitherto discharged by Mr Arthur Greenwood.' Attlee was able to write to reassure Morrison that 'the reception of the first changes was excellent and there was no attempt in any quarter to represent this as in any way derogating from your position. It was inevitable, given the journalist's mind, that they should exaggerate Stafford's position. You know well how the need for making a story operates.'[37] On the whole, this was true. No newspaper wrote Morrison seriously down. The *Evening Standard* even suggested that the planning job had to go to Cripps since Morrison could not be spared to do it from his crucial position as Leader of the Commons, a part at which Sir Stafford had failed dismally in 1942.[38] But realities were otherwise and any delusions still held by Morrison must have been shattered by a letter he received soon afterwards from his friend Maurice Webb:

> The news of the Cripps 'putsch' did not surprise me. Your own attitude to the affair was highly commendable and worthy. I wonder if the PM recognizes just how loyal and decent you have been to him personally. I thought the announcement of the new appointments could be held back until your return. I was surprised when the papers carried the news yesterday. I suppose Cripps pressed for it to be got out, but I know Willy was anxious to hold it all up until you got back.
>
> I must say that I am very disturbed by it all. I do not like the erosion of your own power. I am both surprised and disturbed by it. I suppose it has all been done with your consent. But, even so, I wish you had not yielded up so much in the economic field to Cripps. I fear the terms of the announcement will be commonly interpreted as notice of your withdrawal from the highest places. Indeed, from talks I have already had, I must tell you that that is how it is being generally regarded. I suppose this means the end of Morrison is a typical comment made to me. It distresses me to hear that sort of thing and I wish the thing had been handled so as to avoid such ideas arising. A lot of pressmen have been on to me about your position. Needless to say, I have done all I could to knock out of their heads any idea that you were withdrawing in any way from your own personal position of authority in the Party . . . I do hope you will see that any suggestion of your decline and fall is quickly nipped in the bud.[39]

Webb was Chairman of the parliamentary party, with close contacts in his old Fleet Street haunts. He was well placed to register erosions of power and political reputations moving into decline. Certainly, the new overlord of Britain's economic affairs was in no doubt as to the significance for Morrison of these changes: he wrote to Dalton: 'I hear that Herbert has agreed, but I only hope he understands what it means. . . .'[40]

Section X: Finishing the Job, 1947–1951

Chapter 32

Mid-Term Miscellany

Morrison returned from his Guernsey holiday in autumn 1947 to take up his reorganized duties for the second half of the Labour Government. With the loss of economic co-ordination he was not now responsible for any central policy area.* He was able to concentrate on political management at which he was so adept: as chairman of Cabinet committees, as Leader of the House of Commons, and in helping to manage the Labour Party both in Parliament and in the country at large.† He could also now find more time for the miscellaneous responsibilities which came within his territory, for science, for the nascent project for a Festival of Britain in 1951, for the whole field of information, especially the press and the BBC. He still worked incredibly hard and slept remarkably little, but his treadmill was less punishing than before. He had more time to reflect on the government's general approach – and about its tactics and prospects for the next general election due by the summer of 1950.‡

A number of urgent problems faced the administration before the new autumn session of 1947. Most immediately they had to finalize the emergency Budget made necessary by the convertibility crisis. The main legislation for the coming parliamentary session would be gas nationalization and the proposal to reduce the powers of the House of Lords. Each of these items was on the agenda for a pre-session conference of leading ministers at Chequers over the weekend of 18–19 October. Wives were invited and Margaret Morrison went along. Mrs Bevin was absent ill and Ruth Dalton was otherwise engaged. It was cold and uncomfortable at Chequers, but neither Margaret Morrison

* Nicholson continued to advise Morrison on economic matters and to represent him on the new Economic Planning Board, but it was a nominal representation, with no detailed initiative or real power in economic policy-making. (Interviews, M. Nicholson, Lord Plowden.)

† Morrison remained on the NEC and on its Policy and its Elections sub-committees.

‡ Curiously this whole period until 1950 figures scarcely at all in Morrison's *Autobiography*.

nor her two companions, Vi Attlee and Lady Cripps, were renowned for their concern with the comforts of life. Their husbands agreed the main lines of the coming Budget as well as discussing the tactics for Lords reform. The Morrisons left after dinner on the Sunday and drove back to London with Dalton.[1]

The problem of the Lords had exercised Morrison since his return from illness earlier in the year. His PPS, Patrick Gordon Walker, had urged quick action in May, pointing out that any reform must be passed more than two years before the next election, in order to survive the Lords' existing power of delay.[2] Morrison spent some time listening to the Lords discuss the Transport Nationalization Bill on 17 June – when the government was defeated three times. Significantly, next day he addressed a dinner of metropolitan Labour Mayors and remarked in relation to the Lords' treatment of the Transport Bill, 'we shall have to consider our future constitutional policy'. The lobby correspondent of the *Daily Express*, who was usually close to Morrison, also carried a report that the Cabinet planned to curb the Lords.[3]

What worried Morrison was not the specific treatment of the Transport Bill in the Upper House but, as he told a mass meeting of his Lewisham constituents the weekend after his Chequers visit, the general fear that the Lords could paralyse Labour's whole legislative programme during the last two years of this Parliament.[4] So far the Lords had in fact behaved very reasonably. They had presented many amendments, but the vast majority were constructive and acceptable to the government. Until recently, of course, the Conservative Opposition was demoralized and quiescent. Now it was perking up as Labour blundered into trouble and the Tories' own electoral prospects improved. Ahead lay the controversial steel nationalization, threatening some of the deeper vested interests among Conservative supporters; Labour itself was divided on this issue and the electorate not noticeably enthusiastic. Morrison suspected that their Lordships might be tempted to flex their remaining elegant muscles. Their existing power of two-year delay, exercised after the summer of 1948, would carry beyond the end of this Parliament, in effect constituting a veto. Now that steel had been postponed till the 1948–9 session, it was essential to neutralize this prospective veto.

The bill to limit the Lords' power of delay was quickly ready[5] and Morrison moved its second reading on 10 November 1947. A month later he wound up on its third reading.[6] The debates were poorly attended and provoked no fireworks. Such difficulties as arose came from the government's own back-benches, where there was pressure to curb the Upper House more drastically than proposed in the bill, either by reducing its powers of delay to one month or by total abolition of the second chamber.[7] Morrison firmly resisted, through the Liaison Committee and in the parliamentary party. But the Lords could, of course, still apply their existing powers of delay to the present bill itself and some tricky waters lay ahead to test his parliamentary skills.

Morrison's exhausting political life occasionally enjoyed a lighter side. He went to the palace in November with Attlee, Jowitt and Chuter Ede to present a gift from the Cabinet to Princess Elizabeth for her wedding to the young Battenberg prince. It was a sofa table in amboyna wood.[8] Morrison was made a Freeman of Lambeth. Flanked by two other distinguished Lambeth 'old boys' – Montgomery of Alamein and Archbishop Fisher – he sat in the Town Hall where he was once a young newspaperman and received his scroll in a casket made of oak from his old school in Stockwell Road, which had been bombed in the 1940 blitz. Morrison liked these ceremonies. The documents, letters and invitations relating to them were among the few papers he preserved to the end of his life.

At Christmas he went away with Margaret to stay at Treharrock Manor, near Port Isaac in North Cornwall. The Manor, which had beautiful views over miles of Cornish coastline and was blessed with very mild weather in all seasons, belonged to Dr Edmund Hambly, a Harley Street orthopaedic surgeon. It had been in the Hambly family in the seventeenth century. Now Hambly and his wife, also a doctor, had bought it back and converted it into a hotel. Hambly had attracted Morrison's attention in the war. When Hinley Atkinson, Labour's London agent, broke his hip in 1944, Morrison went to see Hambly and begged him to get Atkinson fit in double quick time to be ready for the coming election battle. Hambly did it. He was a Labour supporter and Jim and Mabel Raisin tried to persuade him to run for Parliament. He declined, but agreed to run for the LCC instead and won a seat in East Lewisham, Morrison's new constituency. Henceforward, Morrison saw a lot of Hambly.[9]

Maurice Webb and his wife went with Morrison to Cornwall, as did the Raisins. Hambly recalled that even on holiday Morrison and Webb 'would talk into the early hours of the morning about their projects and proposals. . . . They looked a really ugly pair, the one with one eye, the other with one leg.' They drank a good deal of whisky together. Hambly never saw Morrison drunk, 'but for his age he drank far too much, perhaps because he was so worried and stayed up such long hours'. Part of the pressure came from the ceaseless flow of boxes of official papers 'brought by messengers on motorcycles at all hours – two and even three o'clock in the morning'.[10] One of these messengers, arriving in the black of night, got lost and ended up with his red boxes in the cowshed. Another arrived hammering on the outer doors at 6.30 on Christmas morning itself. When Webb stumped along to Morrison's bedroom later 'there was Herbert, propped up in bed, starting his Christmas Day by opening his box and getting down to work on the dispatches from Downing Street'.[11] Morrison celebrated his birthday in similar fashion: 'His first birthday gift was a box of Cabinet documents. He read them alternately with a thriller about low life in Ireland.'[12] Even when out for a walk he was never really off political duty. Hambly recalled how 'he would preach socialism and try to convert the local grocers in the shops'. Webb described how 'throughout our holiday we struggled hard to keep politics at a distance, but somehow they got through our defences. There was the trip to Port Isaac. It is said to be a quaint and picturesque little spot. It may well be. I cannot say. For our intended investigation of Port Isaac became an investigation of conditions in the fishing industry. The fishermen, under the leadership of the Harbour Master, gathered round on the town "platt". And, propped up on the stern of a herring boat, the Lord President went over the whole range of fishing economics.'[13] On 30 December he addressed a public meeting in St Austell. He was in Liberal country and the heart of his speech was an appeal to 'progressive Liberals' to join the Labour Party.[14]

Morrison did relax at times. He went for some walks with Margaret, who was most interested in the sub-tropical vegetation which grew in that mild climate. He played darts in the bar. He also joined in with the traditional hand-bell ringers who visited the hotel on Christmas Eve and New Year's Eve. Asked for his New Year's resolution, Morrison replied: 'Well, I've been reading Thurber's *Let Your Mind Alone*.' On his birthday, after the day's diet of Cabinet papers, he exchanged telegram greetings with Attlee. In the evening he had a Cornish pasty for supper and then, with a gale blowing outside, retired early to bed, to read Churchill's *The Gathering Storm*.[15]

The year 1947 had ended better for the Labour government than had seemed possible in August – and better for Morrison than seemed likely when he was close to death in the spring. No further economic or political crisis threatened, at least for the moment. The winter had so far been mild. Morrison was fit and fully active again. He returned to London from Cornwall on 4 January, the day after his birthday. One more ritual remained to complete the familiar cycle of his turn-of-the-year celebrations. Burns Night coincided with a by-election in Camlachie, Glasgow's slum east end, so he was conveniently able to be in Scotland for the festivities on 24 January. He arrived wearing a tie which he described as 'reasonably like my clan colour'.[16] He first went to the luncheon of the Burns Federation in Glasgow where he proposed the toast of 'The Immortal Memory' of the poet. He went out of his way to deny rumours that his father had been a policeman from Aberdeen. But in his love for Burns he yielded to no one. 'Cockney though I be – and proud of it – I am no less proud to affirm myself a devoted student and admirer of Scotland's great poet. My admiration for his writings is absolute, positive and even aggressive.'[17] His admiration still, apparently, unsated by the lunch, Morrison later went to the Burns dinner at the Scottish Co-operative Wholesale Society. Next day he came down to earth, walking the windy site of the new town at East Kilbride, and then campaigning – unavailingly, as it turned out at the poll – in the slums of Camlachie.

In the House of Commons Morrison experienced snags with his parliamentary programme for 1948. The first bill to run into difficulties was the reform of the Lords. Early in the year the Conservatives, with the support of the Liberals, had suggested that there should be all-party conversations to discuss the whole broad area of the future of the second chamber. The government agreed and discussions took place between leaders of the three parties, though without formal authorization from their followers to commit themselves to specific changes. Morrison, as the Labour Party's leading constitutional expert, was one of its most active representatives in the discussion. Broad agreement was reached on the desirable future composition of the House of Lords. They would recommend establishing paid life peers, allowing women members, and permitting hereditary peers to opt not to enter the Upper House. Morrison was particularly keen to get at least the first two of these reforms. Paid life peers would help Labour to strengthen its ranks in the Upper House and he had always supported on principle encouraging more women into Parliament. But the conference became deadlocked over what delaying powers should be given to the reformed Lords. The Conservatives wanted the period of delay to remain effectively what it had been since 1911, covering two full sessions. Labour insisted that no Upper House should be in a position to wreck the last two sessions of a radical government.* Morrison and his colleagues were prepared to compromise marginally over the delaying period in order to secure the other reforms they wanted, but the Conservatives remained rigid in their insistence on a full two years' delay, and there the discussions finally broke down (although the proposed changes in composition were to be introduced on an *ad hoc* basis in the years ahead).

The Lords vetoed the Parliament Bill in June and Morrison responded by announcing an extraordinary session of Parliament in September to force it through more quickly.[18] The special session was a sharp and effective device in the circumstances. It did, however, reflect Morrison's parliamentary machine running a little less smoothly than before. He ran into more difficulties over the Criminal Justice Bill, where a back-bench Labour amendment to abolish capital punishment was sprung on the government at the report stage. Morrison personally supported the death penalty – with arguments which one close colleague who tried unsuccessfully to convert him to abolition described as 'rational, calm and yet reactionary'.[19] He proposed to put on a three-line whip to defeat the amendment, but found himself under heavy fire. Cripps, Bevan and all the Law Officers indicated that they would disobey the whip. Chuter Ede, who was sponsoring the bill, gave his own under-secretary permission to abstain.[20] Morrison was forced to climb down and allow a free vote – which he still assumed would reject the amendment. To his surprise and embarrassment it was firmly approved.[21] The amended bill went to the Lords who, however, voted overwhelmingly to delete the suspension clause on 2 June. The government tried to compromise, inserting a clause which retained the death penalty but applied it only for certain categories of murder committed with 'express malice'. The Lords again rejected it.[22] Morrison was now in a very difficult position, since if the House of Commons insisted on the clause, then the Lords would reject the whole bill, and a large

---

* Under the existing bill then before the Lords the proposed delay was of one year between the second reading in the Commons in one session, and the third reading in the Commons in the next parliamentary session.

body of valuable reforms in the field of justice would be lost until the Lords' period of delay had expired. The parliamentary party therefore reluctantly agreed, and the House of Commons voted, to accept the Lords' veto and not to insist on changes in the death penalty. In the crucial divisions in the Commons on 22 July the whips were on.[23] Even so, thirty-four Labour MPs voted against dropping the suspension clause and some two hundred, including several ministers, abstained in the vote for the amended bill.

It was a confused and ragged end to the session and Parliament formally adjourned on 30 July. The loose ends were tied up in the extraordinary short session held in September.* With this extra session the government was able to pass the Parliament Bill through three successive sessions, leaving the statutory two years between the second reading in the first session and the third reading in the third session, by December 1949. This in turn meant that the revised procedures in relation to the Upper House could apply to steel nationalization and enable that bill to go onto the Statute Book before this Parliament was due finally to dissolve in June 1950.

Morrison spent an unusually quiet and relaxed summer in 1948. Attlee went away on holiday to Ireland until the middle of August and Morrison stayed on in London as acting Prime Minister. He called occasional Cabinets, on economic questions or on the Berlin crisis, but few other ministers were around. He was, according to the *Manchester Guardian*,[24] leading the life of a recluse in Downing Street 'silent and withdrawn from the gaze of both press and public'. Morrison had apparently told a friend that 'it's much easier being Prime Minister than Lord President of the Council. All you have to do is delegate the work to somebody else. Why this morning I've done practically nothing but okay the appointment of parsons. Of course, the fact that there is nothing happening here may have something to do with it.'[25] Shortly before going off himself on holiday he went to the barber's and there were reports that his famous quiff had been cut off by mistake. Morrison issued a public denial. He normally had his hair cut by the barber at the House of Commons, but it was shut for the parliamentary recess so he went to the United Services Club. 'The barber put a lotion on my hair and flattened it down,' explained Morrison. 'I always have trouble of this kind with barbers who don't know me. So later I got a comb and fixed my hair myself.' An eyewitness newspaperman was able to report that 'the quiff is still there, undamaged'.[26]

Morrison flew off on the twentieth for a three-week holiday at the French

---

* The special session opened on 14 September with a speech from the Throne. Morrison himself spoke in the opening debate defending the government's action. He again moved the second reading of the Parliament Bill on 20 September, when he argued that Labour would have amended the powers of the Lords even if there were no question of them rejecting steel nationalization in the future. The bill went comfortably through its third reading the next day and Morrison defended it as a typical British measure, proceeding in an evolutionary fashion, step by step, in bringing our political institutions up to date. The bill then went again to the Lords and Parliament was prorogued on 25 September. (*HC Debs*, Vol. 456, Cols 19–33, 522–35.)

Riviera resort of Cavalaire, staying at the villa of his friend, Dr Ernest Whit-field.* The setting was beautiful, among pines overlooking the Mediterranean. Margaret went out a good deal, walking or sailing in the bay, but Morrison spent most of his time in a deck-chair at the villa, sleeping, reading and planning for the coming parliamentary session, which was to be the last full one before the election.[27]

While Morrison was away in France, Attlee fell ill and went into hospital. When he returned in September the Prime Minister was still recuperating and so he once again took over the reins of government.[28] The pressure of office and the passing of years were beginning to ravage the Cabinet. Attlee was in hospital. Bevin suffered periodic heart attacks and remained alive and in working harness only through incredible will-power supplemented by constant medication. Cripps was soon to waste and wither under the crippling attack of an ultimately fatal disease, the physical impact of which is so horribly apparent in photographs of him during 1948–50. Morrison, though fully recovered in the eyes of himself and his medical advisers, had recently trembled close to death and was still considered a serious health risk by most of his political colleagues and ill-wishers. Dalton, booming, hearty, and jog-trotting through the countryside to the discomfort of his friends and visitors, alone appeared aggressively healthy among Labour's top five; even he was soon to prove far from indestructible. The ministers began to gossip about one another's health rather like old village women. Attlee confided to Dalton his deep concern about the frailty of both Bevin and Morrison. Bevin, himself apparently on his last legs, was in turn 'alarmist about Attlee'. He remarked that 'his mind's gone. It isn't eczema he's got, it's shingles.' Bevin reported that his own doctor had diagnosed the Prime Minister from observation and concluded that his 'nerves aren't right'.[29] Cripps also commented disparagingly, early in September, about Attlee's poor health. He remained convinced that it would be 'a disaster if he led us in the next election'. He still preferred Bevin, but Bevin, apparently having been approached again, 'still said no. He didn't like the parliamentary party and said they didn't like him.' Cripps was as adamant as ever in his opposition to Morrison, who, he said, 'couldn't lead either the Cabinet or the party or the country'.[30]

The middle of this Parliament saw the culmination of various disciplinary problems in the parliamentary party, which put mounting pressure on Morrison in his *de facto* role as party manager. Since early in the 1947–8 session, there had been a series of clashes between the party leadership and certain dissident MPs, who in Morrison's eyes were recklessly damaging the party's electoral image. The main focal point of dissent was in the field of foreign affairs. The intensification of the Cold War, with the series of brutal annexations by the Soviet Union in Eastern Europe, and the Labour Government's unequivocal reaction to them, exposed the wide and unbridgeable gap

*Whitfield, later Lord Kenwood, was a Governor of the BBC and a blind musician of international repute.

that existed between a few members on the far left of the Parliamentary Labour Party and the bulk of the party's membership and its leadership. Morrison was actively involved in these episodes. Most of the dissident activities at issue were extra-parliamentary, though they were often linked to developments in the Commons. In either case, Morrison wielded his school-master's stick. As Leader of the House, controller of the Liaison Committee, and the real power behind the Chief Whip, he was the main instigator of discipline in the parliamentary party. Punishment for extra-parliamentary activities came before the National Executive Committee where he took a leading role, perhaps the leading role, on the full Executive, on the Elections committee, and on the Special Committee of Chairmen of Sub-Committees, set up to deal with disciplinary offences.*

Morrison's long-standing dislike for communism and for the Soviet totalitarian regime made him particularly ready to jump on rebels in the foreign policy field. In the confrontation between East and West, he had no doubt where he stood: firmly behind the hard line of his old enemy Bevin. Early in the new year of 1948 he launched a series of speeches attacking Russia and communism. At Leicester on 11 January he addressed the East Midlands Regional Council of the Labour Party and bitterly attacked the Russians for policies which he said impeded the economic recovery of the post-war world and which were always 'running the risk of war at some time'.[31] After the communist coup in Czechoslovakia he warned a meeting at Grimsby of the danger that the British trade unions might equally be used to subvert freedom and concluded: 'Let the socialist simpletons who urge co-operation with Communists take warning.'[32] Morrison's language in the Cold War battles may jar on a later generation, but given the subversion, brutality and cynical opportunism with which the Soviet communists had penetrated and overthrown the regimes of Eastern Europe, his warnings were understandable.

Labour's Cold War intransigence towards communist Russia, and its ever closer alliance with capitalist America, rapidly produced conflicts within the party. The first serious explosion in the party came over the famous, and in some ways ludicrous, incident of the telegram of good wishes sent by three dozen Labour MPs to Signor Nenni, who was the left-wing socialist leader fighting in alliance with the Italian communists. This was a clear challenge to the Labour leadership which had withdrawn its approval from Nenni and transferred its blessing to the Italian moderate socialists. Sixteen of the signatories quickly announced either that they had never actually signed the telegram or that they had done so under a misunderstanding and now wished to withdraw. The remaining twenty-one were written to by the NEC and required to submit a pledge of loyalty to the party. The NEC communication stated that it was 'seriously disturbed by the activities over a long period of time of certain members of the Party which are considered to be subversive of

---

* This Committee of Chairmen was established after the 1947 conference. Morrison was a member by virtue of his chairmanship of the Policy sub-committee.

P

Party policy', and went on to warn that unless they pledged renewed loyalty they would be excluded from membership of the Labour Party.[33] But this was only a momentary truce. Over the next year or so, four Labour back-benchers were expelled from the party.

The first to go was John Platts-Mills, MP for Finsbury. He was a supporter of a number of communist front organizations and attracted the keen interest of the NEC after he described the communist *coup d'état* in Czechoslovakia as 'a great victory for the workers'.[34] In April 1948 the NEC Special Committee of Chairmen summoned him to account for a long list of rebellious activities. Morrison spearheaded the cross-examination and bluntly asked him if there were any issues on which he disagreed with the Communist Party. Apparently, Platts-Mills was unable to answer this question in a satisfactory manner and after further exchanges the NEC decided that in view of his 'general conduct' he must be expelled from membership of the Labour Party.[35] Three others, Leslie Solley, Lester Hutchinson and Konni Zilliacus,* followed into the political wilderness shortly afterwards: expelled for long records of dissident actions and speeches since 1945.[36] According to Zilliacus's published version of his expulsion, Morrison, although taking a leading role, did not seem to be as thirsty for his blood as Attlee, Bevin, Sam Watson and the other trade unionists, and Morrison made 'a perfectly fair summing-up of my attitude', prior to concluding that Zilliacus ought to go.[37]

British policy in the Middle East, and particularly towards the emerging state of Israel, also provoked simmering discontent in the parliamentary party, reaching a peak early in 1949, though here Morrison's approach was strikingly different from that towards the friends of the communist bloc. The bulk of the Labour members were Zionist in sympathy. They objected to Bevin's attempts to bully the Jews, who had so recently suffered the obscene horrors of Nazi tyranny. They also suspected that the hand of the Foreign Office, with its long traditions of pro-Arabism and latent anti-Semitism, lay behind Bevin's policies. Upwards of a hundred back-benchers rebelled in January 1949 and refused to support the government's proclaimed Palestine policy. Morrison, who was made chairman of the special Cabinet Committee on Palestine,[38] was carefully balanced in his outward attitude. It was especially dangerous for him, above all people, to fish in Bevin's territorial waters. He did, however, remain in close and sympathetic touch with the rebel leaders throughout the crisis and they looked to him to see that their viewpoint did not go unheard in the Cabinet.[39] At the parliamentary party meetings he maintained a position of convincing detachment in successfully conciliating the conflicting factions. Personally, however, he had in fact been passionately

---

* MPs for Thurrock, Rusholme and Gateshead East. All four expellees were defeated at the 1950 election. A fifth Labour MP expelled in 1948 was Alfred Edwards, though his deviation was to the right, in opposing Labour's nationalization of steel and he finally joined the Conservative Party and fought as an unsuccessful Conservative candidate in the 1950 general election.

pro-Zionist since his first visit to Palestine with Dov Hos in 1935. He maintained good relations with Zionist leaders, such as Chaim Weizmann, and
regularly attended Jewish and Israeli functions.[40] He went to the Independence
Day Reception at the Israeli Mission on 4 May 1949, accompanied by Nye
Bevan; Ernest Bevin, who had obstinately delayed official recognition of
Israel as long as possible, was a notable absentee because of 'other engagements'.[41] Early in January the following year, addressing a reception given by
the Israeli trade unions, Morrison said: 'In Israel the spirit of human service
exists more sincerely and more in practice than in any other part of the civilized world. Israel is one of the great experiments of the civilized world and
we are glad it has a Labour Government.'[42] Israel, inspired by lofty ideals, yet
tempered by realism and pragmatism based on hard worldly experience,
international in its cultural origins, yet passionately nationalist, dedicated to
the virtues of hard work and efficiency, and also committed politically to social
democracy, was very much Morrison's kind of country. Labour back-
benchers who rebelled in sympathy with it were not likely to suffer at his hands.

A final bout of indiscipline which troubled him much more occurred over
the Ireland Bill on the very day in May 1949 that the expulsion of Zilliacus and
Solley was announced. A clause in the bill established that Northern Ireland
would remain part of the United Kingdom until the Ulster Parliament
decided otherwise. Many Labour members, especially those with Irish
immigrant constituents, understandably objected to this as being a reinforce-
ment for partition and sixty-three of them voted against a three-line whip
at the committee stage. Five of the rebels were PPSs to Labour ministers. Four
of these were removed from their position because of their revolt and a fifth
resigned before he could be sacked.* Morrison led the attack on them, angrily
asserting that an example must be set and parliamentary discipline tightened
up with a general election possibly a year ahead. But the way in which it was
done, in some cases without even first consulting the minister whose PPS was
about to be axed, created considerable irritation.[43] The wounds were finally
bound at the parliamentary meeting on 25 May 1949. After a long discussion
Morrison wound up, dealing with many points raised by individual MPs, and
concluding with an appeal to the party to unite in brotherhood during the last
months of this Parliament.[44]

Morrison's intense absorption in high-level national and party affairs did
not mean that he altogether neglected his old haunts in London local government. He kept in touch with friends and former colleagues on the LCC,†
being available to give advice and regularly helping with their private parliamentary bills, although always careful (at least in the LCC, if not elsewhere)
not to appear to interfere.[45] He also maintained and even strengthened his
more direct links with the London Labour Party. When Latham resigned

---

* Beswick, Mallalieu, Mellish and Rogers were sacked. Blyton resigned.

† Morrison had resigned as an LCC Alderman, due to 'pressure of work' in November
1945, although he was due to continue until 1949 (LCC Minutes, 4 December 1945).

from the treasurership in May 1948, Daines and the new Chairman, Tiffin, decided that Morrison would be the best replacement and they approached him about it. Morrison agreed to serve providing it was understood that his attendances at executive meetings would be irregular because of his other official commitments. The executive approved this in June and he was made Acting Treasurer until formally appointed by the full conference in the following March.[46] In practice, he went along to the executive on average four times a year. He once attended while he was Acting Prime Minister. Cabinet papers were relayed to him in the meeting and 'he went through these signing them, and yet intervening to the point on the committee agenda at the same time'.[47] He liked to keep his finger in all the London pies, sometimes at a curiously petty level. One moment he would be directing affairs of state at 10 or 11 Downing Street, the next he might be interfering with a local borough party – as when he once tried to get a ward chairman sacked.[48] He was always a principal performer at the London party's annual conference in the spring, where his style, pithy and witty in an earthy way, was absolutely right for the audience.[49] He also addressed the mass May Day rallies and took an active part in preparing the organization and propaganda for the critical 1949 LCC elections. At the end of March he plunged into the turmoil of the campaign itself, writing in the local newspapers and addressing meetings throughout London.[50]

As the London campaign reached its peak, Morrison had to leave the field of battle to make an official four-day visit to Germany. His departure was delayed overnight by bad weather, and he sat up listening to the cliff-hanging LCC results. On the flight they were tossed about by appalling storms but Morrison slept soundly through it all, next to his detective who was calmly reading Homer's *Iliad*.[51] While he was in Berlin the final result of the LCC elections came through. Labour and the Conservatives had tied with sixty-four seats each and the Liberal, Sir Percy Harris, held the balance. The swing to the Conservatives was worrying to Labour within a year of a general election. It was also a personal blow to Morrison, being the first time that Labour had not achieved a majority since he first won London fifteen years before. In Berlin he was quoted as saying that the result was 'awkward, difficult and embarrassing'.[52] On his return he was invited to a meeting of the Labour group to discuss how to get out of the deadlock.[53] He advised them not to resort to discreditable tactics to maintain themselves in power.* More local defeats lay ahead. At the borough elections in May the Conservatives made net gains of 805 seats, winning 269 in six London boroughs: in Morrison's own Lewisham they gained 29. He was abroad at that time, in Paris to give a lecture on British parliamentary democracy, his first visit there since April 1940. He and Mrs Morrison dined after his lecture with the French Foreign Minister, Robert

---

* In the event Labour were able to keep control through their aldermanic majority. Hayward determined this policy, in some ways against Morrison's advice. (Interview, Sir Isaac Hayward.)

Schuman. Next day he asked to see the French police system in operation and visited the Sûreté and the Préfecture. He showed particular interest in models of the guillotine.[54]

In the summer of 1949 the Labour Government found itself again faced with economic crisis. Britain had made a rapid recovery from the economic setbacks of 1947 and the disaster of convertibility. The new Chancellor, Cripps, had run the country's finances on a tight rein, though the move away from cheap money and towards a budget surplus had in fact been begun under his predecessor, Dalton. Economic management was certainly now better co-ordinated through the centralized hands of the Treasury than in the earlier days of the loose troika of Morrison, Dalton and Cripps. The real change, however, was in style rather than policy. Cripps's spartan habits and religious fervour coincided more closely with the realities and needs of Britain's desperate economic situation than did the boisterous and relaxed exuberance of Dalton, or the jaunty cockiness of Morrison. Cripps, although lacking in any deep understanding of economic or financial matters, gave an impression of professionalism and dedication. With his powerful legal mind and immense capacity for work, he was superb at mastering his Treasury briefs. By early 1949 Britain's prospects, helped by American Marshall Aid, seemed bright. Labour moved ahead in the Gallup poll for the first time since the 1947 crisis. But fresh difficulties suddenly arose. The American recession damaged export earnings and prospects. The full weight of public expenditure on the new Welfare State, on the rearmament programme, and also on the recent Berlin airlift, now began to be felt. These factors combined with the longer-term over-valuation of Britain's currency to bring massive pressures against sterling from the early summer onwards.

The decision whether to devalue sterling or not, or indeed whether it could be avoided or not, began to divide the government from the beginning of June. At that point Cripps and Dalton, speaking with considerable combined weight as Chancellor and ex-Chancellor, were against devaluation.[55] Gaitskell and Douglas Jay at the Treasury were not yet in favour. Morrison had a memorandum from Dalton[56] setting out the case against devaluation,* but he was holidaying near Ross-on-Wye, on the fruit farm of Lord Jackson, the former Labour MP, when the Economic Planning Committee first discussed it on 15 June. It was an alarming meeting. Cripps reported that all of Britain's reserves might rapidly disappear and there could be 'a complete collapse of sterling'. Attlee showed signs of panic and as they went out remarked to Dalton '1931 all over again'.[57] By the end of the month the crisis was before the full Cabinet. Cripps took the line advocated by the City, the Bank of England, and certain top civil servants, that they should not devalue but should impose a drastically tighter monetary policy, with higher interest rates and cuts in

---

* Morrison still sat on the Economic Policy Committee and he continued to make speeches in the country on economic questions even after he ceased to be in charge of economic affairs.

subsidies.[58] He restated these proposals to a long and contentious meeting of the Economic Policy Committee at the beginning of July. Morrison, whose chief adviser, Nicholson, favoured devaluation,[59] was now present and took the lead against Cripps. He resisted suggestions for cuts in food subsidies, and argued that devaluation might perhaps be the least of evils among the options facing them; for once Attlee was inclined to support him. These arguments wrangled on throughout July as the reserves situation grew worse.

At the end of July the Commons adjourned for two and a half months, having its final meeting on a Saturday morning, the first Saturday meeting since 1939. Morrison was the only Cabinet minister in the chamber. The following week he acted as deputy prime minister with Attlee once again off sick. The sterling crisis continued to boil. Harold Wilson was now lining up with Cripps and Treasury orthodoxy, supporting massive cuts in public expenditure in the hope of avoiding devaluation.* Dalton had meanwhile swung over beside Morrison and the young economists Gaitskell and Jay to the view that devaluation was perhaps inevitable and preferable to a savage axe on Labour's social and welfare programme. Eventually they imposed the parity change on the sick and reluctant Chancellor,[60] though Morrison was not present for the final showdown.[61] He flew to Strasbourg on 8 August to lead the British delegation of eighteen to the first meeting of the Consultative Assembly of the Council of Europe – another example of his increasing involvement in foreign affairs in the latter half of this Labour Government. Dalton was his deputy and the Tory section was led by Churchill and Harold Macmillan.

This Strasbourg meeting was a great opportunity for Morrison to establish himself on the international scene and to take advantage of the growing tide of Europeanism which was leaving so many of his Labour colleagues quite untouched. Somehow, it did not work out. He got off on the wrong foot from the beginning, having a public row in the corridors of the conference hall with Churchill over the payment of expense allowances to both Churchill and his deputy. It was a petty matter, but one which aroused Morrison's almost pathological suspicions about any misuse of public funds. Churchill felt that Morrison was making a mountain out of a very small molehill. With a firm thrust of the fingers he explicitly indicated to Morrison and the watching European politicians where the Labour leader should put his currency allowance.[62] Further hostile publicity was given to an episode at a cocktail party in Strasbourg where Morrison spoke over-long in English to a French audience. Unfavourable comparisons were drawn between Morrison, allegedly uncouth and insular, and the smooth manners and linguistic facility of the Conservative delegation.[63] It was the kind of criticism that Morrison, with

---

* Dalton wrote, with the harshness that increasingly marked his diary comments, that Harold Wilson 'trims and wavers and is thinking more of what senior ministers – or even senior officials – are thinking of him than of what is right'. (Dalton, diary, 12 September 1949, Vol. 37. Douglas Jay had similar recollections. Interview.)

his touchiness and insecurity about his lack of education, did not easily shrug off. At no point was he treated with quite the respect which his status in the British government and as leader of the British delegation seemed to him to demand. The harsh reality was that Morrison was not well known among the Continentals and he operated at Strasbourg inevitably in the shadows of Churchill, of the other cosmopolitan Conservatives, and of Bevin. He seemed only to gain publicity for his social gaffes.

His treatment by the British press was unfair, reflecting its bias, malice and snobbishness, since in fact Morrison did a serious job of work at the Strasbourg Assembly. He made a major speech on the future of European unity and explained Britain's attitude towards it. He was sympathetic towards any proposals that might achieve greater union, though he did not seem to conceive that he himself or Britain should lend a positive hand in formulating such proposals. He pointed out the diversity of the European peoples, and that unification could only be by consent – 'there can be no question of coercing free peoples and democratic Parliaments into schemes to which they are opposed'. Always electorally conscious, he warned the representatives that they must be honest with themselves, and by that he meant that they must not say anything in Strasbourg by which they would not be prepared to stand or fall before their respective electorates. His own preference was for the functional approach to Europe rather than the federal. Morrison saw Europe in the same way that he saw most political questions in the British Labour movement. He was wary of dogma and preferred pragmatism; he rejected revolution in favour of evolution. 'Very often in public affairs,' he concluded in the Assembly, 'we have to choose between constructive evolution on the one hand and emotional and reckless jumps to we know not where on the other. For myself I believe that constructive evolution, which need not and ought not to lack boldness, is the quickest and surest means of progress.'[64]

Morrison held an important position in these early days of the fledgling United Europe. He must carry some of the blame for not having taken a more positive and imaginative role in moulding that future unity and fashioning a place for Britain within it. But it is a blame that is very widely shared. Britain was simply not ready to contemplate limitations on its national sovereignty so soon after having fought almost to the death to preserve its independence from European aggression. Morrison characteristically voiced, felt and reflected the feelings of his countrymen. He did not view Europe with the hostility of Dalton and Cripps, or with the apathy of Attlee. He was unquestionably concerned to preserve social democracy on the Continent and sympathized with aspirations towards greater unity. But he was temperamentally unsuited to think through to a radically new situation in Europe. Despite his belief in international socialism, he still thought in national concepts and was proudly insular about his own country. He also thought constitutionally in terms of the parliamentary system; as if the British parliamentary form of government was the only ideal towards which others should aspire. When he found that the Strasbourg Assembly lacked the cut and thrust of Westminster debates, his interest declined and he wrote it off as 'a bogus talk shop'.[65] His imagination, which could be fertile in matters of domestic policy, did not at this time encompass a vision of a transformed Europe.

Chapter 33

'Consolidation' and the 1950 Election

As the Labour Government moved towards the end of its term, Morrison spent more and more time planning for the next general election. He had in fact begun preparations within a year of the 1945 victory, discussing the future election programme with his Policy sub-committee of the NEC.[1] Early in 1948, this committee changed its name to the Policy and Publicity Committee[2] and it thenceforward devoted itself to drafting the future programme. Seven sub-committees were established to consider various aspects of policy; Morrison was chairman of two concerned with the existing nationalized industries and with proposals for future nationalization and was a member of a third examining private industry.[3]

To Morrison the problems and necessary tactics of the next election were clear. He assumed that Labour would keep its solid working-class support. The crucial test was whether it could retain and even win more floating voters from the middle ground of politics: the housewives, the professional middle classes, the rural vote, and the Liberals of radical inclination. He believed these could be attracted to Labour only if the party appeared to be non-doctrinal and classless in its approach. In his speeches and other pronouncements, Morrison had long tried to appeal to what he called 'all the useful people'.*

Now he set out to strengthen this bid for the middle ground by attempting to fashion Labour's future policy commitments in a way that he believed would not alienate the floating voters. In particular, he became attached to

---

* At the Gravesend by-election in November 1947, when Morrison was rushed into the battle at the last minute because of the government's fear about the result, he told an enormous gathering of three thousand people in the Market Hall that they should support Sir Richard Acland, the Labour candidate, partly because he stood for 'the useful people' among the better off. (*Daily Herald*, 26 November 1947.) In a party political broadcast in December 1947, Morrison went out of his way to make sympathetic references to the middle classes. Again, early in March of 1948, he spoke at Grimsby and pointed out that the middle classes could never form their own party and went on: 'I say to them – do not stand aside. Do not merely sulk and grumble. Come into the Labour Party.' (*Observer*, 7 March 1948.)

the concept of 'consolidation', which meant that Labour should not pursue further nationalization, but should devote itself to digesting the reforms it had already introduced and especially to creating a better image for the existing nationalized industries.

The 1948 conference held at Scarborough in May had provided the first opportunity and a public glimpse of the way in which Morrison's mind was working. It was a quiet, solid and constructive conference. The sun shone all the week,[4] and Morrison had an excellent time by the sea. He stayed in Scarborough ten days, arriving before the conference to address the agricultural workers, and remaining four days after it closed, resting, and addressing two rallies, one of the National Union of Public Employees, and the other the Inland Revenue Staff conference. At the conference ball he was dancing as enthusiastically and exhaustingly as ever with one partner after another, stretching from the tiny Mrs Shinwell to the lofty Dr Summerskill.[5]

The serious side of Scarborough, in the conference debates, saw Morrison's message coming over strong and clear. Hugh Dalton noted in his diary at the start that the word 'consolidation' was going the rounds for the next Parliament.[6] Morrison took an early opportunity to air his views, when speaking for the NEC on their plans for the next election. He argued that although the next programme would consider more public ownership, it must also leave time to consolidate, develop and make more efficient the industries already socialized. He elaborated this point next day in the debate on production. Opening the morning session he said that there was no point in just passing further legislative acts and establishing new institutions for their own sake. A time comes when 'advance must be followed by detailed consolidation, and by exploiting the territory that has been gained. That is the state which we are now reaching. And if we go on always stretching our hands for more and not making good the gains we have claimed only disaster can follow.'[7] The press was quick to point out that Morrison was already fashioning the tactics for the next election.[8] Some delegates disliked what was afoot and attacked Morrison for an alleged retreat from socialism.[9] Nor were all of his Cabinet colleagues happy. Dalton met Attlee shortly after the conference and told him that 'Morrison's idea of having no new socialization measures in the next Parliament would never do.'[10] Attlee, as always, appeared to agree. But Morrison was now launched on his mission, with all the energy and determination which characterized his political endeavours.

Projecting the Labour Party's image for the coming election was to be his main preoccupation over the next eighteen months. For good or ill, the party did come to reflect his views more than those either of Dalton or of dogmatists on the left. As so often before, Morrison had sensed the direction in which broader public opinion was moving. He constantly hammered his message home. He talked repeatedly of 'consolidation' in his speeches on a tour of south-west England and Wales in mid-June 1948.[11] In an interview in the Labour Party quarterly, *Forum*, in July, he explained that 'consolidation' was 'not a plea for going backwards in any sense of the term. It was a plea for laying firm and secure foundations on which further progress can be made. . . . We have got to take into account the opinions of all sections of the community. Let us not forget the one, two, or more millions of voters, "the floaters" who in the end will in all likelihood determine whether there is a Labour Government or not.' Morrison was being his usual pragmatic self. As he earlier wrote in the *London News*, 'Labour's business is to remain sensible, rational and public-spirited. . . . We won the last election by a sound British combination of idealism and realism.'[12] If Morrison had chosen an epitaph for his own career it would have been that he had always shown a sound British combination of idealism and realism. The one troubling question at this time was whether the previously sound combination had not begun to alter in balance; whether with advancing years the idealism was draining away and realism was being interpreted too readily as a static consolidationism.

The bill to nationalize iron and steel lying before the new session of Parliament in the autumn of 1948 focussed public attention on the problems of the nationalized industries and, to Morrison's way of thinking, seemed to underline the potential electoral liability of the Labour Party's nationalization commitments. There was little evidence of public or party enthusiasm for the steel measure. There was much evidence of doubt in Labour's own ranks. Almost hysterical antipathy arose from the Conservative opposition, whose morale was perceptibly rising. When the bill went through its second reading on 17 November, Morrison closed for the government amid noise and confusion, and the opposition vote of 211, including the Liberals, was the biggest so far in the Parliament.[13]

The dominant theme of his public speeches at this time was the impact of nationalization on Labour's electoral chances in the country at large.[14] On the NEC, his special committee examining the existing nationalized industries met three times between September and November 1948 in his room at 11 Downing Street, covering the structures, efficiency, and industrial relations in the various public industries very thoroughly.[15] Having completed its agenda, the committee held a special meeting with the economic committee of the TUC at Transport House at the end of November. The attendance from the parliamentary side was poor and Morrison felt constrained to apologize for the ill-mannered absence of so many on his side. Flanked only by Morgan Phillips and two officers from Transport House, and facing the big battalions from the TUC including Deakin, Lincoln Evans, Lawther, Tanner, Williamson and Woodcock, Morrison summarized for them the conclusions they had reached in favour of more flexible structures and ways to increase efficiency. From his personal point of view, he said that in the end he had concluded that 'the real problem in nationalization was not who was to appoint members of boards, but that of industrial democracy at lower levels'. It was a point of view that many people well to the left of Morrison would have agreed with, though not all of them perhaps would have expected him, with his image as a right-wing bureaucrat, to take such a position.

Morrison went again with Margaret to Cornwall for Christmas 1948, and the New Year, staying with the Hamblys at Treharrock Manor. Maurice Webb and his wife travelled with them. Morrison enjoyed himself as before, though he spent even more time working. Cabinet boxes continued to flood in by dispatch rider at all hours of the day and night. He was heavily involved with collating the various reports from the sub-committees of his Policy and Publicity Committee into a first draft of the next election programme for the 1949 conference at Blackpool. He was also thinking out the changes in personnel which he believed were necessary to revitalize the administration prior to asking for a new mandate. He wrote to Attlee from Treharrock setting out his suggestions for an extensive reshuffle.[16] 'I feel more than ever convinced that a major reconstruction should take place. The country and the Party expect and want it. The *aim*, I think, should be to make it run to and over the General Election. Which means boldness and special care. . . . The Government needs strengthening, so I hope for real changes.' Naturally his friends and protégés figure prominently among the lists of suggested promotions: Maurice Webb as Minister of Food, of Works or at the GPO; Hartley Shawcross at Works or as Secretary of State for War; Dick Stokes again possibly at Works. His present PPS, Stephen Taylor, and Taylor's two predecessors, Patrick Gordon Walker and Christopher Mayhew, were also put up for high promotion.* Morrison believed in looking after his own. Attlee replied suggesting a talk when Morrison returned, but the necessary reshuffle did not take place.[17]

On his return from Cornwall Morrison plunged into the election build-up. He visited the North East in freezing mid-January to urge the Northern Regional Council of the Labour Party to rise up and do battle. While there he slipped off for an evening to the village of Morley Hill in County Durham to attend their weekly dance and to celebrate Labour's great 1945 victory, keeping a promise he had made to them three years earlier.[18] Next month he returned even further north, to Glasgow and North Lanark, arousing the party faithful (and dealing skilfully and authoritatively with the interruptions of the Scottish Nationalists). At the North Lanark meeting he once again cast his party line to the middle classes. 'It should never be forgotten,' he asserted, 'that the Labour Party stands for the well-being of all the useful people in society . . . it is its duty to cultivate the support of the rural community. It is necessary to spread wise and vigorous Socialist propaganda among the middle classes.'[19]

* Gordon Walker as Secretary of State for Commonwealth Relations or for Air, Mayhew as Minister of State at the Foreign Office.

Morrison's Policy and Publicity Committee approved a draft programme for the next election, based on the sub-committee reports and entitled *Labour Believes in Britain*, in mid-January 1949.[20] This draft was then discussed by the top echelons of the Labour movement at a special conference at Shanklin, Isle of Wight, on the last weekend of February.[21] Morrison travelled with his Cabinet colleagues and with the National Executive Committee on a special four-coach electric train from Waterloo. They crossed by steamer from Portsmouth to Ryde and then travelled in fourteen taxis to the Manor House Hotel, which stood in its own grounds high above the outskirts of Shanklin and was, typically, unlicensed.[22]

Morrison himself opened the proceedings with a long speech introducing the draft programme. The subsequent working sessions went well from Morrison's point of view with general approval for his consolidation approach. On the Saturday evening, with their work complete, the Labour leaders relaxed at dinner. Afterwards, Morrison and Attlee made short speeches and then the whole occasion slipped into informality. Morrison recited a verse from Omar Khayyam, Professor Laski sang 'Poor Old Joe', Tom Williams sang 'Ilkley Moor', and there was general singing with Albert Alexander playing the piano. Next day they returned to London by ferry and by train.[23]

The revised draft of *Labour Believes in Britain* was finally settled by the NEC in March.[24] Morrison had worked to keep the emphasis on consolidation and on the need to improve the functioning of the existing nationalized industries. But he did not win every point. A small list of proposed nationalizations was inserted despite his opposition. He tried particularly hard to get the nationalization of industrial assurance dropped from the manifesto and after a series of meetings with the Co-operative Insurance union representatives, who were sympathetic to his position, achieved a compromise to support mutualization rather than full nationalization.[25]

Labour's conference at Blackpool in June 1949 was the last before the general election. Morrison addressed one of the two big eve-of-conference rallies, held on the Sunday afternoon, 5 June. He indulged in some easy and much appreciated Tory-bashing, denouncing Churchill as irresponsible and suggesting that if elected to be Prime Minister he would cause more industrial strikes. Next day Churchill issued a public protest against Morrison's allegations.[26] The NEC elections announced on Tuesday showed Morrison holding his position comfortably in fourth place, behind Bevan, Foot and Griffiths. That evening he did not make his usual appearance at the Annual Delegates' Ball in the Empress Ballroom. He went to bed early to be in good shape for his major speech on the general election manifesto the next day. It was perhaps also a reminder of the passing of time that the gossip columnists began to write of a new generation of conference dancers: the Minister of Fuel, Hugh Gaitskell, for instance, and Harold Wilson, the young President of the Board of Trade.[27]

Morrison's power to dominate conference, however, was in no way diminished. His speech was strong and rousing and received a great ovation. Presenting the draft manifesto *Labour Believes in Britain*, he pointed out that the next election manifesto would be distilled from this document and he asked for a fair degree of discretion in shaping it. The proposals were a balanced mixture of consolidation and further progress. On the nationalized industries he repeated themes he had already outlined in earlier speeches and at committee meetings. He also introduced what he called 'a new application of socialism and of socialist doctrine. It is called competitive public enterprise . . . aiming at total economic efficiency . . . within a proper field competition between private and public enterprise will be good both for the public and the private sectors of industry.' When he turned to the few areas of industry then suggested for nationalization – sections of food processing and distribution, meat wholesaling, sugar and cold storage, cement, parts of chemicals – it is interesting that he described them in the context not of public ownership but of the need to give consumers a fair deal and to keep the cost of living low.[28]

The debate continued for two days. Morrison replied for the NEC on the Friday. He concluded with great fervour, lifting the eyes of the party faithful to the mighty battle that lay ahead. Once more he reminded them of the need to win the support of the middle classes, the agricultural areas, and the housewives. 'We do not want to be a narrow Party, we want to be the party of all the useful people, the Party of the Nation.' He then summoned them to their election action stations. 'Let us go through that struggle with a sterling determination and coolness but also with a religious zeal and enthusiasm so that when the "all clear" goes it will be an "all clear" for British Labour, British Democracy, British Socialism to go ahead towards another five years of creative effort in the building of a great and prosperous land.'[29] With the rapturous acclamation of his appeal the last Labour conference of this government came to a tumultuous end.

After conference, Morrison returned to his campaign themes. He went to Derby to woo the housewife at a rally of Labour women.[30] The following Sunday, he travelled to Yarmouth to address a mass rally of the Eastern Region of the National Union of Agricultural Workers. It was estimated that up to a hundred thousand farm workers poured into Yarmouth by special trains and coaches over the weekend and the town's cafés stayed open all Saturday night plying them with tea and sandwiches. Morrison had long gone out of his way to cultivate the farm workers' vote. 'I look to the rural constituencies to give us many Labour gains at the next General Election,' he said. 'Go out to smash Tory reaction in the agricultural areas of Britain. . . . We have got the right Government, the first to treat you properly for a hundred and fifty long and tragic years. Keep it.'[31]

The rest of the summer of 1949 Morrison spent dealing with the politics of devaluation, at the Strasbourg Council of Europe, and afterwards on holiday in the South of France. He flew back from the Riviera on 21 September. The dire deed of devaluation had been executed in his absence. Cripps and Bevin were dispatched to Washington to negotiate assistance from the Americans and ministers were already launched on the familiar path of inter-departmental haggling over the harsh consequential economic measures. The Cabinet was not a happy family when Morrison returned. Bevan told Dalton that Cripps 'now had a persecution mania and was taking very hard charges of dishonourable conduct over devaluation'. The Chancellor was demanding reductions in public expenditure of some £700 millions. Bevin and Alexander were threatening to resign if the full weight of these cuts fell on defence; Bevan was threatening to resign if the weight fell on social expenditure; Cripps, who was suffering from insomnia and deteriorating in general health, was threatening to resign unless all agreed with him. Morrison and Attlee desperately worked to find a compromise which would hold the Cabinet and the party together. Finally, on 21 October, the Cabinet agreed a programme of reductions in capital investment and government expenditure having a total deflationary effect of some £250 millions.[32] When Attlee announced them to the Commons on the twenty-fourth he did so to a completely silent House and sat down in front of benches of openly dispirited supporters. It was hardly auspicious with an election no more than nine months, and in reality barely three months, ahead.

Immediately on his return from the South of France, Morrison resumed his electioneering, travelling into the country and making speeches on the now familiar themes with repeated appeals for middle-class support.[33] He also began to attack the iniquities of the Conservative Party's fund raising and the dishonesty of their refusal to disclose the big business sources of their income. Morrison was here not just attacking the opposition party, but was particularly concerned with the activities of Tate and Lyle, the sugar monopoly, which Labour was proposing to nationalize and which in retaliation was spending vast sums of money on anti-Labour propaganda. Slight hysteria in fact developed on Labour's side, with Morrison among the most agitated, about the anti-nationalization campaigns then being promoted by various sections of industry. Morrison gave a public warning that company expenditure for political purposes would be investigated in relation to breaches of the electoral law, and early in December the Attorney-General, Hartley Shawcross, told the Commons that he had instructed the Director of Public Prosecutions to be prepared to institute proceedings.*

The imminence of the election was now dominating the government's thinking and tactics. The parliamentary decks had by the year's end been cleared of the last obstacles to a quick dissolution. The Parliament Bill completed its third and final course in a listless House with members forced to go

---

* Morrison and Shawcross consulted closely about their joint attack on backstairs expenditure in support of the Tories. Morrison even asked Shawcross to vet his speeches for libel as 'I can't afford an action'. (Morrison to Shawcross, 8 December 1949 and 17 November 1949. Shawcross to Morrison, 21 November 1949, 8 December 1949, 14 December 1949, 13 January 1950, 16 January 1950. Morrison–Boon papers.)

over the same old arguments again and again, though Morrison as chief pilot
was unrelenting in pressing home the government's case.* With steel nationalized, Labour had now ticked off the last of its promises from the 1945
election manifesto. It had been a major achievement. Much of the credit
rests with Morrison. With hindsight it could be said that steel nationalization,
the most contentious and least popular measure, should have been put through
earlier and longer before the next general election – though Morrison could,
of course, argue that his 1947 compromise proposal would have secured that
tactical objective without abandoning any basic principles. Such quibbles
apart, Morrison had masterminded an unprecedented programme of reform
restructuring British society, surpassing even that of the Liberal government
before the First World War. His guiding hand was evident everywhere, in
Cabinet, in committee, in Parliament, in the parliamentary party and on the
National Executive.

The problem of the precise timing of the next general election had exercised
Labour's leaders since the middle of 1949. The government could legally wait
until June 1950, but few supported that course and there was some pressure
to dissolve much before. Attlee summoned a council of war to discuss the
timing of the next election on 19 July 1949, assembling Morrison, Bevin,
Bevan, Dalton and the Chief Whip. Cripps was absent in Zürich getting medical treatment, but he sent a letter for Attlee to read to the meeting. The
Chancellor wanted an immediate dissolution and an election in the middle of
the August holidays. The Prime Minister commented drily that Cripps was
obviously not in good shape when he wrote. Bevan, who had long agreed with
his friend, Cripps, on the need for an early election, if not an immediate one,
spoke strongly for getting it over and done with at least before the year was
out. He was afraid of a loss of momentum as their legislative programme
wound down and particularly feared the electoral consequences of the next
Budget, which he rightly saw as needing to be even tougher and less popular
than the last. Attlee, Bevin and Dalton all agreed on the need to dissolve
before the next Budget, though they were willing to wait until February 1950
at the latest. Morrison, who had a reputation for wisdom and good intuition
on electoral matters, was uncharacteristically uncertain and sat on the fence.[34]
He feared that the party machine was not yet tuned up and argued that 'the
country might think we were running away if we dissolve now'. Another

---

* Ironically, the new Parliament Act and its provisions for reduced Lords' delaying
powers were not in the end used to speed up the nationalization of steel – mainly because
this would have meant delaying the election until the last moment in June 1950. The Lords
had, as expected, amended the Nationalization Bill, particularly to postpone the vesting
date of the new industry from 1 May 1950 until July 1951 – in other words, until well after
the next election. The Government partly capitulated, putting up a compromise suggestion,
whereby the vesting date would be delayed until New Year 1951, earlier than the Lords
suggested, but still after the election. The best summary of the complexities of iron and
steel nationalization is in H. Morrison, *Government and Parliament*, (1959), pp. 172 and
180–4.

special meeting was held at 10 Downing Street in the middle of October and they divided as before. Morrison, who had previously genuinely been open-minded, was now firmly for delay.[35] He did not like running away from difficulties. He honestly believed that to dissolve now because the economic situation would get worse later was to deceive the electorate. He also found it easy to take up a position opposed to Bevan and Cripps, who had begun to replace Bevin as his enemies in the Cabinet. Attlee eventually came down on the side of Morrison and Bevin and they then carried a majority of the Cabinet in this view, though Cripps and Bevan continued to speak against delay, and Harold Wilson was 'half-way against'.[36] After this Cabinet on 13 October a statement was issued, in order to end speculation and uncertainty, that there would be no election in 1949.[37]

The senior ministers reached their election conclusions at a special conference late in the afternoon of 7 December at 10 Downing Street. Bevin was absent at Eastbourne, none too well, but sent a message saying he was prepared to leave the decision to them and could offer no firm advice since he was 'no politician'. The choice before them effectively was February or June 1950. All except Morrison plumped for February. Cripps in particular showed signs of panic, arguing it was impossible to hold sterling beyond February. Morrison was uncertain, inclining towards facing the Budget first and delaying the election until 'later', but he was clearly not specific, then or subsequently in his *Autobiography*,[38] precisely when 'later' ought to be. He probably sensed that Labour would do disappointingly in an early election – only two days later on 9 December Labour's majority in the South Bradford by-election was halved. He believed that bad weather would damage Labour's chance since the cold and fog of February would force the old and the sick among the party's working-class supporters, especially in rural areas, to stay at home by the fireside.[39] But Cripps was absolutely determined not to put another Budget before this Parliament. Attlee now finally came down on the side of his Chancellor. So they decided for 23 February, with a public announcement on 17 January and dissolution on 3 February.[40]

With the election decision effectively taken* – though full Cabinet approval had not yet been sought – Morrison went away for Christmas to relax and to prepare for the heavy fight ahead. This year he and Margaret went to an old-world hotel, the Hayburn Wyke Hotel, on the coast six miles north of Scarborough. Maurice Webb, who organized the whole expedition, his wife and son, Leslie Hunter and Dr Jeger, the MP for St Pancras, with his wife Lena, made up the party, occupying all the rooms in the isolated hostelry. It

---

* In his *Autobiography* Morrison oddly ignores these meetings and conclusions before Christmas and simply states that Attlee took the election decision during the Christmas holidays while ministers were away from 'official business for a day or two and relaxed with their families' (p. 268). That was unfair to Attlee. The Prime Minister did determine the final timing, but as on most major decisions he was careful to consult his leading colleagues, getting advice, securing commitment, sharing blame if it went wrong.

was an oddly assorted gathering, for the Jegers were far from being good friends of Morrison. It was also sadly ill-fated: the Webbs' son died within weeks, and both his parents, Leslie Hunter, Dr Jeger and Margaret Morrison were to die within a few years while still relatively young.

Morrison insisted to all the press that he had gone simply for a rest and not to make politics. 'We have no political plots to hatch under this roof,' he told one newspaperman. 'I shall be spending the holiday walking, reading and catching up on a lot of lost sleep.'[41] It was claimed that 'politics as conversation are barred. There is a howl from everyone when politics are mentioned.'[42] The holiday certainly had its lighter side. Morrison always enjoyed joining in at parties and festivities. On Christmas Day, after a dinner of turkey and plum pudding, he played Father Christmas, presenting the gifts from the Christmas tree to the workers and staff of the hotel and its adjoining farm. The biggest cheer came when he took down a gift for himself inscribed 'From the Treasurer of Beverley Conservative Association'. After this ceremony Morrison and his colleagues and their wives played at waiters and served the staff with their Christmas dinner, Morrison marching in wearing a chef's hat and carrying the Christmas pudding aflame with burning brandy.[43] Morrison walked quite a lot, sometimes with Margaret, and spent the evenings mostly sitting gossiping in the hotel lounge. Apart from his favourite detective and mystery stories, he was, as always, ostentatiously reading a 'prestige' book relevant to his current job – this time, J. E. Neale's study of the Elizabethan House of Commons. Often while he stayed at the hotel resting, Margaret rambled over the moors with Lena Jeger, revealing her remarkable knowledge of wild flowers, and curiously losing all trace of her normally paralysing stutter when discussing them.[44]

Morrison welcomed the New Year, and another birthday, in the North. He received a gift of a tobacco jar and a cigar case from the PLP, and exchanged greetings telegrams with Attlee. He left for London on the fourth, nursing the secret of the coming dissolution date.[45] The following Tuesday, 10 January, the full Cabinet confirmed 23 February as polling day and agreed to make a public announcement next day, a week earlier than originally planned. This meant an unusually long election campaign of six weeks. But it was essential to end speculation. An early announcement was also a convenient way, under the electoral law, to bring to an end the anti-nationalization propaganda and anti-Labour expenditure of firms such as Tate and Lyle.

Morrison was again chairman of the NEC special campaign committee, which prepared the literature and budgeted funds for the electoral campaign ahead,[46] though he felt that he never played the same central role in 1950 that he had in 1945. This time he was given only a small room at the top of Transport House. He saw little of the publicity officer who was kept firmly under the Secretary's thumb. Morrison was convinced that Phillips, resentful of the publicity given to Morrison as the architect of the 1945 victory,[47] was now deliberately freezing him out. 'The isolation was psychological as well as physical. I felt ineffective and frustrated.'[48]

Despite these limitations on his formal role, Morrison's burden of work in the 1950 campaign was still enormous. In the space of three weeks he conducted some eighty meetings around the country, travelling constantly to the provinces, from Pudsey to Plymouth, regularly returning to London to Labour headquarters, and also meeting heavy speaking obligations in his own constituency.* He was Labour's election handyman. Having played an influential role in carrying through the policies in the last Parliament and in fashioning the policy manifesto for the new election, he now carried a major burden in taking that message to the party faithful throughout the country. His ceaseless perambulations, sometimes addressing great mass meetings in large halls, sometimes shouting hoarsely above the traffic to scattered spectators at street corners, had much in common with the work done by George Brown in the general elections of 1966 and 1970. The Labour Party needed, from its leadership, a man of the people to go to talk to the people. With Bevin ill, and neither Attlee nor Cripps quite fitting the role, the burden fell on Morrison.

Morrison's own constituency was now South Lewisham. As a result of the boundary revision carried out under the Labour government, Lewisham was given an extra seat (Hackney lost one!) and his former constituency of East Lewisham was divided: the north part, which was safely Tory, was hived off into the North Lewisham constituency and the southern part, which was much more safely Labour, with many transport workers and dockers living there, became Morrison's domain. His local party continued to thrive and had the largest membership of any Labour constituency party in the country. He opened his campaign with a mass meeting of his constituents at Lewisham Town Hall. Their enthusiasm was tremendous. The hall was packed, crowds of people remained in the streets outside and the traffic was brought to a halt.[49]

Public interest mounted ever higher. At Bournemouth, a Tory stronghold, a queue of people extended over half a mile to hear Morrison speak.[50] At Harrow on 13 February the hall was packed with a thousand people inside and an estimated two thousand locked out. The corridors were jammed, and people clambered on the window-sills outside. There were constant interruptions and heckling but Morrison enjoyed being the master of such hurly-burly and dealt with everything that was thrown at him in a good humour for nearly an hour.[51] But the next night at Clapham he was forced to complain angrily that the Tory disruption, the noise and chanting, was of such a systematic kind that it had clearly been organized to prevent his making himself heard. He spent the last week of the campaign in London and the home

---

* The originals of forty-six speeches he delivered are on file in the Morrison–Boon papers. In many cases Boon or Nicholson wrote the first drafts, but Morrison usually made his own additions.

counties, dashing from meeting to meeting, occasionally snatching a plateful of fish and chips in a café beforehand. Usually he rang the changes on his speeches – from foreign to domestic affairs, social welfare, the economic situation, or the general viciousness of the Tories. When he did on one occasion make the same speech at two different meetings the *Daily Telegraph* felt called upon to comment that it was 'unusual for him'.[52] At the Chatham Empire, where he was speaking for Arthur Bottomley, the lions performing in the circus currently appearing at the theatre constantly roared throughout Morrison's address. Every time there was applause they roared under the impression that it was their turn to perform next. Their loudest roars came after Morrison had read an extract from the Labour manifesto.[53] Morrison told Bottomley to go and shut them up and immediately he left the stage they quietened. 'What a candidate!' Morrison exclaimed.[54]

At an eve-of-poll press conference at Transport House, Morrison made his final appeal to the Liberals and the middle-class voters, specifying the professional class, the technicians and the housewives, claiming 'they are a useful and valuable element in our society'. According to one observer 'he lacked some of his usual sprightliness and the quiff was undeniably at half-mast'. Pressed on his drooping hair, Morrison quipped back that 'in view of all the strain and stress of the election, not to mention the experience I had with the lions, I think my old quiff is standing up to it very well, and I hope it will stand higher on Friday'.[55] As a prediction on the result he said 'it looks good, feels good, and smells good'.[56]

Morrison finished his campaign on his own doorstep, making speeches at Deptford, Greenwich, Woolwich and finally in Lewisham. The Woolwich meeting was an exchange arrangement with Bevin, set up by their agents. Mabel Raisin negotiated direct with Bevin, who said 'I'll come for you, Mabel, but not for that so-and-so candidate of yours'. Morrison was delighted at this campaign coup, with the possibility of reconciliation – though he was less pleased when the advertising posters put Bevin's name in bigger print than his own.[57] The meeting was a public success, though nearly a disaster behind the scenes when Bevin had another heart flutter and Morrison's friend Dr Edmund Hambly had to help resuscitate him.[58]

Morrison had travelled over two thousand miles in the damp, cold February weather and was now very hoarse and visibly exhausted. For the last two years he had worked towards this moment, fashioning, moulding and arguing about Labour's policies in committee, at party conference, and on platforms throughout the country. He did not believe in leaving things to chance. He believed in hard work, homework and good management. Now it was up to the British people, in whom he always had genuine and unhypocritical trust.

Polling day started fine, but it ended, as Morrison always feared, in pouring rain. He went that night to Lewisham Town Hall for the declaration of his result. When his victory was announced the Tories and the Communists (whose candidate lost his deposit with a derisory 635 votes) booed for many minutes and he was for some time unable to make the customary vote of thanks to the returning officer. Finally, making himself heard, he reprimanded them sharply.[59] His victory by a comfortable margin of fourteen per cent demonstrated the wisdom and fortune of his move to Lewisham in 1945. It also reflected the organizing skill of his agent, Mabel Raisin, who secured for him the highest voting turn-out in the area (both the other Lewisham seats were lost).

Morrison left Lewisham Town Hall and travelled across the river to Transport House to follow the other election results then coming in on the tape machine and on a screen set up there. By the time he went home to bed the situation looked quite promising. Labour had a large lead in the urban seats. The ominous significance of a general swing of some three per cent against Labour in terms of *votes*, rising to five per cent in Morrison's beloved London area, was not then appreciated by politicians unfamiliar with the refinements of psephology.[60] Labour leaders went to sleep contentedly assuming a majority of upwards of a hundred, providing a good proportion of the suburban and rural seats won in 1945 held firm. But the following day a series of disasters in suburbia and the shires of England flooded in, at one point entirely eliminating Labour's majority, and by late Friday leaving the government with a thin lead of ten with six constituencies still to declare. When the final results arrived from the distant islands the margin was down to five.

The traditional faithful had not failed the party. In a massive turn-out Labour increased its vote to record proportions. But the Tories had recovered dramatically, especially in the dormitory areas; opinion polls suggested that Labour's share of the middle-class vote had fallen from twenty-one per cent to sixteen per cent, despite Morrison's ceaseless wooing. Redistribution of constituency boundaries, executed by Labour with masochistic honesty to eliminate many of its strongholds in the centre of great industrial towns, was responsible for the loss of a good proportion of the 1945 majority. Only eighty constituencies retained their 1945 boundaries and in the LCC area alone the number of seats was cut from 62 to 43. The introduction of the postal vote, less comprehensible to and less exploited by the working people than the more educated classes, also tipped the scales against Labour in some marginal seats. Labour secured a substantial majority of votes cast, nearly three per cent more than the Conservatives, but too many of them were wasted in solidly safe seats. Tory support was more evenly spread and over the country as a whole there was a swing to them of 3·3 per cent.[61]

Morrison was again at Transport House following the nerve-racking ebb and flow of Labour's fortunes on the Friday after the poll, as during the great triumphant hours of 26 July 1945. He took the blows philosophically. 'The British people are wonderful,' he told one lobby correspondent. 'They didn't mean to chuck us out, only to give us a sharp kick in the pants. But I think they've overdone it a bit.'[62] Late on Friday the Cabinet met to discuss the situation and decided to carry on in government. It was to be tough, exhausting, sometimes demoralizing, but Morrison and his colleagues still had nearly two years of high office ahead.

Chapter 34

More Consolidation 1950-1951, and Farewell to the Lord Presidency

After the 1950 election Morrison was deeply involved in the post-mortem on Labour's setback. He was blamed by many on the left who believed that Labour had lost support because it had diluted its socialist objectives. Morrison replied, at a Labour jubilee rally at Clapham, appealing for an end to recriminations: 'The unity of the Labour Movement is imperative at this time. Any of our people who engage in quarrelling in public will be rendering ill service to the cause of Labour, Socialism, and progress.'[1] He also drew up a memorandum for the NEC and the party's Campaign Committee in which he analysed the recent election and set out what he saw as the implications and lessons to be drawn for the future. It was an interesting statement of his own political position. It was also to prove important in the debates and battles ahead between those who wished the Labour Party to cling to its traditional sentiments and fundamentalist principles and those who wished in some way or other to 'modernize'.*

Morrison opened cautiously with the view that 'the result of the Election gives the Labour Party occasion for no extreme rejoicing and no extreme depression'. Analysing the vote by class groups, he drew attention to Labour's good performance in the agricultural working-class areas (as opposed to rural dormitories). He proposed that 'we should collaborate with the trade unions catering for agricultural workers for the purpose of assisting them in extending their membership and in promoting political information within the branches concerned'. He thought that Labour too readily blamed the defection of women, but taken with the clear loss of middle-class support it meant that 'the needs of the consumer and the problems of the housewife must be recognized as a real factor in politics, and Party policy and propaganda should take account of it'.

* There were two drafts of the memorandum, one dated 22 March 1950 for submission to the NEC, and a revised version for the Joint Meeting of the NEC and Ministers 19–21 May 1950. Copies are in the Morrison papers. All quotations are from the second draft.

His proposals for improving Labour's electoral organization were sensible and up to date. He wanted the party to concentrate on key marginal constituencies and 'make as heavy a concentration as possible both in money and personnel upon them *from now on*. . . . We are faced by a strong organization which works electorally *between elections*. We too must try to strengthen our work during these intervening periods. . . . For a sum of about £20,000 a staff of 100 to 120 workers could be employed for six months. This force, concentrated in the right places and carrying out the direct orders of the Regional Staff, might well produce results of a decisive character.' He also strongly urged greater attention to the postal vote, which he estimated as having gone ten to one against Labour in most constituencies

Drawing some policy conclusions from his analysis, he saw Labour's broad economic approach – pursuing full employment and 'fair shares' by means of planning and controls – as a 'winner of importance' provided that 'we do not urge economic planning and control merely for the sake of it'. Other policy areas he saw as on the whole satisfactory, with one exception – nationalization. 'It is, I think, quite clear that the majority of the electorate are not disposed to accept nationalization for the sake of nationalization.' He claimed that the public at the polls, and many Labour supporters talking to him, had expressed the view that 'it was more important to pay attention to making effective and efficient the existing socialization rather than to proceed with a further nationalization programme *at the present time*. . . . As the Executive knows that, in principle, has been my own belief for the last two or three years.'

Morrison interpreted the election setback as confirming his belief that Labour should 'consolidate' rather than attempt further nationalization and he argued that this should be made absolutely clear to the electorate. 'At the last election we were in difficulty because we tried to meet the differing views of the members of the Executive and this weakened the consistency of our programme. . . . We rather "invented" a further socialization programme of odds and ends. . . . What we need is a comprehensive policy that is coherent as a whole and not a patchwork of compromises, and the line of policy should, I suggest, be settled now – before drafting begins.'

The fundamentalist left wing on the NEC was bound to be incensed by these proposals. Morrison met them head on. There was, he wrote, 'a school of thought in the Party which takes the view that the electorate having apparently not been keen on a further socialization programme at this stage, the remedy is to extend and feature those proposals in bigger type than ever, and that if we only bang at them hard enough the electors will become enthusiasts for such a policy. I do not follow this line of reasoning, and I believe it to be unrealistic. In effect, it will lead to reaction and defeat.'

In conclusion Morrison called on his executive colleagues to thrash out the whole question democratically with the party's rank and file and then to be open and frank with the public. 'It is absolutely vital that we show our readiness to adapt ourselves to the pressing needs of the time. This involves no abandonment of socialist principle. Rather we are called upon to both re-assess and reassert the fundamental ethics and economics of our Movement.' It was a strikingly vigorous and combative analysis, a rallying call to moder-ates in the party. Morrison's political antennae had sensed the public mood, just as in the war his reconstruction speeches were close to the pulse of public feeling. But his position fell short of 'revisionism'; that awaited the radical rethinking of Labour's younger generation: Crosland, Gaitskell, Jenkins, Healey and their sympathizers. Morrison opened the battle to abandon traditional dogma. He summoned the party to rethink its principles and policies in a world rapidly changing from that of Keir Hardie and the *Clarion*, in a society of full employment and clamouring consumers. But that was now the extent of his vision: pause and consolidate. He could not manage the intellectual leap into the new society he saw emerging. At least he had the sense to see, and the courage to say, that the leap had to be made.

Morrison put his views and his memorandum to the National Executive on 22 March 1950,[2] to the National Council of Labour in late April,[3] and then to a weekend assembly of the Cabinet, the NEC, the TUC and Co-operative leaders held at Beatrice Webb House, Dorking, from 19–21 May.[4] He gained approval for much of his analysis. One informed and sympathetic com-mentator reported the Dorking summit meeting as 'a peak of triumph for Mr Herbert Morrison. The party manager got his way on all major issues, with surprisingly little opposition.'[5] But it was not as cut and dried as that. Such an issue, involving moving a great mass movement from long entrenched positions and sentiments, could not be settled at one leadership meeting.

Morrison had meanwhile taken his case to the rank and file in the country. At High Wycombe at the end of April he talked about his approach to nationalization, describing public ownership as 'only one of several possible ways of working together'.[6] The press quickly picked up the significance of what he was doing. 'Mr Morrison, perhaps the most resourceful among prac-tising English socialists,' said the *News Chronicle*, 'seems to be groping his way cautiously towards new solutions which are not so far precisely defined in his own mind, which are not identifiable with orthodox Socialism, but which will make for greater flexibility and freedom in the conduct of British in-dustry.'[7] The *New Statesman*, not always his best friend among socialist journals, also praised his High Wycombe speech: 'Herbert Morrison is almost the only Cabinet Minister whose speeches give the impression that he is not too busy to think. His speech . . . at High Wycombe showed that he has taken to heart the plain evidence of recent months that the Labour programme of public ownership and control in industry needs thinking out afresh.'[8]

Morrison returned to his theme in another major speech at Perth in early June. He took his wife and Leslie Hunter on a five-day tour of the Scottish Highlands and back through northern England. Hector McNeil, the Secretary of State for Scotland, also accompanied them for part of the time. It was meant to be a holiday but Morrison addressed meetings along the way in Ross and Cromarty, Inverness, Perth and Huddersfield. His Perth speech was titled 'Socialism Today' and he began with the explicit claim that his object was to re-define socialist objectives in the light of twentieth-century experience.[9] 'We must not be rigid', he insisted. Giving what he termed a 'new definition of Socialism in the light of experience in Labour Government since 1945' he said: 'Socialism means the assertion of social responsibility for matters which are properly of social concern.' More specifically, he defined 'matters of social concern' into ten categories, of which public ownership was only one, though the first.*

The left-wing weekly, *Tribune*, immediately reacted to Morrison's Perth speech which it saw as having 'in effect initiated a public debate on the shape [Labour's] policy should take'. *Tribune* accepted the challenge, rejecting Morrison's re-definition of socialism as having been determined solely by electoral expediency. To *Tribune*, in a moderate and well-reasoned leader, the real lesson of 1945–50 was that 'reformism' was not enough and Labour must redistribute capital so that the power élites of Conservatism would be weakened.[10] Morrison made more concrete progress towards winning the party to his viewpoint at the NEC in July, when they discussed the policy statement for the next conference, but he was forced to compromise short of complete victory.[11] A formula was devised to bridge, at least temporarily, the gap between himself and Bevan. It was agreed that the next election manifesto would threaten nationalization of industries operating against the public interest, but there would be no schedule of named victims. For Morrison this was a successful advance from the embarrassing shopping list of nationalization candidates which he had denounced so scathingly in his post-mortem analysis of the 1950 election.† But it fell far short of the explicit commitment

* 1 The public ownership of natural or almost inevitable local or national monopolies, such as postal services, electricity, gas, broadcasting, water, civil aviation and central banking; and of certain basic industries such as coal mining, inland transport and iron and steel. [In other words, the existing public sector plus water.]
  2 Town and Country Planning.
  3 Municipal rented housing.
  4 Social services including education.
  5 Economic planning and the wise exercise of economic controls to secure social ends and full employment.
  6 Intervening in private industry to assist good enterprise, to promote competition and to end monopoly.
  7 Setting up Development Councils to assist growth and research in private industry.
  8 Protection of consumer rights, against public or private industry.
  9 Assisting agriculture and the development of agricultural co-operatives.
  10 Promoting international peace, co-operation and economic development, particularly among the Colonies and Commonwealth.

  † This compromise specifically strengthened Morrison in his efforts to withdraw from the 1950 commitment to nationalize Tate and Lyle, which had waged a vigorous and successful anti-Labour campaign before the last election. Any legislation to implement this promise was bound to be defeated in the Lords. Morrison preferred instead to take into full public

not to undertake any further nationalizati ons which Morrison had requested in his May memorandum. The 'national interest' formula allowed everything or nothing, and Bevan was happy to settle for that vague compromise, for the time being at least.*

In addition to his efforts to limit Labour's electoral commitments to socialize any new industries in the future, Morrison continued his work to improve the functioning of the existing nationalized sector. Evidence of dissatisfaction with nationalization, on the part of workers in the industries as well as from consumers, flowed in to Morrison and his colleagues. The Amalgamated Engineering Union conducted a questionnaire survey of its district secretaries and produced from their answers a depressing report: complaints recurred of bureaucracy, favouritism, the continuance in power of the old bosses with new hats, or over-centralization and top-heavy staffs.[12] As Pimlott commented to Morrison, the survey was 'chiefly interesting because of the striking way in which it confirms the information which you had from other sources, about the causes of dissatisfaction in the socialized industries'.[13] A similar tale of mismanagement and woe came from the Dorset Federation of Divisional Labour Parties, which held a special conference on the problem in February 1951. All five prospective Labour candidates signed a letter to the Chief Whip (and passed on to Morrison) asserting their fear that 'not only the Labour Government may fall on account of the failure of the nationalized industries, but that the Labour movement, which has championed nationalization for so long, may receive a blow from which it would be slow to recover, and all our socialist ideals and ambitions would be lost for years to come'.[14]

Morrison threw himself into the task of remedying the faults of nationalization and avoiding the political disaster feared by the Labour men in Dorset. In this he was following up the work done by his NEC sub-committee since the 1948 conference.† In March 1950 he drafted a paper for Cabinet discussion on 'Efficiency and Public Accountability of Socialized Industries'. One of his main conclusions was that a Common Efficiency Unit should be set up. He also suggested that special committees of inquiry into each nationalized industry might be held periodically.[15] At one point Attlee reacted with sharp

---

ownership the British Sugar Corporation, a hybrid corporation which was still partly in private hands, and to end the refining agreement which limited the amount of sugar which the Corporation could refine and so gave Tate and Lyle a commercial advantage. In this way the government would in his words 'squeeze 'em a bit'. (Morrison to Davies, 11 October 1950. Davies to Bevin, 12 October 1950. Papers in possession of E. Davies.)

* The final formula, as expressed in the 1951 manifesto, was: 'We shall take over concerns which fail the nation and start new public enterprises wherever this will serve the national interest.' It was assumed that industries which were demonstrably inefficient, monopolistic or essential to national planning would fall within 'national interest' nationalization. For Morrison's argument that the party's refusal to take his full position on nationalization was responsible for the electoral setbacks of 1950–1, see his *Autobiography*, pp. 287–8.

† See above, pp. 443–6.

hostility to the Efficiency Unit suggestion. Morrison felt that his personal status and authority in relation to the other ministers responsible for nationalized industries had been 'made difficult. Indeed my very continuance in Government was difficult unless situation [sic] could somehow be put right.' Attlee smoothed over the difficulty, denying that he had intended to make any 'assault' on Morrison, and 'we left it there,' noted Morrison, 'after further talk in which I made my unhappiness about such a relationship between Prime Minister and deputy Prime Minister clear.'[16]

Morrison's proposals were then passed down for detailed consideration by the Socialization of Industry Committee, of which he was chairman, and which held discussions in July 1950 with the chairmen of the nationalized boards. 'The purpose of the Government's proposal,' as explained to Ernest Bevin, was 'to assure Parliament that there was some external and independent check over the Boards' activities. It was considered that in this way pressure for a greater measure of control by Parliament could be held off.'[17] The proposal for an Efficiency Unit was far from radical. The Unit was to be responsible to the Boards and there was no suggestion of publishing the results of any investigations. Yet the Board chairmen, and especially Citrine, objected strongly to the Unit proposal and, to Morrison's surprise, argued that they would, if forced to choose, prefer a parliamentary select committee to a panel of management consultants. Morrison's view, which he maintained for many years to come (even after the 1956 Select Committee on Nationalized Industries had proved itself a success), was that such a committee was highly undesirable. Morrison's basic objections were that such a committee could never be properly informed, would inflate minor issues and lose sight of big ones, would be used by anti-nationalizers as a stick to beat the nationalized industries, and would inhibit the corporation's management from taking necessary commercial risks. But in view of the statement by the chairmen, and growing public criticism of the nationalized industries, he foresaw that a select committee might be forced upon them by Parliament – 'though as far as I am concerned, it would be very much a last resort'.[18] In the hope of winning the board chairmen round, Morrison asked Ernest Davies, who was a junior minister at the Foreign Office as well as personally assisting Morrison on these nationalization issues, to persuade Bevin to intervene. Bevin was sympathetic at first and offered to help, but after talking to Attlee had second thoughts and decided to do nothing.[19]

The question of efficiency now rested in deadlock. Morrison felt strongly that the intransigence of the board chairmen was over the long run highly damaging to their own industries. But he could not force it against their wishes.[20] He turned, with little prospect of greater success, to the thorny question of worker-management relations in the nationalized sector. His Socialized Industries Committee set up in December 1950 a sub-committee to investigate this particular problem.* It reported back in April 1951, admitting

* It was called the Sub-Committee on Relations with Workers in the Socialized Industries.

a great deal of discontent among workers in the nationalized industries. In terms of concrete proposals and solutions the report[21] was not very helpful to Morrison in his task of improving the image and working of the nationalized industries. One possible approach – workers' control – remained unacceptable to him. As he concluded in his final report to the NEC in April 1952: 'socialists reject the idea of trade union ownership and management as expressed in the syndicalism held by many French trade unionists. Experiments in Guild Socialism, although interesting, have met with only partial success.'[22] He remained committed to the concept of consultation, although its failings in current application were depressing and he had no alternative solutions other than vague recommendations for more good will and education on all sides. What is to Morrison's credit is that he was, more than any other Labour colleague, concerned with improving the performance of the nationalized industries and, despite the oppressive weight of other problems pressing upon him, he worked unsparingly to find remedies and improvements.

As leader of the new Parliament in 1950 Morrison had the tricky job of managing a razor-thin government majority. With the help of the whips, he continued to work through meetings of the Liaison Committee on Tuesday afternoons, usually in his room at the House, followed by the weekly meeting of the parliamentary party on Wednesday mornings. The party meetings now usually began on a macabre note, with reports on the sick and the dying.[23] The Liaison Committee was no longer quite such a cosy group of old friends and disciples as after 1945. Glenvil Hall replaced Maurice Webb as chairman of the PLP when Webb joined the government. A second vice-chairman was deemed desirable and Tony Greenwood was elected from the left of centre. The government was proposing little new legislation of any substance. Anything controversial would fall to the Lord's veto, although the delaying period was now reduced, and might not even survive the Commons committee stage unscathed. It was just a question of hanging on in order to keep the Tories out and in the hope of a recovery at the next election, which might be precipitated at any time and could not be very far away. When the new parliamentary party gathered before the opening of the 1950 session its mood was subdued, with none of the jubilation of 1945. Morrison stressed the importance of discipline if they were to maintain Labour in government. He proposed still to rely on self-discipline and to continue the suspension of standing orders. His flock responded with remarkable self-restraint and he was given little trouble. In some ways the narrowness of the majority assisted party management by forcing even the most rebellious spirits to follow the party line. Dissent was mainly confined to early day motions or simple verbal criticisms. The most serious revolt came early in the session, in March 1950, over the government's decision to withdraw recognition from the Bamangwato chieftain, Seretse Khama, who had married a white English girl. Sensing a colour bar, backbenchers pressed for a full party debate. Morrison, with one of his few lapses into heavy-handedness, at first resisted calling a special meeting, and then when forced to hold one, created hostility by his attempts to close the meeting prematurely. Seven Labour MPs rebelled in the division lobbies after the subsequent debate but Morrison and the whips prudently decided to take no action against them.[24] Back-bench abstentions brought the government its first defeat, on 29 March 1950, when the Tories forced a snap division on an adjournment motion about the inferior quality of coal supplies. Morrison sensibly again treated it lightly, mildly rebuking the Labour absentees at the next party meeting, and later to his constituents dismissing the Tory 'school-boy conspiracy' as 'childish and irrelevant'.[25] There were four other minor defeats in this Parliament.[26] The opposition also periodically held the government under pressure late at night with filibustering and parliamentary guerilla warfare against delegated legislation.

With illness and deaths taking their toll in the summer and following winter, Morrison had to call for 'a tightening of the ranks'.[27] He handled the party and led the House with great skill and experience. At times it was desperately close, with dramatic scenes as Labour rushed its sick and aged into the lobbies at the last moment. When the Tories sprang a surprise division late in the evening of 1 May, on a motion criticizing Labour's road haulage policy, Labour whips had to rally the troops from all over London by telephone and hand messages. Soon the yard of the Palace of Westminster was jammed with cars spilling members into the lobbies. Morrison was seen dashing around, a pink rose in his lapel, encouraging the whips, marshalling his men, nipping into Attlee's room to keep him informed. The result was in doubt till the end. One Liberal went out of the lobbies to take a telephone call and missed voting with the opposition. The tellers reported 278 to 278, the first dead-heat since the division on Palestine in April 1938. The Deputy Speaker gave his casting vote to the government, and Labour survived again.[28] Some objected to the Tory tactics as not really playing the game; after this latter episode several Labour back-benchers put down a motion censuring the opposition for its snap divisions. But Morrison would not give it time for debate. 'It would be a pity,' he stated, 'if the House as a corporate body sought to control the tactics of any political party in the House of Commons.'[29]

This was the true House of Commons man speaking. The vigour of Parliament mattered more than the temporary comfort of himself, as manager of the government's tiny majority. Apart from that, he had never suffered from the curious but widely-held delusion that the Tories were gentlemen where political power was concerned, so he did not share the shocked surprise of some of his more naïve colleagues.

In June 1950, the communists of North Korea invaded the South, beginning a war which was to prove the fatal crisis for the Labour government. Britain readily joined the United States and their other allies in supporting a defensive action under the common flag of the United Nations. The scramble for raw materials rocketed prices and swung the terms of trade dramatically against Britain. A sudden, massive, in fact excessive, rearmament programme pushed the already extended British economy towards a runaway inflation. The hard-won economic recovery engineered by Cripps was jeopardized, and hopes for greater social expenditure were to be deferred.

That full economic reckoning lay a year ahead. In the summer of 1950 Morrison shared the national indignation at the aggression by the communists. It also provided him with further opportunity to move into the field of international affairs, increasingly left void by the ailing Bevin. He was in Manchester for a mass party rally at Belle Vue on Sunday, 2 July. He told the thousands in the audience that he would abandon his prepared speech and turn instead to Korea. 'I sincerely believe,' he said, 'that only by showing that the free democracies will take a stand can we hope to convince disturbers of the peace that aggression just does not pay. . . . By accepting this fresh challenge I have every hope that a world war can be averted. That is the only way to preserve the peace. Otherwise we shall slip along the slippery slope that led to the war of 1939; a war that could have been prevented if the nations of the world had had the courage to act in earlier years.' (Given his own position in the 1930s, Morrison presumably understood that the situation had been then – and was again now – more complex than just a question of courage.) He denounced the 'naked aggression' of the communists in South East Asia but constructively argued that the Western response should not be simply a negative military resistance. He stressed that the only long-term remedy was 'to remove the causes of Communism by alleviating the malnutrition and misery affecting so many millions of people, particularly throughout Asia'.[30]

Morrison's political star was now very much in the ascendant. He was remoulding the party's policy position. He continued at the heart of the party organization through his power bases on the NEC* and on the London Labour Party. The party in Parliament was effectively under his leadership for its day-to-day operations. In the Cabinet his position was enhanced as Bevin, Cripps and Bevan declined. As yet the younger generation, and especially Hugh Gaitskell, had not properly emerged in their full stature. Had Attlee given up the leadership now, it would have been very difficult to stop Morrison getting the succession as by natural right. But this peak was his last, and brief. The Foreign Office lay around the corner. Even now as he staked his claim he gave intimations of troubles to come. Returning from the triumphant acclamations of Belle Vue, Morrison closed for the government in the Commons foreign affairs debate on 6 July. (Bevin was ill in the London Clinic.) Usually when he wound up at the end of a debate – taking points from previous speeches, mixing serious conclusions with knockabout humour, riding the clamour from a well-dined Opposition, slipping inside interruptions and counter-punching – Morrison was at his parliamentary

* He was chairman of the Policy and Publicity Committee and member of the Elections Committee and of the Special Committee of Chairmen.

best. But he failed dismally, seeming ill-informed and boring the House.[31] 'This', said the *Daily Telegraph*, 'was one of Mr Morrison's rare parliamentary failures' and it predicted few would hear him debate on foreign affairs again.[32] Another commentator dismissed his speech as 'enough to wind up any ambitions to be Mr Bevin's successor. For he was plainly lost in far away places.'[33]

Parliament adjourned at the end of July and Morrison was able to relax on holiday. He went with Margaret and the Raisins to Sweden. Jim Raisin had long talked of holidaying in Scandinavia but at first Morrison was un-enthusiastic, asking why he 'wanted to go to that perishing cold place'. Raisin argued that he wanted to see another socialist government at work and Morrison swung round and decided to go.[34] They intended to have a quiet and restful holiday and booked it through the Workers' Travel Association. The Swedes, however, learned that Morrison was coming and laid on an official reception at Gothenburg. Morrison's party then moved on to a small village resort in south-east Sweden. Morrison walked, bathed – wearing grotesque knee-length swimming trunks – and read. He told the press that his holiday literature this year was 'Robbie Burns and various lives of Queen Elizabeth'.[35] His rest was interrupted by a communication that the Swedish Prime Minister, Tage Erlander, wanted to see him. Margaret was not at all keen to go, dis-liking all official occasions and resenting their intrusion into her holiday. Jim Raisin worked hard to persuade Margaret, while Mabel ironed her dresses for her. In the end she gave way and the party set off in style with Erlander to the palatial residence of the Governor of the province. Morrison was treated with great respect and deference. Erlander viewed this meeting as a significant step in the official *rapprochement* between Britain and Sweden since their breach over Sweden's wartime neutrality. The party also visited Erlander's own home. The Swedish Foreign Minister was there and suggested that Morrison might like to visit their defences on the northern border with Russia, but the offer was declined since it might have infringed Bevin's territorial waters.[36] Morrison's journalist friend, Leslie Hunter, arrived to spend a couple of days with them and Maurice Webb, now Minister of Food, who was staying across the Kattegat as guest of the Danish government, also came across to visit them. Morrison was still unable to take a complete holiday from politics; to him it was simply an opportunity to approach politics differently, with more time to read, to reflect and to plan ahead. Scandinavia impressed and interested him particularly as a successful example of social democracy, of social reform-ism stripped of Marxist dogma, where the moderate left wing were almost permanently in power. It was a living example of Morrison's recent speeches. It was also rather expensive by Morrison's frugal standards. When he returned and addressed the Anglo-Swedish Society in London the first thing he told them was that he had just received his holiday bill and 'it has been a bit of a shock'.[37]

While Morrison was in Scandinavia the NEC had published its policy

statement, *Labour and the New Society*, to put before the October party conference as a basis for the next election manifesto. It reflected Morrison's
influence, with its attempt to re-define British democratic socialism. But it
was primarily an attempt to bridge the left and right positions. The tensions
within the party were growing as the price of the new rearmament programme
emerged. In September Parliament was recalled in emergency session to pass
the National Service Bill extending compulsory military service from eighteen
months to two years. The press was full of rumours that Bevan was in rebellion
against the cost of the arms programme[38] though his discontents did not
finally erupt into the open for another six months.

The annual conference met at Margate in the first week of October. Bevan
came comfortably top in the NEC elections. Morrison was third. The two
successful newcomers, Barbara Castle and Ian Mikardo, were both from the
left, certain to support Bevan in any tussle with Morrison. In public the
conference held together surprisingly happily. Morrison introduced *Labour
and the New Society*, looking dapper in his pinstripe suit, red tie and red
carnation.[39] It was a good speech, appropriate to the situation, in general
terms and full of good humour. He went out of his way to insist that the
previous proposals to nationalize sugar, cement and industrial assurance had
not been dropped. The compromise formula was brought into play: all
industries were eligible and potential candidates. Conference was informed
that the NEC had not included any specific proposals for nationalization
because the statement was designed to expound the fundamental principles
and purpose of the Labour movement. 'It is therefore not necessary . . . to
particularize on certain industries.'[40] Bevan was able to wind up without
dissent. The split in the party appeared, for the time being at least, happily
bridged.[41] But in private the animosities were as sharp as ever. A friendly
journalist, enjoying a martini with Morrison before dinner on the eve of the
conference, found him 'increasingly sensitive and increasingly angry at any
suggestion that he and Bevan were in any way on equal terms'. Morrison
pointed out his greater ministerial experience and seniority in the party, and
denounced Bevan violently. 'Power, that's all he wants, power for himself and
he doesn't care what happens to the party so long as he gets it.'[42]

Shortly after the conference Cripps was finally forced to resign from the
Chancellorship. His worsening illness made this move inevitable and for some
time previously there had been speculation about the succession. Attlee sent
for Shinwell, who recommended Morrison, but Attlee rejected the idea on the
ground that Morrison knew too little about finance and revealed his own
preference for Gaitskell, who had been a great success deputizing for Cripps.[43]
Dalton also spoke against Morrison and for Gaitskell,[44] but others, who did
not doubt Gaitskell's economic skills, were worried that he did not yet have the
political weight to carry the Exchequer through the difficult times ahead.
Edwin Plowden, the chief economic planner, was privately deputed to
approach Morrison. Plowden personally questioned Morrison's qualifications

Q

but saw the arguments about the need for political weight and therefore he went to ask if Morrison would be willing, in principle, to take on the Treasury. Morrison reacted quite firmly. 'I listen to Stafford explaining those figures,' he said humbly, 'and I just know I could not do it.'[45] Bridges also pressed Morrison to take it. Bridges thought Morrison would have proved a good Chancellor: 'he was clear, decisive and didn't mind saying no'. Morrison didn't waver. He knew he didn't understand economics and was frightened by the technical jargon of economists.[46] His experience as economic planner in 1947 had left its mark. He feared he might burn his fingers again.[47] Gaitskell's appointment was announced on 19 October.

In retrospect it can be seen that Morrison might have been wiser to press his own claim. He was no master of financial intricacies, but he knew how to work well with expert advisers, and would have been good on the political implications of budgetary decisions. The backing of the most powerful department in Whitehall would have strengthened him politically, though under the pressure of rearmament the Exchequer was bound to be a tricky task for any Labour Chancellor. Certainly it would have saved him from having to take the Foreign Office shortly after and enter a much less suitable field. In this sense it was an important turning point, possibly a fatal one in his career, the moment at which he may have lost the party leadership. Morrison cannot be blamed for not seeing that far ahead. At this time he was happy and successful in his own job and was quite content to see young Gaitskell, who he considered a friend and political ally, promoted – and Bevan kept out. He certainly did not realize that Gaitskell's elevation was the crucial step in a meteoric rise which would conclude with the leadership, and his own final humiliation.

Morrison spent Christmas, the New Year of 1951 and his sixty-third birthday on the Isle of Wight. At the end of January he made another visit to Scotland – officially to review arrangements for the Festival of Britain there – which again fortunately coincided with a Burns' Supper at Greenock. Next day he watched football at Paisley, heavily guarded by police after persistent rumours that Scottish nationalists would kidnap him. In the evening he addressed a big meeting in Edinburgh and made a major foreign affairs speech. He savagely attacked Soviet Russia for its despotism at home and imperialism over its neighbours, and denounced the British Communist Party in similar tones for so slavishly following the Russian line.[48]

Morrison had always been careful not to enter Bevin's departmental field. He often referred wryly to 'Ernie retiring behind his Chinese wall' or to not infringing 'the Foreign Secretary's three-mile territorial waters'. But the East–West confrontation was an exception. Ever since the full outburst of the Cold War Morrison had been licensed to back up Bevin's hard line. His long-standing role as scourge of the British communists equipped him well for the task. As trouble brewed in the parliamentary party over rearmament and the extended military call-up, and Morrison struggled to keep the back-bench ranks in line with his usual mixture of moderate reason and tough threats, his involvement in defence and foreign affairs matters inevitably increased. By now he had an additional interest. Bevin was clearly dying on his feet, and the weeks before he finally resigned on 9 March 1951 were full of rumours and speculation about the succession in which Morrison himself was inevitably involved. Attlee told Dalton as early as 19 February that he was going to move Bevin from the Foreign Office to a post without portfolio. Dalton argued strongly against Morrison taking over. They agreed that Shawcross and Noel-Baker were unsuitable and Hector McNeil and Kenneth Younger were too inexperienced. They inclined, as did Bevin, towards James Griffiths at this stage, particularly as Attlee wanted a trade unionist in the job.[49]

Shinwell and Gaitskell, however, strongly pressed the Prime Minister to appoint Morrison, who was rumoured in the press as being happy to take the job.[50] While Attlee dithered about the succession, Morrison seemed to be reinforcing his own claim with a series of major foreign affairs speeches: at Brighton in late February 1951 and in Leeds and Hull at the beginning of March.[51] These latter speeches were part of a tour of the North East. While there he stayed again with his friends, the Bacons. 'If you can choose between staying at a posh hotel or at a miner's house in Normanton,' he said, 'you choose the latter. The farther you move north from London the better time and the better food you have.'[52] The north-country warmth of the Bacon home contrasted with his frigid life in Archery Road. When he married again in a few years' time, Morrison looked north for these home comforts.

Morrison canvassed his friends and associates on whether he should go to the Foreign Office.[53] Bartholomew of the *Daily Mirror* advised him to take it, as did his political colleagues Shinwell and Gordon Walker. From the opposition, Anthony Eden approached him after an official dinner and conveyed his own and Churchill's opinion that he was the best Labour man for the job and he should do it in the country's interest. Others – Jim Raisin, Richard Coppock, George Deer, George Brown, Alice Bacon and even his civil service secretary, Downes – pressed him not to. When Arthur Bottomley went to plead with him to turn it down, Morrison replied angrily that he was fed up with being the government's dogsbody and wasn't going to continue being it any longer.

His own mind was not in fact as clearly made up as his response to Bottomley suggested. He dithered and left differing impressions of his personal feelings among the widening circle of people he chose to consult. Some were convinced he wanted it, others were just as certain that he didn't.* Attlee remembered none of what Leslie Hunter described as 'the long period of

---

* Raisin, Bottomley, Alice Bacon, Maclellan, Coppock and his 'ghost' autobiographer, F. G. Kay, all received the impression from talking to Morrison that he wanted the job, as did Noel-Baker and Jim Griffiths who was a candidate for the job. Those directly told by Morrison that he did not want it included: Nicholson, Boon, Bartholomew, Ernest Davies, George Isaacs and his personal detective, A. Black.

heart-searching and the grave misgivings with which Morrison had, in the end, accepted the Foreign Office'.[54] Attlee asserted baldly: 'He seemed to want it badly and turned down every other suggestion I made to him, so in the end I appointed him. Rather bad luck for him, as it turned out.'[55]

There seems little doubt that Attlee's recollection is misleading. Morrison was genuinely in doubt, wavering from one view to another, the balance of his preference altering as he talked to one person after another. In the end, as he made clear in his frequent and most frank discussions with Hartley Shawcross (himself a possible candidate for the office), he saw no alternative to himself succeeding Bevin.[56] He realized the risks in leaving his present post, for which he was ideally suited and at which he was immensely successful, to take on a responsibility outside his main field of experience or interests.[57] But 'he felt that if he turned down the number two position in the Government he would disqualify himself for the leadership succession'.[58] He had held neither of the two great departments of state, the Exchequer and the Foreign Office, and saw the appointment as a final step necessary to complete his qualifications for the leadership. There was also the satisfaction of replacing his old enemy Bevin and getting the chance to show that he could do the job just as well. Most immediate was the need to keep out Bevan. Morrison and Bevan were the only two senior ministers with the ability, stature and good health to carry the Foreign Office. Bevan was a close rival to Morrison's own ambitions and also a bitter antagonist. He seemed arrogant, irresponsible, emotional, egocentric, lustful for personal power, full of the rhetoric of the left without any real ability to effect radical government. Morrison disliked and mistrusted prima donnas. For all of these characteristics, which were in Bevan but were certainly not the whole man, Morrison thought him a dangerous politician and clashed with him increasingly in Cabinet. Bevan had to be stopped from achieving greater power. Bevan was 'getting all the publicity now', Morrison is reported to have complained, 'it's time I had a break'.[59]

Morrison's appointment was announced from 10 Downing Street on the evening of 9 March. Lord Addison, who was eighty-one and had first been elected as a Liberal MP in 1910, replaced him as Lord President of the Council. Chuter Ede, who was sixty-eight, became Leader of the Commons, and Bevin, who was celebrating his seventieth birthday when he heard the sad news of his own departure from the Foreign Office, moved reluctantly over to be Lord Privy Seal. (Addison and Bevin took over Morrison's Cabinet committees.) With Attlee sixty-nine and Morrison sixty-three, the government looked very old at the top. Everyone involved in this reshuffle had been growing up before Gladstone formed his last administration. It was hardly a youthful and vigorous crew to face the dreadful storms which lay ahead.

Morrison had been Lord President and Leader of the Commons for over five and a half years, even longer than he was Home Secretary, and he had held the office with equal success. On his giving up leading the House, the distinguished political correspondent of the *Manchester Guardian* wrote that 'friend and foe alike would agree that he has done it with superb skill. Indeed, if he had done nothing else in these six years he would have made for himself a high reputation in parliamentary annals and established a strong claim on the lasting gratitude of his own party. . . . No doubt Mr Morrison has been a little arbitrary on occasion but he has largely prevailed through a combination of flexibility and humour, and, at bottom, a deep respect for the traditions of Parliament. . . . Mr Morrison is a House of Commons man through and through, and members are going to miss him exceedingly from the day to day business of Parliament.'[60] It was a final peak of success and acclaim for Morrison. Ahead lay storms of trouble, the sting of criticism and the taste of failure.

Chapter 35

Herbert Morrison in 1951: The Peaks Behind

The Herbert Morrison who left the Lord Presidency for the Foreign Office in March 1951 was in many respects little changed from the Morrison of 1945. Passing time had of course left its mark. His figure was thicker. The famous quiff of hair was now white and less springy. His face looked noticeably fatter. As he sat listening to those around him, his head on one side, his good eye cocked high and bright, he looked rather like a pigeon contemplating a piece of bread. He wore better quality suits, though they were still always baggy. The *Tailor and Cutter* had attacked him earlier because of his ill-fitting clothes, objecting particularly to his short trouser legs, with 'the left leg a little more so than the right'.[1] Morrison proudly bought his clothes from the Royal Arsenal Co-operative Society, which sponsored him as a parliamentary candidate, and refused to take his custom elsewhere. He did at one point switch to a more expert Co-op tailor than previously but he never looked elegant. It was simply not in his character to think much about sartorial style – and anyway few suits, however beautifully cut, would have survived unscathed the constant stuffing of papers into every pocket which Morrison's clothes suffered.

The black Homburg hat, the developing taste for whisky, the frequent cigar, meals at high quality restaurants, with the Caprice, the Ivy, Mon Plaisir and the Café Bleu among his favourites, all added a new flavour of the successful political tycoon. But it was never a complete or convincing change of life-style. Even now after sixteen years in high office, and five as deputy prime minister, Morrison's attitudes and tastes were still those of the ordinary man from the lower middle class of south London. His approach to personal spending, for instance, remained distinctly cautious. He kept his money in a small purse and carefully scrutinized and occasionally questioned his bill in the House of Commons dining room.[2] In Lewisham he never contributed a penny to his (admittedly prosperous) constituency party and the agent could not remember him ever actually buying anyone a drink.[3] This may have been to avoid all taint of corrupting the electorate, though certainly some felt it was because he was, as one fellow MP recalled, 'a tight-fisted bugger'.[4] Yet others close to him found Morrison normally hospitable. As a guest he was often generous with presents, particularly when visiting homes with little children.[5] But past years of existing on a small salary, coupled with the uncertain financial future of any politician, conditioned him to be cautious. As in many other private matters, he lacked easy generosity; financially, as emotionally, he remained 'a bit tight'.

He still worked an immensely long day. He was constantly on the move, from the Foreign Office to Cabinet or Cabinet committees in Downing Street, and on to lunch; back to No. 11 for his afternoon catnap if he could manage it, or straight to the Commons for questions and debate; to meetings of the parliamentary party at the Commons, of the National Executive Committee at Transport House,* of the London Labour Party Executive in his room or at County Hall. At some point in the late afternoon or early evening he always tried to return to 11 Downing Street to keep appointments there, and to bathe and change his clothes if he was going out to an official dinner. Apart from such official functions, his supper was often just a sandwich snatched at the House of Commons canteen or fish and chips on the way to a political meeting. He often had to be back at the Commons for the vote at the close of parliamentary business. Providing there was not an all-night sitting, he went to bed, sometimes out to Eltham, more often at the Howard Hotel, to finish his paperwork for the coming day, his light rarely going off before 2.30 a.m.[6]

Ethel Donald continued to organize his party activities, the perfect chatelaine at 11 Downing Street. Although in no way a sophisticated woman, and sometimes overheard in rather crude verbal contretemps with Morrison, she had now been with him so long that she instinctively understood his needs. She mothered him, watching, protecting, seeing that he received his party briefs, arranging that important people saw him quickly, and others not at all. Through his succession of offices she was the permanent tiger at the gate and it was not possible to imagine Morrison at work efficiently without Miss Donald.[7]

His *pied-à-terre* at the Howard Hotel, just a bedroom and a lounge, remained a useful retreat for private discussions and negotiations as well as social entertaining. It was quickly accessible to his offices, but also distant from the prying eyes of Westminster and Whitehall, and thus provided the social facilities which other men more fortunate than Morrison in this respect found in their own homes. When its existence was exposed in April 1950 by the *Sunday Express*, which pointed out that Morrison's 'friend and henchman' Maurice Webb also lived there, along with Webb's PPS, the Midland businessman Stanley Evans, Morrison was furious, and complained to Beaverbrook that letters were being addressed to him at the Howard and 'even people with evil intentions might be tempted which gives just a little anxiety to my

* Morrison remained chairman of the Policy and Publicity sub-committee of the NEC and a member of the Elections sub-committee.

detective'. Beaverbrook wrote back a charming letter of apology from the South of France, concluding that 'my regard and esteem for your personal qualities increase in every year. Politics should not divide us.'[8]

At the weekends when not on speaking tours, Morrison rested either at home in Eltham or in the country with friends, such as Leslie Hunter and his wife in Kent or the Shawcrosses in Sussex. He sometimes stayed in bed for twenty-four hours at a time to recover from the exhaustion of the week. By now television was beginning to make its impact in Britain and Morrison, who had a set at home, would watch with Margaret when he was free on Sunday evenings. Most of the rest of the time Margaret led her own life quite separate from her husband's packed days in Whitehall and Westminster. Occasionally she lunched in the West End or joined social functions for ministers' wives, where Lady Cripps was her preferred companion. She still loved the ballet and the theatre and went whenever she could persuade Morrison to join her. Most of her life, however, was spent at home, alone, very simple, spending her time reading and gardening and obsessively cleaning the already spotless house. She refused to have coal fires because of the dirt. She would allow only two journals, the *New Statesman* and the *Radio Times*, downstairs. All other papers, everything to do with her husband's working life, were pushed upstairs into his study in the ceaseless process of dusting and carpet-sweeping.[9] Few friends or colleagues ever set foot in the house.

Of the rest of Morrison's family, his sister Edie remained closest to him. He also kept in touch with his eldest brother Harry and his wife Kitty, occasionally inviting them to dinner at the House of Commons or to an official function.[10] His relations with his daughter Mary had never been close, which is strange in view of the warmth and friendship he showered on other people's little children.[11] He was usually too busy and away from home too often to give her enough affection when a child. She was not interested in his political activities and felt that he was disappointed in her modest educational achievements. Her divorce in 1947 upset him greatly, especially since it was from the son of a Labour ministerial colleague.[12] He never liked any aspects of his personal or family life emerging in public light and was always, almost pathologically, worried by anything which might reflect damagingly upon him or his career.

In no respect could Morrison be said to enjoy a full and satisfying family life. His wife had developed an antipathy to sex since her nervous reaction to her daughter's birth and Morrison had little physical relationship, possibly none at all, with her over that quarter of a century.[13] The resulting sexual frustration of a man as naturally vigorous as Morrison must have been disturbing even now that he had turned sixty. It perhaps partly explains his desire to exhaust himself on an endless treadmill of work. The dam against any emotional-sexual expression within the marriage may also have caused, or accelerated, the aridity of his personal relations with most other people except on a purely job-functional basis. Hence many people felt that they never really came close to him and that though he had a wide circle of friendly acquaintances he had few, if any, deep and close personal friends.

He certainly, however, felt the need for female relationships and built up an extensive network of lady friends, usually buxom and maternal women. He escaped periodically to the warmth of their homes in search of affection and domestic comfort. It is unlikely that he formed continuing sexual relationships with them, though this is a field of investigation where, without visible off-spring, compromising letters, photographs, or written affidavits, the historian's evidence is inevitably intangible and inconclusive. Many contemporaries were genuinely convinced that Morrison was having an affair with Miss X, Mrs Y or Lady Z, but none has so far produced proof, only surmise. Morrison himself went to great lengths to cover the tracks of his flirtations, rarely if ever contacting any of his female friends in writing. 'I never put anything intimate onto a piece of paper' he told one lady friend.[14] In a rare unguarded moment he once said to another, 'women have been very good to me, my dear',[15] which left her the impression at the time that he had enjoyed *affaires*. It would have been remarkable if a man in his situation, given the unquestioned need and the inevitable opportunities, did not sometimes have intimate relation-ships. Certainly at times he was driven to make none-too-elegant passes at casual female acquaintances.[16] But it would be inappropriate to build too much on speculations about this side of Morrison's life. He totally lacked the style and flair for widespread success in such activities and was certainly inhibited by a mixture of puritanical guilt and terror at exposure which might damage his career, and especially his chances of succeeding Attlee. His sexual activity – the lack of it within marriage and the possible furtive excursions outside – are only of relevance to his biography because they are part of the pattern of his whole life: unrelieved tension, caution, compulsive secrecy, the lack of ultimate fulfilment.

Signs of advancing years – though not in themselves necessarily signs of decline – multiplied in Morrison's life. He was more frequently invited to speak at jubilees or at birthdays of living ancients, and there he tended to reminisce. He proposed the health of George Robey at his eightieth birthday party at the Dorchester. He was guest speaker at a dinner to mark the fiftieth anniversary of the publication of Sir Ebenezer Howard's *Garden Cities of Tomorrow*; he recalled the early days at Letchworth and Welwyn Garden City.[17] He attended a reception for London's twenty-eight Mayors at Hackney – mainly as a chance to see Gwen Carter (formerly Butler) who had organized the clerical side of his election campaigns in South Hackney and was now Mayoress. A week later he was a guest of honour, along with Ike Hayward and Emil Davies, at a dinner for thirty retiring members of the LCC.[18] Some of his old friends and colleagues were now coming to the peak of their achievements, others – a nagging reminder of passing time – moved into decline. In late 1949 he attended the memorial service for Albert Stanley, Lord Ashfield, reviving memories of those battles over London Transport. Bevin was not at the service.

Some of the growing diary of nostalgia was more personal. In the spring of 1949 he went back to Brixton and with his sister Edie strolled for several hours among the streets of his childhood. They visited the spot where he was born, but the house was no longer there. They went to see the shop which used to sell 'farthing dips', 'jumbo-chains' of liquorice, and another old favourite, 'pat-wack'; but they were disappointed again, finding a greengrocer's store there now. They wandered on to Mordaunt Street, where the Morrison family moved after leaving Ferndale Road.[19] London had changed, but the echoes continued. He told the Blackheath Licensed Victuallers dinner on 3 October 1949: 'I feel very much at home in this gathering because I worked in a brewery in 1910 – as a thirty shilling a week telephone operator.' Next day at a publisher's lunch he retold the story of how the phrenologist who analysed his bumps told him to read better books and so he went straight home to read Macaulay's *History of England*. He also confessed to an almost capitalist sense of property about books. He said he was still looking for the man who borrowed two of his Matthew Arnold volumes long ago. 'People who socialize my books,' he said, 'I'll fight them to the death.'[20] At the sixtieth birthday celebrations of the National Society of Operative Printers and Assistants, he again plunged into the past, recalling the 'exciting times and extraordinary long hours' on the *Daily Citizen*.[21]

The past was living and vitally important to Morrison. Not because of sentiment for the people he had known and worked with: he seemed worryingly able to cast off old associates when their interests no longer overlapped with his. The past was important because it had formed him and had produced the Labour Party. About those early political years he could be moved to a flowery eloquence far from his customary down-to-earth style. When dedicating two seats in Battersea Park to the memory of Robert Blatchford and Alex Thompson of the *Clarion* he declared: 'The vision was theirs. They bequeathed to us the responsibility of translating their hope and teaching into achievements. . . . We need a new Blatchford now. . . . How he would have loved to see the healthy well-fed children of Britain in 1950. . . . All the activities which grew from the *Clarion* – the scouts, the cycling clubs, the clarion vans and the rest – were permeated with a simple and friendly gaiety. We must recapture and foster that spirit. It was the spirit of hope and youth and purpose.'[22] It was also a spirit worlds away from the problems of Britain in the 1950s.

However much, with the aid of hindsight, the first signs of age may be detected, the hardening mould, the mind hankering backwards and less often leaping ahead, the increasing repetition of old ideas and attitudes, there was no question that at the beginning of 1951 Morrison's abilities appeared barely diminished and his reputation and political stature remained high. He had by now been a central pillar of British government for ten of the most dramatic and testing years in the country's modern history, and had run the world's largest municipal administration for six years before that. The rub of experience and success had toned down his earlier cocky brashness and obsessive desire to project a public image. With the right departmental servicing and personal assistance supplementing his own wide skills and hard application, and working within a domestic field suited to his talents, Morrison operated with immense authority in Westminster and Whitehall. 'Maybe I wasn't born to rule,' as he observed on more than one occasion, 'but I've got used to it.'[23]

He was always in demand as guest of honour at big social and political functions. In the Cabinet his relative stature seemed for a time to grow as his colleagues declined, Cripps and Bevin struck down by illness, Bevan brought into discredit by his personal waywardness. A profile in the then very right-wing *Sunday Times* reflected the respect with which the whole serious press treated him:

What makes a man a political leader? Character, brains, energy, resolution – and, no doubt, an admixture of cunning. Mr Morrison has all these qualities plus a sense of humour and the common touch. When it comes to talking the language of working people he has few equals and no superiors. ... Mr Morrison is neither a demagogue, nor, at heart, a dictator, despite an occasional display of Napoleonic arrogance which infuriates his opponents and sometimes seems designed for just that purpose. A socialist statesman of the first rank, who has graduated triumphantly from the bottom to the top, he has ideals, knows his own mind, and is never afraid to act according to his convictions. These are essential qualities in national leadership and unfortunately rare at the highest level of public life in which Mr Morrison moves.[24]

In terms of intellect, Morrison did not compare with, say, Cripps among his contemporaries or Gaitskell of the younger generation. He lacked broader intellectual interests and was definitely philistine in artistic and aesthetic questions. His conversation was almost totally of politics. But he did know his intellectual and educational limitations and his skill and perception lay in surrounding himself with people who could remedy his short-comings. Indeed he probably over-compensated by giving an excessive valuation to high educational distinction and qualifications. The members of his coterie all had a professional contribution to make. By 1950 Nicholson, Raisin, Webb, Gordon Walker, Hartley Shawcross, Leslie Hunter and his new PPS, Eddie Shackleton, were among his most frequent companions and advisers. This 'travelling circus of middle-class intellectuals', essential to Morrison's role and success in party and in government policy-making, provoked hostility. It especially upset the older-style working-class MPs who suspected Morrison of social climbing and his companions of being careerists on the creep for preferment. These resentments and suspicions were unfair to Morrison, since he remained, despite occasional irritating vanities, still at this point of time touchingly ordinary and unspoiled by success. But it was one factor in the erosion of back-bench support for him by the time of the 1955 leadership battle.[25]

In terms of political ideology Morrison was no longer in any sense a doctrinaire socialist. He shared the broad aims of most democratic socialists and social democrats in the West: peace in the world, an increasing standard of living for all, full employment, greater social justice and equality, an active and vigorous democracy. He did not, however, seem concerned to seize and alter the balance of economic power in Britain. That ambition remained socialist doctrine and was not immediately achievable. He was interested in the achievable, the practical reform; doctrine only interested him in a remote way, as one more echo from his youth. 'I believe the only purpose of life is to be socially useful,' he told an interviewer. 'As for success, well I think it is being able to do a job well. And I don't care tuppence whether the job is that of a Cabinet Minister or a road sweeper. I have always tried to do a good job. When I was an errand boy working about 80 hours a week for less than a penny an hour I had to do it hard and well. And when I became assistant in the grocer's shop I used to take a pride in window dressing. I felt I had achieved something. The sight of that attractive looking window brought me almost as much pleasure as pulling off in the House today a successful duel with Winston Churchill.'[26]

He believed passionately in getting the things done through the democratic process. The government should behave 'responsibly' and be governed by the wishes of the people, never pressing change beyond the pace acceptable to the electorate. As he told the 1950 Labour Party conference: 'The art of Government is not making general propositions and running them like a steam-roller over all the members of the population. We are dealing with human beings . . . if we seek to build a new society successfully . . . what is desirable is the conscious and willing co-operation of the population. . . . Indeed that is democracy; any other system is not democracy.'[27] This view applied to local as well as to central government. Addressing the Metropolitan Labour Mayors – not all men of lofty vision – he argued that 'the municipality is not an instrument of bureaucracy, regulations, bye-laws and red-tape, but of public service, calculated to make better and sweeter the lives of the people and to bring beauty and health into our local life'.[28] Local government was a living organism to him because its purpose, in his mind, was to improve the lives of people. He also liked the fact that in local government a politician could see the tangible results of his work. He once complained about his Cabinet job that 'you never see the result of your work. On a local council if you have only put up a lamp-post you can always go and look at it.'[29]

Often he left the impression of being just an operator of party and government machinery, a technocrat of Transport House and County Hall. When

Nye Bevan was later asked if he had indeed described Morrison as just a third-rate Tammany Hall boss, the Welshman denied it indignantly: 'I never said anything of the kind, boy,' he rapped back at Harold Wilson. 'I said he was a fifth-rate Tammany boss.'[30] Yet the closer one looks at Morrison, the less adequate this description appears. Corruption was a central feature of the Tammany system and Morrison was incorruptible. The other imputations of 'Tammany' – that Morrison was more interested in power manipulation than in the ideals and policy ends of politics, and that in his manipulations he was devious and deceitful, if not plain dishonest – have some foundation but are very far from being the whole truth of the man. His reputation for deviousness arose inevitably from the tactical role he played so long as party manager. He was the man who fixed situations and people and therefore he was a 'fixer' – 'always up to his tricks' as Bevin used to complain. Yet in Labour Party politics this job has to be done and is not dishonourable. The most that can be held against Morrison is that he so obviously relished being a successful political 'wheeler-dealer'. 'It would be unkind to call him a fixer,' as one colleague kindly remarked, 'but he did like to arrange things.'[31] Certainly he was not dishonest. Most people who worked closely with Morrison found him absolutely straight to deal with. 'Absolutely straight' is the phrase that recurs again and again in their recollections.[32] They always knew where they stood with him. He told them what he wanted and how he was trying to achieve it. He did not break a bargain or go back on a position taken in committee. He was, admittedly, as his second wife affectionately recalled, 'warmly calculating' in his approach to a situation, and would compromise to reach a settlement, but he would not trim on basic objectives or deceive either an opponent or a friend.

He was certainly above all a power politician, with a mastery of the party and governmental machine unequalled in Labour history. Against him – and this, among other things, offended Bevan – it must be admitted that Morrison rarely in these later years talked about issues in a large way and did not seem to approach them with any philosophy of what life is or ought to be about. Perhaps in over-reaction to the wilder utopianism of many he had met in the Labour movement, he seemed more interested in whether a solution was practical than in whether it was right and conveyed the impression that he lacked any deeper strain of idealism. His common-sense concern with any policy proposal was: 'Will it work? Will it help? Is it fair? What will it cost? How do you do it? What will be the consequences?' Having satisfied himself on these aspects, he would urge 'don't rush it, think about it'.[33] Then if potential friends had to be persuaded on the issue, or potential enemies discouraged, he would arrange that the appropriate pressures were brought to bear. Yet he was more than just a political-machine man, a manipulator in smoke-filled rooms. In the Labour Party he always tried to look and think ahead, as his constructive activity in party policy-making over many years demonstrates. The machinery of government did fascinate him and he loved exercising his skill at working it, but he was a creative administrator and not just impersonally mechanistic. Significantly, Parliament, the most human of British institutions of government, not any bureaucracy, was now the centre of his public life. To him Parliament was alive, wilful, quixotic. He once related how he could always 'sense the temper of the House and when I get on my feet and feel that the temper of MPs is a bit on the ragged side I tell myself, perhaps some of them have had rows with their wives . . . or have had a meal which has disagreed with them. Others may be burdened with private worries and I go steady . . . at other times you sense that there's a real deep feeling in the House. Perhaps a great principle is at stake or a genuine grievance of the people. Then the House is at its best and it has to be taken seriously. . . . You've got to have a sense of humour. A great thing this, especially in Parliament. Hundreds of times it has come to my aid in difficult situations. Often in the House a joke cracked at the right time will ease an awkward situation.'[34] At times, pushing through Labour's massive programme of reform, Morrison gave the impression of being dictatorial, too much of the 'boss', but this never destroyed his longer-term image as a true House of Commons man. As Lord President he once reprimanded a minister who consulted him on how best to dress up an embarrassing parliamentary statement: 'Never, never lie to the House of Commons.'[35] And at the Foreign Office one reason for his unpopularity with officials was his obsessive concern with keeping the Commons informed and with its reactions to his policies.

Above all, Morrison was a complete *professional*. As a statesman, even at his peak, he was short of the highest stature. But by 1951 he certainly had to his credit outstanding achievements as a minister in Whitehall and as a party manager in Westminster, Transport House, the LCC and the London Labour Party. He was without doubt the most professional politician the Labour Party had so far produced. It was his tragedy that all these achievements came to mean so little to him in terms of personal satisfaction because he thought increasingly of only one objective – the party leadership. Failure in that single ambition was to turn all his other successes to ashes in his mouth.

Chapter 36

Foreign Secretary: Humiliations, Resignations and Defeat, 1951

Morrison's promotion to the Foreign Office in March 1951 was widely acclaimed. In the light of later criticism of his performance it is worth noting that there was little sign at the beginning, in public at least, of doubts about Morrison's ability or suitability for his new job. *The Times* welcomed him to foreign affairs as 'possessed of boldness and imagination' and said 'nobody can interpret better than he the reaction of ordinary men and women to international policies'.[1] The *Manchester Guardian* described him as strong and knowledgeable: 'his is perhaps the acutest mind in the House of Commons at the moment: it is certainly the nimblest.'[2] Lord Beaverbrook wrote 'a message of good wishes on your entering into the Kingdom of the Foreign Office. I know you will have a real triumph there.'[3] Beaverbrook's pleasure, both at Morrison's promotion and Bevin's demise, was certainly sincere. The new Commonwealth shared with the old Empire this pleasure at Morrison's elevation. Krishna Menon, Indian High Commissioner and perhaps the most outstanding living Indian socialist, wrote privately to Morrison shortly after he took over urging him to try to mediate a reduction in East–West tension. 'I am a very old friend of yours,' he said, 'and very devoted to you as you know. Since I am writing to you personally I have great hopes that in spite of what the newspapers say, that before the year is out your personal efforts will make a difference to the ominous situation that exists in the world, and find a way out of the cross-currents, as I know you are a man of peace. Between ourselves, my Prime Minister has told me that if in any way we can help Mr Morrison we must do so. . . . This letter is *purely and strictly personal* from Krishna to Herbert. Please do not put it on the file or let any of your ruddy civil servants see it!' Menon also proposed a private meeting between Morrison and a senior Russian representative, to which Morrison agreed.[4]

One of the 'perks' of the Foreign Office was the right to use the flat recently built for the Foreign Secretary at No. 1, Carlton Gardens. Morrison did not rush the Bevins to move out. This was partly out of consideration for his dying colleague, but also certainly reflected the wishes of Margaret. She hated the idea of moving into the imposing splendour of the ten-roomed apartment, with the publicity and responsibilities as hostess. She preferred to stay quietly out of the limelight and travel up for official receptions which she could not avoid.[5] Their first banquet at Carlton Gardens was four days after Morrison took over, for the Italian Prime Minister De Gasperi, on a three-day visit to London to discuss international matters and especially Trieste.[6] By then Morrison had been to the Palace to receive the seals of office and had established himself in his majestic new office overlooking Horse Guards Parade and the Park. He spent the first Sunday afternoon discussing the Paris meeting of the Big Four deputies with his Minister of State, Kenneth Younger, and his Under-Secretary, Ernest Davies, who had just flown back from the French capital.

Morrison went off on his first mission, to Paris for a two-day meeting of the Committee of Ministers of the Council of Europe, by the night ferry twenty-four hours after the banquet with the Italians. The main item on the Paris agenda was whether the Council should be authorized to discuss defence questions. The more enthusiastic 'Europeans' were pressing for this as a way of strengthening the Assembly, as one more step towards a federal Europe. The British position was distinctly hostile, both because such discussions might be seen as infringing the sovereignty of Parliament and also because Britain saw defence as an Atlantic question, not just European. Britain wanted the Assembly to be purely consultative within a limited range of issues.

The Labour government's attitude to the emerging European community had if anything hardened over the previous twelve months.[7] Bevin, who had worked hard to promote co-operation between the continental Europeans, never assumed that Britain would be part of any resulting European organization. He envisaged a close association of sovereign European states working with Britain and the Commonwealth and supported by the United States within a basically Atlantic framework. Recent European moves towards union left him with no positive policy, only a negative reaction, and this was the official position Morrison inherited. Bevin had circulated a memorandum (prepared by Ernest Davies) to the Labour Party International Committee in April 1950 setting out the case against Britain getting involved in what were described slightingly as 'regional organizations'.[8] The memorandum stated bluntly that 'the Labour Party Executive should approach with caution all proposals for increased co-operation in the Council of Europe. . . . Despite its belief in internationalism and its desire to extend co-operation among like-minded nations, the Executive must accept the fact that any union with Europe entailing the least surrender of sovereignty must, unless all participating European governments have similar Socialist economies, be a potential threat to the Socialist planned economy of this country.'[9] Bevin and Dalton fully endorsed these views – which still found loud echoes in the Labour Party twenty years later.

This was the suspicious and cautious frame of mind in which the British government had received the sudden news in May 1950 that a European conference was being summoned to discuss the Schuman plan for a European Coal and Steel Community. Morrison was acting Prime Minister at the time. The evening when the invitation to Britain arrived, carrying the clear implication that participation in the conference meant accepting the principle of supra-nationalism, and with the request from the French for a prompt British answer, the only minister available at the Foreign Office was Kenneth Younger. Bevin was in hospital preparing for an operation, Attlee was away from London and Morrison, temporarily in charge of the government, was not in Westminster or Whitehall. Younger went in search of Morrison, accompanied by Edwin Plowden, who was in charge of the economic planning questions involved in the Coal and Steel Community. They finally tracked him down, eating in the Ivy restaurant after an evening at the theatre, and called him into a side corridor to point out the need for an urgent decision. Morrison thought a while and then shook his head. 'It's no good,' he said, 'we cannot do it, the Durham miners won't wear it.'[10] Afterwards he consulted Bevin in hospital. Apart from these fears about the domestic political reactions, he objected both to the supra-national principle involved and to the French insistence on accepting this broad principle even before entering into the proposed discussions on detail. Bevin's and Morrison's main concern, it was later reported, was 'how to keep out of this embarrassing offer'.[11] Morrison himself later recalled that the Schuman proposal 'came to the British Government without prior consultation and with a request for an immediate reply. This procedure did not help the situation and the invitation was declined.'[12] There is no evidence to suggest that had the invitation been dispatched with more diplomatic consideration, it would have received a different response.

The Cabinet which Morrison called formally to approve his and Bevin's cool reaction was thinly attended, with the Prime Minister and the Chancellor away on holiday and the Foreign Secretary still in hospital. But given the known views of the senior absentees, and especially the sharp hostility of Cripps, it is unlikely that a full meeting would have concluded otherwise. The NEC, on which Morrison was an active member, issued a declaration on 13 June 1950 firmly opposing British participation in a European economic union.[13] Attlee, in his explanatory statement to the Commons on the same day, expressed sympathy with the Schuman plan, but made it clear that Britain, having a different constitution and different interests from the Europeans, could not take part. With these insular reactions from the Labour government and movement, the initiative in European affairs now slipped away from Britain to the emerging Franco-German axis.

Morrison, whose personal experience of the Council of Europe had not been happy, for a time grew increasingly hostile to the Europeans. In Cabinet on 18 January 1951, while still Lord President, he had 'expressed the view, with which I think some of our colleagues had a good deal of sympathy, that the

United Kingdom gains little by its membership of the Council of Europe and would be well out of it'.[14] Bevin himself shared Morrison's general irritation, but urged him not to be 'too precipitate about any action which might lead to the collapse of the Council of Europe'. Bevin thought a better 'moment for standing up frontally to the pretensions of the Strasbourg Assembly' would come after they had secured West Europe's military defences, after Germany was safely in NATO, and once the relationship between NATO and OEEC had been sorted out. It was undesirable, he felt, to 'look as if we were sabotaging two European institutions at the same time'. Bevin felt they should give the Council another twelve months to see these objectives achieved. Morrison was unconvinced and continued to argue for Britain's immediate withdrawal rather than agree to allow defence questions to be raised at the Council. On the day he resigned as Foreign Secretary, Bevin submitted a final memorandum to the Cabinet restating the argument he had put against over-hasty action in his earlier letter to Morrison. Dalton now joined the fray, arguing to Attlee the inexpediency and unnecessary rigidity of Morrison's position, in view of the fact that the Assembly was only consultative, and could not take decisions on defence.[15] Morrison eventually climbed down a month later.[16] Neither Dalton nor Bevin were 'pro-European', but on the question of the Council of Europe at least, Morrison was opening his tenure at the Foreign Office with a position more hostile than either of them. He was not opposed to allying with European partners on many functional questions; practical economic and military co-operation might be fruitful. But the European Assembly, and even more the Coal and Steel Community, threatened to introduce the dogma of federalism, which he totally rejected. If the European Parliament ever had powers, it would be an intolerable derogation from British sovereignty; while it did not, it was a time-wasting talking-shop. Either way, he was against it. His position had hardened since his visit to Strasbourg in 1949. Then he had seemed interested enough to want to convert them to the virtues of good British parliamentarianism. By March 1951 he had, for the time being at least, lost patience. He had grown a little more jingoistic, more blimpish, less tolerant. 'Land of Hope and Glory' in the new Royal Festival Hall, with the monarchy inside and the eternal Thames flowing outside: these were closer to Morrison's mood in the spring of 1951 than the immediate prospect of cosmopolitan squabbling and the visions of ultimate unity in the Council of Europe.

He did not fully reveal his hostility to the thirteen-nation committee of ministers when he addressed it in Paris on Saturday 17 March. This was his bow on the international stage and he was properly conciliatory in tone. He refused, however, to give ground, speaking firmly against allowing the Assembly any say on defence matters, rejecting as 'repugnant' the suggestion that the Assembly should be able to make member governments put its proposals to their national parliaments, and clashing with Mollet over whether or not to discuss the Schuman plan. At this time had they known the true feelings of Morrison – and of Attlee, Bevin, Dalton and Cripps – the Europeans might have been excused for feeling that they did not need enemies while they had the British Labour government for allies.

Towards the end of his Foreign Office tenure, Morrison's attitude towards Europe definitely softened. Although, like most of his colleagues, he was then unaware of the longer-term significance of the current moves towards closer European unity and of the ultimate dangers to Britain of relying upon her own diminished power and the diminishing asset of the 'special relationship' with the United States, his pronouncements on Europe grew friendlier. One junior minister found his attitude to the Europeans became more flexible than Bevin's had ever been.[17] When he went to Strasbourg at the beginning of August 1951, for the meeting of the Committee of Ministers of the Council of Europe, his approach was noticeably more positive. The British delegation gave the impression of being more interested in European development. The Europeans were particularly pleased when Morrison announced that Hugh Gaitskell, the British Chancellor, would attend the Consultative Assembly in October to discuss OEEC affairs.[18]

Morrison's involvement in discussions on European defence, and especially on German rearmament, may have drawn him into closer sympathy with continental political developments. He knew that the widespread European hostility to rearming Germany could be overcome only within a framework of co-operation and alliance which promised to constrain any renascent German nationalism. Assurances of greater British participation were essential to set at rest the fears of Germany's long-suffering neighbours. Morrison was prepared to swallow a little Europeanism in order to bolster the Western defences against Russia. Unfortunately, some of his colleagues were as opposed to rearming Germany as they were to Britain participating more in Europe. In early July Dalton sent a warning shot across the new Foreign Secretary's bows, writing of his deep concern at recent menacing developments across the Rhine and insisting that German rearmament should not be brought to the Cabinet as a *fait accompli*.[19] Morrison was then working with Shinwell on a paper setting out the arguments for, and possible means of effecting, the proposed German military contribution. He circulated this paper and introduced it at Cabinet on 30 July. The Cabinet had accepted the principle of German rearmament in the previous autumn, since it was a necessary condition of persuading the Americans to send troop reinforcements to Europe, but Morrison was one of the few ministers – Pakenham and Jowitt were others – who positively wanted to make quick progress on the issue. Apart from Dalton's outright opposition, Attlee and several others who accepted the principle still tried to play it slowly, and the Cabinet never reached satisfactory conclusions on the timing, manner and degree of German rearmament before the election in the autumn.[20] This issue was to plague Labour openly for some years in opposition. Morrison's position, and that of his main Cabinet antagonists, was, however, clearly taken in these last few months in office.

In Paris in March Morrison stayed with the Ambassador. On his first evening a formal dinner was arranged for him to meet leading French ministers. At the end of the banquet he privately suggested to his close associates an informal expedition for a drink at a boulevard café. His horrified Foreign Office advisers tried to deter him but he insisted. He headed for the Rue Royale, dragging a reluctant private secretary with him. There his personal detective, walking back from an evening off at Harry's bar, found Morrison, sitting happily at a pavement table drinking and watching Paris go by.[21]

He returned from Paris to London by the night ferry immediately after the March meeting of the Council of Ministers concluded. He immersed himself in departmental problems. At this point Morrison was undoubtedly working vigorously and enthusiastically to master his new brief, just as when beginning the other jobs in his career. He had talked extensively to the visiting Italians. He now took the chance to see Sir Oliver Franks, just back from the Washington Embassy, and to talk to the British Ambassador in from Cairo. He met the heads of the various Foreign Office departments and then began the long and tedious process of receiving members of the diplomatic corps in London.

The first crisis had already blown up. The Prime Minister of Persia, Razmasa, who had resisted nationalist demands to expropriate British oil assets, had been assassinated forty-eight hours before Morrison's appointment and succeeded by Dr Mossadeq, an extreme nationalist. Tension was also mounting in Egypt against Britain's privileged position there. The Egyptians had for the past year been threatening to abrogate unilaterally the 1936 Anglo-Egyptian Treaty, unless their demands for the withdrawal of British troops from Suez and for the annexation to Egypt of the Sudan were met. Bevin in his fading months had delayed on this as on other issues. Morrison put up fresh British proposals shortly after taking over, but the Egyptians now rejected them and in the summer broke off all further negotiations. Further east, in Korea, as the communist armies were rolled back towards the thirty-eighth parallel, fears arose on both sides of the Atlantic that the United Nations forces might push on recklessly to attack Red China. Morrison began to urge peace initiatives,* and to express concern about the behaviour of Douglas MacArthur, the controversial American Commander-in-Chief. War in Korea, threats of war in the Middle East, deadlock with Russia, dramatic movements towards European unity, the prospect of a rearmed Germany, and of formal peace with our other former enemy Japan – major issues of foreign policy crowded onto Morrison's new desk. The problem was whether he would have the time to deal with them.

Before Morrison had settled properly into his new office he was faced by the biggest internal political crisis of this Labour Government, dominating his time, attention and energies through until late April. Attlee went into St

* Truce talks began in July and dragged on until long after Morrison left office.

Mary's Hospital, Paddington on 21 March, because of his duodenal ulcer.[22] Morrison took over as deputy prime minister. At this very time the Chancellor was putting to Cabinet his controversial scheme to impose charges for the supply of false teeth and spectacles under the National Health Service. Gaitskell needed to restrain public expenditure. The Health Service under Bevan was widely believed to have been spendthrift and a Cabinet committee had been set up in 1950 to keep its expenditure under constant review. This was one ministry where any Chancellor was bound to look for economies.[23] Gaitskell's proposed charges could not be seriously criticized as breaking any fundamental principle of socialist faith enshrined in the National Health Act. Bevan himself as Minister had legislated to authorize a charge for prescriptions (not specifically for teeth and spectacles, but the principle was clearly established). Even so, Gaitskell was handling dynamite. The party was demoralized. It was exhausted by the constant efforts to maintain a majority in the Commons; it suffered defeats in late February, early in March and again at the beginning of April. Rearmament was arousing discontent, both in relation to the broad principle of armaments and to the particular economic costs and social consequences for Britain. Party meetings on 31 January and 7 February had been taken up with long discussions on the international situation and Britain's defence requirements.[24] At the former meeting Morrison, then still Lord President, had to intervene to make a strong appeal to Labour members to remain united and not to fall into dissension and rebellion in the House.

The focal point of dissension, in the Cabinet as in the parliamentary party, was Aneurin Bevan. Always volatile and volcanic in temperament, Bevan had been rumbling with discontent throughout the winter. He nearly resigned in protest against the post-devaluation emergency Budget.[25] He made great difficulties for Attlee when changing office. He was jealous and annoyed that Gaitskell was given the Exchequer the previous October. He was himself offered the Ministry of Labour at the time, but 'turned up his nose at it', and tried to get the Colonial Office.[26] The negotiations dragged on. Attlee did not give Bevan what he wanted, yet seemed afraid of taking a firm line with him, no doubt sensing that the Welshman was beginning to look for an excuse for resignation. Finally, in January Bevan accepted the Ministry of Labour. Shortly afterwards, when the Foreign Office came vacant, he again had expectations, which were frustrated by Morrison. The tensions between him and Morrison had built up into a battle for the soul of the party. In the debates about nationalization the struggle had been simplified into one between Morrison's consolidationism and Bevan's socialist fundamentalism. Personal animosities, differences of temperament, jealousies over promotion, disagreements over policies and principles, longer-term rivalries for the future leadership of the Labour Party – all interwove to create a pattern of tension between the two. Gaitskell also clashed abrasively with Bevan for similar reasons. Bevan's frustrations and irritations had so far been generalized, lacking focus. They now could be rationalized into a coherent critique of the whole government. In simple, socialist terms, social services were good, rearmament was bad. Labour was now, it could be urged, sacrificing the good for the bad. Bevan had already asked some of his sympathizers if they would stand by him should he make an issue, and even resign, over the rearmament question. Wilson, Freeman, Strachey and some others indicated they would.[27]

Morrison was in the chair on 22 March when the Cabinet discussed Gaitskell's proposals – for a ceiling on health expenditure, to charge for dentures and spectacles, and to increase old age pensions. Morrison announced his own support for them, reported that Attlee agreed, and asked for the Cabinet's approval. Bevin, half-asleep in his chair, Dalton, Addison, Marquand (the new Health Minister), McNeil and Summerskill all followed this lead. Bevan now made his stand. He argued that this meant giving up the great principle of the 'free health service' and asked why they should boggle at £23 million out of a total budget of £3,000 million. Why should it not come off the military estimates? But only Harold Wilson spoke up for Bevan. Morrison was able fairly to sum up that the general view supported Gaitskell. Bevan then warned that he could not usefully take part in any more proceedings of the Cabinet. Gaitskell in turn told the Cabinet that he could not go on without their unequivocal approval.[28] The lines of confrontation were clear: either Bevan or Gaitskell had to climb down, or one of them would go. Gaitskell was not by temperament someone who climbed down easily. Bevan was not one to jib at resignation. The dispute became public on 3 April, when Bevan assured a meeting of heckling dockers at Bermondsey Town Hall that 'I will never be a member of a Government which makes charges on the National Health Service for a patient.'[29]

The outcome was perhaps determined from the beginning. But it was to be long drawn out and agonizing for the party – and Morrison was once again sitting in the hot seat. His troubles at this point were almost too much for any man to bear. The Persian crisis was exploding on his Foreign Office desk. Closer to home, Margaret Morrison went into University College Hospital on 2 April. Morrison called in briefly to see her on the way to making his first major public speech as Foreign Secretary at Dudley. He missed the train at Paddington, dashed to Euston for another, and kept the audience of 1,400 waiting half an hour. Next morning he returned earlier than planned from Birmingham, and again rushed round to see Margaret. She had been operated on – the press said for a gastric ulcer. Morrison now learned that his wife had advanced and malignant cancer of the stomach.[30] For the rest of his time in office his wife was a dying invalid. Morrison kept it to himself.

The Cabinet spent most of the following Monday, 9 April, thrashing over Gaitskell's proposals, which were to be presented to Parliament the following afternoon. After the Chancellor had explained his Budget, Bevan intervened to object and there flowed back and forth across the table in front of Morrison 'a flood of arguments and appeals'. Gaitskell was looking weary. Bevan's 'hatred of him glared out all the time, and of Herbert Morrison'. Morrison had a delicate task holding them together. Gaitskell offered his resignation and promised to retreat to the back benches without attacking the government. He countered one of Bevan's better arguments by stating that even if he could save the £23 million from the services estimates, he would not use it to keep spectacles and false teeth free, but would use it to increase family allowances and old age pensions. The wrangling went on late into the evening. Morrison reported that he and the Chief Whip had visited Attlee in hospital, presumably early in the afternoon in the break between the two Cabinet meetings, and the Prime Minister had supported the Chancellor's line and insisted that 'a very heavy responsibility would rest on anyone who split the Government and the Party'.[31] Among Morrison's papers is a memorandum in his hand, signed and dated 'St Mary's Hospital 9.4.51', which appears to set out five points which Attlee supported against Bevan:

> *P.M.:* 1 Must be give and take in budgets. No one can say any particular estimate sacrosanct. Lord Randolph Churchill only one who never recovered.
> 2 Must think of the Movement – not himself.
> 3 Crisis at this moment sheer stark folly. Electoral conditions. . . . Party divided – smashed.
> 4 Voters would say we can't govern. Tories in for ten years. A.B. would have done it.
> 5 We must stand by Chancellor of Exchequer – as Cabinet decided with PM in chair.

After Attlee's absent voice had been brought in to support the worried majority, Morrison finally, around nine in the evening – they had first met at 10.30 in the morning – collected opinions. Only Bevan and Harold Wilson stood firmly against.* That evening, to rub in the salt, the Tories sprang a surprise vote against the proposed cut in the cheese ration, from three ounces to two ounces a week, and won. Morrison had to announce that the Government would accept the decision of the House.[32] It had been a bad day.

Gaitskell's Budget speech went well, with little outward signs of the swirling currents beneath the smooth surface of Cabinet solidarity. There was no outcry in the chamber at the health charges. The Chancellor himself, though young in parliamentary experience, already spoke with the clarity and conviction which was always to give him authority on big occasions. His toughness in this crisis was typical, and an interesting prelude to future battles in the party. Gaitskell simply did not bend very easily. He told Dalton next day that he had never been certain up to the last moment that he would be the Chancellor making the Budget speech. He implied that Attlee especially – 'and even Morrison once' – had suffered cold feet about the health charges, although the Chief Whip, Whiteley, was solid as a rock. In any case, he would

---

* John Freeman and John Strachey were also believed to be ready to resign with Bevan from posts outside the Cabinet. (Dalton diary, 9 April 1951, Vol. 40.)

not have compromised, and so he always considered resignation a firm possibility.[33]

The crisis dragged on, with Bevan fuming and threatening but still not certain of resignation. He and Wilson went to see Attlee in hospital on Budget day. Attlee persuaded them 'not to take any steps until after the party meeting tomorrow morning'.[34] Freeman also saw Attlee in the evening, sitting on the side of his bed, his bare feet swinging, sipping a glass of milk. He discussed the issue quite calmly but with an almost total lack of interest, making no serious attempt to persuade the young minister to stay in his administration.[35] Attlee was exhausted by the constant comings and goings and he declined a request from Morrison to see him that same evening. He kept in touch by telephone and arranged to talk to him after the party meeting next day.[36]

Bevan clashed with Morrison at the party meeting on Wednesday and at Thursday's Cabinet but he never actually specifically threatened to resign.[37] Bevan and Wilson also went off to try to recruit the assistance of Ernie Bevin against Morrison and Gaitskell, but Bevin died, on the following Saturday, before he could take any part on either side.[38] A week later they at last reached the edge of the abyss. Bevan announced that he would resign on the third reading of the Health Charges Bill. At this point Shinwell initiated a compromise move. He suggested that it be announced that the health charges were only temporary. Bevan seemed to welcome this lifeline – though, according to Chuter Ede, he at the same time threw a note across the table to Harold Wilson claiming 'We've got them on the run'. By that evening Bevan's ever-changing mood had hardened again. He was offered the compromise formula – a ministerial announcement to the Commons that the charges were temporary and could be altered or abolished in due course simply by an affirmative order – but refused to agree to anything short of the withdrawal of the bill.[39]

Bevan did, apparently, have one last private moment of doubt, contemplating withdrawing his resignation during a meeting with Wilson and Freeman at his flat in Cliveden Place, but they, and especially Wilson, strengthened his resolution, while insisting that the issue must be made broader than the narrow protest at charges for teeth and spectacles with which Bevan had so far been primarily concerned.[40] From this point 'Bevanism', as a wide argument with and dissent from whole areas of the existing Labour leadership's policies, began to be systematically formulated.*

Morrison escaped to the country that final weekend of the crisis to stay with Leslie and Margaret Hunter at Brockham. Morrison always arrived for the weekend looking as though he was on the edge of a breakdown, recalled Hunter. 'In bed by ten, he would sleep round the clock and beyond, until at last a cheerful "Hi!" from his bedroom would announce that he was ready for a light breakfast of a boiled egg, pot of tea and a slice of toast. A leisurely

---

* Dissent had, of course, long existed and the Keep Left group had given it some coherence. From this point in April 1951 it acquired serious leadership and went into unofficial opposition to develop and campaign for its alternative policies.

session in the bathroom would be enlivened with excerpts from *Annie get your Gun* or some other musical. . . . Looking between ten and fifteen years younger than the night before and quite capable (as in fact he was) of facing another week with an average of four hours' sleep a night, he would now take a turn round the green and endear himself to Mrs Miller, the landlady, by popping into the Royal Oak to tell everyone what a lovely village they had.'[41] There was little other relaxation that weekend. The Foreign Office car arrived with its inevitable quota of boxes. He read papers and wrote memoranda. He spent hours on the 'scrambler' telephone especially installed for the weekend in a little room at the end of the house. He arranged, without warning the Hunters, that the Shawcrosses would phone up and invite themselves to coffee. 'It was just one more example of the old technique we knew so well by which Morrison always did his best to keep his fingers from knowing what his thumbs were doing.'[42] Morrison wanted to discuss the coming Cabinet reshuffle, and especially to persuade Shawcross to switch from being Attorney General (at £10,000 a year) to become a Cabinet co-ordinating minister as Lord Privy Seal (at £5,000 a year). He probably wanted to re-create the influential co-ordinating role which he had himself carried out when Lord President, with one of his loyal lieutenants in the post. It did not quite work out that way. Shawcross was subsequently offered by Attlee a choice of Lord Privy Seal or the Board of Trade and preferred to take Harold Wilson's place at the latter post.[43] At the Hunters', Morrison was far from depressed by the prospective resignations. He regretted Freeman's departure, but was pleased to see the back of Bevan and apparently did not think the loss of Wilson was of great consequence.[44] He thought that the promotions of Shawcross and Robens, two old friends whom he had helped to attract into the Labour movement before the war,[45] would definitely strengthen the Cabinet.*

Bevan's resignation statement to the Commons on Monday, the twenty-third, was needlessly intemperate. Harold Wilson followed the next day with a much more impressive exposition of the rebel case.[46] He argued – and time and reflection tend to confirm his position – that the proposed rate of re-armament was indefensible: if the defence estimates were in fact spent then they would inflate the economy into ruin; if not (and he rightly predicted that they would not be spent) then there was no point in restraining social expenditure to remain within budgetary ceilings which would anyway prove meaningless. John Freeman completed the trio of resignations, though he admitted afterwards that 'nothing could have done more to influence me the other way than Nye's outburst' in the Commons.[47] The break was complete. Morrison again went dutifully to see Attlee to report on the damage.[48]

Next morning the battered parliamentary party met for two hours in Westminster Hall. Bevan shocked the meeting with an hysterical outburst, attacking Gaitskell in vituperative personal terms. According to Dalton,

---

* Robens replaced Bevan at Labour and Morrison's friend Dick Stokes became Lord Privy Seal.

Bevan 'was sweating and shouting and seemed on the edge of a nervous breakdown'.[49] Another prominent young Labour minister present reported to a
journalist afterwards that: 'He was hysterical. He bawled, and his Welsh voice,
at times, rose almost to a scream.'[50] A message appealing for unity from Attlee
failed to calm the meeting. Morrison did not speak. Chuter Ede, who was in
the chair, wound up and referred to the scandalous style of one of the earlier
speeches, making comparisons with Oswald Mosley. Jennie Lee leapt to her
feet protesting and Bevan started to shout shrilly from the floor.[51] From this
hysteria they went with relief across to the calm of the Abbey for Ernest
Bevin's memorial service.* With Bevin dead, Cripps dying in a Swiss sanatorium, Attlee ailing in hospital, Bevan stumping off into the political wilderness, the main pillars of Labour's great administration were crumbling to the
ground. Morrison alone was left from that generation of leaders, temporarily
occupying the top seat in the crisis, desperately trying to hold the government
together.

He was criticized for his handling of the Bevan crisis. Attlee later asserted
that Morrison 'lost Bevan and Wilson' and implied that, had he not been in
hospital, he could have saved the party from much of the blood-letting that
occurred.[52] Certainly, Morrison took a very firm line throughout. Other
colleagues felt that he was being more than usually authoritarian in his handling of the Cabinet at this time.[53] The question is whether he was unnecessarily
and damagingly rigid. To sustain this criticism it has to be believed that a
compromise was ever possible. Harold Wilson himself was convinced that
Morrison and Gaitskell had conspired 'to put the needle into Nye' and
intended not to compromise under any circumstances. He believed, and
believes, that Attlee might have rescued the situation.[54] Freeman at the time
also felt that someone less rigid than Morrison might have produced a
compromise, but subsequently came to the conclusion that probably no
formula of words could have healed the split, since Bevan in fact wanted to
go.[55] Morrison argued strongly in his *Autobiography* that there was in reality
no way of bridging the wide gap between Gaitskell and Bevan.[56] This is on
the whole convincing. We know that Gaitskell would not give way. Would
Bevan? He occasionally wavered, but it is difficult to see how Attlee or anyone
else could have devised a formula which would enable Bevan to stay without
forcing Gaitskell to go. All possible appeals to unity were made, by Attlee as
strongly as by others. Shinwell's compromise formula was pursued, but
Bevan refused; it is hard to escape the conclusion that he 'wanted out'.
Morrison certainly did not overly exert himself to keep the rebels in the
government. There is no evidence that he ever approached Bevan to persuade
him to reach a compromise. He only once spoke to Harold Wilson, then
warning him savagely that if he resigned he would be finished in Labour
politics for twenty years.[57] He never spoke a word to John Freeman – though

* Bevin died on 14 April. Morrison – ironically in view of their mutual dislike – made the
Commons tribute to him on the sixteenth.

when he heard vague rumours that Freeman was having second thoughts he did suggest to Attlee that promotion to the Board of Trade might be an incentive.* Morrison saw the situation as offering a brutal choice between Gaitskell and Bevan. Like most of the Cabinet, he thought Gaitskell was right, and of the two protagonists preferred not to lose him. Attlee may have had doubts, but whenever he was pressed by Morrison for a clear statement he came down on Morrison's side. Wavering is not the same as an achieved compromise, any more than Morrison's firmness meant that he was tactlessly rigid. Anyway, what compromise would a more flexible leader have found?

With the Bevan crisis settled, though scarcely solved, Morrison was able to pay a little more attention to his Foreign Office responsibilities. He flew off to Paris – his second visit in a month – on 26 April to liaise with the British delegation to the Big Four talks. By the time he returned to London the new Persian government had passed its legislation cancelling the Anglo-Iranian Oil Company's forty-year lease concessions and nationalizing the British oil assets. Riots were flaring up in the oilfields, with two British soldiers killed there. Morrison struggled to get on top of the job, but already the press was complaining that he had too many non-departmental interests and was neglecting foreign affairs. Early impressions leave a long impact and Morrison foolishly on his first parliamentary day as Foreign Secretary, in March, had left the Foreign Office questions to his junior minister, Younger, while he answered most of the questions about the Festival of Britain.[58] The day before leaving for Paris in April he cancelled a meeting with the Egyptian Ambassador in order to go to report to Attlee in hospital on Cabinet developments. Early in May he again took the Festival of Britain questions, instead of leaving them to Stokes, the minister responsible. The Tory press was highly critical that Morrison should be bothering with the price of bananas in Battersea Park at a time when the Middle East seemed to be rising in rebellion against Britain.[59] Anthony Eden expressed disquiet in the Commons over Morrison's order of priorities and rebuked him with the suggestion that he, 'having taken over responsibilities of unparalleled importance, might want to concentrate on them'. Morrison snapped back that he did not share Eden's 'superior view' of the Foreign Office.[60] 'Rarely,' observed the *Daily Telegraph* next day, 'with so few words can a Foreign Secretary have so wilfully raised so many doubts about his capacity for that office.'[61] It was not a good start.

---

* Freeman was summoned by the Chief Whip and approached by unofficial emissaries from Morrison's camp, but, at this late stage, was not impressed or attracted by the offers. (Interviews, J. Freeman, Lord Shackleton.) Dalton also tried to dissuade Freeman, but found him firm and consistent throughout in his genuine concern over the social consequences of the proposed defence expenditure. (Dalton diary, various dates, Vol. 40.)

The problem was that Morrison really cared about the Festival of Britain; it was in so many ways his pet project and he could not bear to let go at the very moment of its glorious triumph. He had taken over formal responsibility for the proposed Festival back in 1947* and had nurtured it through many difficulties. To him it was a great symbol of national regeneration. Announcing the government's intentions in December 1947, he recalled the Paris Exposition of 1878, which celebrated France's recovery from the defeat of 1870, and said that Britain now needed to demonstrate to the world that she had recovered from the exhausting victory of 1945. He appointed a Council of distinguished advisers – including such prominent artistic figures as T. S. Eliot, Malcolm Sargent and John Gielgud – with General Lord Ismay, one of Churchill's war-horses from 1940, as Chairman[62] and Gerald Barry as Director General. After examining many possibilities, including Hyde Park, the Council chose the south bank of the Thames between Waterloo Bridge and County Hall as its central exhibition site. There the story of Britain and its peoples was to be represented in a series of pavilions, each devoted to a significant aspect of national life – the home, school, industry, transport, the countryside etc. Local exhibitions and festivities were also organized throughout the country, making it a national jamboree with virtually every community involved.

Morrison was naturally delighted with the choice of the south bank site, between his beloved County Hall and his Waterloo Bridge. He had long wanted to see that bedraggled southern riverside turned into something of credit to London and pleasure to Londoners, especially south Londoners. When he personally first suggested it as the best location it was turned down as being too small. Barry was ideally looking for somewhere much larger than this thirty acres. Certain Council members – especially R. A. Butler and Walter Elliot – continued to press for the riverside, and when it was realized that the LCC independently wished to build a concert hall there, which would provide a permanent Festival asset at little cost to the government, the choice was made.[63] Morrison jubilantly announced their decision to the Commons on 10 February 1949, claiming that the South Bank was the only site sufficiently spectacular, central and in keeping with the Festival theme of the 'new Britain springing from the battered fabric of the old'.[64]

The construction programme had sticky patches, suffering from shortages

* The idea for a great Exhibition of 1951, to celebrate the centenary of the 1851 Exhibition, had been raised privately with the government by the Royal Society of Arts as early as 1943. It was given public impetus in an open letter from Gerald Barry to Stafford Cripps, as President of the Board of Trade, published in the *News Chronicle* in September 1945. Soon afterwards the government set up the Ramsden Committee to examine the proposal and the Committee decided in support of an international exhibition. Further consideration led the government to pare down its intentions to a less ambitious national fair, and, having lost its international trading aspects, Cripps insisted that responsibility for it be taken from the Board of Trade – and it went to Morrison.

of materials* and from labour disputes. Morrison at one point called in his old LCC colleague Richard Coppock to sort out industrial troubles on the site. Bevin was upset at not being consulted but Morrison was so pleased with Coppock's success at troubleshooting that he promised him a knighthood as a reward – and delivered it.[65] He made few other ministerial interventions: once to remove mention of free school meals from the schools pavilion, because it might prove politically contentious; once to get Barry to inspect – and exonerate – a statue which had been commissioned for the South Bank and was rumoured in the press to be indecent; once to reorganize the Board for the separate Festival Gardens and funfair in Battersea Park, after it sank into financial chaos with projected losses rising from £1½ million to £2½ million, and the chairman and managing director resigned; and once to introduce a special bill to legalize Sunday opening of the Festival including the funfair. He failed in this latter endeavour. The bill was heavily rejected at the committee stage – a curious repetition of Morrison's previous defeat at the hands of Britain's roundheads when he tried in 1941 to legalize the opening of theatres on Sundays.[66] Apart from these occasional direct interventions, Morrison, who always believed in delegation, generally left Barry and the official organizers to get on with the details of the job.†

Morrison was of course not unaware that party political benefits might be derived from the Festival celebrations. He was politician enough to appreciate Disraeli's dry comment a century earlier, that 'this exhibition will be a boon to the Government, for it will make the public forget its misdeeds'. But his main feeling certainly was that the British people had earned the chance of a little frivolity after eleven years of crisis. When the Exhibition opened he wrote: 'I want everyone in Britain to see it, to take part in it, to enjoy it. I want to see the people happy. I want to hear the people sing.'[67] He 'convinced the Cabinet that we ought to do something jolly', recalled one colleague. 'I can almost hear him now saying "we need something to give Britain a lift".'[68] His personal identification with the Festival – in his own and in other people's minds – was total. When a Tory MP with a felicitous slip of the tongue referred to him as 'the Lord Festival' it seemed appropriate and stuck.[69]

He attended an eve-of-Festival dinner on 2 May, at the elegant home of Political and Economic Planning in Queen Anne's Gate, and claimed, beaming with pleasure, that 'to have organized the Festival now may be madness but it is the sort of madness that has put us on the map and is going to keep us there'.[70] Morrison ought really to have been attending the Committee of

---

* The Festival Hall itself had to be changed from its original steel girder construction because of steel shortages. When a national cement famine developed in 1950, Morrison's Festival scheme was frequently blamed.

† Beneath the Festival Council there was an executive committee of officials to carry out the detailed planning and to co-ordinate the contributions of the various departments of government. The financial vote for the Festival came under Morrison's responsibility.

Ministers of the Council of Europe at Strasbourg, but he could not leave London at this time; he sent his junior minister, Lord Henderson, instead. Next day was the opening concert in the new Festival Hall. With orchestra, massed choirs, and royalty present among an excited audience, Morrison sat high up in a box, proud and moved as 'Land of Hope and Glory' reached its crescendo. The weather was fickle and it poured all next day when he took the King and Queen on a ninety-minute tour of the South Bank, but his spirits were strikingly undampened and undampable. In the evening he was in crackling good humour as guest of honour at the Lord Mayor's dinner to celebrate the Festival.[71] 'This,' remarked the *Observer* that weekend, 'has been Mr Herbert Morrison's week and he has enjoyed it to the full. His speeches have been full of his special cockney humour. . . . What he has most enjoyed has been giving Mr Barry and his younger colleagues a chance. Some of the consequences – and especially the sculpture – have surprised him, but he has refrained from even the most avuncular protest.'[72]

Morrison left behind the London festivities and went away to the Isle of Wight for Whitsun. He and Margaret stayed at Nettlestone Priory, a Workers' Travel Association guest house near Ryde. But he did not get his needed rest. On Whit Monday evening he was interrupted at dinner by a call on his scrambler telephone. The Foreign Office reported further deterioration in the Persian crisis. Morrison cancelled plans to inspect the Festival of Britain ship *Campania* at Southampton next day. He spent his time instead drafting a new note to the Persians, consulting his officials and Attlee by telephone at Chequers, and planning to mobilize United States support.[73] By mid-week he was back in London and again conferred with the Prime Minister and Cabinet before sending another sharp note to the Persians, warning them not to nationalize by force, and offering to send out a mission to negotiate compromise. The government also decided to submit the case to the International Court of Justice at The Hague on the grounds that the Persians had unilaterally broken a freely-entered agreement and had refused to discuss or negotiate the dispute under the arbitration articles provided in the oil company's 1933 agreement. He then left for a six-day visit to Germany and Austria which had been previously arranged for Bevin. Morrison at first did not want to go, feeling the need to get to grips with the Persian problem, but he was persuaded he could not back out.[74] Attlee took over the Foreign Office while he was away, but Morrison was in constant touch about Persia, and was ready to return at an hour's notice if the Middle East erupted.

His German visit was acknowledged to be a considerable success, both by the British and the Germans. Chancellor Adenauer referred to it at a press conference on the twenty-first as opening 'a new phase in Anglo-German relations'. *The Times* described the trip as 'both timely and successful'.[75] He spent his first day in Bonn talking to Adenauer, discussing German rearmament, the Schuman plan, and especially the proposed formal ending to the

State of War with Germany.* He slept the night of 20 May in a Rhineland castle, lunched next day with Schumacher and the Social Democratic Party leaders, and returned in the evening for dinner with Adenauer at the Palais Schaumberg. He finished his tour with a visit to Austria. He addressed the British occupation troops, met first the Vienna politicians at the Rathaus and then the Austrian Chancellor, Dr Figl, and then insisted on inspecting a block of municipal flats.[76] He was the first British Foreign Secretary to visit Austria since Castlereagh, 136 years earlier. At the evening reception at the Embassy he was in high spirits and shocked some of the stiffer diplomats by asking the Ambassador to roll back the carpet so that he could dance with the ladies. The side of the Foreign Office which suited him was the whirlwind tour, the quick man-to-man talks on broad problems, off-the-cuff speeches, hearty receptions, slipping off to see the natives at play. He was less at home with the formality and etiquette. His response was to plough straight on through it, rolling up the red carpet to dance. But ageing Viennese diplomats, like his smooth officials from the Foreign Office, were not always impressed and were often left feeling uncomfortable.[77]

He flew back from Klagenfurt airport to Northolt in a York aircraft of Transport Command and walked across the runway from the plane munching a jam tart. He enjoyed bringing the Foreign Office down to earth. He told the assembled reporters chirpily that he had enjoyed his visit, would have loved to stay longer, 'but I decided that my King, my country and the newspapers needed me'.[78]

The Foreign Office was, if anything, even more frantic on his return. Alarm had been growing for some time about leakages of secret information to the Russians. The security services had been investigating for two years before Morrison took over.[79] By mid-April suspicion was falling on Donald D. Maclean, a specialist in atomic energy questions who had attended Anglo-American atom conferences. On 17 April, at the height of the Bevan crisis, Sir William Strang had cleared with Morrison that Maclean should be closely investigated. When Morrison came into the office on 25 May after returning from Germany, Strang reported the provisional results of their inquiries and proposed that the Security Service be authorized in advance to interview their suspect next month. Morrison agreed. That very evening Maclean, together with his friend Burgess, left England for France and thence to Russia. Morrison curiously was not informed of their flight until the middle of the following week. He then immediately directed that vigorous action should be taken to recover the missing spies, if necessary by arrest in friendly countries. By 7 June he and his advisers had to confess that the birds had almost certainly flown to safety. Requests to allies to arrest Burgess and Maclean on sight were withdrawn. That same day the story was first revealed to the public in the *Daily*

---

* The State of War with Germany, officially in existence since 3 September 1939, was terminated six weeks later. Morrison announced it to the Commons and thirty-nine other allied governments declared peace at the same time. (*HC Debs*, Vol. 490, Col. 39.)

Express. Morrison immediately set up a Committee of Inquiry, under Sir Alexander Cadogan. He was also forced to make a public statement. He reported to the Commons on 11 June, but had – genuinely – nothing to add to the facts already known.[80]

The scandal of Burgess and Maclean was a hammer blow to Morrison. It reflected, quite properly, on the laxity of the Foreign Office. He, as Foreign Secretary, shared the blame, as always under the British system of ministerial responsibility. Had his reputation been currently unsullied, had the government been flying high in public esteem and popularity, he could have ridden this scandal with little damage. The government, however, was stumbling from disaster to disaster. Morrison had already attracted criticism for allegedly neglecting his departmental affairs. This episode seemed symptomatic of laxity and neglect. But it was certainly unfair to blame Morrison. The leakages had occurred before he took over. The incompetent security vetting system was one he inherited and had had no time to test or change. On the three main occasions when the matter of Maclean was raised with him he responded immediately with decisions for action: to authorize investigating Maclean, interviewing him, and arresting him. He had not been told of any prior suspicions about Burgess. He promptly set up a Committee of Inquiry, and vigorously initiated improvements in the security system. He could get public credit or excuse for none of this; in the public eye the spy scandal was just one more thing going wrong at the Foreign Office, and Herbert was the man holding the can. Fortunately, the 'Philby' side of the story was as yet unrevealed. Again, Morrison was not culpably involved – he was never told that Philby was suspected of tipping off Maclean to run, nor of the financial settlement made with Philby when he resigned in July 1951.

The Burgess–Maclean scandal was for Morrison an unpleasant diversion from the Persian situation, which was rapidly escalating out of control into a major crisis.[81] The Persians demanded seventy-five per cent of all oil revenue to the Abadan refinery since nationalization on 20 March, offering the remaining quarter as compensation to the Anglo-Iranian Company for the expropriated assets. From the end of May the Cabinet were willing to concede the principle of nationalization providing the details were settled by negotiation and in the meantime the flow of oil was guaranteed. An Anglo-Iranian Oil Company mission was sent to negotiate direct with the Persian Finance Minister. They offered immediate higher dues and an interim payment while a compromise settlement was agreed. The Persians rejected this proposal and the talks collapsed. Morrison had to find a way out of the impasse. He was trying to take a tough line. A paratroop brigade and extra naval forces were dispatched to the East Mediterranean and air-bases in Iraq were reinforced. The Cabinet also agreed that the refinery operations should be halted and all personnel withdrawn unless the Persians compromised. This would punish the Persians, who needed the revenue, but it was a double-edged weapon and contained an element of bluff: Britain took a third of her petrol from Abadan and a prolonged rupture in supplies would make rationing inevitable.

Morrison made a brief statement to the Commons on 20 June, reporting the breakdown of talks, that the negotiating mission would be recalled, and expressing concern at the gravity of the crisis. He said the government would make a further application to the International Court at The Hague and promised direct military intervention if British lives were in danger. He did not get a sympathetic hearing. He seemed unsure, evasive, leaving no clear impression whether or not a decision had been taken to evacuate or not. The opposition was unhappy, smelling a scuttle. Churchill and Eden urged that there should be no evacuation without first consulting the Commons. They pressed successfully for an emergency debate next day.[82] This went badly for the government and the Opposition really had their tails up. Morrison, to the surprise of many, did not open for the government but chose to wind up, at which he was normally supreme. He never mastered the House this night, lacking authority and being constantly drowned by interruptions. He unwisely used the tactic of aggressively denouncing the Tories as imperialists, thereby inflaming partisan passions, instead of appealing for unity and responsibility in a national crisis. One Tory back-bencher, Harry Legge-Bourke, was made to withdraw from the chamber by the Speaker when he threw a penny at Morrison, demanding that the Foreign Secretary put on another record.[83] The Labour back-benchers were glum and dispirited. They remained silent when Morrison sat down.

The following weekend's press and speeches were full of reports on Morrison's disappointing performance. Some of these comments were simply attempts to exploit the government's difficulties with an eye to a coming election. But even such moderate Conservatives as R. A. Butler and Anthony Eden felt driven to strong criticism. Butler said Morrison's performance was 'disgraceful' and Eden asserted 'there never has been in my judgment a speech more unworthy of the office'.[84] The quality press joined in the criticism.[85] The *Daily Telegraph* – admittedly biased, but usually informed and not too unfair – described Morrison's performances that week as 'so bad as to mark a constitutional landmark – or perhaps abyss is the word – of its own ... manifestly he is not happy at the Foreign Office'.[86] Even the usually friendly *Observer* remarked that Morrison had lost his earlier jaunty cheerfulness: 'he has not been quite his usual sunny self, and it may be that Mr Morrison, always an unconventional worker, has grown a little irked by the rather rigid methods of the Foreign Office.'[87]

Morrison's reputation at the Foreign Office never had time to rise from the widespread criticism of him at the end of June. He tried to recover the lost ground. He took a tougher line in public, pledging protection for all Britons in Persia and dispatching the cruiser *Mauritius*. He was even stronger behind the scenes, complaining in Cabinet that Britain was being 'too United Nations-y' and playing with the idea of sending in troops to take the Abadan refinery and hold it indefinitely. His Foreign Office advisers found him 'more

R

hawkish than we had expected'.[88] He had always been tough-minded and not easily browbeaten. To this was added a touch of jingoism in his later years. 'Morrison very petulant. Quite a little Pam,' reported Dalton cattily on the Cabinet discussions. 'I said [to Attlee] Morrison must not try to compensate himself for having been a conscientious objector in World War I and against arms before World War II.'[89] The more jingoistic press became kinder to the new 'hard-line' Foreign Secretary. In June the *Daily Express* had been calling him 'Mumbo Jumbo Morrison'. By 3 July he had become 'The Man of the Hour' because he was refusing to scuttle.

Such fickle friends were of little consolation or significance compared to the alarming and continuing disintegration of Britain's policy and position in the Middle East. The Egyptians had joined in the game of twisting the old lion's tail. As part of their campaign to force re-negotiation of the Anglo-Egyptian Treaty relating to British military rights in the Suez zone, and to annex the Sudan, a mob of Egyptians boarded and looted a British merchant ship heading for Akaba. In the parliamentary discussions[90] Morrison again sat down to a silent House. He appeared ill-informed and insensitive to the strong feelings in the House that this country should not allow itself to be pushed around much longer. Morrison himself in fact shared precisely those feelings, but he could do nothing about them and ended up leaving the 'jingoes' with the impression that he was too soft, and the moderates and the left wing with the impression that he was a paralysed Palmerston. Not until three weeks after the incident were British warships ordered to protect all British shipping on the Suez–Akaba route. By then the incident had fizzled out of public interest, and attention was back on Abadan; but the additional dents in the Foreign Secretary's image were permanent. Morrison was getting increasingly irritated with his inability to produce a concrete solution of any of the problems on his desk. At one point he told a distinguished American journalist: 'Foreign Policy would be okay except for the bloody foreigners.'[91] At another he said wistfully to an assistant, 'I wish I was Lord Palmerston.'[92] He was by now definitely unhappy in his new job. He was irritated by his civil servants as well as by foreigners and fumed to friends about the iniquities of the Foreign Office.[93] Dancing at a party with a lady who asked him how he liked being Foreign Secretary, he replied, bitterly and not too soberly, that he used to be much happier as a poor young man sitting in the street reading a newspaper.[94]

Through July Morrison was repeatedly on the rack at question time in the Commons. The Conservatives were suspicious of an impending 'sell-out' and pushed him to give assurances that Britain was not withdrawing; his answers were evasive, reflecting Cabinet confusion. The Labour left pressed him for assurances that Britain would not, as the right-wing press and much of the opposition was demanding, intervene with troops; he gave the assurances, but without conviction, since he himself hankered after military action.[95] Morrison went to the miners' gala at Durham and denounced the Tories for 'war-mongering'. Churchill replied savagely in the Commons debate on the

Middle Eastern situation a week later. 'Here is the new Foreign Secretary,' rumbled the Tory leader, 'who shows all the world that his main thought in life is to be a caucus boss. . . . It is tragic indeed that at this time his distorted, twisted, malevolent mind is the one to which our foreign affairs are confided.'[96] Morrison usually relished the rough stuff of parliamentary politics, but he had lost his appetite as his confidence was whittled away. The Tories roared with laughter when he mispronounced the river 'Euphrates', giving it only two syllables with the accent on the first.[97] He was justified to complain that this was typical silly snobbery. (Both Bevin and Churchill amused the House frequently with esoteric pronunciations.) But to many it seemed just one more example of his lack of qualification for foreign affairs. Once the doubt was established, there were no excuses, only confirmations.

There was still a faint hope of salvaging the disaster. Morrison sent an emergency mission to the Persians, under Richard Stokes, the eccentric Lord Privy Seal. But time was running out; on 31 July the Abadan refinery ceased working. During early August, while the Stokes mission was negotiating on the spot in Teheran and most other ministers were holidaying away from London, Morrison assiduously cultivated the friendship of Middle Eastern leaders. He entertained the Foreign Minister and the Ambassador of Saudi Arabia and lunched with first the Egyptian Ambassador and then the Regent, Emir Abdul, of Iraq.[98] Britain needed friends in that part of the world as never before, for the Egyptian situation was rapidly boiling up into a crisis paralleling that in Persia. On 6 August the Egyptian Foreign Minister said that there seemed to be no point in further discussions between the two countries. Before leaving on holiday Morrison approved placatory notes urging the Egyptians to negotiate and promising a new British initiative shortly. But tension increased. Rioters demonstrated outside the British Embassy in Cairo. The Egyptians announced on 26 August that unless the British made a new and constructive move before the end of the parliamentary session they would unilaterally abrogate the 1936 Treaty.[99]

Morrison took his summer holiday, as the year before, in Scandinavia. He toured the Norwegian fiords and cruised north of the Arctic circle to see the midnight sun. While on board ship off the Norwegian coast he received an urgent request from the Foreign Office to return to Whitehall immediately. The Middle East crisis had deteriorated further and the Russians were promising new initiatives in relation to the signing of the Japanese Peace Treaty in San Francisco next month. He sat on his cabin bunk with Jim Raisin and they composed a naughty reply to the effect that although the Foreign Office had killed Bevin, they were not going to kill him, and so they must make use of the Minister of State standing in during his absence.[100] The highlight of his journey was a visit to the far north of Norway, where he inspected the barbed wire marking the desolate border with Russia. He also travelled around rural Norway in ordinary country buses. At the end he told Norwegian reporters that 'it has been the best holiday I have ever had'.[101] It was not all holiday of course. Politics as ever intruded: he spent a day at the end of his visit talking with the Swedish premier, Tage Erlander, at Halvistad in south-west Sweden.[102] When he returned at the beginning of September there were pointed questions about his absence from duty while the Middle East crisis was erupting. Morrison answered that 'subordinate Ministers have been acting with the Prime Minister while I have been away'.[103] The impression remained, however, that he was still not giving his full attention to the Foreign Office. It was not diminished in the weeks ahead. On the contrary, he was absent from London for virtually the whole of September. Most of the time he was on Foreign Office business, in San Francisco for the Japanese Peace Conference, in Washington for the Foreign Ministers' Conference, and in Ottawa for the NATO discussions. But the attention of the nation was on Suez and Persian oil, not on Europe and the Pacific.

The three days between Morrison's arrival from Norway and his departure for the USA were spent desperately catching up on office business. Climbing into the aeroplane at London Airport, he tried to reassure the press: 'I am pretty cheerful, but in foreign affairs it is never wise to be cocksure. . . . I have given a lot of decisions and I am leaving with the feeling that the Foreign Office is in pretty tidy condition.'[104] There were certainly no grounds for being cocksure, and few for being cheerful. That day, 6 September, the Persian crisis reached a new depth, with the Stokes mission recalled in despair of reaching agreement.

Morrison's transatlantic tour covered thirteen thousand miles in twenty days. He went first to San Francisco for the formal signing of the Japanese Peace Treaty.* He was expected there earlier but due to his refusal to cut short his holiday, Kenneth Younger, the Minister of State, was dispatched at short notice to make the opening speech on Britain's behalf.[105] Morrison arrived on the Friday evening and next morning, immediately prior to the signing ceremony, he was introduced from the platform by the Conference President, Dean Acheson. After the ceremony he returned to his hotel and coming out of the lift met Stan Deacon, who had shared a dingy room with him above the shop where they worked together as shop assistants some forty-five years earlier. Deacon had emigrated to Canada and then moved to Oakland, California, where he was now chief accountant at an automobile factory. He had driven to San Francisco especially to see Morrison. 'Glad I could get along, Bert,' he said at the end of their chat together. 'It's been good to see you, Stan,' said Morrison, moving off to lunch with the United States Secretary of State.[106]

Next morning after breakfast he flew to Washington for talks with the Foreign Ministers of the Western Alliance. Germany was the main item on the agenda, though the Americans took the opportunity to press on Morrison

---

* The Japanese Treaty led Morrison to form a profound distrust of Foster Dulles, who he believed had double-crossed him over recognition of China by the new Japan. When Anthony Eden took over the Foreign Office in 1951 Morrison sent him a note warning him not to trust Dulles. (Interview, Earl Avon.)

a more conciliatory line towards Persia and Egypt. It was clear that there would be little transatlantic help if Britain decided to intervene militarily. He renewed contact with President Truman, then in residence at Blair House while the White House was being rescued from beetle and rot. At the end of his four-day visit he addressed the Washington Press Club and courageously defended Britain's decision to recognize communist China and to increase trade with the Soviet Union.[107] He then flew from Washington to join Hugh Gaitskell and Shinwell at the NATO talks in Ottawa. The proposed arrangements for handing over more sovereignty to Western Germany again dominated the agenda. Morrison was tired and struck the American Secretary of State Acheson as low in spirit, constantly carping at the recent developments towards European unity. 'There was nothing buoyant about Morrison,' recalled Acheson later. 'He could be counted on to deepen the gloom that surrounded our talks.' He told them that 'the United Kingdom was impatient with the irresponsibility of the Council of Europe and could not accept the Schuman Plan. So far, the political containment of the Soviet Union had been a success. He would not deny that. But it could go too far and precipitate world war. So far as Germany was concerned, he discerned a tendency to exploit the allies, to squeeze them into paying occupation expenses that Germans should carry.' Acheson added that 'Morrison's unfortunate manner constantly rasped our patience.'[108] Clearly much of the stuffing had been knocked out of him and there was now little trace of the jaunty Morrison who approached his job and problems with so much relish not long before.

On 19 September, three days before Morrison and Shinwell were to sail home from New York in the *Queen Mary*, Attlee informed a thin Cabinet that he proposed to dissolve and call a general election. Morrison did not hide his surprise and dismay from journalists in Ottawa, though he properly declined to make any public comment. Shinwell was apparently equally disturbed. Reports quickly appeared in the press that Attlee had reached the decision either without consulting his deputy prime minister or even against his explicit advice to the contrary.[109] In his *Autobiography* Morrison repeats the accusation of non-consultation, though allowing that Attlee did inform him of his intention to dissolve shortly before the announcement was made. Morrison and Shinwell agitatedly cabled to Attlee urging him to delay any announcement until they 'could return to discuss the matter'.[110] After what Dalton reported as 'a peevish exchange of telegrams across the Atlantic',[111] Attlee went ahead.

Morrison was clearly indignant, giving the impression that Attlee had deviously and without warning taken the opportunity of his absence to produce a *fait accompli*. It was a curious reaction, not easy to reconcile with certain evidence among his own papers. Of particular relevance is a letter from Attlee as early as 27 May informing Morrison that he proposed to hold the election in October. He felt that they should get it over before the King went to Australia in February:

Therefore I think that we ought to go to the country this year. The real decision is whether to go before or after the Autumn Recess. There are three factors militating against the earlier date. The Festival of Britain, Wakes Weeks and our own state of readiness and popularity. I gather that while our position is improving, it is not very good and the local elections confirm this. There is a good prospect of improved meat supplies and a possibility of better weather over the holidays. There may be a change in the Korean and Persian positions. Something may emerge from the Four Power talks. In my view everything points to having an election in the autumn and as early as possible having regard to the late harvest this year.

Late September and early October are best for our campaigning. The Party Conference falls awkwardly. It might be best to make our announcement in time for turning this into a short electoral Conference and a kick-off to the election campaign, but this will need careful thought. If my reasoning is sound we must consider carefully our tactics in the House and in the country.

I have set out these considerations with a view to an early talk with you. I would like to consider with you what other colleagues to bring into consultation.

Yours ever,
Clem.[112]

Attlee privately approached other ministers around the same time and most approved of an October election.[113] The economic situation was deteriorating. The strain of working with a tiny majority, dependent on the support of the rebellious Bevanites, was crushing the ageing administration.

Morrison saw Attlee about his letter of 27 May and suggested that a meeting of a few senior ministers should be called to discuss it. Nothing happened and he wrote to Attlee early in July proposing 'a meeting of a chosen few about it. Time is passing, as I said the other day and it is undesirable that the meeting should be further delayed.' Morrison then gave a hint that he might prefer to delay dissolution until 1952. He acknowledged the importance of Attlee's argument that the King must know either way before he went to Australia in February 1952, but added that 'for the sake of the country and the world, a victory for Labour is of prime importance. As you know, I was unhappy about the 1950 date as to which Stafford and Nye were wrong. I don't want us to make another mistake, though it is a very difficult thing to be sure about.'[114] Once again, as in 1949, he had doubts about proposals for an early election, but it could hardly be said that he was making a very firm stand for a later date. Certainly he could not claim not to have been warned well in advance of Attlee's intentions. A more justified complaint would have been that Attlee did not keep Morrison informed of his continuing intention to dissolve, as he informed Dalton and the King.[115] The consultations which Morrison proposed do not appear to have taken place and Attlee may well have deliberately avoided discussions with a colleague he suspected would take a different position. But he had no reason to be surprised when the dissolution came precisely as Attlee had originally proposed.

Morrison and Shinwell sailed from New York in the *Queen Mary* on 22 September. A state room in the great liner was converted into an office for their use. Morrison was able to rest and relax for a few days on the Atlantic, though his eye had begun to trouble him and it was examined daily by the ship's doctor and bathed night and morning by a nurse.[116] He again ran into protocol trouble with his advisers, who told him that he must give an official party for all the important people on board ship. Morrison at first resisted, disliking the whole idea, and pointing out that anyway their view of who were the important people might not coincide with his own. In the end a compromise was reached and two parties were arranged: one formal cocktail party for the 'important' people and one, more relaxed, for the secretaries, typists and other rank and file who had been working on the American trip.[117] One evening Morrison joined the dancers in the public ballroom. Among his partners was Betta St John, a beautiful American actress, travelling to England to take part in the musical *South Pacific*. Afterwards she reported that 'he is a good dancer and he was gay and lively all the evening, as if he hadn't a care in the world'.[118] While he was on the Atlantic, apparently carefree, the NEC of the Labour Party met in London and decided that the final draft of the election manifesto should be produced by Morgan Phillips, and that Bevan, Dalton and Sam Watson should help with revisions.[119] Not for over a quarter of a century had Morrison (who was still chairman of the Policy sub-committee of the NEC) been so far removed from a manifesto which Labour put before an electorate.

He landed at Southampton on the twenty-sixth and sped to London by Foreign Office car. He had three days of frenzied government business before leaving for the Labour Party conference at Scarborough. Persia, where the remaining British employees were now under threat of forcible expulsion, remained at the top of his agenda. At Cabinet on his first morning back in Whitehall, Attlee reported that President Truman had declined to offer support for any British military action at Abadan. The Prime Minister made it clear that he personally opposed such military action and preferred to work through the United Nations. Morrison then intervened to disagree, asserting that the United Nations was not a serious organization in this context. His Minister of State, who had turned up to the Cabinet in case Morrison was not back in time, was astounded to hear him argue that Britain should send in troops and that this could be done despite the lack of support from the United States. This junior minister had come along with a much less belligerent Foreign Office brief, and later was told that a senior Office adviser, whose interventionist line had been overruled, had privately 'got at' the Foreign Secretary since he landed at Southampton.[120] Shinwell, as Defence Minister, supported Morrison, though adding that the military would prefer to have the British civilians evacuated from Abadan first. Morrison and Shinwell received little support from ministerial colleagues. The Law Officers doubted the legality of force in these circumstances.[121] The Truman veto weighed heavily with several other ministers, coming at a time when Britain's dollar shortage was critical and American financial help was needed desperately. The Cabinet decided on a more pacific and international line, submission to the Security Council of the United Nations. This was done on 1 October, though the matter was then, as Morrison had feared, delayed, the relevant resolution emasculated, and the whole issue remained unresolved for the rest of Labour's term of office.

Morrison was losing on all fronts. To much of the press and public opinion he seemed to be weak, selling out Britain's oil interests to the despised 'wogs'. In Cabinet he was almost alone in support of military intervention, earning disapproval as a 'poor man's Palmerston'. During his prolonged absences in recent weeks, political direction of foreign policy had increasingly been taken by Attlee. Attlee told Dalton on 16 September: 'I am handling Persia. I have made it quite clear that troops are to go in only to save lives.'[122] Morrison, however, was certain to be blamed when things went wrong.

Labour's three-day conference at Scarborough was meant to be a great rally of the faithful before the election. It did not succeed as such. The Persian threat abroad, the economic crisis at home, the Bevanite disaffection within the party – the clouds were gathering ominously. Morrison reached Scarborough on 30 September to address the eve-of-conference rally. With him were a group of Foreign Office officials. A scrambler telephone was installed in his room and he kept frequent contact with Whitehall. 'He seems too busy for lobby gossip' complained one correspondent.[123] During Alice Bacon's address next morning a black box was handed to Morrison sitting on the platform and he studied the official papers in it before passing the box back to his secretary. Morrison concentrated on Persia in his eve-of-conference speech, denouncing 'the semi-hysteria of the Tory back-benchers in the House of Commons. . . . We had to stand up for legitimate British rights; we must at the same time keep our heads. In these circumstances let me tell you with all sincerity that I tremble for the cause of peace if the Conservative temperament and warlike excitability were predominant in Parliament.'[124] Next day the Foreign Office announced that all Abadan staff were being withdrawn, under the threats of forcible expulsion by the Persians. Morrison was immediately subject to a massive attack for capitulation by Churchill at Liverpool.[125]

The NEC elections reflected the success of the Bevanites with the party activists who influenced the votes for the constituency section. Bevan extended his lead at the top of the list. Barbara Castle shot into second place. Driberg and Mikardo showed large gains in third and sixth place. Morrison's vote fell by 76,000 and he slipped from third to fifth out of seven. Griffiths and Dalton lost even more votes, and Shinwell was pushed off the NEC. Shinwell walked out of the conference in anger and left Scarborough, despite Morrison's pleas for him to stay.[126]

Conference closed on 3 October with a major speech by Morrison and a final uninspiring appeal for electoral unity by Attlee. Morrison's performance was praised even by his political enemies.[127] He sat up half the previous night rewriting, after getting details of Churchill's Liverpool speech late on the Tuesday evening.[128] He defended the withdrawal of the refinery staff and asked Churchill bluntly to tell the British people whether he was personally willing to go to war over Abadan. 'As long as I am Foreign Secretary,' he declaimed, possibly to the astonishment of his colleagues who had been present in Cabinet only a week earlier, 'I will not be . . . party to a war which is not necessary and can possibly be avoided. I do not accuse the average Conservative of being a war-monger and thirsting for the shedding of blood. . . . I do not say that and I advise you not to say that, because it would not be fair and would not be true. But it is their temperament; it is the background of their mental outlook, this old imperialist outlook . . . if the country wants peace it had better vote for the people who can be most surely relied upon to preserve peace.'[129] The audience rose and cheered him. It was the last time he was to hear them cheer him as a minister.

Morrison returned directly to London for the prorogation of Parliament on the fourth. That day the first of the refinery staff flew in from Persia. The press was full of allegations that the oilmen felt bitter against Morrison for humiliating them, that they did not wish to leave Abadan, and that Morrison had fallen for Mossadeq's bluff. All, apparently, were going to vote Tory in protest.[130] The General Manager of the Abadan refinery immediately published his 'story of defeat and humiliation'. He blamed Morrison and the government for bungling the whole affair, for basing its policy on the assumption that Mossadeq could be toppled from office by one imperial puff of British power, and failing to appreciate his enormous popularity in Persia.[131] It was 'foolish to rattle a sabre one knows one cannot use', commented the *Observer*, 'our fault was not excessive meekness but empty bullying. . . . Mr Morrison is rightly blamed for his disastrous mishandling of the Persian oil crisis.'[132] The *Sunday Times* compared the Abadan débâcle to Munich, describing it as 'the worst defeat suffered by Great Britain during the present century in the field of foreign affairs'.[133] Some of the press hostility can be explained away in terms of a systematic attempt to discredit the Labour government before the general election. Some derives from the failure of many political commentators, especially those on the right, even as late as 1951, to grasp the true strength of nationalism in the under-developed countries and the irrecoverable decline in Britain's imperial power. It was no longer possible to send in a gunboat and troops to protect Britain's economic interests and restore order among the restless natives. Britain and France, the old imperial powers, were doomed to suffer in the 1950s a succession of humiliations from rampant nationalism in the Middle East and elsewhere. In due course informed opinion appreciated that withdrawal should not always be mourned as national humiliation. In 1951 many lacked the vision to appreciate the broad flow of world events. Even with these failings of bias and perception, however, commentators were not guilty of grave injustice in criticizing Morrison. His approach to the Persian issue was confused and shared some of their own weaknesses. He appreciated the sources of nationalism among the poorer peoples and genuinely denounced exploitation of them by imperialist economic interests. Yet his own reaction when British interests were at stake was primitive and lacking in subtlety. While attacking the Tories in public for their warlike and imperialist temperament, he privately advocated the use of force. In reality, with the Prime Minister, his leading colleagues, and the United States opposed to force, there was little prospect of military intervention, yet the alternatives through negotiation were progressively closed. In the end Britain's policy towards Persia was reduced to the assumption that Mossadeq was bluffing and would capitulate, or be overthrown, before a threat of force. But Britain's threat itself was mere bluff, and Mossadeq called it.

For Morrison it can be said in mitigation that the Persian crisis was in no way of his making and that it was, by now at least, insoluble. The battle had already been lost by the Anglo-Iranian Oil Company, which should have made a fairer deal with the Persians at an earlier stage. The Company's officials lacked political perception, allowed a major crisis to develop, and then left the government to pick up the pieces. The Foreign Office under Bevin's slackening grip had (as with the Egyptian problem) been slow to act. When the final crisis had broken, shortly after Morrison took over, a senior member of the Royal Family is reported to have written to him, suggesting that Britain should react swiftly by welcoming nationalization and sending out a mission to co-operate in making it work. Morrison, however, was then absorbed in the Bevanite crisis and appears not even to have raised the point with the relevant Cabinet committee.[134] By the summer certainly nothing could be done. The only alternatives then open were force, independent arbitration from the United Nations and the International Court, or total capitulation. Morrison certainly was in a minority, along with Shinwell, Alexander and Jowitt, who inclined to using troops. The majority were sensibly against this desperate course, but had no enthusiasm for the other alternatives. Eventually they resorted to the Hague Court and the United Nations, but it is not clear that these were other than political disguises for capitulation. Both these institutions were at early stages of their development. From an internationalist viewpoint it was helpful and worthy that such a major power as Britain should use them rather than resort to force. But Morrison's impatient argument that they would produce no practical solution on this issue to Britain's benefit was unanswerable then and proven in due course.

Looking back at the Persian débâcle it is difficult to escape the conclusion that Morrison lacked both judgment and control in his conduct of policy.[135] Allowances must be made for the almost insoluble complexities of the problem, and the difficulties of policy-making in the last months of an old and collapsing administration. Even so, Morrison in his prime would have done better. He would certainly have failed with more style and better grace.

Morrison was scheduled to begin his election campaign in the second week of October, but the Middle Eastern crisis, with attention now switching to Egypt, interrupted his plans. He had sent a message to the Egyptians on 6 October promising that new British proposals would be ready by the tenth. The Egyptians did not want more negotiations towards any compromise settlement and on the eighth they presented a bill to abrogate the 1936 Treaty; it was passed on the fifteenth. They were also planning to annex the Sudan.[136] Morrison had held his opening campaign meeting in his Lewisham constituency on the eighth. He now cancelled all but two evening meetings in the next six days and retired to the Foreign Office with his officials and the military Chiefs of Staff.[137] They decided as a conciliatory gesture to invite the Egyptians to join with Britain, America, France and Turkey in the new Middle Eastern military command then under discussion. Egypt was also warned not to allow violence against British persons and property and that Britain intended to keep a military presence in the Suez zone until a new Treaty was negotiated. Egypt rejected Britain's proposals out of hand on the fifteenth.[138] Morrison, who had resumed electioneering by then, told meetings at Acton and next day at Lewisham how much he deplored the Egyptian intransigence and that he would send more troops to support his firm line.[139]

He tried to prevent relations with Egypt being made even more tense by opposing the savage characterizations of the portly and amorous King Farouk then current in the British press. After one particularly unflattering sketch by the cartoonist Giles in the *Daily Express*, Morrison wrote direct to Beaverbrook to complain: 'As you know, it is hard enough to maintain sanity in Anglo-Egyptian relations and I am afraid that the Ambassador is right in thinking these attacks a special irritant.' He urged Beaverbrook 'to discourage the newspapers under your control from making King Farouk personally the butt of their criticism and humour. . . . I am, of course, solely concerned with the public interest and write to you in the spirit of one Privy Councillor to another.' Beaverbrook's delicious answer put poor Morrison lightly but firmly in his place. 'I am always happy to have a letter from you,' he replied, 'because it brings back to my mind the days when we exchanged letters on a more intimate basis than of one Privy Councillor to another. They were, for me, agreeable days indeed, even if we did not always speak with respect about the heads of foreign states. . . . It seems to me that King Farouk, an able and vigorous young man, not long ago married to an innocent and beautiful bride, takes an active part in international affairs and is, therefore, a legitimate target. . . .' Morrison was not to be deterred and wrote again to ask Beaverbrook to reconsider his attitude towards Farouk.[140] He also complained to the *Daily Herald* about a Low cartoon.[141] It is curious that he – so long a master at handling the British press, by the delicate process of slipping working journalists titbits of news wrapped up with items helpful to himself – should now try suppression through a heavy approach to proprietors. He was losing his touch.

Morrison eventually extricated himself sufficiently from the Middle Eastern morass to begin electioneering properly during the final eight days of the campaign, though he never made the effort or the impact of the previous two post-war elections. His earlier influence at Transport House campaign headquarters had now been completely whittled away by Morgan Phillips. He toured Lancashire, his only expedition outside the London area, on the last weekend before polling day, visiting Manchester, Preston and Bolton. He was still a draw for Labour crowds: seven thousand filled the King's Hall, Belle Vue, and thousands of others overflowed outside.[142] But there was an ominous lack of enthusiasm from the rank and file. The Tory supporters were more optimistic and extrovert; they vigorously heckled his meetings on the last three days back in London. In his constituency on Tuesday evening, after a very rough ride at Wembley the night before, he appealed for more tolerance. 'I have already spoken twice,' he pointed out, 'and I hope you will give me a fair hearing because I have to go home and work for some hours on Foreign Office papers in the interests of the country.'[143] He seemed tired and without some of his usual buoyancy – 'he was perhaps a little less cocksure than usual'.[144] The responsibility of the Foreign Office almost visibly weighed on his shoulders. He took his big black dispatch box to meetings and set it down wearily next to the water on the rostrum. He also had a scrambler telephone installed in the back room of his Lewisham party headquarters for rapid contact with his officials.[145] He slept at the Foreign Office; Margaret was in the South of France recuperating from what the press called her 'operation for duodenal ulcer'. Apart from a few public meetings he did virtually no personal canvassing in his constituency. He relied on his seven thousand majority and the organizing genius of Mabel Raisin, who had nearly doubled the local membership in the past two years, winning the London Labour Party Membership Trophy in both 1949 and 1950.[146]

When the result was declared at Lewisham Town Hall on Thursday night, 25 October, there were repetitions of the disorderly scenes of the previous year. Morrison had slightly increased his majority. He stepped forward to the microphone to propose a vote of thanks to the returning officer, but his voice was drowned by booing and shouting from local Tories and communists. He stood back, folding his arms and sucking his pipe angrily, until shouts of 'We want Herbert' brought him back to the microphone. Again, his opponents drowned his words, so that he refused to continue and left the communist candidate (who had lost his deposit) to move the thanks.[147]

The next day it was clear that Labour was out of office. It was no landslide. In fact, Labour polled a quarter of a million more votes than their opponents, but there was an average swing of 1·1 per cent to the Conservatives, who won twenty-one seats, giving them a narrow but adequate majority of seventeen. The working-class strongholds remained loyal, but suburbia, especially in the south, continued to return to its Conservative loyalties. Former Liberals, now with fewer candidates to support, were believed to have swung right despite Morrison's repeated attempts to woo them.*

Morrison left the Foreign Office, his last ministerial post, under a cloud of failure, which blotted out for many his great record of achievement in County Hall, Whitehall and Westminster throughout the years since 1934. When he took over from Bevin in March – 'the born manager' replacing the 'Corsican concept of public business'[148] – most commentators welcomed the change and the press was almost universally generous and optimistic. Seven months later he was unanimously written off as a failure. Attlee confided that had Labour won the election he would not have sent Morrison back to foreign affairs.[149] The most that can be said in mitigation is that he was Foreign Secretary for only a very short time, and during that period he was very unlucky with the succession of crises which struck British policy. Abadan, Egypt, Burgess and Maclean – each was really a situation inherited from Bevin. Morrison reaped the whirlwind. His Conservative counterpart, the most distinguished British Foreign Secretary of that generation, generously but firmly assessed Morrison as being in no way miscast in the job but simply 'desperately unlucky' to take over for a brief and difficult period in a collapsing and accident-prone government.[150] But the reality was failure. How can this dismal finale be explained?

Advancing years inevitably played a part. He seemed less agile mentally and to have lost some of his earlier uncanny political flair and judgment. He mishandled his House of Commons business in 1951 in a way that would have been unthinkable a few years earlier. On policy he was less clear about desirable alternatives, with less feel for the practical solution which he used rapidly to sense at the heart of the most complex issues. He allowed himself to get isolated in the Cabinet. Perhaps he was getting out of touch with the feelings of his younger colleagues: he remarked to Arthur Moyle,† around this time that he had never properly understood the post-war parliamentary party.[151]

* See his speeches at Tain, 6 June 1950; Manchester, 1 July 1950; Durham, 15 July 1950; and his election article in the *Star*, 23 October 1951. Morrison had also been engaged in discussions for a Lib.-Lab. alliance since the spring of 1951, dealing with Edgar Granville, Tom Reid and his old friend, Megan Lloyd George, the Liberal deputy leader. Desultory negotiations for an election deal in the constituencies continued until the opening of the election campaign, but nothing concrete was achieved. Megan Lloyd George finally switched to the Labour Party in April 1955. Dalton diary, 15 March, 15 July, 21 September 1951, Vols 39, 41 and 42.

† PPS to Attlee.

Age then was almost certainly a factor. Yet it is too easy to look at a man growing old, analyse his failure in a job, and decide that the one adequately explains the other. In Morrison's case the coincidence of failure with his term at the Foreign Office is too precise. There were certainly other explanations. One frequently canvassed is his alleged 'insularity', that he knew nothing of the world beyond London. In any literal sense, this accusation does not stand up to examination. Morrison had travelled widely and for many years he was one of the party's major spokesmen on international questions. His obsession with the communist menace may have stemmed from parochial animosity at their subversive activities in the London Labour Party, but it led him to follow closely the movements of international communism, the policies of the Soviet Union, and the plight of social democracies threatened by this menace (as by the fascist menace) overseas. His weakness was not any irremediable ignorance of international politics. Nor did it really matter that his geography and foreign pronunciations were sometimes astray: Bevin showed that eccentricity and was loved the more for it. Morrison's deficiency was less tangible. He gave the impression that he lacked any international sense, that his otherwise superb antennae were simply not tuned to the broader movements of history and destinies of nations. Whereas Bevin could see the great themes, he seemed to get bogged down in political minutiae. It would be too harsh to conclude that Morrison was just a municipal politician – 'an excellent Lord Mayor in a vintage year', to modify a description used deprecatingly about Neville Chamberlain. But he did not easily think internationally, and was not basically interested in foreigners or things foreign for their own sake. His later attachment to Norway, Sweden and Israel was mainly because they were successful examples of his kind of political and social democracy.

Advancing years seemed also to cause a distinct narrowing of his political vision, an increasingly conservative outlook which was particularly unfortunate for the Foreign Minister of a democratic socialist government in the post-war world. His instinct now too often coincided with those on the Tory benches opposite. He grew increasingly attached to long-standing British institutions, such as the monarchy and Empire, and revered them in an almost Kiplingesque way. He had always been a patriot in the best sense. Now he became something of a little-England jingo. Within twenty-four hours of taking office he asked for a life of Palmerston, and ostentatiously carried Guedalla's volume around with him for weeks afterwards.[152] He had no real interest in the new developing nations: the African and Asian continents barely entered his view of the world. He maintained an unwavering antipathy towards communism in all its manifestations, understandable in the circumstances of 1951, but over the longer run much too constrictive for the creative conduct of Britain's foreign policy. He therefore faced the two most dynamic, if often unsavoury, forces in international affairs from a position of either lack of interest or positive hostility. His irritation with the United Nations and with the Council of Europe arose partly and understandably because he saw them as impractical talking-shops, but it was sharpened by a lack of sympathy with their supra-nationalism. He strongly disliked certain UN agencies, and especially UNESCO, which he quite rightly criticized as being flagrantly wasteful of public money, but also because he was sadly less and less interested in its international-cultural aims. He even attacked the International Labour Organization, resenting the idea of civil servants living abroad and, as he saw it, doing little worthwhile work in return for large tax-free salaries. In Cabinet he argued for withdrawing financial support from the International Labour Organization, thereby nearly precipitating the final Bevin heart attack.[153] At home he grew ever more impatient of liberal opinion and even contemptuous of those he saw as 'namby-pamby do-gooders'. Perhaps he really was trying to live down his Letchworth past. He certainly could not bear to have admirals and generals, and especially Winston, accuse him of scuttling.

More tangible causes of Morrison's failure were his frequent diversions away from foreign affairs and his inability to adjust his ministerial methods to the particular needs of the Foreign Office. The diversions have been documented in the narrative above. The Bevanite crisis, the Festival of Britain, his long holiday in Scandinavia, the election pressures, all absorbed his time and attention away from Whitehall. Even his brief trip to Strasbourg in August and his three-week visit to North America in September, though on vital Foreign Office business, diverted him from the Middle Eastern crisis, where his reputation was being destroyed. Only for three months, in May, June and July could he be said to have concentrated on foreign affairs with no more than normal diversions. 'The Foreign Office,' as one of his junior ministers observed, 'was too big for a half-time minister.'[154]

The oddest feature of Morrison's tenure of the Foreign Office was his failure to master and to win the respect of his department. Officials at his previous posts were unanimous in their praise of him as a departmental minister. At the Ministry of Transport, the Home Office and the Lord President's Office he was viewed as the civil servant's ideal boss. The same qualities were recalled again and again: diligence in reading his papers, willingness to listen to his officials' advice, speed and good judgment in reaching decisions, great skill in defending and advancing the departmental position in committee, in Cabinet and in the Commons. The Foreign Office was different. He never really got on top of the job there and his officials did not hold him in high regard. For his part, many aspects of protocol and routine working at the Foreign Office irritated him. He thought the lack of delegation of authority and the assumption that the Foreign Secretary should see and respond to virtually all telegrams were wasteful of an important and busy minister's time. He resented intensely the practice of the night duty officer ringing him up at any late hour to say yes or no to some routine telegram. He argued that subordinates left in charge should be familiar with official policy and should apply it accordingly. He swore that he would revolutionize the system of delegating duties, but he never found time.[155]

He did not find his officials personally congenial. The breed of smooth men working at the Foreign Office brought out his sense of educational inferiority and put him ill at ease, especially when he had no hard policy successes to boost his confidence in compensation. He believed that they were snobs; and they believed that he was over-sensitive, coming to the Foreign Office with preconceived ideas about them.[156] Perhaps as a reflection of this, he handled ambassadors in a casual and off-hand way. He often received them – and kept them waiting – in his room at the House of Commons, leaving the unfortunate but not misleading impression that his prime loyalty and interest lay there rather than with the Office.[157] His relations with his private staff were never quite satisfactory. It was probably a mistake to take over Bevin's private secretary and towards the end there were behind-the-scenes moves to get changes.[158] It was not, however, simply a question of incompatible personalities. Morrison had grown accustomed to his own very personal method of operating a department. He liked to work closely with a small team and to have familiar faces around him. Maxwell, Pimlott, Johnstone, Nicholson, Downes, Leslie, Boon, Gordon Walker, Shackleton – for most of his ministerial life in the 1940s Morrison was leaning on a few men; each knew how to get the best out of one another. At the Foreign Office official policy meetings were larger and impersonal. He never had the time, or the will, to select and weld together another small personal team from among them: perhaps the Foreign Office is not amenable to such an approach. He tried to take part of his previous team with him, urging Nicholson to move across. Nicholson talked to Strang at the Foreign Office, but sensed that there was no chance of re-creating the former intimacy and informality and decided not to go. He was surprised that Morrison appeared not to realize fully how different life was going to be there.[159] At the Home Office and at the Lord President's Office, when Morrison had a major speech to give, his inner circle would meet some days or even weeks ahead to discuss a suitable theme. One of them would then produce a draft, and after further discussions and amendments with Morrison adding his own touches, a final version would emerge which was completely 'Morrisonian' in style: lively, factual, but humorous. At the Foreign Office his speeches were written for him by officials with no sense of, or concern for, his personal style. Addressing the Commons his speeches, therefore, sounded and read like departmental memoranda – which indeed they were, turgid and lifeless.

Foreign Secretaries must adhere to carefully constructed texts in order to avoid diplomatic gaffes and at this time they tried to adopt a bi-partisan approach. The Foreign Office serves all its ministers with deathless prose and unless particular care is taken to rewrite and revivify their speeches, Foreign Secretaries do tend to bore the Commons. Morrison lacked the time, energy, commitment and knowledge of the subject to do something to liven up and impose a personal stamp on his speeches. Perhaps his brain had deteriorated, disguised till now by his earlier speech-writing team. More certainly he was hindered by not having himself properly mastered his subject and so not being absolutely clear in his own mind. The House of Commons and the press quickly sensed this uncertainty and were surprised as well as bored by the poor quality of his speeches. 'He knew it, lost confidence and lost the mastery of the House.'[160]

The Foreign Office, perhaps understandably, never really took to Morrison and so they lacked the enthusiasm to remedy his deficiencies and try to make him more of a success. His officials were irritated from the very first day, when he summoned them and delivered the standard Morrison lecture on how civil servants and ministers should work together. They also resented his casual and part-time approach to their work. Bevin was their hero and for many years Bevin had left them in no doubt that Morrison was no good. They were quick, perhaps too quick, to see any confirmation that Bevin was right and that his successor was inferior. Morrison struck them as slower to take decisions: 'he wrote a lot of comments in the margin, but no decision. With Bevin you just got a simple yes to one alternative and no to the others.'[161] This may have been part of Morrison's method of involving the department in a dialogue with its minister. The Foreign Office did not want a dialogue; they wanted rapid decisions. His dilatory approach also certainly reflected his unfamiliarity with the subject matter and his inability to cope with the enormous volume of paper-work that flowed before him. He often complained to his private secretary that he was putting too much work in his night box and told him to cut it down.[162] His one eye suffered strain under the burden. He was forced to ask his personal staff to summarize relevant papers for him and to use wider type-spacing.[163] For the first time in his life Morrison was unable to do his homework properly – which was why he became so dependent on his departmental briefs.

Another of Bevin's alleged virtues, which Morrison lacked, was that he shared the Foreign Office's impatience and even distaste for Parliament. Morrison loved the House of Commons and was always looking over his shoulder to assess how MPs would react to some aspect of foreign policy. At times, he upset his officials by seeming more concerned with approval from the Commons and the press than with what was right. 'Bevin took perhaps too little interest in the House of Commons,' commented Sir Roderick Barclay, private secretary to each of Labour's Foreign Secretaries, 'Morrison took too much.'[164]

For these various reasons, one of the best British departmental ministers of the twentieth century and a very high-calibre departmental machine simply did not mesh. It is arguable that, given more time and application, Morrison would have mastered this job as he had mastered Transport, the LCC, the Home Office and the Lord President's Office before. A number of close associates while he was at the Foreign Office were convinced that in time 'he could have worked it up'.[165] Certainly, there is no rational reason to believe that a man of his previous experience and continuing ability and common sense, with the full support of a distinguished department of state, could not have emerged with a record of at least average competence. The problem was that his appetite for work was declining and he was simply getting more and more exhausted. This would probably have limited the extent to which he would, even with more time and in more favourable circumstances, have 'worked it up'. Beyond that, however, it is difficult to escape the conclusion that Morrison lacked the supreme qualities of vision and style, as well as luck, necessary to succeed as Britain's Foreign Secretary in 1951.

Chapter 37

Recriminations and More Defeats, 1951-1953

Labour was in full opposition for the first time since September 1939 and Morrison out of high public office for the first time in seventeen years. The experiences of 1951, with failure at the Foreign Office and the setback at the general election, had seriously damaged his political career. Where 1947 had halted its triumphant upward momentum, 1951 set it into reverse. Morrison was never fully to recover. The next four years, in his eyes at least, finally turned to ashes a lifetime's political achievements and hopes. His private life also slumped into even deeper gloom, though this at least was later to recover a gleam of happiness.

Defeat and loss of government office is an unpleasant personal trauma for most politicians. Deep down is the wound of public rejection. A multitude of material comforts which have come to be taken for granted also disappear overnight: the chauffeured saloon available at any hour, the highly efficient office with many unseen hands organizing the minister's life, removing the irritations of how to travel, where to eat, whom to see. Suddenly there is nobody thinking ahead on his behalf, to smooth out difficulties before they arise. Nobody, except his long neglected family, is there to bolster him when his spirits are low. People do not automatically spring to attention when he enters a room or visits a town. He queues for meals and drinks and travels on buses or tube trains again. He has to prepare his own speeches, reply to his own letters and pay out of his own pocket for secretarial help. Cinderella-like, the beautiful trappings disappear at a stroke and the ex-minister becomes a very ordinary mortal again.

Morrison was inevitably hurt by the pace and pain of the change in his life-style, though he was not demoralized as some in that position are. He mainly missed the work, the responsibility of government, the simple exercise of power. His vanity, growing with the years, was also wounded at no longer being so important. For some time after November 1951 he continued to carry around his old red official boxes, as if physically holding on to the last remnants of former glories. The material deprivations hurt him less. His salary dropped from five thousand pounds to one thousand, but he had never become incorrigibly extravagant and he could get by on very little. His earnings were anyway supplemented from broadcasting and journalism though his hopes of joining the *Daily Mirror* as a highly-paid editorial consultant were dashed just before Christmas when his old friend Bartholomew was removed from the chairmanship in a coup led by Cecil King. Public transport or eating cheaply were no strange imposition since even when in office he had frequently preferred to travel from Westminster by tube or had slipped out for fish and chips. He was forced to make greater use of his private car, which was a burden – and a constant threat to other road-users. His sense of direction was not good and he had no mechanical flair at all. Once in winter he complained to a friend that he was having difficulty starting his car in the cold mornings. The friend advised him to cover up the engine at night with a blanket. Next day he came to complain that when he started the car that morning pieces of wool were flying out from under the bonnet.[1] Apart from such minor inconveniences however, he was able to adjust. The change even had compensations. He was able to spend more time at home with his wife. He enjoyed the unfamiliar pleasure of lying in bed regularly on Sunday mornings reading the newspapers. In the week he sometimes left the Commons early to go home to listen to the radio: his taste was still for light music or thrillers. He and Margaret went more often together to the local cinema. 'We pay 2/1d for the seats,' he reported, 'and my wife sees we time it so that we don't have to queue.'[2]

Others who had worked close to Morrison were affected by the change in his life. Miss Donald shifted out of Whitehall back to the Palace of Westminster to run his affairs with the same devoted efficiency. Puck Boon, his loyal public relations adviser since the start of the Labour Government, was now out of a job and Morrison arranged with the *Daily Mirror* to take him on[3] – a kind personal gesture which also gave him another useful contact at the most influential pro-Labour newspaper. His personal detective, Alex Black from Newtonmore in Scotland, who observed and later remembered his minister's activities with shrewd perception, was moved on to other pastures by Scotland Yard. 'I came to respect and admire him and would have done anything for him,' recalled Black.[4] Morrison in turn remained friendly towards his former assistants and was always happy to see Black or Boon for a drink at the Commons in the years ahead.

Morrison's engagement diary now looked a little less forbiddingly black. He still attended official functions and travelled to address meetings – to Norwich in March 1952, to Denmark as guest of the Danish Socialist Party in June, to Cumberland and to Scotland twice in the high summer – but his programme was much less taxing than when in office. Shortly before Christmas 1951 he went to the palace to receive the insignia of the Order of the Companions of Honour.[5] Among less select, but more comfortable and appropriate company, he also at this time attended the closing ceremony of the pleasure gardens in Battersea Park. It was a misty autumn evening and a crowd of over sixty thousand packed the fair, taking the total attendance over the eight million mark. Bands played, the crowd joined in community singing, green and pink flares lit up the lake and rockets burst in the sky above to signal the end. Morrison could feel proud. Despite all the attacks and denigration from his political opponents, the Festival and the fair had success-fully met his objectives – to give pleasure to the ordinary people of Britain after the long years of war and austerity. The crowds present at the closing cheered him in affectionate gratitude. 'You must simply believe me,' recalled one witness, 'I have never seen so spontaneous a demonstration for a poli-tician.'[6] That night he urged the Tory government to continue the pleasure gardens in future summers. 'I believe the gardens have contributed to the happiness and joy of life for our people.'[7] The government conceded. 'Out of our love for you we are going to do what you wish,' wrote Churchill gener-ously, and then with a sting in the tail added ' – also try to to get a little of the money back that was wasted.'[8]

Morrison's political activity was now concentrated in the parliamentary party and the National Executive. He still regularly attended the NEC, was chairman of the Policy and Publicity committee and the new Financial and Economic Policy committee, and continued on the Elections committee. On the Policy committee he was soon engaged in preparing a draft policy state-ment to put before conference, and continued to chair the special committee reviewing the nationalized industries.[9]

He was re-elected deputy leader on 1 November. Emrys Hughes attempted to nominate Bevan against him but the rebel leader, biding his time, declined to stand.[10] In the parliamentary committee he took the foreign policy portfolio and was the Shadow Cabinet's representative to the party foreign affairs group. He was, if anything, even less happy with the job in opposition than in office. His only serious parliamentary intervention before the Christmas recess was in the big two-day foreign affairs debate and he was not impressive, simply agreeing with most of what Eden had said before him. He fared even worse against Churchill in late February 1952. 'Herbert Morrison spoke for an hour so badly that people shuffled and groaned,' wrote Nigel Nicolson to his father. 'It made a deplorable effect, and Winston's case was won before he got up.'[11] The constraints of a bi-partisan policy are never helpful to any opposition spokesman on foreign policy and this disadvantage was com-pounded by the continuing lack of sparkle or authority in Morrison's pro-nouncements. 'Mr Morrison has suddenly lost his old position,' commented the *Observer* with apparently sincere regret after the February debate. 'What does he do – quickly retire from foreign affairs with the loss of prestige? Continue as he is and hope for the best? Last week's debate is an unmistakable warning.'[12] Morrison was not unaware of the danger. Stanley Evans urged him to move over to the home policy front where his touch was more sure, and Morrison agreed but felt it would not be seemly to do it straight away.[13]

Hugh Gaitskell pressed similar advice in the spring and summer of 1952.[14] He was not formally moved until after the 1955 election, but in practice he quickly began to disengage from the foreign affairs field. He left Younger to carry much of the day-to-day burden in the Commons and Robens was sent to lead the British delegation to the Council of Europe.[15] Morrison looked for a chance to move back into familiar domestic territory. The government's proposed increase in London bus fares was a made-to-measure opportunity and he grasped it with both hands. 'He was back on his wicket and he dominated the House,' reported a colleague, who afterwards quipped to Morrison's annoyance that he should draw the conclusion – 'Leave foreign affairs and stick to bus fares.'[16] The government's White Paper on the denationalization of road transport in May 1952 gave him a further opportunity to re-establish some of his former parliamentary prestige. He led the Labour opposition to it and attracted comment on his restored vigour and revived skill.[17] He was chairman of a special joint committee of the PLP and the TUC, set up to campaign against the Transport Bill.[18] He broke his summer holiday on the Isle of Wight to address the TUC rally against the bill at Margate in August,[19] and also addressed regional trade union conferences on the same theme in September.[20] By the autumn of 1952 another White Paper, foreshadowing the denationalization of steel, gave him further opportunities to refurbish his image in policy areas where his knowledge and judgment were still unsurpassed in the party. By then however, the central question in the Labour Party did not concern the ability and success of its shadow ministers. Labour politics were dominated by the rebellion against the established leadership of the party, by Bevan and his supporters, fighting to change its policies, domestic and international, and ultimately to make Bevan the next leader.

Morrison was inescapably in the middle of this political warfare, as both the architect of many of the current policies and the heir-apparent to Attlee. He had become, since Bevin's death and his own commitment to 'consolidation', the main *bête noire* of the left. He frequently clashed bitterly with Bevan and now deeply disliked him. Once he was sitting on the terrace of the House of Commons dictating to a secretary when Bevan came by and Morrison said to the young lady, 'don't ever trust that man, he is wicked'.[21]

The Bevanite rebellion was already in full swing by early March 1952, when they mustered fifty-seven votes for their motion to reject outright the Conservative defence policy.[22] The Shadow Cabinet reacted by recommending the PLP to reimpose standing orders. Morrison took a leading role in the reimposition, as he had in their suspension six years earlier. There was now no point in relying on 'the good sense and good fellowship' of the party: each commodity was in very short supply. The Bevanites tried to resist the move back to stricter discipline by proposing a delay at the party meeting, but Morrison leaped in to bring the middle-of-the-road men behind the hard line.[23]

The Bevanite problem was too deep to be solved by a superficial change in the disciplinary rules. The party was suffering a civil war that involved people and emotions at all levels. The disasters and consequent demoralization of the last months in office had spread disenchantment. The existing leadership was old and discredited by failure. The disaffected on the left, having acquired a leader with ability, prestige and charisma, saw the opportunity for change. They built up support in the parliamentary party and also campaigned in the constituencies, addressing and organizing activists, and using *Tribune* as their main propaganda vehicle. Their immediate political target was to win control of the constituency section of the National Executive Committee. The annual conference at Morecambe at the end of September was the first test of their battle strength.

Morrison went to Morecambe knowing that the Bevanite ticket would certainly make big gains and he might even be knocked off the Executive. Since midsummer the press had carried depressing predictions of the extent of the Bevanite success in the constituencies.[24] There were already rumours that Morrison assumed defeat in advance and would stand against Greenwood for the treasurership, with trade union support, as a way of re-establishing himself on the NEC.[25]

Morrison spent some of his first day walking alone back and forward along the blustery promenade.[26] The weather was cold, wet and windy for most of his time there. Morecambe was not an ideal location. Accommodation was dispersed and not always very good, adding to the prevailing bad temper of delegates.[27] The conference hall was too small and ill lit. It was packed to hear the votes for the constituency section early in the morning session of 30 September. Morrison sat with the outgoing Executive at a long table on the stage. Aneurin Bevan again came top of the list, increasing his vote by over 100,000. Mrs Castle, Tom Driberg and Ian Mikardo all strengthened their positions and two of their political associates, Harold Wilson and Richard Crossman, won seats on the NEC for the first time. The Bevanites, who had carefully organized and concentrated their votes, had six out of the seven winning places. The only successful non-Bevanite was James Griffiths, in fourth place. Morrison was defeated, coming eighth with 580,000, forty thousand below Crossman, though well ahead of Dalton who also lost his place. He had held his vote remarkably well: it declined by only eleven thousand compared with 1951 and in most other years it would have secured comfortable re-election.* Defeat also meant his losing the chairmanship of the key Policy sub-committee of the NEC.† He showed no sign of emotion at this hammer blow, taking it right on the chin, just sucking his unlit pipe and doodling on his agenda paper.[28] His opportunity to reply came that afternoon when he wound up the debate on party policy on behalf of the old

---

* In 1948 Morrison came fourth with 580,000 votes.

† He was replaced by James Griffiths. Harold Wilson replaced him as chairman of the Financial and Economic Policy sub-committee.

NEC. As he rose the conference hall erupted into thunderous applause which went on for several minutes. Morrison, obviously moved, responded on absolutely the right note. He disposed of the underlying emotional issue with great dignity in his three opening sentences, which made many in the packed hall feel more than a little ashamed of what they had done to him. He quietly thanked them for their reception, 'which I know conveys a message. Let me assure you that, whatever may have been announced this morning, I shall continue, with all sincerity and loyalty, my work for the Labour Party and Socialism, my work in loyal co-operation with Clement Attlee as Deputy Leader of the Labour Party, and I will do all I can to help our cause. I will allow no bitterness to poison my soul.' Then he moved on to defend the official party policy, on the way warning against the easy temptations of Utopian dreams. He ranged over the whole policy field, analysed the problems of the nationalized industries, denounced cheap anti-Americanism, and stressed that much more remained for a reforming party to do in Britain.[29] He sat down to prolonged cheering and applause. Apart from his loyal constituency supporters, many of those now applauding were trade unionists who had no opportunity to vote for the constituency section but wanted Morrison to know that they were with him. Others may have voted against but still wanted to express appreciation for a life's work in the party. The message which Morrison received was certainly one of immense sympathy, reflecting his claim upon the gratitude of the party. It was also nostalgic, containing more than a hint of farewell, quite different from the sharp glint of steel among the ranks which rose to Gaitskell's trumpet call to fight and fight again eight years later at Scarborough.

That evening Morrison attended the Conference Ball, even joining in the dancing, but he was not feeling well. For the rest of the week he was confined to his hotel room with a cold.[30] He cancelled his speaking engagements. Morecambe was a miserable experience for him in every way.

If Morrison himself showed no bitterness in public, others reacted more strongly and more openly to his defeat. The big trade union leaders were shocked and enraged. Arthur Deakin, general secretary of the mighty Transport Workers, and that year's delegate bringing fraternal greetings from the TUC, used the occasion to make a very unbrotherly attack on the Bevanites, warning them to give up their conspiratorial activities or face the dire consequences.[31] Another big union leader had stormed out of the hall after the NEC vote shouting furiously that 'after this there'll be no more bloody money for this bloody party'. With the force of these expletives his false teeth flew out on to the carpet of the corridor outside. His tirade continued, though less distinctly, and an onlooker picked up the dentures and handed them back saying 'I believe these belong to you'. The union boss slapped them back into his mouth without acknowledgement and continued to denounce the irresponsibility of the party.[32] 'The unbelievable irresponsibility,' said a leading article in the steelworkers' union journal, 'that makes the abilities, services and importance of Herbert Morrison as of less account to the party than any of those who were chosen instead of him, will take some explaining to the average trade unionist.'[33] To the orthodox trade union establishment typified by Tom Williamson, Morrison was now 'the kingpin in the Labour Party. The unions had more to do with him than anyone else. Attlee was very distant.'[34] Morrison's authority, common sense and management was still felt essential to keep the Labour movement on a sane course. The unionists looked for ways, however drastic, to repair the damage and restore him to the NEC. They discussed altering the conference voting system – by, ironically, abolishing the constituency votes which Morrison had himself introduced and which had now struck their creator down.[35] Another union caucus, with Tom O'Brien among its chief organizers, approached Bevan to discuss the immediate removal of Attlee from the leadership, with Morrison taking over and Bevan as his deputy. But Bevan would not play.[36]

Others in the parliamentary party, and especially the younger members of the radical right wing, were also bent upon turning back the Bevanite tide. Morrison's defeat proved a rallying point.* Hugh Gaitskell, the outstanding leader of this younger generation of 'revisionists', launched the counter-attack with his famous Stalybridge speech in the week after Morecambe. 'The defeat of Herbert Morrison,' said Gaitskell, 'is not only an act of gross political ingratitude, but a piece of blind stupidity. Members of the National Executive know well that he has been the principal architect of efficient organization and realistic policy. The loss of his services in this policy-making year is a heavy if not a crippling blow. Members of the Labour Government who worked with Herbert know well what a loyal colleague, wise counsellor and fearless administrator he is.' Gaitskell also drew attention to what he alleged was clear communist infiltration among the delegates at Morecambe. Gaitskell concluded, in fighting language strikingly similar to that he used in 1960, that 'it is time to end the attempt at mob rule by a group of frustrated journalists and restore the authority and leadership of the solid, sound, sensible majority of the movement'.[37] The gloves were off.

Morrison, the focal point of the struggle, was himself curiously uncertain what role to play. His dilemma was understandable. If he stepped into the arena as a leader of the anti-Bevanite campaign he would lose all claim to being above the battle, straddling the conflicting factions, which had been one of the main strengths of Attlee's leadership. By remaining tactically neutral, however, apart from it being foreign to his whole temperament and record, he risked isolation in the parliamentary party and the alienation of the union bosses. The right centre of the Labour movement, its traditional power base, might be driven to abandon him and to turn to the new generation of leaders then emerging. He tried to play it delicately, maintaining his alliance with the

* A Gallup poll at this time showed that 40 per cent of Labour voters were sorry at Morrison's defeat and only 11 per cent pleased; among party members the figures rose to 55 per cent and 22 per cent respectively. (*News Chronicle*, 24 October 1952.)

right and fighting the Bevanites in the parliamentary party, but in public he appeared in a unifying role. In his first major speech after returning to London from Morecambe he was moderate and constructive, arguing that Labour was basically a healthy and united party and pledging himself to carry on the work of rethinking its policies and to help get it back into power. He also disso-ciated himself from the allegations then being made of communist infiltration at Morecambe.[38] During 1953 he continued to stress the need for policy reappraisal and in Parliament returned to his attack on the government's Transport Bill, moving amendment after amendment in committee, and pressing vigorously against the imposition of the guillotine.[39] The parliamen-tary warfare grew more bitter in the spring of 1953 as Labour's morale rose. Morrison's vigour and procedural skill in outmanoeuvring the government whips received praise.[40] His political stock was rising again after three long years of decline. He took charge of the Shadow Cabinet in late March and much of April, while Attlee was again ill in hospital. 'In the weeks of Attlee's absence,' observed the *Daily Mirror*, 'Mr Morrison has made it certain that the succession will fall to him when Mr Attlee retires. He has led the party with the buoyancy and vigour and skill of a man half his age.'[41]

Unfortunately internal strife continued to divide Labour. The parliamen-tary party passed a resolution calling on the Bevanites to disband their formal organization and urging all members to cease personal recriminations, but the atmosphere remained bitter. 'Nothing is getting better,' wrote Dalton. 'More hatred and more love of hatred, in our party than I ever remember. Nye's defects of character . . . are growing on him. Arrogance, conceit, personal animosities. . . .'[42] Attlee held on to the reins but gave little guidance or direc-tion to his unruly team. His coldness and vacillation constantly irritated Morrison. 'I am no closer to him today after working with him all these years,' he complained to a colleague, 'than I was when we first became acquainted. He trusts nobody. He confides in no one. I do not understand the man. He is peculiarly middle class. He has no real contact with the working class. He wants the middle of the road all the while – the best of both worlds, but sometimes you have to come down off the fence and fight. He won't do that.'[43]

Morrison himself no longer had his former stomach for a fight. To the surprise and dismay of his friends he decided in the spring of 1953 not to contest the constituency section of the NEC that year.[44] Morrison had never before been accused of lacking courage, certainly not on controversial public policies. On more personal issues he was less forthright and secure. He now seemed afraid to expose himself to the humiliation of a second defeat.[45] His confidence had been sapped by the setbacks of recent years. He was also now tempted by the possibility of regaining his place on the NEC *ex officio* by getting the treasurership of the party.

Sam Watson of the Durham miners was the main author of this scheme.[46] He mobilized the support of his union's president, Will Lawther, and of the two giants, Arthur Deakin and Tom Williamson, and they brought in the steelworkers' leader, Lincoln Evans. This powerful caucus went into action on Morrison's behalf. They hoped to persuade Greenwood to retire gracefully, but he refused. Early in July Lawther announced that the mineworkers would nominate Morrison for the treasurership and had secured his assent. The Transport Workers and the Municipal Workers then quickly followed suit, as did the London Labour Party. This gave Morrison around two million votes to start with. The union steamroller seemed about to make its familiar and usually unstoppable impact on party conference.

Morrison left the problem behind for a while and went again to Scandinavia for his summer holiday, this time to Finland as well as Sweden and Denmark. He grew to like this part of northern Europe more and more. He particularly appreciated that the Scandinavians were closest to Britain 'in their practice of a healthy parliamentary democracy and rational and constructive Labour movements'.[47] He returned in September and set off at the end of the month for the Margate conference. The last time he had been in Margate was in 1950, when he was deputy prime minister and Lord President and was surrounded by all the glamour and appurtenances of a leading minister of the crown. This year he was not even on the NEC and had to stay in a very modest side-street hotel.[48]

The outcome of the treasurership election remained in the balance. Support had begun to rally to Greenwood during the summer. Some, such as that from communist-dominated constituencies and unions such as the electricians was ideologically anti-Morrison. In addition Greenwood had been promised the support of the railwaymen, the shopworkers and the engineers, and in all could muster some two million votes by the eve of conference. This reaction represented a sentimental attachment to Greenwood. All sections of the party felt genuine affection for 'old Arthur'. This year was to be his conference as he was Chairman. In fact he was in poor physical condition. Now seventy-three, almost voiceless and visibly sagging under the impact of years of illness and drink, there were genuine doubts about whether he was capable of presiding over the conference. Some feared that the announcement of his defeat would kill him on the stage before conference's eyes. Many more bitterly resented the move to humiliate him and throw him out of office at the end of a life's service to the movement.

That weekend Morrison dithered about whether to let his nomination go forward. The decision had to be made and announced by Sunday evening. Sam Watson and Stanley Evans were with him much of the time producing lists of estimated votes. On Saturday it seemed very evenly split. Next day the agricultural workers submitted to hard persuasion and swung behind Morrison. On an optimistic assessment his majority then promised to be around a quarter of a million, but that contained too many doubtfuls to give absolute confidence. At seven in the evening the *News Chronicle* industrial correspondent, who was a close friend, called on him. Though obviously harrowed by doubt, he confirmed to her that he would definitely stand. She filed this report and it was printed and dispatched in the first edition going to the outer parts of the United Kingdom.

Within two hours the story had to be killed.[49] On his final tally Stanley Evans could not guarantee a majority. Morrison, sitting quietly with a book in the dingy hotel room, asked Watson's advice. Watson recommended withdrawal. If Morrison won and Greenwood collapsed, then he would get the blame for killing 'poor old Arthur'. To lose in such an unpopular enterprise would subsequently appear a disastrous miscalculation. Williamson still wanted him to stand but felt similar misgivings. Morrison, who shared these same fears, also now knew of the possibility of another less painful route back to the NEC. The National Union of Seamen had put forward a resolution to amend the constitution so that the Deputy Leader would become an *ex officio* member of the Executive.* This proposal attracted Morrison as an easy way out of his dilemma. It also made his victory less likely if he stood for the treasurership. Many delegates wanted him back on the NEC but did not want to hurt Greenwood. The seamen's amendment, which the NEC discussed on the Sunday evening and decided to support, offered the solution: delegates would be able to vote for the constitutional change, thus getting Morrison on the Executive, and for Greenwood as treasurer, thereby avoiding the pain and embarrassment of his defeat. The more who took this path, the less likely was Morrison to win in a contest which anyway now seemed unnecessary. He told his assembled friends that he wanted to withdraw, but was worried that Deakin would hold it against him after all the work he had done. Tom Williamson went round to inform Deakin and get his approval. Deakin agreed, though he was furious. 'Jesus Christ, that's the bloody last time,' he said to Lawther. He told Margaret Stewart that Morrison was simply yellow.

The news that Morrison would not stand, announced at a press conference at nine on the Sunday evening, delighted most conference delegates. Next morning Greenwood was able to make his opening address to the relieved cheers of a guiltless audience. Morrison walked in during the ovation and joined in the clapping while taking his seat down among the rank and file in the hall.[50] Conference approved the seamen's amendment; he was back on the NEC and next year he would be sitting up on the stage again. But he no longer had any institutional base of popular support in the mass party. He was neither elected by the constituency parties, as in his previous decades on the NEC, nor by the whole conference, as victory for the treasurership would have entailed. His narrow constituency was the 194 MPs who voted him Deputy Leader at Westminster. Even worse, the first doubts had arisen among the trade union leadership whether Morrison had lost his nerve and even whether he could beat Bevan in any future conference vote. They would support Gaitskell for the treasurership next year, when it would certainly be

* The constitution could be amended every three years and 1953 was a triennial year.

vacated by Greenwood and would probably be contested by Bevan.[51] That step, giving Gaitskell a seat on the NEC and a chance to speak for the first time from the stage at conference, was an important move in his rise to the leadership, although for some time yet Morrison remained the union leaders' choice to succeed the weak and disastrously vacillating Attlee.

Chapter 38

Rising from Despair, 1953-1955

During these political buffetings between Morecambe and Margate Morrison also suffered private bereavement. Margaret's stomach cancer grew worse during the spring and summer of 1953. She could no longer eat, and she rapidly wasted away and died on Saturday 11 July. Towards the end he visited her daily in Brentford Hospital.[1] He received the customary condolences, with messages of sympathy from the Queen, from Churchill and from Attlee. It is not easy to assess Morrison's real private feelings. Theirs had not been a happy and fulfilled relationship. Margaret was certainly a very good person, of limited but fine qualities. Yet she did not give him a warm home, satisfying sex, or the large and loving family which he later often said he would have liked. She was not helpful in his political career, either as a partner or as a hostess. He in turn gave little to her. He did not share her interests or show her affection. Like many Labour and trade union wives, she was neglected, rarely benefiting from socialist principles of fellowship and equality in the home, occasionally subject to almost capitalistic exploitation. At some time long ago each had no doubt provided something the other needed. For very many years since, they had lived separate lives, his very public, hers very private.

In a sense Margaret's death was a release – or certainly would have been had it occurred many years earlier when he was in his prime and most needed a wife who could satisfy him physically and support him in his career. Writing to Beaverbrook afterwards he characteristically made no reference to his own feelings: 'She suffered much discomfort during recent years and I knew the end must come. . . . Fortunately there was not much acute pain.'[2] Yet he was deeply saddened to lose her,[3] one more in the series of blows which in the past two years had progressively stripped him of public, party and private attributes. She was cremated at Honor Oak at noon on 15 July. Morrison seemed genuinely moved as he saluted farewell to the coffin.[4] The Attlees and the Gaitskells were among the hundreds of mourners present. The chapel was crowded and the service was relayed to those overflowing into the beautiful gardens outside.[5]

Morrison naturally stayed away from the meeting of the parliamentary party on that afternoon but sent a request through Attlee to wind up in the foreign affairs debate next week. Bevan objected on the grounds of Morrison's absence from recent party meetings. Gaitskell exploded with anger at this insensitivity, pointing out that 'he has been burying his wife this morning', and Bevan was properly swept aside.[6]

Morrison was very lonely and dreaded going back to the empty house in Archery Road. He had no idea how to look after himself and became quite sloppy in his habits and appearance. Various lady friends tried to help, washing his socks, ironing his shirts and generally making him presentable. His neighbour Mrs Downei often popped in to help him.[7] When possible he went away to someone else's home. He frequently visited old friends such as Lady Allen of Hurtwood.[8] He cultivated newer friends, such as George Rogers and his wife, and would telephone out of the blue to invite himself to tea.[9] He grew especially close to Mrs Melman who worked as a secretary to the Parliamentary Labour Party. He often stayed overnight at the Melmans' home in Brixton and kept a spare pair of pyjamas especially for his visits. He loved to sit in front of their coal fire (Margaret had forbidden coal fires because of the dirt) and watch television with their little boy. He also liked being tucked up in bed and would say 'pack me up like a parcel, dear'. Mrs Melman would take him hot milk and whisky and tuck him in.[10] After all those spartan years he simply wanted to be spoilt with some home comforts. In a way it was sad, almost childish, a symptom of decline. Yet it was touchingly human. In these private friendships, outside the pressures of public office or personal family, a quite different Morrison emerged, relaxed, affectionate, generous, funny. He would sometimes telephone Mrs Melman at her home from the House of Commons and would open by saying 'Attlee here', in a sharp clipped voice, and continue with the imitation, trying to put the wind up her. When finally forced by her banter to admit it was Herbert again, he said 'one of these days it will be that bugger Attlee and then you will get the bloody sack'. He remained secretive and was especially afraid that Miss Donald would find out about his visits to the Melmans; if he needed to contact her at the office he would go out into the street to a public call box so that she would not be able to trace the call back. When he took Mrs Melman out for lunch he often removed his glasses and straightened his quiff in the hope of not being recognized.

He needed help when dressing for formal occasions. On one occasion when he was going to the palace from the Commons he was assisted in dressing by a junior member of the party staff – who was apparently too careless or too shy for the job. Next day Morrison complained to Mrs Melman that while standing in line at the palace he noticed that all his trouser front was open, and quickly had to hide behind a distinguished lady visitor and adjust his dress. 'You tell your young blonde she nearly sent me before my monarch with my flies undone.'[11]

Morrison desperately tried to persuade any one of a number of available ladies to marry him. He proposed to Lady Allen of Hurtwood, pointing out that it might damage his career 'getting involved with a MacDonaldite, but never mind, I'll do it'. She understandably replied 'well, if that's how it is, we'd better not'.[12] After similar lack of success elsewhere Morrison dejectedly visited a friend and complained 'womankind has rejected me'.[13]

One escape from his domestic misery that gave him enormous pleasure at this time was to Nuffield College, Oxford. He had been made a Visiting Fellow there in 1947 but while in government had found little time to enjoy the benefits. Shortly after the 1951 defeat he discussed with Norman Chester a project – first suggested by Max Nicholson – for a book on British government and politics. It was agreed that Nuffield would pay for research and secretarial assistance and for Morrison's travel and lodging expenses.* He went up frequently for weekends, usually staying at the Mitre or the Royal Oxford Hotel. He worked in close co-operation with Chester. They first discussed pre-arranged topics, for which Chester had done any necessary detailed work in advance, and then Morrison would retire to his room to dictate. His drafts, which were very loose and conversational, were then hammered into publishable shape by Chester and others.[14] The text was completed in 1953, with Morrison adding some finishing touches shortly before the Margate conference, and the book, *Government and Parliament*, was published by the Oxford University Press in late April 1954.

The press reception to launch the book was held in one of the high, panelled House of Commons committee rooms overlooking the Thames. Morrison, pipe in hand, struck others present as 'so obviously at home. He put his hands in his pockets, held his head high and expanded. He was a fellow talking to his friends in his own parlour.'[15] He told them he had at first been 'a bit shy and nervous of all the brainy people and intellectuals – but now I've reached the point where I'm not afraid of anyone at Oxford. ... I wouldn't mind spending my time writing books at a University.' He acknowledged the valuable assistance of his Oxford helpers and especially of Norman Chester.[16] The book itself was to have considerable academic and commercial success. It became for some years a standard introduction to British institutional politics in universities and schools in Britain and overseas. It was then, and for long after, the best textbook on British government by a twentieth-century British politician. Its faults were typically Morrisonian. It was very orthodox and conventional in approach, taking the existing institutions and constitutional conventions as somehow permanent and perfect and not as the glorious but brief and temporary product of late nineteenth-century liberalism. It was also perhaps too impersonal; Morrison primly refused to reveal any inside stories about Labour politics and rejected Chester's pleas that he include more practical examples from his own personal experience of working the machinery

* Morrison in addition drew his fifty pounds per annum Fellowship honorarium and was later dismayed to be taxed on it. Nuffield papers, Morrison File I, Memorandum EC 3/52.

of party and government in Britain.[17] From the author's financial viewpoint the sales – twenty-four thousand copies in hardback and twenty thousand in paperback – brought a welcome improvement to his bank balance.

Morrison was re-elected deputy leader of the parliamentary party at the start of the 1953–4 session. He beat Bevan comfortably 181 to 76, though each candidate had lost a few votes since the previous year. The rise in abstentions to thirty-five certainly reflected increasing irritation with the endless warfare among the older generation of candidates. Morrison went back *ex officio* onto the NEC and on to the Policy sub-committee, though he did not regain the chairmanship now held by James Griffiths. He continued an active force in Parliament, the real opposition leader against the Tories while Attlee remained ineffective. On the Queen's Speech in November 1953, on rents in December, and especially on the government's commercial television proposals from the end of 1953 throughout 1954, Morrison proved that his debating skills were undiminished providing that they were exercised in familiar policy areas.[18] Commercial television was particularly provocative to him. He accused the Tories of abandoning one of their few virtues, their aristocratic culture, in favour of capitalist commercialism. He also smelled corruption and was incensed that some Tory MPs, and possibly even ministers, who were now defending commercial television overtly on grounds of the Conservative philosophy of competition, might in reality be more attracted by the prospects of future personal gains from the profits. Corruption in public life was still to Morrison among the gravest political sins and this suspicion fed his indignation against the bill throughout 1954. In the second reading debate he had sternly warned that Labour might scrap the whole apparatus of commercial television without compensation to the contractors. It was to prove an empty threat, as Labour voters, like Morrison himself, came to show a preference for ITV over the BBC, but it gave heart to Labour back-benchers. He campaigned on through the committee stage in April and May and almost single-handed forced the government to resort once again to the guillotine.[19]

Within the Labour Party the main issue in 1954 was the question of rearming Western Germany and it proved something of a personal triumph for Morrison. He had supported German rearmament since before he was Foreign Secretary. He had always believed that vindictiveness towards a beaten Germany was the great mistake of 1918 which must not be repeated this time. Germany should be reintegrated into the European community of nations as soon as possible.[20] On a more concrete level he also believed that a German contribution was essential to counterbalance the Russian military menace. As Foreign Secretary he had pursued this policy and the Cabinet had agreed in principle, though reserving its position on details and certain conditions. In opposition, as twenty years later on the Common Market issue, deeper antagonisms, previously held in check by the constraints of Cabinet unity and the responsibility of government, broke to the surface and the party was split. German rearmament touched deep emotions in all sections of the

s

Labour Party, including some of Morrison's normally loyal supporters, though it was particularly taken up and used by the Bevanites in their battle to overthrow the Attlee–Morrison leadership.

During 1952 Morrison's had been a minority position in the Shadow Cabinet. He declined to participate in the Commons debate on German rearmament in July 1952 because he did not feel he could honestly act as spokesman for the more hostile attitude to Germany, led rabidly by Dalton and supported by Bevan, then adopted by the party.[21] By 1954 opinion had moved a little more in Morrison's direction. In February when the Foreign Affairs group of the PLP put a resolution to the full party supporting German rearmament, it managed to scrape through by 113 to 104.* Bevan, Dalton, Callaghan and Chuter Ede were among leading figures voting in the minority. When the NEC met next day to approve the PLP decision, the Bevanites renewed their attack, supported by a number of trade unionists. Morrison 'made an impassioned plea' in support of the new PLP position and his view prevailed fourteen to ten.[22] He then went from Transport House across to Westminster to lead for the opposition in the debate on the recent Berlin Conference. Following Eden, he was at his very best, skilfully beginning by putting the case of his colleagues who had doubts about Germany, doubts which he presented as being sincere and worthy of respect. He then went on to explain modestly why he did not share their position but broadly agreed with that of the government.[23]

Foreign affairs continued to dominate Labour's attention with the commencement of hydrogen bomb tests. Morrison again led in the H-bomb debate in April 1954, this time clearly distinguishing himself from the government's position with a severe attack on Churchill for not having imposed on our American allies the strict obligation to consult Britain before using this terrible new weapon.[24] In the following week a Commons discussion on the government's policy towards South-East Asia provoked a fresh explosion from Bevan. Seeming flushed from a good lunch, Bevan intervened in the debate to present a sharply different line from that of his own leader.[25] After further clashes in the parliamentary party, Bevan resigned from the Shadow Cabinet.[26] He was replaced by Harold Wilson, runner-up at the previous election, despite Bevan's firmly expressed view that this act betrayed himself and their cause. The party was split wide open again and the Bevanites themselves were showing signs of disintegration. On May Day Morrison was the main speaker at the huge rain-swept rally in Hyde Park; he was ceaselessly and systematically barracked by left-wing hecklers, some chanting 'We want Bevan'.[27]

Morrison struck back shortly afterwards with uncharacteristic rashness and found himself in very hot water. He wrote a leading article in the May issue of *Socialist Commentary* attacking Bevan, Bevanism, and the Bevanites in very sharp language. The parliamentary party was thrown into turmoil. Morrison

---

* Harold Wilson's critical amendment was defeated by only two votes. (*The Times*, 25 February 1954.)

had clearly broken the PLP resolution of 23 October 1952 which forbade personal attacks and which he had himself championed as a gag on the Bevanites. The left were delighted. *Tribune* gleefully rebuked Morrison for giving comfort to the Tories by his disruptive action, but expressed understanding for his dilemma and pleaded for more freedom of speech on all sides. The centre of the party was upset that the deputy leader seemed to have opened the door to a fresh wave of vitriolic recriminations. 'And now *back in the shit* once more!' noted Dalton, not without a little pleasure at Morrison's discomfort.[28]

Attlee was extremely embarrassed. Morrison had shown him the offending article beforehand but Labour's leader admitted that he did not know that *Socialist Commentary* – an influential journal of the revisionist right – was a publication on general distribution. He thought that it was only circulated privately. The matter was disposed of at meetings of the NEC and the Shadow Cabinet on 18 May and at a full parliamentary party meeting on the nineteenth. Morrison and Bevan both defended themselves and there was the customary bickering, but no vote was taken.[29] Morrison had emerged uncensured, though the episode was no help to his reputation.

The German rearmament question was finally resolved at the 1954 conference, meeting at Scarborough at the end of September. Morrison had played an active role throughout the year in trying to educate the rank and file out of its anti-German prejudices. He delivered major speeches at Exeter in February, at Oxford in March, at Bradford in June and at Manchester in July, all stressing the case for German participation in European defence.[30] The issue remained in doubt, however, until the end. At the TUC a fortnight earlier – which Morrison addressed as fraternal delegate from the Labour Party – there was a perilously narrow margin in favour.*

Emotions were running very high at Scarborough. Bevan had rashly forfeited his safe seat on the executive to contest the treasurership,† and was heavily defeated by Gaitskell. He now again had no office in the party and his more ambitious followers began to lose hope that he would ever discipline his wilful ego sufficiently to gain the power they sought. He became embroiled in a public shouting match with Deakin and then walked ostentatiously out of the hall as Morrison rose to wind up for the NEC against a critical amendment condemning 'all proposals for German rearmament'. Morrison again struck the moderate and conciliatory note which he had adopted so successfully in the Commons. Firmly for rearmament, he treated the opposing view wih respect, appealing to the dissenters not to throw the party into chaos by a defeat on this issue. The hall was tense with excitement as the voting figures were passed from Morgan Phillips to Wilfred Burke, the chairman. The leadership just squeezed through.[31] With the help of a last-minute switch by

---

* 4·01 million against 3·62 million. (*TUC Report 1954*, pp. 413 and 432ff.)

† Greenwood had died on 9 June 1954.

the Woodworkers' Union, the critical amendment was defeated,* and the official motion in favour was passed even more narrowly.† Victory, however narrow, was decisive. When the Shadow Cabinet and the parliamentary party met in November[32] to discuss Labour's attitude to the recent Paris Agreements for West German sovereignty, much of the earlier resistance crumbled, thus leaving the Bevanites in a minority with the small group of genuine pacifists.‡ Morrison could claim considerable credit for having moved the party so far from its earlier antipathies. His political fortunes seemed to be picking up.

Morrison's personal life also altered, dramatically, for the better in 1954. The Raisins had taken him on holiday in August to Switzerland for a change of scene from his familiar Scandinavia. At their hotel in Davos Morrison met a handsome Lancastrienne, Edith Meadowcroft, who was twenty years younger than he. She was a keen golfer and had won some prizes which were due to be presented at an evening barbecue. She had no one to accompany her to the celebration and Morrison quickly offered to go. She accepted but did not in fact know who he was, thinking that perhaps he was associated with the agency which arranged holidays to that hotel. They enjoyed the barbecue, liked one another, played golf together in the following days and were close friends by the end of the holiday.[33] Morrison arranged to see her a few times after their return, once taking her on a tour of south London. He excitedly showed friends her photograph and discussed with them whether to propose to her.[34] At Labour's Scarborough conference in September, his more perceptive colleagues realized a romance might be in the wind when they noticed Morrison refusing his breakfast in order to slim.[35] He went to the United States lecturing in October and on his return finally took courage and proposed and Edith accepted. The forthcoming marriage was announced a week before Christmas. Morrison proudly told the press about his prospective bride as he left London for Amsterdam, where he was due to address a meeting of the Socialist International to try to persuade the German Social Democrats to accept rearmament.[36] He described Edith as an outdoor woman with little interest in politics – though he mentioned defensively that she had been a member of the Workers' Educational Association, possibly to counter in advance the widespread suspicion that she was, or at least had been, a Tory supporter.[37]

The wedding was in Rochdale Parish Church on Thursday 6 January, three days after his sixty-seventh birthday. He travelled up to Manchester by train (third class) on the Wednesday with his sister Edie, Jim Raisin, who was to be his best man, and Mabel. Thousands lined the route to the church, braving

---

* By 3·281 million to 2·91 million.
† 3·27 to 3·02 million.
‡ Seven back-benchers rebelled against the party decision to abstain and voted in the lobbies, one for and six against, and had the whip removed. (R. Jackson, *Rebels and Whips* (1968), pp. 124–5.)

a bitter, cold wind in the late afternoon, for what the press had already decided even so early on was definitely the wedding of the year. Morrison was resplendent in morning suit and white carnation. A full choir sang at the service, where Eddie Shackleton, his former PPS, and Ernest Thornton helped officiate.* The Attlees were not invited. The reception was at Rochdale Town Hall, Victorian and solidly bourgeois, with the Mayor and Mayoress as guests. Morrison beamed with happiness.[38] There was something about the warmth and homeliness of northern English people which always attracted him. Although he was a Londoner to his fingertips – quick, cocky, ambitious, capable of being devious, not over-generous – there was a side to him which could easily fit into the northern style of life. This was the jolly Morrison, loving warm and friendly homes, sing-songs, brass bands, informal parties with no stuffiness or 'side', socialist fellowship applied in everyday personal lives. He looked to Edith and Rochdale – home, after all, of the Co-operative pioneers – to cushion him in his last years, and he was not disappointed. They went to Morecambe, scene of less happy events in 1952, for a brief honeymoon, returning to Rochdale on the Saturday to watch the home side beat Charlton, his London team, in a Football Association cup-tie. Everybody noticed what good form he was in. When he entered the Commons for the first time after his marriage, on 25 January, MPs cheered and Morrison smiled and bowed in acknowledgement.[39] He took Edith with him to Bathgate, West Lothian, for his annual Burns' Night dinner and to waltz among the three hundred guests afterwards.[40] Morrison was buoyantly renewed. The air of defeat, demoralization and physical slovenliness which hung about him through the depressing years since 1951 faded. This improved morale and domestic bliss was good for him politically, yet it was also a threat, making the seamier side of politics less tolerable, providing an insidious pressure to withdraw into the novel pleasures of his comfy sitting room.

Morrison's new wife had a rapid introduction to Labour politics, seeing him involved in a major row with Bevan and then plunging into the general election campaign at his side. Bevan reopened old wounds in February and March. He first put down an unofficial motion in the Commons calling for summit talks contrary to a party decision. For this he was formally rebuked. He took an independent line in the debate on the government's defence White Paper, interrupting Attlee when the latter was winding up.[41] He then led sixty-one rebels in abstaining from supporting Labour's censure motion. At this the Labour right wing rose in anger and howled for Bevan's blood. Many right-wing MPs, including Morrison, urged on especially by Arthur Deakin and his associates from the unions, were pressing for the ultimate punishment of expulsion from the party.[42] At the Shadow Cabinet, when Attlee declined to give a lead, Morrison stepped in with a strong speech recounting Bevan's many past misdeeds and he swung the meeting firmly behind a resolution recommending the parliamentary party to withdraw the

* MPs for Preston South and Farnworth, respectively.

whip. This was approved by the PLP. At the NEC, however, Attlee proposed that Bevan be given one last chance to apologize. This was narrowly passed fourteen to thirteen with Morrison and Gaitskell in the unyielding minority.[43] Bevan grasped the lifeline and made his peace, but the public impression on the eve of the general election was of a party still completely divided and therefore unfit to govern. Few doubted that Eden would get the bigger majority he sought and that Labour would remain picking its sores in opposition.

The impending dissolution was announced in April and the election held at the end of May. The government had just handed out Budget concessions in the form of tax cuts. The economy was anyway booming at full blast. The next economic crisis loomed – as Morrison presciently warned a Labour rally at Scarborough[44] – a few months ahead, but still far enough away to leave the electorate lulled in prosperity.

There was little if any over-all political control of Labour's 1955 election campaign. Morrison himself was even further removed from influence than in 1951; now he was no longer chairman of the Policy sub-committee. Morgan Phillips ran the machine from Transport House, and the politicians went their own ways. The party's leaders – Attlee, Morrison, Gaitskell, Griffiths – never once met to discuss strategy. Morrison addressed rallies in big cities such as Leeds and Portsmouth, made tours of East Anglia – still seeking the elusive agricultural vote – and throughout Lancashire, finishing there with a packed meeting in Rochdale Town Hall.[45] The last week of the campaign he spent as usual in London – Dulwich, Peckham, Catford, Lewisham, Harrow, Hendon, Uxbridge, Rochester, back to Lewisham – a familiar figure, in his purple bow tie and big rosette, on familiar stamping grounds. In fact, this was the last time he would canvass them as an MP; it was not a memorable farewell. The crowds were small, the atmosphere subdued, the outcome inevitable.[46] Morrison was safely home in Lewisham, where Mabel Raisin maintained membership at record levels. But Labour lost a further sixteen seats and the Tories had a comfortable majority of sixty over all parties. Two of Morrison's close associates, Maurice Webb and Eddie Shackleton, were among those who lost their seats. Afterwards he took a characteristically phlegmatic attitude to the result. 'John Bull has spoken,' he said on television, 'I have too high a regard for the British electorate to be bad tempered with it even when the party of which I am proud to be a member has had a setback. . . . We shall start again straight away, and prepare for victory in the next election.'[47] One prerequisite for such a victory was, of course, a change in the leadership. Election defeat had the compensation that it meant the dithering finally had to stop and the change be made. Morrison might at last, so he believed, come into his own.

Chapter 39

The Final Bid, 1955

Clement Attlee had continued as leader of the Labour Party long beyond the time when he could make any positive contribution in that role. Certainly he showed little interest in the reforming domestic policies to which the Labour Party was committed. His sole achievement after 1951 – negative but of long-run importance in his own and others' eyes – was to retain the leadership until Morrison was disqualified from the succession by age.[1] He was assisted in holding on to office by the divisions within the party about alternatives. Morrison had been the obvious heir apparent for twenty years, but he was increasingly disliked by the left, while as each year passed an increasing number of his natural supporters on the right and in the crucial centre were worried that he was getting too old. Even so, had Attlee been prepared to step down at any time until the 1955 election there is little doubt that Morrison would have won the succession, if only through lack of any serious alternative. Bevan had his band of supporters, but his and their behaviour ruled him out as far as the bulk of the party was concerned. Hugh Gaitskell had made a major impact as a minister, and built growing support on the right in opposition, but he was very young in the parliamentary party, needed time to consolidate his position, and anyway personally supported Morrison for the succession until late in 1955. Until Gaitskell finally emerged with a sudden accretion of broad support, Attlee soldiered on.

Morrison would or could do little to precipitate the issue and grasp the leadership for himself. Many MPs had assumed that Attlee would retire when seventy. Robens and Gaitskell convened occasional dinners at the House in 1952 to discuss the state of the party, including the leadership, and the general view was that Attlee's seventieth birthday in January 1953 would be an appropriate time to say farewell. Their assumption was that Morrison would then succeed and would lead the party into the next election. If he won, he would become Prime Minister for a while before handing on to a representative of the next generation, such as Gaitskell. If he lost, then the younger man ought to take over straight away. Robens and Gaitskell were themselves deputed to put the birthday proposal to Attlee, and when he saw them he assured them that he intended to do as they suggested.[2] The birthday came and many of the published good wishes contained barely disguised hints that this was a suitable exit point.[3] Richard Stokes, who was also holding similar political dinners at his Belgravia home, wrote a brief congratulatory birthday letter to Attlee which directly requested him 'to move over and give Herbert a chance'. Attlee replied that he was personally willing but that his friends would not allow him.[4] Robens and Gaitskell returned to ask their leader why he had not retired as promised and he explained, not wholly convincingly, that the party was by now in such turmoil that he had to stay on to save it from splitting asunder.[5] So he clung on and on, justifying his continuance on the grounds that the succession of either of the only two possible alternatives, Morrison or Bevan, would throw the party into violent open dissension. In fact, in his hands, it was suffering a more insidious demoralization and disintegration.

Morrison remained the most likely next Labour leader through into 1955. The union big battalions and the parliamentary party's right wing were still committed to him and the centre had no viable alternative who could beat Bevan. Stanley Evans, a friend of Morrison's and also something of a political operator in a small way, arranged a lunch for Gaitskell and Arthur Deakin of the Transport Workers' Union at the St Ermin's Hotel on 21 December 1954. They agreed that Morrison was entitled to the succession and each pledged himself to support him.[6] Gaitskell's own star was, however, already rising with dramatic rapidity. After trouncing Bevan for the treasurership at the 1954 conference, he came equal top in the Shadow Cabinet elections at the beginning of the parliamentary session. More people began to discuss him in terms of the leadership. Roy Jenkins, Tony Crosland and Woodrow Wyatt, among the outstanding young intellectuals of the revisionist right, wrote to Gaitskell in March 1955, arguing that a leader must have centre support, 'which Herbert has not got'.[7] Gaitskell, however, continued loyal to his pledge to support Morrison's claims throughout the summer of 1955 and rejected any suggestions of himself as an alternative.[8]

After the 1955 general election defeat the pressures grew for changes at the top of the Labour Party. Dalton wrote to Attlee, and published, a letter calling for the retirement of all the older generation in the Shadow Cabinet, clearly including Morrison but with the diplomatic exception of Attlee himself. Dalton's intention was to prepare the way for Gaitskell's emergence as leader.[9] At the parliamentary party meeting on 9 June, Whiteley, faced by candidates competing for his job as Chief Whip, announced his retirement, unwillingly. He was deeply saddened that Attlee, whom he had served devotedly for ten years, did not lift a finger to support him.[10] Morrison, Whiteley's colleague in the team which so capably managed the Commons from 1945 to 1951, spoke of him with praise and regret. Chuter Ede, Shinwell and Glenvil Hall also decided not to stand again for the Shadow Cabinet. Attlee reported that the Shadow Cabinet had urged him to stay on but added that he would not continue beyond the end of this session. Bevan, knowing that every passing day counted against Morrison, spoke up begging his leader to carry on without a time limit. Others cheered in support of delaying the issue and Attlee once again graciously conceded. For Morrison, who was duly elected deputy leader unopposed, this delay was a harsh blow, since he would be nearly sixty-nine by the end of the session. His hopes revived in the summer when Attlee suffered a stroke and he once more deputized as leader. It involved little since politics was in its midsummer siesta. At the end of July he went on holiday with Edith, back to Davos, to the Hôtel Beau Séjour, where they had met a year before.[11] Asked why his quiff was so much shorter, he explained that 'my wife is making me have it cut much more often. I can't do what I like you know. I get my orders in a broad Lancashire accent. It's worse than being in politics.'[12]

The Labour Party spent the autumn of 1955 painfully and publicly resolving its leadership problem. Attlee gave a newspaper interview in mid-September in which he asserted his desire to retire. Among the sprigs of platitudes about having 'had a long innings', etc., was concealed the inevitable wicked thorn to hurt Morrison's grasp. 'We must have men brought up in the present age, not as I was in the Victorian age,' he added.[13]

Annual conference met at Margate in the second week of October. It was dominated by off-stage discussion of the succession. On stage, Morrison was very active trying to recover support. He made five major speeches: at the eve-of-conference rally, opposing resolutions for unilateral disarmament, summing up for the NEC on the Wilson report on party organization, defending the record of the PLP, and in the debate on automation.[14] The contrast between Morrison and Attlee, who was still listless from his thrombosis, was striking. The press felt that Morrison's skill and renewed vigour had snatched back the succession. The trade union leaders were expressing increased impatience with Attlee for prolonging his departure and were still for Morrison as successor.[15] Attlee 'will be succeeded by Mr Herbert Morrison', concluded a prominent political correspondent.[16] Morrison, accompanied by Edith at her first Labour conference, glowed with his success and allegedly 'looked like a bridegroom on his way to the florist's'.[17] Gaitskell, however, consolidated his strength with a powerful speech about why he was a socialist. He was emotional and completely personal, removing rank and file worry that he might be just 'a desiccated calculating machine'. Ominously for Morrison, Gaitskell received the greatest ovation of the week.[18]

As the parliamentary party reassembled for the new session, Morrison's friends pressed him to force the issue with Attlee and promised him full support. He refused. As so often before, he was not really adept at raising the knife on his own behalf.[19] The tide now began perceptibly to swing away from him. Perhaps his last chance to recover came when he opened the debate on Labour's motion of censure against the government's autumn emergency Budget, introduced to pay for its pre-election excesses. But he lacked the necessary economic expertise and flair. He rambled on at great length, seemingly bored by the subject and in turn boring the House.[20] He was now widely written off in the leadership stakes. 'He has taken a sudden dive out of the running for the succession,' said the *Sunday Times* and it was 'impossible' for him to recover from this catastrophic flop.[21] Other commentators reached similar conclusions.[22]

Gaitskell had by now finally agreed to stand for the leadership, under great pressure from many colleagues who feared that Morrison would not beat Bevan. Gaitskell genuinely had to be drafted, being reluctant to oppose an old friend.[23] He went straight away to tell Morrison, who seemed to accept the news stoically, fairly recalling that twenty years earlier he had joined Greenwood in opposing Attlee. Privately, however, he resented Gaitskell's intervention, feeling strongly that the younger man should have shown more patience and first served an apprenticeship under him.[24]

These were agonizing days for Morrison. After twenty years, the prize he had always sought was becoming available, and now at the last moment he saw it slipping away. Gaitskell's bandwagon gathered momentum. Some who joined it were the enemies Morrison had inevitably made in his long career in politics. Others leaping aboard were young MPs who had entered the House since 1950 and had never seen Morrison in his great years, only in decline. Even those who had long supported Morrison now began to desert him, including some of the younger men and women whom he had helped and guided, such as Patrick Gordon Walker, Christopher Mayhew and Freda Corbet. This hurt him deeply. Their dilemma was, however, very real. Whatever gratitude they felt for past friendship and assistance, they had to vote for the future good of the party, not from past sentiment for individuals. Morrison would certainly be over seventy by the next general election. Gaitskell was forty-nine and just coming into his prime. They believed that Gaitskell was already the better man for the job and that he alone had scope for more intellectual growth.[25]

Several colleagues in the party now tried to persuade Morrison not to expose himself to humiliation but to announce even before Attlee's resignation that he was not a candidate, that he would support Gaitskell and would serve under him as deputy. Sir Hartley Shawcross and Richard Stokes, two of his closest associates in recent years, and two veteran colleagues, George Isaacs and Sam Viant, pressed this point of view on Morrison, without effect. George Brown warned him bluntly that he would get few votes and was in danger of completely ending his political influence. Morrison took this very ill. When Christopher Mayhew explained why he would vote for Gaitskell, he stalked angrily away, terminating their relationship on the spot. Bob Mellish had a similar sharp experience. George Strauss never received acknowledgement of his letter saying that he was sorry on personal grounds but felt that he must vote for the younger man. When Alfred Robens saw Morrison in a corridor of the Commons and urged him to withdraw with honour and without pain, 'he turned on me, the only time he was ever cross with me, and said bitterly "you are another one" '.[26]

Morrison's calculation, on which he remained optimistic against all the contrary advice from his friends, was that Gaitskell might well come top on the first ballot, with himself next and Bevan bottom, but that there would certainly not be an over-all majority for Gaitskell. On the second ballot he expected the Bevanites to switch to him as the lesser evil. This latter assessment was not unreasonable since he was old enough to offer Bevan hope of another crack of the whip before too long.[27] Morrison did not contemplate the possibility that Gaitskell would win an outright majority, or that he could conceivably come bottom of the poll. As to serving under Gaitskell, his view was that the party should elect him as leader or not have him at all, and he made this publicly clear.[28] Curiously, for such an experienced political operator, he did little to mobilize support among his own section of the party. He asked, unsuccessfully, Bob Mellish to help Charles Gibson to canvass the trade unionists.[29] He left Shinwell and Stokes to approach people around the corridors and tea-rooms of the Commons. He did not have anything which could really be described as a campaign on his behalf; he simply waited for the leadership to drop into his lap.

Attlee kept Morrison stretched on the rack a little longer, watching his friends desert, reading in the press of his disqualification by age, listening to counsels of despair. Then, on the morning of Wednesday, 7 December, Attlee announced his retirement, first to the Shadow Cabinet and afterwards to the parliamentary party. Until the end he gave no prior warning to Morrison, who took over the chair at the party meeting, moved a motion accepting the resignation, and proposed a vote of thanks for Attlee's splendid service. Barely half the Labour MPs were present to sing 'For he's a jolly good fellow' and, not without relief, to cheer Attlee on his way.[30] The election was to be a week later, and nominations had to be in by Friday morning at eleven. Early the next day Morrison went to see his tailor at the Woolwich Co-op.[31] Westminster opinion, however, suggested that he would not need his new suit, for Gaitskell was widely described as now unbeatable. Some commentators already foresaw that Morrison was even in danger of coming bottom of the poll.*

The following evening, by when the three expected nominations were in, there was a curious and desperate manoeuvre to stop Gaitskell's otherwise inevitable succession. Bevan was approached by letter from ten Labour MPs asking him to withdraw and to allow Morrison to be returned unopposed – providing 'other nominees' also withdrew.† The ten contained two of Morrison's most active supporters, Shinwell and Stokes, a couple of Bevanites and a number of old warriors who believed that long service should always have

* The *Sunday Times*, 4 December 1955 and *Daily Telegraph*, 9 December 1955, both predicted correctly the order of the result. *The Times* and the *Daily Express* on the tenth forecast that Gaitskell would win on the first ballot.

† The ten were: D. Grenfell, D. T. Jones, C. R. Key, C. L. Hale, F. Messer, W. Monslow, W. Paling, E. Shinwell, R. Stokes, S. Viant.

its due reward. Bevan, who certainly knew in advance of their approach, had nothing to lose and everything to gain by the manoeuvre. He immediately issued a statement to the press declaring his willingness to stand down providing Gaitskell did the same.

The origins of this move are not wholly clear. Leslie Hunter, whose ear was very close to the Westminster ground, asserts with absolute confidence that it originated with Emanuel Shinwell, who was campaigning on Morrison's behalf and desperate to keep out Gaitskell.[32] Shinwell himself later declined to claim credit for the abortive scheme, but he and Stokes were certainly closely involved, not only as signatories themselves but apparently in persuading others to sign.[33]

Morrison and Bevan were themselves without doubt personally implicated. These two bitter enemies met over dinner at the House and discussed the plan to stop Gaitskell in front of a mutual friend.[34] Subsequently, Morrison asked George Rogers to canvass support for the proposed deal, but Rogers refused.[35] It anyway could not get off the ground without Gaitskell's co-operation and that was not forthcoming. He was not approached by the ten signatories, but was simply confronted by the public announcement. Harold Wilson, no longer on good terms with Bevan, went immediately to see Gaitskell and urged him not to play ball, warning that he would put himself forward if Gaitskell stood down. Gaitskell made it absolutely clear that he had no intention of falling into the trap set for him.[36] He followed Bevan's announced willingness to withdraw with a brief statement that the party must have an opportunity to choose and that he would, therefore, still stand. The only consequence of this futile plot was to generate resentment towards Morrison for having associated himself with such intrigues. More of his potential supporters may have been driven away; certainly, some who secretly intended to desert, now felt that they had a decent excuse.[37]

For these last few days between Attlee's retirement and the election Morrison was acting leader of the party. He moved into the Labour leader's room, next to that of the Prime Minister, with its giant fireplace, its green leathered chairs and the battery of telephones on the big dark oak chest. He certainly still refused to believe that defeat was inevitable.[38] Jim Raisin saw him in his room a couple of days before the ballot and Morrison claimed that he would win or at least finish an honourable second. When Raisin replied with the blunt warning 'You will get rolled in the mud', Morrison began shouting angrily.[39] He based his hopes wholly on the loyalty of his friends and the gratitude of the party. He did not claim to have much more to give creatively in the future. Indeed, by threatening to resign as deputy leader if defeated and arguing that 'I think I've done my bit',[40] he was in a way conceding that he was claiming his due for past services rendered. His position, deaf to the ticking of the clock, struck many as tragic and pathetic. The 'loyal old friends' were reported to be still defecting in droves.[41] 'Those who owe everything to Mr Morrison,' commented the *Observer*'s political correspondent, 'who would not even be in the House without his patronage, have deserted to Mr Gaitskell. No doubt they have their reasons, but it is not a pleasant spectacle and it is not a pleasant fact to record.' Morrison faced not only defeat but the end to his career. 'Even those who have no cause to love him must feel compassion.'[42]

The evening before the result was declared Morrison went with Edith to the royal première of the film *Richard III*.[43] He was up early in Eltham next morning and drove in to Transport House for a meeting of the NEC. Afterwards he walked across from Smith Square to the Commons, where the ballot boxes had just closed at noon.[44] The scrutineers – Charles Gibson, Sam Viant and Kenneth Robinson – began counting at 5.00 p.m. Party members packed into Committee Room Fourteen for the result to be announced at seven. Morrison was in the chair when the scrutineers brought in the figures. Gaitskell had achieved an over-all majority comfortably, with 157. Bevan polled seventy, roughly the same support which he attracted back in 1952. Morrison trailed last with a derisory forty votes.* In fact, he had already been told the bad news by Carol Johnson, the party secretary. Johnson, who greatly admired Morrison, was 'so horrified at how badly Morrison had done that I went straight away to see him in his room and warned him in advance. I didn't want him to go to the party meeting and hear it unprepared. Morrison asked "Is it very bad?" and I answered "Yes". He was clearly expecting to do better.'[45] At least he had a few minutes to prepare for the blow. He scribbled some notes for his farewell statement and then went up to Room Fourteen. Robens sat close to him as the meeting was about to open, saw the gist of his proposed speech, and begged him not to deliver it but to announce his willingness to stay on as deputy leader. Morrison replied: 'Do you think I am going to take this after all the disappointments I have had?'[46] After the announcement of the result, Morrison formally congratulated Gaitskell on his success. He then said he would ask for an opportunity to make a statement on his own position later. Gaitskell moved into his place in the chair, and after thanking the meeting, made a powerful personal appeal to Morrison to stay on and work with him. He said that the result of the ballot reflected one thing only, over which they had no control, namely, the difference in their ages. 'Herbert, there is nothing but the years between us.' He expressed his admiration for Morrison and the tremendous job he had done for the party in so many ways. He said that Labour still needed Morrison† and he begged him not to carry out his

---

* Among those who certainly voted for Morrison were Emanuel Shinwell, Charles Gibson, George Brown, George Wigg, Arthur Lewis, Arthur Bottomley, George Rogers, Richard Stokes, George Pargiter, and Sir Hartley Shawcross. Others believed to have done so were Somerville Hastings, Tom Williams, John Hynd, and O. G. Willey. (Interviews, D. Jay, C. Gibson, G. Brown, A. Lewis, P. M. Williams, A. Bottomley, G. Rogers, Lord Shawcross, G. Deer, Lord Shinwell and Lord Wigg.)

† Gaitskell apparently considered creating a new post for Morrison, as permanent head of the mass party and its spokesman outside of Parliament, and also discussed getting him the party treasurership, though Morgan Phillips, the party secretary, opposed this. (Interview, J. W. Raisin.)

earlier threat to resign from the deputy leadership if defeated.[47] At this point the Scottish accent of one of Morrison's prominent supporters was heard to hiss 'don't take it, don't take it'.[48]

Morrison did not need urging. He had firmly decided in advance to retire if defeated, and the humiliating size of his vote reinforced that intention. He realized that this meant leaving the Shadow Cabinet, the National Executive and many important sub-committees, but he felt that the stinging emphasis with which the party had decided he was unfit to be leader also involved his position as deputy. He asked Gaitskell's leave to withdraw and walked despondently to the door. Gaitskell then brought the assembled gathering to its feet in a final acclamation as he left the room. The press was clamouring outside, including such old friends as Leslie Hunter, but Morrison pushed them aside without a word. Arthur Lewis accompanied him along the corridor and downstairs to his room. George Wigg took him afterwards for a consoling drink. Lucy Middleton later met him in the lobby and he seemed completely shattered, with tears in his eyes.[49] He declined to attend the subsequent press conference, where Gaitskell devoted over half of his statement to a tribute to Morrison's work for the Labour movement. Edith drove him home to Archery Road. He brushed past the newspapermen on the steps, saying 'I've had enough', and sat in the lounge while his wife went into the kitchen to make him a cup of tea.[50]

Chapter 40

Nursing His Wounds, 1955-1959

The leadership battle and defeat left Morrison deeply scarred. It was not just a setback. 'I suppose what happened last week was the greatest disappointment of all,' he wrote immediately afterwards, 'because there was a melancholy finality about it. My greatest handicap, it has been said, was age. Time will not lighten that.'[1] The strain took its toll of his health and he saw Dr Maclellan frequently. Visiting him immediately after defeat Morrison slumped down with none of his usual chat and good cheer. 'He just felt he had been hit in the heart, particularly because the young men he had brought on had all voted against him.'[2] Morrison was stricken with a nervous rash over much of his body.[3] He did not return to the Commons until February 1956, the Tories considerately providing him with a guaranteed 'pair'. He received stacks of letters of condolence, too many to answer personally, and he issued a general notice of thanks and appreciation through the press.[4] He spent a quiet family Christmas with Edith and her mother in Rochdale, but he was still so 'flattened' that his wife felt she had to get him away from politics and took him to Austria in the New Year for a winter sports holiday.[5] He could not face any Burns' Night celebrations.[6]

Bitter resentment at his treatment by the party gnawed at Morrison for years after 1955. He cut old friends in public and in private – some, such as Leslie Hunter, banished for ever. At a reception in Australia House he walked straight past Tom Williamson, and another time rebuked him because many trade union MPs had supported Gaitskell.[7] In the tea-rooms at Westminster he occasionally made snide comments, revealing that the defeat still rankled.[8] He puzzled over who had voted for and who against him. Freda Corbet had informed him of her own choice, but he did not hear properly, and for long afterwards he worried about whether she had said she voted for 'you' or for 'Hugh'.[9] Cecil King wrote him a conciliatory letter of condolence but received a savage reply blaming the *Daily Mirror* for his defeat.[10] Gaitskell offered a peerage as an olive branch but was coldly refused.[11] Attlee never again received the ritualistic telegram of congratulations on his birthday.[12] Morrison was, at least in public, a lone and not very attractive figure at this time. His sensitivity and vulnerability showed again in early 1957 when a newspaper published articles based on the second volume of Dalton's memoirs, including the author's critical but not too misleading account of Morrison's attempts to remove Attlee in 1945. Within hours of publication Morrison issued a long statement to the press. 'The story is very inaccurate and unreliable,' he alleged, adding 'I cannot comment on Mr Dalton's own lively activities on the telephone and otherwise, as I stated to him. I do not propose to answer Mr Dalton. The Labour Party – which I have sought to serve loyally, selflessly and to the best of my ability for many years – would be likely to be hurt as a result.' Dalton replied confidently and briefly, quoting from Abraham Lincoln that 'None of us can escape history'.[13] Morrison's scars were clearly still not healed, and he could only suffer more from so exposing them in public.

Fortunately, he had the comforts of home to cushion him. Edith had made the house in Archery Road much brighter and cosier. Morrison gave her a free hand to do what she liked with it providing anything purchased and any painting and decorating was from the Co-op. She coddled him and provided the warmth which had been missing from most of his private life. He wallowed in the novel delights of domestic bliss, proudly showing visitors around the home and repeatedly drawing attention to the virtues of his new wife.[14] His weekly routine was simple. Some mornings they would play golf together, though he never approached her proficiency. Edith often went to visit friends or to play golf again in the afternoons, leaving him to sleep and read and even sometimes to make his own lunch. On Sundays she always cooked roast beef and Yorkshire pudding and usually made him a currant cake for tea.[15] For recreation, apart from golf, Morrison walked a lot and swam often at the Eltham or Bexley baths. He took Edith frequently to the cinema and also liked stage musicals. He regretted not having become an orchestral conductor, instead of a politician. He 'always went to bed singing' and often sang 'The Happy Wanderer' in his sleep. He hoped some time to write for the Labour Party a replacement for 'The Red Flag', which he said 'gives me the shivers'; but he never got round to it.[16]

Home life with Edith provided the balm for his political wounds, but inevitably it cut him off from old friends. Some, including his immediate family, felt that they were being deliberately excluded.[17] He did, however, keep in touch with some of his former haunts. When Edith went away on her monthly trips to stay with her mother, first in Rochdale and later in Lytham St Anne's, he would slip around to the Melman family for a chat and to watch *Coronation Street* or *Perry Mason* on television. He resisted all pressure to stay the night as in former times. He also made it clear that he preferred them not to tell anyone else of his visits, which continued discreetly right up to the end of his life.

As an elder statesman with time on his hands, Morrison received his share of invitations to conferences, lectures, social functions and, most enjoyable of all, to tour overseas. He visited Malaya with a parliamentary delegation in March 1956, and over the following months was on circuit through the London Embassy cocktail parties of various Far Eastern nations.[18] In the autumn he sailed with Edith on the *Queen Mary* for a three-month lecture tour in the United States. He travelled some thirty-five thousand miles and delivered forty lectures in twenty-five states, with his talks on 'The Battle for Peace' and 'The Loyal Opposition' particularly well received. Together with articles he sent back to the English press on the current American presidential elections, the tour was financially very rewarding. It was also a great pleasure. As he told his Lewisham constituents afterwards: 'I am always at home with the Americans, and they with me.'[19] In 1957 he opened a Jewish youth club in Stamford Hill, went to Norfolk for the hundredth birthday party of a farm labourer – an echo of his earlier years cultivating the East Anglian agricultural vote – and attended the civic dinner in Hull in honour of his appointment as High Steward. He made speeches to Labour audiences in Manchester, Beckenham, Monmouth, Cardiff, Belper and Oxford. He lunched with the Queen.[20] He also continued to enjoy his regular trips as Visiting Fellow of Nuffield College. An old LCC friend met him on a college barge during 'Eights Week' and he glowed with pride at being a part of Oxford.[21]

Morrison's interventions in Westminster politics were now intermittent. He chose to sit on the back benches, establishing his own place in the third row below the gangway.[22] His first speech as a back-bencher for over twenty-five years was suitably dramatic. In the debate on capital punishment* he announced that, having 'wrestled with my mind, as usual as with my conscience and with my emotions' since the issue was last discussed in 1948, he had finally swung to support abolition. 'I feel it in my bones that this change will come,' he warned the House.[23] His was a late conversion. As Home Secretary he had experienced no qualms about sending the convicted to the gallows.[24] In 1948 he was still firmly against abolition. By November 1955, under constant pressure from younger friends of liberal sentiment, he had moved into a more neutral position, finding the arguments evenly balanced.[25] He finally switched to abolition a week before the Commons debate. He still had no doubts about those hanged while he was Home Secretary: 'I considered the persons executed very bad, nasty people and that society did not lose by their departure.' He was greatly influenced by Sir Ernest Gowers, chairman of the Royal Commission on Capital Punishment, who became converted to abolition and for whom Morrison had enormous respect. 'He is not over-emotional or sentimental. No thoughtful person could afford to ignore his judgment.'[26]

The Suez invasion was the major event in British politics in 1956. Morrison was lecturing in the United States when the affair reached its climax in October and November, but he had made his position clear in the Commons before

* The abolition motion was passed 292 to 246.

leaving. Drawing on his own experience as Foreign Secretary dealing with the Persians and Egyptians, he urged Eden's government to take a firm stand against Nasser and if need be to proceed to military action without the United States. He believed that John Foster Dulles, the American Secretary of State, was completely untrustworthy and that the United Nations was irrelevant to the issue.[27] Morrison was passionately pro-Israel and in recent years had spoken up strongly in her defence, urging the British government to guarantee her frontiers and supply her with sufficient arms to deter the surrounding Arab states which constantly boasted of her impending genocidal annihilation.[28] Before leaving for the United States in September he called on Eden at 10 Downing Street, to restate his support for the government's tough policy. Eden himself felt that if Morrison had been in England when the crisis broke he 'would have been a steadying influence' and that the Prime Minister's own relations with the Labour Opposition would have been much better.[29]

He made few other major contributions on public issues in the Commons before his retirement in 1959. His most serious intervention was to oppose the Committee of Privileges in its defence of his old colleague, George Strauss, who had been in conflict with the London Electricity Board. Morrison felt that the protection of privilege had been stretched too far, to the detriment of private liberty, and he mobilized a majority for his amendment to reject the committee's ruling. It was a kind of victory, and he no doubt believed in the issues at stake, but it was against a colleague and a one-time friend. His support came almost wholly from the Tory benches and his action did not endear him to many on his own side of the House.[30]

Morrison's withdrawal from active politics to nurse his wounds was least pronounced in London. His first attachment remained his most lasting. His attendance at the London Labour Party executive soon picked up again and he never wholly lost interest in the *London News*. Donald Daines had fallen seriously ill in December 1955, and for most of the following year his assistant, Peter Robshaw, formerly with Transport House, was effectively Secretary. Daines died in October 1956, and Morrison was active in securing the post for Robshaw, even against the disapproval of such an old friend as Jim Raisin. Morrison perhaps thought he saw in young Robshaw a future version of himself. He also probably hoped to have somebody amenable to his own views in the office. He later kept in frequent touch with the new Secretary, inviting him for drinks in the Commons, and regularly telephoning to discuss items on the Executive agenda. But he could not any longer dominate the London party.[31] A new generation was on the Executive, people such as Dick Edmonds, Bob Mellish and Michael Stewart, who had their own independent views. Over Suez, for instance, they passed a resolution completely denouncing the government's actions – and hence Morrison's own position.[32] In any case, the London Labour Party was itself in decline, no longer the great electoral machine it had been in the years of Morrison's dominance. Membership fell in the mid-fifties, though not dramatically; in fact the party's decline was more fundamental and less tangible than just a question of membership figures. The London Labour Party was very much Morrison's creation and, like himself, reflected and symbolized a phase in the growth of Labour to a mass national party, adding the superstructure of urban local government to the original trade union foundations. That stage was now over, as the core of working-class communities dissolved under the social and economic pressures of a more affluent and mobile society. The effective life of the London Labour Party, like that of the old LCC, appropriately spanned Morrison's life and no more.

His personal contribution to the London Labour Party was properly commemorated with the purchase of a new headquarters, to be named Herbert Morrison House. The old offices in Westminster Bridge Road were requisitioned by the LCC for redevelopment. The new premises in Walworth Road, SE17, then known as the Robert Browning Settlement, contained considerably more office space, and cost far less rent and rates, so the move made good financial sense. The property was purchased – with the help of a favourable loan of six thousand pounds from the Amalgamated Society of Woodworkers – in June 1958, and they moved in August.[33] The official opening of the renamed Herbert Morrison House was on Saturday 13 December. The meeting room, named after Donald Daines, was packed. Gaitskell and his deputy, Jim Griffiths, were there, Morgan Phillips for the NEC, Len Williams, the national agent, Tewson from the TUC and older London figures such as Harold Clay and Lord Latham. Hugh Gaitskell made the main speech, full of obviously sincere respect and praise for Morrison, describing his drive and his achievements, and referring to him as 'above all a great Socialist and a great Democrat'.[34] Morrison replied with gratitude and with personal recollections of the London party in earlier days. This happy occasion, with leading representatives of the Labour movement gathered to pay tribute to him and to his life's work, was a watershed for Morrison. It marked the beginning of the end of his period of sulking bitterness. The warmth of Gaitskell's praise and the acclamation of all around him began the process of drawing Morrison back into the full Labour community. The recuperation would take some time yet but at least the scars of rejection were healing.[35]

The next stage in Morrison's political recovery was, paradoxically, his retirement from the House of Commons. Leaving it, he put behind him the scene and memories of his recent failures and was able to move to the House of Lords, where he enjoyed a political Indian summer. His departure had often been rumoured, but he dithered until well into 1959. Mabel Raisin pressed him to make up his mind, since she would need time to run in a new candidate before the next election, and he finally decided to go in June. Sadly his relations with the Raisins had deteriorated in recent years. They were upset by his support for Robshaw at the London Labour Party. They also differed with him over the possible reorganization of London local government. Morrison and Mabel each began to suspect the other of hostile intrigues. She told him directly that she wished their friendship to end and he in turn insisted that an exchange of letters between them should be read out to their embarrassed party activists.[36] It was petty and humiliating and very sad considering the long years of friendship and political collaboration between them.

In his letter of retirement to the chairman of the South Lewisham Labour Party Morrison wrote: 'In view of my long service in Parliament and Local Government and the Labour Party and my desire to give more time if possible to writing I have come to the conclusion that I am entitled to a rest from my parliamentary labours. I shall be sorry for, as you know, I love the House of Commons. It has been an honour and a pleasure for me to serve East and South Lewisham as their first Labour MP. Proud of being of the working class, I have been pleased to serve my fellow workers in public affairs and, if I may say so – I hope that my successor may be of the working class too.'[37] The press quizzed him about moving to the Upper House but he was adamant that he would not take a peerage. 'Several times I could have accepted a viscountcy,' he told the *Daily Mail*, 'but all my life I've been of the working class and that's how I'd like to stay.'[38] This working-class theme recurred often at this time. He said more than once that the Labour Party had gone too far in attractting the middle classes – a process which he admitted he had personally encouraged. Behind this was the feeling that these middle-class recruits had deserted him in 1955 and that his own working-class virtues were no longer sufficiently appreciated. His final intervention in Labour politics while still an MP was of a similar kind. He sent a telegram to Frank Cousins,[39] the left-wing leader of the Transport Workers, in July 1959, congratulating him for attacking the retreat from nationalization by the present Labour leadership. Ironically Morrison had, more than anybody, prepared the way in the late forties and early fifties for the effective abandonment of the party's commitment to massive nationalization. He had not now really changed his views* and he certainly had little in common with the dogmatic and militant Cousins – except this sense of shared class origins, attachment to Labour's past and alienation from the middle-class intellectual revisionists dominating the present party. When Gaitskell, flanked by the NEC, the Shadow Cabinet and the whips formally said goodbye to the outgoing MPs on 22 July – to Tom Williams, Jean Mann, George Isaacs, Hugh Dalton and others, all having a place in Morrison's and Labour's great past – Morrison did not attend. He 'seems almost purposeful', said one observer, 'in his determination to sidle out of Westminster and the Socialist Party like a ghost without a bone'.[40] This was the last sediment of his sour spirits. He did attend the final meeting of the parliamentary party a week later and was presented with a morocco writing case and a television set in appreciation of his services.† Gaitskell again spoke warmly in his praise.

* Morrison had first attacked Labour's new policies in the journal *Forward* in August 957, and at the subsequent party conference.

† Subscribed for by a levy of ten shillings a head on all Labour MPs.

The Conservative government's fortunes rapidly recovered during 1959, aided by another timely if excessive reflation of the economy, and Macmillan felt sufficiently confident to call a general election in October. Morrison still played his part for Labour, addressing fourteen meetings in the London area and also travelling to speak at Rochdale, Manchester and Stalybridge. He found it a difficult campaign to assess and never sensed that the Conservatives would win a massive majority of over one hundred.[41] Looking back afterwards, he felt that the leadership had made errors: in having too many and too detailed policies, in seeming to make rash promises, and in giving the impression that 'in overseas affairs the British are almost always bound to be wrong. If they are, we must say so, but we must not look as if we are enjoying it.' He concluded that the party leadership must study and decide 'what sort of people these British people are'.[42]

Shortly before the dissolution of the old Parliament and the start of the election campaign, Morrison received a letter from the Prime Minister. 'I am proposing,' wrote Macmillan, 'to issue a small Dissolution Honours List on September 19th, and it would give me and, may I say, a great many other people, much pleasure to include your name for a Viscountcy. I would be glad to know if this proposal is agreeable to you.'[43] Morrison, who had clearly been informally 'sounded out' beforehand, immediately replied, thanking him, but saying that he would prefer to be a life peer.[44] Macmillan agreed and Morrison's elevation was published on 19 September. Morrison was then on holiday in Torquay. He obviously felt guilty about it, conceding to 'a lack of logic about taking a title' and insisting that 'I still don't like it very much'.[45] He admitted to the farewell gathering of his constituents that he felt 'a bit of a humbug' in accepting after saying 'No' so often, and reassured them that they could still call him Herbert when he was 'walking around dressed up as a Lord'.[46] Morrison had genuinely been in a dilemma about the peerage. He 'wobbled all over the place' as he admitted.[47] His basic instincts and prejudices were against it for himself – it somehow did not seem to be him.[48] Yet he did approve of the life peerage system. His wife and sister shrewdly pointed out that it was desirable for his morale to remain active in politics, keeping his mind alive and still giving him a worthwhile job to do.[49] He was also worried about the loss of his parliamentary salary and saw that a title would bring not only remuneration for attendance at the Lords but also other opportunities for earning money.[50] 'I did think that the Life Peerage presented a way out,' he wrote to Norman Chester, 'especially as I received a great deal of pressure to go to another place.'[51]

He experienced difficulty in choosing a title. He wanted to be 'Lord Morrison of London'. 'I'm a Londoner and I've done a lot of work on the County Council,' he pointed out. 'I love that Council and I don't think anybody is more entitled to be called "London" than I.'[52] But the Garter King of Arms would not allow it. London was too large for a mere Baron to use as a territorial designation; only Dukes and Earls could take whole counties. 'Lord

Herbert Morrison' was also rejected because only the younger sons of Dukes and Marquesses were allowed to include their first names in the title. He did not wish to be 'Lord Morrison of Lewisham' because of the association and possible confusion with Lady Lewisham. In the end he settled for 'Baron Morrison of Lambeth, Lambeth in the County of London'* and was so officially gazetted on 3 November.[53] He took his seat in the Lords a fortnight later. Dressed in his scarlet robes trimmed with ermine and wearing his tricorn hat, he was introduced by his old friends, Lord Taylor and Baroness Wootton. He knelt at the feet of the Lord Chancellor, Kilmuir, with the red leather Lords Bible in his hand, and slowly read out the traditional oath. He then signed the scroll, bowed three times to the Wool sack, and went in jaunty procession around the chamber, stopping periodically to bow and doff his cocked hat. As he walked out past the throne, a fully fledged peer, a warm cheer went up from all sides. He asked the press not to take any photographs – 'I look a bit of a pantomime.'[54] In 1947 Morrison had described himself as 'bursting to limit the power for mischief of this institution with which we have to live'. Now he was part of the mischief.

* He did not have a coat of arms because of the expense – £131. (*News Chronicle*, 10 November 1959.)

Chapter 41

Light and Shadows, 1959-1965

Morrison made his maiden speech in the Lords on 26 November 1959, welcoming the Marshall Scholarships Bill, and subsequently contributed on an enormously wide range of topics.[1] He was usually statesmanlike in tone, fitting in quickly and well to the cosy and relaxed style of the Upper House. Occasionally he livened the chamber with flashes of his old fire. Opposing the government's plans to reorganize the transport system, he savagely attacked the minister, Marples, for allegedly being biased against the railways, accused him of being a pawn of the road haulage lobby, and implied he was unfit for the job. This was strong stuff for the Lords, but Morrison claimed 'it is not a bad thing for your Lordships to have a bit of a dust-up now and again'.[2] He had become a firm supporter of British entry to the Common Market – a pronounced swing from the scepticism he displayed as Foreign Secretary. He joined with Roy Jenkins and a small group of pro-Marketeers in 1961–2 in trying to prevent Labour from dividing Parliament against Britain's application, but failed. He sharply rebuked his party colleagues, including Attlee, for their insularity: 'it is no good socialists . . . saying "workers of all countries unite" and then adding "but not with the French under De Gaulle or the Germans under Adenauer; not with the United States under their capitalist Government".'[3] On most issues his position was unchanged from earlier years: criticizing the commercialism of television when supporting the Pilkington Report on Broadcasting, or defending London's green belt from property developers, or pointing out, over the Vassall spy scandal, that a certain distance should exist between a minister and a civil servant.[4] He enjoyed life in the Lords and missed as few debates as possible.[5] He never tried to usurp the existing leadership of Alexander and Silkin. 'He settled down quickly', recalled the latter, 'and was always willing to do any job he was asked to do. He didn't put on airs and just became one of us.'[6] His mastery of parliamentary procedure and tactics was highly valued by his colleagues in the group of Labour peers.[7] He did not, however, grow any closer to Attlee and the two never sat next to one another on the front bench.[8]

During the first two years Morrison was in the Lords, the Labour Party was deeply divided over the issue of nuclear disarmament, a division which broadened into an offensive by the left wing to convert the party to neutralism, and above all to eject Hugh Gaitskell from the leadership. Morrison remained aloof from most of this battle. He firmly and publicly rejected the arguments of the nuclear disarmers. 'We do not want the cold war,' he told a Foyles literary lunch, with Gaitskell sitting in the audience, 'but by God we value our liberty and freedom and if necessary we are prepared to fight for them. Personally I would sooner be dead than a slave under a totalitarian state. Some people wouldn't. I don't admire their taste.'[9] But he would not step into the arena to defend Gaitskell's leadership. When the supporters of Gaitskell organized the Campaign for Democratic Socialism and issued their manifesto of principles, Morrison declined to join Attlee, Dalton and others in declaring their approval for its objectives. 'I find this manifesto a bit too much on the right in some respects. I've had a long left-wing life myself, getting things done and changing things.' He was above all relieved not to be involved in the blood-letting. 'I am glad to be out of the other House', he commented, 'I regard it as a depressing affair.'[10] He supported the parliamentary party in refusing to accept as binding the 1960 Scarborough conference decision in favour of unilateralism but he deplored the animosities which were aroused. He looked back nostalgically to 'the exciting, and as a whole glorious days of the Clarion Fellowship' when 'an outstanding slogan was "Fellowship is Life: Lack of Fellowship is Death" . . . Socialism means sweetness and light. Cattiness among us, whether on the part of men or women, is not fellowship and is inimical to sweetness and light and to Socialist ethics.'[11]

Apart from the House of Lords, his main political interest still lay with the London Labour Party. In 1960 and 1961 he attended virtually every Executive Committee meeting.[12] He remained on the advisory board of *London News*. He went to annual conference in the spring of 1960 and to the reunion dance at the Lyceum in October. He danced with several girls, but complained about the modern style of dancing individually apart. 'I like to get a girl really in my arms,' he told a reporter.[13] He was active in the 1961 LCC election campaign, addressing meetings and making eve-of-poll broadcasts on both radio and television. Labour lost many seats and lost control of Middlesex, but managed to hold onto the LCC. Morrison was, however, very much a relic of an earlier age. The London Labour Party Executive, once a family gathering of his political associates and protégés, was now full of unfamiliar faces. Brandon had retired from the chairmanship in 1960.* A new alien generation was thrusting up. Ominously, in 1961 there were other nominations for the job as treasurer. Morrison decided to go before he was pushed out and in June he informed the Executive that he would not stand for re-election in

* R. Mellish succeeded.

1962. 'I have enjoyed enormously my many years' association with the London Labour Party,' he wrote, 'from the difficult pioneering days to the successes in the LCC. . . . But I really feel that I should now retire. Forty-six years is a long time.'[14] At the annual conference at St Pancras Town Hall on Sunday 25 March the final motion, moved by Sir Isaac Hayward, was in appreciation of Morrison's work for the London party. Peter Robshaw then presented him with an illuminated address containing the words of the motion inscribed on vellum. Morrison rose to reply with tears in his eyes. He blew his nose and told them always to be meticulously honest, sensible and socialist. 'We exist not to be masters of London, nor even of our country. We exist to serve.' After a few reminiscences about the London party in the twenties, he said his farewell and sat down to a standing ovation.* He now held no office in the Labour Party.

Changes affected Morrison's personal life. He and Edith moved from Archery Road in October 1960. They bought a smaller house, fully detached with three bedrooms, in Colepitts Wood Road, Eltham. Morrison allowed his wife to choose the house providing it was in the Woolwich area.[15] His attachment to this part of London remained as strong as ever.

The Morrisons entertained in their new house on most weekends and some of the friendships which had been broken off in the bitter days of 1955 were now resumed over a meal and drink.[16] He continued to be in demand for various kinds of social functions. He occasionally addressed political clubs, including the Young Conservatives at Rochdale.[17] He attended the annual dinners of the parliamentary press gallery, the Anglo-German Association and the Scottish Club of Rochdale on Burns' Night.[18] In Lewisham he opened a new health centre for the handicapped and handed over the key of the two-hundred-thousandth house built by the LCC.[19] He took Edith to Torquay for the Conference of the Royal Society of Health, and Gracie Fields, another Rochdale lassie, to dinner at the House of Lords.[20] He appeared on television

---

* LLP papers 15365. *Manchester Guardian*, 26 November 1962; *Daily Herald*, 26 November 1962. The motion stated: 'That this conference places on record its high appreciation of the distinguished services rendered to Labour over many years by the Treasurer of the London Labour Party, Lord Morrison of Lambeth, Socialist and Statesman.

'Conference recalls particularly his services as Secretary of the London Labour Party from 1915–1940, first Labour Leader of the London County Council, and his outstanding contribution towards Labour's victory in the London County Council Election of 1934, and the laying of sure foundations which has enabled Labour to retain its majority on the London County Council for 30 years.

'On national and international levels, Herbert Morrison's contribution to the Labour Movement has been universally recognized and acclaimed.

'In thanking him for so much, Conference extends to Lord Morrison of Lambeth its best wishes for an active, healthy and lengthy future, pledging itself to strive with undiminished vigour to secure the aims which have inspired his lifetime of service to Labour, London and the nation.'

in a *Face to Face* interview with John Freeman: much old mud was again stirred in the water and all his resentment against Attlee still showed through. Overseas lecture tours took him to India in February 1961, to North America in the autumn of that year, and back there again in the following spring. He was remarkably active and sprightly for a man in his mid-seventies and clearly enjoyed his busy and varied life. He even resumed his friendship with Beaverbrook, going to dinner with him at Cherkley in June 1962.[21] He spent August and early September holidaying in Switzerland and Italy and on his return opened the 'Lord Morrison of Lambeth' public house in Wandsworth Road. Whitbread's had taken considerable trouble to collect old photographs, cartoons and mementoes as decorations.[22]

An interesting and rewarding development in Morrison's life was his appointment in June 1960 as President of the Board of Film Censors. The cinema industry wanted as President someone with good contacts with Parliament, with the Home Office, which was responsible for film legislation, with the local authorities which licensed cinemas, and who was skilled at handling the press. Morrison fitted the bill ideally and he was suggested both by John Trevelyan, the Board Secretary, and by Sir Austin Strutt at the Home Office. He was invited to lunch at the Connaught with key figures in the industry and the presidency offer was dangled before him. Afterwards he telephoned Strutt, who had worked under him in the early years of the war, and said 'I'm in a quandary. Do you know any reason of politics, ethics or morals, why I should decline the Presidency of the Board of Film Censors?' Strutt, who then revealed he had already been consulted, did not and Morrison quickly decided to accept.[23] The £3,000 a year salary more than replaced the recent loss of his income as an MP.

Morrison was no stranger to the film industry, which was his responsibility when Lord President. He had set up the Radcliffe Committee of Inquiry into the future of the British Film Institute in December 1947 and had initiated the reorganization of the Institute along the lines of the Radcliffe recommendations in 1948–9. He personally loved going to the pictures, though his taste did not extend much beyond thrillers or musicals. He often attended West End film premières when a minister and later took Margaret and then Edith regularly, if in more humble style, to the local cinema in Eltham.

As President of the Board, Morrison was responsible for the broad lines of policy and was also called on for a decision if the other examining members disagreed. He usually went into the Soho Square offices on Wednesday mornings to view any film of particular interest or difficulty. He also dropped in to consult with Trevelyan at other times and attended film premières and industry dinners and conferences. It was not a heavy load and what there was he enjoyed immensely.[24] One especially pleasant 'perk' of the job was a six-week trip to the United States with Edith in April and May 1962. The main purpose was to visit Hollywood. He saw films being made at the studios of Warner Brothers, Columbia and MGM, went to Disneyland, was guest of honour at a luncheon given by the Association of Motion Picture Producers, and had tea with Mr and Mrs Sam Goldwyn. His schedule was nicely relaxed and he found time to stop off in Memphis, St Paul, Dallas and Mississippi, as well as resting for a week with friends on Long Island, lecturing in New York and paying a formal visit to President Kennedy at the White House. It was an exciting sweep through the glamorous New World – though he did not wholly forget politics in the Old. In mid-tour he appealed to Soho Square for tele-graphed results of the London metropolitan borough elections.[25]

He was moderately successful in his film job, particularly when called upon to resolve difficult internal political situations. He managed the other Board members with his old skill, though his relations with Trevelyan, the mercurial Board Secretary, were patchy. Morrison saw himself in the role of minister with Trevelyan as the civil servant; Trevelyan assumed he himself had more executive responsibility, like a managing director in relation to his company chairman. The reality was closer to Trevelyan's view, which led to some irritations after 1962 when Morrison, with time on his hands after giving up the London Labour Party, tried to get more involved in day-to-day affairs at Soho Square. Ironically, he was never once used in the role for which he was originally selected, to provide access to and influence in Whitehall, West-minster and with the local authorities.[26]

As film censor Morrison was inevitably drawn into the growing debate on 'the state of morals' in Britain and the alleged excesses of the so-called per-missive society. He really had little sympathy with the developing libertarian-ism. Although he repeatedly claimed 'I am no puritan', this was usually the preface to some expression disapproving of the loosening moral climate around him. He was as always calm and showed none of the hysteria of some others in the older generation who shared his repressive instinct. He was certainly embarrassed by the enthusiasm with which his appointment was welcomed among some guardians of morality. 'My Lord, you know how wrong all this output by the professional purveyors of ideas and advertisers is and how wicked,' wrote one well-wisher from St John's Wood. 'I wish you the strength of Hercules and final success in this job of restoring Mental Hygiene to London and making the film industry an asset instead of a poison.'[27] His was no easy job, attempting to maintain general standards in a rapidly changing moral climate.* 'I'll try to be a kindly uncle,' he said at the outset, 'There are no rules in this job. You have to use your common sense.'[28] Broadly that is what he did, though he was never absolutely clear what were the dictates of common sense and always declined to take part in public

---

* The Board's own declared aim is 'to exclude from public exhibition anything likely to impair the moral standards of the public, by extenuating vice or crime or by deprecating social standards, and anything likely to give offence to any reasonably-minded members of the audience'.

debates on the role of censorship.[29] He simply followed his instincts, which led him, for example, to press for major cuts even in *West Side Story*. Outside the film industry he denounced the court decision in favour of the book *Lady Chatterley's Lover*, suggesting that it was a mistake to trust the decision to a jury rather than the Home Secretary, who he felt was a more reliable custodian of the nation's liberties and morality.[30] To the end of his life he claimed that *Lady Chatterley* should be suppressed – also adding to his black list *Fanny Hill*, claiming it was 'certainly pornographic' while pointing out that he had read it 'only as a parliamentary duty'.[31] He argued against relaxing the law relating to homosexuals and in favour of stiffer control of Soho clubs. 'Private clubs on the loose and exhibiting salacious posters on the public highway,' he wrote, 'are likely to be damaging to the nation's morals and have the wrong kind of stimulus. We must be careful not to let the British go to the devil.'[32]

Shortly after taking over as film censor, Morrison published his autobiography. These memoirs had been a long time in gestation. Odhams, his publishers, had periodically tried to spur him into action, offering to provide a ghost-writer and putting at his disposal an office, a dictaphone and a secretary. He dictated a few early draft chapters but nothing substantial came of it until after 1956, when semi-retirement and financial needs pushed him into action. He at first wanted Norman Chester of Nuffield to assist him, as he had with the earlier book, *Government and Parliament*. Chester was willing, but only if it was intended to produce a serious and substantial contribution to the study of politics and history. After preliminary discussions it was clear that Morrison had no such intention and Chester withdrew. Instead a professional ghost-writer was employed, F. G. Kay, who had already successfully 'ghosted' the autobiography of Manny Shinwell. Kay travelled regularly to Eltham. Morrison gave him the basic material and Kay drafted the book. They did not get on very well together, in what must always be a difficult relationship, and neither ended up with a great respect for the other. Kay found Morrison certainly still intellectually vigorous, with a remarkable memory for detail, recalling the names and even the addresses of minor officials in the Social Democratic Federation before the First World War. But his secretiveness, occasional vanity and outbursts of bitterness as they went back over the years of 'carrying the can' for Attlee made it none too easy a task. Morrison would not give Kay access to what then appeared to be a large and well-ordered collection of papers in the room he used as an office. At the end of their association Morrison asked him to return any papers he had been using or any notes he had taken.[33]

The autobiography was published in September 1960. During the previous spring the *Sunday Times* had serialized six extracts, for which Morrison received a payment of £9,500, plus another £500 in advance of overseas syndication rights.[34] Taken together with his film censor salary, this meant that Morrison's financial position dramatically improved in 1960, and explains the surprising size of his estate on death.* Just before the serial appeared, Morrison toned down the existing sharp criticisms of Attlee and specially asked the *Sunday Times* not to suggest in its headlines or advertisements that the articles contained any personal attacks on Attlee or Bevan.[35] Two alterations were also introduced at the suggestion of Sir Norman Brook at the Cabinet Office, who read the manuscript to ensure that there were no breaches of the Official Secrets Act. Neither alteration really involved the nation's security: one removed a little detail relating to the two occasions when Morrison differed from King George VI on the question of reprieve for murder, the other deleted a sentence which 'might be read as implying that Treasury Officials were taking a view about the date of the next [1950] election'.[36] The press reviews of the book understandably lacked enthusiasm. In substance it contained little that was new. It was flat in style and sour in tone. It was sad that such a remarkably full and varied life, involving so much that was important to the history of the Labour movement and Britain, was boiled down to something so grey and boring. Morrison does not emerge from it as a living person, and some of the most important people in his life – his first wife Margaret, his daughter Mary, Jim and Mabel Raisin – are not mentioned at all. No doubt the book had suffered from the uneasy working partnership which had produced it. But it was symptomatic of something deep in Morrison, the persistent caution and secretiveness about all political, personal and private matters, and the unhappiness he felt at the lack of fulfilment in his own career, that he simply could not produce an autobiography worth reading, let alone worthy of the man.

After giving up his London Labour Party work in 1962 Morrison devoted even more time than previously to the House of Lords. He continued to contribute in a wide range of debates, including some issues of long-standing interest to him. He followed closely and broadly supported the 1963 television legislation, though strongly disapproving of the appointment of Charles Hill, a Conservative politician, as Chairman of the ITA. 'I cannot say less than that I think it is a public scandal,' he asserted, '. . . if ever there was a job for the boys, it is this one . . . the whole thing smells from beginning to end. It is shameful.'[37] He opened a transport debate by calling attention to the problems of public transport in Britain, arguing that all private cars should be banned from central London and pointing out in passing, possibly to the relief of south London pedestrians, that he had himself given up driving to Westminster.[38] He launched another savage attack on the Transport Minister, Marples, arguing that he was 'utilizing his prerogative not for the public good but to protect the allies of his political party in the field of private enterprise. I think he is doing it for an ulterior purpose, in order to build up the profits

* £28,600.

of private undertakings ... this man is unfit to hold office in public administration. The Prime Minister ought to get rid of him and let him go back to speculative building where his philosophy would have ample opportunity of being expressed and coming out.'[39] Other peers protested at this attack. It was not really typical of his usual Lords style. This topic did arouse a particularly combustible combination of his passions, arising from his past experience as Transport Minister, his lifelong devotion to public transport and his strongly puritanical feeling that service in government should never seem to be tainted by outside interests.

The issue which above all dominated his attention during these last two years of his life was the government's proposal to reorganize London local government, by abolishing his beloved LCC and establishing a new Greater London authority. This question had simmered for the past forty years, as the effective metropolis had spread far beyond the boundaries of the original LCC. Morrison had altered his position since he gave evidence in favour of creating a larger authority to the 1922 Royal Commission. He bitterly and successfully opposed recommendations for such a larger authority from committees of the London Labour Party, one in the war and another in 1953, and then led the fight against the 1957 White Paper on local government reorganization.[40] He now argued that London was a special case which should be exempted from any national pattern of reform. The proposed GLC was to him far too large for efficient administration and he pleaded for retention of the LCC as at least a proven success in the area it covered.

Some London Labour politicians – including Jim Raisin and Les Hilliard from Fulham – saw that change was inevitable and advocated co-operation in order to have influence on any new arrangements, but Morrison worked to freeze them out of the London party's decision-making.[41] When a Royal Commission on Local Government Reorganization was set up in June 1958, Morrison wrote an article headed 'I Love London Town' arguing that no change was required in the present LCC.[42] In his presidential address to the Association of Municipal Corporations he warned, with macabre prescience, that 'there are people about who would want to convert London into a series of county boroughs. They would do it over my dead body.'[43] Morrison opened the debate on the Royal Commission report in 1960, defending the LCC as 'a great authority, incorruptible, clean and with a high quality administration', and he asked 'what has London done to deserve this abortion'.[44] In April 1961 he resigned from the presidency of the AMC in protest against the Association's support for the findings of the Royal Commission. His savagely worded resignation was deliberately timed for the eve of the LCC elections and appeared in the press before the Association's secretary, Sir Harold Banwell, received Morrison's letter. The AMC, which had never used Morrison in the role of high-level contact man, as originally intended, chose Attlee as his successor, perhaps not consciously intended as revenge but certainly a painful riposte.[45]

When the government announced in late 1961 that the LCC would disappear on 1 April 1965 Morrison declared in the Upper House 'My Lords, the Government is mad'. The government spokesman, Lord Jellicoe, declined to answer a number of Morrison's barbed points because of their 'intemperate language'.[46] In March 1962 he announced 'I will stump London and we will fight in London to denounce the Government for this piece of political job-bery' and accused the Tories of being 'madder than ever. It is really insane ... this wicked attempt ... this contemptible plot, I almost said a corrupt plot.'[47] He travelled with Lord Longford by launch up the Thames from Greenwich to Hampton Court, stopping at piers and handing to local Mayors – of Deptford, Woolwich, Bermondsey, East Ham, Poplar, Stepney – forms for the collection of protest signatures. He angrily withdrew from an engage-ment to address a public meeting in local Woolwich because the borough council had offered to give evidence on reorganization, even though it was in principle against the scheme.[48]

Morrison took the proposed reforms almost as a deliberately personal attack on himself and when the London Government Bill came before the Lords in the spring and summer of 1963 he fought it to the end with the same vigour and tenacity with which he had so often supported changes in his younger days. He intervened frequently at each stage of its slow progress. His fellow Labour peers organized a systematic campaign of opposition which forced the Lords to extend its sitting hours from seven till ten in the evening and sometimes even later into the night. Many joined in as much out of loyalty to Morrison as from conviction on the issue. He did not manage the Labour campaign. His role was more that of a personal crusade, fanatically, sadly, almost pathetically, fighting a doomed battle to preserve one of the great symbols of his life's political work.[49]

Morrison and his wife went away to Italy in the summer of 1963 to rest from the rigours of the recent parliamentary session, which had been the heaviest for him since the early 1950s. He visited the Film Festival at Venice and relaxed on the beach appreciating the beautiful women drifting by.[50] At this point in time he still enjoyed remarkably good health considering his age. Apart from a collapse in 1960, when he was rushed to University College Hospital with a suspected heart attack (which he kept secret from the press and his political colleagues), he had maintained his physical vigour and undimin-ished interest in life.[51] He continued to play an active part in his film censorship job and also attended various public functions in the winter of 1963–4 includ-ing officially opening the new Strand underpass, a traffic improvement scheme which he had long advocated.[52] He went to Beaverbrook's eighty-fifth birthday dinner at the Dorchester in May 1964, surrounded by other political relics from the 1940s and earlier. He still attended the Lords regularly and contrib-uted to its debates. He also tried to get more radio work and pressed hard, but in vain, to appear on the programme *Desert Island Discs*, even having his list of records chosen in readiness, headed by a Vera Lynn song and a Welsh Labour Choir singing 'Jerusalem'.[53]

In the autumn of 1964, however, the retina of his good left eye suffered a disease which proved progressive and could not be checked by any treatment.[54] Despite this affliction he went on a parliamentary delegation to the West Indies in November; a lady colleague helped him to pack and unpack his cases and also rehearsed his speeches aloud to him so that he could speak from memory, because he could no longer read his notes. He refused to let it depress him and companions found him 'amazingly courageous and brave'.[55] On his return he had to ask Warden Chester of Nuffield to deal with the Oxford University Press over the latest edition of *Government and Parliament*. 'My trouble is such,' he communicated to Chester, 'that at the moment I cannot read. However, the one eye has been a very good friend to me for 76 years.'[56] He still went to the Lords, once turning to Citrine during a debate and whispering, 'Walter, what time is it?' He could not see the clock only a few feet away.[57] At home Edith read to him, his correspondence, the newspapers, Hansard, books.[58] This sight failure most directly affected his work as film censor since he simply could not see the films. The Kinematograph Manufacturers' Association had anyway decided not to renew his five-year contract, which ended in 1965. They had found that in practice they did not make use of his political influence, as initially envisaged, and they were also worried by his recent deterioration in vigour. The decision not to renew his appointment was conveyed to Morrison before Christmas 1964 and he took it badly, feeling that he had been sacked.[59] From this point his spirit sagged. He spent his last, sad, Christmas and his seventy-seventh birthday with Edith in Rochdale. He occasionally dropped into the Lords in the new year, but early in February he fell ill and was taken to the Queen Mary Hospital, Sidcup, for observation. He was suffering from an inflammation of the large intestine, which was painful and uncomfortable but treatable with antibiotics. For a time he improved and was able to sit up and enjoy a cigar with brandy. His private doctor was encouraged and told him he would be well enough to go home within a week. Morrison put his head quizzically on one side and asked 'what have I got to recover for? I cannot see. I've lost my job on the Film Censors' Board. There is nothing for me in politics.'[60] Subsequent visitors found him lying in bed, his eyes closed, suffering no pain but showing no interest in anything. He died on Saturday evening, 6 March 1965. The hospital stated the cause of death as cerebral haemorrhage.[61] His personal doctor concluded 'if you ask me what he did die of, I don't know. He just died because he saw no further point in living.'[62]

Morrison was cremated on 11 March at the tiny crematorium in Eltham. It was a cheery occasion, as he wanted. The pearly king and queen were present on a beautiful spring day, with the daffodils and tulips ablaze in the crematorium grounds. Inside the chapel the Salvation Army band, led by General Coutts, played the jolly music which Morrison had requested in his will – 'there is enough sadness in the world' he added. The chapel doors were left open so that the crowds of Londoners outside could enjoy the rousing brassy renderings of 'Onward Christian Soldiers' and 'Sweeping through the gates to the New Jerusalem'.

He also asked in his will that his remains 'be scattered into the high tide of London's river from the terrace of County Hall where I was privileged to render several years of happy service to the people of London'. On the morning of the memorial service at the Abbey, 30 March, when the new Labour Prime Minister read the lesson, the Thames was at low tide. The funeral urn was therefore taken from the festival pier on board an LCC fireboat, *Firebrace*.[63] As the tiny red and black boat sailed slowly past County Hall, where not many hours later the LCC was to hold its last meeting before oblivion, Morrison's ashes were scattered on the rising stream to be carried under Westminster Bridge and past the Houses of Parliament.

Notes

PART ONE

Chapter 1 The Beginning

1 The sources for Morrison's childhood are mainly: Lord Morrison of Lambeth, *An Autobiography* (1960) (cited later as *Autobiography*); M. Edelman, *Herbert Morrison* (1948); M. Webb, 'The Rt. Hon. Herbert Morrison, MP', in H. Tracey (ed.), *The British Labour Party*, Vol. III (1948), pp. 29–40; and interviews with his sister, Mrs E. Richards; his sister-in-law, Mrs C. S. Morrison; and his boyhood playmates, Mrs 'Dolly' Reynolds and Mr H. E. England. Mr S. Richards, his nephew, provided much family information.

2 *Autobiography*, p. 19.

3 C. Booth (ed.), *Life and Labour of the People in London, 3rd Series, Religious Influences*, Vol. 6 (1902), Map, p. 96. Brixton was described by Sir Walter Besant as consisting of 'exceedingly uninteresting and drab streets, where middle-class people of many types make their homes in the midst of the most nondescript architecture'. The houses were mainly terraced with a scattering of larger detached ones, mostly built from the 1860s. Sir Walter Besant, *London South of the Thames* (1912), p. 169. Paul Thompson calculated that in Brixton the middle class formed about 52·5 per cent of the population. P. Thompson, *Socialists, Liberals and Labour, the Struggle for London 1885–1914* (1967), p. 300. Henry Pelling characterized Brixton as possessing a prosperous, predominantly middle or upper class electorate, with a Conservative vote over the six elections between 1885 and 1910 of 58·6 per cent. H. Pelling, *Social Geography of British Elections, 1885–1910* (1967), pp. 30, 34–5.

4 Note to the author from W. E. Jackson.

5 *The Valuation and Rating Book*, Lambeth 1890, gave it a gross value of £26 per annum and a rateable value of £21.

6 *Hackney and Kingsland Gazette*, 2 July 1924.

7 Speech at Conference of Institute of Municipal Treasurers and Accountants, 1960. *Report*, p. 89.

8 *Autobiography*, p. 19.

9 *People*, 15 June 1947.

10 *John Bull*, 9 November 1946; also *News Chronicle*, 6 December 1939.

11 P. Jenkins, 'Maybe it's because he's a Londoner', *The House of Whitbread*, Vol. 22, January 1963, p. 20. He recalled that he always had trouble with his feet. 'We were rather poor at home and replacement of shoes was a problem for a growing boy.' *Daily Mail*, 18 December 1959.

12 See *Sunday Post*, 15 March 1959.

13 *Spectator*, 14 August 1964.

14 Possibly J. Millot Severn; died 1942 aged eighty-two. *Daily Express*, 21 July 1942.

15 *Reader's Digest*, April 1956, pp. 61–3.

16 This episode is described best by P. Johnson in the *Star*, 12 March 1936. See also M. Edelman, op. cit., pp. 18–20.

17 So impressed was Morrison by phrenology that when leader of the LCC 1934–40, he used to consult a Conservative councillor, who was a leading figure in the Phrenological Society, about his own and his colleagues' characteristics. Interview, R. C. D. Jenkins. He also referred often to the significance of his confrontation with the phrenologist, e.g. *Daily Express*, 28 September 1934: 'I started to read in earnest, and have kept it up.'

18 He said: 'This literature was without doubt the basic reason why my thoughts began to turn towards socialism.' *Autobiography*, p. 24.

19 He wrote in his diary: 'As Socialism is very dear to me I cannot agree with the policy of the Parliamentary Labour Party. Moreover, the PLP is affiliated to the Labour Party, and that Party is certainly not a Socialist Party.' *Autobiography*, p. 36.

20 *Spectator*, 14 August 1964; also *Hackney and Kingsland Gazette*, 11 July 1921.

21 Preface to P. C. Hoffman, *They also Serve: The Story of the Shop Worker* (1949), p. vi.

22 *John Bull*, 9 November 1946; M. Edelman, op. cit., p. 48; *Star*, 12 March 1936; *People*, 10 November 1946.

23 Interview, J. Pretty.

24 See *IMTA Conference Report*, 1960, p. 90.

25 *Reader's Digest*, April 1956, p. 62.

26 *Sunday Post*, 15 March 1959.

27 These early grammar books which include Morrison's notes are now in the library of the London Labour Party.

28 Morrison recalled: 'The bulk of the pre-war shop assistants were notoriously snobbish. When I was a shop assistant I considered myself a proletarian. I am so still.' *Daily Express*, 2 August 1932.

29 M. Webb, op. cit., p. 32.

30 *Spectator*, 14 August 1964.

31 BBC radio broadcast, 'Talks for Sixth Forms', 29 June 1962.

Chapter 2 The Politician Emerges

1 See *Justice*, 8 August 1908.

2 *Autobiography*, pp. 45–6.

3 *Autobiography*, pp. 50–51.

4 *The Times*, 1 July 1929, and BBC radio broadcast, 'Talks for Sixth Forms', 29 June 1962.

5 *Star*, 12 March 1936, and unpublished Memoir by Miss A. Sayle.

6 *Time*, 29 July 1946, and interview, Mrs C. S. Morrison.

7 *Justice*, 5 June 1909.

8 *Justice*, 10 July 1909.

9 See Sydney O. Nevile, *Seventy Rolling Years* (1958), p. 244.

10 Interview, Mrs D. Reynolds.

11 *Belfast Telegraph*, 15 March 1946.

12 *Time*, 29 July 1946.

13 Interview, Mrs R. Penna.

14 Unpublished Memoir by Miss A. Sayle, and *Tit-Bits*, 18 February 1950.

15 *Justice*, 24 October 1908.

16 *Justice*, 23 October 1909.

17 *Justice*, 26 June 1909.

18 Interviews, H. J. Stenning and Sir Frederic Osborn; and *Borough of Lambeth Gazette*, 12 March 1909.

19 *Borough of Lambeth Gazette*, 4 December 1908.

20 *Autobiography*, p. 30.

21 *Daily Worker*, 26 June 1954.

22 See *Borough of Lambeth Gazette*, 12 March 1909, and *Brixton Free Press*, 30 July 1909, 13 August 1909.

23 *Daily Worker*, 26 June 1954.

24 *Justice*, 20 February, 27 March 1909.

25 Interview, Mrs E. K. Goodrich.

26 *Brixton Free Press*, 20 May 1910.

27 *Labour Leader*, 11 December 1913.

28 *Brixton Free Press*, 14 April 1911.

29 Draft autobiographical notes. Morrison papers, Nuffield College, Oxford. Cited later as draft autobiography.

30 *Daily Herald*, 4 March 1935. Interviews, H. J. Stenning, C. W. Gibson, Mrs I. Hudson, D. Dixon, Lord Brockway, Dame Mabel Crout, Mrs E. K. Goodrich, G. Finch.

31 Letter of Morrison to Mylles's daughter, 10 June 1964.

32 *Autobiography*, p. 41.

33 *Lewisham Journal*, 1 February 1935.

34 Interview, Mrs R. Penna.

35 *Justice*, 21 May 1910; *Labour Leader*, 29 April 1910.

36 *Reynolds News*, 4 January 1953.

37 *Labour Leader*, 27 October 1911.

38 Documents of the London and Southern Counties Divisional Council of the ILP, ILP Papers, IV C No. 6, document 108. LSE.

39 NAC Minutes, February 1911, and February 1912. LSE.

40 *Autobiography*, p. 52.

41 M. Edelman, *Herbert Morrison* (1948), p. 22.

42 *John Bull*, 9 November 1946.

43 *Clerk*, March 1912.

44 *Clerk*, February 1913.

45 *Clerk*, August 1912.

46 *Brixton and Lambeth Gazette*, 22 September 1911.

47 *Clerk*, July 1913.
48 F. Hughes, *By Hand and Brain* (1953), p. 36.
49 *Brixton and Lambeth Gazette*, 16 February 1912.
50 *Labour Leader*, 1 December 1911.
51 Much later he recalled that he learned dancing 'at sixpenny hops at the Lambeth Baths when I was 18.' *Evening News*, 24 May 1945.
52 Interviews, Mrs E. K. Goodrich, Mrs I. Hudson, D. Dixon, T. J. Fisher, C. W. Gibson.
53 *Labour Leader*, 24 May 1912. His report of the work of the Federation for 1913 to 1914 is preserved in ILP papers, IV B (iii), 8 March 1914, LSE, where he lists the demonstrations, missions, visits and reunions he organized.
54 *Labour Leader*, 5 April 1912.
55 *Daily Mail*, 18 December 1959.
56 *Labour Leader*, 11 December 1913; and 3 May, 27 June, 9 September 1912, 28 August 1913, 23 January 1914.
57 *Labour Leader*, 31 October 1912.
58 See *Labour Leader*, 12 May, 8 December 1911.
59 *Autobiography*, p. 54.
60 *Labour Leader*, 29 December 1911.
61 *Autobiography*, p. 53.
62 The minute book from 1910 to 1916, together with papers, are in the ILP papers collection, IV A, No. 6, LSE.
63 *Autobiography*, p. 35.
64 *Autobiography*, p. 47.
65 *Golders Green Gazette*, 16 November 1934; and speech on accepting freedom of the borough. *Presentation document*, 31 October 1947.
66 *Autobiography*, p. 48.
67 *Brixtonian*, 29 March 1912.
68 *Borough of Lambeth Gazette*, 22 September, 6 October 1911.
69 *Brixton Free Press*, 28 April 1911.
70 *Labour Leader*, 12 May 1911.
71 *Brixton Free Press*, 27 September 1912.
72 Memoir, Miss A. Sayle. Interviews, C. W. Gibson, Mrs E. K. Goodrich, D. Dixon.
73 *Autobiography*, p. 49.
74 *Labour Leader*, 14 November 1912.

Chapter 3   The Young Activist

1 Interview, Lord Brockway.
2 He could now complain that colleagues in private concerns had sold themselves to serve capitalists. Interview, D. Dixon.
3 Interview, T. J. Fisher.
4 A. Marwick, *Clifford Allen: The Open Conspirator* (1964), p. 16.
5 *Daily Herald*, 19 February 1948.
6 Interview, Mrs R. Penna, Morgan's daughter.
7 *Star*, 7 May 1930.
8 Interviews, F. Foster and Mrs H. Wrattan.

9 F. Brockway, *Bermondsey Story* (1949), p. 50. Also interview, Lord Henderson.

10 *Star*, 12 March 1936.

11 *Star*, 7 May 1930.

12 *Star*, 12 March 1936.

13 Memoir by H. J. Stenning. See also *News Chronicle*, 4 April 1960.

14 Quoted in the *Guardian*, 8 March 1965.

15 *Labour Leader*, 22 January 1914.

16 See R. I. McKibbin, 'The Evolution of a National Party: Labour's Political Organization, 1910–24.' Unpublished D. Phil. thesis, Oxford, 1970, pp. 111–19.

17 *Daily Citizen*, 3 March 1915.

18 See *Labour Leader*, 8 January 1914; and interview, Mrs M. Brown.

19 Interview, Mrs R. Penna.

20 Interviews, T. J. Fisher and daughter.

21 R. Blatchford, *The Dolly Ballads* (1950), preface by Morrison. See also *Labour Woman*, May 1913 for Morrison telling a story to a two-year-old.

22 Interviews. The drawing of Morrison by Pogany in 1911 depicts a head that can be called grotesquely ugly.

23 Beatrice Webb's diary, 17 January 1932 and 27 November 1935, Passfield papers, LSE.

24 Interview, Mrs E. K. Goodrich.

25 *Brixton Free Press*, 28 October 1910.

26 *Brixton Free Press*, 15 March 1912.

27 *Labour Leader*, 24 May 1912.

28 *Labour Leader*, 17 February 1911.

29 Interviews, Mrs E. K. Goodrich and Dame Leah Manning.

30 *Labour Woman*, January 1914.

31 Ibid.

32 *Evening Times*, Glasgow, 22 January 1954. See also *Sunday Post*, 15 March 1959.

33 *Brixton and Lambeth Gazette*, 6 October 1911. See J. Mann, *Woman in Parliament* (1962), p. 93, for a description of Morrison's early experiences in Scotland.

34 Interviews, Mrs E. K. Goodrich, Mrs Creech Jones, Mrs R. Penna, H. J. Stenning.

35 *Daily Sketch*, 7 November 1919.

36 *Labour Leader*, 8 January 1914.

37 *Labour Leader*, 10 June 1915.

38 J. T. Murphy, *Labour's Big Three* (1948), p. 15.

39 *Belfast Telegraph*, 15 March 1946.

40 F. Brockway, op. cit., p. 50; interview, Lord Brockway. Also interviews, Mrs Creech Jones, C. Brandon, Mrs D. J. Bolton, T. J. Fisher, H. J. Stenning, C. W. Gibson, D. Dixon, Sir Frederic Osborn.

41 *Daily Sketch*, 7 November 1919.

42 *Brixton Free Press*, 18 June, 16 July 1909, 7 October 1910.

43 *Brixton Free Press*, 19, 26 August, 2, 9 September 1910.

44 *Labour Leader*, 6, 20 January, 3, 17 February, 3, 17 March, 7 April, 21, 28 July, 22 September, 6 October, 22 December 1911.

45 *London News*, October 1926 and September 1932.

46 *Labour Leader*, 21 May 1914. See also *Labour Leader*, 17 July, 24 December 1913, 1 January 1914.

Chapter 4   Time of Turmoil

1 Interview, Mrs R. Penna.

2 E.g. *Labour Leader*, 10 June 1915.

3 *Report of ILP Annual Conference*, April 1915, p. 94.

4 *Labour Leader*, 21 January and 21 October 1915.

5 *Labour Leader*, 18 November 1915.

6 Interview, Dame Margaret Cole.

7 *The Times*, 26 February 1919.

8 See F. Brockway, *Bermondsey Story* (1949), p. 141.

9 P. Thompson, *Socialists, Liberals and Labour, the Struggle for London, 1885–1914* (1967), *passim*.

10 *London News*, April 1934, November 1935, February 1936.

11 P. Thompson, op. cit., p. 289, states that Morrison was elected because the BSP was split over its attitude to the war.

12 *Report of LLP Executive*, 1917–18.

13 *LLP Circular*, May 1917.

14 *Report of LLP Executive*, 1917–18.

15 *LLP Circular*, August 1917.

16 *Report of LLP Executive*, 1915–16.

17 *Report of LLP Executive*, 1916–17.

18 See *Autobiography*, pp. 60–64. Interviews, Lady Allen of Hurtwood, Mrs Creech Jones and Dame Margaret Cole. Also *Daily Record and Mail*, 6 January 1937 for David Kirkwood's recollection of Morrison in Scotland.

19 *Yorkshire Post*, 4 June 1917, and A. Bullock, *The Life and Times of Ernest Bevin*, Vol. I (1960) pp. 73–6.

20 *Autobiography*, p. 69.

21 F. Brockway, op. cit., p. 65.

22 Interview, Mrs E. K. Goodrich.

23 Morrison signed a letter protesting at the penal conditions imposed on conscientious objectors in Home Office camps and called for a scheme of useful social service. D. Boulton, *Objection Overruled* (1967), p. 217.

24 Interview, D. Dixon.

25 The sources for his time at Letchworth are interviews with Mr and Mrs D. Brunt, Mr and Mrs K. H. Kent, Mrs A. Muir, Sir Frederic and Lady Osborn, Lady Tewson and Mrs K. H. Frankl.

26 Mrs Fisher introduced Morrison to Rose whom she had met at Mrs Ramsay MacDonald's sewing circle in Lincoln's Inn Fields.

27 Opposite p. 208.

28 T. E. Naylor, 'Herbert Morrison: The Man and His Work', *Labour Magazine*, October 1929, pp. 243–5.

29 *Autobiography*, p. 71.

30 'I have been a supporter of the Garden Cities and New Towns ever since I left and worked in Letchworth Garden City in the first World War. There I met Ebenezer Howard and he much influenced me.' Morrison to Sir Frederic Osborn, 22 October 1964. Osborn reckoned that his own talks with Morrison on town planning were equally influential.

Chapter 5   On Hackney's Borough Council, 1920–1925

1 Over all London Labour won 39 per cent of the vote, the Municipal Reformers (Conservatives) 38 per cent and the Progressives (Liberals) 23 per cent. See table (c) in the appendices.

2 Labour won only 27 per cent of the vote in the whole borough.

3 See above Chapter 2 and below Chapter 8.

4 See *Hackney Spectator*, 15, 22, 29 October, 12 November 1920. Cited later as *HS*.

5 *Hackney and Kingsland Gazette*, 8 October 1920. Cited later as *H and KG*.

6 'He is a "Red Flagger" of the full-blown order, with red tie to match.' *HS*, 12 November 1920.

7 *The Magazine of the Metropolitan Labour Mayors' and Ex-Mayors' Association*, March 1955, p. 4.

8 *HS*, 15 April 1921.

9 *Autobiography*, pp. 83–4.

10 Interview, Dr R. H. Tee.

11 *Autobiography*, p. 83, and *Daily Herald*, 26 March 1953.

12 In 1917 Morrison had been scornful of royalty in soup kitchens, and in 1919 had called on the Prince of Wales to hand over the estates of the Duchy of Cornwall in London to the LCC and to stop living off the backs of the poor. He objected to paying taxes to provide the Prince with an income when he performed no useful service. *London Labour Chronicle*, July 1919.

13 *H and KG*, 2, 4 May 1921.

14 *H and KG*, 15 April, 17 June 1921.

15 *H and KG*, 13 January 1922.

16 *H and KG*, 29 June, 15 July 1921. See also *H and KG*, 15 September 1922.

17 *H and KG*, 17, 19, 26 November 1920.

18 *HS*, 26 November 1920.

19 Letter to Lloyd George, 4 December 1920 quoted in *H and KG*, 8 December 1920.

20 *H and KG*, 12, 16 September, 7 December 1921.

21 *H and KG*, 26, 30 September 1921.

22 *News Chronicle*, 6 December 1948. Also R. J. Cruikshank, *Roaring Century 1846–1946* (1946), p. 251. A verbatim record of the meeting on 22 September 1921 at Gairloch is preserved in the papers of the LLP Folios 3839–48. A description from the Labour side is in *London Labour Chronicle*, October 1921. See also *Daily Telegraph*, 28 September 1921.

23 *HS*, 28 October 1921; interview, Dr R. H. Tee.

24 *H and KG*, 30 November 1921.

25 *H and KG*, 11 November 1921.

26 *The Magazine of the Metropolitan Labour Mayors' and Ex-Mayors' Association*, March 1955, p. 4.

27 *H and KG*, 11 November 1921.

28 Interviews.

29 *Report of IMTA Conference*, 1960, p. 90.

30 In the maps in Sir Hubert Llewellyn Smith (ed.), *New Survey of London Life and Labour* (1934) Clapton is noted as 'wealthy and middle class'.

31 *H and KG*, 4 February 1924.

32 Interview, W. Southgate.

33 See *H and KG*, 28 January 1924.

34 *London News*, July 1927.

35 This was a view he had held in Lambeth in 1912. See his borough council election address.

36 *HS*, 22 September 1922.

37 Tee put 'God's fear into his staff'. Interview, J. Manning.

38 Interview, Dr R. H. Tee.

39 Interview, C. A. Halcrow.

40 Interview, A. Cullington.

41 Interviews, Dr R. H. Tee and A. Villiers.

42 See *Report of IMTA Conference*, 1960, p. 84.

43 *H and KG*, 19 January 1925. Also interview, W. E. Loweth.

44 *HS*, 4 November 1921.

45 H. Morrison, 'Labour's Municipal Policy', *Labour Magazine*, October 1923, pp. 246–9.

46 Between January 1921 and July 1922 Morrison was Hackney's representative on the Metropolitan Boroughs' Standing Joint Committee, which he used as a platform from which to expound Labour's views, supporting municipal enterprise, decrying private enterprise, urging higher central grants and protesting at reduced grants. See Minutes of the Metropolitan Boroughs' Standing Joint Committee, 31 January 1921, 25 July 1921, 31 October 1921, 30 January 1922, 3 April 1922. He called for a wide range of municipal activities: farms, kitchens, restaurants, laundries, theatres, dances, banks, the provision of insurance services and information centres, the building of houses, the distribution of milk and coal, the manufacture and distribution of power, electricity and water, the provision of transport by tram, bus, train, tube, taxi and boat.
To advance municipalization Morrison was a supporter of the Labour Party's Local Authorities Enabling Bill, 'The Citizen's Charter', which would have granted general powers to local authorities to do anything a company could do. They would be able 'to establish or purchase or carry on any business or undertaking within their area having for its purpose either the acquisition or gain or the promotion of commerce, art, science, recreation, charity, or any other object which might lawfully be established or carried on by a company'. He felt it was absurd for a local authority to have to go to Parliament and promote a private bill each time it wanted to carry out a simple task for which it had not express statutory authority. See Morrison's LLP pamphlet, *The Citizen's Charter* (1921), explaining the bill, and *The [Woolwich] Pioneer*, May 1925.

47 See *H and KG*, 6 April 1923.

48 *H and KG*, 23 May 1923, 1 December 1924.

49 *H and KG*, 5 May 1922.

50 *H and KG*, 15 December 1922, 26 January 1923, 29 February 1924.

51 *H and KG*, 11 April 1921 and letter to trade unions affiliated to the LLP, 8 April 1921. LLP papers.

52 *H and KG*, 29 February 1924. The local gossip column observed that soon after Morrison went boating on the Lee the Medical Officer of Health found the river contaminated. *HS*, 16 June 1922.

53 Minutes of the Lee Conservancy Board, 26 May, 9 June 1922 and 15 February 1924. Morrison was a member of the Board from March 1922 to April 1925.

54 *H and KG*, 28 July 1922. See also *H* and *KG*, 20 May, 26 July 1922, 1 January 1923.

55 *H and KG*, 12 February, 9 May 1923. In 1923 the LCC tried to prohibit fairs on the Hackney Marshes except at bank holidays. Morrison objected on the grounds of the merriment they provided and the money for hospitals they raised. *H and KG*, 9 February 1923.

56 *HS*, 15 December 1922.

57 *H and KG*, 11 February 1924.

58 See Table (c).

59 *Municipal Circular*, No. 119, 3 November 1922.

60 *H and KG*, 7 October 1925. For a similar occasion see *H and KG*, 15 May 1925.

61 See *H and KG*, 8 June 1923, 27 June, 24 October 1924, 16 January, 30 March, 1 April 1925.

62 Interview, J. Manning.

63 *HS*, 10 March 1922.

64 *H and KG*, 23 July 1923.

65 *H and KG*, 2 November 1923.

66 *H and KG*, 24 April 1925.

67 *Municipal Circular* No. 48, 12 October 1920.

68 *H and KG*, 13 February, 16 October 1925.

69 *H and KG*, 6 April 1923.

70 *H and KG*, 30 October 1925.

71 *H and KG*, 5 October 1923.

72 *HS*, 25 January 1924.

73 *H and KG*, 24 July 1925.

74 *H and KG*, 28 October 1925.

75 See Table (c).

Chapter 6   At the London Labour Party, 1918–1929

1 *London Labour Chronicle*, June 1921.

2 M. Webb, 'The Rt Hon. Herbert Morrison, MP', in H. Tracey (ed.), *The British Labour Party*, vol. III (1948), p. 34.

3 Interview, Dr E. Rickards, a former member of the LLP Executive.

4 Letter, T. O'Connor to G. W. Jones, 16 December 1966. See also T. E. Naylor, 'Herbert Morrison: The Man and His Work', *Labour Magazine*, October 1929, pp. 243–5.

5 See appendices.

6 *Reports of LLP Executive*.

7 D. Daines in *London News*, May 1950.

8 *Report of LLP Executive*, 1918–19.

9 See letters in NEC Minutes, Vol. 20, 14 October 1920; and R. I. McKibbin, 'The Evolution of a National Party: Labour's Political Organisation 1910–1924'. Unpublished Oxford D. Phil. Thesis, 1970, pp. 302–6.

10 *London Labour Chronicle*, March, April and May 1921.

11 NEC Minutes, Vol. 40, 24 November 1926.

12 *London News*, September 1929.

13 *Daily Herald*, 1 August 1929.

14 Interviews, Mrs W. Moore, Mrs D. A. Robinson, Dr E. Rickards, H. Atkinson and J. W. Raisin.

15 Interview, and K. Martin, *Editor* (1968), p. 51.

16 Interview, J. Cliff, former deputy to Bevin at the TGWU; and *Report of LLP Executive*, 1928–9.

17 Interview, Lord Citrine.

18 Interview, C. Brandon; also interviews, C. W. Gibson and Sir Isaac Hayward.

19 *London News*, May 1926.

20 *London Labour Chronicle*, May 1922.

21 Charles Brandon stated that Morrison never sought these increases, but that trade unionists on the Executive urged that he accept the rate for the job.

22 Information on Daines from his widow Mrs S Daines and his brother H. J. Daines.

23 Interviews, Miss J. Bourne, Mrs W. Moore, H. Atkinson, C. Brandon.

24 Interviews, Miss J. Bourne, Mrs W. Moore, Mrs F. Griffiths.

25 Interview, Mrs W. Moore.

26 Ibid.

27 Interviews, Mrs W. Moore and Mrs F. Griffiths.

28 See also *Labour Magazine*, October 1929, pp. 243–5.

29 *London Labour Chronicle*, February 1920; and see *London Labour Chronicle*, January 1924.

30 Interviews.

31 *Report of the LLP Executive*, 1923–4 and 1925–6.

32 Interview, P. Benson and *Star*, 14 January 1938.

33 Interview, Mrs W. Moore.

34 Minutes of the National Joint Council of Labour, Vol. 2, 12 October 1923. Morrison's Memo to Executive of LLP, 31 May 1923. *Report of LLP Executive*, 1926–7. Morrison's activities before the Tribunal can be discovered in *Reports of LLP Executive*, 1923–7; and *LPCR*, 1924, p. 47 and 1927, pp. 36–8. Morrison's report to LLP Executive, 24 June 1926.

35 NEC Minutes, Vol. 50, 27 March 1929.

36 *London Labour Chronicle*, December 1918. See also *London Labour Chronicle*, February 1921, January 1922.

37 *LLP Circular*, May 1918.

38 *London Labour Chronicle*, April 1922.

39 See the Labour Party publications, *Organisation Points*, No. 1, 4 November 1920 and *Labour Party Organisation in London*, 1921, p. 5.

40 *London News*, September 1925.

41 *London News*, August 1925.

42 In 1945 he told the Theatrical Managers' Association that running a dramatic federation 'was past my organising ability'. *Star*, 17 May 1945.

43 See *London Labour Chronicle*, May 1924.

44 *Report of LLP Executive*, 1927–8.

45 *Reports of LLP Executive*, 1927–8 and 1928–9.

46 Letter T. O'Connor to G. W. Jones, 16 December 1966.

47 *Labour Magazine*, June 1929, pp. 66–8.

48 He laid down this line in *London Labour Chronicle*, July 1919.

49 *Report of LLP Executive*, 1916–17.

50 *London News*, December 1924.

51 *Report of LLP Executive*, 1919–20.

52 *Justice*, 22 April 1920.

53 *Report of LLP Executive*, 1919–20.

54 Interviews, E. A. Robinson, A. Cullington, J. Nicholls and D. Frankel.

55 Interview, W. Southgate.

56 He outlined his views notably in the *Labour Magazine*, December 1927, pp. 348–57 and *London News*, March 1929.

57 *Municipal Circular*, Nos 23 (11 May 1920) and 26 (21 May 1920); *Councillor*, No. 2, January 1921.

58 Memo to Labour JPs, 13 April 1926. LLP Papers.

59 They discussed licensing, education, summonses, prison visiting, and gaoling for non-payment of rates because of poverty.

60 Memos to Labour JPs, 10 July 1926, 20 December 1926. LLP Papers.

61 Memo to Executive of LLP, 7 April 1921. LLP Papers.

62 See G. W. Jones, *Borough Politics* (1969), Chapter 8.

63 In 1927 he had argued that decisions on appointments should not be left to a free vote, for fear that 'one of our people may be got at by someone trying to push a man in'. By 1929 he was in favour of free votes on appointments to eliminate party influence.

64 *London News*, January 1926.

65 For example, LLP papers, Folios 70 and 1433, 15 July 1919 and 7 June 1923.

66 Interview, Mrs W. Moore.

67 Interview, K. H. Kent; also C. Brandon. In 1921–2, Clement Attlee was a member of the LLP Executive, nominated by the Stepney Labour Party and Trades Council. Attlee's period on the Executive was brief, a single session, and the minutes suggest that he contributed nothing of importance to the deliberations.

68 *London News*, October 1933.

69 Interview, M. Orbach.

70 Interview, Mrs W. Moore.

71 Morrison's memo to Executive of LLP, 28 October 1926. LLP papers.

72 *London News*, January 1937.

73 *London Labour Chronicle*, September 1919.

74 Letter from Morrison to Local Councils of Action, 1 August 1920, LLP papers; *London Labour Chronicle*, September 1920, and letter sent 28 October 1919 to *Morning Post*, LLP papers.

75 *Daily Express*, 24 February 1921; see also *London Labour Chronicle*, February 1921.

76 *Report of LLP Executive*, 1920–1.

77 *Municipal Circular*, No. 141, 13 January 1926.

78 *Municipal Circular*, No. 148, 4 May 1926.

79 Letter to Secretaries of local parties, 7 May 1926. LLP papers.

80 Draft autobiography. J. Paton wrote that Morrison 'was biting his nails in idleness, no effective use having been found for either himself or the magnificent machine of the London Labour Party'. *Left Turn* (1936), p. 247.

81 *London News*, June 1926.

82 See *London News*, June 1926 and draft autobiography.

83 Minutes of LLP Executive, 4 July 1929.

Chapter 7 On the London County Council in the 1920s

1 *London News*, March 1925.

2 See Table (b).

3 Election Circular No. 3, 7 May 1920, LLP papers.

4 Ibid.

5 Interviews, C. A. G. Manning and Dr C. Brook. Also letter T. O'Connor to G. W. Jones, 16 December 1966.

6 Interviews, Mrs D. A. Robinson and G. Isaacs.

7 Letter, T. O'Connor to G. W. Jones, 16 December 1966.

8 He had been selected as candidate in January 1922, but not without opposition. A Mr Bell mustered twelve votes against Morrison's thirty-five at the selection meeting. Minutes of the Woolwich East General Management Committee, 13 January 1922.

9 See W. H. Barefoot, *Twenty Five Years* (1928); *London News*, October 1925, April 1928, February 1932; and R. Stucke (ed.), *Fifty Years of the Woolwich Labour Party, 1903–53* (1953).

10 *London News*, October 1925.

11 Interview, J. W. Raisin.

12 *London News*, December 1941–January 1942. Interviews, Dame Mabel Crout and Sir Isaac Hayward. Barefoot had been Chairman of the Municipal Mutual Supplies Organization which Morrison had tried to establish.

13 Interview.

14 Interview, Sir Isaac Hayward.

15 See Lord Snell, *Men, Movements and Myself* (1936).

16 Interview, J. W. Raisin.

17 Foreword to R. Stucke, op. cit.

18 In Sir Hubert Llewellyn Smith (ed.), *The New Survey of London Life and Labour* (1934), Eltham was noted on the maps as 'wealthy and middle class'.

19 Interview, Lady Morrison.

20 *Pioneer*, 3 February 1922.

21 The *Pioneer*, July 1923 and August 1923. See LCC, *Council Minutes*, 13 March 1923, for more local issues promoted by Morrison.

22 Interview, Dame Mabel Crout who was a valuable informant on Woolwich history and politics. George Wansbrough recalled that in the 1930s the Woolwich party was 'smashing and efficient', due to Barefoot and Crout, and that so great was Morrison's influence there that he obtained for Wansbrough a parliamentary candidature in Woolwich. Interview. Morrison also found a parliamentary candidature at Woolwich for Sir Stafford Cripps in 1929.

23 Minutes of LLP Executive, 7 July, 4 August 1921 and agenda papers of Executive, 1921–2.

24 *LCC Election Manifesto*, LLP, 1922.

25 See A. G. Gardiner, *John Benn and the Progressive Movement* (1925).

26 *Autobiography*, p. 76.

27 See H. Gosling, *Up and Down Stream* (1927).

28 Morrison always urged members of local authorities to read their documents, for if they did not, they were liable 'to be swept off their feet by gusts of emotion or on the other hand to be chained to unimaginative lines of action by conservative or indifferent officials'. *Labour Magazine*, December 1927, pp. 348–57.

29 Interview, C. A. G. Manning.

30 *Pioneer*, January 1925.

31 Minutes of LCC Labour Party, 10 March 1925 and *London News*, April 1925.

32 *Council Minutes*, 5 May 1925 (cited later as *CM*); *The Times*, 6 May 1925; *London News*, June 1925.

33 *The Times*, 7 May 1925.

34 The following is based on the minutes of the LCC and *The Times*.

35 He also protested at the LCC against handing electricity supply and distribution to a private monopoly.

36 *The Times*, 27 January 1926.

37 *London News*, September 1927.

38 *H and KG*, 9 April 1924; *The Times*, 3 March 1926.

39 *LLP Circular*, February 1918; *London Labour Chronicle*, September 1918.

40 *CM*, 28 November 1924; *The Times*, 29 November 1924; *Daily Herald*, 24 November 1926.

41 *CM*, 23 October 1923 and 4 March 1924; *The Times*, 31 October 1923 and 6 February 1924; *Evening News*, 6 February 1924.

42 *London News*, June 1928.

43 *London News*, May 1928, reference to council meeting on 3 April 1928. In May the debate on the Education Estimates lasted till 1.54 a.m. *London News*, June 1928.

44 Minutes of LCC Labour Party, 10 March 1925.

45 Letter in LLP papers, 7 March 1925.

46 See *Autobiography*, p. 134.

47 Interview, Mrs P. Jay.

48 Interview, Dr E. Rickards.

49 Interviews, Sir Isaac Hayward and C. W. Gibson.

50 Interviews, A. E. Samuels and Dr E. Rickards.

51 *Labour Magazine*, October 1929, p. 245.

52 Interview, Lord Attlee.

53 Minutes of LCC Labour Party, 10 March 1925, 9 February 1926, 25 January 1927, 13 March 1928 and 5 March 1929.

54 M. P. McCarran, *Fabianism in the Political Life of Britain* (1954), p. 439.

55 Interview, C. A. G. Manning.

56 Interviews, Sir Richard Coppock and Sir Isaac Hayward.

Chapter 8   On a Wider Stage

1 *LPCR*, 1918, p. 39.

2 *LPCR*, 1919, p. 128.

3 *LPCR*, 1920, pp. 148–9. See also *London Labour Chronicle*, September 1919.

4 *LPCR*, 1920, pp. 169–70.

5 *LPCR*, 1921, pp. 152–4.

6 *LPCR*, 1922, pp. 181–4.

7 Morrison was at conferences as a delegate of the London Labour Party and was its nominee for the NEC. He refused nomination by trade unions.

8 NEC Minutes, Vol. 44, 6 October 1927. He defeated Miss Susan Lawrence, eleven votes to six.

9 NEC Minutes, Vol. 44, 26 October 1927.

10 NEC Minutes, Vol. 20, 13 October 1920.

11 NEC Minutes, Vol. 31, 24 July 1924.

12 NEC Minutes, Vol. 31, 23 July 1924.

13 NEC Minutes, Vol. 41, 7 February 1927.

14 NEC Minutes, Vol. 36, 24 June 1925.

15 Charles Ammon noted in his diary that the NEC was firm to make arrangements 'for a nominal observance of the Party constitution'. Unpublished diary of Lord Ammon, 24 November 1926.

16 *New Leader*, 28 January 1927.

17 NEC Minutes, Vol. 42, 23 March 1927.

18 The story of the Mosley incident can be followed in the NEC Minutes from November 1926 to March 1927, Vols. 40–2. Also *London News*, February 1927.

19 *LPCR*, 1927, pp. 247–9.

20 *LPCR*, 1928, p. 245.

21 *LPCR*, 1928, p. 204.

22 M. A. Hamilton, *Arthur Henderson* (1938), pp. 262–3.

23 *LPCR*, 1928, p. 207.

24 Columbia Broadcasting System broadcast, New York, 6 April 1938.

25 *London Labour Chronicle*, November and December 1920, and January 1921; and *London News*, June 1926.

26 *H and KG*, 29 November 1920.

27 Interview, W. Southgate. Morrison became so fed up with communists within the Clerks' Union that he resigned, and transferred to NATSOPA, the union of his colleague, George Isaacs. He removed the office staff of the LLP from the NUC and had them join the General and Municipal Workers' Union.

28 Interview, Sir Isaac Hayward.

29 *Labour Magazine*, June 1929, pp. 66–8.

30 Minutes of LLP Executive, 16 September 1920.

31 *LPCR*, 1921, p. 167 and 1922, p. 199.

32 See M. A. Hamilton, *Remembering my Good Friends* (1944), p. 166.

33 *London Labour Chronicle*, April 1923.

34 NEC Minutes, Vol. 29, 31 October 1923.

35 NEC Minutes, Vol. 32, 2 September 1924. In July 1924 the National Agent had met a delegation from the Communist Party seeking affiliation. He reported to the NEC in August that three choices were open. (1) The Morrisonian line, to declare individual communists not eligible as affiliated or individual members, delegates and candidates. He said that this was a drastic course; the affiliated bodies, the trade unions, would not accept it, and in any case it was no protection against penetration by hidden communists. (2) To keep the existing situation. (3) To ban communists only as candidates, but not as members or delegates. This might, he thought, be hard to operate. Report of National Agent, 27 August 1924, in NEC Minutes, Vol. 31.

36 *LPCR*, 1924, pp. 129–31.

37 Quoted in *The Times*, 27 September 1924.

38 Letter to local Labour parties, 11 November 1924; Minutes of LLP Executive, 6 November 1924; *London News*, December 1924.

39 NEC Minutes, Vol. 34, 28 January 1925.

40 *London News*, July 1925.

41 NEC Minutes, Vol. 37, 2 October 1925.

42 Minutes of LLP Executive, 8 October 1925.

43 Letter of Morrison, 9 October 1925.

44 NEC Minutes, Vol. 37, 28 October 1925.

45 Agenda papers of LLP Executive, 23 October 1925.

46 NEC Minutes, Vol. 40, 7 September 1926 and Agenda papers of LLP Executive, 11 February 1926.

47 NEC Minutes, Vol. 38, 2 February 1926 and Vol. 40, 7 September 1926.

48 NEC Minutes, Vol. 47, 25 July 1928.

49 *London News*, February 1926.

50 Minutes and agenda papers of LLP Executive, 1 July 1926.

51 Interview, C. Brandon.

52 Interview, G. Rogers.

53 Letter, 1 March 1928, MacDonald papers, 5/39.

54 Morrison complained to MacDonald that Lansbury's support of communist activities was a deliberate incitement to defy conference decisions. 6 January 1927, MacDonald Papers, 5/38. Even MacDonald was once 'conned' into sending a message of goodwill to the *Hackney Worker*, a communist news-sheet. Morrison complained and MacDonald apologized, although toning down Morrison's draft statement of dissociation. Morrison to MacDonald, 22 April 1927 and MacDonald to Morrison, 31 May 1927, MacDonald papers, 5/38.

55 *Report of LLP Executive*, 1928–9. In the November borough elections, forty-eight open communists ran plus fourteen as candidates of disaffiliated Labour parties. *LLP Election Notes*, No. 6, 22 October 1928.

56 *LLP Election Notes, No. 3*, 19 March 1928, and *Report of LLP Executive*, 1927–8.

57 *London News*, September 1927.

58 *London News*, December 1927.

59 *Report of LLP Executive*, 1928–9.

60 *Labour Magazine*, May 1928, pp. 11–13.

61 *London News*, July 1928. See also *Daily Telegraph* and *Daily Express*, 7 June 1928.

62 *London News*, July 1926.

63 *London News*, June 1925.

64 *Daily Herald*, 15 May 1929.

65 See *London Labour Party Circular*, January 1918 and June 1918.

66 Letter to Executive, 10 July 1922.

67 Morrison memo to Executive of LLP, 20 July 1922.

68 Report of National Agent to NEC, Minutes, Vol. 25, 5 September 1922.

69 *H and KG*, 29 October 1923.

70 Report to Executive, 12 November 1923.

71 Minutes of LLP Executive, 28 November 1923.

72 *Autobiography*, pp. 90–1, and M. Webb, 'The Rt Hon. Herbert Morrison, MP', in H. Tracey (ed.), *The British Labour Party*, Vol. III (1948), p. 35.

73 Interview, J. W. Raisin.

74 *London Labour Chronicle*, December 1923.

75 e.g. *H and KG*, 23 November 1923 and 26 November 1923.

76 M. Edelman, *Herbert Morrison* (1948), p. 36, and *Autobiography*, p. 93.

77 Interview, W. Southgate.

78 *Autobiography*, p. 92.

79 See Table (a).

80 *HS*, 7 December 1923.

81 *H and KG*, 12 December 1923.

82 *Daily Herald*, 2 January 1947.

83 *H and KG*, 12 December 1923.

84 *H and KG*, 10 December 1923.

85 Interview, Sir William Lawther.

86 *H and KG*, 14 April 1924.

87 *H and KG*, 21 July 1924.

88 *H and KG*, 2 April 1924.

89 *Daily Sketch*, 1 July 1924.

90 *Autobiography*, p. 104.

91 *Autobiography*, p. 96.

92 *House of Commons Debates* (Hansard), cited later as *HC Debs.*, Vol. 169, Cols 642–7, 21 January 1924.

93 *HC Debs.*, Vol. 169, Col. 647, 21 January 1924. The Hansard report differs from that recalled by Morrison in his *Autobiography*, pp. 95–6, which rather casts doubt on the other occasions when Morrison professed to recall verbatim what was said.

94 M. Edelman, op. cit., p. 38.

95 *HC Debs*, Vol. 169, Col. 287, 17 January 1924.

96 *HC Debs*, Vol. 169, Cols 291, 725, 1732, 17 January, 12 February, 20 February 1924.

97 *HC Debs*, Vol. 176, Cols 2756–8, 5 August 1924; *H and KG*, 8 August and 13 August 1924.

98 *Daily Express*, 19 March 1924.

99 *HC Debs*, Vol. 173, Col. 2514, 22 May 1924.

100 *H and KG*, 31 March 1924.

101 *H and KG*, 4 April 1924.

102 *HC Debs*, Vol. 173, Col. 2522, 22 May 1924.

103 *HC Debs*, Vol. 171, Col. 1, 17 March 1924. See also *Autobiography*, p. 102; and *HC Debs*, Vol. 176, Cols 1033–4, 21 July 1924.

104 *HC Debs*, Vol. 177, Cols 657–61, 8 October 1924.

105 *H and KG*, 17 October 1924.

106 *HS*, 17 October and 24 October 1924.

107 pp. 107–10.

108 Letter to local parties, 25 October 1924.

109 See Table (a).

110 *H and KG*, 12 November 1924.

111 *H and KG*, 21 November 1924.

112 *LPCR*, 1921, p. 3; 1928, p. 324; and *London Labour Chronicle*, March 1923.

113 *London News*, October and November 1927.

114 *London News*, October 1927. Morrison urged the LCC to examine the system in Cologne. *CM*, 18 October 1927, 31 January, 24 July 1928, 7 May 1929.

115 Memorandum to LLP Executive, 5 April 1928.

116 *London News*, October 1929.

117 *Labour Magazine*, January 1929, pp. 393–5.

118 *Social Democrat*, July 1930.
119 Interview, E. Wimble.
120 *LPCR*, 1925, pp. 238–9.
121 Letter to local Labour parties, 27 August 1919, LLP papers.
122 Leaflets and posters in LLP papers, 4 February 1923.
123 *LPCR*, 1929, pp. 151–2.
124 LLP papers, July 1919.
125 *London Labour Chronicle*, July 1922; see also *LLP Circular*, June 1918.
126 Report on the Demonstration, 5 December 1926, in LLP papers.
127 See speech in 1929 at Labour Party Conference: *LPCR*, p. 152.

Chapter 9   Metropolitan and Public Utility Problems

1 *Royal Commission on London Government*, paper no. 108, 13 June 1922.
2 M. Cole, *Growing up into Revolution* (1949), p. 70.
3 *London Labour Chronicle*, February 1919.
4 *London Labour Chronicle*, March 1922.
5 *LLP Circular*, December 1917. See also *The Times*, 21 January and 28 January 1925.
6 *London Labour Chronicle*, October 1918.
7 See *London Labour Chronicle*, February 1920, May 1920, April 1922, May 1924; *London News*, February 1925; letter of Morrison to local Labour parties, 29 January 1929.
8 Description of his proposals can be seen in *London Labour Chronicle*, February 1920, September 1924. Written memorandum of evidence to the Royal Commission on London Government, paper no. 108, 13 June 1922. Verbal evidence of Morrison, 20 June 1922, pp. 680–96.
9 Letter of Morrison to editors of trade union and party journals in preparation for the 1922 LCC elections. LLP papers.
10 Morrison memorandum, 13 June 1924, LLP folios 1786–8.
11 *Report of LLP Executive*, 1927–8 and *London News*, February 1928.
12 Identical views were expressed in a special 'Transit' issue of the *LLP Circular*, August 1916. See also Morrison's election address in 1912.
13 Quoted in *London Labour Chronicle*, August 1919.
14 *London Labour Chronicle*, August 1923 – article based on a memorandum to LLP Executive, 9 July 1923. Morrison had urged this policy at the Metropolitan Boroughs Standing Joint Committee. Minutes, 7 June 1922.
15 The best study of Ashfield's career is F. A. Menzler, 'Lord Ashfield'. *Public Administration*, 1951, pp. 99–111.
16 LLP papers, May 1923.
17 NEC Minutes, Vol. 28, July 1923.
18 *Report of the Royal Commission on London Government*, Cmd. 1830, 1923.
19 Minutes of LLP Executive, 5 July 1923 and NEC Minutes, Vol. 28, 25 July 1923.
20 See H. Gosling, *Up and Down Stream* (1927).
21 Interview, C. A. G. Manning. MacDonald's daughter Ishbel thought the story likely. Interview. See also M. Edelman, *Herbert Morrison* (1948), p. 38.
22 A. Bullock, *The Life and Times of Ernest Bevin*, Vol. I (1960), pp. 237–42.
23 Cab. 24, 165, C.P. 130 (24), 22 February 1924. Cabinet papers at Public Record Office.

24 Cab. 23, 47, 17 (24), Item 6, 28 February 1924.

25 Cab. 23, 47, 19 (24), Item 1, 12 March 1924.

26 Cab. 23, 47, 17 (24), Item 6, 28 February 1924. Cab. 23, 47, 19 (24), Item 1, 12 March 1924.

27 *HC Debs*, Vol. 171, Cols 1734–43, 28 March 1924.

28 For Morrison's views on the bill, see *London Labour Chronicle*, May 1924; Report of Morrison to the LLP Executive, 1 April 1924; *Report of LLP Executive*, 1923–4; and H. Morrison, *Socialisation and Transport* (1933).

29 See Report on London Traffic Control of the London and Home Counties Group of the Parliamentary Labour Party, drafted by Morrison and sent to MacDonald, 17 February 1924. MacDonald Papers, 1/65.

30 *HC Debs*, Vol. 171, Col. 1742, 28 March 1924.

31 The unions were not unanimous. Cramp of the National Union of Railwaymen supported Morrison. Report on London Traffic Control.

32 H. Morrison, op. cit., p. 190.

33 Ibid.

34 See letter and memorandum of Morrison to representatives of Labour parties attending a conference to discuss the Advisory Committee's report, 1 November 1927; and memorandum to LLP Executive, 10 December 1926 and Minutes of LLP Executive, December 1927 and January 1928.

35 See LCC, *Council Minutes*, 25 January 1927.

36 *London News*, December 1928; interviews, Sir Richard Coppock and Dr E. Rickards.

37 See *Daily Herald*, 8 November 1928.

38 Details of the campaign are preserved in the files of the Executive of the London Labour Party, 1928–9.

39 H. Morrison, op. cit., p. 52.

40 Interview, Lord Hurcomb.

41 *Report of LLP Executive*, 1928–9.

42 *The London Traffic Fraud*, p. 21.

43 E. Estorick, *Stafford Cripps* (1949), pp. 77–8. Morrison reprinted the letters in *Autobiography*, p. 115.

44 E. Estorick, op. cit., p. 79, and *Autobiography*, p. 158.

45 Interview, Dame Leah Manning, the prospective candidate for Bristol South-east, who gave way for Cripps on the promise of another seat.

46 The development of his policy can be seen in *LLP Circular*, February 1918; *London Labour Chronicle*, April 1920, March 1923, May 1924, August 1924, and *Municipal Circular*, No. 104, 1 February 1922. See his introduction to A.E. Davies, *The Story of the London County Council* (1925).

47 *London Labour Chronicle*, June 1924.

48 Agenda paper of LLP Executive, 30 July 1924.

49 MacDonald to Gosling, 17 July 1924. MacDonald Papers, 1/179. See also Morrison's obituary of Gosling, *London News*, December 1930.

50 Cab. 23, 48, 44 (24), Item 1, 30 July 1924. Haldane, for instance, was in favour of making a deal with capitalists if it increased productivity. Beatrice Webb arranged for him to meet Morrison, but no agreement was reached. B. Webb's diary, 23 June 1924.

51 Agenda papers of LLP Executive, including report by Morrison, 25 February 1925. Also *New Leader*, 27 February 1925.

52 *London News*, July 1925. The story of Morrison's role in the battle against the bills can best be seen in the *Reports of LLP Executive*, 1923–4 and 1924–5, and *London Labour Chronicle*, June 1924, September 1924, November 1924, January 1925. His views are clearly put in his pamphlet *London Threatened by Electrical Trust*, originally a memorandum to members of the Parliamentary Labour Party, 1924. See also his speech *HC Debs*, Vol. 176, Cols 2157–66, 30 July 1924, and his article 'Giant Power: Private Monopoly or Public Service?', *Labour Magazine*, August 1924, pp. 150–3.

53 Minutes of the London and Home Counties Joint Electricity Authority, 24 March 1926 and 11 November 1927. He also urged the admittance of the press to meetings of the Authority, 22 May 1929.

54 See *Municipal Circular*, No. 146, 17 March 1926, and his article, 'Baldwin's Electrical Plant', *Labour Magazine*, February 1926, pp. 442–4.

55 Morrison in *London News*, August 1931.

56 Report to Highways Committee, 27 March 1924.

57 The story of the bridge is taken from LCC Council Minutes 1923–9 and minutes of the Highways and Improvements Committees and the Bridges Sub-Committee. Cabinet papers have also been consulted.

58 *New Leader*, 1 January 1926.

59 *The Times*, 11 November 1925.

60 *The Times*, 25 February 1925.

61 *The Times*, 11 November 1925.

62 Royal Institute of British Architects, Society for the Protection of Ancient Buildings, Architecture Club, London Society, Town Planning Institute, Royal Academy.

63 Morrison memorandum to Labour MPs, 17 May 1926 and *Report of LLP Executive*, 1925–6. MacDonald, although aggrieved about Morrison's line, promised not to hold up the bill. MacDonald to Morrison, 8 March 1926. MacDonald papers, 5/37.

64 *The Times*, 23 June 1926; *London News*, July 1926. The Chairman of the Commission had signed a petition against demolition.

Chapter 10   Minister of Transport, 1929–1931

1 LLP 1929 manifesto, 12 April 1929, LLP Folios 3795–7. M. Edelman, *Herbert Morrison* (1948), p. 40. See *Hackney Gazette*, 15 March, 8 May and 24 May 1929.

2 *Autobiography*, p. 103, and H. Morrison, *Government and Parliament* (1964), pp. 181–2. Also draft autobiography.

3 *Government and Parliament*, pp. 134–5, 179.

4 Draft autobiography, and *Government and Parliament*, pp. 52–3.

5 Draft autobiography, and an interview with Morrison in *News Chronicle*, 7 December 1959.

6 Morrison to MacDonald, 21 November 1929. Morrison Papers.

7 MacDonald to Morrison, 21 November 1929. Morrison Papers.

8 Sir Charles Petrie, *The Life and Letters of the Right Hon. Sir Austen Chamberlain*, Vol. II (1940), p. 378.

9 J. H. Thomas, *My Story* (1937), pp. 255–6.

10 Diary, 23 January 1930.

11 *The Times*, 30 March 1931.

12 *News Chronicle*, 23 October 1931. See also P. Snowden, *An Autobiography*, Vol. II (1934), p. 767; *Financial News*, 25 March 1931; Sir Alexander Mackintosh, *Echoes of Big Ben* (1945), p. 116; D. E. McHenry, *The Labour Party in Transition, 1931–38* (1938), p. 148; *Daily Herald*, 27 September 1930, 15 September 1934; *John Bull*, 25 October 1930; *Sunday Express*, 16 February 1930.

13 J. H. Thomas, op. cit., p. 256. Dalton first spotted Morrison's potential at this time. He wrote in his diary, 'a damned able chap. I think he may be a future P.M.' Dalton diary, 30 October 1929, Vol. 13. LSE.

14 Interviews.

15 *Social Democrat*, July 1930. The *Daily Herald* carried a photograph of him cleaning a tram to prove he was not a 'bureaucrat in an office'. 10 March 1931.

16 Sir Oswald Mosley, *My Life* (1968), p. 235. Dalton had heard in November 1930 that Mosley was saying that Morrison was a failure as a minister. To Dalton it showed that Mosley had no sense of real life. Diary, 10 November 1930.

17 Beatrice Webb noted that Morrison was 'trusted and admired and liked by his two aristocratic Undersecretaries – first Russell then Ponsonby'. Diary, 17 January 1932.

18 Morrison had submitted to MacDonald a list of those he thought suitable to be his parliamentary secretary. Top of the list was C. R. Attlee. Morrison to MacDonald, 6 June 1929. MacDonald papers, 2/3.

19 Interview. Also *Labour Magazine*, January 1930, pp. 416–18, and June 1931, pp. 53–5.

20 Minutes of LLP Executive, 4 July 1929 and *Report of LLP Executive*, 1928–9.

21 *London News*, July 1929.

22 Morrison to ILP, 28 June 1929. LLP papers.

23 Morrison letter, 17 June 1929. LLP papers.

24 Minutes of LCC Labour Party, 31 March 1931.

25 See G. W. Jones, *Borough Politics* (1969), Chapter 8.

26 NEC Minutes, Vol. 54, 26 March 1930.

27 NEC Minutes, Vol. 56, 29 August 1930.

28 *LPCR*, 1930, pp. 164–5.

29 *Daily Express*, 19 January 1931.

30 *Report of the Executive Committee of the Labour Party*, 1930–1, in *LPCR*, 1931, p. 8.

31 *Morning Post*, 30 November 1929.

32 *HC Debs*, Vol. 235, Vols 1203–25, 18 February 1930.

33 *LPCR*, 1930, pp. 244–9.

34 Before the Home Affairs Committee of the Cabinet Morrison urged the necessity of increasing the powers of local authorities to run omnibuses in order to counterbalance the loss of their powers to license public service vehicles. Cab. 26(12), HA (30) 29, 6 November 1929.

35 A. Bullock, *The Life and Times of Ernest Bevin*, Vol. I (1960), p. 459.

36 *Glasgow Herald*, 4 August 1930, and draft autobiography.

37 Report of BBC radio broadcast, *The Times* and the *Manchester Guardian*, 1 January 1931. Sir George Stedman said that he drafted the Code after looking at foreign examples. Morrison edited it and made only minor alterations. Interview.

38 *Manchester Guardian,* 7 May 1930.

39 *Daily Express,* 28 October 1930.

40 *Daily Express,* 22 January 1931.

41 *H and KG,* 3 February 1930.

42 *HC Debs,* Vol. 234, Cols 2273–4, 7 February 1930. See also *Star,* 8 February 1930. Also *New Leader,* 14 February 1930.

43 Draft autobiography. When Morrison came to make his appointments there were 3,200 applicants for the twelve positions. He refused to appoint a man whom Wedgwood Benn, Secretary of State for India, urged on him. Merit alone was his test. Morrison to MacDonald, 13 November 1930, MacDonald papers, 2/4.

44 Draft autobiography, and *Government and Parliament,* pp. 188 and 224.

45 *HC Debs,* Vol. 241, Cols 2105–11, 22 July 1930.

46 Memorandum, 12 December 1929. LLP papers.

47 Report of unofficial deputation to Minister of Health, January 1930, LLP papers, dated 4 February 1930.

48 An account of the passing of the bill appears in Morrison's *Socialisation and Transport;* see also E. E. Barry, *Nationalisation in British Politics* (1965), Chapter 12.

49 *Daily Express,* 8 March 1965.

50 Draft autobiography.

51 Morrison to MacDonald, 20 June 1929, MT 46/1. Ministry of Transport papers, 46/1. Cited later as MT. Public Record Office.

52 Cab. 24, 204, CP 170 (29), 24 June 1929.

53 Cab. 23, 61, 25(29), Item 6, 26 June 1929.

54 MT 46/1, Meeting at Ministry of Transport, 4 July 1929.

55 *HC Debs,* Vol. 230, cols. 550–61, 17 July 1929.

56 Reginald Hill recalled: 'At the outset Herbert had not formulated his views. He didn't quite know what he wanted. He got his ideas as he went along.'

57 Cab. 24, 206, CP 251 (29), 20 September 1929.

58 See G. Ostergaard, 'Labour and the Development of the Public Corporation', *Manchester School of Economic and Social Studies,* May 1954, pp. 192–226, and A. H. Hanson, 'Labour and the Public Corporation', *Public Administration,* Summer 1954, pp. 203–9.

59 Cab. 23, 61, 35 (29), Item 2, 25 September 1929.

60 Cab. 27 (401), LT1(29), 2(29), 3(29).

61 Cab. 24, 206, CP 305 (29), Report of Committee on London Traffic, 7 November 1929.

62 e.g. MT 46/1.

63 See memorandum in MT 46/1.

64 Cab. 23, 62, 48(29), Item 6, 14 November 1929.

65 *HC Debs,* Vol. 232, Cols 1929–32, 2 December 1929.

66 Stevenson to Morrison, 21 December 1929. Morrison papers.

67 See E. E. Barry, op. cit., pp. 292–4.

68 Report of interview between Morrison and a Mr Hartley, 24 November 1930. MT 46/1.

69 See A. Bullock, op. cit., p. 459, and *Socialisation and Transport,* p. 212.

70 A. Bullock, op. cit., p. 510.

71 Interview, Lord Francis-Williams.

72 *Socialisation and Transport*, p. 206.

73 *Sunday Express*, 25 June 1933.

74 H. Morrison, *British Parliamentary Democracy* (1962), pp. 41–2, and *Autobiography*, pp. 139–40.

75 W. A. Robson considered that 'the compensation terms were generous beyond the dreams of avarice', and blamed Morrison. *Public Enterprise* (1937), p. 385. However, Ernest Davies appreciated that events outside Morrison's control were responsible for the apparent generosity to the former owners. 'Interest rates had already started to fall when acquisition took place, and they fell steadily for two years more. The result was that what might have appeared reasonable interest when negotiations started became over-generous after the Board had been in operation for a short while. The result was naturally an appreciation in the value of the stocks. The combination of high income and long life, plus the improved credit of the public corporation, has led to a rise in the value of the stocks of the Board far greater than the general market rise of similar securities.' E. Davies, 'The London Passenger Transport Board', in W. A. Robson, op. cit., p. 193.

76 Interview, Lord Hurcomb.

77 A sketch of Pick is in F. A. Menzler, 'Lord Ashfield', *Public Administration*, 1951, pp. 102–3, 107, 110.

78 *LPCR*, 1930, p. 245.

79 G. R. Strauss, 'London Traffic Bill Will Make History', *Labour Magazine*, June 1931, p. 53.

80 Cab. 23, 65, 65(30), Item 24, 29 October 1930.

81 Morrison to Lloyd George, 2 October 1930, MT 46/1.

82 In 1944 he told a deputation of Liberal MPs that he got the idea for a London Transport Board from the Liberal Party's pamphlet *Britain's Industrial Future*. *Evening Standard*, 8 March 1944.

83 *HC Debs*, vol. 250, col. 67, 23 March 1931.

84 *Socialisation and Transport*, p. 171.

85 *HC Debs*, vol. 250, col. 58, 23 March 1931.

86 The tangle of finance is penetrated by E. Davies in W. A. Robson, op. cit., pp. 185–201.

87 Cab. 24, 213, CP 216(30), 23 June 1930.

88 Cab. 23, 64, 33(30), Item 5, 24 June 1930.

89 Cab. 24, 213, CP 247(30), 18 July 1930.

90 Morrison to Snowden, MT 46/1, 18 July 1930.

91 Cab. 23, 64, 44(30), Item 10, 23 July 1930.

92 Cab. 24, 214, CP 277(30), 28 July 1930.

93 Cab. 23, 64, 47(30), Item 8, 30 July 1930.

94 Morrison to MacDonald, 17 September 1930. MT 46/1.

95 MT 46/3.

96 Cab. 23, 65, 53(30), Item 1, 18 September 1930; Cab. 24, 214, CP 297(30), 8 September 1930.

97 On 2 March 1931.

98 He had pointed out earlier to the President of the Board of Trade that if 'the Minister of Transport gets his Bill, you will not get your Coal Bill'. Draft autobiography.

99 Cab. 23, 66, 16(31), Item 2, 4 March 1931.

100 Pethick-Lawrence (Financial Secretary to the Treasury) to MacDonald, 9 March 1931, MacDonald papers, 2/3.

101 Cab. 23, 66, 17(31), Item 9, 11 March 1931.

102 MacDonald to Morrison, Morrison papers.

103 MacDonald to Morrison, 23 March 1931, Morrison papers.

104 *HC Debs*, vol. 250, cols 47–71, 23 March 1931.

105 Interview.

106 Interviews, Sir Reginald Hill and J. W. Raisin.

107 Cab. 24, 222, CP 188 (31), 23 July 1931. Cab. 23, 67, 40(31), Item 12, 30 July 1931.

108 *News Chronicle*, 21 January 1931.

109 *Daily Telegraph*, 7 February 1931; *Daily Express*, 18 March 1931.

110 Draft autobiography. MacDonald was also worried and asked Morrison to intervene. Cab. 24, 206, CP 271 (29), 11 October 1929. Also see H. Morrison, 'The Elected Authority – Spur or Brake', in Royal Institute of Public Administration, *Vitality in Administration* (1957), p. 14.

111 Cab. 24, 220, CP 82 (31), 27 March 1931, and draft autobiography.

112 Cab. 27, 464 (LPT), 15 July 1931; Cab. 24, 222, CP 170 (31), 6 July 1931.

113 Cab. 23, 67, 40(31), Item 14, 30 July 1931.

114 *HC Debs*, vol. 233, col. 529, 11 December 1929; see also *LPCR*, 1930, p. 244.

115 Cab. 23, 67, 38(31), Item 7, 15 July 1931; Cab. 24, 222, CP 171(31), 8 July 1931. Also draft autobiography.

116 Cab. 24, 209, CP 42(30), 8 February 1930.

117 *HC Debs*, vol. 235, cols 1526–40, 19 February 1930.

118 Cab. 23, 64, 25(30), Item 19, 7 May 1930; Cab. 24, 211, CP 148(30), 6 May 1930.

119 Cab. 23, 67, 30(31), Item 8, 3 June 1931; Cab. 24, 221, CP 131 (131, (6 May 1931.

120 Cab. 24, 222, CP 165 (31), 4 July 1931; Cab. 23, 67, 38 (31), Item 2, 15 July 1931.

121 *Daily Express*, 30 July 1931.

122 *London News*, August 1931.

123 *Star*, 5 April 1932.

124 Draft autobiography.

125 *Socialisation and Transport*, p. 105.

126 *News Chronicle*, 28 November 1930. Also *Socialisation and Transport*, pp. 106–7 and p. 291.

127 R. Postgate, *The Life of George Lansbury* (1951), p. 295.

128 *Forward*, 18 January 1936.

129 Morrison to Hurcomb, 18 April 1933, in possession of Lord Hurcomb.

Chapter 11   The 1931 Crisis

1 *Daily Herald*, 1 July 1929.

2 R. Skidelsky, *Politicians and the Slump* (1967).

3 *Manchester Guardian*, 20 October 1930.

4 *London News*, July 1930.

5 The correspondence between Morrison and Snowden has been preserved in MacDonald papers, 1/211. It shows that Snowden resisted all Morrison's claims and yielded only under pressure from the Prime Minister.

6 R. Skidelsky, op. cit., pp. 153–5 and 194–5.

7 See Morrison memorandum, 28 October 1929, Cab. 27 (405), AL 29 (3), Acquisition of Land for Public Purposes Committee. See Sir George Stedman to G. W. Jones, 28 November 1968. At a conference of ministers in May 1930 Morrison gave the example of the Shooters Hill bypass for which money had been voted. 'It was found there was a railway in the way; houses on the route; tramway being built. There are always physical difficulties. Plant has to be shifted about. Negotiations must proceed with churches, allotment holders, residents.' T. Jones, *Whitehall Diary*, Vol. II, 1926–30, ed. by K. Middlemass (1969), p. 257.

8 Morrison reported to the Committee on National Schemes that: 'I feel that any diminution in local responsibility would raise far-reaching political issues and be found on balance to possess grave disadvantages,' and that state control did not automatically mean smooth sailing. Cab. 27 (397), NS 29 (2), 13 November 1929. See also Cab. 27 (390), DU 29 (53), Departmental Committee on Unemployment, 11 September 1929.

9 Morrison memorandum to Departmental Committee on Unemployment, Cab. 27 (390), DU 29 (60), 5 October 1929.

10 *HC Debs*, vol. 246, cols 1101–2, 16 December 1930.

11 Morrison to J. H. Thomas, 2 February 1930. Morrison papers.

12 Ibid.

13 *Observer*, 24 June 1934.

14 Draft autobiography.

15 Morrison to Thomas, loc. cit.

16 *The Times*, 6 December 1930.

17 *The Times*, 13 April 1931.

18 e.g. in *London News*, July 1930, September 1930 and June 1931; *HC Debs*, vol. 240, cols 460–5, 18 June 1930; vol. 244, cols 719–33, 4 November 1930; vol. 246, cols 1101–20, 16 December 1930; and vol. 251, cols 478–86, 16 April 1931. *Forward*, 14 February 1931, report of a talk on BBC radio.

19 *Daily Express*, 16 December 1929. (Manchester edition.)

20 Morrison to Snowden, 9 December 1929. MacDonald papers, 1/211.

21 Conference of Ministers on Unemployment, Cab. 27 (437), CMU 6 (30) 2, 4 June 1930.

22 Morrison memorandum, Cab. 27 (439), UP 30 (45), 20 January 1931.

23 Mosley memorandum to National Schemes Committee, 25 November 1929, Cab. 27 (397), NS (29) 5.

24 See R. Bassett, *Nineteen Thirty-One* (1958). R. Skidelsky, op. cit., chapter 13, and his articles, 'Crisis 1931', *The Times*, 2 December and 3 December 1968.

25 Cab. 24, 222, CP 203 (31).

26 Draft autobiography.

27 Cab. 23, 67, 41 (31), 19 August 1931.

28 Cab. 23, 67, 42 (31), 43 (31) and 44 (31).

29 Cab. 23, 67, 45 (31).

30 Cab. 23, 67, 46 (31).

31 MacDonald, Snowden, Thomas, Sankey, Passfield, Bondfield, Wedgwood Benn, Shaw, Amulree, Lees-Smith, Parmoor (who was absent) were in this group.

32 Henderson, Clynes, Graham, Greenwood, Alexander, Lansbury, Johnston, Adamson, Addison.

33 Cab. 23, 67, 47 (31).
34 H. Morrison, *Government and Parliament*, p. 92.
35 *Autobiography*, pp. 126–7.
36 Harold Nicolson, *King George the Fifth* (1952), p. 467.
37 M. A. Hamilton, *Remembering My Good Friends* (1944), p. 247. He must have also told Maurice Webb that he refused an offer (M. Webb, 'The Rt Hon. Herbert Morrison, MP' in H. Tracey (ed.), *The British Labour Party*, vol. III, (1948), p. 36) and Maurice Edelman who wrote that Morrison 'remained steadfastly with the Party' (M. Edelman, *Herbert Morrison* (1948), p. 46.)
38 M. A. Hamilton, op. cit., p. 168.
39 Morrison to MacDonald, 27 August 1931. MacDonald papers, 5/43.
40 MacDonald to Morrison, 27 August 1931. MacDonald papers, 5/43.
41 Morrison to MacDonald, 28 August 1931. MacDonald papers, 5/43.
42 Thomas had asked his former PPS, George Isaacs, to go with him into the government, claiming that over sixty Labour MPs would follow them. Interview, G. A. Isaacs.
43 Interview, Dame Leah Manning.
44 The *Observer*, 9 October 1966, confirmed in an interview.
45 Interview, A. MacDonald.
46 Interview, Mrs K. H. Frankl.
47 Interview, Lord Shinwell.
48 Interview, G. R. Strauss.
49 Undated carbon copy of a letter from Morrison to Davies, in Morrison papers. Both Clement Attlee and James Griffiths felt that Morrison had wanted to join MacDonald and stayed out only because MacDonald would not have him. They had no evidence, but this was their guess. Interviews.
50 Earl of Swinton, *Sixty Years of Power* (1966), p. 156.
51 Diary of G. R. Strauss.
52 e.g. *John Bull*, 9 November 1946; interview, C. Brandon; Strauss Diary.
53 Interview, Lady Allen of Hurtwood.
54 Interview, Mrs Lucy Middleton.
55 Interview, Mrs E. K. Goodrich.
56 Interview.
57 Interview. Tom Jones, who had attended as a Secretary at the final Cabinet meeting, wrote that MacDonald 'had set him [Morrison] free to go, for his future's sake, but he is very unhappy'. *A Diary with Letters, 1931–1950* (1954), p. 11. Two days later he was, in Strauss's view, 'despondent'. Mary Agnes Hamilton described him at this time as 'troubled and unhappy', op. cit., p. 247, and Hannen Swaffer noted that 'No man feels it more than he.' *Daily Herald*, 26 August 1931.
58 *Daily Telegraph*, 25 March 1965.
59 Interview, Mrs I. Peterkin.
60 Interviews, Sir Isaac Hayward, Lord Silkin, Lord Latham, H. Atkinson, C. W. Gibson.
61 This section is based largely on interviews with Malcolm MacDonald, Alistair MacDonald and Mrs Ishbel Peterkin.
62 NEC Minutes, vol. 60, 26 August and 27 August 1931.
63 *Daily Mail*, 28 August 1931.
64 M. Gilbert, *Plough My Own Furrow* (1965), p. 212.

65 For this speech see *The Times*, 8 September 1931 and *London News*, October 1931.
66 Diary, 7 September 1931, vol. 14.
67 *Hackney Gazette*, 28 September 1931 and *The Times*, 28 September 1931.
68 M. Gilbert, op. cit., p. 234.
69 *Daily Herald*, 12 October 1931.
70 *Sunday Express*, 11 October 1931 and *Hackney Gazette*, 12 October 1931.
71 *The Times*, 12 October 1931.
72 Interview, Mrs W. Moore.
73 Minutes of a joint NEC and GC meeting, 10 November 1931. (No vol. number.)
74 *London News*, January 1932 and May 1932.
75 *Daily Express*, 28 February 1933.
76 Interview, Lady Allen of Hurtwood.
77 *Bulletin and Scots Pictorial*, 18 March 1935.

Chapter 12 Morrison the Man

1 Interview, Mrs M. Mandelson.
2 The *Social-Democrat*, July 1930. In January 1932 Beatrice Webb notes: 'He is now a heavy smoker and moderate whisky drinker and meat eater – and he takes no exercise . . . he is puritan in sex.' Diary, 17 January 1932.
3 Interviews, Colonel W. E. Loweth and Dr R. H. Tee.
4 Diary, 2 February 1936.
5 Good descriptions appear in the *New York Times Magazine*, 3 May 1936; the *Bulletin and Scots Pictorial*, 10 January 1935; *Evening News*, 3 May 1937; *Daily Express*, 13 July, 1 August 1933, 16 January 1934, 28 June 1937; *Sussex Daily News*, 15 June 1935; *Manchester Evening News*, 7 September 1940; *English Digest*, October 1943; *Observer*, 10 January 1943; M. A. Hamilton, *Remembering My Good Friends* (1944), p. 167; 'Watchman', *Right Honourable Gentlemen* (1940), p. 183. Also interviews, H. Atkinson, G. Wansbrough, J. Griffiths, A. L. Rowse and Miss P. Jones. Harold Laski wrote a superb profile in the *Daily Herald*, 27 September 1930.
6 'Watchman', op. cit., p. 183.
7 Interview, R. C. D. Jenkins.
8 Interview, Sir George Stedman.
9 Interview, Mrs F. Corbet.
10 Interviews, Mrs D. J. Bolton, G. Jeger, Lady Gater, Dame Joan Vickers.
11 Interviews, K. H. Kent, J. W. Raisin, F. L. Stevens, Mrs W. Moore.
12 Interview, G. Jeger.
13 Diary, 17 January 1932.
14 H. Altman to G. W. Jones, 16 January 1967.
15 Interviews, Mrs M. Mandelson, Lady Cripps and Mrs D. Robinson.
16 Unpublished Memoir of Miss A. Sayle.
17 Interview, Mrs M. Mandelson.
18 Interviews, Mrs H. Butler, Lady Wilmot, Mrs R. Penna, Lady Allen of Hurtwood.
19 Interviews, Mrs E. Richards, Mr S. Richards, Mrs C. S. Morrison.
20 Interview, Mrs M. Mandelson.
21 Interview, J. Griffiths.

22 Interviews, E. Jay, Sir Richard Coppock, T. G. Randall, Dr C. Brook, R. W. Bell, Miss P. Jones.

23 Interviews, D. N. Pritt, Mrs B. Castle, K. Martin.

24 Interviews, Sir Isaac Hayward, H. Atkinson, J. W. Raisin.

25 Interview, Mrs R. Penna.

26 Interview, Lady Allen of Hurtwood.

27 Interviews, Lord Willis, Mrs D. Robinson, Lady Gater.

28 Interviews, Dr B. Homa, Sir George Stedman, F. L. Stevens, M. MacDonald, Mrs L. Middleton, J. W. Raisin, Sir Frederic Osborn, C. A. G. Manning, G. Wansbrough, Mrs F. Corbet, Mrs R. Stanton; *Daily Express*, 13 July 1933, 28 June 1937; the *Observer*, 10 January 1943; M. A. Hamilton, op. cit., p. 167; 'Watchman', op. cit., p. **184**; F. Williams, *The Triple Challenge* (1948), p. 88.

29 Interviews, A. Clark, Lady Gater, Lord Silkin, Sir Richard Coppock.

30 See *Daily News*, 6 August 1929; *Daily Express*, 13 July 1933; interviews, J. Manning, G. Jeger, Mrs F. Griffiths, C. A. G. Manning.

31 *Daily Express*, 1 July 1929. Also *Daily Telegraph*, 17 September 1937.

32 *English Digest*, October 1943; *Daily Herald*, 23 June 1938; 'Watchman', op. cit., p. 186; the *Star*, 16 May 1931; *Daily Dispatch*, 8 April 1935; *Daily Express*, 1 August 1933. W. E. Jackson to G. W. Jones, 12 February 1966; *Star*, 17 December 1937. His politics were, however, in his clothes. In 1936 he told a London audience: 'Dress co-operatively if you want to be smart. Everything in which I stand up has been bought from a Co-operative Society; you should do the same and then you would look as nice as I do ... Even when you are being carried to your last resting place you can reflect, "Well, I'm travelling in a Co-op hearse so I'm carrying my principles to the grave".' *London News*, October 1936.

33 W. E. Jackson to G. W. Jones, 12 February 1966.

34 M. A. Hamilton, op. cit., pp. 168–9.

35 *Daily Mail*, 10 November 1939; interviews, Mrs F. Griffiths, Mrs W. Moore, Mrs R. Stanton, Mrs M. Mandelson, Miss M. McCulloch; Morrison memorandum to LLP Executive, 30 July 1939.

36 Interviews, D. Frankel, Sir Richard Coppock, Sir Isaac Hayward, Mr and Mrs J. W. Raisin, E. Jay, Lord Moyle, Miss M. McCulloch.

37 *Daily Express*, 6 March 1940.

38 Morrison memorandum to LLP Executive, 31 May 1937 and minutes of LLP Executive, 3 June 1937.

39 Interview, E. Jay, and 'Watchman', op. cit., p. 183.

40 *Picture Post*, 13 April 1940. Dr B. Homa, a former LCC councillor, recalled that, when he talked to Morrison at the LCC. Morrison was restless, moving around the room and fingering his papers, although attentive. Interview.

41 *News Chronicle*, 1 November 1935. See also M. Webb, 'The Rt Hon. Herbert Morrison, MP' in H. Tracey (ed.), *The British Labour Party*, vol. III (1948), p. 31; *Manchester Evening News*, 8 November 1935; H. Dalton, *High Tide and After* (1962), p. 201.

42 *Star*, 6 March 1937.

43 Interview, C. A. G. Manning.

44 *Millgate*, January 1940, p. 217.

45 *Gloucestershire Echo*, 29 November 1934.

46 Note to the author from W. E. Jackson, 12 February 1966; interviews, Sir Aylmer Firebrace, Sir Isaac Hayward, R. Stamp. See *Daily Express*, 28 September 1934.

47 F. Williams, op. cit., pp. 87–8. Also interviews, Lady Wilmot and G. Wansbrough.

48 Interviews, E. Jay, Lady Gater, Lady Summerskill, Lady Wilmot, C. A. G. Manning; St John Ervine in *Belfast Telegraph*, 15 March 1946. Also F. Williams, op. cit., pp. 92–3.

49 *Manchester Evening News*, 7 September 1940.

50 See J. T. Murphy, *Labour's Big Three* (1948), pp. 248–9. *Daily Herald*, 1 October 1934; F. Williams, op. cit., p. 93.

51 R. Calder in *Picture Post*, 13 April 1940. Also M. Webb, op. cit., p. 30.

52 *Manchester Evening News*, 7 September 1940. See also 'Watchman', op. cit., p. 186, and M. Webb, op. cit., p. 31, who wrote: 'he must have everything neatly in order, clear-cut, systematically marshalled, and straightforward'.

53 M. Edelman, *Herbert Morrison* (1948), p. 90; F. Williams, op. cit., p. 92; M. Webb, op. cit., p. 31 and p. 33; *Manchester Evening News*, 7 September 1940; *English Digest*, October 1943; interview, H. Atkinson.

54 M. Webb, op. cit., p. 33.

55 *Manchester Evening News*, 7 September 1940.

56 Diary, 17 January 1932.

57 *Manchester Evening News*, 7 September 1940; 6 December 1943; *Star*, 4 March 1937, 13 May 1940; *South Wales Argus*, 8 December 1934; *Daily Herald*, 9 March 1935; *Millgate*, January 1940, p. 216; F. Williams, op. cit., p. 92. Interviews, G. Wansbrough, E. Jay, Mrs D. J. Bolton.

58 Interview, A. L. Rowse.

59 Interview, R. H. S. Crossman.

60 *Picture Post*, 13 April 1940; *Daily Mirror*, 16 January 1940; M. A. Hamilton, op. cit., p. 167, and her article 'Herbert Morrison' in *Britain Today*, January 1946, pp. 5–10, especially p. 6; interviews, S. C. Leslie, J. W. Raisin, G. Wansbrough.

61 See Peter Jenkins, 'Maybe it's because he's a Londoner', *The House of Whitbread*, vol. 22, January 1963, p. 21.

62 See J. Winocour, 'The Lord President', in *Who Runs Britain*, 1949, pp. 2–4.

63 J. Winocour, op. cit., p. 2; M. Edelman, op. cit., p. 10; M. Webb, op. cit., p. 29.

64 Diary, 2 February 1936.

Chapter 13 Changing Gear, 1931–1933

1 See Tables (a), (b), (c).

2 *News Chronicle*, 23 October 1931. See also *The Times*, 12 October 1931 and *Daily Herald*, 12 October 1931.

3 *Manchester Guardian*, 29 October 1931.

4 *London News*, January 1932.

5 Morrison Memorandum, 10 December 1931, LLP papers.

6 e.g. the *Star*, 21 October 1931.

7 Minutes of LCC Labour Party, 23 February 1932.

8 Interviews, Dr E. Rickards, Sir Richard Coppock, Dr C. Brook, D. Frankel, Mrs F. Corbet, Sir Isaac Hayward and Lord Silkin.

9 Minutes of LCC Labour Party, 14 February 1933.

10 The originals are in the LLP papers, January to June 1932. They were published in various Labour journals, e.g. *South Hackney Citizen*, February to July 1932.

11 He wrote in 1932 two Labour Party pamphlets of a theoretical nature, *A New Appeal to the Young* and *An Easy Outline of Modern Socialism*. The latter was reissued in 1935 and 1938. In November 1934 he delivered at Oxford the Sidney Ball lecture on 'Man: the Master or the Slave of Material Things', (Barnett House Papers, No. 18), and in December at the Sorbonne he gave a similar oration to the British Institute (*Morning Post*, 1 December 1934). He talked on BBC radio in 1935 about economic and social freedom (*Listener*, 17 April 1935, pp. 646–7). In 1938 he lectured to the Fabian Society on 'Socialism Today' (in B. Russell et al., *Dare We Look Ahead?* (1938), pp. 120–60).

12 *London News*, October 1931.

13 *A New Appeal to the Young*, Labour Party, 1932, p. 6 and *London News*, September, 1938.

14 *South Hackney Citizen*, May 1933. *Manchester Guardian*, 2 July 1934. In August 1937 one campaigning week was called 'Socialist Crusade Week'. *Forward*, 11 September 1937.

15 Added in the answer in 1938, *South Hackney Citizen*, August 1938.

16 *London News*, July 1933.

17 Fabian Society Lecture, op. cit., p. 142; *New Clarion*, 20 August 1932.

18 H. Morrison, *Socialisation and Transport* (1933), p. 140.

19 Minutes of the Policy sub-committee, 6 December 1931.

20 Dalton, diary, 16 December 1931.

21 H. Dalton, *The Fateful Years: Memoirs 1931–1945* (1957), p. 23.

22 Article to Labour editors, 20 August 1932, LLP papers and *London News*, October 1932.

23 Minutes of the Re-organization of Industry Group, 3 March 1932.

24 See Morrison report to LLP Executive, 7 July 1932.

25 *LPCR*, 1931, pp. 170–3.

26 TUC Report, *The Public Control and Regulation of Industry and Trade*, 1932, and A. Bullock, *The Life and Times of Ernest Bevin*, vol. I (1960), p. 510. Bevin's memorandum of dissent was dated 10 May 1932. He was the sole dissentient when both the draft and the final version were adopted. Minutes of the Economic Committee of the TUC General Council, 19 May and 14 June 1932.

27 NEC Minutes (no vol. no.), 23 June 1932.

28 *The National Planning of Transport* and *The Re-organisation of the Electricity Supply Industry*, LPCR, 1932, pp. 217–25.

29 *LPCR*, 1932, pp. 223–4. He frequently condemned the London Passenger Transport Board. He called it 'the worst form of public control' (A. Bullock, op. cit., p. 510) and attacked the financial psovisions as imposing on the London public as great a burden as the Water Board had twenty years before. *LPCR*, 1933, p. 237. See also A. Bullock, op. cit., pp. 514–15.

30 NEC Minutes, vol. 61, 26 October 1932.

31 *Daily Express*, 25 June and 8 July 1932.

32 Minutes, 9 February, 15 February, 22 February 1933.

33 Minutes of joint meeting of representatives from Economic Committee of TUC and Policy Committee of Labour Party, 8 March 1933 – agreement reported to NEC on 22 March 1933.

34 *LPCR*, 1933, pp. 204–9.

35 *LPCR*, 1934, pp. 163–5 and 197–9 and *Socialisation and Transport*, pp. 244–79.

36 Morrison wrote of Churchill: 'his particular form of fun is to embarrass any Government which has not taken the precaution of including him among its members.' *London News*, January 1933.

37 Interviews, Lord Hurcomb and Sir Reginald Hill. See Cab. 24, 223, CP 214 (31), 31 August 1931, and Cab. 24, 224, CP 270 (31), 10 November 1931.

38 Morrison memorandum to LLP Executive, 15 September 1932.

39 *London News*, August 1932, and *Financial Times*, 16 November 1932, *The Times*, 29 November 1932. He objected to two further alterations in his bill: the prevention of the board from manufacturing rolling stock and vehicles for its own requirements, and the transfer of the power to make orders about travel services and facilities from the Traffic Advisory Committee to the Railway Rates Tribunal which he felt had not sufficient experience of such matters involving questions of public policy.

40 Draft autobiography.

41 *Star*, 24 May 1933.

42 *Star*, 30 June 1933, 23 January, 20 June 1935, and *Daily Herald*, 7 June 1935.

43 *London News*, July 1932; *Socialisation and Transport*, pp. 146–8; and *Forward*, 12 August 1933.

44 *LPCR*, 1937, p. 193. See also *Manchester Guardian*, 2 August 1933. Under Morrison's prompting the LLP Executive in 1932 and 1933 organized a campaign to educate members in socialism. Morrison drew up a course of six lectures: The Rise of the Labour Movement; Capitalism and the World Crisis; Finance and the City; The Limits of Social Reform and the Necessity of Socialism; The Socialization of Industry; and Socialism and the World Order. Lecturers were found, booklists and notes devised. Study circles were established in ward parties and the women's sections, and weekend schools were held. He appealed to members to spread common-sense socialist education among the people. *Reports of LLP Executive*, 1931–2, 1932–3; *London News*, July, September 1932, November 1933; *The Times*, 31 December 1934.

Chapter 14   Leader of the London County Council, 1934–1940

1 H. Morrison, *How London is Governed* (1949), p. 35.

2 Ibid., p. 33.

3 *Manchester Evening News*, 8 November 1935.

4 E.g. in 1947; H. Dalton, *High Tide and After* (1962), p. 243.

5 Interview, Lady Summerskill.

6 E.g. *Daily Herald*, 1 October 1938.

7 Interview, T. G. Randall.

8 Morrison memorandum to LLP Executive, 4 June 1931. Also *London News*, July 1932 and March 1933.

9 *Evening Standard*, 27 February 1934. The press campaign against the Co-operative Movement can be examined in the collection of press cuttings in the Papers of Lord Alexander of Hillsborough, Avar, 10/7. Churchill College, Cambridge.

10 See *Manchester Guardian*, 8 March 1934. *Daily Telegraph*, 9 March 1934, also interviews, Lord Silkin, Sir Isaac Hayward, Dr C. Brook and R. Stamp.

11 Compared with the results in 1931 Labour's share of the vote had risen by eleven per cent, the Municipal Reformers' had fallen by eight per cent and the Progressives' had fallen by three per cent. See Table (b).

12 Interview, J. Griffiths.

13 *Daily Express*, 15 March 1934.

14 *Morning Post*, 2 April 1934. See also *South Hackney Citizen*, April 1934.

15 Interviews, Mrs H. C. Bentwich, Mrs F. Corbet, H. Atkinson.

16 Latham deputized in Morrison's rare absences, e.g. *Daily Herald*, 6 October 1938.

17 This procedure was repeated in 1937. Minutes of the LCC Labour Party, 8 March 1937. Silkin said he stepped down from the Deputyship 'in order to be on the same level as the other two'. Interview.

18 Details of the 'Presidium' are from interviews with Lord Latham, Lord Silkin, Sir Isaac Hayward, C. W. Gibson, Sir Edward Bligh and an unpublished memoir by Miss A. Sayle.

19 Interview, Dr C. Brook.

20 Interview, Sir Richard Coppock.

21 Interview.

22 Interviews, Dr C. Brook, F. J. Powe, Dr E. Rickards and Sir Richard Coppock.

23 Interview, R. W. Bell.

24 Interview.

25 Interview. Also interview, C. W. Gibson, a whip under Morrison for a short time.

26 Interview, Sir Richard Coppock.

27 Interview.

28 Interviews, Mrs H. C. Bentwich, Lady Nathan and Sir Isaac Hayward. In the 1930s he continued to add to his team. He brought John Wilmot in as an alderman and made him Chairman of the Fire Brigade Committee. Interview, Lady Wilmot.

29 Interviews, Mrs D. J. Bolton, Dr C. Brook, J. Cliff, Sir Richard Coppock, Mrs F. Corbet, D. Frankel, Sir Isaac Hayward, Lord Latham, Lady Nathan, Dr E. Rickards, A. E. Samuels, Lord Silkin, G. R. Strauss. The authors were unable to interview either Sir Charles Robertson (Education) or Somerville Hastings (Hospitals). However, members of their committees said that Morrison treated them as he did other chairmen. Interviews, Sir Richard Coppock, D. Frankel and Lady Nathan. *Manchester Evening News*, 8 November 1935. See also *London News*, March and October 1936, for a lecture to the Institute of Public Administration on how he ran the LCC.

30 Interview, A. E. Samuels.

31 Also interview, F. J. Powe.

32 Interviews, Mrs H. C. Bentwich, J. Cliff, Sir Richard Coppock, Sir Allen Daley, Sir Isaac Hayward, Lord Latham, Dr E. Rickards, A. E. Samuels, R. Stamp.

33 Interview, Lord Silkin.

34 Interviews, M. Orbach, Mrs L. Jeger.

35 M. A. Hamilton, *Remembering My Good Friends* (1944), p. 169.

36 Interviews, Sir Isaac Hayward and G. R. Strauss. *London News*, March 1936.

37 Interviews, Mrs H. C. Bentwich, Mrs D. J. Bolton, C. W. Gibson, Sir Isaac Hayward, Lord Latham, Dr B. Homa, Lady Nathan, F. J. Powe, Dr E. Rickards, G. R. Strauss.

38 Interviews, R. W. Bell, Sir Edward Bligh, Sir Allen Daley, Sir Howard Roberts, Sir Aylmer Firebrace, F. W. Holland, W. E. Jackson, and T. G. Randall.

39 Interview, F. J. Powe.

40 Morrison asked Tee to apply for a post as a solicitor at the LCC, pointing out that it was on the route to the Clerkship. Morrison was keen to bring on men and women whose skills he appreciated. Tee refused, not wanting to be too involved in legal work. Interview, Dr Tee.

41 Interviews, T. G. Randall, Sir Edward Bligh, R. W. Bell.

42 Morrison to Gater, 4 March 1937. Gater papers in possession of Lady Gater.

43 Morrison to Gater, 9 November 1939. Gater papers.

44 Interview, Lady Gater.

45 Interviews, R. W. Bell, Sir Edward Bligh, Sir Allen Daley, W. E. Jackson.

46 Interviews, R. W. Bell, J. W. Raisin, Sir Richard Coppock, Dr C. Brook, Dr E. Rickards and Sir Isaac Hayward.

47 Interviews, R. W. Bell, Sir Edward Bligh, F. W. Holland and T. G. Randall.

48 Interview, Lady Nathan.

49 Interviews with numerous elected members and officials who heard Morrison's speeches.

50 Interview, Sir Edward Bligh, and unpublished memoir by Miss A. Sayle.

51 Minutes of the LCC Labour Party, 4 June 1935.

52 Interview, C. W. Gibson. Morrison wanted G. G. Mackenzie to be Chairman of the Public Assistance Committee's Staff sub-committee so as to have no impropriety in appointments. He told Mackenzie to rule out immediately anyone on whose behalf there was canvassing, and it was done strictly as Morrison insisted. Interview, G. G. Mackenzie.

53 *Daily Mail*, 19 July 1935. *London News*, December 1934; *Daily Herald*, 26 November 1934 and 31 January 1938.

54 *London News*, December 1934.

55 Interview, Mrs D. J. Bolton.

56 Memoir by Miss A. Sayle.

57 Note from W. E. Jackson.

58 *Sunday Dispatch*, 18 March 1934; and C. Pearce to G. W. Jones, 15 October 1968.

59 Interviews, Mrs T. Cazalet-Keir, Lord Blakenham, Dame Joan Vickers, R. C. D. Jenkins; C. Pearce to G. W. Jones, 15 October 1968; W. Hornby Steer to G. W. Jones, 16 August 1968.

60 He did just that over civil defence, *Autobiography*, p. 156.

61 *Daily Express*, 10 July 1935.

62 *Sunday Express*, 21 July 1935. See also *Bayswater Chronicle*, 6 April 1935.

63 Interviews, Lord Blakenham, F. J. Powe, T. G. Randall.

64 Interviews, Lord Blakenham, R. C. D. Jenkins and Dame Joan Vickers.

65 Charles Ammon who rejoined the LCC in 1934 after an interval of nine years noted that: 'The Tory party is little changed in personnel. Of the Labour Party there are only about six who were members nine years ago ... The Labour Party are mainly young people.' Diary of Lord Ammon, 18 November 1934.

66 Interviews, R. C. D. Jenkins, Mrs T. Cazalet-Keir, Dame Joan Vickers; C. Pearce to G. W. Jones, 15 October 1968.

67 Interview. Also A. E. Davies, *The London County Council, 1889–1937*, Fabian Tract No. 243 (1937), p. 13 and p. 17.

68 See W. A. Robson, *The Government and Misgovernment of London* (1948); Sir Gwilym Gibbon and R. W. Bell, *History of the London County Council, 1889–1939* (1939); W. E. Jackson, *Achievement: A short history of the London County Council* (1965); B. Barker, *Labour in London* (1946); A. E. Davies, op. cit.; H. Morrison and D. Daines, *London under Socialist Rule* (editions 1934 and 1935).

69 *Report of the LCC Labour Party*, 1933–4. See also *Daily Herald*, 25 January 1935.

70 *Daily Herald*, 26 June 1935.

71 *Daily Express*, 12 March 1965.

72 The opposition was said to consist of Municipal Reformers who did not want an increase in Labour voters, and of residents adjacent to the proposed site. Interview, A. Cullington.

73 *North London Recorder*, 13 September 1935.

74 *Daily Herald*, 8 April 1936.

75 *Daily Herald*, 8 April 1936.

76 *Daily Express*, 23 May 1936.

77 Interview, Sir Allen Daley.

78 Election Notes, 4 February 1937, LLP papers. See also Table (e).

79 Morrison's views were clearly expressed in *Work, Training and Instruction*, a London Municipal Pamphlet, No. 10, 1931, published by the LLP, written by Morrison.

80 Interviews, Sir Isaac Hayward and Sir Edward Bligh. Also Morrison memorandum to LLP Executive, 28 May 1934. LLP papers; and Minutes of LLP Executive, 7 June 1934.

81 Interviews, Sir Isaac Hayward, Sir Edward Bligh and D. Frankel.

82 Interview, Sir Richard Coppock.

83 *Morning Post*, 23 March 1935; *Forward*, 4 September 1937; *Manchester Guardian*, 26 July 1939; *Evening Standard*, 9 May 1936.

84 *Evening Standard*, 30 May 1936; *Daily Express*, 27 June 1936.

85 *News Chronicle*, 28 April 1934.

86 *London News*, November 1934.

87 *Daily Mail*, 30 November 1936.

88 The grants could be up to fifty per cent of the cost of purchase.

89 *Daily Herald*, 4 February 1937.

90 Interview, R. W. Bell.

91 *Daily Herald*, 9 July 1934.

92 Interview, F. J. Powe.

93 Article to Labour editors, 27 July 1934, LLP papers.

94 *Evening Standard*, 8 June 1932.

95 *Daily Express*, 25 October 1933.

96 See Cab. 24, 248, CP 86 (34), 22 March 1934 and Cab. 23, 78, 13 (34), item 6, 28 March 1934.

97 *Daily Herald*, 23 March 1934.

98 *Daily Express*, 23 April 1934.

99 *Evening News*, 20 June 1934.

100 21 June 1934. The *Spectator* (16 March 1934) complained that Morrison had 'an aesthetic blindness amounting to Philistinism'.

101 *The Times*, 10 December 1934.

102 Cab. 24, 262, CP 114 (36), 23 April 1936 and Cab. 23, 84, 34 (36), item 14, 6 May 1936.

103 See Cab. 24, 267, CP 31 (37), 25 January 1937 and Cab. 23, 87, 4 (37), item 10, 27 January 1937.

104 The following version is from a speech to the IMTA Conference in 1960. *Report of Annual Conference of IMTA*, 1960, p. 101. Another version is in *Autobiography*, pp. 151–2.

105 Cab. 24, 271, CP 243 (37), 14 October 1937.

106 Cab. 23, 90, 45 (37), item 15, 1 December 1937.

107 *HC Debs*, vol. 330, cols 1975–7, 22 December 1937.

108 *Star*, 6 July 1937.

109 *Morning Post*, 26 March 1934; the *Star*, 5 April 1932 and *The Times*, 17 February 1932.

110 *News Chronicle*, 26 March 1934.

111 Interview, F. G. Kay.

112 e.g. *South Hackney Citizen*, June 1939. See Table (e).

113 See Table (f).

114 *Evening Standard*, 18 October 1935 and 28 March 1939.

115 *Evening Standard*, 24 February 1937.

116 *Evening Standard*, 8 February 1937.

117 H. C. Bedwell, former County Treasurer of Oxfordshire, guided the authors through the maze of LCC financial statistics.

118 Morrison instigated the production of a book [Sir Gwilym Gibbon and R. W. Bell, *History of the London County Council, 1889–1939* (1939)] to commemorate the fiftieth year of the LCC and watched over its compilation. Interview, R. W. Bell. See B. Webb diary, 30 June and 15 September 1938.

119 See *London News*, June 1934.

120 See F. L. Stevens, *Under London* (1939). In the introduction to this book Morrison wrote: 'there is a general understanding at County Hall that our business is to tell journalists and writers everything we possibly can and to give them all the help within our power.' And 'My view is that people who pay have a right to be told what they are getting for their money, and how the services are conducted.'

121 Interview, T. G. Randall.

122 Interview, P. Benson. His view was confirmed by E. Jay who covered the LCC for the *Daily Herald*.

123 Interviews, R. W. Bell and T. G. Randall.

124 23 November 1936.

125 Interview, C. W. Gibson, S. C. Leslie and T. G. Randall. Minutes of the LCC Labour Party, 19 June 1934 and 26 June 1934.

126 Interview, T. G. Randall.

127 Interviews, Sir Robert Fraser and G. Wansbrough.

128 Interview, S. C. Leslie.

129 Minutes of LLP Executive, 5 November 1936.

130 E.g. in *Daily Express*, 4 March 1937.

131 Interview. Also interview, Lord Francis-Williams.

132 *Picture Post*, 13 April 1940. Morrison's respect for specialists in publicity was further revealed in 1939 during a debate in the Commons, when he advised the Ministry of Information to broaden the scope of its appointments. 'I hope journalists will forgive me for saying this, but on balance advertising and publicity men as such are even more entitled to consideration than journalists because the modern

advertising man has to create an idea or a doctrine and "get it over".' *HC Debs*, vol. 355, col. 745, 6 December 1939.

133 Interviews, G. Wansbrough and G. R. Strauss.

134 LLP financial statistics, LLP papers. Also Strauss to Morrison, 29 May 1937, printed in *Forward*, 5 June 1937.

135 24 February 1937 at 9.40 p.m.

136 *Daily Herald*, 18 February 1937. See the collection of MR election literature at the Guildhall Library.

137 Morrison to Gater, 4 March 1937. Gater papers.

138 See Table (b).

139 *Labour*, August 1937.

Chapter 15   The Party Politician

1 *South Hackney Citizen*, May 1934.

2 *Warrington Examiner*, 23 March 1935.

3 Interviews, H. Atkinson, Mrs F. Griffiths, Miss J. Bourne, Mrs H. C. Bentwich and R. Stamp.

4 Interview, Miss J. Bourne. A secretary, Mrs F. Griffiths, made the same point.

5 Figures from *Reports of LLP Executive*.

6 This section on Morrison and the LCS is based on: *South Hackney Citizen*, November 1932; *London News*, May 1933; *Reports of LLP Executive*, 1932–4; Minutes of National Joint Committee (NEC and Co-op) Vol. 64, 28 November 1933, 5 January 1934, 18 January 1934, 1 February 1934; NEC Minutes, vol. 67, 27 February 1935 and 8 March 1935 including Morrison's memorandum and correspondence; *London News*, February and March 1939; also Morrison's memorandum to Chancellor of the Exchequer, 3 April 1933, LLP papers.

7 Memorandum to LLP Executive, 13 October 1932.

8 *Report of LLP Executive*, 1938–9.

9 Interview, Sir Isaac Hayward.

10 Morrison was keen that LCC members should not be remote from the party, and he urged local parties to invite them to talk about their work on the LCC. Morrison's letter to party secretaries, 25 November 1937, LLP papers.

11 List, 7 July 1938, LLP papers.

12 *Reports of LLP Executive*, 1931–7.

13 Morrison memorandum, 15 March 1938, LLP papers.

14 *Reports of LLP Executive*, 1931–5.

15 *Daily Herald*, 7 May 1934.

16 Daines's memorandum to Executive, 20 October 1938.

17 *Report of LLP Executive*, 1935–6.

18 *Report of LLP Executive*, 1936–7.

19 Interview, E. A. Robinson.

20 *LPCR*, 1936, p. 234; *LPCR*, 1939, p. 223. See also *Manchester Guardian*, 9 October 1936.

21 *Daily Herald*, 5 November 1934.

22 *Evening Standard*, 3 November 1934; *Star*, 3 November 1934.

23 An account is given in *Report of LLP Executive*, 1936–7.

24 Interviews, F. L. Stevens and Lord Francis-Williams.

25 *South London Press*, 5 October 1934, and noted in *London News*, December 1934.
26 *Daily Express*, 27 October 1934.
27 *Evening Standard*, 1 November 1934, and see 3 November 1934.
28 Interview, G. Jeger.
29 Minutes of Election Sub-Committee, 2 November 1934.
30 *Daily Express*, 31 May 1935. See *LPCR*, 1935, p. 141.
31 *London News*, August 1939.
32 J. Bonham, *The Middle-Class Vote* (1954), pp. 154–5.
33 NEC Minutes.
34 8 October 1932, vol. 14. Interviews, Lady Summerskill, Lord Shinwell, P. Noel-Baker, J. Griffiths and Sir William Lawther. See also J. T. Murphy, *Labour's Big Three* (1948), p. 166 and p. 172.
35 See H. Pelling, *A Short History of the Labour Party* (1968), pp. 77–85. Morrison felt that the NCL was too much dominated by the trade unions and by Citrine in particular. He complained to Beatrice Webb that it had been a mistake to link the party and the TUC so firmly together: 'the G.C. of the T.U. ought to keep to the industrial side – and let the labour party take the lead in general politics and foreign affairs.' B. Webb's diary, 2 February 1936.
36 Interview, Lord Citrine; also G. Mackenzie.
37 Similar to the proposals of the Royal Commission on Local Government in England Cmnd, 4040, 1969.
38 *London News*, October 1932. Memorandum No. 28, 4 May 1932. No vol. number. NEC papers. *LPCR*, 1933, pp. 215–16.
39 *Sunday Times*, 7 March 1965. Maurice Webb wrote that: 'the mantle of Arthur Henderson fell upon Morrison. He became . . . Labour's electoral commander-in-chief.' M. Webb, 'The Rt Hon. Herbert Morrison, MP'. In H. Tracey (ed.), *The British Labour Party*, vol. III (1948), p. 29.
40 Interview, J. Griffiths.
41 Interviews, E. Jay, P. Benson, H. Atkinson, Mrs L. Middleton, G. G. Mackenzie, Dame Leah Manning, W. Paling, Lady Cripps. Also J. T. Murphy, op. cit., p. 156.
42 Morrison had spoken on his behalf and applauded his victory as evidence that 'The Socialist spirit of the Labour Party was already rising . . . This is only the beginning.' *Daily Herald*, 25 April 1932.
43 In August 1933 Beatrice Webb noted that the parliamentary leaders, Lansbury, Cripps and Attlee, did not want Morrison, Alexander and Benn back in the Commons. Diary, 5 August 1933.
44 Interview, H. Atkinson.
45 Interviews, Lord Latham, H. Atkinson, J. W. Raisin and Sir Isaac Hayward.
46 *Morning Post*, 13 November 1935.
47 *The Times*, 30 October 1935 and *Manchester Guardian*, 13 November 1935.
48 *News Chronicle*, 13 November 1935.
49 Interviews, J. W. Raisin, W. Nichols, H. W. Butler, Mrs H. Butler.
50 See *South Hackney Citizen*, October 1930, for his holiday in France and his views on the French way of life.
51 Interview, J. W. Raisin.
52 *HC Debs*, vol. 307, cols. 673–4, 9 December 1935.
53 'Watchman', *Right Honourable Gentlemen* (1940), pp. 187–8.
54 *HC Debs*, vol. 342, cols 1660–72, 12 December 1938.

55 *HC Debs*, vol. 309, cols 1595–603, 5 March 1936, and vol. 317, cols 1454–65, 16 November 1936.

56 *HC Debs*, vol. 329, cols 55–71, 15 November 1937; *HC Debs*, vol. 340, cols 411–34, 3 November 1938; *HC Debs*, vol. 342, cols 1660–72, 12 December 1938; *HC Debs*, vol. 344, cols 1316–36, 1 March 1939; *HC Debs*, vol. 345, cols 2653–69, 4 April 1939.

57 *HC Debs*, vol. 313, cols 879–85, 16 June 1936.

58 *HC Debs*, vol. 317, cols. 1956–65, 19 November 1936. As Minister of Transport he had strongly opposed this measure when urged by Mosley.

59 *HC Debs*, vol. 337, cols 602–19, 17 June 1938. He protested in 1938 against increased taxes on petrol in the Finance Bill. *HC Debs*, vol. 337, cols 1127–30, 22 June 1938. See also *HC Debs*, vol. 349, cols 1359–73, 5 July 1939. He opposed driving tests because of their high administrative costs; the placing of arbitrary power in the hands of officials who would be open to temptations of bribery; and their ineffectiveness since only a minority of dangerous or careless drivers would appear to be dangerous or careless in the test. The answer was not to impose restrictions, but to promote courtesy.

60 *News Chronicle*, 31 May 1935.

61 *Stockport Express*, 21 March 1935.

62 He would say to his passengers: 'Keep a look-out on the right. Don't forget I can't see there.' Interview, E. A. Robinson.

63 *HC Debs*, vol. 307, cols 868–73, 10 December 1935; *HC Debs*, vol. 329, cols 529–38, 17 November 1937; *HC Debs*, vol. 357, cols 621–33, 13 February 1940; *HC Debs*, vol. 331, cols 528–35, 3 February 1938; *HC Debs*, vol. 318, cols 466–79, 25 November 1936.

64 *HC Debs*, vol. 328, cols 437–9, 29 October 1937; *HC Debs*, vol. 317, cols 632–43, 9 November 1936. Also *HC Debs*, vol. 307, cols 676–86, 9 December 1935.

65 *HC Debs*, vol. 331, cols 1953–9, 16 February 1938; *HC Debs*, vol 332, cols 1992–2000, 9 March 1938; *HC Debs*, vol. 350, cols 1840–52, 28 July 1939.

66 *HC Debs*, vol. 332, col. 1993, 9 March 1938.

67 *HC Debs*, vol. 352, cols 1846–52, 31 October 1939.

68 *HC Debs*, vol. 329, cols 55–71, 15 November 1937; *HC Debs*, vol. 341, cols 411–34, 3 November 1938; *HC Debs*, vol. 344, cols 1316–36, 1 March 1939; *HC Debs*, vol. 345, cols 2653–69, 4 April 1939; *HC Debs*, vol. 352, cols 2242–58, 2 November 1939.

Chapter 16   Enemies on the Right and on the Left

1 *London News*, July 1934.

2 Memorandum to Joint Consultative Committee of the London Trades Council and LLP, 26 July 1934. LLP papers. Also *London News*, September 1934. Information about the meeting can be found in *Report of LLP Executive*, 1933–4, and *London News*, October 1934.

3 E.g. information for delegates on the deputation to the Home Secretary, 20 October 1936, dated 19 October 1936. LLP papers. Morrison expressed his concern in the House of Commons at the worsening situation. *HC Debs*, vol. 309, cols 1595–603, 5 March 1936.

4 *The Times*, 9 October 1936.

5 *LPCR*, 1936, pp. 164–5.

6 Articles for use of Labour editors, 20 October 1936, nos 71 and 72. The letter to the Home Secretary is noted in the *Daily Herald*, 17 October 1936. An account appears in *Report of LLP Executive*, 1935–6, and *London News*, November 1936.

7 Morrison letter to party secretaries, 6 April 1937. LLP papers. Morrison letter to local parties, 20 September 1937. LLP papers, and *Report of LLP Executive*, 1936–7.

8 *Report of LLP Executive*, 1936–7.

9 Morrison to party secretaries, 30 November 1936. LLP papers.

10 Morrison Memorandum to LLP Executive, 5 June 1937.

11 Accounts of the incident appear in *Daily Telegraph*, 11 March 1939, and *Daily Mirror*, 11 March 1939.

12 Interviews, G. G. Mackenzie, C. Brandon, G. Jeger, G. A. Renshaw. Dame Joan Vickers noticed at the LCC that 'the East End people felt left out of it'. Interview.

13 Interviews, D. Frankel and G. Jeger.

14 *The Times*, 4 November 1930.

15 *Daily Express*, 1 April 1932; see also 21 March 1932.

16 *Daily Express*, 6 May 1935, and *Birmingham Gazette*, 6 May 1935.

17 Morrison's views at various times can be seen from *London News*, May 1933; *South Hackney Citizen*, July 1936; and *London News*, January 1939. Also from his speeches at Labour Party Conferences in 1933, 1934, 1937 and 1939. Letter from Executive, 6 April 1933. LLP papers. Letter to local party 4 May 1933. Also see *Report of LLP Executive*, 1932–3.

18 *London News*, November 1939.

19 *London News*, February 1940. He felt that this issue was a test of principle, and that anyone who justified Russian aggression should be out of the Labour Party. *London News*, April 1940.

20 *London News*, January, February and April 1940.

21 *London News*, May 1933 and H. Morrison, *The Communist Solar System* (1933). *South Hackney Citizen*, March 1939.

22 *LPCR*, 1933, p. 145.

23 *London News*, July 1930, and September 1932.

24 *Daily Herald*, 3 May 1934.

25 *LPCR*, 1934, pp. 137–8; see report in *Daily Express*, 2 October 1934.

26 *London News*, August 1937.

27 *London News*, January 1939 and *News Chronicle*, 3 January 1939.

28 Interview, S. C. Leslie.

29 Interview, Lord Willis.

30 Interviews, M. Orbach and D. N. Pritt. Also D. N. Pritt, *From Right to Left* (1965), p. 81.

31 Interview. Also interview, Dame Leah Manning, and L. Manning, *A Life for Education*, (1970) pp. 108–9.

32 E.g. *Morning Post*, 29 October 1934; *London News*, April 1935.

33 *London News*, January 1937. See *LLP Election Notes*, 8 January 1937.

34 E.g. *London News*, February and October 1935; *Daily Express*, 6 May 1935.

35 Some did find its way into LLP envelopes. Memorandum on 1937 election, LLP papers.

36 Correspondence printed in *Evening Standard*, 13 February 1937. Originals, Pollitt to Morrison, 2 February 1937 and Morrison to Pollitt, 13 February 1937 in LLP papers.

37 *Sunday Express*, 31 January 1937. (Early edition only.)

38 *Evening Standard*, 13 February 1937.

39 *Sunday Express*, 14 February 1937.

40 *Evening Standard*, 16 February 1937, and interview, S. C. Leslie.

41 *News Chronicle*, 17 March 1937, and *Evening News*, 16 March 1937.

42 *Tribune*, 12 March 1937, quoted in *Evening Standard*, 13 March 1937; *Evening News*, 16 March 1937; *The Times*, 17 March 1937; interview, G. R. Strauss.

43 *The Times*, 18 March 1937. See also *Forward*, 20 March 1937, 27 March 1937, 10 April 1937, 24 April 1937. Correspondence, between Morrison and Strauss, printed in *Forward*, 5 June 1937: Originals 14 May, 26 May, 29 May and 31 May 1937 in LLP papers.

44 Morrison memorandum to LLP Executive, 12 January 1933, LLP papers; *London News*, January 1932; *South Hackney Citizen*, January 1935; A. Peacock, *Yours Fraternally* (1945), pp. 22–3; *Daily Herald*, 25 February 1935.

45 *South Hackney Citizen*, October 1936. See also *London News*, September 1938; *Daily Express*, 1 April 1939.

46 Morrison memorandum to LLP Executive, 12 January 1933; Minutes of LLP Executive, 2 February 1933; Morrison memorandum to LLP Executive, 23 February 1933.

47 Interview, Lord Willis; also S. Goldberg.

48 Morrison memorandum to LLP Executive, 23 March 1939; *London News*, July 1939.

49 NEC Minutes, vol. 78, 13 January 1939.

50 NEC Minutes, vol. 78, 18 January 1939. Dalton note, 19 January 1939. Dalton papers, File 14 (ii).

51 NEC Minutes, vol. 79, 25 January 1939.

52 NEC Minutes, vol. 79, 22 February 1939.

53 NEC Minutes, vol. 79, 22 March 1939.

54 B. Webb, diary, 20 March 1939. In his *Autobiography*, p. 166, Morrison wrote that he 'regretted' the expulsion.

55 National Agent to A. Bevan et al., 23 March 1939. Morrison printed the correspondence for a meeting of the LLP Executive, 4 May 1939.

56 See Beatrice Webb to Morrison, 3 March 1939; and Morrison to Beatrice Webb, 16 March 1939. Passfield papers, LSE.

57 *LPCR*, 1939, pp. 297–9.

58 *Morning Post*, 8 November 1934. See also *Daily Herald*, 3 October 1934.

59 Quoted in E. Estorick, *Stafford Cripps* (1949), p. 159.

60 NEC Minutes, vol. 80, 28 June 1939.

61 NEC Minutes, vol. 80, 27 September 1939.

62 NEC Minutes, vol. 81, 20 December 1939 and 28 February 1940.

63 NEC Minutes, vol. 80, 25 October 1939.

64 For instance, the correspondent of the *Daily Express* called his speech to the 1937 conference one of 'brilliant and blasting ridicule' and the correspondent of the *Manchester Guardian*, 'a brilliant piece of destructive raillery'. 6 October 1937.

Chapter 17   Frustrated Ambitions

1 *Autobiography*, p. 294.

2 *Autobiography*, p. 41. See *London News*, May 1932 and *Manchester Evening News*, 7 September 1940. On 'careerism' he said: 'It is a beastly word and I hate it. To shape a career is a cynical operation that is a bad thing and ought not to be.' *Kentish Mercury*, 2 October 1959.

3 Interviews, Lord Henderson, Lady Gater, Lady Summerskill, Lady Wilmot, E. Jay, C. A. G. Manning, Lady Cripps.

4 *Hackney Gazette*, 10 January 1934; *London Electricity*, March 1963; *Autobiography*, p. 163; and M. Edelman, *Herbert Morrison* (1948), p. 50.

5 *Hackney Gazette*, 10 January 1934.

6 M. A. Hamilton, *Remembering My Good Friends* (1944), p. 168.

7 Interview, H. Atkinson. M. Webb, 'The Rt Hon. Herbert Morrison, MP' in H. Tracey (ed.), *The British Labour Party*, vol. III (1948), p. 29.

8 *Daily Express*, 2 September 1930.

9 T. Jones, *A Diary with Letters, 1931–1950* (1954), p. 68.

10 Dalton diary, 1934 review, vol. 16. Also B. Webb, diary, 19 August 1934.

11 B. Webb, diary, 19 August 1934. Dalton noted that at the NEC Morrison was 'frequently anti-Uncle' [Henderson]. Diary, 8 October 1932, vol. 14.

12 B. Webb, diary, 2 September 1934, and 7 October 1934. Interview, H. Atkinson.

13 Interviews, H. Atkinson, Lord Henderson.

14 *Manchester Guardian*, 4 October 1934 and 5 October 1934. Interviews Mr and Mrs D. Robinson. Bevin was responsible for instituting the rule of the incompatibility of being Secretary and an MP. Interviews, G. G. Mackenzie, H. Atkinson, Lord Citrine and A. L. Rowse.

15 *Manchester Guardian*, 4 October 1934. *LPCR*, 1934, p. 191 and p. 208.

16 Interview, A. L. Rowse. See also H. Dalton, *The Fateful Years* (1957), p. 56.

17 *Sunday Express*, 14 October 1934 and *Manchester Daily Dispatch*, 15 October 1934.

18 NEC Minutes, vol. 66, 28 November 1934. The other candidates were: I. D. Harry, A. Creech Jones, G. R. Shepherd, J. A. Webb, A. Woodburn.

19 *Morning Post*, 8 October 1934.

20 NEC Minutes, vol. 67, 23 January 1935. Also *Evening Standard*, 4 November 1938, and interviews, Mr and Mrs D. Robinson.

21 *Evening Standard*, 10 March 1934.

22 E.g. *Sunday Express*, 11 March 1934 and *Daily Telegraph*, 12 July 1934.

23 *Time and Tide*, 6 October 1934.

24 'The most brilliant speech of the Conference', thought the *Yorkshire Observer*, 3 October 1934. See also *Yorkshire Evening Post*, 12 October 1934; the *News Letter*, 13 October 1934.

25 *Sunday Express*, 28 October 1934.

26 *Manchester Guardian*, 5 October 1934 and *Yorkshire Evening Post*, 12 October 1934.

27 *News Letter*, 13 October 1934.

28 Noted in *Sunday Express*, 26 May 1935.

29 *News Chronicle*, 27 May 1935. See also *Daily Mail*, 7 January 1935.

30 *Sunday Express*, 29 September 1935.

31 K. Martin, *Editor* (1968), p. 172. *LPCR*, 1935, pp. 190–3.
32 R. Postgate, *The Life of George Lansbury* (1951), p. 304. Beatrice Webb praised his 'statesmanlike and gracious speech' which she saw as an attempt to bring Lansbury to shore and to stop Cripps committing suicide. Diary, 1 October 1935.
33 2,168,000 votes against 102,000. *LPCR*, 1935, p. 193.
34 Interviews, Sir Isaac Hayward and Sir Trevor Evans.
35 Draft autobiography.
36 *Forward*, 12 October 1935.
37 *Evening Standard*, 25 September 1935. Shinwell noted this move in *The Labour Story* (1963), p. 151.
38 *Morning Post*, 21 October 1935.
39 *News Chronicle*, 31 October 1935.
40 A. Briggs, *The Golden Age of Wireless* (1965), p. 140. Also T. Jones, op. cit., p. 156.
41 Diary, 12 November 1935 and 15 November 1935. Philip Noel-Baker recalled that during the election campaign, Tory speakers frequently referred to the future leadership of the Labour Party: 'When Attlee's name was mentioned there would be a laugh and when Greenwood's name was mentioned there would again be a laugh. But when Herbert's name was mentioned the laughter would be mitigated.' Interview.
42 Article in *Forward*, quoted in *Manchester Guardian*, 23 November 1935, and *The Times*, 25 November 1935. In his *Autobiography*, p. 163, Morrison criticized Attlee in the campaign as not 'forceful enough'.
43 *Daily Mail*, 26 November 1935.
44 Attlee's autobiographical notes, Attlee Papers, 1/14, p. 3. Churchill College, Cambridge.
45 Interview. See also M. Edelman, op. cit., p. 46.
46 Interview. In the 1930s Rowse dedicated two books to Morrison: *Mr Keynes and the Labour Movement* and *Politics and the Younger Generation*.
47 Interview, D. Jay. Also interview, G. R. Strauss.
48 Interview.
49 Interview, and K. Martin, op. cit., p. 51, and K. Martin, *Father Figures* (1966), p. 207.
50 Interview, K. Martin.
51 Interview, D. N. Pritt.
52 B. Webb, diary, 28 September 1935. In her diary for 1935 Beatrice Webb indicated the following as pro-Morrison: Ivor Thomas, Kingsley Martin, F. W. Galton, E. D. Simon, Noel Buxton, John Ramage, A. V. Alexander and the Earl of Listowel.
53 Dalton diary, 27 May 1935, vol. 16.
54 He mentions the Treasury in his memoirs, H. Dalton, *The Fateful Years* (1957), p. 70, but not in his diary.
55 H. Dalton, op. cit., p. 70.
56 This diary entry formed the basis for p. 70 of Dalton's memoirs.
57 Interview, Lord Francis-Williams.
58 Dalton diary, 20 November 1935, vol. 16. The names mentioned were: Watkins, Fletcher, Bellenger, Parker, Kelly, Viant, Creech Jones, Ede, Frankel and Ellen Wilkinson.

59 *Daily Express*, 23 November 1935, and interview, D. Frankel.

60 *Daily Express*, 23 November 1935.

61 Dalton diary, 26 November 1935, vol. 16. See also *Evening Standard*, 23 November 1935.

62 The account of the meeting is taken from NEC and PLP Minutes, vol. 69, 26 November 1935; H. Dalton, op. cit., pp. 81–2; Dalton diary, 26 November 1935, vol. 16; and I. Bulmer-Thomas, *The Growth of the British Party System*, vol. II (1967), pp. 114–16.

63 David Kirkwood claimed to have proposed Morrison in *Daily Record and Mail*, 6 January 1937, but the minutes record that Morrison was nominated by T. Naylor and D. Adams, Greenwood by J. Walker and J. Compton, and Attlee by T. Williams and D. Grenfell.

64 Arthur Hollins.

65 NEC and PLP Minutes, vol. 69, 3 December 1935.

66 E.g. Jennie Lee in the *New Leader*, 12 October 1934.

67 Interview, Lord Longford, who was very left in the early 1930s. See his *Born to Believe* (1953), pp. 79–80.

68 Interview, Lord Henderson.

69 Attlee papers, 1/14, p. 3. Churchill College. James Griffiths and Wilfred Paling agreed. Interviews.

70 p. 164. See H. Dalton, op. cit., p. 82.

71 Interview, W. Paling.

72 William Nield.

73 Dalton diary, 6 April 1938, vol. 19. Miss Phyllis Jones recalled seeing the list in Morrison's office. Interview. The names were – Sir Robert Young, J. Compton, A. Short, Major Milner, J. W. Bowen, Rev. H. Dunnico, Colonel L'Estrange Malone, J. Hayes, W. Henderson, F. O. Roberts, W. Dobbie, B. Tillett, G. Hicks, F. J. Bellenger, Lord Kinnoull, and A. Greenwood.

74 Ibid.

75 Much of the section on the contest of 1935 was based on interviews with W. Paling, D. Frankel, Mrs Lucy Middleton, Miss Phyllis Jones, Mr and Mrs D. Robinson, G. R. Strauss, Lord Henderson, J. Griffiths, G. Eden, also J. T. Murphy, *Labour's Big Three* (1948), pp. 188–9, and R. T. McKenzie, *British Political Parties* (1963), pp. 360–5.

76 Beatrice Webb noted in her diary that Attlee was 'the neutral and *least disliked* member of the front bench'. Diary, 27 November 1935.

77 Earl of Swinton, *Sixty Years of Power* (1966), p. 155.

78 Interview, Mrs Lucy Middleton.

79 Interview, Lord Latham.

80 *Sunday Express*, 31 October 1937.

81 Article by Harold Hutchinson, *Sun*, 8 March 1965.

82 Interview, J. Griffiths.

83 F. Truelove to G. W. Jones, undated.

84 *Daily Record and Mail*, 6 January 1937. Hannen Swaffer said the same, *John Bull*, 24 October 1936.

85 J. Mann, *Woman in Parliament* (1962), pp. 92–3.

86 Interview. John Cliff claimed to have told Herbert to go to the North more since he was not well known outside London. Interview.

87 See Lord Williams of Barnburgh, *Digging for Britain* (1965), p. 100.

88 Interviews, Lord Francis-Williams, G. Jeger, Dame Leah Manning, D. Frankel.

89 Interview, C. Brandon. See also H. Dalton, op. cit., p. 31. Kingsley Martin said they were 'always at loggerheads', *Sunday Times*, 7 March 1965. Lloyd George compared the rivalry of Bevin and Morrison with that of Rosebery and Campbell-Bannerman. T. Jones, op. cit., p. 351.

90 *Observer*, 20 March 1960.

91 F. Williams, *Ernest Bevin* (1952), p. 186.

92 Interview, Sir Trevor Evans; also interviews, C. W. Gibson, G. G. Mackenzie, C. Brandon, H. Atkinson, J. Cliff, Mrs H. Clay.

93 Interview.

94 Interviews, J. Griffiths and Lord Henderson.

95 Dalton diary, 26 November 1935, vol. 16. At the LSE Dalton told the Common Room that Labour had thrown away its chances of being a government. Interview, Lord Chorley.

96 Interview, D. Jay.

97 B. Webb diary, 27 November 1935.

98 Earl of Swinton, op. cit., p. 156. Also Dalton diary, 6 April 1938, vol. 19.

99 Interview, G. R. Strauss.

100 Interview, Lady Gater.

101 7 December 1935.

102 *Manchester Evening News*, 8 November 1935. Also interview, K. H. Kent.

103 B. Webb diary, 2 February 1936.

104 Emanuel Shinwell says that to the best of his knowledge Morrison took no part in these intrigues. *Conflict without Malice* (1955), p. 133.

105 P. Thurtle to G. W. Jones, 13 November 1969, and interview. Also interview, F. Barlow.

106 *Sunday Express*, 15 November 1936.

107 *Sunday Express*, 7 March 1937.

108 A. L. Rowse, 'The Prospects of the Labour Party' (1937), reprinted in *The End of an Epoch* (1947), pp. 103–17.

109 *Daily Telegraph*, 3 January 1938. See also *Sunday Dispatch*, 20 June 1937. The *Manchester Guardian* noted that he was now making 'one of his rare, his all too rare speeches'. 24 June 1937. But in October the *Daily Herald* observed that he never quite came off in the House, and it urged the LCC to release him. 9 October 1937.

110 *Sunday Express*, 31 July 1938.

111 H. Dalton, op. cit., p. 83 and p. 201.

112 Diary, 30 June 1938.

113 Dalton diary, 15 June 1938, vol. 19.

114 Ibid.

115 *Sunday Express*, 1 January 1939.

116 H. Dalton, op. cit., pp. 222–3; also interview Lord Francis-Williams, and *Daily Herald*, 9 June 1939.

117 Dalton diary, 14 June 1939, vol. 20.

118 Ibid. Morrison told Dalton later: 'That was a queer double-meaning debate we had this morning.' Ibid.

119 Dalton, for instance, was now a supporter of Greenwood, since he felt that
Morrison was 'out of the picture at Westminster'. H. Dalton, op. cit., p. 281.
Dalton told Greenwood that he backed him. Dalton diary, 11 September 1939,
vol. 21. He felt that the PLP, 'pending a substantial change of personnel at a
General Election, would not back Morrison'. Diary, December, 1939, vol. 21.
Morrison said that 'the party is against *any leadership*'. Attlee was 'less objectionable because less impressive than the more striking personalities of Cripps,
Dalton and himself'. B. Webb diary, 30 June 1938.
120 *Sunday Express*, 24 September 1939.
121 *Daily Express*, 7 November 1939. See also *Daily Herald*, 13 November 1939.
122 Dalton diary, entry for December 1939, vol. 21.
123 Letter to Dalton, 9 November 1939, together with diary entry for December
1939, vol. 21.
124 Morrison to Edwards, 11 November 1939. Copy in Dalton diary, entry for
December 1939, vol. 21.
125 *Evening Standard*, 15 November 1939.
126 H. Dalton, op. cit., pp. 281–2, based on his diary entry for December 1939.
127 Dalton diary, December 1939, vol. 21.
128 *Forward*, 18 September 1939 and *News Chronicle*, 18 September 1937. See also
Sunday Express, 3 October 1937.
129 B. Webb diary, 2 February 1936.
130 B. Webb diary, 20 October 1936.
131 NEC Minutes, vol. 79, 22 March 1939.
132 W. J. Reader, *Architect of Air Power* (1968), pp. 139–40.
133 *News Chronicle*, 9 January 1935. The other three were Walter Elliott, Lord
Samuel and Leslie Hore-Belisha.
134 *People* and *Observer*, 26 May 1935.
135 *Morning Post*, 27 May 1935.
136 *Reynolds News*, 2 June 1935.
137 T. Jones, op. cit., p. 280.
138 An interview in the *Star*, 25 June 1936 quoted in A. Sampson, *Macmillan* (1967),
p. 42.
139 *Sunday Graphic*, 18 July 1937.
140 *Daily Herald*, 19 July 1937.
141 Dalton diary, 8 April 1938, vol. 19.
142 See H. Dalton, op. cit., pp. 200–3, and Dalton diary, 3, 6 and 12 October 1938,
vol. 19. Also H. Macmillan, *Winds of Change, 1914–1939* (1966), p. 587, and L. S.
Amery, *My Political Life*, vol. 3 (1955), pp. 298–9.
143 Interview, G. Wansbrough.
144 See Dalton diary, 14 June 1939, vol. 20.

Chapter 18 Foreign Affairs in the 1930's

1 See J. F. Naylor, *Labour's International Policy* (1969).
2 *HC Debs*, vol. 339, col. 172, 4 October 1938; *Manchester Guardian*, 29 June 1936;
Forward, 21 March 1936.
3 *Forward*, 20 March 1937; *The Times*, 3 April 1939; *South Hackney Citizen*,
October 1933; *Manchester Guardian*, 12 June 1939; *Morning Post*, 1 July 1935.

4 *Manchester Guardian,* 17 September 1938.

5 *HC Debs,* vol. 328, cols 432–4, 29 October 1937; *London News,* February 1936; *Forward,* 5 March 1938; *London News,* April 1938.

6 *HC Debs,* vol. 309, cols 2077–9, 10 March 1936; *Daily Herald,* 14 March 1935; *LPCR,* 1939, pp. 298–9.

7 E.g. *Manchester Guardian,* 6 December 1937; *South Hackney Citizen,* January 1938; *The Times,* 24 September 1938; *HC Debs,* vol. 339, cols 169–83, 4 October 1938; articles to Labour editors, 22 March 1938, LLP papers.

8 *Daily Express,* 8 January 1937; also *Forward,* 3 October 1936.

9 *Forward,* 5 March 1938; 20 June 1936; 4 July 1936; *London News,* August 1938.

10 *Forward,* 20 December 1935.

11 *Star,* 24 June 1939; *Daily Herald,* 5 February 1938; *News Chronicle,* 6 October 1937.

12 *Daily Express,* 8 January 1937.

13 *Forward,* 3 July 1937; *Manchester Guardian,* 28 February 1938.

14 *Daily Herald,* 28 February 1938; *Manchester Guardian,* 28 February 1938 and 1 March 1938.

15 *Daily Herald,* 4 January 1932; *Star,* 7 April 1933; *The Times,* 18 March 1935; *Forward,* 7 March 1936; *London News,* July 1939.

16 Morrison memorandum to LLP Executive, 20 June 1936; *LPCR,* 1935, p. 191; interview, P. Noel-Baker.

17 *Forward,* 18 July 1936, 29 August 1936 and 9 January 1937; *The Times,* 21 August 1936; *Daily Express,* 3 October 1935 and 7 March 1938.

18 *LPCR,* 1935, p. 192; *Daily Herald,* 1 February 1936.

19 *Forward,* 1 May 1937.

20 *The Times,* 22 August 1936.

21 *South Hackney Citizen,* January 1938.

22 *Forward,* 26 December 1936; *London News,* May 1938.

23 *London News,* May 1938; *Manchester Guardian,* 8 May 1939; *Forward,* 27 March 1937 and 17 July 1937; *HC Debs,* vol. 309, cols 2070–80, 10 March 1936; *HC Debs,* vol. 339, cols 169–83, 4 October 1938; article to Labour editors, 20 January 1936, LLP papers; *Daily Herald,* 19 November 1934.

24 *The Times,* 22 August 1936; *Forward,* 29 August 1936. The speech exists in full in LLP papers.

25 E.g. Zilliacus to Morrison, 10 April 1936, LLP papers.

26 *Labour Magazine,* March 1929, pp. 494–5.

27 *Peace or War in America* (1941), Debate, Upton Sinclair v. P. F. La Follette, p. 27; see also *South Hackney Citizen,* May 1937.

28 Interview, Mrs M. Mandelson. Morrison was also fond of the works of Anatole France.

29 Article to Labour editors, 20 May 1936, LLP papers; *London News,* June 1936.

30 *News Chronicle,* 12 May 1936.

31 *Daily Express,* 17 April 1936.

32 *London News,* June 1937.

33 *Sunday Post,* 15 March 1959.

34 *Evening Standard,* 23 April 1936.

35 *Daily Herald,* 12 May 1936; *Daily Express,* 11 May 1936.

36 *Daily Mail,* 11 May 1936.

37 *News Chronicle*, 12 May 1936.

38 *London News*, June 1937.

39 *Evening Standard*, 23 April 1936; *South Hackney Citizen*, May 1937; *News Chronicle*, 4 May 1937.

40 *New York Times Magazine*, 3 May 1936.

41 *Daily Mail*, 11 May 1936.

42 Cahan to Morrison, 24 December 1934. LLP papers.

43 *South Hackney Citizen*, June 1936.

44 *News Chronicle*, 25 March 1937 and *Forward*, 1 May 1937.

45 *Daily Mail*, 17 April 1937. Morrison recalled this experience in *Government and Parliament* (Third edition 1964), p. 167. 'It was an interesting and fascinating experience: a crowded room, some seated, some standing, including local government officers who had come long distances. The Chairman of the day was evidently hostile to the Bill [Senator Wagner's Housing Bill] and he handled me with some degree of American frankness and hostility. By the time we had reached nearly the last question I was beginning to feel at home and equally frank, so that when he asked me "Well Mr Morrison, what *is* this London County Council, anyway?", I thought I had better be a little boastfully British and I replied, "Sir, it is the greatest municipality in the world – that's what the London County Council is".'

46 *News Chronicle*, 21 April 1938.

47 *Daily Herald*, 28 November 1938.

48 Morrison to Eden, 23 March 1936, LLP papers.

49 *News Chronicle*, 12 May 1936.

50 *Evening News*, 3 May 1937.

51 *Daily Express*, 28 April 1938.

52 *Daily Herald*, 28 April 1938.

53 *Daily Express*, 7 January 1939; also *HC Debs*, vol. 328, col. 429, 29 October 1937, and *HC Debs* vol. 332, col. 309, 22 February 1938; *Manchester Guardian*, 13 October 1937.

54 *The Times*, 19 June 1936.

55 *Daily Herald*, 30 April 1936.

56 *HC Debs*, vol. 332, cols 307–8, 22 February 1938.

57 *South Hackney Citizen*, May 1939.

58 21 September, 22 September, 25 September, 26 September, 29 September, 2 October 1933.

59 He expressed this view again in *Manchester Guardian*, 2 March 1935.

60 He expressed this view again in *Forward*, 11 January 1936.

61 He expressed this view again in *Daily Herald*, 1 December 1936.

62 See *Forward*, 11 January 1936.

63 *Daily Herald*, 2 October 1933.

64 *Daily Herald*, 21 September 1933. Also *Forward*, 25 January 1936.

65 *The Times*, 19 March 1936.

66 *LPCR*, 1933, pp. 231–2; see also *Forward*, 5 December 1936; and *Manchester Guardian*, 23 May 1938. Maisky, the Russian Ambassador in London, told Beatrice Webb that he admired Morrison and regarded him as 'the second best speaker in the House of Commons after Lloyd George'. Diary, 25 July 1937.

67 Draft autobiography.

68 *London News*, September 1939.

69 *Daily Mirror*, 7 December 1939, 29 February 1940.

70 *Jewish Chronicle*, 27 January 1950.

71 S. Levenberg, *The Jews and Palestine* (1945), p. 129, and interview, Dr S. Levenberg.

72 Speech at Labour Party Conference, quoted in *Jewish Chronicle*, 21 May 1948.

73 Interview, Dr S. Levenberg.

74 *HC Debs*, vol. 313, col. 1387, 19 June 1936.

75 *Daily Herald*, 12 September 1935.

76 *Daily Herald*, 22 August 1935.

77 *Jewish Chronicle*, 6 November 1936, also 27 January 1950.

78 *HC Debs*, vol. 313, cols 1387–8, 19 June 1936.

79 *Daily Herald*, 29 October 1936.

80 Interviews, S. Goldberg and Dr S. Levenberg.

81 *Jewish Chronicle*, 6 May 1960.

82 Morrison's views on Palestine can be found in *HC Debs*, vol. 313, cols 1380–90, 19 June 1936; *HC Debs*, vol. 341, cols 1996–2010, 24 November 1938 and *HC Debs*, vol. 347, cols 2129–44, 23 May 1939. Also in *Forward*, 22 January 1938 and *Daily Telegraph*, 26 October 1938.

83 *LPCR*, 1929, p. 153.

84 E.g. *London News*, May 1933; also *Manchester Guardian*, 17 September 1935.

85 Article to Labour editors, 21 November 1938, LLP papers.

86 *London News*, May 1933. In May 1933 Morrison attended Jewish-German protest meetings in Shoreditch and Holborn. Report to LLP Executive, 1 June 1933.

87 *News Chronicle*, 3 April 1933.

88 *Manchester Guardian*, 28 November 1934.

89 *Daily Telegraph*, 16 April 1934.

90 *London News*, January 1932 and May 1933.

91 *Manchester Guardian*, 28 September 1936.

92 *The Times*, 13 September 1935.

93 *Forward*, 9 January 1937 and 19 February 1938; *Star*, 6 September 1938; article to Labour editors, 21 November 1938, LLP papers.

94 *Forward*, 9 January 1937.

95 *Manchester Guardian*, 19 January 1938.

96 *Daily Telegraph*, 16 April 1934; *Manchester Guardian*, 28 November 1934 and 17 September 1935; *Daily Mail*, 24 January 1938.

97 *The Times*, 13 September 1935 and *Forward*, 12 October 1935.

98 *Evening Standard*, 21 October 1935; *LPCR*, 1935, pp. 190–3; *South Hackney Citizen*, February 1936; *London News*, February 1936; *Manchester Guardian*, 29 June 1936; article to Labour editors, 18 December 1937, LLP papers.

99 J. T. Murphy, *Labour's Big Three* (1948), p. 195.

100 Interviews, S. C. Leslie, Lord Shinwell, Lord Brockway and P. Noel-Baker.

101 H. Dalton, *The Fateful Years: Memoirs 1931–1945* (1957), p. 96.

102 *Forward*, 1 August 1936.

103 *Forward*, 10 October 1936.

104 *Millgate*, January 1940, p. 216. (A Co-operative Press publication.) At an NEC meeting in 1938 Morrison opposed the calling of a special party conference on Spain, 'because it would be impossible to prevent it from discussing a "People's

Front".' Sybil Wingate to J. Pole, 27 May 1938. Papers of the Labour Spain Committee, 1/5 (14). Churchill College, Cambridge.

105 Minutes of Joint Meeting of NEC, Executive of PLP and General Council of the TUC, vol. 9, 28 October 1936; *Manchester Guardian*, 28 October 1936; *Forward*, 8 January 1937.

106 *Forward*, 16 January 1937, 20 March 1937 and 12 June 1937; *HC Debs*, vol. 326, cols 1619–32, 15 July 1937.

107 *Forward*, 5 September 1936; *Daily Mail*, 23 September 1936; *HC Debs*, vol. 326, cols 1619–32, 15 July 1937.

108 *Forward*, 27 March and 3 July 1937; *Daily Herald*, 24 January 1939; *South Hackney Citizen*, February 1939.

109 *HC Debs*, vol. 335, cols 546–61, 2 May 1938.

110 *Manchester Guardian*, 12 July 1937; *Daily Herald*,[8 January 1937; *London News*, August 1937.

111 *Daily Telegraph*, 20 February 1939.

112 *HC Debs*, vol. 344, cols 1196–208, 28 February 1939.

113 Dalton diary, 17 September 1938, vol. 19; *The Times*, 19 September 1938; also Lord Citrine, *Men and Work* (1964), pp. 365–6.

114 *The Times*, 9 September 1938 and *Manchester Guardian*, 12 September 1938.

115 *HC Debs*, vol. 339, cols 169–83, 4 October 1938; *Daily Herald*, 11 October 1938; *South Hackney Citizen*, November 1938.

116 Dalton diary, 19 October 1938, vol. 19.

Chapter 19   Defence and War

1 *The Times*, 13 March and 28 October 1935; *Daily Herald*, 7 March 1935; *London News*, November 1935.

2 *LPCR*, 1935, p. 192.

3 *South Hackney Citizen*, July 1935; *News Chronicle*, 11 November 1935; *The Times*, 28 October 1935.

4 *London News*, April 1936.

5 NEC Minutes, vol. 70, 4 March 1936.

6 *LPCR*, 1936, pp. 192–5, 202–3, 206.

7 *Manchester Guardian*, 7 October 1936; *Daily Express*, 7 October 1936. The final vote was 1,738,000 for the NEC and 657,000 against. *LPCR*, 1936, p. 207.

8 *Forward*, 31 July 1937.

9 *Forward*, 26 December 1936.

10 *Daily Express*, 23 July 1937.

11 *Daily Herald*, 26 July 1937.

12 Dalton diary, 15 June 1938, vol. 19.

13 H. Dalton, *The Fateful Years: Memoirs 1931–1945* (1957), pp. 134–5 and 138–9.

14 E.g. *The Times*, 22 March 1938; *Daily Herald*, 25 June 1938; *The Times*, 22 June 1939.

15 *The Times*, 26 January 1939.

16 *LPCR*, 1939, pp. 281–9.

17 NEC Minutes, vol. 78, 16 December 1938.

18 Article to Labour editors, 21 October 1938. LLP papers.

19 *London News*, May 1939.

20 *London News*, July 1939.

21 Minutes of the NEC, Executive of PLP and General Council of the TUC, 27 April 1939. NEC Minutes, vol. 79, 9 May 1939. *Daily Express*, 2 May 1939. *Evening Standard*, 31 May 1939. *LPCR*, 1939, pp. 281–9.

22 *London News*, August and October 1935; *Daily Herald*, 12 July 1935; *Forward*, 27 July 1935, 28 September 1935 and 7 December 1935; *Report of LLP Executive*, 1934–5; *Municipal Circular* (of LLP) 196, 17 July 1935.

23 *The Times*, 2 December 1935. See also *LPCR*, 1935, p. 200.

24 Memorandum of H. J. Hodsall, 26 September 1935. Hodsall papers, 4/1. No. 19. Churchill College, Cambridge.

25 Minutes of the LCC Labour Party, 16 July 1935, 22 October 1935. Some borough parties grumbled against the Morrison line as late as 1939 (Morrison letters to party secretaries, 13 December 1938 and 4 February 1939) even going so far as to try to set up an association of like-minded parties, but Morrison was able to crush them.

26 See *County Councils Gazette*, August and December 1937; *Minutes of Executive Council of County Councils Association*, 27 October 1937, p. 198 and 24 November 1937, p. 202. Also *Daily Express*, 16 November and 17 November 1937, and *London News*, December 1937.

27 *London News*, November 1938.

28 Ibid.

29 *HC Debs*, vol. 340, cols 411–34, 3 November 1938, which formed the basis for an LLP pamphlet, *London Undefended* (1938). Also see *Daily Herald*, 27 October 1938.

30 B. H. Liddell Hart, *The Memoirs*, vol. II (1965), pp. 163–4 and 167–8. Also Dalton diary, 14 September and 23 September 1938, vol. 19.

31 H. Dalton, op. cit., p. 182.

32 *HC Debs*, vol. 344, cols 1316–36, 1 March 1939; *London News*, August 1939.

33 *HC Debs*, vol. 345, cols 2653–69, 4 April 1939; *London News*, May 1939; *Report of LLP Executive*, 1938–9, and *News Chronicle*, 5 July 1939.

34 *London News*, July 1939. Also *Daily Telegraph*, 31 August 1939; *News Chronicle*, 5 July 1939.

35 Morrison memorandum to LLP Executive, 11 April 1939. LLP papers.

36 T. Johnston, *Memories* (1952), p. 134. See also *Star*, 7 February 1939; *Daily Telegraph* and *Daily Mail*, 8 February 1939. In January 1938 Hodsall had suggested that Morrison be appointed chairman of an ARP Committee for Greater London. Hodsall noted that Morrison seemed agreeable, if he could have 'a free hand' and if his LCC officials could be taken into the confidence of the ARP department at the centre. However, Morrison pointed out that there would be political difficulties to his open participation in a government policy. H. J. Hodsall to H. S. Hutchinson, 29 January 1938. Hodsall papers, 4/39.

37 *Manchester Guardian*, 17 May 1939. See *London News*, May 1939.

38 *The Times*, 12 July 1939; *Manchester Guardian*, 17 May 1939.

39 *The Times*, 28 August 1939.

40 *London News*, October 1939.

41 *HC Debs*, vol. 352, col. 2247, 2 November 1939; *London News*, November 1939.

42 *Picture Post*, 13 April 1940. His room is also described in *Star*, 1 November 1939.

43 *Daily Mail*, 10 January 1939.

44 *Star*, 1 November 1939.

45 *Municipal Circular*, no. 229, 18 October 1939. LLP papers.

46 *London News*, December 1939. Also *Daily Mirror*, 23 November 1939.

47 *London News*, January 1940. Usual practices were also restored in the boroughs. *London News*, February 1940.

48 Morrison to Sir John Anderson, 14 September 1939, quoted in *Municipal Circular*, no. 227, 26 September 1939, and *HC Debs*, vol. 352, cols 2244–5, 2 November 1939.

49 *London News*, June 1940.

50 NEC Minutes, vol. 80, 2 September 1939.

51 *London News*, October 1939.

52 Peake to Cadogan, 2 December 1939. Halifax papers, vol. 17; FO 800, 325; Document XL/19. Public Record Office.

53 *London News*, October 1939.

54 H. Dalton, op. cit., p. 270.

55 *Daily Mirror*, 12 October 1939. He parted company with *Forward* in 1939 as it took an increasingly anti-war line.

56 *HC Debs*, vol. 352, cols 2242–58, 2 November 1939 and *HC Debs*, vol. 355, cols 741–55, 6 December 1939.

57 *Daily Mirror*, 16 January 1940.

58 Peake to Cadogan, loc. cit.

59 *Daily Worker*, 29 November 1939.

60 *Evening Standard*, 29 December 1939.

61 See *London News*, November 1939.

62 *Report of LLP Executive, 1938–9;* Morrison letter to party secretaries, 21 September 1939, LLP papers. *London News*, October 1939.

63 *Report of LLP Executive*, 1939–40; Minutes of LLP Executive, 2 November 1939.

64 See *HC Debs*, vol. 356, cols 1309–25, 1 February 1940 and *HC Debs*, vol. 357, cols 621–33, 12 March 1940 and *Daily Mirror*, 15 February 1940. He also urged more vigorous action from the Minister of Information. *Daily Herald*, 24 April 1940.

65 *Evening Standard*, 4 May 1940.

66 E.g. 30 March 1940.

67 E.g. 24 April 1940.

68 *HC Debs*, vol. 358, cols 1523–41, 15 March 1940.

69 Interview.

70 *Autobiography*, p. 171.

71 *Hackney Gazette*, 12 April 1940.

72 Draft autobiography and *Autobiography*, p. 172.

73 See J. Harvey (ed.), *The Diplomatic Diaries of Oliver Harvey, 1937–40* (1970), pp. 352–3.

74 9 May 1940.

75 *HC Debs*, vol. 360, cols 1251–65, 8 May 1940.

76 *Sunday Post*, 15 March 1959.

77 The majority fell to eighty-one. Forty Conservatives voted against the government and eighty abstained.

78 Sir Oliver Harvey noted in his diary that 'Herbert Morrison's was most effective attack on the Government . . .' J. Harvey (ed.), op. cit., p. 355.

79 *Autobiography*, p. 172.

80 *Autobiography*, p. 173.

81 Interview.

82 *A Prime Minister Remembers* (1961), p. 30.

83 H. Dalton, op. cit., p. 305 and Dalton diary, 8 May 1940, vol. 22.

84 Attlee to Thompson, 19 July 1965. Thompson papers.

85 Williams to Thompson, 26 August 1965. Thompson papers. See L. Thompson, *1940* (1966), p. 77.

86 L. Thompson, op. cit., p. 78.

87 *Autobiography*, p. 174.

88 Interview.

89 p. 175.

90 *Autobiography*, p. 177.

91 *Autobiography*, p. 178. See also W. S. Churchill, *The Gathering Storm* (1960), p. 588.

92 Sir Horace Wilson to L. Thompson, 10 January 1965, Thompson papers; and H. Dalton, op. cit., pp. 309–10. Also the Earl of Birkenhead, *The Life of Lord Halifax* (1965), p. 455.

93 Attlee autobiographical notes, Attlee papers, 1/16.

94 Attlee to Thompson, 18 December 1964. Thompson papers. Dalton recorded in his diary for 9 April that at the Parliamentary Executive meeting which discussed joining the government no one, not even A. V. Alexander who had previously been keen, would serve at this stage under Chamberlain.

95 Attlee papers, loc. cit., 1/16. NEC Minutes, vol. 82, 10 May 1940. Minutes of the NEC, Executive of PLP and General Council of the TUC, vol. 82, 12 May 1940.

96 Dalton claimed to have drafted it; H. Dalton, op. cit., p. 310.

97 *Autobiography*, p. 177.

98 Attlee to Thompson, 18 December 1964. Thompson papers.

99 NEC Minutes, vol. 82, 10 May 1940.

100 Attlee to Thompson, 18 December 1964. Thompson papers.

101 Attlee papers, loc. cit., 1/16. They did not learn this news from the door-keeper at No. 10 Downing Street as Dalton claimed. H. Dalton, op. cit., p. 312.

102 M. Webb, 'The Rt Hon. Herbert Morrison, MP' in H. Tracey (ed.), *The British Labour Party*, vol. III (1948), pp. 37–8.

103 NEC Minutes, vol. 82, 11 May 1940.

104 Interview, G. G. Mackenzie.

105 H. Dalton, op. cit., pp. 313–14.

106 NEC Minutes, vol. 82, 11 May 1940. The dissenter is unknown.

107 NEC Minutes, vol. 82, 12 May 1940.

108 NEC Minutes, vol. 82, 12 May 1940.

109 L. Thompson, op. cit., p. 73.

110 *Daily Mail*, 6 May 1940. See also L. Thompson, op. cit., pp. 73–4.

111 Harcourt Johnstone to Lloyd George, 9 May 1940. Beaverbrook Foundation: Lloyd George papers, G/10/11/6.

112 The Earl of Birkenhead, op. cit., p. 453; and L. Thompson, op. cit., p. 83. Also Lord Butler, *The Art of the Possible* (1971), p. 83.

113 Peake to Cadogan, loc. cit.

114 W. S. Churchill, op. cit., p. 588.

115 H. Dalton, op. cit., p. 311 and p. 314. Attlee noted that 'I had more or less agreed with A.G. as to whom to suggest for the Government'. Attlee papers, loc. cit., 1/16.

116 Morrison to LLP Executive, 14 May 1940. LLP papers.

117 *London News*, June 1940.

118 *The Times*, 23 May 1944. In his *Autobiography* (p. 211) Morrison also recalled the following exchanges: 'When he invited me to become Minister of Supply I asked him, before I accepted the office, if he intended to eliminate the influences behind the scenes which we of the Labour Party had reason to believe had slowed down the war effort. His answer was forthright, and untrammelled by any apologies or denials of my charges. "Certainly they will go," he said. "May I also ask if the powers for mobilization of war production effort and the emergency powers for mobilizing the whole nation will be enforced?" I next asked. His answer was an emphatic "yes". He assured me that in the prosecution of the war he would know no party or political prejudices. Whatever was necessary for victory would be done.'

119 *Autobiography*, p. 178.

120 Minutes of LLP Executive, 23 May 1940.

PART TWO

Chapter 20   Supply and the Blitz Begins

1 *Autobiography*, p. 178.

2 *Daily Herald*, 13 May 1940, *Star*, 13 May 1940, *Daily Express*, 15 May, 21 August 1940. Interview, Lord Chandos.

3 Memorandum on the Munitions Situation, 29 August 1940, Cab. 66/11, WP (40) 339.

4 *Autobiography*, pp. 178–82. H. Macmillan, *Memoirs*, vol. II (1968), pp. 103–5, also see pp. 87–92, 114–15, 118–20, 130–2.

5 *HC Debs*, vol. 362, cols 627–38, 27 June 1940. *Autobiography*, pp. 178–86. Interviews, S. C. Leslie and H. Stedman.

6 *Daily Telegraph*, 21 May 1940.

7 *Daily Express*, 23 May 1940.

8 Churchill to Morrison, 5 July 1940. Morrison papers. See also Morrison's Memorandum on Purchase of Machine Tools in America, 21 September 1940, Cab. 67/8, WP (G) (40) 240.

9 *Daily Telegraph*, 25 June 1940 and 22 July 1940.

10 *Daily Telegraph*, 29 July 1940.

11 *The Times*, 6 August 1940.

12 *The Times*, 16 August 1940.

13 Interviews, E. Jay and Mrs H. C. Bentwich.

14 Memorandum on the Munitions Situation, see above.

15 Interview, Lord Avon.

16 *Daily Herald*, 4 October 1940.

17 Cab. 65/8, WM 229 (40), 16 August 1940. Cab. 65/9, WM 239 (40), 2 September 1940. Cab. 65/9, WM 244 (40), 6 September 1940.

18 K. Young, *Churchill and Beaverbrook* (1966), pp. 160–1. Beaverbrook declined because of his asthma. See Lord Avon, *The Reckoning* (1965), pp. 144–5.

19 Interviews, Lord Attlee, Lord Chandos, Lord Citrine, Sir Trevor Evans, D. Jay, S. C. Leslie, Sir Miles Thomas, G. Wansbrough.

20 The most readable account of the blitz on London is in C. Fitzgibbon, *London's Burning* (1971).

21 C. Fitzgibbon, op. cit., p. 151. See also R. Calder, *New Statesman*, 21 September 1940, p. 276. Interview K. Martin. K. Martin, *Editor* (1968), p. 295.

22 N. Nicolson (ed.), *H. Nicolson, Diaries and Letters 1939–45* (1967), p. 114.

23 E. D. Idle, *War Over West Ham* (1943), pp. 6–7.

24 Interview, D. Frankel.

25 S. Orwell and I. Angus (eds.), *Collected Essays etc. of George Orwell*, vol. II (1968), p. 374.

26 *People*, 21 June 1959. Also *World Press News*, 23 December 1955.

Chapter 21   The Home Office and Home Security

1 *Evening Standard*, 30 December 1940.

2 T. H. O'Brien, *Civil Defence*, History of Second World War, UK Civil Series (1955), pp. 117 and 173–5.

3 Cab. 73/2, Civil Defence Committee (40) 45, 4 December 1940. Also HO 186/634.

4 *Autobiography*, pp. 183, 206–7.

5 Interview, S. C. Leslie.

6 Interview, Sir Aylmer Firebrace.

7 Among those convinced that Ellen Wilkinson was Morrison's mistress were Kingsley Martin and Dame Leah Manning. (Interviews.) Some people close to the two politicians were convinced otherwise. (Interviews, Miss M. McCulloch, S. C. Leslie, Lord Robens.)

8 Interview, Sir Austin Strutt.

9 Interview, Sir Austin Strutt.

10 Interviews, A. Bottomley, Sir Austin Strutt. *Autobiography*, p. 218.

11 Cab. 65/9, WM 266 (40), 4 October 1940.

12 *Daily Herald*, 5 October 1940. *Daily Mail*, 5 October 1940.

13 *Daily Herald*, 7 October 1940.

14 Interview, Sir Austin Strutt.

15 *Daily Herald*, 4 October 1940.

16 *The Times*, 5 October 1940.

17 *HC Debs*, vol. 365, cols 389–464, 495–568, 9 October 1940.

18 The interim recommendations of the Horder Committee on shelter conditions, set up in September 1940, were published as White Papers in November 1940. The Committee continued reporting to Morrison until late 1941.

19 Cab. 67/9, WP (G) (41) 7, 15 January 1941.

20 Cab. 65/9, WM 280 (40), 30 October 1940. Also see Morrison's memorandum on Air Raid Shelter Policy, Cab. 67/8 WP (G) (40) 275, and for general shelter policy between 1940–42 see HO 186/1213.

21 'Minister's Broadcast', Cab. 67/8, WP (G) (40) 280.

22 *Evening News*, 17 December 1940.

23 S. Orwell and I. Angus (eds.) *Collected Essays etc. of George Orwell*, vol. II, (1968), p. 399, 6 May 1941.

24 *Autobiography*, p. 186.

25 Interview, Sir John Baker. This story is recorded in HO 191/203, pp. 112–14.

26 Interview, Sir John Baker.

27 Cab. 65/17, WM 7 (41), 16 January 1941. Also Morrison's memorandum on Air Raid Shelter Policy, WP (G) (41) 7, 15 January 1941.

28 *Daily Express*, 12 February 1941.

29 HO 186/580 and HO 186/883.

30 Morrison to Baker, 27 July 1943, copy in Morrison papers.

31 Interview, Sir John Baker.

32 Interview, John Parker.

33 N. Nicolson (ed.), *H. Nicolson, Diaries and Letters 1939–45* (1967), p. 164.

34 Interview, Sir Austin Strutt.

35 HO 186/626. Also 186/556 and 603.

36 Interview, Sir Austin Strutt.

37 Interview, Sir Austin Strutt. *Daily Express*, 16 November 1940. *Evening Standard*, 18 November 1940.

38 Interview, Sir Austin Strutt.

39 See the many references in the War Cabinet Minutes in Cab. 65/9, Cab. 65/10 and following.

40 Cab. 65/10 WM 290 (40), 18 November 1940. For censorship on reporting of air raids see HO 186/584 and 885.

41 See below, pp. 297–300.

42 Cab. 65/10 WM 298 (40), 28 November 1940. Also Lord Reith, *Into the Wind* (1949), p. 438.

43 Interview, Sir Austin Strutt. HO 186/608.

44 For greater detail on the civil defence reorganization see T. H. O'Brien, op. cit., *passim*.

45 For the official report of 'Lessons of Recent Heavy Air Raids' see HO 186/608, 609 and 626. Also Civil Defence Committee (41) Cab. 73/4, 1 January 1941, 8 January 1941 and 15 January 1941.

46 *Evening Standard*, 26 December 1940.

47 Cab. 65/10, WM 309, 311 and 312 (40), 23, 30 and 31 December 1940. Also Cab. 65/17, WM1 (41), 2 January 1941.

48 *Daily Express*, 2 January 1941.

49 *The Times*, 1 January 1941.

50 *The Times*, 20 January 1941.

51 Cab. 65/17, WM 5 (41), 13 January 1941. Also HO 186/498, 500 and 809.

52 See for example *Daily Herald*, 21 January 1941; the *Star*, 22 January 1941.

53 HO 186/502 and 507. *TUC Conference Report 1941*, pp. 312–13. NEC Minutes, vol. 83, 7 May 1941.

54 There were meetings with the TUC on 30 June, 10 July and 25 August 1941. HO 186/501 and 503.

55 *The Times*, 21 September 1941.

56 Interview, Sir Austin Strutt.

57 HO 186/608.

58 *Autobiography*, p. 184.

59 Interview, Sir Austin Strutt.
60 The Regional Commissioner reported that the Plymouth Emergency Committee was 'entirely hopeless' and that the exodus of population was creating great difficulties in surrounding rural areas. Report by Inspector General in HO 186/625.
61 A. Firebrace, *Fire Service Memories* (1949), pp. 204–5.
62 Cab. 65/18 WM 48 (41), 8 May 1941. WP (41) 97, 6 May 1941.
63 Interview, Sir Austin Strutt.
64 Cab. 65/43 WM 96 (44), 26 July 1944. Cab. 65/43 WM 99 (44), 31 July 1944. *HC Debs*, vol. 402, cols 761–7, 26 July 1944, 1209–28, 1 August 1944. Interview, Lady Allen. H. Morrison, *Government and Parliament* (1959), pp. 321–3.
65 *Autobiography*, p. 185.
66 *The Times*, 15 July 1941.

Chapter 22   Civil Liberties: Newspapers, Aliens and Mosley

1 Cab. 65/9, WM 267 (40), 7 October 1940.
2 *HC Debs*, vol. 352, col. 1849, 31 October 1939.
3 Cab. 65/9, WM 268 (40), 9 October 1940. Cab. 66/13 WP (40) 402, 8 October 1940.
4 Cab. 65/9, WM 272 (40), 16 October 1940. Cab. 65/10, WM 282 (40), 4 November 1940.
5 See Cecil King, *Memoirs* (1969), p. 117 and *With Malice Towards None: a War Diary* (1970), pp. 94–107. M. Edelman, *The Mirror, a Political History* (1966), esp. p. 106.
6 Cab. 65/10, WM 310 (40), 27 December 1940. Cab. 65/21, WM 5 (41), 13 January 1941. WP (41) 7, 11 January 1941.
7 *Autobiography*, p. 225.
8 *Evening Standard*, 24 January 1941. *The Times*, 29 January 1941. NEC Minutes, vol. 83, 4 February 1941. *HC Debs*, vol. 368, cols 185–7, 463–534, 22 January 1941.
9 *News Chronicle*, 2 October 1941; *Daily Telegraph*, 13 October 1941.
10 NEC Minutes, vol. 86, 5 June, 24 June, 22 July 1942. *LPCR*, 1942, pp. 158–60. Cab. 65/18 WM 62 (41), 23 June 1941. Cab. 65/30, WM (42), 30 June 1942. Cab. 65/31 WM (42) 101, 1 August 1942.
11 *Sunday Pictorial*, 26 October 1941.
12 Cab. 65/19, WM 106, (41), 27 October 1941.
13 Cab. 65/20, WM 110, (41), 10 November 1941. WP (41) 262.
14 Cab. 66/19, WP (41) 269. Also Cab. 65/20, WM 115 (41), 17 November 1941.
15 Cab. 65/25, WM 32 (42), 9 March 1942. Cab. 65/25, WM 35 (42), 18 March 1942. Another defence regulation, 2C, could have been invoked, but it involved action through the courts after due warning and so did not meet the desire of Cabinet 'hawks' for speedy suppression.
16 *Autobiography*, pp. 222–4. M. Edelman, op. cit., pp. 117–18. C. King, *With Malice Towards None* (1970), p. 165. Interviews, S. C. Leslie, Sir Austin Strutt. *HC Debs*, vol. 378, cols 1665–9, 19 March 1942.
17 NEC Minutes, vol. 85, 25 March 1942. *Daily Herald*, 26 March 1942.
18 *HC Debs*, vol. 378, cols 2233–308, 26 March 1942. *Evening Standard*, 27 March 1942.
19 *Sunday Express*, 12 April 1942.

20 *HC Debs*, vol. 379, cols 21–5, 13 April 1942.

21 *Daily Express*, 12 March 1942. Interview, Sir Austin Strutt. *HC Debs*, vol. 379, cols 23–4, 13 April 1942.

22 Interview, Lord Chorley.

23 *Manchester Guardian*, 23 March 1942.

24 *The Times*, 2 April 1942.

25 There is a well-informed biography of Fisher in the *Dictionary of National Biography*, written by H. Hamilton of the Treasury.

26 Dalton diary, 3 April 1942, vol. 26.

27 HO 186/821 and 822.

28 HO 186/1155.

29 Cab. 65/10, WM 293 (40), 21 November 1940. Also WP (G) (40) 308 and 309.

30 Interview, Sir Austin Strutt.

31 Interviews, K. Martin, Mrs F. Laski, K. Martin in *Sunday Times*, 7 March 1965.

32 See Morrison's memorandum on Members of the British Union detained under 18B. Cab. 67/8, WP (G) (40) 309, 19 November 1940.

33 *HC Debs*, vol. 376, col. 186, 18 November 1941. 671 were still detained out of 1766 interned. See also Cab. 65/20, WM 116 (41), 20 November 1941.

34 *HC Debs*, vol. 381, cols 1426–1518, 21 July 1972.

35 See Mosley's autobiography, *My Life* (1968), p. 404.

36 *Autobiography*, p. 221.

37 Ibid., p. 222.

38 Cab. 65/36, WM 156 (43), 17 November 1943. Annex Cab. 65/36, WM 163 (43), 29 November 1943. A. Bullock, *The Life and Times of Ernest Bevin*, vol. II (1967), pp. 286–7.

39 Interview, Miss J. Nunn.

40 *Daily Express*, 19 November 1943.

41 *The Times*, 20 November 1943; *Manchester Guardian*, 22 November 1943, 26 November 1943; *Daily Telegraph*, 23 November 1943; *Daily Express*, 24 November 1943; *Daily Mail*, 25 November 1943.

42 *HC Debs*, vol. 393, cols 1428–33, 23 November 1943. *Star*, 23 November 1943; *Evening Standard*, 23 November 1943.

43 *The Times*, 24 November 1943; *Daily Express*, 24 November 1943.

44 NCL Minutes, 23 November 1943. *News Chronicle*, 24 November 1943; *Daily Express*, 24 November 1943; *Daily Mail*, 25 November 1943.

45 *Daily Express*, 25 November 1943.

46 NEC Minutes, vol. 88, 24 November 1943. *Daily Express*, 25 November 1943; *Daily Mail*, 25 November 1943. Dalton diary, 24 November 1943, vol. 29.

47 *Manchester Guardian*, 25 November 1943.

48 *The Times*, 26 November 1943; *Manchester Guardian*, 25, 26 November 1943; *Daily Express*, 26 November 1943. Dalton diary, 25 November 1943, vol. 29.

49 26 November 1943.

50 *People*, 28 November 1943.

51 J. Parker, G. Dagger and G. Woods.

52 *HC Debs*, vol. 395, cols 395 and 461–76, 1 December 1943.

53 William Barclay in *Daily Express*, 2 December 1943.

54 2 December 1943.

55 *HC Debs*, vol. 395, cols 475–8, 1 December 1943. *The Times*, 1, 2 December 1943.

56 *The Times*, 6 December 1943.

57 *TUC Annual Report*, 1944, p. 186. *Daily Express*, 23 December 1943.

58 *Daily Mail*, 12 January 1943.

59 Interview, Miss J. Nunn.

60 Interviews, Sir Philip Allen, Miss J. Nunn.

Chapter 23   Into the War Cabinet

1 Cab. 73/9, CDC (E) (41) 2, 3 October 1941. Cab. 71/2, LP (41) 49, 24 October 1941. Cab. 67/9, WP (G) (41) 134, 21 November 1941. Cab. 71/2, LP (41) 56, 2 December 1941. Cab. 65/28, WM 163 (42), 1 December 1942. Cab. 65/28, WM 167 (42), 11 December 1942. Cab. 65/35, WM 102 (43), 22 July 1943. Cab. 65/35, WM 164 (43), 1 December 1943. Cab. 71/11, LP (43) 77, 31 December 1943. HO 186/1102.

2 *The Times*, 25 September 1942. *TUC Annual Report* 1942, pp. 110 and 206.

3 Interviews, M. Nicholson, Sir Austin Strutt.

4 *The Times*, 15 July 1943.

5 Interview, M. Nicholson.

6 Cab. 65/44, WM 153 (44), 22 November 1944. Cab. 65/49, WM 21 (45), 19 February 1945. J. A. F. Watson, *Which is the Justice* (1969), pp. 154–67. Interview, Lady Allen of Hurtwood.

7 Interview, Sir Austin Strutt.

8 Cab. 71/11, LPC (41) 10, 17 January 1941. Cab. 65/17, WM 15 (41), 10 February 1941. Cab. 71/11, LPC (41) 32, 24 February 1941.

9 *HC Debs*, vol. 370, col. 962, 1 April 1941.

10 Cab. 65/17, 48/12/1, 26 March 1941.

11 For his later change of position see below, p. 545.

12 Interview, Lady Wilson.

13 Interview, Mrs J. Melman.

14 *Autobiography*, pp. 226–8. For general background interviews, Sir Philip Allen, Sir Austin Strutt.

15 Interview, Sir Philip Allen. The rest of this section has been helped greatly by interviews with Sir Austin Strutt and Lady Reading and by Pimlott memorandum, 26 July 1945, copy in Morrison papers.

16 Interview, Sir Austin Strutt.

17 Interview, Sir Austin Strutt.

18 Interview, Sir Austin Strutt.

19 Interviews, Sir Philip Allen, Miss J. Nunn, S. C. Leslie.

20 Interview, P. Benson.

21 Interview, Sir Austin Strutt.

22 For this section, interviews K. H. Kent, F. J. Powe, Sir Austin Strutt. Morrison did visit Margaret for their silver wedding anniversary in March 1944. Morrison to Churchill, 8 March 1944. Morrison papers.

23 Interview, Lord Chorley.

24 Interview, Sir Robert Fraser.

25 Interview, Lady Allen of Hurtwood. Also interviews, Sir Robert Fraser, Sir Austin Strutt, Dr E. Maclellan.

26 Lord Avon, *The Reckoning* (1965), pp. 342, 352. Morrison, draft autobiography, war chapter, pp. 43–5. Morrison papers.

22 Interview, S. C. Leslie. *The Times*, 30 October 1942; *Daily Herald*, 30 October 1942.

28 *Daily Mail*, 31 October 1942; *The Times*, 2 November 1942.

29 *The Times*, 19 November 1942.

30 *Autobiography*, p. 216. Interview, Sir Austin Strutt.

31 *Daily Express*, 23 November 1942.

32 *Reynolds News*, 29 November 1942.

33 Beaverbrook to Morrison, 23 November 1943. Copy in Beaverbrook Foundation: Beaverbrook papers.

34 Interview, Lord Citrine.

35 Churchill to Morrison, 21 November 1940, 18 July 1942, Morrison papers.

36 Beaverbrook to Morrison, 3 December 1941, Morrison papers. Other colleagues praised the quality of Morrison's contributions in Cabinet. Interviews, Lord Avon and Lord Chandos.

37 See below, p. 319 and 338.

38 Interviews, Sir William Murrie, Lord Chandos. *Autobiography*, pp. 212–18.

39 A. Bullock, *The Life and Times of Ernest Bevin*, vol. II (1967), pp. 117–18.

40 Interviews, Lord Avon, Lord Chandos, Sir Austin Strutt. Dalton diary, 23 October 1944, vol. 31.

41 Cab. 65/28, WM 159 (42), 26 November 1942.

42 Dalton diary, 15 November 1942, vol. 28. Also Lord Beveridge, *Power and Influence* (1953), p. 327. Interviews, Dr E. Maclellan, Sir Austin Strutt.

43 Cab. 87/13, PR (43) 2, 20 January 1943. Dalton to Morrison, 24 January 1943. Morrison to Dalton, 29 January 1943. Dalton papers (1943–4).

44 Cab. 76/13, PR (43) 2, 20 January 1943.

45 Cab. 65/33, WM 28 (43), 12 February 1943.

46 Dalton diary, 16, 17 February 1943, vol. 28.

47 *Evening Standard*, 17 February 1943.

48 Interview, D. N. Chester.

49 Dalton diary, 18 February 1943, vol. 8. *Daily Express*, 18 February 1943. *The Times*, 19 February 1943.

50 Interview, S. C. Leslie.

51 Interviews, D. N. Chster, S. C. Leslie, Sir Austin Strutt. Pimlott memorandum, 26 July 1945. Morrison papers.

52 *Daily Express*, 19 February 1943.

53 *The Times*, 19 February 1943; *Daily Telegraph*, 19 February 1943.

54 Edward Turnour (Lord Winterton), *Orders of the Day* (1953), p. 291. *The Times*, 19 February 1943.

55 Interview, J. Griffiths.

56 Dalton diary, 18 February 1943, vol. 28.

57 See below, pp. 327–9.

58 See above, pp. 287.

59 *Daily Telegraph*, 20 March 1943.

60 *The Times*, 6, 8 March 1943.

61 *HC Debs*, vol. 387, col. 669, 10 March 1943. *The Times*, 11 March 1943.

62 Cab. 65/34, WM (43) 48, 5 April 1943. Cab. 66/35, WP (43) 137, 5 April 1943. Cab. 73/7, CDC (43) 5, 15 April 1943. The Home Security papers on Bethnal Green are in HO 206/6.

63 Baker versus Bethnal Green Borough Council, 18 July 1944. Kings Bench Division. Appeal 8 December 1944. Court of Appeal.

64 *HC Debs*, vol. 407, cols 504–7, 19 January 1945.

65 *HC Debs*, vol. 408, col. 2204, 8 March 1945.

66 Interview, D. Sandys. T. H. O'Brien, *Civil Defence*, History of Second World War, UK Civil Series (1955), p. 645. David Irving, *The Mare's Nest* (1964), *passim. Autobiography*, pp. 193–4.

67 Interviews, Sir Martin Flett, Lady Allen of Hurtwood. Cab. 73/7, CDC (43) 35, 28 December 1943.

68 Cab. 66/43, WP (43) 520 and 535, 25 November 1943.

69 Cab. 65/42, WM (80) (44), 19 June 1944.

70 Cab. 73/8, CDC (44), 1 and 18 January 1944. Cab. 65/43, WM 85, 89 and 93, 3, 10 and 24 July 1944. WP (44) 377, 5 July. Cab. 65/43, WM 104(44), 9 August 1944.

71 Interview, D. Sandys.

72 Interview, S. C. Leslie.

73 Cab. 66/51, WP (44) 348, 27 June 1944.

74 Cab. 65/43, WM 89, 93, 97, 98 and 113 (44), 10, 12, 27, 28 July and 31 August 1944. Cab. 65/46, WM 82 (44), 26 July 1944. WP (44), 412, 27 July 1944.

75 Cab. 65/43, WM 116 (44), 4 September 1944. Cab. 65/43, WM 117 (44), 5 September 1944. Cab. 65/43, WM 118 (44), 7 September 1944.

76 *The Times*, 8 September 1944.

77 *Daily Express*, 12 April 1945.

78 *HC Debs*, vol. 413, cols 182–8, 17 August 1945. Interviews, R. Jeune, W. Krichevsky, Sir Austin Strutt. Cab. 65/49, WM 26, 37 (45), 6 and 28 March 1945.

79 Interview, Sir Philip Allen.

Chapter 24 Labour Politics, Post-War Reconstruction and the 1945 Election

1 Interviews, Mrs D. J. Bolton, Sir Isaac Hayward, Mrs D. Jay, Dr E. Rickards.

2 Interview, Miss J. Bourne.

3 LLP papers 9111, 12 September 1942; 9514, 21 September 1944; 9550, 26 October 1944; 9562, 16 November 1944; 9485–92, 15 June 1944.

4 See the Minutes of the NEC and of these sub-committees in vols. 82–8.

5 NEC Minutes, vol. 84, 25 June 1941.

6 Interview, Lady Bacon.

7 *LPCR*, 1942, pp. 145–6.

8 *People*, 31 May 1942.

9 Churchill to Morrison, 29 May 1942. Morrison papers.

10 Memorandum, 10 January 1943, copy in Dalton papers, 1943.

11 A. Bullock, *The Life and Times of Ernest Bevin*, vol. II (1967), pp. 188–9, 287.

12 Interview, S. C. Leslie.

13 *Daily Express*, 18 January 1943.

14 *Daily Mail*, 12 December 1940.

15 See his speeches to the Foreign Press Association on 6 June 1941, to the British Association on September 1941, at Sheffield on 12 October 1941, at Bradford on 5 March 1942, to the London Labour Party on 14 March 1942, and to the Cheshire Regional Labour Party in September 1942. *London News*, November 1941, April

1942, *The Times*, 7 June 1941, 27 September 1942; *Manchester Guardian*, 13 October 1941.

16 *Autobiography*, pp. 229–30.

17 Dalton diary, 28 October 1942, vol. 27.

18 *London News*, January/February 1943.

19 *Manchester Guardian*, 12 January 1943. On these speeches see *The Times*, 21 December 1942, 15 and 25 February 1943; *Evening Standard*, 18 December 1942; *Daily Herald*, 21 December 1942.

20 Interviews, S. C. Leslie, Sir Austin Strutt.

21 Interview, Lord Chorley.

22 *Sunday Times*, 9 May 1942.

23 NEC Minutes, vol. 83, 7 May 1941.

24 NEC policy committee minutes, 23 May, 4 July 1941. NEC emergency committee minute 20 June 1941. Vols 84, 85.

25 NEC reconstruction committee minutes, vol. 84, 30 July 1941.

26 NEC Minutes, vol. 87, 23 March 1943.

27 *LPCR*, 1943, pp. 126–7.

28 *Evening Standard*, 14 June 1943.

29 Beverley Baxter in *Evening Standard*, 9 April 1943.

30 *Daily Express*, 15 October 1943.

31 LLP papers 9177, 25 February 1943.

32 Dalton diary, 11 June 1943, vol. 28.

33 A. Bullock, op. cit., pp. 244–5.

34 Dalton diary, 13 June 1943, vol. 28.

35 NEC Minutes, vol. 88, 14 June 1943.

36 Dalton diary, 14 June 1943, vol. 28.

37 Dalton diary, 15 June 1943, vol. 28. *Daily Express*, 16 June 1943; *Daily Mail*, 16 June 1943.

38 *LPCR*, 1943, pp. 165–6. *Daily Express*, 17 June 1943.

39 Interview, D. Frankel.

40 *People*, 20 June 1943.

41 *Manchester Guardian*, 16 July 1943. On this section also interviews, J. Parker, S. Elliott, and *London News*, August 1943.

42 *London News*, August 1943. *The Times*, 28 June 1943.

43 Dalton diary, 2 November 1943, vol. 29. *Autobiography*, pp. 232–3.

44 Cab. 87/13, WP G (43), 15, 22 February 1943.

45 Cab. 65/36, WM 144 (43), 21 October 1943. Cab. 65/42, WP (43) 465, 467.

46 Annex Cab. 65/40, WM 140 (43), 14 October 1943. See also Morrison's Memorandum on Social Insurance in Cab. 66/52, WP (44) 357, 30 June 1944.

47 Quoted in A. Bullock, op. cit., p. 337.

48 Ibid, p. 338.

49 Dalton to Morrison, 24 October 1944, copy in Dalton papers, 1944. Dalton diary, 22 November 1944, vol. 31.

50 Morrison memorandum, 22 November 1944. Morrison papers.

51 NEC Minutes, vol. 90, 16 May 1944.

52 Dalton diary, 26 July, 13 September 1944, vol. 31.

53 *LPCR*, 1944, pp. 160–9, esp. p. 163. H. Dalton, *The Fateful Years* (1957), pp. 421 ff.

54 *Daily Herald,* 16 December 1944.

55 NEC Minutes, vol. 89, 22 March 1944. Dalton diary, 22 March 1944, vol. 30. Interviews, Mrs L. Middleton, Lady Phillips, Sir William Lawther, Mrs D. Robinson. *Evening Standard,* 27 November 1943.

56 Dalton diary, 11 April 1945, vol. 32.

57 NEC policy committee minutes 23 January, 27 February, 27 March 1945, vol. 91. *Autobiography,* p. 232. *The Times,* 20, 23 January 1945.

58 *Autobiography,* p. 232.

59 Dalton diary, 11 April 1945, vol. 32. NEC campaign committee minutes 19 March, 11 April 1945, vol. 91.

60 *The Times,* 30 April 1945.

61 *Star,* 22 May 1945. *LPCR,* 1945, p. 89.

62 *Daily Express,* 23 May 1945; *The Times,* 23 May 1945; *News Chronicle,* 23 May 1945.

63 *Evening News,* 24 May 1945.

64 Dalton diary, 10 April 1945, vol. 32.

65 Lord Chandos, *The Memoirs of Lord Chandos* (1962), p. 322.

66 E. Turnour (Lord Winterton), *Orders of the Day* (1953), p. 311.

67 H. Dalton, *The Fateful Years* (1957), p. 458.

68 *Autobiography,* p. 234. A. Bullock, op. cit., pp. 375, 328–9, 371. H. Dalton, op. cit., p. 458. Lord Avon, *Memoirs: The Reckoning,* vol. II (1965), p. 453.

69 Dalton diary, 16 September 1943, vol. 29. *Evening News,* 3 January 1944.

70 See for example his speeches to the Pavior's Company on 22 May 1944 and to the Yorkshire Area Labour Conference on 2 December 1944. *The Times,* 23 May 1944, *Sunday Dispatch,* 3 December 1944. Also Dalton diary, 11 May 1945, vol. 32. Avon, op. cit., pp. 524–5.

71 *HC Debs,* vol. 404, cols 662–8, 31 October 1944.

72 Copies in Dalton papers, 1945, printed in H. Dalton, op. cit., p. 457. Dalton diary, 10 May 1945, vol. 32.

73 Churchill issued a statement giving his version of these events on 12 June 1945 and Attlee published his version on 13 June. *The Times,* 14 June 1945. Lord Attlee, *As It Happened* (1954), pp. 132–8. Dalton diary, 18 May 1945, vol. 32. A. Bullock, op. cit., p. 375.

74 F. Williams, *A Prime Minister Remembers* (1961), pp. 63–4.

75 A. Bullock, op. cit., pp. 375–7. *Autobiography,* p. 235. Dalton diary, 18 May, 19 May 1945, vol. 32. NEC Minutes, vol. 91, 20 May 1945.

76 H. Dalton, op. cit., p. 459. F. Williams, op. cit., p. 68. A. Bullock, op. cit., p. 377.

77 *Evening Standard,* 26 May 1945. *The Times,* 28 May 1945. *Manchester Guardian,* 26, 28 May 1945.

78 *HC Debs,* vol. 411, cols 28 and 36, 29 May 1945.

79 *Autobiography,* p. 289. Interviews, Lord Henderson and J. W. Raisin.

80 *Sunday Pictorial,* 3 June 1945. *Reynolds News,* 1 July 1945.

81 *Daily Herald,* 5 June 1945.

82 See above, pp. 297–300.

83 Interview, S. Elliott.

84 LLP papers, 9675, 31 May 1945.

85 *Daily Worker,* 21 July 1944; *Star,* 17 August, 24 October 1944.

86 *The Times,* 10 January 1945; *Star,* 10 January 1945; *Reynolds News,* 11 February

1945; *Sunday Express*, 11 February 1945; *Evening Standard*, 12 February 1945; *News Chronicle*, 9 February 1945.

87 *The Times*, 10 January 1945. *Autobiography*, pp. 238–9.

88 Interview, J. W. Raisin.

89 Interviews, Sir Isaac Hayward, J. W. Raisin. Dalton diary, 5 April 1945, vol. 32.

90 *News Chronicle*, 12 January 1945; *Daily Worker*, 11 January 1945.

91 Interviews, Mrs H. Butler, A. Cullington, W. Nichols.

92 Interviews, H. Atkinson, A. Cullington.

93 LLP papers 9307, March 1943; 9315, 28 October 1943.

94 Morrison in *Punch*, 16 September 1964. Interview, H. Atkinson.

95 Interview, D. Frankel.

96 Interviews, Mrs H. Butler, Mr H. Butler.

97 LLP papers 9112, 24 September 1942.

98 This section is based on national and local press coverage from 1 June to 5 July 1945. Also see Morrison's own recollections in *Punch*, 16 September 1964.

99 Interview, G. Rogers.

100 Interview, J. W. Raisin.

101 Interview, Mrs D. Baker. *Daily Telegraph*, 21 June 1945.

102 Interview, J. W. Raisin.

103 *Daily Express*, 5 July 1945.

104 *Daily Telegraph*, 5 July 1945.

105 *Daily Mirror*, 1 August 1945.

106 Interview, J. W. Raisin.

107 *Autobiography*, p. 242.

Chapter 25   Labour Into Power, July 1945

1 *Autobiography*, pp. 242–3.

2 Interview, C. Johnson.

3 *The Times House of Commons 1945*, pp. 130, 153. R. B. McCallum and A. Readman, *The British General Election of 1945* (1947), p. 264.

4 H. Dalton, *The Fateful Years* (1957), p. 468.

5 F. Williams, *A Prime Minister Remembers* (1961), pp. 3–4.

6 Ibid., p. 3.

7 H. Dalton, op. cit., p. 468.

8 Dalton diary, 12 and 28 October 1942, vol. 27. Also see Francis Williams, *Nothing So Strange* (1970), p. 211.

9 Interview, G. R. Strauss. Bevan stayed with Strauss at this time and had several telephone conversations discussing the leadership question in which his preference for Morrison emerged.

10 *Daily Express*, 31 May 1945; *Daily Mirror*, 5 October 1944.

11 Dalton diary, 20 May 1945, vol. 32.

12 H. Dalton, op. cit., p. 467. F. Williams, *Ernest Bevin* (1952), pp. 238–9. Interview, Lord Attlee.

13 *Evening Standard*, 15 June 1945.

14 *Autobiography*, p. 236.

15 Interview, Mrs D. Baker.

16 *Star*, 27 July 1945.

17 Interview, R. Boon.

18 Interview, J. Parker.

19 Interview, G. Isaacs.

20 Francis Williams also advised Attlee to go to the Palace as quickly as possible. Interview.

21 Dalton gives a contrary impression but the authors are satisfied from private information that Morrison did intervene in this way. H. Dalton, op. cit., p. 469. Interview, C. Johnson.

22 *LPCR*, 1933, pp. 8–10. Interview, F. Barlow.

23 *LPCR*, 1933, p. 8.

24 This interpretation is made in R. T. McKenzie, *British Political Parties* (2nd ed. 1963), p. 32 n. I.

25 Dalton diary, 27 July 1945, vol. 33. Interview, C. Johnson.

26 F. Williams, *A Prime Minister Remembers* (1961), p. 4.

27 There is little doubt that in recent years Morrison had been the dominant electoral figure in the parliamentary party. Lord Francis-Williams, who was close to Attlee at this time and also knew the Labour Party well, believed that Morrison would have won a leadership contest in 1945. Interview.

28 *Autobiography*, pp. 245–6.

29 Interview, J. W. Raisin. H. Dalton, op. cit., p. 474.

30 Draft autobiography, vol. 1/17. Attlee papers.

31 Ibid. Also H. Dalton, op. cit., p. 474.

32 *Autobiography*, pp. 246–7.

33 George VI, Richard Crossman, Francis Williams and Edward Bridges have been described as giving the decisive advice. J. Wheeler-Bennett, *George VI* (1958), p. 638. H. Dalton, op. cit., p. 472. Interview, D. Jay.

34 F. Williams, *A Prime Minister Remembers* (1961), p. 5.

35 Interviews, Lord Citrine, Lord Williamson, J. W. Raisin, R. Boon.

36 Frank Owen in *Daily Express*. 10 March 1951.

37 Interview, C. Brandon.

38 Interview, Sir Trevor Evans.

39 F. Williams, *Nothing So Strange* (1970), p. 218.

40 Interview, C. Mayhew.

41 Interview, Lord Francis-Williams.

42 Interview, C. Mayhew.

43 Interview, Lord Robens.

44 Interview, Lady Summerskill.

45 Interview, Dame Leah Manning.

46 Interview, C. Johnson.

Chapter 26 At Work as Lord President

1 Interview, A. Bottomley.

2 Interviews, C. Mayhew, J. Christie.

3 Interview, Lord Stow Hill.

4 On the respective roles of Attlee and Morrison in developing the committee system to service the Labour Cabinet's work programme, see H. Morrison, *Government and Parliament* (1964), pp. 18, 35.

5 Interviews, D. Jay, M. Nicholson, Lord Plowden.

6 See below pp. 359–60 and 421.

7 Interviews, C. Mayhew, P. Gordon Walker.

8 R. S. Sayers, *Financial Policy 1939–45*, History of the Second World War, UK Civil Series (1956), p. 486.

9 Morrison was at least once referred to as the 'economic Chancellor of the Exchequer' to distinguish him from Dalton as the 'financial' Chancellor. *Evening Standard*, 15 January 1947. Interview, Lord Bridges. See also J. Dow, *The Management of the British Economy 1945–60* (1968), pp. 1–29.

10 Interview, Lord Bridges.

11 Interview, G. Isaacs.

12 H. Morrison, *Government and Parliament*, p. 296.

13 Lecture to Institute of Public Administration, 17 October 1946.

14 4 November 1946.

15 Interview, Sir Alexander Johnstone. This view was shared by Downes, Plowden and, with qualifications, by Nicholson. Interviews.

16 Interview, D. Jay.

17 Interview, M. Nicholson.

18 Interviews, Lord Bridges, Sir Alexander Johnstone, M. Nicholson, Lord Plowden.

19 H. Morrison, *Government and Parliament*, pp. 247–8.

20 Interview, Lord Shinwell.

21 Interview, Sir Trevor Evans.

22 Interview, Lord Reith.

23 Interviews, J. Cliff, Sir Reginald Hill, S. S. Wilson.

24 Lord Reith, *Into the Wind* (1949), pp. 390–1, and interview.

25 See below, Chapter 30, pp. 400–4.

26 Interviews, Sir William Murrie, Sir Charles Harris.

27 Interview, D. Jay.

28 H. Morrison, *Government and Parliament*, pp. 222, 242.

29 Ibid., pp. 234–5.

30 Interview, M. Nicholson.

31 Interviews, P. Benson, G. Eden, Sir Trevor Evans, D. Keir, Lord Shackleton, Lady Wilson.

32 Interviews, C. Mayhew, Lord Shackleton.

33 These files are in the Morrison–Boon papers.

34 See Morrison's speech to the National Council of Labour, 27 January 1948, and miscellaneous related documents in Morrison–Boon papers.

35 J. G. Crowther, *Fifty Years with Science* (1970), pp. 252–3, 273.

36 H. Morrison, *Government and Parliament*, pp. 330–3. M. Nicholson, *The Environmental Revolution* (1970), p. 159. Reith Lectures, 1969. *Listener*, 11 December 1969, p. 819.

37 Interview, G. Isaacs.

38 Interview, G. Isaacs.

39 Interview, Sir Alexander Johnstone.

40 Interview, Lord Attlee.

41 Interview, J. Griffiths.

42 Interview, J. Griffiths.

w

43 Interview, Lord Robens.
44 Interviews, Lord Attlee, G. Isaacs.
45 Interview, M. Nicholson.
46 Interview, Lord Bridges.
47 Interview, Sir Alexander Johnstone.
48 Interviews, G. Downes, Sir Martin Flett, D. Henley, Sir William Murrie, Sir David Stephens.

Chapter 27   Managing Parliament and the Party

1 Interview, M. Nicholson.
2 Interview, J. Christie.
3 Interview, D. Jay.
4 Interview, W. Paling.
5 H. Morrison, *Government and Parliament* (1964), pp. 117–20.
6 Interview, Sir Edward Fellowes.
7 H. Morrison, *Government and Parliament*, p. 170.
8 *HC Debs*, vol. 413, cols 133–74, 16 August 1945.
9 *HC Debs*, vol. 413, col. 984, 24 August 1945.
10 Parliamentary Papers: *First Report from the Select Committee on Procedure*, pp. 14–16 and Appendix.
11 H. Morrison, *Government and Parliament*, p. 211.
12 Ibid., pp. 209–12.
13 Ibid., p. 213.
14 *HC Debs*, vol. 415, col. 2398, 15 November 1945.
15 H. Morrison, *Government and Parliament*, p. 220, also pp. 207–20.
16 Ibid., p. 210.
17 Calculated from *The Times House of Commons 1945*.
18 Interview, C. Johnson.
19 Interview, C. Johnson.
20 H. Morrison, *Government and Parliament*, p. 124. Interview, C. Johnson.
21 Interviews, C. Johnson, G. Isaacs, F. Barlow.
22 Interview on BBC Television, 9 September 1969.
23 *Autobiography*, pp. 254–5.
24 Dalton diary, 24 July 1944, vol. 31. These earlier groups are in fact referred to in H. Morrison, *Government and Parliament*, p. 124. Interview, C. Johnson.
25 *Autobiography*, pp. 254–5.
26 Interview, C. Johnson.
27 Interview, C. Johnson.
28 *Sunday Express*, 30 September 1945.
29 *Autobiography*, p. 254.
30 H. Morrison, *Government and Parliament*, p. 165.
31 Ibid., p. 130.
32 R. Jackson, *Rebels and Whips* (1968), pp. 313–14. Interview, C. Johnson.
33 *The Times*, 31 January 1946. Interview, C. Johnson.
34 For details see below Chapter 32, pp. 432–5.
35 *News Chronicle*, 18 October 1945. Interview, C. Johnson.
36 See below, Chapter 28, pp. 387–8.

37 Interview, Lord Avon.
38 Interviews, J. Christie, G. Downes, D. Henley.
39 Interviews, J. Christie, G. Downes, D. Henley, Sir Alexander Johnstone, M. Nicholson, Sir David Stephens.
40 Interview, Sir Alexander Johnstone.
41 Interview, C. Johnson.
42 Interview.
43 Interview, C. Johnson.

Chapter 28   On the Treadmill, 1945–1946

1 *Daily Express*, 2 August 1945.
2 R. R. James (ed.), *Chips: The Diaries of Sir Henry Channon* (1967), p. 409.
3 *Autobiography*, p. 241.
4 *Daily Herald*, 15 August 1945.
5 R. R. James, op. cit., p. 411.
6 Interview, C. Johnson. See above, Chapter 26, pp. 356–8.
7 H. Dalton, *High Tide and After* (1962), pp. 24–31.
8 *The Times*, 10 December 1945.
9 *Manchester Guardian*, 8 and 11 December 1945.
10 *Manchester Guardian*, 1 February 1946.
11 *HC Debs*, vol. 418, col. 1109, 31 January 1946.
12 *Manchester Guardian*, 1 February 1946.
13 *HC Debs*, vol. 421, cols 969–73, 1 April 1946.
14 *HC Debs*, vol. 421, cols 2217–58, 15 April 1946.
15 Dalton diary, 1 August 1946, vol. 34.
16 *HC Debs*, vol. 416, col. 958, 31 January 1946.
17 *Sunday Express*, 24 March 1946.
18 *Daily Telegraph*, 7 May 1946; *The Times*, 7 May 1946.
19 *HC Debs*, vol. 423, col. 1114, 28 May 1946.
20 *HC Debs*, vol. 423, col. 662, 23 May 1946.
21 *HC Debs*, vol. 423, col. 664–7, 23 May 1946. *Daily Express*, 24 May 1946.
22 *Daily Herald*, 13 September 1945.
23 *Star*, 29 September 1945.
24 *Daily Telegraph*, 8 January 1946.
25 *Daily Telegraph*, 10 January 1946.
26 *Daily Telegraph*, 11 January 1946. See also *News Chronicle*, 28 December 1945; *Star*, 2 January 1946; *Daily Herald*, 5, 8 January 1946; *Sunday Times*, 6 January 1946; *Sunday Express*, 6 January 1946; *The Times*, 7 January 1946.
27 *Daily Telegraph*, 12 January 1946. *The Times*, 12 January 1946.
28 *The Times*, 14 January 1946; *Daily Herald*, 14 January 1946.
29 *Daily Telegraph*, 15 January 1946; *Daily Express*, 15 January 1946.
30 *Sunday Times*, 20 January 1946.
31 *Daily Telegraph*, 17 January 1946; *Sunday Times*, 20 January 1946.
32 *Sunday Express*, 24 March 1946; *The Times*, 18 April 1946.
33 *Daily Herald*, 19 June 1946; *The Times*, 1 July 1946.
34 F. Williams, *A Prime Minister Remembers* (1961), pp. 136–48.
35 *Autobiography*, pp. 205–6.

36 *Sunday Chronicle*, 12 May 1946; *Sunday Dispatch*, 12 May 1946.

37 *Evening Standard*, 11 May 1946.

38 Interview, M. Nicholson.

39 *Daily Express*, 13 May 1946.

40 *Autobiography*, p. 256.

41 *Daily Express*, 16 May 1946.

42 *Daily Express*, 16 May 1946.

43 *Daily Telegraph*, 18 May 1946.

44 *Manchester Guardian*, 18 May 1946. *HC Debs*, vol. 423, col. 556, 23 May 1946.

45 *Observer*, 19 May 1946; *Daily Express*, 18 May 1946.

46 *Daily Telegraph*, 22 May 1946.

47 *HC Debs*, vol. 423, col. 545, 23 May 1946.

48 *Daily Express*, 25 May 1946.

49 *Sunday Express*, 26 May 1946.

50 *HC Debs*, vol. 423, col. 1163, 29 May 1946.

51 Dalton diary, 15 May 1946, vol. 34.

52 Trevor Evans, in *Daily Express*, 10 June 1946.

53 *Daily Mail*, 13 June 1946.

54 *LPCR*, 1946, p. 169.

55 Ibid., p. 174.

56 Ibid., p. 177.

57 *Star*, 13 June 1946.

58 *News Chronicle*, 15 June 1946.

59 *London News*, October 1945.

60 On 24 June 1946.

61 *HC Debs*, vol. 424, col. 2333, 4 July 1946.

62 *Daily Graphic*, 9 July 1946.

63 See e.g. *HC Debs*, vol. 416, cols 1543–5; vol. 427, cols 363–5; vol. 431, cols 2183–91.

64 *Daily Mail*, 23 March 1948.

65 H. Dalton, op. cit., p. 93.

66 *Liverpool Daily Post*, 12 September 1946; *Star*, 13 September 1946; *Daily Graphic*, 16 September 1946; *Daily Telegraph*, 17 September 1946.

67 *Daily Herald*, 16 October 1946.

68 Interviews, R. Boon, D. Jay.

69 *The Times*, 19 October 1946.

70 *Observer*, 1 December 1946.

71 *Daily Telegraph*, 2 December 1946.

72 *HC Debs*, vol. 430, col. 526, 18 November 1946.

73 R. Jackson, *Rebels and Whips* (1968), pp. 54 ff. Also for above see *Daily Express*, 14 November 1946; *Daily Telegraph*, 14, 29 November 1946; *Daily Worker*, 29 November 1946.

Chapter 29   The First Setback

1 *HC Debs*, vol. 431, cols 2068–84, 18 December 1946.

2 H. Dalton, *High Tide and After* (1962), p. 201.

3 *Star*, 3 January 1947.

4 *Daily Herald*, 2 January 1947. Part of this quotation is also used in chapter 8, p. 106.

5 Dalton diary, 17 January 1947, vol. 35.

6 *Daily Herald*, 11 January 1947.

7 *Autobiography*, p. 257.

8 Interview, Dr E. MacLellan.

9 *Star*, 16 January 1947.

10 *Daily Telegraph*, 18 January 1947.

11 Dalton diary, 17 January 1947, vol. 35.

12 *Daily Telegraph*, 18, 22 January 1947.

13 *News Chronicle*, 1 February 1947; *Daily Express*, 1 February 1947; *Star*, 4 February 1947; *Evening Standard*, 11 February 1947.

14 Interview, Dr E. Maclellan.

15 H. Dalton, op. cit., p. 203.

16 Interviews, Miss M. McCulloch, S. C. Leslie, Lord Robens.

17 Interview, Lady Morrison.

18 Interview, S. C. Leslie.

19 Letter from Dr Edward Maclellan to the author.

20 Interviews, Dr E. Hambly, J. W. Raisin.

21 *Autobiography*, p. 257.

22 Interview, J. Christie.

23 Interview, P. Gordon Walker.

24 *Autobiography*, p. 258.

25 Interview, Lord Shinwell.

26 *Daily Herald*, 5 March 1947.

27 Interview, Lady Allen of Hurtwood.

28 *Evening Standard*, 4 March 1947; *Sunday Express*, 9 March 1947; *Star*, 26 March 1947; *News Chronicle*, 26 March 1947.

29 Interview, Sir Allen Daley. *Daily Express*, 26 March 1947.

30 Interview, Sir Allen Daley.

31 *Sunday Express*, 6 April 1947; *Evening News*, 10 April 1947. Interview, Dr E. Maclellan.

32 Morrison to Attlee, 8 April 1947. Morrison papers.

33 Attlee to Morrison, 5 April 1947. Morrison papers.

34 Morrison to Attlee, 8 April 1947. Morrison papers.

35 Whiteley to Morrison, 16 April 1947. Morrison papers.

36 Attlee to Morrison, 16 April 1947. Morrison papers.

37 H. Dalton, op. cit., pp. 237, 158–9, 200–1.

38 *Daily Express*, 17 April 1947.

39 *Daily Herald, Daily Telegraph, Star*, 25 April 1947.

40 *Daily Herald, Daily Telegraph, Daily Express, Star*, 25 April 1947.

41 Interview, P. Gordon Walker.

42 *Daily Telegraph*, 30 April 1947.

43 Frank Owen in *Daily Mail*, 2 May 1947.

44 *HC Debs*, vol. 436, col. 2174, 1 May 1947. *The Times*, 28 April, 2 May 1947; *Daily Telegraph*, 2 May 1947; *Manchester Guardian*, 2 May 1947.

45 Interview, J. W. Raisin.

46 *Evening Standard, Daily Express, Daily Mail*, 2 May 1947.

47 *Star*, 8 May 1947.

48 LLP papers, 9724, 9769, 2 August 1945 and 27 September 1945.

49 LLP papers 10183, 28 November 1946; 10219, 19 December 1946; 10300, 29 March 1947; 10425, 18 September 1947. *Daily Herald*, 18 December 1947.

50 Interview, P. Noel-Baker.

51 Interview, Dr E. Maclellan.

52 *Daily Herald*, 30 June 1947; *News Chronicle*, 30 June 1947.

53 *LPCR*, 1947, pp. 134–7. *Daily Express*, 26 May 1947; *Evening Standard*, 28 May 1947.

54 *HC Debs*, vol. 437, col. 1102, 12 May 1942.

55 *HC Debs*, vol. 440, col. 599, 17 July 1947.

56 *Daily Express*, 22 May, 5 June, 1947.

Chapter 30   The Storm

1 H. Dalton, *High Tide and After* (1962), p. 138.

2 Ibid., pp. 138–9.

3 Ibid., p. 248.

4 Dalton diary, 8 August 1947, vol. 35.

5 Interview, P. Gordon Walker.

6 Interview, Lady Wilson.

7 Interview, D. Jay.

8 Interview, J. Christie.

9 Draft chapter on 'War', p. 62. Morrison papers.

10 Interview, Lord Chandos.

11 *Autobiography*, p. 296.

12 On this whole episode see Dalton diary, 31 July 1947, 8 August 1947, vol. 35, parts of which are printed in H. Dalton, op. cit., pp. 249 ff.

13 *Autobiography*, p. 296. H. Dalton, op. cit., p. 249.

14 H. Dalton, op. cit., pp. 250–1.

15 H. Dalton, op. cit., p. 252. *Daily Express*, 12 August 1947; *Daily Mail*, 12 August 1947.

16 H. Dalton, op. cit., p. 252.

17 Ibid., p. 252.

18 Interview, Lord Attlee.

19 Interview, Lady Wilmot.

20 H. Dalton, op. cit., p. 193.

21 Ibid., p. 195.

22 Dalton to Attlee, 20 July 1947, printed in H. Dalton, op. cit., pp. 195–8.

23 J. Dow, *Management of the British Economy 1945–60* (1968), p. 22.

24 See P. Einzig, *In the Centre of Things* (1960), p. 265.

25 *HC Debs*, vol. 439, cols 2063–5, 8 July 1947.

26 For contemporary editorial comment on the crisis see especially *The Economist*, 12 July, 9 August, 20 September 1947, and *New Statesman*, 9 August, 11 October 1947.

27 *Sunday Express*, 30 March 1947. H. Dalton, op. cit., p. 212.

28 *Daily Herald*, 19 June 1947. Also *The Times*, 17 May 1947; *Daily Herald*, 5 June 1947; *Daily Express*, 3 July 1947.

29 *HC Debs*, vol. 439, col. 1804, 7 July 1947. *The Times*, 8, 22 July 1947.
30 Dalton diary, 2 May 1947, vol. 35.
31 Bridges to Morrison, 5 July 1947. Morrison papers.
32 Morrison to Bridges, 6 July 1947. Copy in Morrison papers.
33 H. Dalton, op. cit., p. 237.
34 *HC Debs*, vol. 439, col. 2066, 8 July 1947.
35 *Daily Express*, 9 July 1945.
36 H. Dalton, op. cit., p. 292. Also Dalton diary, vol. 35, especially 9 August 1947.
37 Dalton diary, 29 July 2947, vol. 35.
38 *Evening Standard*, 29 July 1947.
39 Dalton diary, 4 April 1948, vol. 36.
40 Dalton diary, 30 July 1947, vol. 35.
41 Dalton diary, 31 July 1947, vol. 35.
42 *Daily Express*, 2 August 1947.
43 *Daily Mail*, 2 August 1947.
44 *HC Debs*, vol. 441, cols 1794–1887; *The Times*, 5, 6, 9, 13 August 1947.
45 *Manchester Guardian*, 25 July 1947.
46 *Star*, 25 August 1947; *Daily Herald*, 29 August 1947; *Sunday Express*, 10 August 1947.
47 *News Chronicle*, 18 August 1947; *Daily Express*, 18 August 1947.
48 Dalton diary, 17 August 1947, vol. 35.
49 Dalton diary, 17, 19 August 1947, vol. 35.
50 *Daily Herald*, 21 August 1947; *Daily Express*, 21 August 1947.
51 Dalton diary, 25 August 1947, vol. 35. *The Times*, 22 August 1947; *Daily Mail*, 22 August 1947.
52 *The Times*, 27 August 1947.
53 *Star*, 25 August 1947.
54 *Daily Herald*, 29 August 1947.
55 *Autobiography*, p. 260. Hugh Gaitskell apparently put the main blame on the Treasury and the Bank of England and especially on the advice Dalton received from Eady. (Interview, P. M. Wil ams.)
56 Dalton diary, 14 December 1947, vol. 37.
57 Dalton diary, 19 July 1949, vol. 37.

Chapter 31   The Putsch

1 F. Williams, *A Prime Minister Remembers* (1961), pp. 222–3.
2 H. Dalton, *High Tide and After* (1962), pp. 236–7.
3 Dalton diary, 15 May 1947, vol. 35.
4 Dalton diary, 29 March 1946, vol. 34.
5 Attlee draft autobiography, f. 1/17.
6 H. Dalton, op. cit., p. 238.
7 Interview, Sir William Lawther.
8 Dalton diary, 26 July 1947, vol. 35.
9 H. Dalton, op. cit., pp. 239–40.
10 Interview, C. Mayhew.
11 Dalton diary, 17 August 1945, vol. 35.
12 Interview, C. Mayhew.

13 *Daily Mail*, 20 August 1947.
14 H. Dalton, op. cit., pp. 240–1.
15 Dalton diary, 5 September 1947, vol. 35. Interview, Lord Plowden.
16 Dalton diary, 5 September 1947, vol. 35. H. Dalton, op. cit., pp. 241–2.
17 H. Dalton, op. cit., pp. 241–2.
18 He discussed the situation with Patrick Gordon Walker, who helped him to draft the letter to Cripps. Interview, P. Gordon Walker
19 Copy in Morrison papers.
20 Morrison papers.
21 H. Dalton, op. cit., p. 244–5.
22 Copy in Morrison papers.
23 H. Dalton, op. cit., p. 245.
24 Ibid., p. 245.
25 *Autobiography*, p. 260.
26 *The Times*, 11 September 1947; *Evening News*, 10 September 1947.
27 Morrison to Attlee, 19 September 1947. Copy in Morrison papers.
28 *Daily Herald*, 27 September 1947.
29 *Daily Telegraph*, 23, 24, September 1947.
30 Dalton diary, 10, 18 September 1947, vol. 35.
31 Copy in Morrison papers.
32 Morrison papers.
33 H. Dalton, op. cit., p. 247.
34 Morrison to Attlee, 19 September 1947, copy in Morrison papers.
35 H. Dalton, op. cit., p. 253.
36 Attlee to Morrison, 23 September 1947. Morrison papers.
37 Attlee to Morrison, 3 October 1947. Morrison papers.
38 *Evening Standard*, 30 September 1947.
39 Webb to Morrison, 1 October 1947. Morrison papers.
40 H. Dalton, op. cit., p. 246.

Chapter 32   Mid-Term Miscellany

1 Dalton diary, 18–19 October 1947, col. 35.
2 Gordon Walker to Morrison, Memorandum 6 May 1947. Morrison papers. Gordon Walker also here suggested the creation of Life Peerages.
3 *Daily Express*, 19 June 1947; *The Times*, 20 June 1947.
4 *The Times*, 28 October 1947.
5 Miscellaneous papers on the Parliament bill in Morrison papers. Also interview, Sir Alexander Johnstone.
6 *HC Debs*, vol. 444, cols 36–54, 10 November 1947; *HC Debs*, vol. 445, cols 1074–86, 10 December 1947.
7 *The Times*, 11 November, 11 December 1947.
8 *The Times*, 7 November 1947.
9 Interviews, Dr E. Hambly, J. W. Raisin.
10 Interview, Dr E. Hambly.
11 Maurice Webb writing in *Daily Herald*, 1 January 1948.
12 *Daily Herald*, 4 January 1948.
13 Ibid.

14 *Financial Times*, 31 December 1947.

15 *News Chronicle*, 3 January 1948; *Evening News*, 3 January 1948; *Evening Standard*, 29 December 1948.

16 *Evening News*, 23 January 1948.

17 *Manchester Guardian*, 26 January 1948; *The Times*, 26 January 1948; *Daily Express*, 27 January 1948. According to his Scottish detective, Morrison's knowledge of Burns stood up to rigorous and highly sceptical examination. (A. Black, Memorandum to the author.)

18 H. Morrison, *Government and Parliament* (1964), pp. 187–8. *HC Debs*, vol. 452, col. 1568, 24 June 1948.

19 Interview, M. Nicholson.

20 Interview, K. Younger.

21 By 245 to 222 on 14 April 1948. *HC Debs*, vol. 449, col. 1094, 17 April 1948.

22 *HL Debs*, vol. 157, col. 1072, 20 July 1948.

23 H. Morrison, op. cit., pp. 184–7.

24 *Manchester Guardian*, 11 August 1948.

25 *Manchester Guardian*, 12 August 1948.

26 *Evening Standard, News Chronicle*, 18 August 1948.

27 *Evening News*, 27 August 1948.

28 Attlee to Morrison, 1 September 1948. Morrison papers.

29 Dalton diary, 15 September 1948, vol. 36.

30 Dalton diary, 11 September 1948, vol. 36.

31 *The Times*, 12 January 1948.

32 *Daily Express*, 27 February 1948; *Observer*, 7 March 1948; *The Times*, 14 March 1948.

33 R. Jackson, *Rebels and Whips* (1968), pp. 65–6. NEC Minutes Special Committee of Chairmen of Sub-Committees, vol. 95, 21 April 1948.

34 R. Jackson, op. cit., p. 203.

35 Ibid., p. 204. NEC Minutes Special Committee of Chairmen of Sub-Committees, vol. 95, 13, 23 April 1948.

36 Ibid., pp. 207–11. NEC Minutes, vol. 97, 23 February, 18 May 1949. Zilliacus, it should be noted, was a more independent character than the others, occasionally diverging from the line adopted by communists, and he later rejoined the Labour Party.

37 K. Zilliacus, *Why I was Expelled* (1949), pp. 40 and 50.

38 Interview, J. Christie.

39 Interview, R. H. S. Crossman.

40 Interview, S. Goldberg.

41 *Daily Express*, 5 May 1949. See also C. L. Sulzberger, *A Long Row of Candles* (1969), especially p. 312.

42 *The Times*, 25 January 1950; *Manchester Guardian*, 27 January 1950.

43 Interviews, G. Rogers, G. R. Strauss, R. Mellish.

44 Interview, C. Johnson. *Daily Express*, 26 May 1949.

45 Interviews, Sir Isaac Hayward, Dr E. Hambly.

46 LLP papers 10607, 17 March 1948; 10672, 25 May 1948; 10683, 10 June 1948; 10719, 8 July 1948.

47 Interview, A. Lewis.

48 Interview, R. Mellish.

49 Interview, R. Edmonds.

50 LLP papers 10735, 2 September 1948; 10517, 26 January 1949; 10875, 9 December 1948. *Star*, 25 March 1949; *Manchester Guardian*, 20 March 1949; *The Times*, 31 March 1949.

51 Memorandum, A. Black to author. *The Times*, 9 April 1949.

52 *News Chronicle*, 9 April 1949; *The Times*, 9 April 1949; *Daily Express*, 11 April 1949.

53 Interviews, Mrs H. C. Bentwich, C. W. Gibson, Sir Isaac Hayward.

54 *The Times*, 7 May 1949; *Daily Herald*, 10 May 1949.

55 Cripps to Dalton, 6 June 1949. Dalton papers.

56 Memorandum, 1 June 1949. Dalton papers.

57 Dalton diary, 15 June 1949, vol. 37.

58 Dalton diary, 29 June 1949, vol. 37.

59 Interview, M. Nicholson.

60 Interviews, D. Jay, M. Nicholson. Gaitskell sent Morrison a copy of his memorandum recommending devaluation in August. Gaitskell Papers, p. 22.

61 Cripps was also abroad receiving treatment in a Swiss sanatorium.

62 H. Dalton, op. cit., pp. 321–2. *Autobiography*, p. 279. According to one witness, Churchill had anyway misheard and misunderstood Morrison and later sent a latter of apology. A. Black, memorandum to the author.

63 H. Dalton, op. cit., p. 323.

64 *Manchester Guardian*, 18 August 1949.

65 *Daily Mirror*, 22 August 1949.

Chapter 33   'Consolidation,' and the 1950 Election

1 NEC Minutes, vol. 93, Policy Sub-Committee, 27 May 1946.

2 NEC Minutes, vol. 95, Policy Committee, 15 March 1948.

3 NEC Minutes, vol. 96, Policy and Publicity Committee, 7 July, 19 July, 13 September 1948.

4 Dalton diary, May 1948, vol. 36.

5 *Evening Standard*, 19 May 1948.

6 Dalton diary, 13 May 1948, vol. 36.

7 *LPCR*, 1948, pp. 121–2, p. 130.

8 *Daily Express*, 19 May 1948.

9 On the other hand, R. H. S. Crossman communicated to Morrison's PPS that he was very much impressed by the consolidation theme. S. Taylor to Morrison, 8 June 1948. Morrison papers.

10 Dalton diary, 13 May 1948, vol. 36.

11 *Daily Telegraph*, 14 June 1948.

12 *London News*, June 1947.

13 *HC Debs*, vol. 458, cols 481–94, 17 November 1948.

14 *Daily Telegraph*, 27 November 1948; *Sunday Express*, 17 October 1948; *Manchester Guardian*, 18 October 1948.

15 Interview, E. Davies. NEC Minutes, vol. 96, Policy and Publicity Committee, 17 January 1949.

16 Morrison to Attlee, 29 December 1948. Morrison papers.

17 Attlee to Morrison, 2 January 1949. Morrison papers.

18 *Daily Herald, Daily Mirror*, 17 January 1949.

19 *The Times*, 7 February 1949.

20 NEC Minutes, vol. 96, Policy and Publicity Committee, 17 January 1949. The draft was written by Michael Young.

21 NEC Minutes, vol. 97, 23 February 1949.

22 *Daily Express*, 26 February 1949.

23 *Daily Express*, 24, 25, 26, 28 February 1949; *The Times*, 28 February 1949; *Sunday Times*, 27 February 1949; *Daily Herald*, 28 February 1949.

24 NEC Minutes, vol. 97, 23 March 1949. Dalton diary, 23 March 1949, vol. 37.

25 NEC Minutes, vol. 98, 27 July 1949, 23 November 1949, 21 December 1949. Policy and Publicity Committee, 27 July 1949, 17 October 1949, 14 November 1949, 12 December 1949, 13 December 1949.

26 *The Times*, 6, 7 June 1949.

27 *Evening Standard*, 8 June 1949.

28 *LPCR*, 1949, pp. 152–212.

29 Ibid., p. 212. *The Times*, 9, 11 June 1949; *Evening Standard*, 4 June 1949; *Sunday Express*, 5 June 1949.

30 *Manchester Guardian*, 20 June 1949.

31 *Sunday Express*, 26 June 1949; *The Times*, 27 June 1949.

32 Dalton diary, 10, 11, 12, 21 October 1949, vol. 37.

33 *Manchester Guardian*, 24 September, 3 October 1949; *News Chronicle*, 24 September 1949; *Daily Herald*, 12 October 1949; *Daily Telegraph*, 27 November 1949.

34 Dalton diary, 19 July 1949, vol. 37. F. Williams, *A Prime Minister Remembers* (1961), p. 228.

35 Dalton diary, 11 October 1949, vol. 37.

36 Dalton diary, 13 October 1949, vol. 37. *Daily Express*, 13 October 1949.

37 *The Times*, 14 October 1949.

38 *Autobiography*, p. 268. Also Dalton diary, 7 December 1949, vol. 37.

39 F. Williams, op. cit., p. 228.

40 Dalton diary, 7 December 1949, vol. 37. Also see D. Jay in W. T. Rodgers, (ed.), *Hugh Gaitskell* (1964), esp. p. 95.

41 *Evening News*, 24 December 1949.

42 *Evening Standard*, 28 December 1949.

43 *Daily Herald*, 31 December 1949; *Evening News*, 28 December 1949; *Evening Standard*, 28 December 1949.

44 Interview, Mrs L. Jeger.

45 *News Chronicle*, 4 January 1950.

46 NEC Minutes, vols. 98, 99, Campaign Committee, 26 July, 27 September, 25 October, 22 November 1949, 23 January 1950.

47 Interviews, E. Jay, Lady Phillips.

48 *Autobiography*, p. 289.

49 *Daily Telegraph*, 17 January 1950; *Evening Standard*, 17 January 1950.

50 *Manchester Guardian*, 11, 13 February 1950; *Observer*, 12 February 1950; *Daily Herald*, 13 February 1950.

51 *Daily Express*, 14 February 1950; *Evening Standard*, 14 February 1950.

52 *Daily Telegraph*, 17 February 1950.

53 Interview, A. Bottomley. *The Times*, 20 February 1950; *Manchester Guardian*, 20 February 1950; *Daily Mail*, 20 February 1950.

54 Interview, A. Bottomley.
55 *Yorkshire Post*, 22 February 1950; *Evening News*, 21 February 1950.
56 *Manchester Guardian*, 22 February 1950.
57 Interview, J. W. Raisin.
58 Interview, Dr E. Hambly.
59 *Daily Express*, 24 February 1950.
60 H. G. Nicholas, *The British General Election of 1950* (1951), pp. 306–7.
61 Ibid.
62 Wilfred Sendall, in *News of the World*, 7 March 1965.

Chapter 34   More Consolidation 1950–1951

1 *Daily Telegraph*, 28 February 1950.
2 NEC Minutes, vol. 99, 22 March 1950.
3 *Daily Telegraph*, 26 April 1950.
4 NEC Minutes, vols 99, 100, 19 May 1950, 24 May 1950.
5 Trevor Evans in *Daily Express*, 22 May 1950.
6 *The Times*, 29 April 1950.
7 *News Chronicle*, 29 April 1950.
8 *New Statesman*, 6 May 1950.
9 *The Times*, 9 June 1950.
10 *Tribune*, 16 June 1950.
11 NEC Minutes, vol. 100, 12 and 26 July 1950.
12 Amalgamated Engineering Union, Report to Executive Council on Nationalized Industries, Workers' Participation and Control, 19 January 1951. Papers in possession of E. Davies.
13 Pimlott to Morrison, 23 February 1951. Papers in possession of E. Davies.
14 Dorset Federation of Labour Parties to W. Whiteley, April 1951. Papers in possession of E. Davies.
15 Davies to Morrison, 5 April 1950. Morrison to Davies, 13 April 1950. Papers in possession of E. Davies.
16 H. Morrison memorandum, 21 April 1950. Morrison papers.
17 Davies to Bevin, 6 August 1950. Papers in possession of E. Davies.
18 Morrison to Davies, 1 August 1950. Papers in possession of E. Davies.
19 Davies to Bevin, 6 August 1950. Papers in possession of E. Davies.
20 *Autobiography*, p. 288. H. Morrison, *Government and Parliament* (1959), p. 274. Interview, Lord Longford.
21 Copy in Morrison papers.
22 Copy in Morrison papers.
23 Interview, C. Johnson.
24 R. Jackson, *Rebels and Whips* (1968), pp. 89–90.
25 Ibid., pp. 88–9. *HC Debs*, vol. 473, col. 527, 29 March 1950. *Manchester Guardian*, 1 April 1950.
26 R. Jackson, op. cit., pp. 88–9.
27 Ibid., p. 89.
28 *HC Debs*, vol. 474, col. 1536, 1 May 1950. *Daily Express*, 2 May 1950.
29 *HC Debs*, vol. 474, col. 1904, 4 May 1950.
30 *The Times*, 3 July 1950.

31 *HC Debs*, vol. 477, cols 586–95, 5 July 1950.
32 *Daily Telegraph*, 7 July 1950.
33 *Sunday Express*, 9 July 1950.
34 Interview, J. W. Raisin.
35 *News Chronicle*, 23 August 1950. Interview, Lady Stewart.
36 Interview, J. W. Raisin.
37 *Manchester Guardian*, 22 November 1950; *News Chronicle*, 7, 23 August 1950; *Daily Herald*, 8 August 1950; *Newspaper World*, 10 August 1950.
38 *Observer*, 24 September 1950. *Daily Express*, 23, 25 September 1950.
39 *Daily Herald*, 5 October 1950.
40 *LPCR*, 1950, pp. 111–33.
41 *Daily Herald*, 5 October 1950.
42 L. Hunter, *The Road to Brighton Pier* (1959), pp. 24–5.
43 Interview, Lord Shinwell.
44 Dalton diary, 27 January 1950, vol. 38.
45 Interview, Lord Plowden.
46 Interview, Lord Bridges.
47 Interviews, M. Nicholson, G. Downes.
48 *Daily Herald*, 4, 29 January 1951; *The Times*, 29 January 1951.
49 Dalton diary, 19 February 1951, vol. 39.
50 Interview Lord Shinwell. Gaitskell diary, 16 February 1951. *Daily Mirror*, 9 February 1951; *Daily Mail*, 23 February 1951; *News Chronicle*, 1 March 1951; *Financial Times*, 29 January 1951.
51 *Star*, 24 February 1951; *Manchester Guardian*, 26 February 1951; *Sunday Times*, 4 March 1951; *The Times*, 5 March 1951.
52 *Daily Mail*, 5 March 1951.
53 The following section is based on interviews with: Lord Attlee, Lord Avon, Lady Bacon, R. Boon, A. Bottomley, C. Brook, George Brown, Sir Richard Coppock, E. Davies, G. Deer, G. Downes, P. Gordon Walker, J. Griffiths, Dr E. Hambly, G. Isaacs, R. Jenkins, F. Kay, Dr E. Maclellan, R. Mellish, M. Nicholson, P. Noel-Baker, C. Pannell, J. W. Raisin, Lord Shackleton, Lord Shawcross, Lord Shinwell, Sir David Stephens, Lord Francis-Williams, Lady Wilson, H. Wilson.
54 L. Hunter, op. cit., p. 30 and pp. 28–9.
55 F. Williams, *A Prime Minister Remembers* (1961), p. 243. Interview, Lord Attlee.
56 Interview, Lord Shawcross.
57 Gaitskell diary, 16 February 1951.
58 Interview, Lord Shawcross. Also interview with Morrison in *News Chronicle*, 9 December 1959.
59 Dalton diary, 12 March 1951, vol. 39.
60 *Manchester Guardian*, 10 March 1951.

Chapter 35   Herbert Morrison in 1951: The Peaks Behind

1 *Tailor and Cutter*, November 1946.
2 Interviews, A. Bottomley, R. Mellish, C. Pannell.
3 Interview, J. W. Raisin.
4 Interview, C. Pannell.
5 Interviews, Mr and Mrs Melman, J. Christie, Lord Shackleton.

6 Memorandum from A. Black to the author.

7 Interviews, R. Boon, J. Christie, A. Downes, J. Griffiths, Sir Isaac Hayward, Mrs W. Moore, Mrs E. Richards, Lord Shackleton, Sir Austin Strutt.

8 Morrison to Beaverbrook, 24 April 1950. Beaverbrook to Morrison, 28 April 1950. Beaverbrook Foundation: Beaverbrook papers. *Sunday Express*, 23 April 1950.

9 Interviews, R. Boon, Mrs M. Mandelson.

10 Interview, Mrs C. S. Morrison.

11 Interviews, Sir Robert Fraser, Mrs J. Melman.

12 Interview, Mrs M. Mandelson.

13 Interviews, J. W. Raisin, Mrs J. Melman.

14 Interview, Lady Allen of Hurtwood.

15 Interview, Mrs J. Melman.

16 Interviews, Lord Chandos, J. Trevelyan, private information from other interviews.

17 *Manchester Guardian*, 7 October 1948.

18 *Daily Herald*, 8, 16 February 1949.

19 *Star*, 17 May 1949.

20 *Evening Standard*, 4 October 1949; *Daily Herald*, 5 October 1949.

21 *Daily Herald*, 19 October 1949.

22 *Daily Herald*, 15 May 1950.

23 *Observer*, 15 January 1950.

24 *Sunday Times*, 17 July 1949.

25 Interviews, G. Deer, A. Lewis.

26 *People*, 15 June 1947.

27 *LPCR*, 1950, p. 112.

28 *Daily Herald*, 7 April 1951.

29 Interview, R. Boon.

30 Interview, H. Wilson.

31 Interview, Sir William Murrie.

32 Interviews, Lady Allen, Lord Avon, Lord Bridges, J. Christie, G. Downes, Lady Emmet, P. Gordon Walker, D. Jay, Sir Alexander Johnstone, Lord Shackleton, H. Stenning.

33 Interview, Lord Stow Hill.

34 *People*, 15 June 1947.

35 Interview, Lord Plowden.

Chapter 36   Foreign Secretary, 1951

1 *The Times*, 10 March 1951.

2 *Manchester Guardian*, 10 March 1951.

3 Beaverbrook to Morrison, March 1951. Copy in Beaverbrook Foundation: Beaverbrook papers.

4 Menon to Morrison, 1 May 1951. Morrison papers.

5 *Star*, 10 March 1951.

6 *Evening Standard*, 14 March 1951.

7 For general analyses of this subject see: M. A. Fitzsimons, *The Foreign Policy of the British Labour Government 1945–1951* (1953); A. H. Robertson, *The Council of*

Europe (2nd edition 1961); A. J. Zurcher, *Struggle to Unite Europe 1940–1958* (1958); P. Calvocoressi, *Survey of International Affairs 1951* (1954); R. B. Mandelson-Jones, 'American Attitudes towards Britain's Relations with Western Europe 1947–1956', unpublished thesis at London University.

8 Davies to Dalton, 28 April 1950. Dalton papers.

9 Memorandum, 25 April 1950. Dalton papers (Miscellaneous 1952).

10 Interview, K. Younger.

11 L. Hunter, *The Road to Brighton Pier* (1959), p. 13.

12 Morrison to A. Short, 1 May 1963. Copy in Morrison papers.

13 *The Times*, 14 June 1950.

14 Bevin to Morrison, 22 January 1951. Copy in Dalton papers (1952 Box).

15 Dalton to Attlee, 14 March 1951. Copy in Dalton papers (1952 Box).

16 Dalton diary, 19 April 1951, vol. 40.

17 Interview, E. Davies. *Le Monde*, 23 October 1951. Morrison himself later recalled the change in his attitudes while at the Foreign Office in his letter to A. Short, 1 May 1963. Copy in Morrison papers.

18 *The Times*, 3, 4 August 1951.

19 Dalton to Attlee, 10 July 1951. Copy in Morrison papers.

20 See the summary in Dalton diary, August 1951, vol. 41.

21 Memorandum, A. Black to the author.

22 *The Times*, 22 March 1951.

23 Interview, D. Jay. Morrison interview in *News Chronicle*, 8 December 1959.

24 *The Times*, 1, 8 February 1951.

25 Interview, H. Wilson.

26 Dalton diary, 30 October 1950, vol. 38.

27 Interview, J. Freeman.

28 Dalton diary, 22 March 1951, vol. 39.

29 *News Chronicle*, 4 April 1951.

30 Interview, Dr E. Maclellan. *Manchester Guardian, Daily Telegraph, Evening News*, 3 April 1951.

31 Dalton diary, 9 April 1951, vol. 40.

32 *HC Debs*, vol. 486, cols 777–81, 9 April 1951.

33 Dalton diary, 11 April 1951, vol. 40.

34 Attlee to Morrison, 10 April 1951. Morrison papers.

35 Interview, J. Freeman.

36 Attlee to Morrison, 10 April 1951. Morrison papers.

37 *Daily Express*, 12 April 1951. Dalton diary .12 April 1951, vol. 40.

38 Interview, H. Wilson.

39 Dalton diary, 19, 20 April 1951, vol. 40.

40 Interview, J. Freeman.

41 L. Hunter, op. cit., pp. 34–5.

42 Ibid., p. 36.

43 Interview, Lord Shawcross.

44 Interviews, Lord Shawcross, Lady Wilson.

45 Interviews, Lord Robens, Lord Shawcross.

46 *HC Debs*, vol. 487, cols 34–43, 228–31, 23 April 1951.

47 Freeman to Dalton, 23 April 1951. Dalton papers.

48 *Daily Express*, 24 April 1951.

49 Dalton diary, 24 April 1951, vol. 40.
50 Boon memorandum, 24 April 1951. Copy in Morrison papers.
51 Dalton diary, 24 April 1951, vol. 40.
52 Interview, Lord Attlee.
53 Interviews, G. Isaacs, Lord Shinwell.
54 Interview, H. Wilson.
55 Interview, J. Freeman.
56 *Autobiography*, pp. 266–7.
57 Interview, H. Wilson.
58 *HC Debs*, vol. 485, cols 1059–63, 12 March 1951.
59 *Evening Standard*, 10 May 1951; *Daily Mail*, 10 May 1951; *Sunday Dispatch*, 13 May 1951.
60 *HC Debs*, vol. 487, cols 1953–4, 9 May 1951.
61 *Daily Telegraph*, 10 May 1951.
62 Lord Ismay, *Memoirs* (1960), pp. 448–52.
63 Interviews, Dr E. Hambly, M. Nicholson. Morrison interview in *Daily Mail*, 9 May 1951.
64 *HC Debs*, vol. 461, col. 546, 10 February 1949.
65 Interview, Sir Richard Coppock.
66 See above, p. 309.
67 *Sunday Pictorial*, 29 April 1951.
68 Interview, Lord Robens.
69 *Daily Express*, 16 November 1950.
70 *Daily Express*, 3 May 1951.
71 *The Times, Daily Telegraph, Daily Express*, 5 May 1951.
72 *Observer*, 6 May 1951.
73 *The Times, Daily Express, Evening Standard*, 15 May 1951.
74 Interview, Lord Henderson.
75 *The Times*, 25 May 1951.
76 Interview, Lord Henderson.
77 Interview, Sir Roderick Barclay.
78 *Daily Express*, 25 May 1951. Also *Sunday Times*, 20 May 1951; *Evening Standard*, 21 May 1951; *The Times*, 22, 23, 24 May 1951; *Daily Express*, 24 May 1951; *Manchester Guardian*, 25 May 1951; *Daily Herald*, 25 May 1951.
79 For this episode see Memorandum, 19 July 1963, in Morrison papers.
80 *HC Debs*, vol. 488, cols 1669–70, 11 June 1951.
81 See: E. Windrich, *British Labour's Foreign Policy* (1952); A. Ford, *Anglo-Iranian Dispute 1951–2*(1954); J. Frankel, 'The Anglo-Iranian Dispute', in Keeton G. W. and Schwarzenberger G., eds., *The Year Book of World Affairs*, vol. 6 (1952), pp. 56–74.
82 *HC Debs*, vol. 489, cols 519–26, 21 June 1951.
83 *HC Debs*, vol. 489, cols 827–8, 21 June 1951.
84 *Sunday Times*, 24 June 1951.
85 *The Times, Yorkshire Post, Daily Telegraph*, 23 June 1951.
86 *Daily Telegraph*, 23 June 1951.
87 *Observer*, 17 June 1951.
88 Interview, Sir Roderick Barclay.
89 Dalton diary, 2 July 1951, vol. 41.
90 *HC Debs*, vol. 490, cols 424–8, 11 July 1951.

91 C. L. Sulzberger, *A Long Row of Candles* (1969), p. 574.

92 Interview, R. Boon.

93 Memorandum, A. Black to the author. Interview, Lady Wilson.

94 Interview, Sir Austin Strutt.

95 *HC Debs*, vol. 490, cols 835–42, 16 July 1951; vol. 491, col. 34, 23 July 1951. *Daily Telegraph*, 9 July 1951.

96 *HC Debs*, vol. 491, col. 989, 30 July 1951.

97 *HC Debs*, vol. 491, col. 695, 30 July 1951. Apparently Morrison asked his secretary to write phonetic pronunciations of foreign words in the margin – and this is what he misread. (Interview, Sir Roderick Barclay.)

98 *The Times*, 9 August 1951; *Evening Standard*, 13 August 1951; *Evening News*, 13 August 1951; *Daily Telegraph*, 15 August 1951.

99 *The Times*, 7, 23, 27 August 1951.

100 Interview, J. W. Raisin.

101 *News Chronicle*, 7 September 1951; *Evening Standard*, 18 August 1951; *Sunday Times*, 19 August 1951; *Daily Worker*, 1 September 1951.

102 *Evening News*, 31 August 1951.

103 *Daily Telegraph*, 4 September 1951.

104 *Manchester Guardian*, 7 September 1951; *News Chronicle*, 7 September 1951.

105 Interview, K. Younger.

106 *Daily Herald*, 10 September 1951. Memorandum, A. Black to the author.

107 *Daily Telegraph*, 11, 14 September 1951.

108 D. Acheson, *Present at the Creation* (1969), pp. 556, 559.

109 *News Chronicle*, 20 September 1951; *Sunday Express*, 23 September 1951.

110 *Autobiography*, p. 283.

111 Dalton diary, 19 September 1951, vol. 42.

112 Attlee to Morrison, 27 May 1951. Morrison papers.

113 Dalton diary, 29 May, 1, 26 June, 2 July 1951, vol. 41.

114 Morrison to Attlee, 6 July 1951. Copy in Morrison papers.

115 Dalton diary, 4, 16 September 1951, vol. 42. J. Wheeler-Bennett, *George VI* (1958), pp. 791–2.

116 Memorandum, A. Black to the author.

117 Ibid.

118 *Sunday Chronicle*, 30 September 1951; *Evening Standard*, 27 September 1951; *Daily Telegraph*, 29 September 1951.

119 NEC Minutes, vol. 103, 24 September 1951. Dalton diary, 24 September 1951, vol. 42.

120 Interview, K. Younger.

121 Dalton diary, 27 September 1951, vol. 42.

122 Dalton diary, 16 September 1951, vol. 42.

123 *Evening Standard*, 1 October 1951.

124 *The Times*, 1 October 1951.

125 *The Times*, 2, 3 October 1951.

126 *Daily Express*, 3 October 1951.

127 *Daily Telegraph*, 4 October 1951.

128 *Evening Standard*, 5 October 1951.

129 *LPCR* 1951, p. 129. *The Times*, 4 October 1951.

130 *Daily Telegraph*, 5, 6 October 1951. *Daily Express*, 6 October 1951.

131 *Sunday Express*, 7 October 1951.

132 *Observer*, 7 October 1951.

133 *Sunday Times*, 7 October 1951.

134 Interview, K. Younger.

135 On this section: interviews with E. Davies, P. Gordon Walker, Lord Henderson, Lord Stow Hill, K. Younger and a senior Foreign Office official.

136 P. Calvocoressi, *Survey of International Affairs 1951* (1954), pp. 260–92.

137 *Daily Mail*, 10 October 1951; *Evening Standard*, 12, 16 October 1951.

138 *Survey of International Affairs 1951*, pp. 260–92.

139 *Evening Standard*, 16 October 1951; *The Times*, 17 October 1951.

140 Morrison to Beaverbrook, 6 September, 8, 15 October 1951. Beaverbrook to Morrison, 12 September, 11 October 1951. Beaverbrook Foundation: Beaverbrook papers.

141 *Daily Herald*, 11 October 1951.

142 *Sunday Times*, 21 October 1951; *The Times*, 22 October 1951.

143 *Daily Telegraph*, 24 October 1951.

144 *Manchester Guardian*, 25 October 1951.

145 *Daily Mail*, 10 October 1951; *Evening Standard*, 12, 16 October 1951. *Daily Express*, 16 October 1951; *The Times*, 17 October 1951.

146 Interview, J. W. Raisin. LLP papers 11269, 20 April 1950; 11272, 20 April 1950; 11530, 1 February 1951; 11538, 1 February 1951.

147 *Daily Express*, 26 October 1951; *Evening Standard*, 26 October 1951.

148 Frank Owen in *Daily Express*, 10 March 1951.

149 Dalton diary, 16 September 1951, vol. 42.

150 Interview, Lord Avon.

151 Information communicated by P. M. Williams.

152 Interview, K. Younger.

153 Interviews, P. Noel-Baker, K. Younger.

154 Interview, Lord Henderson.

155 Memorandum, A. Black to the author.

156 Interviews, Sir Roderick Barclay, Sir Geoffrey Furlonge.

157 Interviews, Lord Bridges, G. Rogers, Lord Silkin.

158 Interviews, Lord Shackleton, Sir Roderick Barclay.

159 Interview, M. Nicholson.

160 Interview, C. Johnson. For this general analysis, interviews with Lord Avon, Sir Roderick Barclay, R. Boon, Sir Geoffrey Furlonge, P. Gordon Walker, C. Mayhew, P. Noel-Baker, Lord Shackleton, Lord Shawcross, K. Younger.

161 Interview, Sir Roderick Barclay.

162 Interview, Sir Roderick Barclay. Also interviews, Lord Avon and P. Gordon Walker.

163 Interview, E. Davies.

164 Interview, Sir Roderick Barclay.

165 Interviews, Lord Henderson, G. Isaacs, G. Rogers, Lord Stow Hill, and a senior Foreign Office official.

Chapter 37 Recriminations and More Defeats, 1951–1953

1 Interview, Mrs J. Melman.

2 Morrison interview in *Daily Mirror*, 11 January 1952.
3 Interview, R. Boon.
4 Memorandum, A. Black to the author.
5 *Daily Telegraph*, 30 November, 14 December 1951.
6 Henry Fairlie in *Daily Mail*, 22 June 1959.
7 *Daily Herald*, 5 November 1951.
8 Churchill to Morrison, 12 November 1951. Morrison papers.
9 NEC Minutes, vols 104, 105 and 106. Policy and Publicity Sub-Committee, 3 December 1951, 18 February, 17 March, 21 April, 23 June 1952. Financial and Economic Policy Sub-Committee, 1 July, 16 September 1952.
10 Dalton diary, 1 November 1951, vol. 42.
11 3 March 1952, printed in N. Nicolson (ed.), *H. Nicolson, Diaries and Letters*, vol. III (1968), p. 222. *HC Debs*, vol. 494, cols 54–71, 19 November 1951, and vol. 496, cols 945–63, 26 February 1952.
12 *Observer*, 2 March 1952.
13 S. Evans Memorandum, 12 February 1952, copy in possession of the author.
14 Dalton diary, 1 May 1952, vol. 43.
15 Interviews, Lord Robens, K. Younger.
16 Interview, C. Pannell.
17 *News Chronicle*, 29 April 1952; *Manchester Guardian*, 9 May 1952; *Yorkshire Post*, 10 May 1952.
18 NEC Minutes, vol. 106–11, 1952–3, Transport Joint Sub-Committee.
19 *Manchester Guardian*, 1 September 1952; *Daily Herald*, 11 September 1952.
20 *The Times*, 15 September 1952.
21 Interview, Mrs J. Melman.
22 R. Jackson, *Rebels and Whips* (1968), p. 116.
23 *News Chronicle*, 20 March 1952; *Daily Telegraph*, 20 March 1952.
24 *Daily Express*, 17 June 1952; *Yorkshire Post*, 7, 9 August 1952; *People*, 17 August 1952. Dalton diary, 31 May 1952, vol. 43.
25 *Daily Telegraph*, 16 August 1952.
26 *Evening Standard*, 29 September 1952.
27 Dalton diary, September 1952, vol. 44.
28 Interview, C. Pannell.
29 *LPCR*, 1952, pp. 107–12.
30 *Evening Standard*, 1 October 1952; *Evening News*, 6 October 1952.
31 *LPCR*, 1952, p. 127.
32 Interview, Sir Trevor Evans.
33 *Man and Metal*, 13 October 1952.
34 Interview, Lord Williamson.
35 Interview, Lord Williamson.
36 Interview, H. Wilson.
37 *The Times*, 6 October 1952.
38 *Manchester Guardian*, 11 October 1952.
39 *HC Debs*, vol. 508, cols 1586, 1593, 1708, 1710, 3 December 1952; vol. 509, cols 261, 574, 678–9, 734, 749, 751, 8 December 1952 and 11 December 1952.
40 *Daily Express*, 24 April 1953.
41 *Daily Mirror*, 25 April 1953.
42 Dalton diary, 24 October 1953, vol. 44.

43 S.Evans Memorandum, 12 February 1952. Also *Autobiography*, pp. 249 and 194–5.
44 See disparaging comment in *News Chronicle*, 13 April and 9 June 1953, and in *Manchester Guardian*, 13 April 1953.
45 Interview, S. Evans.
46 This section is based on interviews with S. Evans, Sir Trevor Evans, P. Gordon Walker, Sir William Lawther, Lord Williamson, Lady Wilson. Also see L. Hunter, *The Road to Brighton Pier* (1959), pp. 66–70.
47 *London News*, November 1953.
48 L. Hunter, op. cit., p. 69.
49 Interview, Lady Wilson. L. Hunter, op. cit., p. 68.
50 *Evening Standard*, 28 September 1953.
51 Interviews, Sir William Lawther, Lord Williamson.

Chapter 38   Rising from Despair, 1953–1955

1 Interview, K. H. Kent.
2 Morrison to Beaverbrook, 29 July 1953. Beaverbrook Foundation: Beaverbrook papers.
3 Interview, Dr E. Maclellan.
4 Interview, Lady Summerskill.
5 *Lewisham Journal and Borough News*, 17 July 1953.
6 Dalton diary, 15 July 1953, vol. 45.
7 Interview, Mrs G. G. Downie.
8 Interview, Lady Allen of Hurtwood.
9 Interview, G. Rogers.
10 Interview, Mrs J. Melman.
11 Interview, Mrs J. Melman.
12 Interview, Lady Allen of Hurtwood.
13 Interview, Mrs J. Melman.
14 Interview, D. N. Chester.
15 *Daily Express*, 29 April 1954; *Daily Herald*, 29 April 1954.
16 *Manchester Guardian*, 29 April 1954.
17 Interview, D. N. Chester.
18 *HC Debs*, vol. 520, cols 156–71, 4 November 1953;
   HC Debs, vol. 521, cols 1061–70, 1 December 1953;
   HC Debs, vol. 522, cols 65–87, 14 December 1953.
19 *HC Debs*, vol. 525, cols 1457–74, 25 March 1954;
   HC Debs, vol. 527, cols 204–9, 304–6, 314–17, 489–93, 1035–45, 4 and 11 May 1954;
   HC Debs, vol. 531, cols 245–6, 292–6, 367–70, 27 July 1954.
20 See Morrison's article in *Daily Sketch*, 12 June 1953.
21 Dalton diary, 15, 24, 28, 29 July 1952, vol. 44.
22 NEC Minutes, vol. 112, 24 February 1954. *Daily Express*, 25 February 1954.
23 *HC Debs*, vol. 524, cols 417–33, 25 February 1954.
24 *HC Debs*, vol. 526, cols 134–51, 5 April 1954.
25 *HC Debs*, vol. 526, col. 971, 13 April 1954.
26 Dalton diary, 13, 14 April 1954, vol. 46. L. Hunter, *The Road to Brighton Pier* (1959), pp. 75–6.
27 *Manchester Guardian*, 3 May 1954.

28 Dalton diary, 5 May 1954, vol. 46.
29 *Daily Express*, 19, 20 May 1954. See also Dalton diary, 5, 6 May 1954, vol. 46.
30 Speeches, 27 February, 5 March, 6 June, 24 July 1954, copies in Morrison-Boon papers.
31 *LPCR*, 1954, pp. 106–8. *Daily Express*, 29 September 1954.
32 Dalton diary, 9, 11 November 1954, vol. 46. *Daily Express*, 12 November 1954.
33 Interviews, Lady Morrison, J. W. Raisin. *Evening Standard*, 18 December 1954.
34 Interview, Mrs J. Melman.
35 Interview, Lady Wilson.
36 *Manchester Guardian*, 20, 21 December 1954; *The Times*, 21 December 1954.
37 *News Chronicle*, 18 December 1954; *Daily Express*, 12 July 1958.
38 *Yorkshire Post*, 1 January 1955; *Evening Standard*, 3 January 1955; *Daily Express*, 6, 7, 10 January 1955; *Daily Mail*, 7 January 1955.
39 *Evening Standard*, 25 January 1955.
40 *Observer*, 30 January 1955.
41 *HC Debs*, vol. 537, col. 565, 17 February 1955.
42 On this episode see: R. Jackson, *Rebels and Whips* (1968), p. 128; L. Hunter, op. cit., pp. 93–113. Dalton diary, 7, 15, 16 March 1955, vol. 47. *Daily Express*, 17, 24 March 1955.
43 NEC Minutes, vol. 116, 23 and 30 March 1954. L. Hunter, op. cit., pp. 107, 120.
44 *Manchester Guardian*, 21 April 1955.
45 *Yorkshire Post*, 3 May 1955; *The Times*, 7 May 1955; *Daily Mail*, 9 May 1955; *Daily Telegraph*, 14, 17 May 1955.
46 *Daily Telegraph*, 19, 20, 25 May 1955; *Daily Mail*, 20 May 1955; *Observer*, 23 May 1955; *London News*, June 1955.
47 *The Times*, 29 May 1955.

Chapter 39 The Final Bid, 1955

1 Interview, Lady Wilson. L. Hunter, *The Road to Brighton Pier* (1959), p. 123. Hunter's book, often denounced by contemporary Labour politicians, is a lively and not inaccurate record of the party's troubles at the time.
2 Interview, Lord Robens.
3 See especially *Reynolds News*, 4 January 1953.
4 Interview, C. Pannell and Pannell memorandum to the author, 28 October 1968. Interview, Lord Shawcross.
5 Interview, Lord Robens.
6 Interview, S. Evans.
7 21 March 1955, Gaitskell papers.
8 Dalton diary, 31 March, 7 April 1955, vol. 47.
9 H. Dalton, *High Tide And After* (1962), pp. 415–6. L. Hunter op. cit., pp. 115–6. *Daily Express*, 4 June 1955; *Daily Telegraph*, 6 June 1955.
10 L. Hunter, op. cit., p. 121. H. Dalton, op. cit., pp. 421–2.
11 Diary, 29 July 1955. Morrison papers.
12 *Sunday Express*, 28 August 1955.
13 *News Chronicle*, 15 September 1955; *Daily Express*, 16 September 1955; *Observer*, 18 September 1955. L. Hunter, op. cit., pp. 133–6.
14 *LPCR*, 1955, pp. 149–51, 162–4, 204.
15 L. Hunter, op. cit., pp. 137–43. *Manchester Guardian*, 10 October 1955.

16 *Daily Express*, 14 October 1955.
17 *Evening Standard*, 12 October 1955; *Evening News*, 10 October 1955; *Observer*, 16 October 1955.
18 L. Hunter, op. cit., pp. 142–3.
19 Ibid., pp. 147–8.
20 *HC Debs*, vol. 545, cols 683–700, 31 October 1955.
21 *Sunday Times*, 6 November 1955.
22 *Observer*, 6 November 1955; *Daily Telegraph*, 1 November 1955; *Daily Express*, 1 November 1955. Dalton diary, 31 October 1955, vol. 47.
23 Interview, D. Jay. See also L. Hunter, op. cit., pp. 164–7. *Daily Herald*, 12 November 1955.
24 Interviews, Mrs J. Melman, Lady Morrison, J. W. Raisin.
25 Interviews, Mrs F. Corbet, P. Gordon Walker, C. Mayhew, Lord Robens, G. R. Strauss, Lord Williamson. Dalton diary, 3 November 1955, vol. 47. *Yorkshire Post*, 2 December 1955; *Sunday Times*, 4 December 1955.
26 Interviews, G. Brown, G. Isaacs, C. Mayhew, R. Mellish, Lord Robens, Lord Shawcross, G. R. Strauss.
27 L. Hunter, op. cit., pp. 167–8.
28 Interviews, Mrs F. Corbet, G. Isaacs, C. Mayhew, Lord Shawcross.
29 Interview, R. Mellish.
30 *Evening Standard*, 7 December 1955; *Observer*, 11 December 1955.
31 Diary, 8 December 1955. Morrison papers.
32 L. Hunter, op. cit., pp. 173–4.
33 Sir Frederick Messer to the authors, undated, 1969. Dalton diary, 2 March 1956, vol. 48.
34 Interview, Mrs L. Jeger.
35 Interview, G. Rogers.
36 Interview, H. Wilson.
37 Interviews, C. W. Gibson, P. Gordon Walker, G. Rogers.
38 Interview, C. Pannell.
39 Interview, J. W. Raisin.
40 Interview in *Sunday Express*, 11 December 1955.
41 *Sunday Express*, 11 December 1955.
42 *Observer*, 11 December 1955.
43 *Daily Express*, 14 December 1955.
44 *Star*, 14 December 1955; *Evening Standard*, 14 December 1955.
45 Interviews, F. Barlow, C. Johnson.
46 Interview, Lord Robens.
47 Memorandum, C. Pannell to the author, 28 October 1968.
48 Interview, J. Parker.
49 Interviews, F. Barlow, C. Johnson, A. Lewis, Mrs L. Middleton, Lord Wigg.
50 *The Times, Daily Express, Daily Herald, Manchester Guardian*, 15 December 1955. This whole section was assisted by interviews with: Lord Attlee, F. Barlow, A. Bottomley, G. Brown, D. N. Chester, Mrs F. Corbet, R. H. S. Crossman, G. Deer, S. Evans, M. Foot, J. Griffiths, Lady Gaitskell, P. Gordon Walker, Dr E. Hambly, G. Isaacs, D. Jay, E. Jay, Mrs L. Jeger, C. Johnson, A. Lewis, C. Mayhew, R. Mellish, Mrs J. Melman, Mrs L. Middleton, Lady Morrison, I. Mikardo, C. Pannell, J. Parker, J. W. Raisin, Mrs E. Richards, Lord Robens, G. Rogers, Lord Shawcross, Lord Shinwell, G. R. Strauss, Lord Williamson, H. Wilson.

Chapter 40 Nursing His Wounds, 1955–1959

1 *Daily Express*, 19 December 1955.
2 Interviews, Dr E. Maclellan, Lady Morrison.
3 Interview, Mrs E. Richards.
4 *Daily Telegraph*, 21 December 1955; *The Times*, 14 February 1956
5 Interview, Lady Morrison. *Daily Express*, 24 December 1955.
6 Morrison to Boon, 3 December 1955. Morrison–Boon papers.
7 Interview, Lord Williamson.
8 Interview, C. Pannell.
9 Interview, Mrs J. Melman.
10 C. King, *Memoirs* (1969), p. 130.
11 Dalton diary, 16 October 1959, vol. 51.
12 *Daily Express*, 19 January 1959.
13 *Evening Standard*, 11 March 1957; *Daily Express*, 12 March 1957. Dalton diary 11 March 1957, vol. 49.
14 Interviews, F. G. Kay, Lady Reading, Mrs E. Richards.
15 Interview, Lady Morrison. Profile in *Daily Herald*, 29 November 1955.
16 Interview, Lady Morrison.
17 Interviews, Mrs G. G. Downie, Mrs M. Mandelson, Mrs J. Melman, Mrs C. S. Morrison.
18 *Daily Mail*, 24 March 1956; *Evening Standard*, 30 April, 4 May 1956.
19 *London News*, February 1957; *Daily Express*, 22 December 1956, 4 January 1957.
20 *Daily Herald*, 20 November 1957; *Evening Standard*, 13, 23 February 1957; *Star*, 14 June 1957.
21 Interview, Mrs H. C. Bentwich.
22 Dalton diary, 2 February 1956, vol. 48. *Daily Mail*, 3 February 1956, 13 May 1959.
23 *HC Debs*, vol. 548, col. 2579, 16 February 1956.
24 Interview, Mrs J. Melman.
25 See his article in *News of the World*, 20 November 1955. Interview, Mrs J. Melman.
26 *Empire News*, 19 February 1956.
27 *HC Debs*, vol. 557, cols 1653–61, 2 August 1956.
28 *HC Debs*, vol. 529, col. 18, 21 June 1954; *HC Debs*, vol. 545, col. 673, 31 October 1955.
29 Interview, Lord Avon.
30 *HC Debs*, vol. 591, cols 222–36, 8 July 1958. H. Morrison, *Government and Parliament* (1959), pp. 357-61. Interview, G. R. Strauss.
31 Interviews, R. Edmonds, P. Robshaw.
32 LLP papers, no. 13304, 2 November 1956.
33 LLP papers no. 13825, 3 July 1958. *Star*, 12 December 1958; *Daily Telegraph*, 13 December 1958.
34 *London News*, January 1959.
35 Interviews, A. Richman, P. Robshaw.
36 Interviews, R. Edmonds, Lady Morrison, J. W. Raisin, Mrs M. Raisin, P. Robshaw.
37 *Daily Telegraph*, 20 June 1957. His successor was Carol Johnson, previously secretary to the parliamentary party.

38 *Daily Mail*, 22 June 1959; *News of the World*, 20 June 1959; *The Times*, 25 June 1959.

39 *Daily Telegraph*, 9 July 1959; *The Times*, 8 July 1959.

40 *Daily Mail*, 23 July 1959.

41 *Manchester Guardian*, 26 October 1959.

42 *Daily Express*, 10 October 1959; *Daily Telegraph*, 24 October 1959; *Manchester Guardian*, 26 October 1959.

43 Macmillan to Morrison, 10 September 1959. Morrison papers.

44 Morrison to Macmillan, 11 September 1959. Copy in Morrison papers.

45 *Daily Herald*, 27 October 1959.

46 *Daily Express*, 25 September 1959.

47 Ibid.

48 Interviews, Sir Richard Coppock, Dr E. Maclellan, Lady Morrison.

49 Interviews, Sir Richard Coppock, Lady Morrison, Mrs E. Richards.

50 Interview, C. W. Gibson.

51 Morrison to Chester, 20 October 1959. Nuffield papers, Morrison File I.

52 *Daily Mail*, 4 November 1959.

53 *Evening Standard*, 21 October 1959; *Daily Telegraph*, 22 October 1959.

54 *News Chronicle*, 18 November 1959; *Daily Express*, 18 November 1959.

Chapter 41   Light and Shadows, 1959–1965

1 Among the subjects on which he spoke during 1959–62 were: scientific policy, telephone tapping, foreign affairs, cinema taxation, relations with the Irish Republic, departmental reorganization, security arrangements, office conditions, economics and taxation, prisons, Covent Garden Market, the press, the channel tunnel, immigration, the new Cunard liner, and various local authority matters. See *HL Debs*, vol. 219, cols 983–6; vol. 220, cols 205–11, cols 529–32; vol. 222, cols 1094–1102; vol. 223, cols 1061–5; vol. 224, cols 832–41; vol. 225, col. 30; vol. 226, cols 66–76, cols 460–7; vol. 227, cols 482–7; vol. 229, cols 1096–7; vol. 230, cols 142–5, cols 1356–7; vol. 231, cols 536–8, cols 1261–8; vol. 232, cols 127–8, cols 296–7, cols 1213–16, col. 711; vol. 233, cols 327–89, cols 1174–90, 1038–47; vol. 234, col. 551; vol. 235, cols 235–42; vol. 237, cols 223–4; vol. 242, cols 851–4; vol. 244, cols 32–3; vol. 245, cols 1103–1113.

2 *HL Debs*, vol. 227, cols 62–78, 174–8, 7 December 1960.

3 *HL Debs*, vol. 234, cols 173–8, 2 August 1961. Also his article in *Sunday Pictorial*, 3 February 1963.

4 *HL Debs*, vol. 242, cols 618–30, 18 July 1962; *HL Debs*, vol. 244, cols 646–50, 14 November 1962.

5 Interview, Lady Morrison.

6 Interview, Lord Silkin.

7 Interview, Lord Willis.

8 Interview, Lord Longford.

9 *Daily Mail*, 27 September 1960; *Daily Telegraph*, 27 September 1960; *Daily Express*, 3 October 1960.

10 *Daily Express*, 25 October 1960.

11 *London News*, August 1961.

12 LLP papers, 14096, 1 February 1960; 15178, 21 December 1961.

13 *Daily Sketch*, 19 October 1960.
14 LLP papers, 14938, June 1961.
15 Interview, Lady Morrison. *Daily Herald*, 26 September 1960; *Daily Mail*, 25 October 1960; *Evening News*, 26 October 1960.
16 Interviews, G. Deer, R. Edmonds, R. Mellish, G. Rogers.
17 *Daily Telegraph*, 4 November 1959, 18 June 1960.
18 *Daily Mail*, 12 March 1960; *Evening Standard*, 15 November, 14 December 1960. Morrison to R. Brown, 17 January 1962. Morrison papers.
19 *Evening Standard*, 11 November 1959.
20 *Daily Mirror*, 24 March 1960; *Daily Express*, 29 April 1960.
21 Beaverbrook to Morrison, 1 and 8 June 1962. Morrison to Beaverbrook, 30 May, 6 June 1962. Beaverbrook Foundation: Beaverbrook papers.
22 *Evening Standard*, 16 October 1962.
23 Interviews, J. Trevelyan, Sir Austin Strutt.
24 Interviews, Lady Morrison, J. Trevelyan.
25 Morrison to Trevelyan, 12 May, 17 April 1962. Board of Film Censors papers. Also *Daily Mirror*, 3 May 1962; *Daily Express*, 3 May 1962.
26 Interview, J. Trevelyan.
27 18 May 1960. Board of Film Censors papers.
28 *Daily Herald*, 16 June 1960.
29 Morrison to Lew Grade, 17 April 1963. Board of Film Censors' papers.
30 *Daily Mail*, 7 November 1960.
31 *HL Debs*, vol. 260, cols 569–74, 852–3, 24 July 1964.
32 *Daily Mail*, 7 November 1960.
33 Interview, F. G. Kay.
34 D. Barker to Morrison, 10 February 1960. Morrison papers.
35 Morrison to L. Russell, 24 February 1960. Copy in Morrison papers.
36 Normanbrook to Morrison, 18 and 24 March 1960. Morrison papers.
37 *HL Debs*, vol. 251, cols 1320–1, 9 July 1963.
38 *HL Debs*, vol. 255, cols 1112–3, 26 February 1964; *HL Debs*, vol. 257, cols 492–501, 15 April 1964.
39 *HL Debs*, vol. 257, cols 322–4, 13 April 1964.
40 *HC Debs*, vol. 574, cols 1130–45, 30 July 1957.
41 Interviews, R. Edmonds, J. W. Raisin.
42 *London News*, June 1958.
43 *The Times*, 18 September 1958.
44 *HL Debs*, vol. 227, cols 1025–51, 21 December 1960.
45 Interviews, Sir Harold Banwell, Sir Francis Hill, P. Robshaw. *Daily Telegraph*, 12, 21 April 1961; *London News*, June 1961.
46 *HL Debs*, vol. 235, cols 1147–51, 29 November 1961.
47 *HL Debs*, vol. 238, cols 170–89, 241, 300–4, 14 March 1962.
48 *Guardian*, 3 November 1962.
49 Interviews, Lord Henderson, Lord Longford, Lord Silkin, Lord Willis.
50 *Daily Express*, 2 September 1963.
51 Interviews, F. G. Kay, Lady Morrison.
52 *Daily Telegraph*, 22 January 1964.
53 Interview, Lord Willis.
54 Interview, Dr E. Maclellan.

55 Interviews, Lady Summerskill, Dame Joan Vickers.

56 Morrison to Chester, 26 November 1964. Nuffield papers, Morrison File II.

57 Interview, Lord Citrine.

58 *Sunday Express*, 6 December 1964.

59 Interview, J. Trevelyan. Morrison to Trevelyan, 2 January 1965, Trevelyan to Morrison, 4 January 1965. Board of Film Censors papers.

60 Interview, Dr E. Maclellan.

61 *The Times*, 8 March 1965.

62 Interview, Dr E. Maclellan.

63 *Evening Standard*, 30 March 1965. Interview, P. Robshaw.

Appendices

1 *General Tables:*

Table (a): Parliamentary Elections in London.
Table (b): LCC Elections.
Table (c): Metropolitan Borough Elections.
Table (d): Labour and the Boards of Guardians.

2 *LCC Tables:*

Table (e): Expenditure on Rate Services.
Table (f): Rate in the £ levied.
Table (g): Capital Expenditure of Year.
Table (h): Debt Charges from the Rates.

1 *General Tables*

Table (*a*)   *Parliamentary Elections in London*

Date	Labour		Conservative		Liberal		Total Vote
	Votes	Seats	Votes	Seats	Votes	Seats	
1918	109,800	2	375,000	44	182,500	15	751,300
1922	323,400	9	577,700	43	308,500	9	1,255,200
1923	424,100	22	429,000	29	331,000	11	1,184,100
1924	568,600	19	682,100	39	187,800	3	1,459,600
1929	784,600	36	754,200	24	353,900	2	1,907,700
1931	562,500	5	1,106,800	51	86,800	4	1,816,800
1935	759,500	22	1,131,500	39	57,505	1	1,970,300

Table (b)

LCC Elections

Date	Labour			Municipal Reform (Conservative)			Progressive (Liberal)			Communists	Fascists	Total Vote	Poll
	Votes	C	A	Votes	C	A	Votes	C	A				
1919	54,100	15	2	59,000	68	12	38,700	40	6			152,800	16·6%
1922	194,200	17	3	285,800	82	12	100,300	25	5			583,900	36·8
1925	230,200	35	4	274,100	83	13	53,500	6	3	2,500		559,500	30·6
1928	250,600	42	6	284,500	77	12	97,000	5	1	11,600		649,300	35·6
1931	214,300	35	6	284,000	83	13	32,300	6	—	3,100		542,600	27·8
1934	341,400	69	11	298,500	55	9	22,900			7,700		675,900	33.5
1937	446,100	75	12	402,700	49	8	10,800				7,700	881,200	43.4

C = Councillors
A = Alderman

Table (c)   *Metropolitan Borough Elections*

Date	Labour		Municipal Reform (Conservative)	Progressive (Liberal)	Communist	Fascist	Total Vote	Total Seats
	Votes	Seats						
1919	185,600	572	179,100	111,400			476,100	1,362
1922	210,700	259	342,300	48,700			601,700	1,362
1925	294,700	364	441,700	31,500			767,900	1,366
1928	253,700	459	284,700	45,600	3,800		587,900	1,376
1931	198,100	257	374,900	23,200	6,100		602,300	1,385
1934	332,900	729	300,100	17,200	4,600		654,800	1,386
1937	353,000	778	306,000	16,000	1,800	6,400	683,100	1,371

Table (d)   *Labour and the Boards of Guardians*

Date	Seats
1913	21
1919	143
1922	112
1925	233
1928	231

2 LCC Tables

Table (e)

Expenditure on Rate Services (Source LCC Financial Abstracts)

In £000s.

	Total	Education	Hospitals	Housing	Public Assistance	Ambulances	Civil Defence	Fire Brigade and Fire Protection	Main Drainage	Means of Communication, Bridges, Tunnels, etc.	Mental Deficiency and Mental Hospitals	Parks and Open Spaces	Public Health	Welfare of the Blind	Administration
1931–2	27,506	6,811	2,039	331	7,454	53	—	761	729	625	581	310	187	85	788
1932–3	25,994	7,164	3,551	325	5,939	45	—	709	694	533	618	253	142	91	766
A 1933–4	25,905	7,212	3,954	311	5,862	48	—	694	676	578	670	255	137	98	759
1934–5	27,108	7,314	4,128	392	5,928	52	—	734	678	632	715	268	140	113	824
1935–6	28,509	7,600	4,316	447	5,851	45	—	774	716	564	787	321	164	141	868
1936–7	29,445	7,561	4,511	503	5,782	48	—	780	722	723	854	344	166	149	884
B 1937–8	30,377	7,838	4,906	594	5,719	50	2	797	774	751	882	353	184	156	941
Difference between A and B	4,472	626	952	283	−143	2	—	103	98	173	212	98	47	58	182
% increase	17	8.5	24	91	−2.4	4	—	15	15	30	32	38	34	59	24
1938–9	31,114	7,845	5,394	686	5,530	56	67	904	785	709	905	368	196	222	925
C 1939–40	35,694	6,974	4,686	730	5,336	152	300	1,169	781	702	886	370	198	239	861
Difference between A and C	9,789	−238	732	419	−526	104	—	475	105	124	216	115	61	141	102
% increase	38	−33	18	132	−9	220	—	68	16	21	32.5	45	44.5	142	13

Table (f)
Rate in the £ levied
(Source LCC Financial Abstracts)

1931–2	79·5d.
1932–3	78·5
A 1933–4	75·5
1934–5	73·5
1935–6	84·0
1936–7	87·5
B 1937–8	87·5

Difference between	
A and B	12
% increase	16
1938–9	93·5
C 1939–40	93·5

Difference between	
A and C	18
% increase	24

Table (g)
Capital Expenditure of Year
(Source LCC Financial Abstracts)
In £000,000s.

	Total	Housing
1931–2	4·8	3.2
1932–3	2·2	1·3
A 1933–4	2·1	1·5
1934–5	3·0	2·0
1935–6	5·8	3·1
1936–7	6·9	4·6
B 1937–8	6·8	4·6
Difference between		
A and B	4·7	3·1
% increase	225	206
1938–9	7·8	4·6
C 1939–40	5·8	3·1
Difference between		
A and C	3·7	1·6
% increase	176	106

Table (h)
Debt charges from the Rates
(Source LCC Financial Abstracts)

		In £000s
	1931–2	2,047
	1932–3	2,058
A	1933–4	2,387
	1934–5	2,132
	1935–6	1,947
	1936–7	2,122
B	1937–8	2,762

Difference between	
A and B	375

% increase	16

	1938–9	2,833
C	1939–40	2,942

Difference between	
A and C	555

% increase	23

Index

Note: Herbert Morrison is referred to as 'HM' throughout the index